Jewish Life and Thought among Greeks and Romans

Zodiac, mosaic floor, Hammath Tiberias synagogue, fourth century.

Jewish Life and Thought among Greeks and Romans

PRIMARY READINGS

Edited and Introduced by

LOUIS H. FELDMAN

and

MEYER REINHOLD

T&T CLARK
EDINBURGH

Published in the United States of America by
Augsburg Fortress
426 S. Fifth Street, Box 1209
Minneapolis, MN 55440

This edition published under licence from Augsburg Fortress by
T&T Clark Ltd
59 George Street
Edinburgh EH2 2LQ
Scotland

First published 1996

ISBN 0 567 08525 2

British Library Cataloguing-in-Publication Data
A catalogue record for this book is available from the British Library

Typeset by Waverley Typesetters, Galashiels
Printed and bound in Great Britain by Biddles Ltd, Guildford

Contents

Acknowledgments

"Aaron at the Temple," from the assembly room in the synagogue at Dura-Europos. Princeton University Press/Art Resource, New York. Used by permission.

"The Pharos Lighthouse of Alexandria." Foto Marburg/Art Resource, New York. Used by permission.

Bust of Julius Caesar, Museo Archeologico Nazionale, Naples, Italy. Alinari/Art Resource, New York. Used by permission.

"Joseph, Potiphar's Wife, and Asenath," Vienna Genesis. Österreichische Nationalbibliothek, Vienna. Used by permission.

Inscription from Aphrodisias, including God-fearers, New York University Excavations at Aphrodisias. Used by permission.

We are grateful to the following publishing firms for permission to use selections from copyrighted material of translations:

E. J. Brill for Jack Lightstone's translation in Jacob Neusner's edition of *Christianity, Judaism and Other Greco-Roman Cults*.

Cambridge University Press for Henry Chadwick's translation of Origen's *Contra Celsum*.

Doubleday Dell Publishing Group Inc. for Theodor H. Gaster's translation of *The Dead Sea Scriptures*, Christoph Burchard's translation of *Joseph and Aseneth*, and the Anchor Bible Dictionary.

E. P. Dutton for Abraham Cohen's translation in *Everyman's Talmud*.

HarperCollins for translations by Sidney Tedesche of 1 and 2 *Maccabees* and by Moses Hadas of the *Letter of Aristeas*.

Harvard University Press for translations from the Loeb Classical Library and the *Corpus Papyrorum Judaicarum*, edited by Victor Tcherikover, Alexander Fuks, and Menahem Stern.

Hebrew Union College Press for Bernard J. Bamberger's translation in his *Proselytism in the Talmudic Period*.

Israel Academy of Sciences and Humanities for translations by Menahem Stern in his *Greek and Latin Authors on Jews and Judaism*.

Israel Exploration Journal for Naphtali Lewis' translation of *Papyrus Yadin 18.*

Thomas Nelson and Sons for selections from the Revised Standard Version of the New Testament.

Oxford University Press for Augustine Fitzgerald's translation of Synesius, Edwin H. Gifford's translation of Eusebius, D. A. Russell's translation of Longinus, Richard Walzer's translation of *Galen on Jews and Christians,* and Yigael Yadin's translation of the *Scroll of the War of the Sons of Light against the Sons of Darkness.*

Random House for Yigael Yadin's translation of the Bar-Kochba letters.

Scholars Press for Carl R. Holladay's translations in his *Fragments from Hellenistic Jewish Authors* and Jacob Neusner's translations from *Lamentations Rabbah* and *Song of Songs Rabbah.*

The Soncino Press for translations from the Talmud and Midrash.

Wayne State University Press for selections from Amnon Linder's *The Jews in Roman Imperial Legislation.*

Yale University Press for selections from Jacob Neusner's translation of *The Mishnah.*

Preface

The present source book endeavors to present representative selections from Greek and Latin literature, the Apocrypha, the New Testament, Dead Sea Scrolls, Graeco-Jewish writers (notably Philo and Josephus), Roman imperial legislation, the rabbinic corpus, inscriptions, papyri, and coins. It attempts to illustrate the political (with special attention to the revolts against Rome), religious (with special attention given to the various movements within Judaism and the degree of Hellenization), economic, social, and cultural life of the Jews in both Palestine and the various countries of the Diaspora for the period of approximately a thousand years from the time of Alexander the Great in the fourth century BCE to the sixth century CE. The focus, in particular, is on the relations of Jews with their neighbors – governments (especially Rome), the masses, and intellectuals. To a considerable degree the passages are an extended historical commentary on the anti-Judaism, philo-Judaism, and conversion to Judaism of this period. In most cases there are brief introductions, bibliographies of items in English on the most significant passages (arranged chronologically, so that the last item is the most recent scholarly treatment of the topic), and very brief notes explaining points requiring elucidation. In addition to the highly selective general bibliography, a list of topics for further study has been added. The sophisticated student will, we believe, realize the importance – and the excitement – of reading and analyzing the documents and drawing his or her own conclusions from them and not merely relying upon scholars, whatever their reputations may be, especially in those many instances where there is a sharp difference of opinion in published scholarship. Because the focus of the volume is on the relations between Jews and non-Jews, the reader will find striking relevance to the situation of Jews in the world today, with similar problems of anti-Judaism, terrorism, dual allegiance, assimilation, intermarriage, and conversion from Judaism, as well as the phenomena, likewise paralleled in the modern world, of philo-Judaism, ecumenism, and conversion to Judaism.

A few caveats are in order. The student should be aware that as grateful as we should be for what has survived from Greek and Latin literature, the great majority of literary sources have perished, though a very sizeable percentage of what has remained pertaining to the Jews has been included, taken, for the most part, from Menahem Stern's magnificent collection. We must always ask, nevertheless, whether what has survived is truly representative or whether it reflects the interests – and prejudices – of those who decided what should be kept.

Great as is the historical value of inscriptions and documents on papyri, in that they are usually contemporary with the people and the events to which they refer and reflect a broader spectrum of the population – ranging from the poorest in the Roman catacomb inscriptions to the wealthiest donors – than is to be found in the literary texts, yet those pertaining to synagogues, for example, generally reflect the wealthier class who could afford to build or improve the structures and who presumably held the offices in them. Only a very small percentage of the surviving inscriptions has been included. The picture is skewed, inasmuch as more than a third of those that we have found come from a single location, Rome, which had perhaps 1 per cent of the total Jewish population of the Diaspora. They give us precious little information about the beliefs and practices of the Jews. In fact, the average inscription contains no more than between ten and twenty words. Most are fragmentary, and reconstructions are often uncertain. Errors in the texts abound, since they are often chiseled by the less learned and since they are generally copies of a first draft on wood or papyrus. Seldom is there reference to an actual date, and sometimes the possible range of dates is several centuries. This is especially true when inscriptions are discovered away from their original site. Frequently there is a real question as to whether the inscription is that of a Jew or of a non-Jew, whether pagan or Christian. The names of the people involved are not necessarily conclusive, inasmuch as the Jews very often had non-Jewish names. As for the papyri, almost all of them come from Egypt and they cover a period of a thousand years. The reader will note that they are almost always in fragmentary, often in extremely fragmentary, condition. They are included not merely to shed contemporary light upon events but also to indicate the difficulties – and the tantalizing and challenging possibilities – in working with just such sources, valuable as they are, even in their mutilated condition.

As to the laws that are quoted, they were not always enforced, especially during the chaotic third and fourth centuries CE; and one is particularly suspicious when a provision is affirmed and reaffirmed over and over again.

In the case of rabbinic sources (and only a very small percentage of what has remained is included here), we must realize that they were not codified and reduced to writing until, in most cases, several centuries after the lifetime of those rabbis who are cited; but at the same time there is some reason to think – though this is admittedly vigorously disputed by many modern scholars – that those rabbis who preserved the statements of their teachers and other predecessors did so with reverence and with care. But the Talmud is a kind of Congressional Record, full of debates, 319 of which are never finally resolved; and one must, in any case, always differentiate between a rabbinic opinion and a law. Moreover, there were many groups in opposition to the Pharisees, so that one rabbinic tradition mentions that there were twenty-four sects at the time of the destruction of the Temple in 70 CE.

We must constantly be aware of the time-frame of the sources, inasmuch as considerable changes occurred over the course of the approximately thousand years covered in this collection. We must also be aware that we have much more information for certain periods, for example the reign of Herod (37–4 BCE) and the great revolt of 66–74, than for other periods, for example the two centuries before Alexander the Great and the period after 74. In the case of the Jews, the numerous wars fought in Palestine and the major revolts of 66–74 and 132–5 had an obvious impact both upon the Jews and upon their relations with the great powers and with non-Jews generally. There is a vast difference between the favor shown the Jews by Julius Caesar, especially because of the aid that they had given him in his civil war with Pompey, and the attitude of the Christian emperors in the fourth and later centuries.

On the question of how much Hellenization occurred in Palestine there is a tremendous debate among scholars; a major question is whether commercial contact brought with it a cultural and religious impact as well. Here, too, there are differences, depending, in part, whether Judaea was under the Ptolemies, Seleucids or Romans or was independent or quasi-independent; and there are regional differences not only between Judaea and Galilee but even between upper and lower Galilee. We must also not forget that there were large numbers – though a minority in the general population – of non-Jews, including Samaritans, in Palestine; and there were considerable fluctuations in the tensions between them and the Jews. There is a great deal of debate as to how much influence the Pharisees had in Palestine, whether this influence was direct or indirect, and how it was affected by events, notably the destruction of the Temple in 70 CE. Indeed, the great scholar Elias Bickerman once suggested that the greatest religious reformer in history was none other than the Roman general Titus, who effected a religious revolution, in effect, by destroying the Temple and thus putting an end to the sacrificial system. Even if we take the mass of rabbinic literature into account, we know precious little about the beliefs, practices, and thoughts of ordinary people. Moreover, a great debate rages in scholarly circles today as to how successful Jews were in winning proselytes and "sympathizers;" and, of course, there are vast differences in various countries and periods. Finally, we must be aware that our most extensive authority for the period from Alexander to the end of the Great Revolt in 74 is Josephus, about whom a great debate rages in scholarly circles as to his reliability and fairness; the prevailing current opinion seems to be that we should respect but suspect him.

As to the Diaspora, we must realize that we have far less information than we have for Palestine. Thanks to Philo we have a fair amount of information about Egyptian Jewry in the first half of the first century, though he, too, has his limitations because of his aristocratic bias: but for Asia Minor and Syria, which apparently had very large Jewish populations, we have very little indeed, though this is now supplemented by recently discovered inscriptions.

Although we have included a number of selections dealing with the attitude of pagans – whether governments, intelligentsia, or the masses – toward the Jews and of Jews toward them, we have not included passages dealing with the attitude of the New Testament, Church Fathers, and Church Councils toward Jews because of the magnitude and complexity of the topic and because there are source books dealing with those issues.

We should like to take this occasion to thank Professor E. P. Sanders for very many helpful suggestions; Donna J. Rawls for assistance in proofreading; and Mary Jane Frisby for preparation of the indices.

L.H.F. and M.R.

Sources

(Pseudo-)Acro: A collection of scholia (marginal comments) in Latin on Horace. His date is unknown but is thought to be about 400 CE.

Acts of the Alexandrian Martyrs: A collection of papyri, written in Greek, now in fragmentary form, dating from the first two centuries CE, written by extremely anti-Jewish Alexandrian patriots.

Agatharchides: A learned scholar of the second century BCE, originally from Cnidus (in Asia Minor), who was a follower of Aristotle and who lived in Alexandria. He is the author of a *History of Asia* and a *History of Europe*, in Greek, preserved in extracts and in an epitome.

Alexander Polyhistor: Greek writer from Miletus (in Asia Minor) who lived in the first century BCE. He is the author of a work *On Jews*, brief fragments of which are quoted by the Church Father Eusebius.

Ammianus Marcellinus: Historian born in Antioch *ca.* 330 CE who wrote in Latin a continuation of the histories of Tacitus in thirty-one books, of which we have eighteen. They cover the period from 353 to 378. He served under the Emperor Julian in the campaign against the Persians.

Antonius Diogenes: Author of unknown date, but thought to have lived at the end of the first century CE, who wrote a romance in Greek, extant only in fragments, in which the hero and heroine meet each other at the edge of the world in Thule.

Apion: Greek of Egyptian origin who lived in the first half of the first century CE, well-known as a Homeric scholar and the author of a work on the history of Egypt. He represented the Greeks of Alexandria when the Alexandrian Jews were accused before the Emperor Gaius Caligula.

Apocrypha: A collection of thirteen works (*Epistle of Jeremiah, Tobit, Judith, 3 Ezra, Additions to Esther, Prayer of Azariah and the Song of the Three Young Men, Susanna, Bel and the Dragon, 1 Baruch, Ecclesiasticus (Ben Sira), Wisdom of Solomon, 1 Maccabees,* and *2 Maccabees*) dating from approximately 300 BCE to 70 CE. They are not included in the canon of the Hebrew Bible but are regarded as canonical by Roman Catholics, though not by Protestants. All are preserved in Greek, but all, except for *Wisdom of Solomon* and *2 Maccabees*, were written in a Semitic language.

Apollonius Molon: Greek rhetorician who lived in the first century BCE and taught on the island of Rhodes, among his pupils being Cicero and Caesar. He wrote a book about the Jews, fragments of which are quoted by Eusebius.

Appian of Alexandria: Author of a history of Rome, written in Greek about the year 160 CE, in twenty-four books, of which we have approximately half. As a native of Egypt he took pride in the Ptolemies but also was very pro-Roman.

Apuleius: Lucius Apuleius, who flourished in the middle of the second century CE, was born in North Africa and wrote, in Latin, an *Apologia*, defending himself against the charge that he had won a rich widow in marriage by the use of magic. His most famous work is his *Metamorphoses* or *Golden Ass*, a romance in eleven books which tells of the transformation of a certain Lucius into an ass and of his eventual return to human shape through the intervention of the goddess Isis. He is also the author of *Florida*, a collection of passages from his speeches.

Aristides: Aelius Aristides, writer during the second century CE, in Greek, of speeches as well as of letters and prose hymns. His style, imitative of classic Attic Greek, was much admired in later times, so that fifty-five of his compositions have survived.

Aristotle: Greek philosopher (384–322 BCE), tutor of Alexander the Great, pupil of Plato, founder of the Peripatetic school of philosophy. Most of his treatises are lost, but of those that survive the following are the most famous: his logical treatises, *Physics*, *Metaphysics*, *Nicomachean Ethics*, *Politics*, *Rhetoric*, and *Poetics*.

Arrian: Greek from Asia Minor (*ca.* 95–175 CE) who served as an officer in the Roman army and as a Roman administrator in Asia Minor. A great admirer of Xenophon, he wrote *Anabasis*, an account of Alexander the Great's campaigns; *Encheiridion*, a manual of the philosophy of the Stoic Epictetus; as well as treatises on hunting, geography, and tactics. His histories of Parthia and Bithynia are lost, except for fragments.

Artapanus: Historian, generally assumed to be Jewish, who flourished in Egypt before the middle of the first century BCE and who wrote in Greek an account, fragments of which survive, embellishing the biblical accounts of Abraham, Joseph, and Moses. These excerpts show a good deal of syncreticism with pagan traditions.

Artemidorus: Author in the second half of the second century CE of a work in Greek in five books on the interpretation of dreams.

Augustine: Church Father (354–430 CE), born in North Africa, teacher of rhetoric, wrote in Latin various philosophical, theological, and polemical works. His most famous works are his *City of God*, a monumental theology of history, and *Confessions*, his intellectual and religious autobiography.

Avoth de-Rabbi Nathan: Tractate, which has been transmitted in two versions, appended to the Talmud after the tractate *Avoth*. It is a homiletic commentary in Hebrew on the Mishnah *Avoth* ascribed to the second-century CE Rabbi Nathan of Babylonia but more probably written at an unknown later date. It contains many ethical sayings attributed to various rabbis, as well as a number of anecdotes.

Babylonian Talmud: see *Talmud, Babylonian*

Ben Sira: see *Ecclesiasticus*

Cagnat, René: see *Inscriptiones Graecae ad Res Romanas Pertinentes*

Cassius, Dio: see *Dio Cassius*

Celsus the Encyclopedist: Aulus Cornelius Celsus, who lived in the early part of the first century CE, author of an encyclopedia in Latin on agriculture, philosophy, medicine, and other subjects. Only his eight books on medicine survive.

Celsus the Philosopher: Author in Greek in the second century CE of *The True Doctrine* attacking Christianity. Considerable parts of his work, otherwise lost, are included in Origen's reply, *Against Celsus*.

Chaeremon: First-century CE Egyptian priest who succeeded Apion as librarian in Alexandria and wrote, in Greek, a history of Egypt, fragments of which have survived. His anti-Jewish views may be seen in his account of the exodus of the Israelites from Egypt as cited by Josephus.

Cicero: Marcus Tullius Cicero (106–43 BCE), the greatest Roman orator, held the consulship in the year 63 BCE and wrote numerous orations and rhetorical and philosophical treatises in Latin. He was murdered by the agents of Mark Antony.

Claudius Iolaus: Author of a work (in perhaps the first century CE) in Greek on Phoenician history, of which fragments are preserved.

Clearchus of Soli: Philosopher from Soli on Cyprus, who apparently flourished *ca*. 300 BCE, pupil of Aristotle, author in Greek of a dialogue *On Sleep*, in which Aristotle is one of the speakers. Josephus preserves a fragment of this work.

Clement of Alexandria: Church Father (*ca*. 160–215 CE), author, in Greek, of *An Exhortation to the Greeks*, *Paidagogos* (a course of religious instruction), and *Stromateis* ("Coverings," "Miscellanies," attempting to reconcile faith and reason).

Cleodemus Malchus: Jewish historian (though there is a question as to whether he was Jewish), who apparently lived before the middle of the first century BCE. He wrote a work in Greek of unknown title which is lost except for a fragment quoted by Alexander Polyhistor (who refers to him as "the prophet"), who in turn is quoted by Josephus.

Cleomedes: Stoic, author, in the first or second century CE, of a work in Greek on astronomy.

Code of Justinian: see *Justinian, Code of*

Corpus Inscriptionum Iudaicarum [*CII*], 2 vols, ed. Jean-Baptiste Frey (Rome: Pontificio Istituto di Archeologia Cristiana, 1936–52) (reissued with a critical prolegomenon by Baruch Lifshitz; New York: Ktav, 1975, pp. 21–107): A collection of inscriptions, in Greek and Latin (with a few in Hebrew and Aramaic), concerning Jews among the Greeks and Romans, dating from the third century BCE to the seventh century CE. It contains a French translation of the inscriptions and very brief comments.

Corpus Inscriptionum Latinarum: A multi-volume collection of all inscriptions in Latin found throughout the Roman world.

Corpus Papyrorum Judaicarum [*CPJ*], 3 vols, eds. Victor A. Tcherikover, Alexander Fuks, Menahem Stern (Cambridge, Mass.: Harvard University Press, 1957–64): A collection of papyri and ostraca concerning Jews among the Greeks and Romans, covering the Ptolemaic period (from 323 BCE) through the early Byzantine period (641 CE). It contains an English translation of the documents, which are in Greek, together with extensive bibliographies for each papyrus, considerable introductions, and often extensive commentary.

Damascius: Pagan Neoplatonic philosopher (a follower of Proclus) from Damascus, who lived in the first half of the sixth century CE and who wrote in Greek. Fragments of his *Life of Isidorus* (he succeeded Isidorus as the head of his school in Athens) have been preserved by the ninth-century Photius and the tenth-century Suda. His chief treatise is *Difficulties and Solutions of First Principles*, on the attributes of God and on the human soul.

Damocritus: Author, perhaps in the first century CE, of a book in Greek about the Jews of which we have only fragments, as well as a book about tactics.

Deuteronomy Rabbah: see *Midrash*

Digest: see *Justinian, Digest of*

Dio Cassius: Cassius Dio, generally known as Dio Cassius (*ca.* 160–230 CE), author of a *Roman History* in Greek in eighty books, of which twenty-six survive, covering the period from the foundation of Rome until the year 229. Though Dio was rhetorical and not always critical, he brought to his work the political expertise of a long public career as senator and provincial administrator.

Dio Chrysostom: Stoic philosopher and orator (*ca.* 40–*ca.* after 113 CE), surnamed the "golden-mouthed," author of a series of popular lectures in Greek. Born in Bithynia in Asia Minor, he lived in Rome under Domitian, who banished him, whereupon he traveled widely.

Diodorus the Sicilian: Author, in the latter part of the first century BCE, of a highly unoriginal universal history in forty books (of which fifteen survive) in Greek. He has been termed by Macaulay "a stupid, credulous, prosing old ass."

Diogenes Laertius: Author (*ca.* 200–50 CE) of a collection of biographies of eighty-two eminent philosophers (from Thales to Epicurus) in Greek in ten books.

Ecclesiasticus: A work in the Apocrypha by Ben Sira written originally in Hebrew in Palestine during the early second century BCE. It is modeled on the biblical book of Proverbs and contains ethical maxims as well as theological and philosophical reflections.

1 Enoch: A work composed between the fourth century BCE and the beginning of the Common Era, included in the Pseudepigrapha, extant in an Ethiopic translation of a Greek translation of an Aramaic original (portions of which have been found among the Qumran manuscripts).

Epictetus: Stoic philosopher (*ca.* 60–140 CE), originally a slave, from Phrygia in Asia Minor, author of lectures in Greek on popular Stoicism, as well as a brief manual on Stoicism, which have been preserved by Arrian.

Eupolemus: Jewish historian (though there is a question as to whether he was Jewish) who wrote, presumably in the Land of Israel, in Greek in the middle of the second century BCE a work *Concerning the Kings in Judaea.*

(Pseudo-)Eupolemus: An anonymous historian, perhaps a Samaritan, who wrote in Greek in the first half of the second century BCE in the Land of Israel.

Eusebius: (265–340 CE), bishop of Caesarea in Palestine, author of a summary in Greek of universal history, as well as a history of the Church (to 314 CE) and *Preparation for the Gospel*, which includes a survey of the philosophies and religion of the Greeks.

Exodus Rabbah: see *Midrash*

Ezekiel the Tragedian: Jewish author, in the middle of the second century BCE, of a tragedy (largely influenced in style by Euripides) in Greek on the Exodus, considerable fragments of which are quoted by Alexander Polyhistor, who, in turn, is quoted by Eusebius.

4 Ezra: Jewish work, also known as *The Apocalypse of Ezra* or *2 Ezra*, included by Protestants in the Apocrypha, written at the end of the first century CE. Originally written apparently in Hebrew, it is extant only in Latin, Syriac, Ethiopic, Arabic, Armenian, Georgian, Slavonic, Romanian, and fragments in Greek and in Coptic, and was very popular in the early Christian churches. A major apocalyptic work, it is concerned with the theological problems arising from the destruction of the Temple in Jerusalem.

Firmicus Maternus: Christian author, in Latin in the first half of the fourth century CE, of an astrological treatise in eight books and of a treatise *On the Error of Profane Religions*.

Frey, Jean-Baptiste: see *Corpus Inscriptionum Iudaicarum*

Frontinus: Sextus Julius Frontinus (*ca.* 40–104 CE), consul, governor of Britain, author of a work in Latin on military strategy in three books, written as a sequel to his lost work on the art of war, as well as an extant work on aqueducts.

Gabba: *Iscrizioni greche e latine per lo studio della Bibbia*, ed. Emilio Gabba (Turin: Marietti, 1958): Greek and Latin inscriptions relating to Jewish and Christian life in the Roman Empire.

Galen: Famous Greek physician (*ca.* 129–200 CE), from Pergamum in Asia Minor, author of numerous medical writings, over 100 of which survive, as well as works on philosophy, literature, and grammar, which are lost except for fragments.

Genesis Rabbah: see *Midrash*

Greek and Latin Authors on Jews and Judaism: see *Stern*

Hecataeus of Abdera: Author (*ca.* 300 BCE) of a history of Egypt in Greek, now lost, which served as a major source for the history by Diodorus, who has preserved an excursus of some length concerning the Jews. He was a pupil of Pyrrho the Skeptic.

(Pseudo-)Hecataeus: Historian, generally assumed to be a Jew, of the second century BCE, author in Greek of *On Abraham* and *On the Jews*, now lost but fragments of which survive in the works of Josephus.

Hermippus of Smyrna: Adherent of the Peripatetic school of Aristotle, author (*ca.* 200 BCE) in Greek of a collection of biographies of philosophers, including Pythagoras, only fragments of which survive.

Herodotus: Author (*ca.* 480–*ca.* 425 BCE), from Halicarnassus in Asia Minor, of a history in Greek, in nine books, of the wars between the Persians and the Greeks (490–478 BCE). He was termed by Cicero "the father of history."

Historia Augusta: see *Scriptores Historiae Augustae*

Horace: Quintus Horatius Flaccus (65–8 BCE), major poet in Latin, author of *Odes*, *Epodes*, *Satires*, *Epistles* (including *Ars Poetica*), and *Carmen Saeculare*. His patron was Maecenas, who admitted him to the circle of Augustus.

Horbury and Noy: see *Jewish Inscriptions of Graeco-Roman Egypt*

Iamblichus: Neo-Platonist philosopher who was born in Syria and lived in the third century CE. He was a pupil of Porphyry and wrote a work on Pythagorean philosophy in Greek, part of which survives.

Inscriptiones Graecae ad Res Romanas Pertinentes, ed. René Cagnat *et al.*, 4 vols (Paris, 1901–27): A collection of Greek inscriptions dealing with Roman affairs.

Jerusalem Talmud: see *Talmud, Jerusalem*

Jewish Inscriptions of Graeco-Roman Egypt: With an Index of the Jewish Inscriptions of Egypt and Cyrenaica, ed. William Horbury and David Noy (Cambridge University Press, 1992): Corrects and supplements Frey's *Corpus Inscriptionum Iudaicarum* in many respects.

Joseph and Aseneth: A work of unknown authorship in the Pseud-epigrapha dating perhaps from the first century BCE or the first century CE and telling of the sincere repentance and conversion of the non-Jewish Aseneth to Judaism and her marriage to Joseph, the son of Jacob.

Josephus: Josephus Flavius (Joseph ben Mattityahu Ha-Kohen) (37–*ca.* 100 CE), a highly educated Jew, hostile to the extreme Jewish nationalists and convinced of the need to collaborate with Rome. He served as a general for the Jewish forces in Galilee at the beginning of the war against the Romans in 66 but surrendered to the Romans. After the destruction of the Temple in 70 he lived in Rome and was granted Roman citizenship. All his works, written in Greek, are extant: *The Jewish War*, in seven books, describing in great detail the rebellion of the Jews against the Romans in 66–73/4; *Jewish Antiquities*, in twenty books, a history covering the period from creation to the outbreak of the war against the Romans; *Life*, presenting his autobiography, with emphasis on his role in the war against the Romans; and *Against Apion*, in two books, a defense of Judaism against various anti-Jewish writers.

Julian: Born in 331 CE, Julian became Roman emperor in 360 and was killed in battle with the Persians in 363. Raised as a Christian, Julian rejected Christianity, became a vigorous proponent of paganism, was attracted particularly to the worship of the solar god Helios, and adopted the theurgy of Maximus of Ephesus and the Neoplatonism of Iamblichus. In his treatise, written in Greek, *Against the Galileans*, preserved in sizable fragments by Cyril of Alexandria, he bitterly attacks Christianity, while showing respect for Judaism as a traditional religion. He gave orders to rebuild the Temple in Jerusalem, but fires cut short this effort.

Justin: Author, in the third or fourth century CE, of an epitome in Latin of Pompeius Trogus' *Philippic Histories*.

Justinian, Code of: Part of the *Corpus Juris Civilis* of Justinian, first appeared in 529 CE; a revised version appeared in 534. It is a compendium in Latin, compiled under the editorship of Tribonian, of the decrees of the emperors, starting with the time of Hadrian, together with their answers to various legal questions submitted to them.

Justinian, Digest of: A collection, forming part of the *Corpus Juris Civilis*, issued between 529 and 535 CE by a commission of jurists headed by Tribonian, consisting of fifty books containing the views of the most famous classical jurists, notably Gaius, Paulus, Ulpian, Modestinus, and Papinian.

Justinian, Novellae of: Ordinances on various subjects, nearly all published in Greek, issued by the Eastern Roman Emperor Justinian between 534 and 565.

Juvenal: Decimus Junius Juvenalis (*ca.* 60–*ca.* 130 CE), Roman satirist whose sixteen poems, highly rhetorical, present a detailed, grim, bitter, pessimistic picture in Latin of Roman life.

Lamentations Rabbah: see *Midrash*

Letter of Aristeas: A letter, included in the Pseudepigrapha, ostensibly by a non-Jewish courtier of Ptolemy Philadelphus, written in Greek to Aristeas' brother Philocrates, which relates how Ptolemy, about the year 270 BCE, requested that a translation of the Pentateuch be made into Greek for his library in Alexandria. In actuality it was more probably written in the second century BCE by a Jew in Alexandria for apologetic purposes.

Leviticus Rabbah: see *Midrash*

(Pseudo-)Longinus: Unknown author of a treatise in Greek *On the Sublime* in the first or second century CE, analyzing what constitutes sublimity in style and finding it in grandeur of ideas, a capacity for strong emotion, and dignity and nobility of phraseology. He is particularly critical of bombastic and tasteless writers.

Lucian: Writer (*ca.* 115–200 CE) in Greek, from Samosata in Syria on the Euphrates, of parodies and satirical dialogues. His criticisms of shams in religion and philosophy are particularly clever and witty.

Lydus: John Lydus, fifth-century CE writer in Greek of *On Omens, On Roman Magistrates,* and *On Months.*

Lysimachus: Graeco-Egyptian author, dating from perhaps the second or first century BCE, of a history of Egypt in Greek, of which only fragments remain.

Maccabees: Four Apocryphal books, included in the Septuagint, and extant in Greek. *1 Maccabees,* covering the years 175 to 135/134 BCE, was written in the Land of Israel *ca.* 100 BCE and is a history of the Maccabean revolt and the Hasmonean dynasty. It is a Greek translation of a Hebrew original and was written from a pro-Hasmonean viewpoint. *2 Maccabees,* covering the years 175 to 160 BCE, was written in Greek in 124 BCE for the edification of Egyptian Jews and is an abridgement of a work in five books by Jason of Cyrene. It is an example of "tragic" historiography. *3 Maccabees,* despite the title, nowhere refers to the Maccabean struggle against the Syrian Greeks. Like the first and second books of *Maccabees*, it tells of a persecution of the Jews by a Hellenistic king (Ptolemy IV Philopator, who ruled Egypt 221–204 BCE) and of their miraculous rescue. It is an example of "pathetic" or "tragic" history in highly rhetorical language. It was written *ca.* early first century BCE. *4 Maccabees*, composed *ca.* first century CE, falsely ascribed to Josephus, deals with the martyrdom of the aged sage Eleazar and of a mother and her seven sons. Writing in a highly rhetorical style, the author is well versed in Greek philosophy but aims to show that the faculty of reason, so prized by the Greeks, is actually compatible with obedience to the precepts of the Torah.

Macrobius: Ambrosius Theodosius Macrobius, who lived in the first half of the fifth century CE, grammarian and antiquarian, author of *Saturnalia*, a work in Latin in seven books presenting the discussions, particularly about the works of Virgil and religious matters, of some scholars at a dinner.

Manetho: Egyptian priest of the third century BCE who wrote a history of Egypt in Greek, fragments of which remain.

Manual of Discipline: One of the first Dead Sea Scrolls discovered in 1947 at Qumran, in cave 1. It is otherwise known as the *Rule of the Community* (1 QS). It was apparently composed in the second century BCE. Written in Hebrew, it contains the rules of the sect, the entrance requirements, and the penalties for violation of the rules.

Martial: Marcus Valerius Martialis (*ca.* 40–104 CE), born in Spain, author of a collection of short, witty, satirical epigrams in Latin in fourteen books, affording a humorous glimpse, with a considerable amount of sheer obscenity, of almost every aspect of life in Rome.

Megasthenes: Greek who *ca.* 300 BCE was sent several times on embassies to the Indian king Chandragupta and who wrote a work in four books about India, containing a good deal of reliable information mixed with fable. Only fragments remain.

Mekilta: Rabbinic midrash in Hebrew interpreting the Book of Exodus chapter by chapter and verse by verse, existing in two versions, that of Rabbi Ishmael and that of Rabbi Simeon ben Yoḥai, both probably redacted not earlier than the fifth century CE.

Meleager of Gadara: Poet from the city of Gadara (just east of the River Jordan), who lived from the end of the second century to the beginning of the first century BCE (?), grew up in Tyre and spent his old age in Cos. His best poems, written in Greek, are succinct epigrams about love and death. He also edited an anthology of epigrams.

Menander of Laodicea: Rhetorician from Asia Minor at the end of the third century CE who wrote rhetorical treatises and commentaries in Greek.

Midrash: Rabbinic literature written in Hebrew and Aramaic, sermonic in nature, interpreting the Scriptures, both the legal and non-legal portions, and going beyond, often far beyond, the literal meaning. The redaction of the various midrashic treatises (Genesis Rabbah, Exodus Rabbah, Leviticus Rabbah, Numbers Rabbah, Deuteronomy Rabbah, Lamentations Rabbah, Song of Songs Rabbah, Midrash Psalms) dates, variously, from the fifth century to the thirteeenth century CE.

Mishnah: A codification in Hebrew of six sections (orders) of the Oral Law (Seeds, Appointed Times, Women, Damages, Holy Things, and Purity), divided into sixty-three tractates, made by Rabbi Judah the Prince (*ca.* 220 CE), which, according to tradition, was divinely transmitted through Moses to the Israelites. It is more a textbook than a code and often records conflicting opinions.

Mnaseas of Patara: Traveller and geographical writer in Greek (*ca.* 200 BCE), from Asia Minor, a pupil of the famous geographer Eratosthenes.

Modestinus: Herennius Modestinus (*ca.* 250 CE), famous Roman jurist, a pupil of Ulpian, writer in Latin, often cited in Justinian's *Digest*.

Nepotianus: Januarius Nepotianus, fourth- or fifth-century CE epitomator in Latin of Valerius Maximus' *Memorable Deeds and Sayings*.

Nicarchus: Author, in Greek, of a monograph about the Jews in the first century CE.

Nicolaus of Damascus: Non-Jewish author (*ca.* 64 BCE to beginning of the first century CE) in Greek of a universal history in 144 books (now lost except for fragments), Aristotelian philosopher, famous orator, confidant of Herod.

Novellae: see *Justinian, Novellae of*

Numbers Rabbah: see *Midrash*

Numenius of Apamea: Platonist (*ca.* 150–200 CE), precursor of the Neoplatonists. His works, written in Greek, are lost except for fragments. He greatly admired eastern religions.

Origen: Church Father (185–253 CE), voluminous and learned writer in Greek of treatises (especially commentaries on the Bible), homilies (best-known for their allegorical interpretations), letters, and dialogues, born in Alexandria and lived in Caesarea in Palestine.

Ovid: Publius Ovidius Naso (43 BCE–18 CE), poet, author in Latin of love poetry and a handbook of mythology in epic verse. He was exiled by Augustus, apparently because of the immorality of his poem *The Art of Love* or because of his influence upon the Emperor's grand-daughter Julia.

Palestinian Talmud: see *Talmud, Jerusalem*

Papyrus Yadin: Papyrus, dating from the year 128 CE, found in the Cave of Letters in Naḥal Ḥever in Israel and containing a marriage contract in Greek.

Paris, Julius: Fourth-century CE epitomator in Latin of Valerius Maximus' *Memorable Deeds and Sayings*.

Paulus, Julius: Roman jurist, who lived during the first half of the third century CE and wrote a book of legal *Opinions* in Latin.

Persius: Aulus Persius Flaccus (34–62 CE), author of six satires in Latin imbued with Stoic preaching.

Pesiqta Rabbati: Medieval (*ca.* ninth century CE) sermonic midrash on the festivals of the year.

Petronius: Gaius Petronius (died *ca.* 65 CE), author, in Latin, of a satirical picaresque novel, the *Satyricon*, in prose interspersed with poetry, only a portion of which remains.

Philo: Philo of Alexandria (*ca.* 15 BCE–40 CE), a member of a distinguished and wealthy Jewish family, headed the delegation of Alexandrian Jews that met with the Roman Emperor Gaius Caligula. His vast literary output, in Greek, reveals a man deeply influenced by Hellenism but devoted to his ancestral Judaism. Many of his treatises seek to reconcile Greek philosophy, especially Platonism, with Judaism and, in particular, the Bible, especially through the method of allegory. His pamphlets *Against Flaccus* and *Embassy to Gaius* were written in defense of Alexandrian Jews against their enemies. His view of the Logos as an intermediary between God and man is partially paralleled by the Fourth Gospel of the New Testament.

Philostratus: Sophist who lived from the second half of the second century CE to the 40s of the third century CE and who wrote, in Greek, a biography of the first-century CE Pythagorean mystic and wonder-worker Apollonius of Tyana.

Photius: Erudite patriarch of Constantinople (*ca.* 820–91 CE), author in Greek of *Library*, a collection of extracts from 280 books of classical authors, many of the originals of which are lost.

Pliny the Elder: Gaius Plinius Secundus (23–79 CE), Roman governor in Gaul, Africa, and Spain, author, in Latin, of *Natural History*, a veritable encyclopedia in thirty-seven books, dealing particularly with the sciences.

Plutarch: Prolific author (*ca.* 46–120 CE), in Greek, of parallel biographies of famous Greeks and Romans and of numerous essays on religious, philosophical, scientific, and literary subjects.

Pompeius Trogus: Author (dating from the end of the first century BCE to the beginning of the first century CE) of *Philippic Histories*, a universal history (focusing on the Macedonian–Hellenistic states) in Latin in forty-four books. The work is lost; but an epitome, composed by Justin in the third or fourth century, has been preserved.

Porphyry: Neoplatonic philosopher (232–ca. 301 CE), a pupil of Plotinus; author, in Greek, of a biography of his teacher, a biography of Pythagoras, a history of philosophy, and a number of essays, as well as a treatise against the Christians.

Preisigke, Bilabel, Kiessling: see *Sammelbuch griechischer Urkunden aus Ägypten*

Psalms of Solomon: A collection of eighteen psalms in the Pseudepigrapha dating from the first century BCE, preserved in Greek and Syriac.

Pseudepigrapha: A modern collection of sixty-five ancient works dating from 250 BCE to 200 CE. They are not included in the biblical canon by either Jews or Christians. Most were written by Jews, some by Christians, and some by Jews but expanded or rewritten by Christians. The name is derived from the fact that some of the works are incorrectly (pseudepigraphically) ascribed to such authors as Adam, Enoch, Noah, Abraham, Jacob, Joseph, Moses, David, Solomon, Elijah, Isaiah, Jeremiah, Ezekiel, Daniel, Ezra, and Job.

Ptolemy the Astronomer: Claudius Ptolemaeus, famous astronomer, who lived in Alexandria in the second century CE. His work, *System of Mathematics*, written in Greek and later translated into Arabic, and known as the *Almagest*, became the most influential work on astronomy from antiquity. He also wrote works on geography and astrology.

Ptolemy the Historian: Perhaps to be identified with the grammarian Ptolemy of Ascalon, who lived apparently at the end of the first century BCE and who wrote, in Greek, a life of Herod.

Rutilius Namatianus: Rutilius Claudius Namatianus, a pagan native of Gaul who lived at the beginning of the fifth century CE, wrote a poem *On His Return* in Latin commemorating his return from Rome to Gaul.

Sammelbuch griechischer Urkunden aus Ägypten, ed. F. Preisigke, F. Bilabel, E. Kiessling (Strasbourg, Berlin, Heidelberg, etc., 1913–): A collection of papyri in Greek found in Egypt and in the Land of Israel.

Scriptores Historiae Augustae: A collection of lives in Latin of various emperors from Hadrian (117) to Numerianus (284) ostensibly by diverse authors, modeled on Suetonius, seemingly written between 284 and 337 but probably dating from the end of the fourth century.

Semaḥoth: One of the minor tractates, edited, it is thought, in the middle of the eighth century CE and generally appended to the Babylonian Talmud. The title, "Rejoicings," is euphemistic, since it deals with death and mourning.

Seneca the Younger: Lucius Annaeus Seneca (*ca.* 4 BCE–65 CE), Stoic philosopher, author, in Latin, of *Dialogues*, *Moral Epistles*, various moral treatises, *Natural Questions* (on natural phenomena), *Apocolocyntosis* (a burlesque satire on the death of Claudius), and nine tragedies. He was tutor and adviser to the Emperor Nero.

Septuagint: The translation of the Pentateuch into Greek, undertaken, according to the *Letter of Aristeas*, by seventy-two Palestinian Jews at the behest of the Egyptian king Ptolemy Philadelphus *ca.* 270 BCE. Most scholars, however, believe that the translation was done at a somewhat later date at the behest of the Jewish community of Alexandria, perhaps for synagogue and instructional use.

Sextus Empiricus: Physician who, in the latter part of the second century CE, wrote, in Greek, *Pyrrhonean Sketches* and *Against the Mathematicians*, defending the view of the Skeptic philosophers and attacking the other schools.

Sibylline Oracles: A collection of twelve quasi-prophetic books in Greek, variously of pagan, Jewish, and Christian origin, included in the Pseudepigrapha, dating from the second century BCE to the fourth century CE. The themes are Messianic and eschatological.

Sifre: Exegetical halakhic Midrash, in Hebrew, on the biblical books of Numbers and Deuteronomy, apparently edited in the Land of Israel but not before the end of the fourth century CE.

Solinus: Gaius Julius Solinus (third century CE?), grammarian, author of a Latin work, *Collections of Memorable Things*, a miscellany of items of history, religion, and natural history.

Song of Songs Rabbah: see *Midrash*

Stephanus of Byzantium: Author of a geographical dictionary in Greek in the sixth century CE, fragments of which are preserved.

Stern: *Greek and Latin Authors on Jews and Judaism*, ed. Menahem Stern, 3 vols (Jerusalem: Israel Academy of Sciences and Humanities, 1974–84). A collection of all references to Jews and Judaism in Greek and Latin literature from the fifth century BCE to the sixth century CE in the original languages, with important variant readings, English translations, introductions, notes, and bibliographies.

Strabo: From Pontus in Asia Minor (*ca.* 64 BCE–*ca.* 20 CE), author, in Greek, of a history in forty-three books coming down to his own day, only fragments of which remain, and of a geographical work in seventeen books, most of which is extant, covering the whole known world of his time.

Suda (Suidas): Tenth-century CE author of a work in Greek which is a combination of dictionary and encyclopedia containing many quotations from ancient works.

Suetonius: Gaius Suetonius Tranquillus (*ca.* 69–*ca.* 150 CE), secretary to the Roman Emperor Hadrian and author of *Lives of the Caesars*, which are biographies in Latin of twelve Roman rulers from Julius Caesar through Domitian. Despite their anecdotal, antiquarian, and scandal-mongering interest, these lives contain much valuable data, though his comments are of unequal value. His sources are uncertain, but he is critical within his limits.

Sulpicius Severus: Christian writer (*ca.* 363–*ca.* 425 CE), from Aquitania (France), author, in Latin, of a sacred history from creation to his own time, with the omission of events recorded in the Gospels and Acts.

Supplementum Epigraphicum Graecum (Leiden, 1923–): Greek inscriptions, newly discovered or revised, reported periodically.

Synesius: Christian (*ca.* 373–414 CE), bishop of Cyrene in Libya, Neoplatonist, author, in Greek, of philosophical works, speeches, hymns, and letters.

Tacitus: Cornelius Tacitus (*ca.* 56–120 CE), eminent Roman lawyer, senator, and historian. His *Annals*, in perhaps eighteen books, cover, in the extant portion, the history of the Roman Empire from the death of Augustus (14 CE) to the death of Nero (68 CE). His *Histories*, in perhaps twelve books, cover, in the extant five books, the years 69–70 (the year of the four emperors), and include a relatively extensive excursus about the origins, history, and customs of the Jews. He claims to be impartial, but his highly rhetorical style, his frequent epigrammatic and highly quotable moralizing, and his deep cynicism betray a strong bias against the imperial system.

Talmud, Babylonian: Codification of Oral Law in sixty-three tractates, consisting of the Mishnah in Hebrew, as codified by the patriarch Rabbi Judah the Prince *ca.* 220 CE, and the Aramaic discussions thereon as codified in Babylonia *ca.* 500 by Ravina and Ashi. Only thirty-six tractates are extant. It is generally regarded as the more authoritative of the two Talmuds.

Talmud, Jerusalem: Codification of Oral Law in sixty-three tractates, consisting of the Mishnah in Hebrew, as codified by the patriarch Rabbi Judah the Prince *ca.* 220 CE, and the Aramaic discussions thereon as codified in Tiberias in the Land of Israel *ca.* 400. Thirty-nine tractates are extant.

Tanḥuma: A name given to various homiletical midrashic compilations on the Pentateuch, written in a mixture of Hebrew and Aramaic, ascribed to a certain Amoraic Rabbi Tanḥuma but apparently not edited before 800 CE.

Tcherikover, Fuks, and Stern: see *Corpus Papyrorum Judaicarum*

Testaments of the Twelve Patriarchs: A work dating perhaps from about 100 BCE in the Pseudepigrapha, giving the last words of the twelve sons of Jacob to their descendants. Although there are Christian interpolations in it, it is generally regarded as being of Palestinian Jewish origin and having been composed originally in Greek. Fragments of it have been found among the Dead Sea Scrolls.

Theodosian Code: A codification, promulgated in sixteen books in Latin in 438 CE, by the Emperor Theodosius II, of all laws issued since 315 CE.

Theodotus: Poet, usually thought to be a Samaritan, who wrote an epic in Greek in the second century BCE, presumably in the Land of Israel, *On the Jews*.

Theophrastus: Greek philosopher (372–288 BCE), successor to Aristotle as head of the Peripatetic school. He also wrote important treatises on religion, on stones, and on botany.

Timagenes: Alexandrian who lived in the first century BCE and taught rhetoric in Rome. He wrote a history of kings in Greek which is extant only in fragments.

Torah: The Hebrew Pentateuch (Genesis, Exodus, Leviticus, Numbers, Deuteronomy), according to tradition, revealed by God through Moses to the Israelites.

Tosefta: A work in Hebrew organized like the Mishnah in six sections (orders) and supplementing it. It was composed in the Land of Israel but not edited apparently until the end of the fourth century CE.

Valerius Maximus: Compiler in Latin at the beginning of the first century CE of a collection of anecdotes, *Memorable Deeds and Sayings*, for the use of orators. It is extant in two epitomes, one by Julius Paris (fourth century?) and the other by Januarius Nepotianus (fourth or fifth century).

Varro: Marcus Terentius Varro (116–27 BCE), "the most learned of the Romans" according to Quintilian, author of over 600 books in Latin on grammar, science, philosophy, antiquarian lore, poetry, satire, and law, most of them no longer extant.

The War Scroll: One of the Dead Sea Scrolls found in Qumran, also known as the *War of the Sons of Light against the Sons of Darkness*, dating from the end of the first century BCE or the early first century CE and written in Hebrew. It apparently foresees an eschatological war against the Romans.

Zosimus: Author in Greek of alchemical, magical, and mystical writings. Born in Panoplos in Egypt, he flourished at the end of the third century or possibly in the fourth century CE. His main work was an encyclopedia of the chemical arts in twenty-eight books. He is the earliest writer on alchemy of whom we have genuine writings.

Abbreviations

Books and Periodicals

ABD	*Anchor Bible Dictionary*, ed. David N. Freedman
AJA	*American Journal of Archaeology*
AJP	*American Journal of Philology*
AJSL	*American Journal of Semitic Languages and Literature*
AJSR	*Association for Jewish Studies Review*
AJT	*American Journal of Theology*
Alon	Gedaliah Alon, *The Jews in Their Land in the Talmudic Age (70–640 CE)* (1980)
ANRW	*Aufstieg und Niedergang der römischen Welt*
AS	*Ancient Society*
ASTI	*Annual of the Swedish Theological Institute*
ATR	*Anglican Theological Review*
AUSS	*Andrews University Seminary Studies*
BA	*Biblical Archaeologist*
BAR	*Biblical Archaeology Review*
Baron	Salo W. Baron, *A Social and Religious History of the Jews*, vols 1 and 2 (1952)
BASOR	*Bulletin of the American Schools of Oriental Research*
BETL	*Bibliotheca Ephemeridum Theologicarum Lovaniensium*
BIOSCS	*Bulletin of the International Organization for Septuagint and Cognate Studies*
BJRL	*Bulletin of the John Rylands Library*
BT	*Bible Translator*
CBQ	*Catholic Biblical Quarterly*
CCARJ	*Central Conference of American Rabbis Journal*
CII	*Corpus Inscriptionum Iudaicarum*, ed. Jean-Baptiste Frey
CJ	*Conservative Judaism*
CP	*Classical Philology*
CPJ	*Corpus Papyrorum Judaicarum*, ed. Victor Tcherikover, Alexander Fuks, and Menahem Stern
CQ	*Classical Quarterly*
CRINT	*Compendia Rerum Iudaicarum ad Novum Testamentum*
CTJ	*Calvin Theological Journal*
CTSR	*Chicago Theological Seminary Register*
E-I	*Eretz-Israel*
EJ	*Encyclopaedia Judaica*

Feldman	Louis H. Feldman, *Jew and Gentile in the Ancient World: Attitudes and Interactions from Alexander to Justinian* (1993)
Gager	John G. Gager, *Moses in Greco-Roman Paganism* (1972)
GCAJS	*Gratz College Annual of Jewish Studies*
GR	*Gordon Review*
Gray	Rebecca Gray, *Prophetic Figures in Late Second Temple Jewish Palestine: The Evidence from Josephus* (1993)
GRBS	*Greek, Roman, and Byzantine Studies*
Hengel	Martin Hengel, *Judaism and Hellenism: Studies in Their Encounter in Palestine during the Early Hellenistic Period*. 2 vols (1974)
HJ	*Historia Judaica*
Holladay	Carl R. Holladay, *Fragments from Hellenistic Jewish Authors*, vol. 1 (1983); vol. 2 (1989)
HSCP	*Harvard Studies in Classical Philology*
HT	*History Today*
HTR	*Harvard Theological Review*
HUCA	*Hebrew Union College Annual*
IBS	*Irish Biblical Studies*
IEJ	*Israel Exploration Journal*
JBH	*Josephus, the Bible, and History*, ed. Louis H. Feldman and Gohei Hata
JBL	*Journal of Biblical Literature*
JC	*Jerusalem Cathedra*
JEA	*Journal of Egyptian Archaeology*
JES	*Journal of Ecumenical Studies*
JJC	*Josephus, Judaism, and Christianity*, ed. Louis H. Feldman and Gohei Hata
JJML	*Journal of Jewish Music and Liturgy*
JJP	*Journal of Juristic Papyri*
JJS	*Journal of Jewish Studies*
JQR	*Jewish Quarterly Review*
JR	*Journal of Religion*
JRH	*Journal of Religious History*
JRS	*Journal of Roman Studies*
JS	*Jewish Spectator*
JSJ	*Journal for the Study of Judaism*
JSNT	*Journal for the Study of the New Testament*
JSOR	*Journal of the Society of Oriental Research*
JSoS	*Jewish Social Studies*
JSS	*Journal of Semitic Studies*
JTS	*Journal of Theological Studies*
Kasher	Aryeh Kasher, *The Jews in Hellenistic and Roman Egypt: The Struggle for Equal Rights* (1985)
Kindler	Arie Kindler, *Coins of the Land of Israel* (1974)
LCL	Loeb Classical Library
Linder	Amnon Linder, *The Jews in Roman Imperial Legislation* (1987)

Mikra	*Mikra: Text, Translation, Reading and Interpretation of the Hebrew Bible in Ancient Judaism and Christianity*, ed. Martin J. Mulder (1988)
Millar	Fergus Millar, *The Roman Near East 31 BC–AD 337* (1993)
Modrzejewski	Joseph Mélèze Modrzejewski, *The Jews of Egypt from Rameses II to Emperor Hadrian* (trans. Robert Cornman) (1995)
Moore	George Foot Moore, *Judaism in the First Centuries of the Christian Era: The Age of the Tannaim*, 3 vols (1927–30)
NT	*Novum Testamentum*
NTS	*New Testament Studies*
NTT	*Nederlands Theologisch Tijdschrift*
OS	*Oudtestamentliche Studien*
OTP	*The Old Testament Pseudepigrapha*, ed. James H. Charlesworth, 2 vols (1983, 1985)
PAAJR	*Proceedings of the American Academy for Jewish Research*
PEQ	*Palestine Exploration Quarterly*
PQ	*Philological Quarterly*
RB	*Revue Biblique*
REJ	*Revue des Etudes juives*
RQ	*Revue de Qumran*
RTR	*Reformed Theological Review*
Sanders	E. P. Sanders, *Judaism: Practice and Belief 63 BCE–66 CE* (1992)
SBLSP	*Society of Biblical Literature Seminar Papers*
Schürer	Emil Schürer, *The History of the Jewish People in the Age of Jesus Christ (175 BC–AD 135)*, ed. Geza Vermes and Fergus Millar, 3 vols (1973–86)
SCI	*Scripta Classica Israelica*
SE	*Studia Evangelica*
SH	*Scripta Hierosolymitana*
Smallwood	E. Mary Smallwood, *The Jews under Roman Rule: From Pompey to Diocletian* (1976)
SP	*Studia Patristica*
SPA	*Studia Philonica Annual*
SR	*Studies in Religion/Sciences Religieuses*
ST	*Studia Theologica*
Sterling	Gregory E. Sterling, *Historiography and Self-Definition: Josephos, Luke–Acts and Apologetic Historiography* (1992)
Stern	Menahem Stern, *Greek and Latin Authors on Jews and Judaism*, 3 vols (1974–84)
TAPA	*Transactions of the American Philological Association*
Tcherikover	Victor Tcherikover, *Hellenistic Civilization and the Jews* (1959)
TDNT	*Theological Dictionary of the New Testament*, ed. Gerhard Kittel and Gerhard Friedrich
TE	*Theologia Evangelica*
TS	*Theological Studies*
TU	*Texte und Untersuchungen*

TZ	*Theologische Zeitschrift*
USQR	*Union Seminary Quarterly Review*
VC	*Vigiliae Christianae*
VT	*Vetus Testamentum*
Wacholder	Ben Zion Wacholder, *Eupolemus: A Study of Judaeo-Greek Literature* (1974)
YCS	*Yale Classical Studies*
ZAW	*Zeitschrift für die alttestamentliche Wissenschaft*
ZNW	*Zeitschrift für die neutestamentliche Wissenschaft*
ZPE	*Zeitschrift für Papyrologie und Epigraphik*

Names of Translators

A.C.	Abraham Cohen
A.Ca.	Alexander Carlebach
A.F.	Augustine Fitzgerald
A.L.	Amnon Linder
B.J.B.	Bernard J. Bamberger
C.B.	Christoph Burchard
CPJ	*Corpus Papyrorum Judaicarum*, 3 vols, ed. Victor A. Tcherikover, Alexander Fuks, and Menahem Stern (Cambridge: Harvard University Press, 1957–64)
C.R.H.	Carl R. Holladay
D.A.R.	D. A. Russell
E.H.G.	Edwin H. Gifford
G.B.G.	George Buchanan Gray
G.H.B.	George H. Box
H.C.	Henry Chadwick
H.C.K.	Howard C. Kee
H.T.A.	Herbert T. Andrews
I.H.	Isaak Heinemann
J.L.	Jack Lightstone
LCL	Loeb Classical Library (Cambridge: Harvard University Press)
L.H.F.	Louis H. Feldman
L.H.S.	Lawrence H. Schiffman
M.H.	Moses Hadas
M.R.	Meyer Reinhold
M.S.	Menahem Stern
N.L.	Naphtali Lewis
R.H.C.	Robert H. Charles
R.P.	Raphael Patai
RSV	Revised Standard Version of the Bible
R.W.	Richard Walzer
Soncino	Soncino translation of the Talmud (ed. Isidore Epstein; London: Soncino Press, 35 vols, 1935–52) and Midrash (ed. Harry Freedman and Maurice Simon, 10 vols; London: Soncino Press, 1977)

S.T.	Sidney Tedesche
T.H.G.	Theodor H. Gaster
W.H. and D.N.	William Horbury and David Noy
Y.Y.	Yigael Yadin

Illustrations

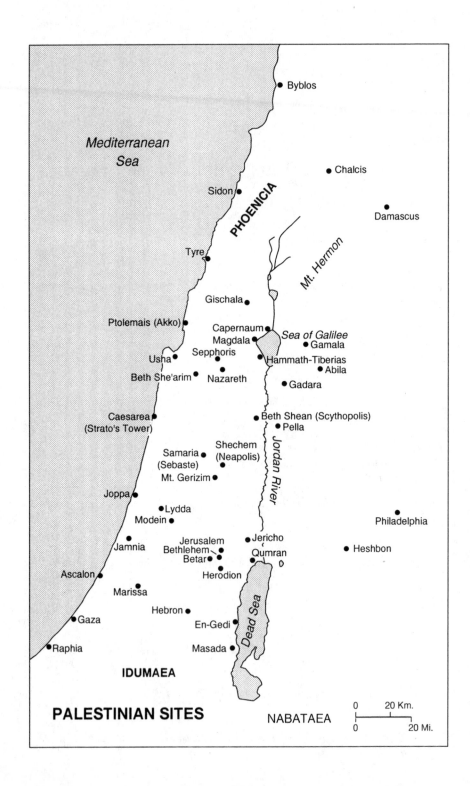

Byblos

Mediterranean Sea

Chalcis

Sidon

PHOENICIA

Damascus

Tyre

Mt. Hermon

Gischala

Ptolemais (Akko)

Capernaum

Sea of Galilee

Magdala

Gamala

Usha

Sepphoris

Hammath-Tiberias

Abila

Beth She'arim

Nazareth

Gadara

Caesarea
(Strato's Tower)

Beth Shean (Scythopolis)

Pella

Shechem
(Neapolis)

Samaria
(Sebaste)

Jordan River

Mt. Gerizim

Joppa

Lydda

Modein

Philadelphia

Jericho

Jamnia

Jerusalem

Qumran

Heshbon

Bethlehem

Betar

Ascalon

Herodion

Dead Sea

Marissa

Hebron

Gaza

En-Gedi

Raphia

Masada

IDUMAEA

PALESTINIAN SITES

NABATAEA

0   20 Km.

0   20 Mi.

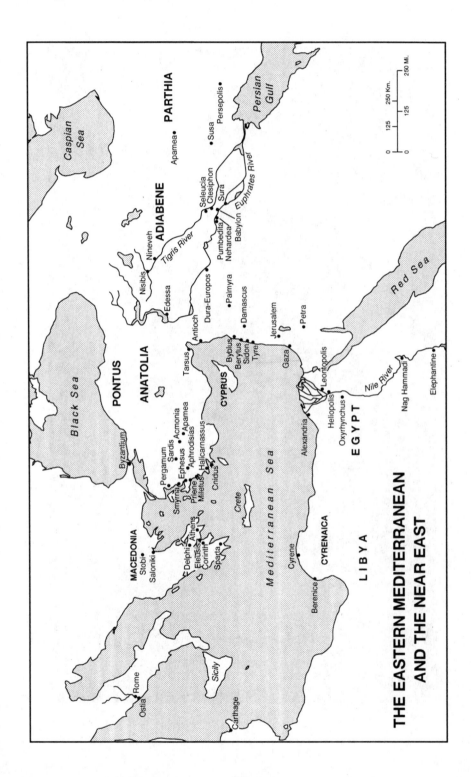

THE EASTERN MEDITERRANEAN AND THE NEAR EAST

Aaron at the Temple, from the assembly room of the synagogue at Dura-Europos, ca. 250 CE.

1

❦

The Greeks Discover the Jews

Contacts between Greeks and Jews go back at least to biblical times. Japheth (whose name reminds us of Iapetos, the father of Prometheus), one of the sons of Noah (Gen 6:10), is the father of Javan (reminiscent of Greek Ion, the ancestor of the Ionians of Asia Minor), who is said, for example, by Josephus (*Jewish Antiquities* 1.124), to be the ancestor of all the Greeks. Moreover, it is probable (2 Sam 20:23, 1 Kgs 1:38) that in the tenth century BCE King David employed mercenaries from the island of Crete. The discovery of Greek pottery in such sites as Samaria indicates commercial contacts as early as the eighth century BCE. As early as the fifth century BCE Jews minted coins with the characteristic Athenian emblem of the owl. A Greek poet named Choerilus is cited by Josephus (*Against Apion* 1.172–3) as referring to Jews in the army of the Persian king Xerxes during his invasion of Greece in 480 BCE.

The Jewish people survived the destruction of their nation of Judaea by the Babylonians in 586 BCE, though it is estimated (in view of the destruction of the ten tribes constituting the Kingdom of Israel in 722–721 BCE and the great losses in numerous wars) that their number had been reduced to a mere 150,000.[1] After its restoration under the Persians by Cyrus the Great's edict in 538 BCE, as mentioned in Isa 44:28 and Ezra 1:2–4, Judaea became, in effect, a theocratic state (under Persian rule) centered around the Temple in Jerusalem.

Alexander (356–323 BCE) and the Jews

BIBLIOGRAPHY

Ralph Marcus, "Alexander the Great and the Jews," Appendix C, in his translation of Josephus, vol. 6 (LCL, 1937), 512–32.
Tcherikover (1959), 41–50.
Cecil H. R. Martin, "Alexander and the High Priest," *Transactions of the Glasgow University Oriental Society* 23 (1969–70), 102–14.
Arnaldo Momigliano, "Flavius Josephus and Alexander's Visit to Jerusalem," *Athenaeum* 57 (1979), 442–8.
Shaye J. D. Cohen, "Alexander the Great and Jaddus the High Priest according to Josephus," *AJSR* 7–9 (1982–3), 41–68.
Modrzejewski (1995), 47–55.

A truly new era opens with the conquest of Judaea by Alexander the Great in 332 BCE. As an indication of the high regard which the Jews had

---

1. Salo W. Baron, "Population," *Encyclopedia Judaica* 13 (1971), 869.

for him it is said that they named all baby boys born in that year Alexander. Many are the stories in rabbinic literature about him, particularly noting the honor that he gave to the high priest Simeon the Just, the special privileges that he granted to the Jews, and his rejection of the Samaritans.[2]

1.1 Babylonian Talmud, *Yoma* 69a (edited *ca.* 500 CE)

The following excerpt from the Talmud (which mentions no specific rabbi as its source) illustrates the high regard that Alexander is said to have had for the high priest and his rejection of the Samaritans, who are here referred to as Cutheans, so called from the district of Cuthah in Mesopotamia from which they are said to have emanated, and who had rebelled against Alexander (as we also learn from the first-century Roman writer Curtius Rufus [*History of Alexander the Great* 4.8.34.9]). Samaritan papyri found in 1962 in caves at Wadi Daliyeh west of the River Jordan and dating from this period may, it is thought, belong to Samaritan fugitives from this abortive rebellion.

The twenty-fifth of Tebeth is the day of Mount Gerizim,[3] on which no mourning is permitted. It is the day on which the Cutheans demanded the House of our God from Alexander the Macedonian so as to destroy it, and he had given them the permission, whereupon some people came and informed [the high priest] Simeon the Just.[4] What did the latter do? He put on his priestly garments . . . ; some of the noblemen of Israel went with him carrying fiery torches in their hands; they walked all the night . . . until the dawn rose.

When the dawn rose he [Alexander] said to them [the Jewish noblemen]: 'Who are these [the Samaritans]?' They answered: 'The Jews who rebelled against you.' As he reached Antipatris,[5] the sun having shone forth, they [Alexander and Simeon] met. When he saw Simeon the Just, he descended from his carriage and bowed down before him. They [the Jewish noblemen] said to him: 'A great king like yourself should bow down before this Jew?' He answered: 'His image it is which wins for me in all my battles.' He said to them: 'What have you come for?' They said: 'Is it possible that star-worshippers should mislead you to destroy the House wherein prayers are said for you and your kingdom that it should be never destroyed?' He said to them: 'Who are these?' They

---

2. The Bible (2 Kings 17) describes the Samaritans as descendants of the heathen from Mesopotamia whom the Assyrian king Sargon II settled in Samaria after the destruction of the Kingdom of Israel. The Samaritans themselves assert that they are the direct descendants of the Joseph tribes, Ephraim and Manasseh. They do not accept the validity of the Oral Torah (as codified in the Talmud) but only the written Torah, the Pentateuch, their text of which differs in many places from the Masoretic Text. Their sacred temple is not in Jerusalem but on Mount Gerizim in Samaria.

3. The site where the Samaritans had their temple.

4. According to Josephus (*Ant.* 12.43) Simeon is to be identified with Simeon I (died *ca.* 270 BCE), the son of Onias I and the grandson of Jaddua, who was the high priest in the days of Nehemiah (Neh 12:11, 22). According to the Talmud (*Menaḥoth* 109b), he is to be identified with Simeon II, the father of the Onias who built the temple at Leontopolis in Egypt *ca.* 175 BCE.

5. A city on the northern boundary of the territory of Judaea.

said to him: 'These are Cutheans who stand before you.' He said: 'They are delivered into your hand.' At once they perforated their heels, tied them to the tails of their horses and dragged them over thorns and thistles, until they came to Mount Gerizim, which they ploughed and planted with vetch, even as they had planned to do with the House of God. And that day they made a festive day. (Soncino)

1.2 Josephus, *Antiquities* 11.331–9

The following account, which parallels the above passage in the Talmud, likewise illustrates Alexander's regard for the high priest and mentions the special privileges that Alexander gave to the Jews both in Judaea and in the Diaspora. Of particular interest is the statement that many Jews joined Alexander's army and while serving therein were permitted to observe their traditional Jewish practices.

When Alexander while still far off saw the multitude in white garments, the priests at their head clothed in linen, and the high priest in a robe of hyacinth-blue and gold, wearing on his head the mitre with the golden plate on it on which was inscribed the name of God, he approached alone and prostrated himself before the Name and first greeted the high priest. Then all the Jews together greeted Alexander with one voice and surrounded him, but the kings of Syria and the others were struck with amazement at his action and supposed that the king's mind was deranged.

And Parmenion[6] alone went up to him and asked why, indeed, when all men prostrated themselves before him, he had prostrated himself before the high priest of the Jews, whereupon he replied, 'It was not before him that I prostrated myself but the God of whom he has the honor to be high priest, for it was he whom I saw in my sleep dressed as he is now, when I was at Dium in Macedonia; and, as I was considering with myself how I might become master of Asia, he urged me not to hesitate but to cross over confidently, for he himself would lead my army and give over to me the empire of the Persians. Since, therefore, I have beheld no one else in such robes, and on seeing him now I am reminded of the vision and the exhortation, I believe that I have made this expedition under divine guidance and that I shall defeat Darius and destroy the power of the Persians and succeed in carrying out all the things which I have in mind.'

After saying these things to Parmenion, he gave his hand to the high priest and, with the Jews running beside him, entered the city [of Jerusalem]. Then he went up to the Temple, where he sacrificed to God under the direction of the high priest, and showed due honor to the priests and to the high priest himself. And when the book of Daniel was shown to him, in which he had declared that one of the Greeks would destroy the empire of the Persians,[7] he believed himself to be the one indicated; and in his joy he dismissed the multitude for the time being, but on the following day he summoned them again and

6. Macedonian general, second in command to Alexander.
7. Presumably a reference to Dan 8:21.

told them to ask for any gifts which they might desire. When the high priest asked that they might observe their country's laws and in the seventh year[8] be exempt from tribute, he granted all this. Then they begged that he would permit the Jews in Babylon and Media also to have their own laws, and he gladly promised to do as they asked. And when he said to the people that if any wished to join his army while still adhering to the customs of their country, he was ready to take them, many eagerly accepted service with him. (LCL)

Rights Given by Alexander to Jews in Alexandria

BIBLIOGRAPHY
Kasher (1985), 168–91.

   1.3 Josephus, *Against Apion* 2.33, 34–5, 37–40, 42–4

When Alexander the Great founded the city of Alexandria in 332 BCE, he sought to make it a center of Greek civilization. Realizing that Greeks and Macedonians constituted only a small portion of the population, he invited the Jews of Judaea to help found the city and even, according to Josephus (although this is disputed by scholars), granted them citizenship. The Jews flocked to the city, which soon became the greatest commercial and cultural center of the Mediterranean, displacing even Athens. Their privileged position, according to Josephus, was confirmed by Alexander's successor in Egypt, Ptolemy I. There was no ghetto, but in the first century BCE the Jews predominated in two of the five sections of the city, numbering, it is estimated, 200,000 of the half million inhabitants. In the passage below Josephus is refuting the charge of the first-century anti-Jewish Egyptian, Apion, that the Jews are not citizens of Alexandria.

Let us look at the terrible and shocking things with which Apion has charged the Jews living in Alexandria. 'They came,' he says, 'from Syria and settled by a seacoast without a harbor . . .' [But] the seaboard is part of the city as all agree, the best residential quarter. If the Jews occupied this by force and remained there subsequently, that is evidence of their valor. But in fact Alexander granted them this district as residence,[9] and they obtained privileges equal to those of the Macedonians. . . . If Apion had read the letters of King Alexander and of Ptolemy son of Lagus, if he had come upon the documents of the kings of Egypt after him, if he had seen the stele standing in Alexandria containing the rights granted the Jews by [Julius] Caesar the Great; if then, I say, he knew these documents and had the nerve to write the opposite, he was a scoundrel; if he had no knowledge of them, he was ignorant.

   8. The sabbatical year (*shemittah*, Lev 25:2), when Jews must allow the land of Palestine to lie fallow.
   9. It was, in fact, not Alexander but Ptolemy I Soter, the reputed son of Lagus, who made this grant.

And his being astonished that Jews should be called Alexandrians[10] reveals similar ignorance. All those invited to join a colony, even if they differ widely in their nationality, receive their name from the founders. Why must one speak of other peoples? Those of us who reside in Antioch are called Antiochenes, for they were granted citizenship by the founder Seleucus. Similarly, those at Ephesus and throughout the rest of Ionia have the same name as the native citizens, a right granted by the successors of Alexander. Have not the generous Romans shared their name with almost all mankind, not to individuals only, but to entire great peoples? . . .

This privilege [of joining in the founding of Alexandria] was granted to our people by Alexander, who, after careful scrutiny approved our valor and fidelity. Indeed, he honored our people, as Hecataeus[11] also says about us, in that, in recognition of the goodwill and loyalty which the Jews showed him, he added [to Judaea] possession of the region of Samaria, free from tribute.

Alexander's opinion of the Jews residing in Alexandria was shared by Ptolemy son of Lagus.[12] As a matter of fact, he entrusted the fortresses of Egypt to them, thinking that they would guard them loyally and bravely. And when he wished to strengthen his hold on Cyrene and the other cities of Libya, he sent out a part of the Jews to settle in them. (M.R.)

Earliest References to the Jews in Greek Literature

Herodotus

BIBLIOGRAPHY
Stern, vol. 1 (1974), 1–5.

1.4 Herodotus (*ca.* 480–*ca.* 425 BCE) 2.104.2–3

The earliest mention of the Jews in Greek literature is to be found in the historian Herodotus, though, to be sure, he calls them Syrians of Palestine and does not mention them by name. Despite his great interest in the customs of various peoples, he apparently never visited Judaea and refers only to their being circumcised, a practice which, according to Herodotus, the Syrians of Palestine learned from the Egyptians.

The Colchians[13] and Egyptians and Ethiopians are the only nations that have from the first practiced circumcision. The Phoenicians and the Syrians of Palestine acknowledge of themselves that they learnt the custom from the Egyptians. (LCL)

10. At issue is whether the Jews were citizens of the city of Alexandria and whether "Alexandrians" denoted residents of Alexandria or citizens of that city.
11. Hecataeus of Abdera, fourth century BCE Greek historian, extant only in fragments, who incorporated a relatively extensive and favorable account of the Jews in his history of Egypt.
12. Ptolemy I, founder of the dynasty of the Ptolemies, ruled Egypt as satrap from 323 BCE, when Alexander died. He assumed the title of king in 305 BCE, and remained in power until his death in 283 BCE.
13. A people who lived at the eastern end of the Black Sea.

Aristotle

BIBLIOGRAPHY

Eisig Silberschlag, "The Earliest Record of the Jews in Asia Minor," *JBL* 53 (1933), 66–77.

Hans Lewy, "Aristotle and the Jewish Sage according to Clearchus of Soli," *HTR* 31 (1938), 205–35.

Stern, vol. 1 (1974), 47–52.

> 1.5 Aristotle (384–322 BCE), cited by Clearchus of Soli (*ca.* 300 BCE), *On Sleep*, quoted by Josephus, *Against Apion* 1.176–82

Most scholars suspect that the incident, here recounted, of Aristotle's meeting with a Jew in Asia Minor, is apocryphal. But whether the meeting ever took place or not, the fact that Clearchus, a pupil of the famous Aristotle, could have thought that it occurred indicates that a high opinion of the Jews as a nation of philosophers, related to the famed philosophers of India no less, seemed plausible.

Clearchus, a disciple of Aristotle, and in the very first rank of Peripatetic philosophers, relates, in his first book *On Sleep*, the following anecdote told of a certain Jew by his master. He puts the words into the mouth of Aristotle himself. I quote the text: 'It would take too long to repeat the whole story, but there were features in that man's character, at once strangely marvelous and philosophical, which merit description. I warn you, Hyperochides,' he said, 'that what I am about to say will seem to you as wonderful as a dream.' Hyperochides respectfully replied, 'That is the very reason why we are all anxious to hear it.' 'Well,' said Aristotle, 'in accordance with the precepts of rhetoric, let us begin by describing his race, in order to keep to the rules of our masters in the art of narration.' 'Tell the story as you please,' said Hyperochides.

'Well,' he replied, 'the man was a Jew of Coele-Syria.[14] These people are descended from the Indian philosophers. The philosophers, they say, are in India called Calani,[15] in Syria by the territorial name of Jews; for the district which they inhabit is known as Judaea. Their city has a remarkably odd name; they call it Hierusaleme. Now this man, who was entertained by a large circle of friends and was on his way down from the interior to the coast, not only spoke Greek, but had the soul of a Greek. During my stay in Asia, he visited the same places as I did, and came to converse with me and some other scholars, to test our learning. But as one who had been intimate with many cultivated persons, it was rather he who imparted to us something of his own.' These are the words of Aristotle as reported by Clearchus, and he went on to speak of the great and astonishing endurance and sobriety displayed by this Jew in his manner of life. Further information can be obtained, if desired, from the book itself; I forbear to quote more than is necessary. (LCL)

14. Southern Syria, including Judaea.
15. Calanus was the name of a Brahman Indian sage who burnt himself to death in the presence of Alexander's army (Plutarch, *Alexander* 65), thereby, according to one report, creating such an impression that the Indians referred to all wise men as Calani.

Theophrastus

BIBLIOGRAPHY

Max Radin, *The Jews among the Greeks and Romans* (1915), 81–4.

Werner Jaeger, "Greeks and Jews: The First Greek Records of Jewish Religion and Civilization," *JR* 18 (1938), 127–43.

Menahem Stern and Oswyn Murray, "Hecataeus of Abdera and Theophrastus on Jews and Egyptians," *JEA* 59 (1973), 159–68.

Stern, vol. 1 (1974), 8–17.

1.6 Theophrastus (372–288 BCE), *On Piety*, quoted by Porphyry (third century CE), *On Abstinence* 2.26

Theophrastus, whose primary interest was botany, succeeded his teacher Aristotle as the head of the Peripatetic school of philosophy in Athens. In the fragment cited below from his otherwise lost treatise on piety, he expresses disapproval of animal sacrifice but notes that though the Syrians, of whom the Jews constitute a part, actually instituted such sacrifices they did so only under compulsion and, in any case, follow a method different from that of the Greeks. Like Aristotle, he offers the Jews the extreme praise of referring to them as philosophers by race. His description of Jewish sacrifices is the earliest that we have outside of the Bible; but it contains a number of errors: sacrifices were made during the day, not at night; honey and wine were not used; humans were not sacrificed; there was no cult of stars.

Among the Syrians the Jews, following primitive practice, even now . . . sacrifice live victims. If one ordered us to sacrifice in the same manner, we would shrink from the practice. Indeed, they do not eat the sacrificial victims, but sacrifice whole burned offerings at night, and, pouring much honey and wine over them, they complete the sacrifice swiftly, so that the sun may not be witness to the horror. And they do this while fasting on intervening days. All this time, being a race of philosophers, they converse with each other about divinity; and during the night they view the stars, turning their eyes to them and invoking God with prayers. They were the first to sacrifice both other animals and also humans, doing this out of necessity and not from any inclination for it. (M.R.)

Hecataeus of Abdera

BIBLIOGRAPHY

Werner Jaeger, "Greeks and Jews: The First Greek Records of Jewish Religion and Civilization," *JR* 18 (1938), 127–43.

Peter M. Fraser, *Ptolemaic Alexandria*, vol. 1 (1972), 496–505.

Gager (1972), 26–37.

Menahem Stern and Oswyn Murray, "Hecataeus of Abdera and Theophrastus on Jews and Egyptians," *JEA* 59 (1973), 159–68.

Stern, vol. 1 (1974), 20–35.

Doron Mendels, "Hecataeus of Abdera and a Jewish 'Patrios Politeia' of the Persian Period (Diodorus Siculus XL, 3)," *ZAW* 95 (1983), 96–110.

Sterling (1992), 59–78.

1.7 Hecataeus of Abdera (*ca.* 300 BCE), *History of Egypt,* quoted by Diodorus of Sicily (latter part of the first century BCE), *Historical Library* 40.3

The most extensive of extant earliest accounts of the Jews by non-Jews is by a historian named Hecataeus of Abdera (in northern Greece), who visited Egypt and presumably derived his information about Jews from there. Except for the statement that Jews lead an unsocial and intolerant mode of life, the passage is extremely complimentary toward the Jews and, in particular, toward Moses. Even such errors as that Moses founded Jerusalem, that he established the Temple, that the Jews never have a king, and that Moses assigned greater allotments of land to the priests are clearly complimentary in intent. The statement that the Jews were expelled from Egypt because of a pestilence is not anti-Jewish, since they are coupled with such famous Greek mythical leaders as Danaus and Cadmus. According to Hecataeus, the Jews changed their way of life only after contact with other nations during the Persian and Hellenistic periods.

When in ancient times a pestilence arose in Egypt, the common people ascribed their troubles to the workings of a divine agency; for indeed with many strangers of all sorts dwelling in their midst and practicing different rites of religion and sacrifice, their own traditional observances in honor of the gods had fallen into disuse. Hence the natives of the land surmised that unless they removed the foreigners, their troubles would never be resolved. At once, therefore, the aliens were driven from the country, and the most outstanding and active among them banded together and, as some say, were cast ashore in Greece and certain other regions; their leaders were notable men, chief among them being Danaus and Cadmus.[16] But the greater number were driven into what is now called Judaea, which is not far distant from Egypt and was at that time utterly uninhabited.

The colony was headed by a man called Moses, outstanding both for his wisdom and for his courage. On taking possession of the land he founded, besides other cities, one that is now the most renowned of all, called Jerusalem. In addition he established the Temple that they hold in chief veneration, instituted their forms of worship and ritual, drew up their laws and ordered their political institutions. He also divided them into twelve tribes, since this is regarded as the most perfect number and corresponds to the number of months that make up a year. But he had no images whatsoever of the gods made for them, being of the opinion that God is not in human form; rather the Heaven that surrounds the earth is alone divine and rules the universe. The sacrifices that he established differ from those of other nations, as does their way of living, for as a result of their own expulsion from Egypt he introduced an unsocial and intolerant mode of life.

16. According to the usual form of the myth, told in Aeschylus' tragedy, *Suppliants,* Danaus had fifty daughters, and his brother Aegyptus had fifty sons in Egypt. The brothers quarreled, and Danaus fled with his daughters to Argos in Greece, where he became king. Cadmus (who is usually said to have been king of Phoenicia) is known as the founder of the city of Thebes in Greece.

He picked out men of most refinement and with the greatest ability to head the entire nation, and appointed them priests; and he ordained that they should occupy themselves with the Temple and the honors and sacrifices offered to their God. These same men he appointed to be judges in all major disputes, and entrusted to them the guardianship of the laws and customs. For this reason the Jews never have a king,[17] and authority over the people is regularly vested in whatever priest is regarded as superior to his colleagues in wisdom and virtue. They call this man the high priest, and believe that he acts as a messenger to them of God's commandments. It is he, we are told, who in their assemblies and other gatherings announces what is ordained; and the Jews are so docile[18] in such matters that straightway they fall to the ground and do reverence to the high priest when he expounds the commandments to them. And at the end of the laws there is even appended the statement: 'These are the words that Moses heard from God and declares unto the Jews.'[19]

Their lawgiver was careful also to make provision for warfare, and required the young men to cultivate manliness, steadfastness, and, generally, the endurance of every hardship. He led out military expeditions against the neighboring tribes, and after annexing much land apportioned it out, assigning equal allotments to private citizens and greater ones to the priests,[20] in order that they, by virtue of receiving more ample revenues, might be undistracted and apply themselves continually to the worship of God.

The common citizens were forbidden to sell their individual plots, lest there be some who for their own advantage should buy them up, and by oppressing the poorer classes bring on a scarcity of manpower.[21] He required those who dwelt in the land to rear their children,[22] and since offspring could be cared for at little cost, the Jews were from the start a populous nation.

As to marriage and the burial of the dead, he saw to it that their customs should differ widely from those of other men. But later, when they became subject to foreign rule, as a result of their mingling with men of other nations (both under Persian rule and under that of the

---

17. Hecataeus is clearly unaware that the Jews had kings for hundreds of years in Judaea and Israel. His error is apparently derived from the fact that at the time he was writing they were no longer independent.

18. The credulity of the Jews is a frequent motif in pagan literature. Perhaps it derived from the fact that at Sinai, according to the Pentateuch, when offered the Pentateuch, before even knowing its contents, they responded that they would obey it.

19. This sentence is not found at the end of the Pentateuch. Perhaps Hecataeus is thinking of Deut 28:69, somewhat before the end of the Pentateuch: "These are the words of the covenant which the Lord commanded Moses to make with the people of Israel in the land of Moab."

20. Hecataeus' statement is contradicted by the Pentateuch, which states that Levites (and priests) were not allotted a share in the land (Deut 18:1).

21. Presumably Hecataeus is referring to the law (Lev 25:13) that sale of land in Palestine was to be temporary, with the former owner regaining the land in the Jubilee (fiftieth) year.

22. Hecataeus is here contrasting the Jewish attitude with that of the Greeks, who practiced infanticide.

Macedonians who overthrew the Persians), many of their traditional practices were disturbed. Such is the account of Hecataeus of Abdera in regard to the Jews. (LCL)

(Pseudo-)Hecataeus

BIBLIOGRAPHY

John J. Gager, "Pseudo-Hecataeus Again," *ZNW* 60 (1969), 130–9.
Stern, vol. 1 (1974), 35–44.
Wacholder (1974), 266–74.
Holladay, vol. 1 (1983), 277–335.
Robert Doran, "Pseudo-Hecataeus," *OTP* 2 (1985), 905–19.
Sterling (1992), 78–91.

> *1.8* (Pseudo-)Hecataeus (second century BCE), *On the Jews*, cited by Josephus, *Against Apion* 1.186–204

A number of fragments from two works – *On the Jews* and *On Abraham (and the Egyptians)* – attributed to Hecataeus of Abdera and cited by Josephus and Eusebius are generally regarded by scholars as coming from a Jewish author; indeed, Herennius Philo (in Origen, *Against Celsus* 1.15), who lived in the second half of the first century to the first half of the second century CE, had already expressed doubt as to the authenticity on the ground that the remarks were too favorable to the Jews; but the fragments appear to stop short of the kind of glorification that a Jewish forger would have been expected to produce. Though the provenance is unknown, there seems good reason to believe that the work was composed in Egypt, inasmuch as the author gives great prominence to Egypt. The date of composition is most likely at some time around the middle of the second century BCE.

The following excerpt tells of the settlement in Egypt by a group of Jews led by the chief priest Ezechias not long after the death of Alexander the Great. It compliments the Jews for their stubborn adherence to their laws and for their clever refutation of the validity of the Greek rite of augury. It has a highly appreciative description of Jerusalem and of the Temple worship.

Josephus refers to the role taken, according to Hecataeus of Abdera, by the Jews in the campaigns of Alexander the Great. He mentions an incident which Hecataeus himself says he witnessed.

Hecataeus goes on to say that after the battle of Gaza [312 BCE] Ptolemy [I] became master of Syria, and that many of the inhabitants, hearing of his kindliness and humanity, desired to accompany him to Egypt and to associate themselves with his realm. 'Among these (he says) was Ezechias, a chief priest of the Jews, a man of about sixty-six years of age, highly esteemed by his countrymen, intellectual, and moreover an able speaker and unsurpassed as a man of business. Yet (he adds) the total number of Jewish priests who receive a tithe of the revenue and administer public affairs is about fifteen hundred.' Reverting to Ezechias, he says: 'This man, after obtaining this honor and having been closely in touch with us, assembled some of his friends and read to them his whole scroll, in which was written the story of their settlement and the constitution of the state.'

In another passage Hecataeus mentions our regard for our laws, and how we deliberately choose and hold it a point of honor to endure anything rather than transgress them. 'And so (he says), neither the slander of their neighbors and of foreign visitors, to which as a nation they are exposed, nor the frequent outrages of Persian kings and satraps[23] can shake their determination; for these laws, naked and defenseless, they face tortures and death in its most terrible form, rather than repudiate the faith of their forefathers.'

Of this obstinacy in defense of their laws he furnishes several instances. He tells how on one occasion Alexander, when he was at Babylon and had undertaken to restore the ruined temple of Bel, gave orders to all his soldiers, without distinction, to bring materials for the earthworks; and how the Jews alone refused to obey, and even submitted to severe chastisement and heavy fines, until the king pardoned them and exempted them from this task. Again, when temples and altars were erected in the country by its invaders, the Jews razed them all to the ground, paying in some cases a fine to the satraps, and in others obtaining pardon. For such conduct, he adds, they deserve admiration.

Then he goes on to speak of our vast population, stating that though many myriads of our race had already been deported to Babylon by the Persians, yet after Alexander's death myriads more migrated to Egypt and Phoenicia in consequence of the disturbed condition of Syria.

The same writer has referred to the extent and beauty of the country which we inhabit in the following words: 'They occupy almost three million *arourae*[24] of the most excellent and fertile soil, productive of every variety of fruits. Such is the extent of Judaea.'

Again, here is his description of Jerusalem itself, the city which we have inhabited from remote ages, of its great beauty and extent, its numerous population, and the temple buildings: 'The Jews have many fortresses and villages in different parts of the country, but only one fortified city, which has a circumference of about fifty stades[25] and some hundred and twenty thousand inhabitants; they call it Jerusalem. Nearly in the center of the city stands a stone wall, enclosing an area about five plethra long and a hundred cubits broad,[26] approached by a pair of gates. Within this enclosure is a square altar, built of heaped up stones, unhewn and unwrought; each side is twenty cubits long and the height ten cubits. Beside it stands a great edifice, containing an altar and a lamp-stand, both made of gold, and weighing two talents;[27] upon these is a light which is never extinguished by night or day. There is not

23. Perhaps this is a reference to the attempt of Haman, as mentioned in the Book of Esther, to wipe out the Jewish people.

24. An *aroura* was an Egyptian measure of land equivalent to about half an acre. Three million *arourae* would be approximately 2,300 square miles. By comparison, the state of Israel in the pre–1967 borders consisted of approximately 8,000 square miles.

25. A stade was approximately one-eighth of a mile.

26. Five plethra would be about 500 feet. A hundred cubits was about 150 feet.

27. Approximately 120 lb.

a single statue or votive offering, no trace of a plant, in the form of a sacred grove or the like. Here priests pass their nights and days performing certain rites of purification, and abstaining altogether from wine while in the temple.'

The author further attests the share which the Jews took in the campaigns both of King Alexander and of his successors. One incident on the march, in which a Jewish soldier was concerned, he states that he witnessed himself. I will give the story in his own words: 'When I was on the march towards the Red Sea, among the escort of Jewish cavalry which accompanied us was one named Mosollamus, a very intelligent man, robust, and, by common consent, the very best of bowmen, whether Greek or barbarian. This man, observing that a number of men were going to and fro on the route and that the whole force was being held up by a seer who was taking the auspices, inquired why they were halting. The seer pointed out to him the bird he was observing, and told him that if it stayed in that spot it was expedient for them all to halt; if it stirred and flew forward, to advance; if backward, then to retire. The Jew, without saying a word, drew his bow, shot and struck the bird, and killed it. The seer and some others were indignant, and heaped curses upon him. 'Why so mad, you poor wretches?' he retorted; and then, taking the bird in his hands, continued, 'Pray, how could any sound information about our march be given by this creature, which could not provide for its own safety? Had it been gifted with divination, it would not have come to this spot, for fear of being killed by an arrow of Mosollamus the Jew.' (LCL)

Megasthenes

BIBLIOGRAPHY
Allan Dahlquist, *Megasthenes and Indian Religion: A Study in Motives and Types* (1962).
Stern, vol. 1 (1974), 45–6.
Sterling (1992), 92–102.

1.9 Megasthenes (*ca.* 300 BCE), *Indica*, cited by Clement of Alexandria (end of second and beginning of third century CE), *Coverings* 1.15.72.5

Like Theophrastus and Clearchus, Megasthenes compliments the Jews as a race of philosophers; and his comparison of the Jews with the Indian Brahmans is reminiscent of Clearchus' comparison of the Jews with the Indian Calani.

Megasthenes, the writer who was a contemporary of Seleucus Nicator,[28] writes in the third book of his *Indica*: 'All the opinions expressed by the ancients about nature are found also among the philosophers outside Greece, some among the Indian Brahmans and others in Syria among those called Jews.' (M.S.)

---

28. Seleucus Nicator, the founder of the Seleucid dynasty of Syria, accompanied Alexander in his campaigns and won distinction particularly in the campaign in India.

Hermippus of Smyrna

BIBLIOGRAPHY

Stern, vol. 1 (1974), 93–6.

Howard Jacobson, "Hermippus, Pythagoras and the Jews," *REJ* 135 (1976), 145–9.

1.10 Hermippus of Smyrna (*ca.* 200 BCE), *On Pythagoras*, cited by Josephus, *Against Apion* 1.162–5

Pythagoras, the famous Greek mathematician and philosopher who lived in the sixth century BCE, was the founder of a monastic-like brotherhood, bound by strict vows to their leader, in Crotona in Italy. He is said to have traveled in Egypt and the East. Hermippus of Smyrna, an Aristotelian who wrote biographies of philosophers, notes Pythagoras' indebtedness to the Jews.

Now Pythagoras of Samos, who belongs to olden times and is considered to have excelled all the philosophers in wisdom and piety to the divine, evidently not only knew our practices but also became an enthusiastic admirer of them. It is acknowledged that we possess no composition of his, but his views have been recorded by many writers. The most distinguished of these is Hermippus, always a careful historian. Now in the first book of his work on Pythagoras he states that Pythagoras, on the death of one of his disciples, named Calliphon, a native of Crotona, stated that his pupil's soul was with him night and day and counseled him not to pass by a certain spot on which an ass had collapsed,[29] to abstain from thirst-producing water,[30] and to refrain from blasphemy.[31] Then he continued as follows: 'In so doing and in stating these precepts, he was imitating and appropriating to himself the doctrines of Jews and Thracians.' In fact, it is said that that great man actually took over many points of Jewish law into his philosophy. (M.R.)

Antonius Diogenes

BIBLIOGRAPHY

Stern, vol. 1 (1974), 536–7.

1.11 Antonius Diogenes (end of the first century CE), cited by Porphyry (third century CE), *Life of Pythagoras* 11

Antonius Diogenes, who is the author of a romance in which his hero and heroine meet each other at the end of the earth, repeats the tradition that

---

29. Presumably the reference is to Exod 23:5: "If you see the ass of one who hates you lying under its burden, you shall refrain from leaving him with it; you shall help him to lift it up."

30. Perhaps the reference is to the prohibition (Mishnah, *Terumoth* 8:4) against drinking certain liquids that have been left uncovered because they have been poisoned by a snake.

31. Presumably the reference is to Exod 22:27 ("The judges thou shalt not revile; and a ruler among thy people thou shalt not curse") or to Lev 19:16 ("Thou shalt not go up and down as a talebearer among thy people").

Pythagoras traveled in the East. He asserts that Pythagoras borrowed from the Jews his knowledge of the interpretation of dreams, which in antiquity was regarded as the height of wisdom.

He [Diogenes] says that Pythagoras came also to the Egyptians, the Arabs, the Chaldeans, and the Hebrews, from whom he learnt the exact knowledge of dreams.[32] (M.S.)

32. The supposed skill of Jews in interpreting dreams apparently went back to Joseph. See the remarks of Pompeius Trogus below.

The Pharos Lighthouse of Alexandria (reconstruction after Adler), built by Sostratus of Cnidus for Ptolemy II, ca. 280 BCE.

2

꒰ꑦꑦ꒱

The Beginnings of Hellenization in Egypt

Hellenization has been well defined by Goldstein[1] as containing the following ingredients on which all observers, ancient and modern, could agree: (1) some Greeks are present, and the non-Greeks have some contact with them; (2) there must be some knowledge and use of the Greek language; (3) for intellectuals the age is characterized by the development and spread of rational philosophies that are often skeptical of traditional religion; (4) in literature highly emotional epic, dramatic, and lyric poetry are produced; (5) athletic and educational pursuits of the Greek gymnasia are very important; (6) in architecture Hellenism leaves an enduring legacy in the surviving traces of ancient gymnasia, stadia, and theaters.

The Septuagint

BIBLIOGRAPHY

Jacob Freudenthal, "Are there Traces of Greek Philosophy in the Septuagint?" *JQR*, old series, 2 (1889–90), 205–22.

Henry B. Swete, *An Introduction to the Old Testament in Greek*, 2nd ed. (1914).

Ralph Marcus, "Jewish and Greek Elements in the Septuagint," in Alexander Marx *et al.*, eds, *Louis Ginzberg Jubilee Volume* (1945), 227–45.

Gillis Gerleman, "The Septuagint Proverbs as Hellenistic Portrait," *OS* 8 (1950), 15–27.

Henry S. Gehman, "The Hebraic Character of Septuagint Greek," *VT* 1 (1951), 81–90.

Charles H. Dodd, *The Bible and the Greeks*, 2nd ed. (1954), 3–98.

Gillis Gerleman, *Studies in the Septuagint*, III. *Proverbs* (1956).

Elias Bickerman, "The Septuagint as a Translation," *PAAJR* 28 (1959), 1–39; reprinted in his *Studies in Jewish and Christian History*, vol. 1 (1976), 167–200.

Sidney Jellicoe, *The Septuagint and Modern Study* (1968).

Sebastian P. Brock *et al.*, *A Classified Bibliography of the Septuagint* (1973).

Peter Walters, *The Text of the Septuagint: Its Corruptions and Their Emendation* (1973).

Sidney Jellicoe, ed., *Studies in the Septuagint: Origins, Recensions, and Interpretations: Selected Essays* (1974).

Harry M. Orlinsky, "The Septuagint as Holy Writ and the Philosophy of the Translators," *HUCA* 46 (1975), 89–114.

1. Jonathan A. Goldstein, "Jewish Acceptance and Rejection of Hellenism," in E. P. Sanders *et al.*, eds, *Jewish and Christian Self-Definition*, vol. 1: *Aspects of Judaism in the Greco-Roman Period* (Philadelphia: Fortress, 1981), 67.

Sebastian P. Brock, "Aspects of Translation Technique in Antiquity," *GRBS* 20 (1979), 69–87.

Emanuel Tov, "Did the Septuagint Translators Always Understand Their Hebrew Text?" in *De Septuaginta. Festschrift John W. Wevers* (1984), 53–70.

Emanuel Tov, "The Rabbinic Tradition Concerning the 'Alterations' Inserted into the Greek Pentateuch and their Relation to the Original Text of the LXX," *JSJ* 15 (1984), 65–89.

John W. Wevers, "An Apologia for Septuagint Studies," *BIOSCS* 18 (1985), 16–38.

Melvin K. H. Peters, "Why Study the Septuagint?" *BA* 49 (1986), 174–81.

Alan F. Segal, "Torah and Nomos in Recent Scholarly Discussion," *SR* 13 (1984), 19–28; reprinted in his *The Other Judaisms of Late Antiquity* (1987), 131–45.

Schürer, vol. 3 (1986), 474–93.

Emanuel Tov, "The Septuagint," *Mikra* (1988), 161–88.

Melvin K. H. Peters, "Septuagint," *ABD* 5 (1992), 1093–104.

Modrzejewski (1995), 99–112.

Bibliography on *Letter of Aristeas*

Sterling Tracy, "Aristeas and III Maccabees," *YCS* 1 (1928), 239–52.

Moses Hadas, ed., *Aristeas to Philocrates* (1951).

Avigdor Tcherikover, "The Ideology of the Letter of Aristeas," *HTR* 51 (1958), 59–85.

Günther Zuntz, "Aristeas Studies," *JSS* 4 (1959), 21–36, 109–26.

David W. Gooding, "Aristeas and Septuagint Origins," *VT* 13 (1963), 357–79.

Albertus F. J. Klijn, "The Letter of Aristeas and the Greek Translation of the Pentateuch in Egypt," *NTS* 11 (1964), 154–8.

Sidney Jellicoe, "The Occasion and Purpose of the Letter of Aristeas: A Re-examination," *NTS* 12 (1966), 144–50.

Sidney Jellicoe, "Septuagint Origins: *The Letter of Aristeas*," in his *The Septuagint and Modern Study* (1968), 29–58.

George E. Howard, "The Letter of Aristeas and Diaspora Judaism," *JTS* 22 (1971), 337–48.

Harry M. Orlinsky, "The Septuagint as Holy Writ and the Philosophy of the Translators," *HUCA* 46 (1975), 89–114.

Robert J. H. Shutt, "Notes on the Letter of Aristeas," *BIOSCS* 10 (1977), 22–30.

Robert J. H. Shutt, "Letter of Aristeas," *OTP* 2 (1983), 7–34.

Daniel R. Schwartz, "The Priests in Ep. Arist. 310," *JBL* 97 (1978), 567–71.

Naomi Cohen, "The Names of the Translators in the Letter of Aristeas: A Study in the Dynamics of Cultural Transition," *JSJ* 15 (1984), 32–64.

Schürer, vol. 3 (1986), 677–87.

According to tradition, King Ptolemy II Philadelphus of Egypt, about the year 270 BCE, decided to have the Torah (Pentateuch) translated into Greek and to add it to his new library in Alexandria. A more likely or at least an additional reason for the translation was the need of the Jewish community for such a translation, since there is good reason to believe that the children and grand-children of the founders of the community no longer understood the Pentateuch in the original or in an Aramaic paraphrase. The *Letter of Aristeas*, supposedly written by a courtier of the king but, more likely, written by a Jew, contains an account of the making of the translation, supposedly by seventy (hence the name "Septuagint") or seventy-two elders imported from Jerusalem. According to the account which follows, when the translation was completed, the Jewish community of Alexandria deemed it so perfect that it ordained that no changes should be made in it.

2.1 *Letter of Aristeas* (*ca.* second century BCE) 9–11, 121–2, 308–11

When Demetrius of Phalerum was put in charge of the royal library, he was granted large sums for gathering, if possible, all the books of the world. And by making purchases and transcriptions, he carried the king's purpose to completion, as far as was in his power. When he was asked in my [Aristeas'] presence how many thousands of books there were, he replied, 'More than 200,000, O king. And I shall hasten in a short time to round the rest to the number of 500,000. I am informed that the laws of the Jews also are worth transcribing and being in your library.' 'What keeps you,' he replied, 'from doing this? Everything has been granted to you for your needs.' But Demetrius said, 'Translation is needed; for in the land of the Jews they use their own script, just as the Egyptians use their system of writing, just as they have their own language. They are presumed to use Aramaic, but this is not so, for they have another kind.' When the king learned these details, he directed that a letter be sent to the high priest of the Jews, so that the aforementioned might be carried to completion. . . .

[The high priest] Eliezer selected men who were distinguished and outstanding in learning, inasmuch as they were of distinguished parents, men who had acquired expertise, not only in the literature of the Jews but had also devoted more than cursory study to Greek literature as well. Accordingly, they were suitable for being sent on embassies, and they served in this capacity whenever necessary, and they had great talent for meetings and discussions regarding the Law. They cultivated the quality of the mean (for that is best). . . .

When the task reached its conclusion, Demetrius summoned the Jewish community to the place where the translations had been made, and read it to all in the presence of the translators; these received a great ovation from the community. . . . When the books had been read, the priests and the elders among the translators, and some from the corporative body who were the leaders of the community said: 'Since the translation has been well and piously done, and is accurate in every respect, it is proper that it should remain as it is, and that no revision be made.' When all had given their approval to this statement, in accordance with their customs they ordered a curse to be pronounced upon anyone who revises it by adding to, transposing anything in all that has been written, or making any deletion. This was well done by them so that it might be preserved forever imperishable and unaltered. (M.H.)

2.2 Philo, *Life of Moses* 2.6.31–7.44

In the account which follows, Philo tells how King Ptolemy Philadelphus commissioned the translation, how the translators were chosen by the high priest in Jerusalem and how they impressed Ptolemy with their knowledge. Philo, in his account of the translation, indicates that the translators, in the tranquil atmosphere of the island of Pharos off the coast of Alexandria, were actually divinely inspired, so that, though isolated from one another, they arrived at identical and perfect translations. Each year, says Philo, an assembly is held on Pharos, attended by Jews and non-Jews alike, to commemorate the translation.

This great man [King Ptolemy Philadelphus of Egypt], having conceived an ardent affection for our laws, determined to have the Chaldean[2] translated into Greek, and at once dispatched envoys to the high priest and king of Judaea,[3] both offices being held by the same person, explaining his wishes and urging him to choose by merit persons to make a full rendering of the Law into Greek. The high priest was naturally pleased, and thinking that God's guiding care must have led the king to busy himself in such an undertaking, sought out such Hebrews as he had of the highest reputation, who had received an education in Greek as well as in their native lore, and joyfully sent them to Ptolemy. When they arrived, they were offered hospitality, and having been sumptuously entertained, requited their entertainer with a feast of words full of wit and weight. For he tested the wisdom of each by propounding for discussion new instead of the ordinary questions, which problems they solved with happy and well-pointed answers in the form of apophthegms, as the occasion did not allow of lengthy speaking.

After standing this test, they at once began to fulfill the duties of their high errand. Reflecting how great an undertaking it was to make a full version of the laws given by the Voice of God, where they could not add or take away or transfer anything,[4] but must keep the original form and shape, they proceeded to look for the most open and unoccupied spot in the neighborhood outside the city. For, within the walls, it was full of every kind of living creatures, and consequently the prevalence of diseases and deaths, and the impure conduct of the healthy inhabitants, made them suspicious of it.

In front of Alexandria lies the island of Pharos, stretching with its narrow strip of land towards the city, and enclosed by a sea not deep but mostly consisting of shoals, so that the loud din and booming of the surging waves grow faint through the long distance before it reaches the land. Judging this to be the most suitable place in the district, where they might find peace and tranquillity and the soul could commune with the laws with none to disturb its privacy, they

2. Normally Chaldean refers to the Aramaic language; and this would seem to indicate that the translation was made from an Aramaic Targum (or paraphrase); but most scholars assume that Chaldean here refers to Hebrew. In the sixteenth century Azariah dei Rossi, in his *Meor Eynayim*, relied upon this passage to explain the numerous changes made by the translators.

3. Judaea at this time did not have a king. Presumably the reference is to the fact that the high priest, to all intents and purposes, was the leader of the Jewish community.

4. Cf. Deut 13:1: "All this word which I command you, that shall ye observe to do; thou shalt not add thereto, nor diminish from it."

fixed their abode there; and, taking the sacred books, stretched them out towards heaven with the hands that held them, asking of God that they might not fail in their purpose. And He assented to their prayers, to the end that the greater part, or even the whole, of the human race might be profited and led to a better life by continuing to observe such wise and truly admirable ordinances.

Sitting here in seclusion with none present save the elements of nature, earth, water, air, heaven, the genesis of which was to be the first theme of their sacred revelation, for the laws begin with the story of the world's creation, they became as it were possessed, and, under inspiration, wrote, not each several scribe something different, but the same word for word, as though dictated to each by an invisible prompter. Yet who does not know that every language, and Greek especially, abounds in terms, and that the same thought can be put in many shapes by changing single words and whole phrases and suiting the expression to the occasion? This was not the case, we are told, with this law of ours, but the Greek words used corresponded literally with the Chaldean, exactly suited to the things they indicated. For, just as in geometry and logic, so it seems to me, the sense indicated does not admit of variety in the expression which remains unchanged in its original form, so these writers, as it clearly appears, arrived at a wording which corresponded with the matter, and alone, or better than any other, would bring out clearly what was meant. The clearest proof of this is that, if Chaldeans have learned Greek, or Greeks Chaldean, and read both versions, the Chaldean and the translation, they regard them with awe and reverence as sisters, or rather one and the same, both in matter and words, and speak of the authors not as translators but as prophets and priests of the mysteries, whose sincerity and singleness of thought has enabled them to go hand in hand with the purest of spirits, the spirit of Moses.

Therefore, even to the present day, there is held every year a feast and general assembly in the island of Pharos, whither not only Jews but multitudes of others cross the water, both to do honor to the place in which the light of that version first shone out, and also to thank God for the good gift so old yet ever young. But, after the prayers and thanksgivings, some fixing tents on the seaside and others reclining on the sandy beach in the open air feast with their relations and friends, counting that shore for the time a more magnificent lodging than the fine mansions in the royal precincts. Thus the laws are shown to be desirable and precious in the eyes of all, ordinary citizens and rulers alike, and that too though our nation has not prospered for many a year. It is but natural that when people are not flourishing their belongings to some degree are under a cloud. But if a fresh start should be made to brighter prospects, how great a change for the better might we expect to see! I believe that each nation would abandon its peculiar ways, and throwing overboard their ancestral customs, turn to honoring our laws alone. For, when the brightness of their shining is accompanied by national prosperity, it will darken the light of the others as the risen sun darkens the stars. (LCL)

2.3 Babylonian Talmud, *Megillah* 9a (edited *ca.* 500 CE)

The account which follows from the Talmud corroborates Philo's version that the translators were divinely inspired. It adds that Ptolemy Philadelphus did not even tell them why they had been brought together but only, after placing them in separate rooms, asked them to translate the Pentateuch, whereupon they all, though isolated from one another, arrived at precisely the same translation.

Rabbi Judah [bar Ilai, mid-second century CE] said: When our teachers permitted Greek, they permitted it only for a scroll of the Torah.[5] This was on account of the incident related in connection with King Ptolemy [Philadelphus], as it has been taught: 'It is related of King Ptolemy that he brought together seventy-two elders and placed them in seventy-two [separate] rooms, without telling them why he had brought them together, and he went in to each one of them and said to him, "Translate for me the Torah of Moses your master."' God then prompted each one of them and they all conceived the same idea.[6] (Soncino)

Hellenization of the Jews in Egypt in the Third and Second Centuries BCE

BIBLIOGRAPHY

Joseph Mélèze Modrzejewski, "How to Be a Jew in Hellenistic Egypt," in Shaye J. D. Cohen and Ernest S. Frerichs, eds, *Diasporas in Antiquity* (1993), 65–92.
S. Honigman, "The Birth of a Diaspora: The Emergence of a Jewish Self-Definition in Ptolemaic Egypt in the Light of Onomastica," in Shaye J. D. Cohen and Ernest Frerichs, eds, *Diasporas in Antiquity* (1993), 93–127.

Legal and Business Affairs

BIBLIOGRAPHY

Modrzejewski (1995), 107–19.

The Jews who first came to Alexandria in the fourth century BCE spoke Aramaic, as our papyri from that period indicate. But within less than a century the papyri show that the Jews had become Greek-speaking. Their occupations were very varied: most were farmers or craftsmen; others were shopkeepers, sailors, traders, or tax collectors, soldiers or policemen serving the royal establishment. Few were wealthy; a few reached high positions in government or society. Everywhere they were accorded the right to live "according to their ancestral customs." As resident aliens in a Greek city, the Jews were organized in their own quasi-political corporate body (called a *politeuma*, as distinct from the Greek *polis*) under a special royal charter, with their own officials and religious courts.

---

5. I.e., they permitted only the Pentateuch to be written in Greek; they required that other books of the Bible be written only in their original language.
6. Here follow thirteen instances in which the translators deliberately departed from the Hebrew text. Only five of these are to be found in our manuscripts of the Septuagint.

Though we find evidence for the existence of synagogues, the local communal religious and social centers of the Jews everywhere in the Diaspora, we also find Hellenization, notably in the use of the Greek language, Greek personal names, and aspects of Hellenistic law.

The Tobiads

BIBLIOGRAPHY

Chester C. McCown, "The 'Araq el-Emir and the Tobiads," *BA* 20 (1957), 63–76.
Benjamin Mazar, "The Tobiads," *IEJ* 7 (1957), 137–45, 229–38.
Jonathan A. Goldstein, "The Tales of the Tobiads," in Jacob Neusner, ed., *Christianity, Judaism, and Other Greco-Roman Cults: Studies for Morton Smith at Sixty*, Part 3: *Judaism before 70* (1975), 85–123.
Dov Gera, "On the Credibility of the History of the Tobiads (Josephus, *Antiquities* 12, 156–222, 228–36)," in Aryeh Kasher, Uriel Rappaport, Gideon Fuks, eds, *Greece and Rome in Eretz Israel: Collected Essays* (1990), 21–38.

2.4 *CPJ*, nos. 4–5 (257 BCE)

Some Jews during this period went very far in adopting a Greek way of life. One example is the family of the Tobiads, whose influence in political, religious, economic, and social matters dates from the period of Nehemiah in the fifth century BCE. The Zenon Papyri document the activities of Toubias (Tobiah), who was the head of a military colony in Transjordan during the reign of Ptolemy Philadelphus (283–246 BCE). His son Joseph was a tax-farmer during the reign of Ptolemy III Euergetes (246–221 BCE); during his lifetime the family reached the height of its influence, having close connections with the king and being related by marriage with the high-priestly families of Jerusalem.

Below are two letters written by Toubias to Apollonius, the minister of Ptolemy Philadelphus. In the first he indicates that he has sent him four young slaves; in the second he asserts that, in accordance with Apollonius' request, he has sent to the king a number of animals, including some rare ones.

Toubias to Apollonius[7] greeting. If you are well and all your affairs and the rest are as you wish, many thanks to the gods. I too have been well, keeping you in mind ever, as was proper. I have sent you Aineias bringing one eunuch and four house slaves of good stock, two of whom are uncircumcised. I append for you also descriptions of the boys for your information. Farewell, Year 29, Xandikos 10th. [There follow distinguishing characteristics of the boys, aged seven through ten.] ...
    [Address] To Apollonius.
    [Docket] Toubias, regarding a eunuch and four boys sent to him. Year 29, Artemision 16th, at Alexandria.

Toubias to Apollonius greeting. Pursuant to your letter in the month Xandikos asking me to send the king gifts, I sent on the 10th of Xandikos my servant Aineias bringing two horses, six dogs, one wild

---

7. Apollonius was the finance minister of King Ptolemy Philadelphus of Egypt.

mule out of an ass, two white Arab donkeys, two foals out of a wild mule, one foal out of a wild ass. These are tame. I have sent you also the letter written by me to the king concerning the gifts, and likewise a copy of it for your information. Farewell. Year 29, Xandikos 10th.

To King Ptolemy from Toubias, greeting. I have sent you two horses, six dogs, one wild mule out of an ass, two white Arab donkeys, two foals out of a wild mule, one foal out of a wild ass. Farewell. (M.R.)

2.5 Josephus, *Jewish Antiquities* 12.175–89, 208–22

The right to collect taxes was normally sold by the government to the highest bidder. The fact, as indicated in the passage below, that Joseph, the son of Toubias, gained that right without guarantors aroused the jealousy of his rivals. Joseph then proceeded successfully to use strong-arm tactics in collecting taxes. He ate forbidden food and fell in love with a pagan dancing-girl. His son Hyrcanus obtained the contract for tax-farming in place of his father. He is remarkable, as illustrated in the passage below, equally for his cleverness and for his ruthlessness, particularly in his dealings with his father and brothers.

Now when the day came round on which the rights to farm taxes in the cities were to be sold, bids were made by those eminent in rank in the various provinces. When the sum of taxes from Coele-Syria[8] and from Phoenicia and Judaea with Samaria added up to eight thousand talents,[9] Joseph came forward and accused the bidders of having made an agreement to offer the king a low price for the taxes, whereas he for his part promised to give double that amount and send over to the king the property of those who had been remiss toward his house; for this right was sold along with that of farming the taxes. Thereupon the king, who heard him gladly, said that he would confirm the sale of the tax-farming rights to him, as he was likely to increase his revenue, but asked whether he also had some persons to give surety for him; he then answered very cleverly, 'Yes, I will offer persons of the very best character, whom you will not distrust.' And when the king asked him to tell who they were, he replied, 'I offer you, O king, you yourself and your wife as the persons who will give surety for me, each to guarantee the other's share.' At this Ptolemy laughed and granted him the tax-farming rights without guarantors. This act gave great pain to those who had come to Egypt from the cities, for they considered themselves slighted. And so they returned with discomfiture to their respective provinces.

Then Joseph, after getting from the king two thousand foot soldiers – for he had asked to have some assistance, in order that he might be able to use force with any in the cities who treated him with contempt – and borrowing five hundred talents in Alexandria from the friends of the king, set out for Syria. And coming to Ascalon, he demanded

---

8. Probably here refers to Transjordan.
9. It is almost impossible to estimate the equivalent of eight thousand talents in terms of contemporary buying power. That it was a huge sum is clear from the fact that Cicero estimates the total revenue of Ptolemy XI Auletes (80–51 BCE) as 12,500 talents.

tribute from the people of the city, but they not only refused to give him anything, but even insulted him to boot; he therefore arrested some twenty of their principal men and put them to death, and sent their property, which all together was worth a thousand talents, to the king, informing him of what had happened. Thereupon Ptolemy, who admired his spirit and commended his actions, permitted him to do whatever he wished.

When the Syrians heard of this, they were struck with consternation and, having a terrible example of the consequences of disobedience in the execution of the men of Ascalon, they opened their gates and readily admitted Joseph and paid the tribute. And when the inhabitants of Scythopolis also attempted to insult him and would not render him the tribute which they formerly paid without any dispute, he put to death their chief men as well and sent their property to the king. Having thus collected great sums of money and made great profits from farming the taxes, he used his wealth to make permanent the powers which he now had, thinking it prudent to preserve the source and foundation of his present good fortune by means of the wealth which he had himself acquired; and so he surreptitiously sent many gifts to the king and to Cleopatra and to their friends and to all those who were powerful at court, purchasing their goodwill through these gifts.

This good fortune he enjoyed for twenty-two years, becoming the father of seven sons by one wife, and also begetting a son, named Hyrcanus, by the daughter of his brother Solymius, whom he married under the following circumstances. He once came to Alexandria with his brother as he was taking there his daughter, who was of marriageable age, in order that he might marry her to one of the Jews of high rank; and when Joseph was dining with the king, a beautiful dancing-girl came into the banquet-room, and Joseph, having fallen in love with her, told his brother of this and begged him, since the Jews were prevented by law from having intercourse with a foreign woman, to aid in concealing his sin and do him a good service by making it possible for him to satisfy his desire. Thereupon his brother, gladly undertaking to be of service, beautified his own daughter and brought her to him by night to sleep with him. But Joseph in his drunken state did not know how matters really were, and so he had intercourse with his brother's daughter, and when this had happened several times, he fell still more violently in love with her. He then told his brother that he was risking his life for a dancer whom the king would perhaps not allow him to have. But his brother urged him not to be anxious, telling him to enjoy without fear the woman whom he loved, and to make her his wife; and he revealed the truth to him, how he had chosen to dishonor his own daughter rather than see him fall into disgrace, and so Joseph, commending him for his brotherly love, married his daughter and by her begot a son, Hyrcanus, as we said before. . . .

[When he grew up] Hyrcanus paid his respects to the royal pair, who were glad to see him and entertained him in friendly fashion in honor of his father. Then he secretly went to the slave-dealers and bought from them a hundred boys who were well educated and in the prime of youth, at a talent apiece, and a hundred virgins at the same price.

Now once when he was invited together with the leading men of the country to feast with the king, he was placed at the foot of the table, being slighted as still a youth by those who assigned the places according to rank. And all those who reclined at table with Hyrcanus piled up before him the bones of their portions – from which they themselves had removed the meat – so as to cover the part of the table where he reclined, whereupon Tryphon, who was the king's jester and was appointed to make jokes and raise laughter when there was drinking, with the encouragement of those who reclined at the table, stood up before the king and said, 'My lord, do you see the bones lying before Hyrcanus? From this you may guess that his father has stripped all Syria in the same way as Hyrcanus has left these bones bare of meat.' The king then laughed at Tryphon's words, and asked Hyrcanus why there were so many bones lying before him, and he replied, 'It is natural, my lord; for dogs eat the bones together with the meat, as these men do' – and he looked toward those who reclined there, indicating that there was nothing lying before them – 'but men eat the meat and throw the bones away, which is just what I, being a man, have now done.' Thereupon the king, who admired his reply for being so clever, and to show approval of his wit, ordered all to applaud.

But the next day Hyrcanus, going to each of the king's friends and the men powerful at court, and paying his respects to them, inquired of their servants what gift their masters were going to give the king for the child's birthday. And when they said that some were going to give gifts worth ten talents, while of the others, who were of high rank, each would give in accordance with the amount of his wealth, he pretended to be grieved at not being able to bring so large a present, saying he had no more than five talents. Accordingly, when the servants heard this, they reported it to their masters. And they rejoiced at the thought that Hyrcanus would be judged unfavorably and offend the king by the smallness of his present; and when the day came, the others brought their offerings to the king, which in the case of those who believed themselves to be unusually munificent were not worth more than twenty talents, but Hyrcanus brought the hundred boys and hundred virgins whom he had purchased, and giving each of them a talent to carry, presented them, the boys to the king, and the girls to Cleopatra. And while all were astonished at the unexpected lavishness of his gifts, including the royal pair themselves, he also gave to the king's friends and to those who were in attendance on him gifts worth many talents so as to escape any danger from them; for Hyrcanus' brothers had written to them to make an end of him. Then Ptolemy in admiration of the young man's magnanimity directed him to take whatever present he wished. But he asked that the king do no more for him than to write to his father and brothers about him. And so the king, after showing him the highest honor and giving him splendid presents, wrote to his father and brothers and to all his governors and administrators and sent him away. But when Hyrcanus' brothers heard that he had obtained these favors from the king and was returning with great honor, they went out to meet him and do away with him, even though their father knew of it; for being angry with him because of the money which had been spent for the presents, he felt no concern for his safety; his anger at his son had, however, been concealed by Joseph, who feared the king. And when Hyrcanus' brothers encountered him in battle, he killed many of the men with them and also two of the brothers themselves, while the rest escaped to their father in Jerusalem. (LCL)

The Evidence from the Papyri

BIBLIOGRAPHY

CPJ, 3 vols (1957–64).
P. W. Pestman, "Loans Bearing No Interest?" *JJP* 16/17 (1971), 7–29.

Because the sands of Egypt serve as a preservative we have been able to unearth many thousands of scraps, written on papyrus, the paper of that day. Included are several hundred fragments pertaining to Jews. However, in almost every papyrus there are many gaps and many illegible letters. In addition, unless there is specific identification of someone as a Jew it is often very hard to be sure that the person is a Jew, since names are not necessarily a sure criterion.

2.6 *CPJ*, no. 19 (226 BCE)

This papyrus contains the official report of a session of a Greek court, known as the "Court of Ten," in Egypt. What is particularly remarkable is that a trial between a Jew and a Jewess was brought before a Greek tribunal rather than before a Jewish court as would have been required according to Talmudic law. The reference to a Jew of the Epigone, that is, of the military reserve, confirms our information from literary sources indicating the important participation of Jews in the army of the Ptolemies.

In the 22nd year of the reign of Ptolemy, son of Ptolemy and Arsinoe, gods Adelphoi, the priest of Alexander and the gods Adelphoi and the gods Euergetai and the *kanephoros*[10] of Arsinoe Philadelphus being those officiating in Alexandria, the 22nd of the month Dystros, at Crocodilopolis in the Arsinoite nome [district], under the presidency of Zenothemis, the judges being Diomedes, Polycles, Andron, Theophanes, Maeandrius, Sonicus, Diotrephes, Polydeuces, the clerk of the court, having constituted us in accordance with the order sent to him by Aristomachus, appointed *strategos* [administrator] of the Arsinoite nome, of which this is a copy.

To Polydeuces greeting. Heracleia has requested the king in her petition to form and swear in a court for her of all the judges except

---

10. Literally, "basket-bearer," the title of maidens who carried baskets in the processions during religious festivals.

such as either party may challenge in accordance with the regulations. . . .

We have given judgment as below in the action brought by Dositheus against Heracleia according to the following indictment:

'Dositheus son of . . . Jew of the Epigone,[11] to Heracleia daughter of Diosdotus, Jewess. . . . [I state] that on Peritios 22 of year 21, as I with other persons was entering the . . . of Apion . . . from the so-called house of Pasytis which is in Crocodilopolis in the Arsinoite nome [district] opposite the so-called house of Pasytis the . . . you came to that place with Callippus the . . . and abused me saying that I had told certain persons that [you are a . . .] woman, and on my abusing you in return you not only spat on me but seizing the loop of my mantle . . . me and . . . until . . . and the said Callippus . . . as the people present rebuked you and Callippus . . . you ceased your insults . . . to which I have borne witness. Wherefore I bring an action of assault against you for 200 drachmas, the assessment of damages being . . . drachmas . . .'

Whereas this was the indictment, and Dositheus neither appeared in person nor put in a written statement nor was willing to plead his case; and whereas Heracleia appeared with her guardian Aristides son of Proteas, Athenian of the Epigone, and put in both a written statement and justificatory documents, and was also willing to defend her case; and whereas the code of regulations which was handed in by Heracleia among the justificatory documents directs us to give judgment in a . . . manner on all points which any person knows or shows us to have been dealt with in the regulations of king Ptolemy, in accordance with the regulations, and on all points which are not dealt with in the regulations, but in the civic laws, in accordance with the laws, and on all other points to follow the most equitable view; but when both parties have been summoned before the court and one of them is unwilling to put in a written statement or plead his case or acknowledge defeat [?] . . . he shall be judged guilty of injustice; we have dismissed the case. (*CPJ*)

2.7 *CPJ*, no. 20 (228–221 BCE)

For a Jew to lend money to another Jew at interest is strictly forbidden by the Pentateuch (Exod 22:24, Deut 23:20); indeed, even a hint of interest is forbidden by the rabbis (Mishnah, *Baba Metzia* 5:1ff.). Yet, of six papyri mentioning loans by Jews to Jews, one is at interest although we do not know the rate, and four (including this one) are at the usual rate of interest during the Ptolemaic period of 24 per cent per year.

Mousaeus son of Simon, Jew of the Epigone, has lent to Lasaites son of Iz . . . is, Jew of the Epigone, 108 drachmas of copper at par, at interest of 2 drachmas a month. (M.R.)

---

11. Soldiers who settled in colonies and who took wives from among the natives produced a younger generation, called the Epigone, who had a military tradition from their very birth and who grew up in these military colonies.

2.8 CPJ, no. 33 (third century BCE)

The noteworthy point of this document is that it indicates that Jews and Greeks in a village in the Fayum, in northern Egypt, were treated as two separate groups by an official.

. . . to Asclepiades, greeting . . . to be collected from all those who live in Psenyris, for the village granaries, from the Jews and the Greeks, one half drachma per son. Collected through Dicaius the *epistates* [i.e., overseer]. If you agree, please write to Apollonius. . . . (*CPJ*)

2.9 CPJ, no. 38 (218 BCE)

This document contains the complaint of a dealer in wool against a shepherd, Seos, a Jew. Note that the Jew bears an Egyptian name, Seos, and that there is no anti-Jewish intimation in the complaint.

To King Ptolemy from Harmiysis, wool-merchant living at Crocodilopolis, greeting.

I am being wronged by Seos, a Jew living at Alabanthis. He sold me, at four drachmas, five obols, two chalkoi each, the fleece of 118 cross-bred sheep, which I bought on behalf of Amyntas in order to . . . the king's *parabole*.[12] I paid him a deposit of 76 drachmas, undertaking to pay the remainder when I had sheared the sheep. But Seos came upon the flock, washed, . . . and sheared it, and removed the wool for himself, and refuses to return it at my request. Therefore, my king, I beg you, if you will, to order Diophanes the *strategos* to write telling the *epistates* . . . to summon Seos to the *strategos* Diophanes, so that if it appears that he sold the wool and took the deposit, he shall make him give me the wool. If this comes about, I shall no longer be wronged, and Amyntas, for whom I have made other purchases also, [will be able to pay] the taxes which he owes at Alexandria. And thus we shall obtain justice by our appeal to you, impartial savior of all men.

[Endorsed] Year 4, Dios 3, Phamenoth 27.

Harmiysis, wool-merchant, against Seos, about wool. (*CPJ*)

2.10 CPJ, no. 23 (182 BCE)

This loan upon a mortgage is the best-known example of a contract in which both parties are Jews. In form it is very similar to non-Jewish deeds of the Ptolemaic period. This loan, to be sure, is without interest, but even so it is subject to the overtime interest rate of 24 per cent if not repaid within one year.

In the reign of King Ptolemy son of Ptolemy, and of Arsinoe, gods Philopatores, in the 24th year, at the time of the priesthood of Alexander in Alexandria, and of the gods Adelphoi and the gods Euergetae and the gods Philopatores and the gods Epiphaneis and the *athlophoros* [i.e., prize-bearer] of Berenice Euergetes officiating in

12. Apparently the wool bought by Harmiysis was intended to release Amyntas from the king's interdict which could be removed only when a certain amount of wool was delivered to the government.

Alexandria, and the *kanephoros* [i.e., basket-bearer] of Arsinoe
Philadelphus in Alexandria, the priestess of Arsinoe Philopator in
Alexandria, on the 28th of the month Dystros = Thoth 28, in
Crocodilopolis of the Arsinoite nome, Apollonius son of Protogenes,
Jew of the Epigone, twenty-fourth year of the reign of Ptolemy son of
Ptolemy and Arisinoe, gods Philopatores, the priest Alexander and
the gods Adelphoi and the gods Euergetai and the gods Philopatores
and the gods Epiphaneis, and the *athlophoros* [i.e., prize-bearer] of
Berenice Euergetis and the *kanephoros* [i.e., basket-bearer] of Arsinoe
Philadelphus and the priestess of Arsinoe Philopator being those
officiating at Alexandria, on the twenty-eighth of the month of Dystros,
being Thoth twenty-eighth, in Crocodilopolis in the Arsinoite nome.
Apollonius son of Protogenes, Jew of the Epigone, lent to Sostratus son
of Neoptolemus, Jew of the Epigone, two talents and 3,000 drachmas of
copper money for one year without interest, from the above written
date, on security of house and court belonging to him, with all the
appurtenances, at Apias in the division of Themistes.

Sostratus is to repay this loan to Apollonius in one year. If he does
not repay it as specified, it is permitted to Apollonius to lay claim to the
security in accordance with the edict.[13] Sostratus shall guarantee to
Apollonius this security and shall produce it unencumbered, un-
pledged, free from any other debt, and free from royal charges. If he
does not guarantee it or produce it as specified, Sostratus shall at once
forfeit to Apollonius the loan plus one-half again and interest at the
rate of two drachmas a month for the overtime.[14] This contract shall be
valid everywhere. Through Boubakes also called Stheneus.[15]

Apollonius, about 35, good height, fair-haired, with rather bright
eyes, protruding ears.

Sostratus, about 35, middle height, fair-haired ... scar over right
eyebrow.[16] (M.R.)

2.11 *CPJ*, no. 24 (174 BCE)

This document is important for its confirmation of the fact that Jews
served in the armies of the Ptolemies. It was during the reign of Ptolemy
Philometor (181–145 BCE) that Jews achieved particular prominence in the
Egyptian army. As indicated here, soldiers received landholdings and at
times enjoyed a regular rent from their estates. Here, too, the rate of
interest on a loan is 24 per cent.

[A long prescript specifies the date.] Judas son of Josephus, Jew of the
Epigone, has lent to Agathocles son of Ptolemaeus, Jew, of the detach-
ment of Molossus, infantry, stationed in the Heracleopolite nome, who
is paymaster [?], two talents and 500 drachmas of copper money for
twelve months from the aforementioned date, at interest of two

---

13. The reference is to an edict of the king on judicial matters.
14. The rate of interest is 24 per cent per year, the usual rate of interest throughout
the Ptolemaic period.
15. Boubakes was *agoranomos*, i.e., in effect, notary public of the district.
16. This is one of the very few instances where we have a physical description of
Jews of this period.

drachmas a month per mina.[17] This loan is the sum which Agathocles still owed Judas from the five talents which he received from Judas as advance for a partnership in retail trade, according to the contract of agreement of which Ananias son of Jonathan, Jew of the Epigone, is the guardian. Agathocles shall repay to Judas the aforesaid loan and the interest in the month of Mecheir of the 8th year. If he does not repay as specified, he shall repay it increased by one-half again as penalty. The contract is valid.

Witnesses: Deinias son of Aineias, Thraseas son of Sosibus, Theobon son of Phanocles, Samaelus son of Joannes, all four Jews of the Epigone; Theodorus son of Theodorus, also called Samaelus, Nicanor son of Jason, these two Jews who are 80-arourae holders, of the first hipparchy[18] settled by Dositheus.

I, Agathocles, have the aforementioned loan of two talents and 500 drachmas of copper, and I have deposited the agreement as valid, with Deinias keeper of the contract. (M.R.)

2.12 CPJ, no. 43 (second century BCE)

This petition by a Jew seeks to reverse the decision of a scribe who had arbitrarily raised his rent.

To Zopyrus, financial official, from Judas the Jew, son of Dositheus the Jew. I am a farmer near Philadelphia of three arourae of dry ground paying a pre-existing rental per annum of four artabas[19] of wheat per aroura, and have cultivated this land with great suffering and expense, and have completed the payment of rent without complaint annually to the 23rd year. Now Marres, the village secretary, contrary to what is proper, has inscribed me for an account more than the existing rent, in the sum of 5⅔ artabas per aroura, though I have never paid this sum. Therefore, I appeal to your kindness, and ask you, if you so judge, to write to the proper authority to supply you with accurate details, so that if matters are as I have written, then you may make provision that I shall not have to pay anything contrary to what is due, and that I myself may obtain justice. Farewell. (M.R.)

2.13 CPJ, no. 46 (second or first century BCE)

What is significant about this document is that we find here Jews joining in a business venture with non-Jews, namely in the joint use of a pottery. Another interesting feature is that some of the Jews bear Egyptian names. A third feature is that the Jews are illiterate, that is, they cannot sign their names in Greek.

Sabbataeus son of Horus[20] and his son Dosatus, potters from a village of Syrians, Jews, to Petesuchus and his sons Nepherus and Nechthanoupis, greeting. We agree to share with you the pottery at

17. A mina consisted of 100 drachmas.
18. The cavalry, the most aristocratic part of the army, was composed of hipparchies, called by numbers.
19. An *artaba* was a measure of capacity equivalent to 24 to 42 liters.
20. This and the others are Egyptian names.

Nilopolis belonging to Paous son of Sabbataeus, from Tybi 25, Year 7, up to Mesore 30 of the same year, in the following shares: ¼ for me, and for my son ¾ of ¼. We shall pay the tax jointly, each according to his share. But if there is any loss or profit, these shall be joint and shared. It shall not be permitted for us to abandon the pottery during the aforementioned year, and it shall not be permitted for you to turn us out of the pottery. If we do not act as stipulated, we shall pay to the royal treasury a fine of 40 silver drachmas. This contract shall be valid everywhere.

This was written for them by Chaeremon son of Callicrates at their request, since they declare themselves to be illiterate. Year 7, Tybi 25.

Sabaeidon son of Nikon, witness; Nicodromus son of Philippus, witness. (M.R.)

2.14 *CPJ*, no. 151 (5/4 BCE)

This is a petition, extant only in a fragmentary form, from an Alexandrian Jew to the governor of Egypt regarding his civic status. The Jews of Alexandria continued to have their own quasi-civic community, as they had under the Ptolemies, and the age-old privileges accorded them. But when Augustus imposed the poll tax on the population of Egypt, probably in 24/23 BCE, he exempted only two groups: Roman citizens resident in Egypt and the Greeks of Alexandria. This effectively degraded the Jews of Alexandria to the same status in the social hierarchy as Egyptian peasants. The Jews sought in various ways to extricate themselves from this restrictive social position and stigma, thus generating increased friction between themselves and the Greeks.

To Gaius Turranius, from Helenus the son of Tryphon, an Alexandrian,[21] a Jew of Alexandria.

Most mighty governor, although my father was an Alexandrian citizen and I have always lived here, receiving the appropriate education, as far as my father's means allowed, I run the risk not only of being deprived of my native country but also.... For it has happened that Horus, the public administrator, ... of the month Tybi[?] ... on the ground of ... my father to his ancestral gymnasium [?] ... forcibly ... from the ephebate[22] ... Caesar ... written ... poll-tax ... the month Mecheir ... the remaining time for the poll-tax because of the age-limit of sixty. I beseech you, savior of all, not to reject my plea, since I have not been disturbed either by the first governors[23] or by you.... (*CPJ*)

21. This word was deleted and replaced by the designation that follows.

22. A roster of those (called *ephebes*) who had passed through the gymnasium education, necessary for admission to Alexandrian citizenship (which was, in turn, a necessary step before Roman citizenship). Acquisition of Alexandrian citizenship ensured exemption from the poll tax, as well as from the compulsory public services imposed on the population of Egypt, and provided other legal and social privileges.

23. Of the Roman province of Egypt, the first of whom was Cornelius Gallus, appointed by Augustus in 30 BCE.

Jews as Soldiers

BIBLIOGRAPHY

Tcherikover, "Prolegomena," *CPJ*, vol. 1 (1957), 11–15.
Modrzejewski (1995), 83–7.

2.15 *CPJ*, no. 27 (158 BCE)

Literary sources (e.g., the *Letter of Aristeas* 13) indicate that the Jews served as soldiers in Hellenistic armies, but some scholars have disputed the historicity of this evidence on the ground that Jewish observance of the Sabbath would have made such service impossible. A number of papyri, of which the one below refers to a Jewish cavalry officer (the name Iasibis is clearly Hebrew), show that Jews did serve in the Ptolemaic army. This papyrus is a receipt for payment for a house. Iasibis is one of those who arranged the auction at which the house was bought.

[The price of a house] put to sale in Diospolis Magna on the 28th of Coiach of the 23rd year through Ptolemaios the superintendent of the revenues in the Thebais and Theon the royal scribe in the presence of Dionysios himself and Harnouphis the topogrammateus,[24] Imouthes the village-scribe, Megisthenes the phrourarchos,[25] Lichas the archiphylakites,[26] Aristogenes one of the officers serving with Hippalos, Iasibis the epistates[27] of a hipparchy,[28] and many others, through Timarchos the herald of the soldiers. (*CPJ*)

Everyday Life of the Jews in Egypt

Complaint of a Wife

2.16 *CPJ*, no. 128 (218 BCE)

In this fragmentary papyrus a wife (it is not clear whether or not she is Jewish) complains to King Ptolemy IV Philopator against her Jewish husband.

To King Ptolemy greeting from Helladote, daughter of Philonides. I am being wronged by Jonathas, the Jew. . . . He has agreed in accordance with the law of the Jews to hold me as wife. . . . Now he wants to withhold, . . . hundred drachmas, and also the house . . . does not give me my due, and shuts me out of my house . . . and absolutely wrongs me in every respect. I beg you therefore, my king, to order Diophanes, the *strategos* [chief administrator], to write to . . . the *epistates* [subordinate administrator] of Samareia not to let . . . to send Jonathas to Diophanes in order . . . (*CPJ*)

24. An Egyptian official, secretary of a region.
25. Commander of a garrison.
26. Commander of police.
27. Commander or chief.
28. Squadron of cavalry.

A Divorce

BIBLIOGRAPHY

Boaz Cohen, "Concerning Divorce in Jewish and Roman Law," *PAAJR* 21 (1952), 3–34.
Reuven Yaron, "CPJud 144 et Alia," *IURA* 13 (1962), 170–5.

2.17 CPJ, no. 144 (13 BCE)

This is the only deed of divorce involving Jews (the name Sambathion is most probably a Jewish name) that we have found among the Egyptian papyri. It follows the form of Hellenistic non-Jewish divorces and seems to show no indication of the form of divorce known to us from biblical and Talmudic sources. In particular, the husband and wife agree to be divorced, whereas the biblical formula in Deuteronomy (24:1) has the husband divorcing the wife. Moreover, there is no indication of witnesses. It is possible that this is merely the state document of divorce corresponding to the religious document of divorce.

To Protarchus, from Apollonia daughter of Sambathion with her guardian, her mother's brother, Heracleides son of Heracleides, and from Hermogenes son of Hermogenes an Archistrateian.

Apollonia and Hermogenes agree that they have dissolved their marriage by an agreement made through the same court in the thirteenth year of Caesar [Augustus] in the month Pharmouthi. Apollonia agrees that she has duly received back from Hermogenes the dowry of sixty drachmas which he had on her account from her parents Sambathion and Eirene according to the marriage-agreement. They agree therefore that the marriage-agreement is void, and that neither Apollonia nor anyone proceeding on her behalf will proceed against Hermogenes to recover the dowry, and that neither of them will proceed against the other on any matter arising from the marriage or from any other matter arising up to the present day, and that from this day it shall be lawful for Apollonia to marry another man and Hermogenes to marry another woman without penalty, and that whosoever transgresses this agreement shall be liable to the appointed penalty. The seventeenth year of Caesar [Augustus], Phamenoth 14. (CPJ)

Athletics

BIBLIOGRAPHY

Harold A. Harris, *Greek Athletics and the Jews* (1976).
Feldman (1993), 59–61.

One of the major differences between the "true" Greek and the barbarian was the crucial role of athletics in the gymnasium curriculum and in life generally for the former. The games in which students of the gymnasia participated were, however, held at pagan religious festivals. Hence, participation even as a spectator involved a compromise with Jewish orthodoxy. Nevertheless, Philo, who gives every appearance of being an observant Jew in the traditional sense, presents ample evidence of knowledge of athletics – notably, wrestling, boxing, and running – particularly in his figures of speech, as seen in the three passages below.

2.18 Philo, *On Husbandry* 25.111–26.117

Do you then also, my friend, never come forward for a rivalry in badness, nor contend for the first place in this, but, best of all, if possible make haste to run away; but if in any case, under the pressure of strength greater than your own, you are compelled to engage in the contest, do not hesitate to be defeated; for then you, the defeated combatant, will have won a grand victory, and those who have won will be suffering defeat. And do not allow either the herald to announce or the judge to crown the enemy as victor, but come forward yourself and present the prizes and the palm, and crown him ('by your leave, sir'), and bind the headband round his head, and do you yourself make with loud and strong voice this announcement: 'In the contest that was proposed in lust and anger and licentiousness, in folly also and injustice, O ye spectators and stewards of the sports, I have been vanquished, and this man is the victor, and has proved himself so vastly superior that even we, his antagonists, who might have been expected to grudge him his victory, feel no envy.' Yield, then, to others the prizes in these unholy contests, but bind upon your own head the wreaths won in the holy ones. And count not those to be holy contests which the states hold in their triennial festivals, and have built for them theaters to hold many myriads of men; for in these prizes are carried away either by the man who out-wrestled someone and laid him on his back or on his face upon the ground, or by the man who can box or combine boxing with wrestling, and who stops short at no act of outrage or unfairness.

Some give a sharp, strong edge to an iron-bound thong, and fasten it round both hands and lacerate the heads and faces of their opponents, and, when they succeed in planting their blows, batter the rest of their bodies, and then claim prizes and garlands for their pitiless savagery.

As for the other contests, of sprinters or of those who enter for the five exercises, what sensible person would not laugh at them, at their having practiced to jump as far as possible, and getting the several distances measured, and making swiftness of foot a matter of rivalry? And yet not only one of the larger animals, a gazelle or a stag, but a dog or hare, among the smaller ones, will, without hurrying much, outstrip them when running full pelt and without taking breath. Of these contests, in sober truth, none is sacred, and even if all men testify to that effect, they cannot escape being convicted of false witness by themselves. For it was the admirers of these things who passed the laws against overbearing persons, and fixed the punishments to be awarded to acts of outrage, and allotted judges to investigate the several cases. How, then, are these two things compatible? How can the very same persons be indignant at outrages committed in private and have affixed to them inexorable penalties, and at the same time have by law awarded garlands and public announcements and other honors to those who have done so publicly and at State festivals and in theaters? (LCL)

2.19 Philo, *On the Cherubim* 24.80–1

The other kind we find in the case of an athlete in a boxing-match or pancratium[29] for a crown of victory. As the blows fall upon him he brushes them off with either hand, or he turns his neck round this way and that and thus evades the blows, or often he rises on his tiptoes to his full height, or draws himself in and compels his adversary to lay about him in empty space, much as men do when practicing the movements. (LCL)

2.20 Philo, *Every Good Man is Free* 17.110

I know many cases of wrestlers and pancratiasts so full of ambition and eagerness for victory that though their bodies have lost their strength, they renew their vigor and continue their athletic efforts with nothing to help them but the soul, which they have inured to despise terrors, and in this they persevere to their last gasp. (LCL)

The Theater

BIBLIOGRAPHY

Howard Jacobson, *The Exagoge of Ezekiel* (1983).
Louis H. Feldman, "Philo's Views on Music," *JJML* 9 (1986–7), 36–54.
Feldman (1993), 61–3.

In antiquity the theater among Greeks was associated with pagan religion, namely the worship of Dionysus, at whose festivals the plays were performed. At the banquet said, according to the *Letter of Aristeas*, to have been held by King Ptolemy Philadelphus in honor of the translators of the Torah into Greek, the king, in his admiration of their wisdom, asks them a number of questions, in response to one of which one of the translators advises the king to watch plays.

2.21 *Letter of Aristeas* 284–5

The king spoke enthusiastically to the man and asked another 'How ought a man to occupy himself during his hours of relaxation and recreation?' And he replied, 'To watch those plays which can be acted with propriety and to set before one's eyes scenes taken from life and enacted with dignity and decency is profitable and appropriate. For there is some edification to be found even in these amusements, for often some desirable lesson is taught by the most insignificant affairs of life. But by practicing the utmost propriety in all your actions, you have shown that you are a philosopher and you are honored by God on account of your virtue.' (H.T.A.)

---

29. The pancratium was an athletic contest involving both boxing and wrestling.

2.22 Philo, *On Drunkenness* 43.177

In the passage below Philo remarks that he has often been to the theater and noted the impact of the music on various groups of people.

For example, I have often when I chanced to be in the theater noticed the effect produced by some tune sung by the actors on the stage or played by the musicians. Some of the audience are so moved that in their excitement they cannot help raising their voices in a chorus of acclamation. Others are so unstirred that, as far as this is concerned, you might suppose them on a level of feeling with the senseless benches on which they sit. Others, again, are so repelled that they are off and away from the performance, and indeed, as they go, block their ears with both hands for fear that some echo of the music should remain to haunt them and produce a sense of discomfort to irritate and pain their souls. (LCL)

Jewish Literary Activity in Egypt

Demetrius

BIBLIOGRAPHY

Peter M. Fraser, *Ptolemaic Alexandria*, vol. 1 (1972), 690–4; vol. 2, 958–63.

Elias J. Bickerman, "The Jewish Historian Demetrios," in Jacob Neusner, ed., *Christianity, Judaism, and Other Greco-Roman Cults*, vol. 3 (1975), 72–84; rev. ed. in his *Studies in Jewish and Christian History*, vol. 1 (1980), 347–58.

Carl R. Holladay, "Demetrius the Chronographer as Historian and Apologist," in *Christian Teaching: Studies in Honor of Lemoine G. Lewis* (Abilene, Texas: Abilene Christian University, 1981), 117–29.

Holladay, vol. 1 (1983), 51–91.

John S. Hanson, "Demetrius," *OTP*, vol. 2 (1985), 843–54.

Sterling (1992), 153–67.

Modrzejewski (1995), 61–5.

2.23 Demetrius, quoted by Alexander Polyhistor (first century BCE), as cited by Eusebius (end of third and beginning of fourth century CE), *Preparation for the Gospel* 9.21.13–14

Demetrius was a Jewish historian who was particularly interested in chronography and who apparently lived in Egypt during the last quarter of the third century BCE. From his work, *On the Kings in Judaea*, written in Greek, a few fragments survive, most of them as quoted by the pagan Alexander Polyhistor, and presenting a close and exact summary of events as found in the Septuagint of Genesis and Exodus. He is not uncritical and indeed seeks to explain a number of difficulties in the biblical text, for example, as seen below, in the story of Joseph.

But though Joseph had good fortune for nine years, he did not send for his father because he was a shepherd as were his brothers too, and Egyptians consider it a disgrace to be a shepherd.[30] That this was the

---

30. The reason given is an addition by Demetrius.

reason he did not send for him, Joseph himself declared. For when his kin did come, he told them that if they should be summoned by the king and were asked what they did for a living, they were to say that they were cowherds. A crucial question arises as to why Joseph gave Benjamin a five-fold portion at the meal even though he would not be able to consume so much meat. He did this because seven sons[31] had been born to his father by Leah whereas only two sons had been born to him by Rachel his mother. For this reason, he served up five portions for Benjamin and he himself took two.[32] Thus, there were between them seven portions, that is, as many as all the sons of Leah had taken. (C.R.H.)

Philo the Epic Poet

BIBLIOGRAPHY

Joshua Gutman, "Philo the Epic Poet," *SH* 1 (1954), 36–63.
Holladay, vol. 2 (1989), 205–99.

> 2.24 Philo the Epic Poet, *On Jerusalem*, quoted by Alexander Polyhistor (first century BCE), cited by Eusebius (end of third and beginning of fourth century), *Preparation for the Gospel* 9.20.1

Josephus (*Against Apion* 1.218), mentions a Philo the Elder as a Greek (i.e., a non-Jewish) author who is exceptional in his approximation of the truth; but whether this is identical with Philo the Epic Poet has been much debated. It has usually been assumed that Philo's interest in Jerusalem indicates that the poet came from Palestine, but we find a similar focus in the *Letter of Aristeas*, which, it is generally agreed, is of Alexandrian provenance. In view of Philo's affinity with other Hellenistic epics such as Apollonius of Rhodes' *Argonautica* (rather than with Homeric epic), it seems more likely that the poem was written in Alexandria. The style is unusually bombastic and the language is often obscure. His date is unknown, but some time between the end of the third century and the middle of the second century BCE seems most probable. The passage below is an elaborate praise of Abraham and, in particular, of his faith in God when instructed to sacrifice his son Isaac.

> They[33] unloosed the loins for our ancestors just as once
>   [they were commanded] by the [divine] ordinances –
> O Abraham, [you are] renowned through the preeminent
>   seal of the bond(s)[34]
> Radiant [are you], overflowing with glorious thoughts –
> Divinely pleasing gestures.[35] For this one who left the
>   splendid enclosure

31. The Bible (Gen 35:23) lists only six sons by Leah.
32. The question and the explanation are extra-biblical.
33. Perhaps the reference is to "our ancestors."
34. The reference is presumably to circumcision.
35. The reference is to the act of circumcision.

Of the awesome race the praiseworthy one[36] with a
thundering sound prevented [from carrying out] the
immolation.
[And thus] he made his own voice immortal. From then on
The offspring of that awesome child achieved much-
hymned renown. (C.R.H.)

Artapanus

BIBLIOGRAPHY

Martin Braun, *History and Romance in Graeco-Oriental Literature* (1938), 26–31, 99–102.

David L. Tiede, *The Charismatic Figure as Miracle Worker* (1972), 146–77.

Daniel J. Silver, "Moses and the Hungry Birds," *JQR* 64 (1973–4), 123–53.

Hengel, vol. 1 (1974), 90–4.

Carl R. Holladay, *Theios Aner in Hellenistic Judaism. A Critique of the Use of this Category in New Testament Christology* (1977), 199–232.

John J. Collins, *Between Athens and Jerusalem: Jewish Identity in the Hellenistic Diaspora* (1983), 32–8.

Holladay, vol. 1 (1983), 189–243.

John J. Collins, "Artapanus," *OTP*, vol. 2 (1985), 889–903.

Robert Doran, "The Jewish Hellenistic Historians before Josephus," *ANRW* 2.20.1 (1987), 257–63.

Pieter W. van der Horst, "The Interpretation of the Bible by the Minor Hellenistic Jewish Authors," *Mikra* (1988), 532–7.

Arthur J. Droge, *Homer or Moses? Early Christian Interpretations of the History of Culture* (1989), 25–35.

Sterling (1992), 167–86.

2.25 Artapanus, *Concerning the Jews*, quoted by Alexander Polyhistor (first
century BCE), cited by Eusebius (end of third and beginning of fourth
century CE), *Preparation for the Gospel* 9.27.3–10

By the second century BCE Hellenization, at least in literary circles, had
apparently reached the point of syncretism. A case in point is the historian
Artapanus, fragments of whose work have been preserved by the pagan
Alexander Polyhistor, who lived in the first century BCE and who is quoted
by Eusebius. Indeed, he is so syncretistic (note, in particular, in the
passage below, the identification of Moses with the mythical Mousaios
and consequently as a teacher of the famed mythical musician Orpheus,
as well as the statement that Moses introduced the worship of animals as
gods) that some have doubted that he was a Jew; but his glorification of
Jewish heroes is said to make a non-Jewish origin less likely. Moses is
here presented as a great inventor, philosopher, and general.

When he [Moses] became a man, he was called Mousaios[37] by the
Greeks. This Moses became the teacher of Orpheus.[38] When he

36. The reference is to God.
37. Mousaios (Musaeus) was a legendary pre-Homeric Greek poet who is said to
have been a teacher or a pupil of Orpheus.
38. Orpheus is the legendary Greek musician who is said to have been such a
marvelous player on the lyre that he held even wild beasts spellbound by his music.
He was also the founder of the mysteries which took his name.

reached manhood, he bestowed on humanity many useful contributions, for he invented ships, machines for lifting stones, Egyptian weapons, devices for drawing water and fighting, and philosophy. He also divided the state into thirty-six nomes,[39] and to each of the nomes he assigned the god to be worshipped; in addition, he assigned the sacred writings to the priests. The gods he assigned were cats, dogs, and ibises. He set aside as well land exclusively for the use of the priests. He did all these things for the sake of keeping the monarchy stable for Chenephres,[40] for prior to this time the masses were disorganized and they would sometimes depose, sometimes install rulers, often the same persons, but sometimes others. Thus, for these reasons Moses was loved by the masses, and being deemed worthy of divine honor by the priests, he was called Hermes[41] because of his ability to interpret the sacred writings.

When Chenephres saw the fame of Moses, he became jealous and sought to kill him on some reasonable pretext. Thus when the Ethiopians marched against Egypt, Chenephres, supposing that he had found the right moment, sent Moses against them as the commander of a force of troops. He conscripted a band of farmers for Moses, rashly supposing that Moses would be killed by the enemy because his troops were weak. Moses came to the nome called Hermopolis with approximately 100,000 farmers, and he camped there. He commissioned as generals those who would eventually preside as rulers over the region, and they won every battle with distinction. He says that the Heliopolitans report that the war lasted ten years. Thus, Moses and those with him, because of the size of the army, founded a city in this place, and they consecrated the ibis in the city because of its reputation for killing those animals that were harmful to men. They named it 'The City of Hermes.' So then, although the Ethiopians had been enemies, they came to love Moses, and as a result learned from him the practice of circumcising the genitalia – not only they but all the priests as well. (C.R.H.)

Ezekiel the Tragedian

BIBLIOGRAPHY

Gregory M. Sifakis, *Studies in the History of Hellenistic Drama* (1967), 113–35.

John Strugnell, "Notes on the Text and Metre of Ezekiel the Tragedian's *Exagoge*," *HTR* 60 (1967), 449–57.

John J. Collins, *Between Athens and Jerusalem: Jewish Identity in the Hellenistic Diaspora* (1983), 207–11.

Pieter W. van der Horst, "Moses' Throne Vision in Ezekiel the Dramatist," *JJS* 34 (1983), 21–9.

Howard Jacobson, *The Exagoge of Ezekiel* (1983).

Pieter W. van der Horst, "Some Notes on the *Exagoge* of Ezekiel," *Mnemosyne* 37 (1984), 354–75.

39. A nome was a portion of a province of ancient Egypt.

40. The Pharaoh Chenephres was the brother and successor of Cheops and was of the fourth Egyptian dynasty (*ca.* 2500 BCE).

41. Hermes was the Greek god, one of the twelve major divinities on Mount Olympus, who was the messenger of the gods and the conductor of the souls of the dead to Hades.

Ben Zion Wacholder and Steven Bowman, "Ezechielus the Dramatist and Ezekiel the Prophet: Is the Mysterious *zoion* in the *Exagoge* a Phoenix?" *HTR* 78 (1986), 253–77.
Howard Jacobson, "Phoenix Resurrected," *HTR* 80 (1987), 229–33.
Holladay, vol. 2 (1989), 301–529.

2.26 Ezekiel the Tragedian, *The Exodus*, quoted by Alexander Polyhistor (first century BCE), cited by Eusebius (end of third and beginning of fourth century CE), *Preparation for the Gospel* 9.29.4–6

We know of a Jew, Ezekiel, who composed tragedies, considerable fragments of one of which, *The Exodus*, have been preserved. His thorough familiarity with various classical authors, particularly Aeschylus and Euripides, indicates that he was well schooled in Greek literature. The play itself follows the biblical narrative closely, though the dream here mentioned, together with the interpretation by Moses' father-in-law Raguel (Jethro), is non-biblical. There would appear to be significance in the fact that this crucial dream is interpreted by a non-Jew, Raguel.

Ezekiel thus mentions these things in his work *The Exodus* and includes the dream seen by Moses and interpreted by his father-in-law. In the following extract, Moses himself speaks in dialogue with his father-in-law.

'I dreamt there was on the summit of Mount Sinai
A certain great throne extending up to heaven's cleft,
On which there sat a certain noble man[42]
Wearing a crown and holding a great sceptre
In his left hand. With his right hand
He beckoned to me, and I stood before the throne.
He gave me the sceptre and told me to sit
On the great throne. He gave me the royal crown,
And he himself left the throne.
I beheld the entire circled earth
Both beneath the earth and above the heaven,
And a host of stars fell on its knees before me;
I numbered them all.
They passed before me like a squadron of soldiers.
Then, seized with fear, I rose from my sleep.'
His father-in-law interprets the dream thusly:
'O friend, that which God has signified to you is good;
Might I live until the time when these things happen to you.
Then you will raise up a great throne
And it is you who will judge and lead humankind;
As you beheld the whole inhabited earth,
The things beneath and the things above God's heaven,
So will you see things present, past, and future.' (C.R.H.)

42. Scholars differ as to whether God is here represented as a man, an image similar to Daniel's "son of man" or whether, as seems more likely, the figure represents Pharaoh, who here gives up his throne to Moses.

Jewish Philosophers in Egypt: Philo

BIBLIOGRAPHY

Erwin R. Goodenough, *The Jurisprudence of the Jewish Courts in Egypt. Legal Administration by the Jews under the Early Roman Empire as Described by Philo Judaeus* (1929).

Sterling Tracy, *Philo Judaeus and the Roman Principate* (1933).

Erwin R. Goodenough, *By Light, Light! The Mystic Gospel of Hellenistic Judaism* (1935).

Erwin R. Goodenough, *The Politics of Philo Judaeus: Practice and Theory* (1938).

Samuel Belkin, *Philo and the Oral Law: The Philonic Interpretation of Biblical Law in Relation to the Palestinian Halakah* (1940).

Harry A. Wolfson, *Philo: Foundations of Religious Philosophy in Judaism, Christianity and Islam*, 2 vols (1947).

Samuel Sandmel, *Philo's Place in Judaism: A Study of Conceptions of Abraham in Jewish Literature* (1956).

Erwin R. Goodenough, *An Introduction to Philo Judaeus*, 2nd ed. (1962).

Louis H. Feldman, *Scholarship on Philo and Josephus (1937–1962)* (1963), 1–26.

Samuel Sandmel, *Philo of Alexandria: An Introduction* (1979).

Alan Mendelson, *Secular Education in Philo of Alexandria* (1982).

Ray Barraclough, "Philo's Politics: Roman Rule and Hellenistic Judaism," *ANRW* 2.21.1 (1984), 417–553.

Peter Borgen, "Philo of Alexandria," in *CRINT* 2.2 (1984), 233–82.

Peter Borgen, "Philo of Alexandria: A Critical and Synthetical Survey of Research since World War II," *ANRW* 2.21.2 (1984), 98–154.

Earle Hilgert, "Bibliographia Philoniana 1935–1981," *ANRW* 2.21.2 (1984), 47–97.

Samuel Sandmel, "Philo Judaeus: An Introduction to the Man, His Writings, and His Significance," *ANRW* 2.21.2 (1984), 3–46.

David Winston, "Philo's Ethical Theory," *ANRW* 2.21.2 (1984), 372–416.

Louis H. Feldman, "Philo's Views on Music," *JJML* 9 (1986–7), 36–54.

Alan Mendelson, *Philo's Jewish Identity* (1988).

Roberto Radice and David T. Runia, *Philo of Alexandria: An Annotated Bibliography 1937–1986* (1988).

David T. Runia, *Exegesis and Philosophy: Studies on Philo of Alexandria* (1990).

David T. Runia, "How to Search Philo," *SPA* 2 (1990), 106–39.

David Winston, "Judaism and Hellenism: Hidden Tensions in Philo's Thought," *SPA* 2 (1990), 1–19.

Peder Borgen, "Philo of Alexandria," *ABD*, vol. 5 (1992), 333–42.

David Dawson, "Philo: The Reinterpretation of Reality," in his *Allegorical Readers and Cultural Revision in Ancient Alexandria* (1992), 73–126.

David T. Runia, *Philo in Early Christian Literature: A Survey* (1993).

2.27 Philo, *Allegorical Interpretation*, Book 2. 15.53–6, 16.60, 16.64

The interpenetration of Hellenism and Judaism reached its acme in the works of the eminent Jew Philo (*ca.* 15 BCE–40 CE), one of the leaders of the Jewish community in Alexandria in the time of the emperor Gaius Caligula. Steeped in Greek learning and especially music, he strove to rethink Jewish religious traditions in the light of Greek rationalism for his own edification and that of other intellectuals of Alexandria, both Jewish and non-Jewish. As we can see from his frequent allusions, he often attended the theater, was a keen observer of boxing contests, attended chariot races, and participated in costly suppers with their lavish entertainment. Philo tells us nothing of his Jewish education, and his knowledge of Hebrew was apparently minimal,[43] for the Torah he relied on the Septuagint, which he regarded as perfect. Rejecting literal meanings in the Bible as indefensible, he methodically applied an allegorical interpretation. His belief in God as a transcendent God (comparable to Plato's Idea of the Good) led him to posit a mediator for God in the physical realm. This intermediary he called the *Logos* ("Word" [or better, "Communication"] or "Reason"), a term derived from Greek philosophical thought. A similar doctrine was propounded shortly after his time in the opening verses of the Gospel according to John. Philo's philosophical thinking was eclectic, a compound of Platonism, Stoicism, and Neopythagoreanism, but he was not a systematic philosopher–theologian; rather, his thought is presented, for the most part, through commentaries on various biblical personalities and passages. Though he was a religious Jew, devoted to his people and to maintaining the Law, his influence was greatest on early Christianity. Indeed, Jerome included him among the Church Fathers.

The passage that follows illustrates Philo's use of the allegorical method (itself of Greek origin) in explaining the meaning of the nakedness of Adam and his wife.

'And the two were naked, Adam and his wife, and were not ashamed' (Gen 2:25). 'Now the serpent was the most subtle of all the beasts that were upon the earth, which the Lord God had made' (Gen 3:1). The mind that is clothed neither in vice nor in virtue, but absolutely stripped of either, is naked, just as the soul of an infant, since it is without part in either good or evil, is bared and stripped of coverings: for these are the soul's clothes, by which it is sheltered and concealed. Goodness is the garment of the worthy soul, evil that of the worthless.

Now there are three ways in which a soul is made naked. One is when it continues without change and is barren of all vices, and has divested itself of all the passions and flung them away.... What this means is this. The soul that loves God, having disrobed itself of the body and the objects dear to the body and fled abroad far away from these, gains a fixed and assured settlement in the perfect ordinances of virtue.... This is why the high priest shall not enter the Holy of Holies in his robe (Lev 16:1ff.), but laying aside the garment of opinions and impressions of the soul, and leaving it behind for those that love outward things and value semblance above reality, shall enter naked with no colored borders or sound of bells, to pour as a libation the blood of the soul and to offer as incense the whole mind of God our Savior and Benefactor....

This is one form, the noblest form, of stripping or becoming naked. The other is of a contrary nature, a deprivation of virtue due to a turning or change of condition, when the soul becomes foolish and deranged. This kind of stripping is experienced by Noah, who is made naked when he has drunk wine....

---

43. See David Rokeah, "A New Onomasticon Fragment from Oxyrhynchus and Philo's Etymologies," *Journal of Theological Studies* 19 (1968), 70–82.

A third form of producing nakedness is the middle or neutral one. Here the mind is irrational and has no part as yet either in virtue or in vice. It is of this form that the prophet is speaking. In this the infant too is partaker. Accordingly, the words, 'The two were naked, both Adam and his wife,' amount to this: neither mind nor sense was performing its functions, the one being bare and barren of mental action and the other of the activity of sense-perception. (LCL)

2.28 Philo, *On the Confusion of Tongues* 28.146

The following passage illustrates Philo's use of the Logos concept as an angel-like intermediary between God and the world and as God's First-born.

But if there be any as yet unfit to be called a Son of God, let him press to take his place under God's First-born, the Word [*Logos*], who holds the eldership among the angels, their ruler as it were. And many names are his, for he is called 'the Beginning,' and the Name of God, and His Word, and the Man after His image, and 'he that sees,' that is Israel. (LCL)

2.29 Philo, *On the Creation of the World* 4.16

In the following passage Philo clearly shows his indebtedness to Plato's view of the visible world as being a copy or imitation of the Form or Idea of the world, that is, the intelligible world.

For God, being God, assumed that a beautiful copy would never be produced apart from a beautiful pattern, and that no object of perception would be faultless which was not made in the likeness of an original discerned only by the intellect. So when He willed to create this visible world He first fully formed the intelligible world, in order that He might have the use of a pattern wholly God-like and incorporeal in producing the material world, as a later creation, the very image of an earlier, to embrace in itself objects of perception of as many kinds as the other contained objects of intelligence. (LCL)

2.30 Philo, *The Special Laws* 2.15.62–3

In the following passage Philo describes the Sabbath schools of Egypt and their subject-matter, as well as their method of instruction. The emphasis clearly is on ethics. There is no mention of instruction in ritual aspects of Judaism.

Each seventh day there stand wide open in every city thousands of schools of good sense, temperance, courage, justice, and the other virtues in which the scholars sit in order quietly with ears alert and with full attention, so much do they thirst for the draught which the teacher's words supply, while one of special experience rises and sets forth what is best and sure to be profitable and will make the whole of life grow to something better.

But among the vast number of particular truths and principles there studied, there stand out practically high above the others two main heads: one of duty to God as shown by piety and holiness, one of duty to men as shown by humanity and justice, each of them splitting up into multiform branches, all highly laudable. (LCL)

2.31 Philo, *On the Cherubim* 14.48–9

In Egypt, where the mystery cults of Isis and Osiris and of Sarapis were so popular, Philo apparently felt a need to stress that Jews did not have to leave Judaism to find all the elements of a mystery cult. Here, in a rare autobiographical note, he even remarks that he himself was initiated into Judaism's greater mysteries (a term which he borrowed from the most famous pagan mysteries, those of Eleusis).

These thoughts, ye initiated, whose ears are purified, receive into your souls as holy mysteries indeed and babble not of them to any of the profane. Rather as stewards guard the treasure in your own keeping, not where gold and silver, substances corruptible, are stored, but where lies that most beautiful of all possessions, the knowledge of the Cause and of virtue, and, besides these two, of the fruit which is engendered by them both. But, if ye meet with anyone of the initiated, press him closely, cling to him, lest knowing of some still newer secret he hide it from you; stay not till you have learnt its full lesson.

I myself was initiated under Moses the God-beloved into his greater mysteries, yet when I saw the prophet Jeremiah and knew him to be not only himself enlightened, but a worthy minister of the holy secrets, I was not slow to become his disciple. He out of his manifold inspiration gave forth an oracle spoken in the person of God to Virtue the all-peaceful. 'Didst thou not call upon Me as thy house, thy father and the husband of thy virginity?' (Jer 3:4). Thus he implies clearly that God is a house, the incorporeal dwelling-place of incorporeal ideas, that He is the father of all things, for He begat them, and the husband of Wisdom, dropping the seed of happiness for the race of mortals into good and virgin soil. (LCL)

2.32 Philo, *On the Creation* 23.70–1

In the following passage Philo describes in mystic terms the feeling that one has in contemplating the universe created by God and in perceiving the Platonic Ideas. Here Philo's language betokens a borrowing from the spirit of the mystery cults of his day. One is struck by the oxymoronic phrase, "sober intoxication."

When, on soaring wing it [the mind of man, created in the likeness of God] has contemplated the atmosphere and all its phases, it is borne yet higher to the ether and the circuit of heaven, and is whirled round with the dances of planets and fixed stars, in accordance with the laws of perfect music, following that love of wisdom which guides its steps. And so, carrying its gaze beyond the confines of all substance discernible by sense, it comes to a point at which it reaches out after the intelligible world, and on descrying in that world sights of surpassing loveliness, even the patterns and the originals of the things of sense which it saw here, it is seized by a sober intoxication, like those filled with Corybantic[44] frenzy, and is inspired, possessed by a longing for other than theirs and a nobler desire. Wafted by this to the topmost arch of the things perceptible to mind, it seems to be on its way to the Great King Himself; but, amid its longing to see Him, pure and untempered rays of concentrated light stream forth like a torrent, so that by its gleams the eye of understanding is dazzled. (LCL)

Jewish Scientists in Egypt: Maria the Jewess

BIBLIOGRAPHY

Raphael Patai, "Maria the Jewess – Founding Mother of Alchemy," *Ambix* 29 (1982), 177–97.

2.33 Zosimus (end of third and beginning of fourth century CE), *On Apparatus and Furnaces* 1

A certain Zosimus, who lived in Alexandria and who is the most important of the early alchemical authors, states that the sacred art of the Egyptians, and the power of gold resulting from it, was revealed only to the Jews, by fraud, and that they, in turn, disseminated it to the rest of the world. In particular, Zosimus refers to a certain Maria, who seems to have lived in Alexandria in the second or third century CE, who invented the basic alchemical furnaces and apparatus which apparently remained in use until the eighteenth century, and whom he identifies as a philosopher and a Jewess. According to Zosimus, Maria taught that the inner, concealed nature of the metals could be discerned by a complex alchemical process that was revealed to her by God Himself and that was to be transmitted only to the Jewish people.

A great number of constructions of apparatus have been described by Maria; not only those which concern the divine [or sulphurous] waters, but also many kinds of kerotakis[45] and furnaces. (R.P.)

Education of the Jews in Egypt

BIBLIOGRAPHY

Louis H. Feldman, "The Orthodoxy of the Jews in Hellenistic Egypt," *JSoS* 22 (1960), 212–37.
Alan Mendelson, *Secular Education in Philo of Alexandria* (1982).
Alan Mendelson, *Philo's Jewish Identity* (1988).
Feldman (1993), 57–9.

2.34 Philo, *The Special Laws* 2.40.229–30

From several sources (e.g., Philo, *Embassy to Gaius* 44.349) we see how eager Jews were to obtain citizenship in Alexandria; and this was apparently granted only to those who had received a gymnasium (that is,

---

44. The Corybantes were the companions and eunuch priests of the goddess Cybele. They followed her with wild dances and music.
45. A hot plate used by painters and alchemists to keep wax paints hot.

secondary school) education. Such an education combined physical training with mental training in the liberal arts and philosophy. The gymnasium was the center not only of cultural but also of social and religious life.

Further, who could be more truly called benefactors than parents in relation to their children? First, they have brought them out of non-existence; then, again, they have held them entitled to nurture and later to education of body and soul, so that they may have not only life, but a good life. They have benefited the body by means of the gymnasium and the training there given, through which it gains muscular vigor and good condition and the power to bear itself and move with an ease marked by gracefulness and elegance. They have done the same for the soul by means of letters and arithmetic and geometry and music and philosophy as a whole which lifts on high the mind lodged within the mortal body and escorts it to the very heaven and shows it the blessed and happy beings that dwell therein, and creates in it an eager longing for the unswerving, ever-harmonious order which they never forsake because they obey their captain and marshal. (LCL)

The Religious Life of the Jews in Egypt

Synagogues

BIBLIOGRAPHY

John Gwyn Griffiths, "Egypt and the Rise of the Synagogue," *JTS* 38 (1987), 1–15.
Heather A. McKay, *Sabbath and Synagogue: The Question of Sabbath Worship in Ancient Judaism* (1994).
Modrzejewski (1995), 87–98.

Though rabbinic tradition (Targum of Pseudo-Jonathan on Exodus 18:20, *Midrash Yalqut* on Exodus 408), Josephus (*Against Apion* 2.175), and the New Testament (Acts 15:21) all ascribe the origin of the synagogue to Moses, the earliest synagogues whose remains have been discovered are dated from the third century BCE in Schedia and Arsinoe-Crocodilopolis, Egypt (the inscriptions are practically identical). Note that the synagogues are dedicated in honor of the king, the queen, and the royal family of Egypt.

2.35 *CII*, no. 1440 (246–221 BCE) (Schedia)

In honor of King Ptolemy and Queen Berenice, his sister and wife, and their children, the Jews built this house of prayer. (M.R.)

2.36 *CII*, no.1441 (143–117 BCE) (Xenephyris)

In honor of King Ptolemy and Queen Cleopatra his sister and Queen Cleopatra his wife, the Jews from Xenephyris dedicated the portico of the house of prayer, when Theodorus and Achillion were presidents. (M.R.)

2.37 CII, no. 1442 (143–117 BCE) (Nitriae)

In honor of King Ptolemy and Queen Cleopatra his sister and Queen Cleopatra his wife, their benefactors, the Jews in Nitriae dedicated the house of prayer and its appurtenances. (M.R.)

2.38 CII, no. 1443 (second or first century BCE) (Athribis)

In honor of King Ptolemy and Queen Cleopatra, Ptolemy son of Epicydus, commandant of the guards, and the Jews in Athribis dedicate this house of prayer to the Highest God.[46] (M.R.)

2.39 CII, no. 1449 (date uncertain) (Lower Egypt)

By order of the queen and king. In place of the previously dedicated tablet on the occasion of the dedication of the house of prayer the following is to be inscribed. King Ptolemy Euergetes[47] [bestowed the right of] asylum on the house of prayer. The queen and king gave the order.[48] (M.R.)

2.40 Jewish Inscriptions of Graeco-Roman Egypt, no. 126, pp. 214–16 (first or second century CE)

This inscription is remarkable in that it refers to a synagogue built by a single individual, who must have had considerable wealth.

Papous built the house of prayer on behalf of himself and his wife and children. In the fourth year, Pharmouthi 7. (W.H. and D.N.)

2.41 Babylonian Talmud, Sukkah 51b (edited ca. 500)

This is a highly glorified description of the great synagogue in Alexandria. The seating according to occupation may indicate that the synagogue was also the place where the crafts met like guilds to discuss common problems.

It has been taught, Rabbi Judah [bar Ilai, Palestinian, mid-second century CE] stated, He who has not seen the double colonnade of Alexandria in Egypt has never seen the glory of Israel. It was said that it was like a huge basilica, one colonnade within the other, and it sometimes held twice the number of people who went forth from Egypt.[49] There were in it seventy-one cathedras [chairs] of gold, corresponding to the seventy-one members of the Great Sanhedrin,

46. Athribis is modern Beha. It is not certain whether Ptolemy VI Philometor (180–145 BCE) or Ptolemy VIII Euergetes II (145–116 BCE) is meant, or that Epicydus was a Jew.

47. It is uncertain whether Ptolemy Euergetes I (246–221 BCE) or II (145–116 BCE) is meant.

48. The last sentence is in Latin. The editor of *Corpus Papyrorum Judaicarum* thought that the reference was to Queen Zenobia and her son Vaballat who ruled Palmyra in the third century CE.

49. According to the census reported in the Bible (Num 26:51) there were 601,730 men, in addition to 23,000 male Levites (Num 26:62).

not one of them containing less than twenty-one talents of gold, and a wooden platform in the middle upon which the attendant of the synagogue stood with a scarf in his hand. When the time came to answer Amen, he waved his scarf and all the congregation duly responded.[50] They moreover did not occupy their seats promiscuously, but goldsmiths sat separately, silversmiths separately, blacksmiths separately, metalworkers separately and weavers separately, so that when a poor man entered the place he recognized the members of his craft and on applying to that quarter obtained a livelihood for himself and for the members of his family. (Soncino)

The Temple of Onias in Leontopolis

BIBLIOGRAPHY

Edouard H. Naville, *The Mound of the Jews and the City of Onias* (1890).
Samuel A. Hirsch, "The Temple of Onias," in Isidore Harris, ed., *Jews' College Jubilee Volume* (1906), 39–80.
Tcherikover (1959), 275–81, 392–4.
Robert Hayward, "The Jewish Temple at Leontopolis: a Reconsideration," *JJS* 33 (1982), 429–43.
Kasher (1985), 119–35.
Modrzejewski (1995), 121–9.

2.42 Josephus, *Jewish War* 7.423–32

After the outbreak of the Maccabean revolt in 166 BCE, the high priest Onias IV took refuge in Egypt, where with the approval of King Ptolemy Philometor he established a temple at Leontopolis, in the district of Heliopolis near modern Cairo, and where he himself was named commander-in-chief of the Egyptian army. It has been conjectured, based on the passage below, that Philometor welcomed the building of the temple at Leontopolis as a means of propaganda to win the favor of the Jews against the Syrian Seleucids, who controlled the city of Jerusalem, where the original Temple was located. Josephus here presents the theory that Onias hoped, in building the temple, to attract the Jewish multitude away from the Temple in Jerusalem. The temple in Leontopolis, modeled on the Temple in Jerusalem, is mentioned by the Mishnah (*Menaḥoth* 13:10) but is not cited by Philo or by any other Egyptian Jewish writer. It remained standing until it was closed down by the Romans in 73 CE. The place is still called Tell al-Yehudiyya (Mound of the Jews).

Onias, son of Simon, and one of the chief priests at Jerusalem, fleeing from Antiochus, king of Syria, then at war with the Jews, came to Alexandria, and being graciously received by Ptolemy, owing to that monarch's hatred of Antiochus, told him that he would make the Jewish nation his ally if he would accede to his proposal. The king having promised to do what was in his power, he asked permission to build a temple somewhere in Egypt and to worship God after the

---

50. Because of the huge size of the synagogue the precentor's voice could not be heard everywhere.

manner of his fathers; for, he added, the Jews would thus be still more embittered against Antiochus, who had sacked their temple at Jerusalem, and more amicably disposed towards himself, and many would flock to him for the sake of religious toleration.

Induced by this statement, Ptolemy gave him a tract, a hundred and eighty furlongs distant from Memphis, in the so-called nome of Heliopolis. Here Onias erected a fortress and built his temple (which was not like that in Jerusalem, but resembled a tower) of huge stones and sixty cubits in altitude. The altar, however, he designed on the model of that in the home country, and adorned the building with similar offerings, the fashion of the lampstand excepted; for, instead of making a stand, he had a lamp wrought of gold which shed a brilliant light and was suspended by a golden chain. The sacred precincts were wholly surrounded by a wall of baked brick, the doorways being of stone. The king, moreover, assigned him an extensive territory as a source of revenue, to yield both abundance for the priests and large provision for the service of God. In all this, however, Onias was not actuated by honest motives; his aim was rather to rival the Jews at Jerusalem, against whom he harbored resentment for his exile, and he hoped by erecting this temple to attract the multitude away from them to it. There had, moreover, been an ancient prediction made some six hundred years before by one named Esaias,[51] who had foretold the erection of this temple in Egypt by a man of Jewish birth. Such, then, was the origin of this temple. (LCL)

2.43 Josephus, *Jewish Antiquities* 13.62–7

In the passage below Onias petitions King Ptolemy Philometor of Egypt to grant him permission to build a temple in honor of the royal family which will serve to unite the Jews of Egypt.

Now the son of Onias the high priest, who had the same name as his father, was living in Alexandria. He had fled to King Ptolemy called Philometor.... When Onias saw that Judaea was oppressed by the Macedonians [i.e., the Seleucids] and by their kings, wishing to establish for himself eternal fame and glory, he decided to petition King Ptolemy and Queen Cleopatra [II] for permission to build a temple in Egypt similar to that at Jerusalem, and to install Levites and priests out of his own stock. The reason he decided to do so was that he relied especially upon the prophet Isaiah [19:19], who had lived about 600 years before and foretold that there surely was to be a temple in Egypt to the Most High God built by a man who was a Jew.

Onias, inspired by these words, wrote the following letter to Ptolemy and Cleopatra: 'Having with God's help performed many services for you in the course of the war[52] when I was in Coele-Syria and Phoenicia, I then came with the Jews to Leontopolis of the Heliopolite nome and other places where our people live. And then I found that most of them

---

51. The reference is to Isaiah 19:19: "In that day there will be an altar to the Lord in the midst of the land of Egypt, and a pillar to the Lord at its border."
52. We do not know precisely which war is meant.

had temples contrary to what is proper, and that therefore they are hostile to one another, something which has happened also to the Egyptians by reason of the multitude of their temples and of the varying views concerning forms of worship. I found a very suitable place in the fortress named Bubastis in that region; this place abounds in trees of various sorts and is full of sacred animals. I beg, therefore, that you grant me permission to purify this holy place, which belongs to no one, and is fallen into ruins, and to build there a temple to the Highest God in the likeness of the one in Jerusalem and of the same dimensions, in honor of yourself and your wife and children, so that those Jews living in Egypt may have a place to meet together in mutual harmony and serve your interests.'[53] (M.R.)

Mysticism

BIBLIOGRAPHY

Erwin R. Goodenough, *By Light, Light* (1935).
Erwin R. Goodenough, *Jewish Symbols in the Greco-Roman Period*, 13 vols (1953–68).

2.44 *Joseph and Aseneth* 16

In antiquity there were a number of religions in Egypt, Syria, Asia Minor, Persia, and Greece (the most famous being the Eleusinian Mysteries) which emphasized an extraordinary initiation ceremony into a mystery cult whereby the candidate was said to die to his former self and to be born anew and thus to gain salvation. There were also a number of additional ceremonies, all of them secret, including especially a sacred meal. In the passage which follows, the non-Jewish Aseneth, having undergone complete repentance in preparation for her conversion to Judaism and her marriage to Jacob's son Joseph, the vizier to the Pharaoh, is told by the heavenly visitor that the mysteries have been revealed to her. He gives her a piece of honeycomb to eat, which has magically appeared, and tells her, in a passage reminiscent of the later Christian communion, that this is the bread of life and the cup of immortality.

And Aseneth hurried and set a new table before him [the heavenly visitor] and went to provide bread for him. And the man said to her, 'Bring me also a honeycomb.' And Aseneth stood still and was distressed because she did not have a honeycomb in her storeroom. And the man said to her, 'Why do you stand still?' And Aseneth said, 'I will send a boy to the suburb, because the field which is our inheritance is close, and he will quickly bring you a honeycomb from there, and I will set [it] before you, Lord.' And the man said to her, 'Proceed and enter your storeroom, and you will find a honeycomb lying upon the table. Pick it up and bring [it] here.' And Aseneth said, 'Lord, a honeycomb is not in my storeroom.' And the man said, 'Proceed and you will find [one].'

---

53. It should be noted that the authenticity of this letter is dubious.

And Aseneth entered her storeroom and found a honeycomb lying on the table.... . And Aseneth took that comb and brought it to the man.... . And the man ... stretched out his right hand and grasped her head and shook her head with his right hand. And Aseneth was afraid of the man's hand because sparks shot forth from his hand as from bubbling [melted] iron. And Aseneth looked, gazing with her eyes at the man's hand. And the man saw [it] and smiled and said, 'Happy are you, Aseneth, because the ineffable mysteries of the Most High have been revealed to you, and happy [are] all who attach themselves to the Lord God in repentance, because they will eat from this comb. For this comb is [full of the] spirit of life. And the bees of the paradise of delight have made this from the dew of the roses of life that are in paradise of God. And all the angels eat of it and all the chosen of God and all the sons of the Most High, because this is a comb of life, and everyone who eats of it will not die for ever [and] ever.'

And the man stretched out his right hand and broke a small portion off the comb, and he himself ate; and what was left he put with his hand into Aseneth's mouth and said to her, 'Eat.' And she ate. And the man said to Aseneth, 'Behold you have eaten bread of life and drunk a cup of immortality, and been anointed with ointment of incorruptibility.... And the man stretched out his right hand and touched the comb where he had broken off [a portion], and it was restored and filled up, and at once it became whole as it was in the beginning.' (C.B.)

Deviations in Interpretation of the Bible

BIBLIOGRAPHY

Erwin R. Goodenough, *The Jurisprudence of the Jewish Courts in Egypt. Legal Administration by the Jews under the Early Roman Empire as Described by Philo Judaeus* (1929).
Montgomery J. Shroyer, "Alexandrian Jewish Literalists," *JBL* 55 (1936), 261–84.
Samuel Belkin, Philo and the Oral Law (1940).
Feldman (1993), 74–7.

2.45 Philo, *The Confusion of Tongues* 4.9–10

Philo criticizes excessive literalists who, refusing to interpret Scripture allegorically, asked, for example, as in the passage below, what good God had accomplished by the confusion of tongues in the story of the Tower of Babel.

Now Moses, say the objectors, brings his story nearer to reality and makes a distinction between reasoning and unreasoning creatures, so that the unity of language for which he vouches applies to men only. Still even this, they say, is mythical. They point out that the division of speech into a multitude of different kinds of language, which Moses calls 'confusion of tongues,' is in the story brought about as a remedy for sin, to the end that men should no longer through mutual understanding be partners in iniquity, but be deaf in a sense to each other and thus cease to act together to effect the same purposes. But no good result appears to have been attained by it. For all the same after they had been separated into different nations and no longer spoke the same tongue, land and sea were constantly full of innumerable evil deeds. (LCL)

2.46 Philo, *On the Change of Names* 8.61–2

In the passage below, the excessive literalists, refusing to see allegorical significance in the change of names, scoff that God should have added an alpha to Abram's name and a rho to Sara's. Eventually this scoffer hanged himself.

Not long ago I heard the scoffing and railing of a godless and impious fellow who dared to speak thus: 'Vast and extraordinary indeed are the gifts which Moses says come from the hand of the Ruler of all. What a boon He is supposed to have provided by adding a single letter, an alpha, and again by another addition of a rho, for He <turned Abram into Abraham by doubling the alpha, and> Abraham's wife Sarai into Sarah by doubling the rho.' And in a sneering way he ran over the list of such cases without a moment's pause. Well, it was not long before he paid the penalty which his wicked folly called for. For a slight and trivial cause he hastened to hang himself, and thus even a clean death was denied to the unclean miscreant. (LCL)

2.47 Philo, *On the Migration of Abraham* 16.89–92

That Philo was personally observant, at least as he understood the law, seems clear from the following passage in which he vigorously denounces the extreme allegorists, who deviated from the traditional observance of such commandments as those pertaining to the Sabbath and circumcision on the ground that the ceremonial laws are only a parable.

There are some who, regarding laws in their literal sense in the light of symbols of matters belonging to the intellect, are overpunctilious about the latter, while treating the former with easy-going neglect. Such men I for my part should blame for handling the matter in too easy and off-hand a manner: they ought to have given careful attention to both aims, to a more full and exact investigation of what is not seen and in what is seen to be stewards without reproach.

As it is, as though they were living alone by themselves in a wilderness, or as though they had become disembodied souls, and knew neither city nor village nor household nor any company of human beings at all, overlooking all that the mass of men regard, they explore reality in its naked absoluteness. These men are taught by the sacred word to have thought for good repute, and to let go nothing that is part of the customs fixed by divinely empowered men greater than those of our time.

It is quite true that the Seventh Day is meant to teach the power of the Unoriginate and the non-action of created beings. But let us not for this reason abrogate the laws laid down for its observance, and light fires or till the ground or carry loads or institute proceedings in court or act as jurors or demand the restoration of deposits or recover loans, or do all else that we are permitted to do as well on days that are not festival seasons. . . .

It is true that receiving circumcision does indeed portray the excision of pleasure and all passions, and the putting away of the impious conceit, under which the mind supposed that it was capable of begetting by its own power; but let us not on this account repeal the law laid down for circumcising. Why, we shall be ignoring the sanctity of the Temple and a thousand other things if we are going to pay heed to nothing except what is shown us by the inner meaning of things. (LCL)

Intermarriage

BIBLIOGRAPHY

E. W. Brooks, *Joseph and Asenath: The Confession and Prayer of Asenath, Daughter of Pentephres the Priest* (1918).

Victor Aptowitzer, "Aseneth, the Wife of Joseph," *HUCA* 1 (1924), 239–306.

S. West, "Joseph and Asenath. A Neglected Greek Romance," *CQ* 24 (1974), 70–81.

Howard C. Kee, "The Socio-Religious Setting and Aims of 'Joseph and Asenath,'" *SBLSP* (1976), 183–92.

Howard C. Kee, "The Socio-Cultural Setting of Joseph and Aseneth," *NTS* 29 (1983), 394–413.

Christoph Burchard, "Joseph and Aseneth," *OTP* (1985), 2.177–247.

Christoph Burchard, "The Importance of Joseph and Aseneth for the Study of the New Testament: A General Survey and a Fresh Look at the Lord's Supper," *NTS* 33 (1987), 109–17.

Christoph Burchard, "The Present State of Research on Joseph and Aseneth," in Jacob Neusner *et al.*, eds, *Religion, Literature, and Society in Ancient Israel, Formative Christianity and Judaism*, vol. 2 (1987), 31–52.

Randall D. Chesnutt, "The Social Setting and Purpose of Joseph and Aseneth," *JSP* 2 (1988), 21–48.

Feldman (1993), 77–9.

Modrzejewski (1995), 67–72.

2.48 *Joseph and Aseneth* 15

That there was some intermarriage in the Diaspora and that it met with approval in the case where the non-Jewish partner was sincere in converting is indicated by a pseudepigraphic work entitled *Joseph and Aseneth*, dating from perhaps the first century BCE or the first century CE, which some have thought missionary propaganda designed to win Gentiles to Judaism. The work, however, as seen in the excerpt below, more likely emphasizes the need for the convert utterly to repudiate idolatry. Once this is done, the author stresses that the convert is to be received fully into the Jewish community and obtains heavenly endorsement. In the excerpt, the chief of the angels announces that because Aseneth (Asenath) has truly repented of her past she has been accepted as a bride for Joseph, after he had been appointed by Pharaoh to administer Egypt (Gen 41:45).

And she [Aseneth] went to the man [actually, the chief of the angels] into her first chamber and stood before him. And the man said to her: 'Remove the veil from your head, and for what purpose did you do this? For you are a chaste virgin today, and your head is like that of a young man.' And Aseneth removed the veil from her head.

And the man said to her: 'Courage, Aseneth, chaste virgin. Behold, I have heard all the words of your confession and your prayer. Behold, I have also seen the humiliation and the affliction of the seven days of your want [of food]. Behold, from your tears and these ashes, plenty of mud has formed before your face. Courage, Aseneth, chaste virgin. For behold, your name was written in the book of the living in heaven; in the beginning of the book, as the very first of all, your name was written by my finger, and it will not be erased forever. Behold, from today, you will be renewed and formed anew and made alive again, and you will eat blessed bread of life, and drink a blessed cup of immortality, and anoint yourself with blessed ointment of incorruptibility. Courage, Aseneth, chaste virgin. Behold, I have given you today to Joseph for a bride, and he himself will be your bridegroom for ever [and] ever.' (C.B.)

2.49 Philo, *The Special Laws* 3.5.29

Intermarriage was apparently not a major problem in Egypt, since, if it were, we would have expected Philo to have stressed it, especially in view of the sharp condemnation of the practice in Deuteronomy. When Philo does mention the biblical prohibition of intermarriage, he speaks of its consequences not in his own day but rather at some vague time in the future.

But also, he [Moses] says, do not enter into the partnership of marriage with a member of a foreign nation, lest some day conquered by the force of opposing customs you surrender and stray unawares from the path that leads to piety and turn aside into a pathless wild. And though perhaps you yourself will hold your ground steadied from your earliest years by the admirable instructions instilled into you by your parents, with the holy laws always as their keynote, there is much to be feared for your sons and daughters. It may well be that they, enticed by spurious customs which they prefer to the genuine, are likely to unlearn the honor due to the one God, and that is the first and last stage of supreme misery. (LCL)

Apostasy

BIBLIOGRAPHY

Alexander Fuks, "Dositheos Son of Drimylos. A Prosopographical Note," *JJP* 7/8 (1954), 205–9.
Alexander Fuks, *Social Conflict in Ancient Greece* (1984), 307–11.
H. Hauben, "A Jewish Shipowner in Third-Century Ptolemaic Egypt," *AS* 10 (1979), 167–70.
Feldman (1993), 79–83.
Modrzejewski (1995), 56–61.

2.50 Philo, *On the Virtues* 34.182

It was lack of observance rather than actual apostasy that was apparently the chief problem of the Jewish community in Philo's day. It would appear that rabbinic authority outside Palestine was weak; and there was, as we see from the amulets that have been found, a good deal of compromising and syncretism with paganism. However, apostasy was deterred by the high level of anti-Judaism on the part of the masses. The only definite apostates of whom we hear are Dositheus, son of Drimylus (who is probably to be identified with the Dositheus [Josephus, *Against Apion* 2.49] who was named commander-in-chief of the army by Ptolemy Philometor in the second century BCE); Antiochus of Antioch in the first century CE (Josephus, *War* 7.47–60); and the children of Alexander, the son of Tigranes (the grandson of Herod the Great) (Josephus, *Ant.* 18.141). In the passage below, those who deviate from the laws of the Pentateuch are said to be motivated by bodily and sensual desires.

The proselytes become at once temperate, continent, modest, gentle, kind, humane, serious, just, high-minded, truth-lovers, superior to the desire for money and pleasure, just as conversely the rebels from the holy laws are seen to be incontinent, shameless, unjust, frivolous, petty-minded, quarrelsome, friends of falsehood and perjury, who have sold their freedom for dainties and strong liquor and cakes and the enjoyment of another's beauty, thus ministering to the delights of the belly and the organs below it – delights which end in the gravest injuries both to body and soul. (LCL)

2.51 3 Maccabees 1:1–3 (*ca.* early first century BCE)

Dositheos is here described as a Jew who had apostasized from his ancestral religion of Judaism and who saved the life of King Ptolemy Philopator from an assassination plot.

When [King Ptolemy] Philopator [of Egypt] learned from those who returned that the regions that he had controlled had been seized by Antiochus, he gave orders to all his forces, both infantry and cavalry, took with him his sister Arsinoe, and marched out to the region near Raphia,[54] where the army of Antiochus [III] was encamped. But a certain Theodotus, determined to carry out the plot he had devised, took with him the best of the Ptolemaic arms that had been previously issued to him, and crossed over by night to the tent of Ptolemy, intending single-handed to kill him and thereby end the war. But Dositheus, known as the son of Drimylus, a Jew by birth who later changed his religion and apostasized from the ancestral traditions, had led the king away and arranged that a certain insignificant man should sleep in the tent; and so it turned out that this man incurred the vengeance meant for the king.

54. A city in Palestine, three miles from Gaza. The battle of Raphia occurred in the year 217 BCE.

2.52 CPJ 127e (222 BCE)

In this papyrus, referring to a lease of land registered in a village of the Oxyrhynchus district, we see that Dositheos had actually become a priest of the cult of Alexander the Great and the deified Ptolemaic kings of Egypt.

In the twenty-fifth year of the reign of Ptolemy son of Ptolemy and Arsinoe the gods Adelphoi, when Dositheos son of Drimylos was priest of Alexander and the gods Adelphoi and the gods Euergetai, the *kanephoros* ['basket-bearer'] of Arsinoe Philadelphos being Berenike daughter of Pythangelos, in the month Gorpiaios, at Tholthis in the Oxyrynchite nome.

2.53 Josephus, Jewish War 7.46–7

In the passage below we see how far an apostate, Antiochus of Antioch, was ready to go in his detestation of Jews, in bringing about a wholesale massacre of his former compatriots.

Now just at the time when the war had been declared and Vespasian had recently landed in Syria, and when hatred of the Jews was everywhere at its height, a certain Antiochus, one of their own number and highly respected for the sake of his father, who was chief magistrate of the Jews in Antioch, entered the theater during an assembly of the people and denounced his own father and the other Jews, accusing them of a design to burn the whole city to the ground in one night; he also delivered up some foreign Jews as accomplices to the plot. On hearing this, the people [the non-Jewish Antiochenes], in uncontrollable fury, ordered the men who had been delivered up to be instantly consigned to the flames, and all were forthwith burnt to death in the theater. They then rushed for the Jewish masses, believing the salvation of their native place to be dependent on their prompt chastisement. Antiochus further inflamed their fury; for, thinking to furnish proof of his conversion and of his detestation of Jewish customs by sacrificing after the manner of the Greeks, he recommended that the rest should be compelled to do the same, as the conspirators would thus be exposed by their refusal. (LCL)

Social Life in Egypt

The Position of Women

BIBLIOGRAPHY

Jacob J. Rabinowitz, "Marriage Contracts in Ancient Egypt in the Light of Jewish Sources," *HTR* 46 (1953), 391–7.

Ross S. Kraemer, "Non-Literary Evidence for Jewish Women in Rome and Egypt," *Helios* 13 (1986), 85–101.

Dorothy Sly, *Philo's Perception of Women* (1990).

J. Romney Wagner, "Philo's Portrayal of Women – Hebraic or Hellenic?" in Amy-Jill Levine, ed., *"Women like This": New Perspectives on Jewish Women in the Greco-Roman World* (1991), 41–66.

Ross S. Kraemer, *Her Share of the Blessings. Women's Religions among Pagans, Jews, and Christians* (1992).

Our evidence with regard to the position of women in the Diaspora generally and Egypt in particular, is meager. Philo, as the passages below indicate, has an extremely derogatory view of women.

2.54 Philo, *Questions and Answers on Genesis* 4.148 on Gen 25:5–6

In the passage below Philo equates "female" with inferior and unadmirable.

What is the meaning of the words, 'And Abraham gave all that was his to Isaac his son, and to the sons of his concubines he gave gifts'? . . .
So much superior was Isaac to [the sons] of the concubines as are possessions to gifts. Wherefore [Scripture] recently described Isaac as motherless, and it calls those born to the concubines fatherless.[55] Accordingly, those who were harmonious in the father's family are of the male progeny, while the [sons] of the women and those of inferior descent are certainly to be called female and unvirile, for which reason they are little admired as great ones. (LCL)

2.55 Philo, *Questions and Answers on Exodus* 1.7 on Exod 12:5a

Here Philo says explicitly that the female is merely an imperfect male.

Why does [Moses] command [them] to take a 'perfect male sheep of one year'?
[It is to be] perfect in two physical features, [namely] in the sensitive parts of the body and also in the other organs. For an imperfect [sacrifice] is not worthy to be brought to the altar of God. And [it is to be] male, first because the male is more perfect than the female. Wherefore it is said by the naturalists that the female is nothing more than an imperfect male.[56] (LCL)

2.56 Philo, *Hypothetica* 11.14

Here Philo describes women as selfish, jealous, deceitful, and beguiling.

No Essene takes a wife because a wife is a selfish creature, excessively jealous and an adept at beguiling the morals of her husband and seducing him by her continued impostures. (LCL)

---

55. I.e., they were not legitimate sons of Abraham.
56. We find very similar language in both Plato, *Timaeus* 90A ff. and Aristotle, *On the Generation of Animals* 775A.

"A tree of life for all who hold fast to her," fresco over the Torah niche, Dura-Europos synagogue, ca. 250 CE.

3

᷈᷈᷈

Jewish Life in Other Countries of the Diaspora

During the eighty years of the independent Jewish state, Jews continued to emigrate in large numbers to many Hellenistic lands, notably Cyrenaica, Greece and the Aegean, Syria, Rome and the rest of Italy. Apart from Alexandria in Egypt, the largest Jewish community of the Diaspora was in the city of Antioch on the Orontes in Syria, the capital of the Seleucid kingdom.

Jews in Cyrenaica (Libya)

BIBLIOGRAPHY

Shimon Applebaum, "The Jewish Community of Hellenistic and Roman Teucheria in Cyrenaica," *SH* 7 (1961), 27–52.

Shimon Applebaum, "Cyrenensia Judaica – Some Notes on Recent Research Relating to the Jews of Cyrenaica in the Hellenistic and Roman Periods," *JJS* 13 (1963), 31–43.

Shimon Applebaum, "Jewish Status at Cyrene in the Roman Period," *Parola del Passato* 19 (1964), 291–303.

Shimon Applebaum, *Jews and Greeks in Ancient Cyrene* (1979).

Cyrenaica, particularly the city of Berenice (modern Benghazi), was a major center of Judaism in the Diaspora. Though the Jews enjoyed civic equality, they encountered persecution particularly in sending their annual donations to the Temple in Jerusalem. The fact that a leader of the Sicarii named Jonathan (Josephus, *War* 7.437–50) was able to gather considerable support in his attempt to renew the struggle against the Romans after the fall of Jerusalem fits in with our other evidence that there were close ties between the Jews of Cyrene and those of Palestine. We may also note that the revolt of 115–17 against the Romans originated in Cyrene with a messianic figure, Lukuas-Andreas.

> 3.1 Strabo (64 BCE–*ca.* 20 CE), *Historical Memoranda*, cited by Josephus, *Jewish Antiquities* 14.115–16

In this passage, where Josephus quotes Strabo, we see that the Jews of Cyrene apparently constituted a separate class, distinct from the resident aliens, that the rulers (who were the same as those of Egypt under the Ptolemies) encouraged the expansion of the Jews, and that the Jews observed the traditional Jewish laws.

There were four classes in the state of Cyrene; the first consisted of citizens, the second of farmers, the third of resident aliens [metics], and the fourth of Jews. . . . And it has come about that Cyrene, which had the same rulers as Egypt, has imitated it in many respects, particularly in notably encouraging and aiding the expansion of the organized groups of Jews which observe the national Jewish laws. (LCL)

> 3.2 *Supplementum Epigraphicum Graecum*, vol. 16, no. 931 (end of the first century CE)

This inscription records the gratitude of the Jewish community of Cyrene to a benefactor.

3rd year, Phamenoth 5, in the archonship of. . . . When Decimus Valerius Dionysius son of Gaius . . . , a worthy man as ever and benefactor in every way he can both of the community and individually of each of the citizens, and . . . plastered the ground floor of the amphitheater and painted the walls; it was decreed by the archons and the community of the Jews in Berenice to record him in . . . , and that he be exempted from all compulsory public services; likewise, that he be crowned with a wreath by name at each meeting and new moon, with a wreath of olive and woolen fillet. This decree is to be inscribed by the archons on a stele of Parian marble and placed in a most conspicuous place of the amphitheater. Unanimous.

Decimus Valerius Dionysius, son of Gaius, plastered the ground floor of the amphitheater and painted it at his own expense as a contribution to the community. (M.R.)

Jews in Greece and the Aegean

BIBLIOGRAPHY

Paul R. Trebilco, *Jewish Communities in Asia Minor* (1991).

Though we have no literature emanating from Jews in Greece, we do have inscriptions attesting to the existence of Jewish communities. These communities were augmented by Jewish slaves who were freed.

> 3.3 *Supplementum Epigraphicum Graecum* 15.293 (third century BCE)

From the temple of Amphiaraus in Oropus (Boeotia), Greece. A manumitted Jewish slave sets up a thank-offering in a Greek shrine in gratitude for some benefit.

Moschus . . . to be free, not belonging in any way to anyone. If something happens to Phrynides before the time elapses, Moschus is to depart a free man, wherever he may wish. With good fortune!

Witnesses: Athenodorus son of Mnasicon, of Oropus; Biottus son of Eudicus, of Athens; Charinus son of Articharmus, of Athens; Athenades son of Epigonus, of Oropus; Hippon son of Aeschylus, of Oropus.

Moschus son of Moschion, a Jew, having seen it in a dream, at the instruction of the god Amphiaraus and of Hygieia, in accordance with the orders of Amphiaraus and of Hygieia, inscribed it on a stele and set it up next to the altar. (M.R.)

3.4 *CII*, no. 709 (170–157 BCE)

Greek inscription from Delphi. Among the hundreds of manumission inscriptions at Delphi, a few concern Jews.

In the archonship of Archon son of Callias, in the month Endyspoi-tropion, Ateisides, son of Orthaius, sold to the Pythian Apollo three women slaves, whose names are Antigona, of Jewish origin, and her daughters Theodora and Dorothea, at the price of seven silver minas, and he has the whole price. Guarantor, according to the law of the city: Eudoxus son of Praxias, Delphian.

Accordingly, Antigona and Theodora and Dorothea have entrusted the sale to the god, on condition that they be free and unencumbered in every respect all their lives. But if anyone seizes them to reduce them to slavery, the vendor Ateisides and the guarantor Eudoxus shall provide surety. If the vendor and the guarantor do not provide surety for the sale to the god, they shall be subject to suit according to the law. Likewise also, those who meet them shall be empowered to seize them as free persons with impunity and without being subject to suit in respect to all legal process and fines.

Witnesses: the priest of Apollo Amyntas, and the archons Nicarchus, Cleon son of Damothenes, Hagion son of Ecephylus; private persons, Archon son of Nicoboulos, Eudorus son of Amyntas. (M.R.)

3.5 *CII*, no. 710 (162 BCE)

Greek inscription from Delphi. Sale of a Jewish slave to the god Apollo.

In the archonship of Emmenidas son of Callias, in the month Apellaeus, Cleon son of Cleudamus, sold to the Pythian Apollo, with the consent of Zenophanea, mother of Cleudamus, a male slave named Judaeus, of Jewish origin, at the price of four silver minas, on condition that he be free and unencumbered in every respect all his life. As Judaeus has entrusted the sale to the god, he shall be free to do as he wishes.

Guarantors, according to the law of the city: Xenon son of Glaucus, Aristion son of Agon.

Witnesses: the priests of Apollo, Amyntas of Tarentum, and the archons Aristion, Asandrus, Aristomachus.

Private persons: Sodamidas, Theuphrastus, Teison, Glaucus son of Xenon, Menes. (M.R.)

3.6 *CII*, no. 725 (end of the second or early first century BCE)

Greek inscription from Delos. Invocation of the Highest God to punish those responsible for the death of an innocent woman.

I invoke and ask of the Highest God, the lord of souls and all body, against those who treacherously killed or poisoned Heraclea, inflicting on her a premature fate, pouring out her innocent blood unjustly, that punishment may come to those who murdered her or poisoned her, and to her children, O Lord who oversees all, and, O angels of God, before whom every soul on that day[1] humbles itself with supplication, that you may avenge the innocent blood and demand recompense as speedily as possible. (M.R.)

Jews in Syria

BIBLIOGRAPHY

Carl H. Kraeling, "The Jewish Community at Antioch," *JBL* 52 (1932), 130–60.
Wayne A. Meeks and Robert L. Wilken, *Jews and Christians in Antioch in the First Four Centuries of the Common Era* (1978).
Schürer, vol. 3 (1986), 5–38.

3.7 Josephus, *Jewish War* 7.43–5

On the great size of the Jewish community of Antioch, due to their privileged position as citizens and the security granted to them by the kings, and on the attraction of multitudes of Greeks to Judaism.

The Jewish race, densely interspersed among the native populations of every portion of the world, is particularly numerous in Syria, where intermingling is due to the proximity of the two countries. But it was at Antioch that they specially congregated, partly owing to the greatness of that city, but mainly because the successors of King Antiochus[2] had enabled them to live in security. For, although Antiochus surnamed Epiphanes sacked Jerusalem and plundered the Temple, his successors on the throne restored to the Jews of Antioch all such votive offerings as were made of brass, to be laid up in their synagogue, and, moreover, granted them citizen rights on an equality with the Greeks. Continuing to receive similar treatment from later monarchs, the Jewish colony grew in numbers, and their richly designed and costly offerings formed a splendid ornament to the Temple. Moreover, they were constantly attracting to their religious ceremonies multitudes of Greeks, and these they had in some measure incorporated with themselves. (LCL)

Jews in Italy

BIBLIOGRAPHY

Hugo Gressmann, "Jewish Life in Ancient Rome," in George A. Kohut, ed., *Jewish Studies in Memory of Israel Abrahams* (1927), 170–91.
George LaPiana, "Foreign Groups in Rome during the First Centuries of the Empire," *HTR* 20 (1927), 183–403.
Harry J. Leon, *The Jews of Ancient Rome* (1960).

1. I.e., Yom Kippur, the Day of Atonement.
2. Antiochus I Soter, who reigned from 280 to 261 BCE, is apparently meant.

Leonard V. Rutgers, *The Jews in Late Ancient Rome: Evidence of Cultural Interaction in the Roman Diaspora* (1995).

The Jewish community in the imperial capital was the largest in the western part of the Roman Empire, comprising perhaps as many as 50,000 people, most of whom lived across the Tiber in the district now called Trastevere. They did not have a central communal organization. Eleven synagogues are mentioned in the inscriptions, according to Leon, but there are few reliable criteria for dating these inscriptions. Thus the bricks may be contemporary, or second-hand materials may have been employed dating from a much earlier period. Leon, based partly on the masonry, the brick stamps, the mosaic patterns, the artistic decorations, and the names that are inscribed, concludes that they range in date from the first to the third centuries. The most recent student of the subject, Rutgers, concludes that they date from the third and fourth and possibly the early fifth century. In any case, they cover a very considerable period of time, and they may very well not have existed at the same time. The Jews buried their dead in six catacombs; indeed, we have more inscriptions (approximately 570, three-quarters of which are in Greek, almost all the rest in Latin) from the Jews of Rome than from those of any other community of the Diaspora. Though the Jews were Romanized (for the most part, for example, they appropriate non-Jewish names) and made use of contemporary non-Jewish culture, they agreed, on the whole, with the Jews of Palestine in their practice of Judaism and did not seek to be assimilated.

From the Jewish Catacombs in Rome
Dates unknown, but most seem to come from the third or fourth century CE.

3.8 *CII*, no. 68 (Latin)

Tombstone of a proselyte.

[Here lies] Cresces Sinicerius, Jew, proselyte; he lived thirty-five years, laid to rest. His mother did for her sweet son what he should have done for her. Eight days before the Kalends of January. (M.R.)

3.9 *CII*, no. 72 (Latin; on a marble sarcophagus)

Tribute to a pious Jewess.

To Julia Irene Arista, mother, preserved through the grace of God and the devotion of her family, pious observer of the Law. Antonius Tullianus Eusebius, an excellent man, her son, in due devotion. Age 41. (M.R.)

3.10 *CII*, no. 118 (Greek)

Tribute to an official of the synagogue.

I, Zotichus, official [of the synagogue], lie here, having lived a good life, friend of all and known to all for distinction, courage, and assistance. May your sleep be with the just! (M.R.)

3.11 CII, no. 220 (Latin)

Request to be buried next to her husband.

Julia Afrodisia made this for her well-deserving husband, Aurelius Hermias; and she prays and asks that a place be reserved for her, so that she may be placed with her husband when her time comes. (M.R.)

3.12 CII, no. 301 (Greek)

Tombstone of an official of the council of a synagogue.

Here lies Annius, official of the council of the synagogue of the Augustesians. In peace his sleep! (M.R.)

3.13 CII, no. 319 (Greek)

Tribute to the wife of a father of the synagogue.

Here lies Irena, wife from maidenhood of Clodius, brother of Quintus Claudius Synesius, father of the synagogue of the Campenses of Rome. [In Hebrew] Peace! (M.R.)

3.14 CII, no. 321 (Greek)

Tribute to a pious man who died young.

Here lies Lazar, pious, just, lover of his children, lover of his brothers, lover of the synagogue, age 31. In peace his sleep! (M.R.)

3.15 CII, no. 392 (Greek)

Tribute to a devoted wife.

Here lies Rebecca, who had only one husband; she lived forty-four years. May she rest in peace! (M.R.)

3.16 CII, no. 476 (Latin; a metrical inscription)

Tribute to a wife who died soon after marriage.

Here lies Regina, covered by this tomb, which her husband decided was appropriate for his love. After she was twenty, he lived with her one year, four months and eight days. She will live again, and will return to the light again. For one may hope that she will rise to the promised life, as is the true faith, to the worthy and pious; she has deserved to have a place in the hallowed land. This your piety has accorded to you, this your chaste life, this your love of your people, this your observance of the Law, your devotion to your marriage, whose repute was your concern. For all these deeds your hope for a future life is assured. From all of this your sorrowing husband seeks comfort. (M.R.)

3.17 CII, no. 509 (Greek)

Tribute to a synagogue leader who lived an extraordinarily long life.

Here lies Pancharius, father of the synagogue of Elaea, age 110 years, lover of his people, lover of the commandments. He lived a good life. In peace his sleep! (M.R.)

3.18 CII, no. 523 (Latin)

Tribute to a philanthropic proselyte.

Veturia Paulla, happily placed in the eternal home. She lived eighty-six years, six months, proselyte for sixteen years; she was also named Sara. Mother of the synagogue of the Campenses and of the Volumnians. May she rest in peace! (M.R.)

From Elsewhere in Italy

3.19 CII, no. 537 (Greek; from Porto, Rome's harbor)

Tribute to the daughter of a synagogue leader.

Here lies Cattia Ammias, daughter of Menophilus, father of the synagogue of the Carcaresians. She lived a good life in Judaism, having lived thirty-four years with her husband. She saw grandchildren from her children. Here lies Cattia Ammias. (M.R.)

3.20 CII, no. 556 (Latin; from Naples)

Tribute to the former slave of the emperor.

Claudia Aster, captive from Jerusalem, took care of this. Here lies Tiberius Claudius Masculus, freedman of the emperor. I ask you to take care that no one, contrary to the law, removes this inscription of mine. He lived twenty-five years. (M.R.)

Synagogues in the Roman Empire

BIBLIOGRAPHY

Eleazar L. Sukenik, *Ancient Synagogues in Palestine and Greece* (1934).

Eleazar L. Sukenik, "The Present State of Ancient Synagogue Studies," *Bulletin of the Louis M. Rabinowitz Fund for the Exploration of Ancient Synagogues* 1 (1949), 1–23.

M. Floriani Squarciapino, "The Synagogue at Ostia," *Archaeology* 16 (1963), 194–203.

Alf Thomas Kraabel, "Hypsistos and the Synagogue at Sardis," *GRBS* 10 (1969), 81–93.

Joseph Gutmann, *The Dura-Europos Synagogue: A Re-evaluation (1932–72)* (1973).

Joseph Gutmann, ed., *The Synagogue: Studies in Origins, Archaeology and Architecture* (1975).

Samuel Safrai, "The Synagogue," in Samuel Safrai and Menahem Stern, eds, *The Jewish People in the First Century* (CRINT, sect. 1, vol. 2 [1976]), 908–44.

Samuel Safrai, "The Synagogue and Its Worship," in Michael Avi-Yonah and Zvi Baras, eds, *The World History of the Jewish People*, First Series: *Ancient Times*, vol. 8: *Society and Religion in the Second Temple Period* (1977), 65–98.

Abraham Ovadiah, "Ancient Synagogues in Asia-Minor," *Proceedings of the Tenth International Congress of Classical Archaeology 1973*, vol. 2 (1978), 857–66.

Alf Thomas Kraabel, "The Diaspora Synagogue: Archaeological and Epigraphic Evidence since Sukenik," *ANRW* 2.19.1 (1979), 477–510.

Carl H. Kraeling, *The Synagogue (The Excavation at Dura-Europos): Final Report* (1979).

Hershel Shanks, *Judaism in Stone: The Archaeology of Ancient Synagogues* (1979).

Shaye J. D. Cohen, "Women in the Synagogues of Antiquity," *CJ* 34.2 (1980), 23–9.

Eric M. Meyers, "Ancient Synagogues in Galilee: Their Religious and Cultural Setting," *BA* 43 (Spring, 1980), 97–108.

Joseph Gutmann, *Ancient Synagogues: The State of Research* (1981).

Alf Thomas Kraabel, "The Excavated Synagogues of Late Antiquity from Asia Minor to Italy," *Jahrbuch des Österreichischen Archäologischen Instituts* 32 (1981), 227–36.

Lee I. Levine, ed., *Ancient Synagogues Revealed* (1981).

Bernadette Brooten, *Woman Leaders in the Ancient Synagogue* (1982).

Alf Thomas Kraabel, "The Synagogue and the Jewish Community," in George M. A. Hanfmann, ed., *Sardis from Prehistoric to Roman Times* (1983), 168–90.

Jonathan Goldstein, "The Central Composition of the West Wall of the Synagogue of Dura-Europos," *Journal of the Ancient Near East Society* 16–17 (1984–5), 99–142.

Lee I. Levine, ed., *The Synagogue in Late Antiquity* (1987).

L. Michael White, "The Delos Synagogue Revisited: Recent Fieldwork in the Graeco-Roman Diaspora," *HTR* 80 (1987), 133–60.

Kurt Weitzmann and Herbert L. Kessler, *The Frescoes of the Dura Synagogue and Christian Art* (1990).

L. Michael White, *Building God's House in the Roman World: Architectural Adaptation among Pagans, Jews, and Christians* (1990).

James T. Burtchaell, *From Synagogue to Church: Public Services and Offices in the Earliest Christian Communities* (1992).

Heather A. McKay, *Sabbath and Synagogue: The Question of Sabbath Worship in Ancient Judaism* (1994).

Dan Urman and Paul V. M. Flesher, eds, *Ancient Synagogues: Historical Analysis and Archaeological Discovery*, vol. 1 (1995).

Every considerable Jewish community throughout the Roman Empire had one or more synagogues. Rabbinic tradition (*Targum of Pseudo-Jonathan* on Exodus 18:20 and *Yalqut* Exodus 408), Josephus (*Against Apion* 2.175), and the New Testament (Acts 15:21) ascribe the origin of the synagogue to Moses. The Jerusalem Talmud (*Megillah* 3.1) asserts that there were 480 synagogues in Jerusalem alone at the time of the destruction of the Temple in 70, whereas the Babylonian Talmud (*Kethuboth* 105a) gives the number as 394. Moreover, we know of 66 communities in the Diaspora that had synagogues, ranging from the Black Sea region to Syria, Lebanon, Asia Minor, Greece, Crete, Cyprus, Yugoslavia, Hungary, Italy, Sicily, Spain, Egypt, Libya, and Tunisia; but the dates vary very widely. We may note that the synagogue served not only as a house of prayer but also as a place of assembly, a place of instruction in the Law, a hostel for strangers, and a place where slaves might be set free. The synagogues were led not by rabbis or priests but by lay people.

The leading position, that of *archisynagogus*, who served as a patron of the Jewish community, seems to have been held by benefactors, including, most remarkably, several women; but the question of women's participation in the administration of Diaspora synagogues has been hotly disputed. We may also note references to art-work, including painting, in the synagogue, despite the seeming prohibition of such in the Bible. It is of particular interest that we find instances of synagogues contributed by non-Jews. The following is a selection of inscriptions from synagogues. These inscriptions are in Greek, except where otherwise noted.

3.21 CII, no. 690 (from Gorgippias, in the Cimmerian Bosporus, mid first century CE)

The synagogue as a site for the emancipation of a female slave.

To the Highest God, all powerful, blessed be He. In the reign of King Polemon, friend of Germanicus and friend of his country, in the year 338,[3] month Dius, Pothus son of Straton has consecrated in the prayer house, in accordance with his vow, his slave named Chrysa, in such a way that she will be unencumbered and unmolested by every inheritance, [being freed] by Jupiter, Earth, Sun. (M.R.)

3.22 Supplementum Epigraphicum Graecum, vol. 17, no. 823 (found in 1939 at Berenice [modern Benghazi, Libya], 56 CE)

A list of contributors to the building of a synagogue.

Year 2 of the Emperor Nero Claudius Caesar son of Drusus Germanicus, Choiak 5. It was decreed by the synagogue of the Jews in Berenice to record on a stele of Parian marble the names of those contributing to the building of the synagogue: Zenion son of Zoilus, archon, 11 drachmas; Isidorus son of Dositheus, archon, 11 drachmas; Dositheus son of Ammonius, archon, 11 drachmas; Pratis son of Jonathas, archon, 11 drachmas; Carnedas son of Cornelis, archon, 11 drachmas; Heraclides son of Heraclides, archon, 11 drachmas; Thaliarchus son of Dositheus, archon, 11 drachmas; Sosibius son of Jason, archon, 11 drachmas; Protomedes son of Socrates, archon, 11 drachmas; Antigonus son of Straton, archon, 11 drachmas; Cartisthenes son of Archias, priest, 11 drachmas.

Lysanias son of Lysanias, 25 drachmas; Zenodorus son of Theuphilus, 28 drachmas; Marion son of . . . , 25 drachmas; Alexander son of Euphranor, 5 drachmas; Isidora daughter of Serapion, 5 drachmas; Zosima daughter of Terpolion, 5 drachmas; Polon daughter of Dositheus, 5 drachmas. (M.R.)

3.23 CII, no. 766 (from Acmonia, Phrygia [north-west Asia Minor], ca. 60 CE)

Plaques given to donors.

3. Of the Bosporan Era, i.e., 41 CE.

This building, constructed by Julia Severa,[4] was restored by Gaius Tyrronius Clades, head of the synagogue for life; and Lucius son of Lucius, head of the synagogue, and Popilius Rufus, archon, from their own funds and from money contributed[5] the walls and the roof, and they made safe the little doors and all the remaining decorations. These men the synagogue honored with a golden shield on account of their virtuous life and their goodwill and zeal for the synagogue. (M.R.)

3.24 Inscriptiones Graecae ad Res Romanas Pertinentes, vol. 1, no. 881 (from Panticapaeum, in the Crimea, 80 CE)

Manumission of a slave.

In the reign of King Tiberius Julius Rhescuporis,[6] friend of Caesar and friend of Rome, the pious, in the year 377,[7] in the month Peritius the 20th. I, Chreste, formerly wife of Drusus, release at the house of prayer my house-bred slave Heraclas to be absolutely free, according to my vow. He is not to be recovered or disturbed by any heir of mine, but he is to go wherever he may wish, without let or hindrance, as I vowed, except into the house of prayer . . .[8] Assent is given to this also by my heirs, Heraclides and Heliconias, and joint oversight will be provided also by the synagogue of the Jews. (M.R.)

3.25 CII, no. 694 (from Stobi, capital of Macedonia, in the ruins of a synagogue, probably second century CE)

A philanthropist contributes funds for a synagogue in the lower story, while a private owner retains the upper story.

[Claudius] Tiberius Polycharmus also called Achyrius, father of the synagogue in Stobi, who has conducted himself with all the prescriptions of Judaism, in accordance with a vow built the building for the holy place and the dining room, together with the colonnaded hall, from his own funds, without touching in any way the funds of the sanctuary. But the complete right to and ownership of the upper story, I, Claudius Tiberius Polycharmus, reserve for myself and my heirs for life. If anyone wishes to make alterations contrary to my decisions, he shall pay to the patriarch [of the synagogue] 250,000 denarii. This agreement was made by me so that the brick construction of the upper story is to be made by me and my heirs. (M.R.)

3.26 CII, no. 738 (from Phocaea, Ionia, date unknown)

Tribute to a woman philanthropist.

4. Julia Severa, the wife of Lucius Servenius Capito, was a priestess of a municipal pagan cult and, at the same time, a Jewish "sympathizer."
5. Presumably by members of the community.
6. Rhescuporis was a Roman client-king of the Bosporus.
7. Of the Bosporan Era, i.e., 80 CE.
8. The significance of this is unclear.

In honor of Tation, daughter of Straton son of Empedon, who constructed, at her own expense, the assembly-room, and the enclosure of
the open-air courtyard and bestowed it on the Jews. The synagogue of
the Jews honored Tation, daughter of Straton son of Empedon, with a
gold crown and the privilege of a front seat [at functions in the
synagogue]. (L.H.F.)

3.27 *L'Année épigraphique*, 1967, pp. 27–8 (from the only known synagogue
in Ostia, Italy, date unknown)

Tribute to the donor of the ark of a synagogue.

[In Latin] For the safety of the emperor.
  [In Greek] Mindis Faustus built this and made it out of his own funds,
and set up the ark for the sacred Law. (M.R.)

3.28 *CII*, no. 1404 (Jerusalem, date unknown, but before 70 CE)

Tribute to a philanthropist, descendant of philanthropists.

Theodotus, son of Vettenus, priest and archisynagogus,[9] son of an
archisynagogus, grandson of an archisynagogus, built the synagogue
for the reading of the Law and the teaching of the Commandments,
and provided the guest-house and the rooms and the water supplies as
an inn for those who have need when they come from abroad; which
synagogue his fathers founded and the elders and Simonides. (M.R.)

3.29 *CII*, no. 972 (from Kasyoun, Judaea, 197 CE)

Dedication in honor of the Emperor, his wife, and his sons.

For the safety of our lords the Emperor and the Caesars, Lucius
Septimius Severus Pius Parthicus Augustus, and Marcus Aurelius
Antoninus and Lucius Septimius Geta, his sons, in accordance with a
vow of the Jews.
  Also of Julia Domna Augusta. (M.R.)

3.30 Carl H. Kraeling, *The Excavations at Dura-Europos*, vol. 8.1: *The
Synagogue* (1956), pp. 263–4 (from Dura-Europos in Syria; a fragmentary
building inscription in Aramaic, 241–5 CE)

Officers in charge of the construction of a synagogue.

This house was built in the year 556,[10] corresponding to the second year
of Philip Julius Caesar, in the eldership of the priest Samuel son of
Yeda'ya, the archon. Now those who stood in charge of this work were
Abram the Treasurer, and Samuel son of Sapharah, and ... the
proselyte. With a willing spirit they [began to build] in this fifty-sixth
year. ... . Peace to them, and to their wives and children all. [The rest is
fragmentary.] (M.R.)

9. President of the synagogue.
10. Of the Seleucid Era, which began in 311 BCE.

3.31 Louis Robert, *Nouvelles Inscriptions de Sardes* (1964), nos 4, 5. 6, 7 (from the synagogue at Sardis in Asia Minor, medallions in mosaic pavement; second to fifth centuries CE)

Donors to a synagogue who fulfilled their pledges.

Aurelius Eulogius, pious, fulfilled a vow.

Aurelius Polyippus, pious, having made a vow, fulfilled it.

I, Aurelius Olympius of the tribe of Leontii, with my wife and children, fulfilled my vow.

. . . with my wife Regina and my children . . . I have given from the gifts of the all-powerful God all the facing [of marble] . . . of the assembly-hall and the painting. (M.R.)

3.32 Louis Jalabert and René Mouterde, *Inscriptions grecques et latines de la Syrie*, vol. 4 (1955), nos. 1319, 1320 (from Apamea, Syria, 391 CE)

Officers of and donors to a synagogue.

Under the very honored heads of the synagogue, Eusebius and Nemeias and Phineas, and under the president of the council of elders Theodorus, and under the most honored elders Isaac, Saul and others, Ilasius head of the synagogue at Antioch, had the entrance adorned with mosaic [a distance of] 150 feet. Year 703,[11] 7th day of Audnaeus. Benediction to all.

Ilasius son of Isaac, head of the synagogue at Antioch, for the salvation of Photion his wife and his children, and for the salvation of Eustathia his mother-in-law, and in memory of Isaac and of Edesius and of Hesychion his ancestors, made the mosaic of the entrance. Peace and mercy to all your holy community. (M.R.)

Greek Influence in Jewish Art

BIBLIOGRAPHY

Erwin R. Goodenough, *Jewish Symbols in the Greco-Roman Period*, 13 vols (1953–68).

Morton Smith, "The Image of God: Notes on the Hellenization of Judaism with Especial Reference to Goodenough's Work on Jewish Symbols," *BJRL* 40 (1957–8), 473–512.

Michael Avi-Yonah, *Oriental Art in Roman Palestine* (*Studi Semitici*, vol. 5) (1961).

Joseph Gutmann, "The 'Second Commandment' and the Image in Judaism," *HUCA* 32 (1961), 161–74.

Jacob Neusner, "Notes on Goodenough's Jewish Symbols," *CJ* 17 (Spring–Summer, 1963), 77–92.

Morton Smith, "Goodenough's Jewish Symbols in Retrospect," *JBL* 86 (1967), 53–68.

Jacob Neusner, *Early Rabbinic Judaism* (1975), 139–215.

Erwin R. Goodenough, *Jewish Symbols in the Greco-Roman Period*, edited with a foreword by Jacob Neusner (1992).

Feldman (1993), 39–42.

11. Of the Seleucid Era.

Goodenough, in particular, has propounded the thesis that paganism deeply influenced Judaism during the Hellenistic period, that the rabbis had much less control over the people than George Foot Moore had postulated, and that, in fact, there was a "popular" Judaism with a mystic bent, as indicated by the symbolism of Hellenistic Jewish art, which cannot be regarded as merely decorative and which corresponds on the artistic plane to Philo on the literary and philosophical level. Goodenough would thus explain the rapid Hellenization of Christianity, which has usually been posited as a paradox, namely the triumph of Christianity despite its Jewish origins, by declaring that Christianity was the natural heir of a deeply Hellenized Judaism. His thesis, however, is very much debated.

No doubt in the period of the kings of Judah and Israel the Jews were susceptible to pagan influences, as the Bible itself indicates. But, at least in the time of Hecataeus of Abdera (*ca.* 300 BCE), as cited by Josephus (*Against Apion* 1.193), the Jews avoided contact with paganism, to the extent that when pagan temples and altars were erected in Judaea "the Jews razed them all to the ground, paying, in some cases, a fine to the [Persian] satraps and, in others, obtaining pardon." We may note that *1 Maccabees* is the only text dating from this period that speaks of the use of images by Jews for any purpose, and the New Testament does not refer to the subject at all. Nevertheless, with regard to images there was always a range of interpretation. The Temple itself was decorated in part by a vine, grape clusters, and the stars, to say nothing of Herod's eagle. And the Temple preferred Tyrian coins, prominently displaying Melqart, the Phoenician equivalent of Heracles.

During the period after 70 CE there was much symbolism in Jewish art, particularly on gravestones, as noted by Goodenough, in terms of bulls, lions, trees, Victory and her crown, rosettes, wheels, masks, psychopomps, and astronomical symbols. The head of Helios, the Greek sun god, has been found on a sarcophagus, dating from somewhere between the second and fourth centuries CE, in a catacomb at Beth She'arim in Palestine, where rabbinic families are buried; and a representation of Helios appears at the center of the floors of five synagogues found in Palestine. Moreover, various sun-god symbols with Jewish labels appear on numerous amulets of that period. In a synagogue excavated at Hammath-Tiberias in Palestine dating, it is thought, from the beginning of the fourth century, the signs of the zodiac are found with the sun god Helios on his chariot in the center. In the third-century CE synagogue found at Dura-Europos in eastern Syria on the Euphrates, amid various paintings of biblical scenes containing numerous motifs paralleled in the midrashic tradition, there appears the figure of the Greek mythical Orpheus playing his lyre to an eagle and a lion. One of the paintings depicts Moses taken out of the ark by a naked woman who is identified by her peculiar necklace as the goddess Aphrodite. In the depiction of the prophet Ezekiel and the valley of the dry bones, the souls of the dead are portrayed as Greek Psyches with wings of butterflies. Goodenough argues that these are pagan symbols which were fully "alive" during this period and hence indicate pagan influence. Others have argued that they show merely that the Jews were lax at the time in borrowing ornament, and that these figures do not indicate an ideological invasion of Judaism from the pagan world. Apparently, however, to judge from various comments in the Talmudic tractate *Avodah Zarah*, the rabbis were not worried that such decorations would lead to actual idol-worship. Indeed, we have the tradition (*Yoma* 69b, *Sanhedrin* 64a), cited in the name of Rabbi Judah (second century CE) or Rabbi Jonathan (beginning of the third century CE), that all idolatrous impulses had been eradicated from among the people of Israel as early as the beginning of the Second Temple under Ezra in the fifth century BCE, as well as the corroborative statement in Judith (8:18), dating probably from the Maccabean period in the second century BCE, that idol worship had disappeared "in our generation."

Julius Caesar.

4

⚜

Pro-Jewish Attitudes by Governments

Syria

BIBLIOGRAPHY

Aryeh Kasher, "The Rights of the Jews of Antioch on the Orontes," *PAAJR* 49 (1982), 69–85.

After living for more than 100 years as subjects of the Ptolemies, the Jews of Judaea came under the power of the Seleucids of Syria when Antiochus III (the Great) (223–187 BCE) wrested Coele-Syria (including Judaea) from the Ptolemies and annexed it in 198 BCE. Not only was Judaism accorded the traditional religious toleration of the Seleucid state, but the Jews were even granted special privileges.

4.1 Josephus, *Jewish Antiquities* 12.138–53 (198 BCE)

In the letter below we see that Antiochus III assisted the Jews in the restoration of the Temple in Jerusalem, contributed animals for the sacrifices, granted the Jews religious autonomy, relieved them of taxes, freed those who were slaves, and protected the sanctity of Jerusalem. The authenticity of his letters and decrees, cited below, has been disputed, but they are generally regarded as genuine. Because of his confidence in the loyalty of the Jews he directed the transport of two thousand Jewish families to areas of unrest, granting them special privileges.

'King Antiochus to Ptolemy,[1] greeting. Inasmuch as the Jews, from the very moment when we entered their country, showed their eagerness to serve us and when we came to their city, gave us a splendid reception and met us with their senate[2] and furnished an abundance of provisions to our soldiers and elephants, and also helped us to expel the Egyptian garrison in the citadel, we have seen fit on our part to requite them for these acts and to restore their city which has been destroyed by the hazards of war, and to repeople it by bringing back to it those who have been dispersed abroad. In the first place we have decided, on account of their piety, to furnish them for their sacrifices an allowance of sacrificial animals, wine, oil, and frankincense to the value of twenty thousand pieces of silver, and sacred *artabae*[3] of fine

---

1. Ptolemy son of Thraseas, Antiochus' governor of Coele-Syria and Phoenicia.
2. The reference is to the Gerousia, the council of elders which was the chief Jewish legislative and judicial body, corresponding to the later Sanhedrin.
3. The *artaba* was an Egyptian measure, normally about 40 liters.

flour in accordance with their native law, and 1,460 *medimni*[4] of wheat and 375 *medimni* of salt. And it is my will that these things be made over to them as I have ordered, and that the work on the Temple be completed, including the porticoes and any other part that it may be necessary to build. The timber, moreover, shall be brought from Judaea itself and from other nations and Lebanon without the imposition of a toll-charge. The like shall be done with the other materials needed for making the restoration of the Temple more splendid. And all the members of the nation shall have a form of government in accordance with the laws of their country, and the senate, the priests, the scribes of the Temple and the Temple-singers shall be relieved from the poll-tax and the crown-tax and the salt-tax which they pay. And in order that the city may the more quickly be inhabited, I grant both to the present inhabitants and to those who may return before the month of Hyperberetaios exemption from taxes for three years. We shall also relieve them in the future from the third part of their tribute, so that their losses may be made good. And as for those who were carried off from the city and are slaves, we herewith set them free, both them and the children born to them, and order their property to be restored to them.'

Now these were the contents of the letter. And out of reverence for the Temple he also published a proclamation throughout the entire kingdom, of which the contents were as follows: 'It is unlawful for any foreigner to enter the enclosure of the Temple which is forbidden to the Jews, except to those of them who are accustomed to enter after purifying themselves in accordance with the law of the country. Nor shall anyone bring into the city the flesh of horses or of mules or of wild or tame asses, or of leopards, foxes or hares or, in general, of any animals forbidden to the Jews. Nor is it lawful to bring in their skins or even to breed any of these animals in the city. But only the sacrificial animals known to their ancestors and necessary for the propitiation of God shall they be permitted to use. And the person who violates any of these statutes shall pay to the priests a fine of three thousand drachmas of silver.'

He also testified in writing to our piety and loyalty when, on the occasion of his being in the upper satrapies, he learned of revolts in Phrygia and Lydia, and ordered Zeuxis, his governor, and one of his close friends, to send some of our people from Babylonia to Phrygia. He then wrote as follows: 'King Antiochus to Zeuxis, his father,[5] greeting. If you are in good health, it is well. I also am in sound health. Learning that the people in Lydia and Phrygia are revolting, I have come to consider this as requiring very serious attention on my part, and, on taking counsel with my friends as to what should be done, I determined to transport two thousand Jewish families with their effects from Mesopotamia and Babylonia to the fortresses and most important places. For I am convinced that they will be loyal guardians of our

4. The *medimnus* was about 50 liters.
5. "Father" is probably a term of respect for a senior official of the Seleucid Empire. Zeuxis was satrap of Lydia in Asia Minor. The date of the resettlement is *ca.* 210–205 BCE.

interests because of their piety to God, and I know that they have had the testimony of my forefathers to their good faith and eagerness to do as they are asked. It is my will, therefore – though it may be a troublesome matter – that they should be transported and, since I have promised it, use their own laws. And when you have brought them to the places mentioned, you shall give each of them a place to build a house and land to cultivate and plant with vines, and shall exempt them from payment of taxes on the produce of the soil for ten years. And also, until they get produce from the soil, let them have grain measured out to them for feeding their servants, and let there be given also to those engaged in public service sufficient for their needs in order that through receiving kind treatment from us they may show themselves the more eager in our cause. And take as much thought for their nation as possible, that it may not be molested by anyone.' (LCL)

4.2 Plutarch (*ca.* 46–120 CE), *Apophthegms of Kings and Generals* 184 E–F

According to Plutarch, King Antiochus VII of Syria showed such great respect for the Jewish religion that when he was besieging Jerusalem he permitted the transfer of offerings to the priests.

The Jews, when he [i.e., Antiochus VII Sidetes] was besieging Jerusalem [132 BCE], asked for an armistice of seven days for their most important festival [Tabernacles], and he not only granted this, but he also made ready bulls with gilded horns, and a great quantity of incense and spices, and brought all these in solemn procession as far as the gates. Then having transferred the offerings to the hands of their priests, he returned to his camp. The Jews were amazed, and immediately after the festival placed themselves in his hands. (LCL)

Asia Minor

4.3 Josephus, *Jewish Antiquities* 14.247–55 (*ca.* end of second century BCE)

The following decree of the people of Pergamum, influenced by the ancient friendship of the Jews with the Pergamenes, as well as by the alliance of the Jews with the Romans, confirms the freedom of the Jews of Pergamum to engage in commerce.

Decree of the people of Pergamum.
In the presidency of Cratippus, on the first of the month Daisios, a decree of the magistrates.
As the Romans in pursuance of the practices of their ancestors have accepted dangerous risks for the common safety of all mankind and strive emulously to place their allies and friends in a state of happiness and lasting peace, the Jewish nation and their high priest Hyrcanus [I] have sent as envoys to them Straton, son of Theodotus, Apollonius, son of Alexander, Aeneas, son of Antipater, Aristobulus, son of Amyntas, and Sosipater, son of Philip, worthy and excellent men, and have made representations concerning certain particular matters, whereupon the Senate passed a decree concerning the matters on which they spoke, to the effect that King Antiochus [IX Cyzicenus], son of Antiochus [VII

Sidetes], shall do no injury to the Jews, the allies of the Romans; and that the fortresses, harbors, territory, and whatever else he may have taken from them shall be restored to them; and that it shall be lawful for them to export goods from their harbors and that no king or people exporting goods from the territory of the Jews or from their harbors shall be untaxed except only Ptolemy [VII Euergetes II Physcon], king of Alexandria, because he is our ally and friend; and that the garrison in Joppa shall be expelled, as they have requested. . . . (LCL)

4.4 Josephus, *Jewish Antiquities* 14.259–61 (*ca.* 100 BCE)

The following decree of the people of Sardis grants the Jews the privilege of being organized as a community, of having their own courts, and of being permitted to import kosher food.

Decree of the people of Sardis.
The following decree was passed by the council and people on the motion of the magistrates. Whereas the Jewish citizens living in our city have continually received many great privileges from the people and have now come before the council and the people and have pleaded that as their laws and freedom have been restored to them by the Roman Senate and people, they may, in accordance with their accepted customs, come together and have a communal life and adjudicate suits among themselves, and that a place be given them in which they may gather together with their wives and children and offer their ancestral prayers and sacrifices to God, it has therefore been decreed by the council and people that permission shall be given them to come together on stated days to do those things that are in accordance with their laws, and also that a place shall be set apart by the magistrates for them to build and inhabit, such as they may consider suitable for this purpose, and that the market-officials of the city shall be charged with the duty of having suitable food for them brought in. (LCL)

Egypt

The Macedonian–Greek Ptolemies, who ruled Egypt after the death of Alexander, realizing that the Greeks and Macedonians were a minority (perhaps no more than 10 per cent) of the population, almost from the beginning sought to ingratiate themselves with the Jews, who soon became a sizable minority (perhaps 10 per cent of the population). The alleged invitation by Ptolemy Philadelphus *ca.* 270 BCE to translate the Pentateuch into Greek, if it is historical, was clearly intended to flatter the Jews. Likewise, the invitation to Onias in the middle of the second century BCE to build the temple at Leontopolis and to become a commander in Ptolemy Philometor's army continued this trend.

4.5 Strabo (*ca.* 64 BCE–*ca.* 20 CE), *Historical Memoranda*, cited by Josephus, *Jewish Antiquities* 13.284–7

The summit of Jewish influence in Egypt came with Queen Cleopatra III's appointment at the end of the second century BCE of two Jews,

Chelkias and Ananias (the sons of the Onias who had built the temple at Leontopolis), as commanders of her army.

At this time [*ca.* 107 BCE] not only were the Jews in Jerusalem and in the country in a flourishing condition, but also those who lived in Alexandria and in Egypt and Cyprus. For Queen Cleopatra, who was at war with her son Ptolemy, surnamed Lathyrus, appointed as her generals Chelkias and Ananias, sons of the Onias who had built the temple in the nome of Heliopolis.... And having entrusted her army to them, Cleopatra did nothing without their approval, as Strabo of Cappadocia also testifies, when he writes as follows: 'For the majority, both those who came back from exile and those who were later sent to Cyprus by Cleopatra, immediately went over to Ptolemy. And only the Jews of the district named for Onias remained faithful to her, because their fellow-citizens Chelkias and Ananias were held in special favor by the queen.' (LCL)

Rome

BIBLIOGRAPHY

William D. Morrison, *The Jews under Roman Rule* (1890).

Horst R. Moehring, "The 'Acta Pro Judaeis' in the *Antiquities* of Flavius Josephus: A Study in Hellenistic and Modern Apologetic Historiography," in Jacob Neusner, ed., *Christianity, Judaism, and Other Greco-Roman Cults: Studies for Morton Smith at Sixty*, Part 3: *Judaism before 70* (1975), 124–58.

Smallwood (1976).

Tessa Rajak, "Was there a Roman Charter for the Jews?" *JRS* 74 (1984), 107–23.

Tessa Rajak, "Jewish Rights in the Greek Cities under Roman Rule," in William S. Green, *Approaches to Ancient Judaism*, vol. 5: *Studies in Judaism and Its Greco-Roman Context* (1985), 19–35.

Julius Caesar (100–44 BCE)

4.6 Josephus, *Jewish Antiquities* 14.192–95 (47 BCE)

The highly-privileged position of the Jews in the Roman Empire dates back particularly to the privileges granted to them by Julius Caesar, who was especially grateful to them for the aid that they had granted to him militarily. In particular, he rewarded Hyrcanus, who had assisted him in Egypt, with the high priesthood.

I, Julius Caesar, Imperator and Pontifex Maximus, Dictator for the second time, have decided as follows with the advice of the council. Whereas the Jew Hyrcanus, son of Alexander, both now and in the past, in time of peace as well as in war, has shown loyalty and zeal toward our state, as many commanders have testified on his behalf, and in the recent Alexandrian war came to our aid with fifteen hundred soldiers, and being sent by me to Mithridates, surpassed in bravery all those in the ranks, for these reasons it is my wish that Hyrcanus, son of Alexander, and his children shall be ethnarchs[6] of the Jews and shall

---

6. I.e., *de facto* rulers of the people without actually having the title of king.

hold the office of high priest of the Jews for all time in accordance with their national customs, and that he and his sons shall be our allies and also be numbered among our particular friends; and whatever high-priestly rights or other privileges exist in accordance with their laws, these he and his children shall possess by my command. And if, during this period, any question shall arise concerning the Jews' manner of life, it is my pleasure that the decision shall rest with them. Nor do I approve of troops being given winter-quarters among them or of money being demanded of them. (LCL)

4.7 Josephus, *Jewish Antiquities* 14.213–16 (46 BCE)

In the following letter, Caesar writes to the magistrates of Parium in Asia Minor (who apparently exercised local autonomy) urging them to revoke the statutes forbidding the Jews to observe their ancestral customs. He notes the special privileges enjoyed by the Jews in Rome, notably to assemble, to collect contributions, and to have common meals.

Julius Gaius [i.e., Caesar],[7] praetor, consul of the Romans, to the magistrates, council, and people of Parium, greeting.

The Jews in Delos and some of the neighboring Jews, some of your envoys also being present, have appealed to me and declared that you are preventing them by statute from observing their national customs and sacred rites. Now it displeases me that such statutes should be made against our friends and allies and that they should be forbidden to live in accordance with their customs and to contribute money to common meals and sacred rites, for this they are not forbidden to do even in Rome. For example, Gaius Caesar, our consular praetor, by edict forbade religious societies to assemble in the city, but these people alone he did not forbid to do so or to collect contributions of money or to hold common meals. Similarly do I forbid other religious societies but permit these people alone to assemble and feast in accordance with their native customs and ordinances. And if you have made any statutes against our friends and allies, you will do well to revoke them because of their worthy deeds on our behalf and their goodwill toward us. (LCL)

Publius Dolabella (ca. 70–43 BCE)

4.8 Josephus, *Jewish Antiquities* 14.225–7 (43 BCE)

In the following letter sent by Publius Dolabella, Roman governor of Syria, to the magistrates of Ephesus in Asia Minor, he grants the Jews exemption from military service (because of their observance of the Sabbath) and permission to follow their laws and customs.

In the presidency of Artemon, on the first day of the month of Lenaeon, Dolabella, Imperator, to the magistrates, council and people of Ephesus, greeting.

---

7. There is uncertainty with regard to the name.

Alexander, son of Theodorus, the envoy of Hyrcanus, son of Alexander, the high priest and ethnarch of the Jews, has explained to me that his co-religionists cannot undertake military service because they may not bear arms or march on the days of the Sabbath; nor can they obtain the native foods to which they are accustomed. I, therefore, like the governors before me, grant them exemption from military service and allow them to follow their native customs and to come together for sacred and holy rites in accordance with their law, and to make offerings for their sacrifices; and it is my wish that you write these instructions to the various cities. (LCL)

Mark Antony (ca. 83–30 BCE)

4.9 Josephus, *Jewish Antiquities* 14. 320–2 (41 BCE)

In the following letter to the magistrates of Tyre in Phoenicia Mark Antony decrees that whatever possessions had been seized by Gaius Cassius from the Jews should be restored to them and that those who had been taken into slavery should be freed.

Statement of Marcus Antonius, Imperator, one of the triumvirs appointed to govern the republic.

Whereas Gaius Cassius in the late rebellion seized a province which did not belong to him, and after occupying it with armed forces, plundered it and our allies, and forced the surrender of the Jewish nation, which was a friend of the Roman people, we, therefore, having overcome his madness by our arms, do establish order by our edicts and decisions in the territories plundered by him, so that they may be restored to our allies. And whatever was sold belonging to the Jews, whether persons or possessions, shall be released, the slaves to be free, as they were originally, and the possessions to be returned to their former owners. And it is my wish that whoever disobeys my edict shall be brought to trial, and if such a person is convicted, it shall be my concern to prosecute the offender in accordance with the seriousness of his act. (LCL)

Augustus (ruled 27 BCE–14 CE)

BIBLIOGRAPHY

Solomon Zeitlin, "The Edict of Augustus Caesar in Relation to the Judaeans of Asia," *JQR* 55, (1951–2) 160–3.

By 30 BCE all the Jews in the lands around the Mediterranean were under Roman sovereignty. Augustus, in healing the wounds of the civil wars of the previous hundred years and reuniting the Roman Empire, won the allegiance of millions by his policy of religious freedom and protection of established cults, including that of the Jews.

4.10 Philo, *Embassy to Gaius* 23.155–8

In the following passage Philo speaks of the reverence shown by Augustus for Jewish traditions. So great was his respect for the Jews that he ordered that sacrifices should be carried out daily at his expense in the

Temple in Jerusalem as a tribute to the Jewish God. He even granted the Jews the privilege, when monthly distributions of money and food were made at Rome on the Sabbath, of collecting these distributions on the next day.

He [Augustus] was aware that the great section of Rome on the other side of the Tiber is occupied and inhabited by Jews, most of whom were Roman citizens emancipated. For having been brought as captives to Italy they were liberated by their owners and were not forced to violate any of their native institutions. He knew therefore that they have houses of prayer and meet together in them, particularly on the sacred sabbaths when they receive as a body a training in their ancestral philosophy. He knew too that they collect money for sacred purposes from their first-fruits and send them to Jerusalem by persons who would offer the sacrifices.

Yet nevertheless he neither ejected them from Rome nor deprived them of their Roman citizenship because they were careful to preserve their Jewish citizenship also, nor took any violent measures against the houses of prayer, nor prevented them from meeting to receive instructions in the laws, nor opposed their offerings of the first-fruits. Indeed so religiously did he respect our interests that supported by wellnigh his whole household he adorned our Temple through the costliness of his dedications, and ordered that for all time continuous sacrifices of whole burnt offerings should be carried out every day at his own expense as a tribute to the most high God. And these sacrifices are maintained to the present day and will be maintained forever to tell the story of a character truly imperial.

Yet more, in the monthly doles in his own city when all the people each in turn receive money or corn, he never put the Jews at a dis-advantage in sharing the bounty, but even if the distributions happened to come during the sabbath when no one is permitted to receive or give anything or to transact any part of the business of ordinary life, particularly of a lucrative kind, he ordered the dispensers to reserve for the Jews till the morrow the charity which fell to all. (LCL)

4.11 Philo, *Embassy to Gaius* 40.311–17

In the following passage Philo notes that Augustus reaffirmed the right of the Jews to assemble in synagogues (in general, the Romans feared that assemblies by others might be to plot conspiracies) and to send their annual contributions to the Temple in Jerusalem. He stresses that Augustus ordered sacrifices, at his own expense, to be made daily to God.

While I[8] have a great abundance of evidence to show the wishes of your great-grandfather Augustus I will content myself with two examples. The first is a letter which he sent to the governors of the provinces in Asia, as he had learnt that the sacred first-fruits were treated with disrespect. He ordered that the Jews alone should be permitted by

---

8. Philo is addressing the Emperor Gaius Caligula, the great-grandson of Augustus.

them to assemble in synagogues. These gatherings, he said, were not based on drunkenness and carousing to promote conspiracy and so to do grave injury to the cause of peace, but were schools of temperance and justice where men while practicing virtue subscribed the annual first-fruits to pay for the sacrifices which they offer and commissioned sacred envoys to take them to the Temple in Jerusalem. Then he commanded that no one should hinder the Jews from meeting or subscribing or sending envoys to Jerusalem according to their ancestral practice. For these were certainly the substance if not the actual words of his instructions. But there is one letter which I subjoin here to convince you, my lord and master, sent by Gaius Norbanus Flaccus declaring what Caesar [Augustus] had written to him. Here is a transcript of this letter.

'Gaius Norbanus Flaccus, proconsul, to the magistrates of the Ephesians, greeting. Caesar has written to me that the Jews, wherever they may be, regularly according to their old peculiar custom, make a rule of meeting together and subscribing money which they send to Jerusalem. He does not wish them to be hindered from doing this. I therefore write to you to let you know that this is what he orders to be done.'

Is not this a clear proof, my emperor, of the principles which he followed as to the honor due to our Temple? He did not think that the form generally adopted about meetings should be applied to do away with the assemblages of the Jews to which they resort for collection of the first-fruits and their other religious observances.

Another example no less cogent than this shows very clearly the will of Augustus. He gave orders for a continuation of whole burnt offerings every day to the Most High God to be charged to his own purse. These are carried out to this day. Two lambs and a bull are the victims with which he added lustre to the altar, knowing well that there is no image there openly or secretly set up. (LCL)

4.12 Josephus, *Jewish Antiquities* 16.160–5 (ca. 3 CE)

In the following passage, the Emperor Augustus, responding to the complaints of Jews that they were being mistreated by the Greeks in Asia Minor and Cyrene, reaffirms the privileges of the Jews to send monies to Jerusalem, and to be free of appearing in court after the ninth hour on the afternoon before the Sabbath, and inflicts stern penalties on those who steal their sacred books or sacred monies.

Now the Jews of Asia [Minor] and those to be found in Cyrenaean Libya were being mistreated by the cities there, although the kings had formerly granted them equality of civic status (*isonomia*); and at this particular time the Greeks were persecuting them to the extent of taking their sacred monies away from them and doing them injury in their private concerns. And so, being mistreated and seeing no limit to the inhumanity of the Greeks, they sent envoys to Caesar about this state of affairs. And he granted them the same equality of taxation as before, and wrote to the provincial officials letters of which we subjoin copies as evidence of the [friendly] disposition which our former rulers had toward us.

'Caesar Augustus, Pontifex Maximus, with tribunician power, decrees as follows: Since the Jewish nation has been found well disposed to the Roman people not only at the present time but also in time past and especially in the time of my father the commander Caesar, as has their high priest Hyrcanus, it has been decided by me and my council under oath, with the consent of the Roman people, that the Jews may follow their own customs in accordance with the law of their fathers, just as they followed them in the time of Hyrcanus, high priest of the Most High God, and that their sacred monies shall be inviolable and may be sent up to Jerusalem and delivered to the treasurers in Jerusalem, and that they need not give bond (to appear in court) on the Sabbath or on the day of preparation for it [Sabbath Eve] after the ninth hour [approximately 3 PM]. And if anyone is caught stealing their sacred books or their sacred monies from a synagogue or an ark [of the Law], he shall be regarded as sacrilegious, and his property shall be confiscated to the public treasury of the Romans. As for the resolution which was offered by them in my honor concerning the piety which I show to all men, and on behalf of Gaius Marcius Censorinus, I order that it and the present edict be set up in the most conspicuous [part of the temple] assigned to me by the federation of Asia in Ancyra.[9] If anyone transgresses any of the above ordinances, he shall suffer severe punishment.' This was inscribed upon a pillar in the temple of Caesar. (LCL)

Marcus Agrippa (64/63–12 BCE)

4.13 Nicolaus of Damascus (64 BCE to the beginning of the first century CE), *Histories*, cited by Josephus, *Jewish Antiquities* 12.125–7 (16–13 BCE)

Marcus Agrippa, son-in-law of the Emperor Augustus, was a Roman general who was appointed governor of the eastern provinces, which he administered from 23–21 and 17/16–14 BCE. He was an especially close friend of Herod and he visited Jerusalem in 14 BCE. Augustus named him as his successor, but Agrippa died in 12 BCE, long before Augustus' death in 14 CE. In the following passage we read that the non-Jews of Ionia had argued that the Jews were not entitled to be citizens since they did not worship the gods of the Ionians; but Agrippa, convinced by the Jews' advocate, the non-Jew Nicolaus of Damascus, one of Herod's chief counsellors, reaffirms the right of the Jews in Ionia to be citizens.

And we know that Marcus Agrippa[10] had a similar view concerning the Jews, for when the Ionians agitated against them and petitioned Agrippa that they alone might enjoy the citizenship that Antiochus, the grandson of Seleucus called Theos [God] by the Greeks,[11] had given

---

9. The temple of Roma and Augustus at Ancyra, administrative center of the province of Galatia.

10. Marcus Agrippa, son-in-law of the Emperor Augustus, visited the East as his viceroy in 16–13 BCE and was ceremonially feted in Jerusalem in 14 BCE.

11. Antiochus Theos ruled from 262 to 246 BCE.

them, and claimed that, if the Jews were to be their fellows, they should worship the Ionians' gods, the matter was brought to trial and the Jews won the right to use their own customs, their advocate being Nicolaus of Damascus; for Agrippa gave his opinion that it was not lawful for him to make a new rule. But if anyone wishes to learn the details, let him read the hundred and twenty-third and hundred and twenty-fourth books of Nicolaus' *History*. (LCL)

4.14 Josephus, *Jewish Antiquities* 16.167–70 (*ca.* 14 BCE)

Here Agrippa, Augustus' right-hand man, writes to the magistrates of Ephesus in Asia Minor and of Cyrene very strongly protecting the right of the Jews to collect money for transmission to the Temple and to be free from appearing in court on the Sabbath.

Agrippa himself also wrote on behalf of the Jews in the following manner. 'Agrippa to the magistrates, council and people of Ephesus, greeting. It is my will that the care and custody of the sacred monies belonging to the account of the Temple in Jerusalem shall be given to the Jews in Asia in accordance with their ancestral customs. And if any men steal the sacred monies of the Jews and take refuge in places of asylum, it is my will that they be dragged away from them and turned over to the Jews under the same law by which temple-robbers are dragged away from asylum. I have also written to the praetor Silanus that no one shall compel the Jews to give bond [to appear in court] on the Sabbath.' (LCL)

4.15 Josephus, *Jewish Antiquities* 16.169–70 (*ca.* 14 BCE)

Here also Agrippa writes to the local rulers of Cyrene that they should not interfere with the right of the Jews to transmit money to the Temple in Jerusalem.

Marcus Agrippa to the magistrates, council and people of Cyrene, greeting. The Jews in Cyrene, on whose behalf Augustus has already written to the former praetor of Libya, Flavius, and to the other officials of the province to the effect that the sacred monies may be sent up to Jerusalem without interference, as is their ancestral custom, now complain to me that they are being threatened by certain informers and prevented [from sending these monies] on the pretext of their owing taxes, which are in fact not owed. I therefore order that these monies be restored to the Jews, who are in no way to be molested, and if sacred monies have been taken away from any cities, the persons in charge of these matters shall see that amends are made to the Jews there. (LCL)

Publius Petronius, Roman Governor of Syria (40 CE)

4.16 Josephus, *Jewish Antiquities* 19.300–11 (40 CE)

The following passage shows how concerned the Roman administrators were, as a rule, not to offend the religious sensibilities of the Jews, especially when it came to bringing statues of the emperor into a synagogue, even though this must have seemed to some Romans to indicate a lack of loyalty on the part of the Jews. The key to such tolerance in every instance was to reiterate the privileges granted by Julius Caesar and constantly renewed by his successors. Appeals to Roman governors, as here to Petronius, the governor of Syria, against anti-Jewish mob actions normally, as here, produced indignation against such actions and stern warnings, especially when such appeals came from Jewish leaders such as King Agrippa I, who had close personal relations with the Roman imperial family. The Romans were particularly fearful that if they did not take strong measures, the Jews themselves, in desperation, would take the law into their own hands.

A very short time after this, certain young men of Dora,[12] who set a higher value on audacity than on holiness and were by nature recklessly bold, brought an image of Caesar into the synagogue of the Jews and set it up. This provoked Agrippa exceedingly, for it was tantamount to an overthrow of the laws of his fathers. Without delay he went to see Publius Petronius, the governor of Syria, and denounced the people of Dora. Petronius was no less angry at the deed, for he too regarded the breach of law as sacrilege. He wrote in anger to the leaders of Dora as follows:

'Publius Petronius, legate of Tiberius Claudius Caesar Augustus Germanicus, to the leading men of Dora speaks: Inasmuch as certain of you have had such mad audacity, notwithstanding the issuance of an edict of Claudius Caesar Augustus Germanicus [the Emperor Claudius] pertaining to the permission granted the Jews to observe the customs of their fathers, not to obey this edict, but to do the very reverse, in that you have prevented the Jews from having a synagogue by transferring to it an image of Caesar, you have thereby sinned not only against the law of the Jews, but also against the emperor, whose image was better placed in his own shrine than in that of another, especially in the synagogue; for by natural law each must be lord over his own place, in accordance with Caesar's decree. For it is ridiculous for me to refer to my own decree after making mention of the edict of the emperor that permits Jews to follow their own customs, yet also, be it noted, bids them to live as fellow citizens with the Greeks.

As for those who have, in defiance of the edict of Augustus, been so rash as to act thus – at which deed even those who are regarded as eminent among the transgressors are indignant and assert that it was done not because anyone deliberately and personally proposed it, but by an impulse of the mob – I have given orders that they are to be brought before me by Proclus Vitellius the centurion to give an account of their actions.

To the ranking magistrates I give this warning: that, unless they wish to have it thought that the wrong was committed with their consent and intent, they must point out the guilty parties to the centurion, allowing no occasion to occur that could lead to strife or battle. For this,

___

12. A city in Phoenicia.

in my opinion, is precisely what they hope to achieve by such actions. For both King Agrippa, my most honored friend, and I have no greater interest than that the Jews should not seize any occasion, under the pretext of self-defence, to gather in one place and proceed to desperate measures. And, that you may be better informed of his imperial majesty's policy concerning the whole matter, I have appended his edicts that were published at Alexandria. Although they seem to be universally known, my most honored friend King Agrippa read them before my tribunal at the time when he pleaded that the Jews ought not to be despoiled of the privileges granted by Augustus. For the future, therefore, I charge you to seek no pretext for sedition or disturbance, but to practice severally each his own religion.' (LCL)

Claudius (Roman Emperor, 41–54 CE)

BIBLIOGRAPHY

Harold Idris Bell, *Jews and Christians in Egypt: the Jewish Trouble in Alexandria and the Athanasian Controversy, illustrated by texts from Greek papyri in the British Museum* (1924), 1–37.

Henry S. Jones, "Claudius and the Jewish Question at Alexandria," *JRS* 16 (1926), 17–35.

Vincent M. Scramuzza, *The Emperor Claudius* (1940), 64–79.

Angelo Segré, "The Status of the Jews in Ptolemaic and Roman Egypt: New Light from the Papyri," *JSoS* 6 (1944), 375–400.

Harry A. Wolfson, "Philo on Jewish Citizenship in Alexandria," *JBL* 63 (1944), 165–8.

Simon Davis, "The Question of Jewish Citizenship at Alexandria," in his *Race-Relations in Ancient Egypt: Greek, Egyptian, Hebrew, Roman* (1952), 93–112.

Victor A. Tcherikover and Alexander Fuks, eds, *CPJ*, vol. 1 (1957), 39–41, 56–7, 62, 69–74; vol. 2 (1960), 25–107.

Tcherikover (1959), 309–28, 409–15.

Shimon Applebaum, "The Legal Status of the Jewish Communities in the Diaspora," in Samuel Safrai and Menahem Stern, eds, *The Jewish People in the First Century* (*CRINT*, vol. 1, 1974), 420–63.

Kasher (1985), 226–309, 358–64.

Constantine Zuckerman, "Hellenistic *Politeumata* and the Jews: A Reconsideration," *SCI* 8–9 (1985–8), 171–85.

4.17 Josephus, *Jewish Antiquities* 19.278–85 (41 CE)

As the following passage shows, the assassination of Caligula and the accession of Claudius encouraged the Jews of Alexandria. They armed themselves; and apparently fighting began between Greeks and Jews, which Claudius ordered, through the Roman governor of Egypt, to be ended at once. In turn, the emperor issued an edict reaffirming the privileges taken from the Jews by his predecessor Gaius Caligula and enjoining both Jews and Alexandrian Greeks to refrain from disturbances.

About this time, there arose a feud between Jews and Greeks in the city of Alexandria. For upon the death of Gaius, the Jews, who had been humiliated under his rule and grievously abused by the Alexandrians, took heart again and at once armed themselves. Claudius commanded the prefect of Egypt to put down the factional war. In addition, on the petition of Kings Agrippa [I] and Herod,[13] he issued an edict to Alexandria and Syria to the following effect: 'Tiberius Claudius Caesar Augustus Germanicus, holding the tribunician power, speaks. Having from the first known that the Jews in Alexandria called Alexandrians were fellow colonizers from the very earliest times jointly with the Alexandrians and received equal civic rights from the kings, as is manifest from the documents in their possession and from the edicts; and that after Alexandria was made subject to our empire by Augustus their rights were preserved by the prefects sent from time to time, and that these rights of theirs have never been disputed; moreover, that at the time when Aquila[14] was at Alexandria, on the death of the ethnarch of the Jews, Augustus did not prevent the continued appointment of ethnarchs, desiring that the several subject nations should abide by their own customs and not be compelled to violate the religion of their fathers; and learning that the Alexandrians rose up in insurrection against the Jews in their midst in the time of Gaius [Caligula] Caesar, who through his great folly and madness humiliated the Jews because they refused to transgress the religion of their fathers by addressing him as a god; I desire that none of their rights should be lost to the Jews on account of the madness of Gaius, but that their former privileges also be preserved to them, while they abide by their own customs; and I enjoin upon both parties to take the greatest precaution to prevent any disturbance arising after the posting of my edict.' (LCL)

4.18 Josephus, *Jewish Antiquities* 19.286–91 (41 CE)

The Emperor Claudius, petitioned by the Jewish kings Agrippa I and Herod of Chalcis, issued the following edict to the Roman Empire at large requiring that the Jews' privileges be reaffirmed but also enjoining upon the Jews to be more tolerant toward the theological views held by non-Jews.

That [edict of the Emperor Claudius] to the rest of the world ran as follows: 'Tiberius Claudius Caesar Augustus Germanicus Pontifex Maximus, holding the tribunician power, elected consul for the second time, speaks: Kings Agrippa and Herod, my dearest friends, having petitioned me to permit the same privileges to be maintained for the Jews throughout the empire under the Romans as those in Alexandria enjoy, I very gladly consented, not merely in order to please those who petitioned me, but also because in my opinion the Jews deserve to obtain their request on account of their loyalty and friendship to the Romans. In particular, I did so because I hold it right that not even Greek cities should be deprived of these privileges, seeing that they were in fact guaranteed for them in the time of the

---

13. Herod II, grandson of Herod the Great, was the brother of Agrippa I. He was king of Chalcis in Lebanon from 41 to 48 CE.
14. Aquila was governor of Egypt under the Emperor Augustus.

divine Augustus. It is right, therefore, that the Jews throughout the whole world under our sway should also observe the customs of their fathers without let or hindrance. I enjoin upon them also by these presents to avail themselves of this kindness in a more reasonable spirit, and not to set at nought the beliefs about the gods held by other peoples but to keep their own laws. It is my will that the ruling bodies of the cities and colonies and municipia in Italy and outside Italy, and the kings and other authorities through their own ambassadors, shall cause this edict of mine to be inscribed, and keep it posted for not less than thirty days in a place where it can plainly be read from the ground.' (LCL)

4.19 *CPJ*, no. 153 (41 CE)

This letter (some, but not most, scholars have assumed that it is identical with the edict cited above) from the Emperor Claudius to the Alexandrian Greeks is the most important papyrological document dealing with the Jewish question. In it he attempts to be even-handed toward the Alexandrian Greeks and the Jews. In particular, he warns the Jews not to send two embassies in the future, not to participate in the athletic contests presided over by the gymnasiarchs, reminding them that the city is not their own, that is, that they are not citizens (an apparent contradiction to the statement in Josephus [*Ant*. 14.188] that Julius Caesar had declared them to be citizens of Alexandria, as well as in Philo [*Against Flaccus* 7.47], who speaks of Jewish citizens of Alexandria). Moreover, he forbids further immigration of Jews into Alexandria.

With regard to the responsibility for the disturbances and rioting, or rather, to speak the truth, the war, against the Jews, although your ambassadors, particularly Dionysios the son of Theon, argued vigorously and at length in the disputation, I have not wished to make an exact inquiry, but I harbor within me a store of immutable indignation against those who renewed the conflict. I merely say that, unless you stop this destructive and obstinate mutual enmity, I shall be forced to show what a benevolent ruler can be when he is turned to righteous indignation. Even now, therefore, I conjure the Alexandrians to behave gently and kindly toward the Jews who have inhabited the same city for many years, and not to dishonor any of their customs in their worship of their god, but to allow them to keep their own ways, as they did in the time of the god Augustus and as I too, having heard both sides, have confirmed. The Jews, on the other hand, I order not to aim at more than they have previously had and not in the future to send two embassies as if they lived in two cities,[15] a thing which has never been done before, and not to intrude themselves into the games

---

15. Some have suggested that the two Jewish embassies represented two main trends in the Alexandrian Jewish community, those who were more Hellenized and those who were less Hellenized. Others have suggested that there were two separate confrontations of Jews and Greeks before the Emperor Claudius.

presided over by the *gymnasiarchoi* and the *kosmetai*,[16] since they enjoy what is their own, and in a city which is not their own they possess an abundance of all good things. Nor are they to bring in or invite Jews coming from Syria or Egypt, or I shall be forced to conceive graver suspicions. If they disobey, I shall proceed against them in every way as fomenting a common plague for the whole world. If you both give up your present ways and are willing to live in gentleness and kindness with one another, I for my part will care for the city as much as I can, as one which has long been closely connected with us. Barbillus[17] my friend, as I can witness, has always been your champion with me and has now conducted your case with the greatest zeal, and the same is true of my friend Tiberius Claudius Archibios. Farewell. (*CPJ*)

Trajan (Roman Emperor, 98–117 CE)

BIBLIOGRAPHY

R. Loewe, "A Jewish Counterpart of the Acts of the Alexandrians," *JJS* 12 (1961), 105–22.
Modrzejewski (1995), 191–7.

4.20 *CPJ*, no. 157 (script of the early third century CE)

As the fragmentary papyrus cited below indicates, Trajan heard a dispute which took place some time before 113 CE between two delegations, one Jewish and one Greek, the latter including three Alexandrian gymnasiarchs. Trajan's wife, Plotina, influenced Trajan and the members of the Roman Senate against the Alexandrian Greeks. Hermaiskos, the spokesman of the Alexandrians, accuses the emperor of favoring the Jews.

[Trajan:] 'You must be eager to die, having such contempt for death as to answer even me with insolence.'

Hermaiskos said: 'Why, it grieves us to see your council filled with impious Jews.'

Caesar said: 'This is the second time I am telling you, Hermaiskos: you are answering me insolently, taking advantage of your noble birth.'

Hermaiskos said: 'What do you mean, I answer you insolently, greatest emperor? Explain this to me.'

Caesar said: 'Pretending that my council is filled with Jews.'
Hermaiskos: 'So, then, the word Jew is offensive to you? In that case you ought to help your own people and not play the advocate for the impious Jews.'

As Hermaiskos was saying this, the bust of Sarapis[18] that they carried suddenly broke into a sweat, and Trajan was astounded when he saw

16. The *gymnasiarchoi* were the heads of the gymnasia. The *kosmetai* were the magistrates in charge of the ephebes (adolescents).
17. Titus Claudius Barbillus is perhaps identical with the governor of Egypt under Nero (55–9 CE). He championed the cause of the Alexandrian Greeks against Agrippa I during the trial of the anti-Jewish Alexandrian Isidore.
18. Sarapis was a god invented and introduced into Egypt by Ptolemy I (323–283 BCE) in order to unite the Greeks and Egyptians through a common worship.

it. And soon tumultuous crowds gathered in Rome and numerous shouts were heard, and everyone began to flee to the highest parts of the hills. (*CPJ*)

Hadrian (Roman Emperor, 117–38 CE)

4.21 *CPJ*, no. 158 (first half of the second century CE)

In this fragmentary papyrus we have a dispute (*ca.* 119–20 CE) between a Greek delegation (led by Paulus, Theon, and Antoninus) and a Jewish delegation before the newly-crowned Emperor Hadrian, who is here dealing with various complaints connected with the revolt against Trajan led by the pseudo-messianic "king" Lukuas-Andreas in 115–17.

Paulus [spoke] about the king, how they brought him forth and [mocked him?]; and Theon read the edict of Lupus[19] ordering them to lead him forth for Lupus to make fun of the king of the scene and the mime.[20] After we had thus [testified?], the emperor took occasion to remark to Paulus and our people as follows: 'During such disturbances . . . during the Dacian war . . .'[21] The Jews . . . impious. . . .

Caesar answered the Jews; 'I learned. . . .'

The Jews: 'They seized them from the prison and . . . wounded them.'

Caesar: 'I have investigated all these matters [?], and not [all?] the Alexandrians but only those responsible should be prosecuted . . . so that if some were to be exiled from Alexandria, they were none the less not seized by us, as they allege, but by them, and this occasioned a false accusation against us. Now all [the slaves] who had fled to their masters intending to secure complete safety were brought to justice by them and punished.'

The Jews: 'Sir, they are lying: they do not know how many men there were.'

Paulus: 'My only concern is for the grave in Alexandria which I expect to have.[22] Advancing as I am towards this, I shall have no fear in telling you the truth. Listen to me then, Caesar, as to one who may not live beyond the morrow.'

Antoninus: 'My Lord Caesar, I swear by your *genius*[23] he speaks the truth as one who may not live another day. For when we were in such

19. Lupus was governor of Egypt in the last years of Trajan.
20. The grammatical construction of this sentence is very confused. It is not clear who the king is, but it seems likely that Lukuas-Andreas is here referred to. Some have suggested that the reference is to the hero of a farce arranged by the Alexandrians in order to ridicule the Jews and their "king."
21. The reference is probably to the war waged by Hadrian against a Sarmatian tribe in Dacia (modern Rumania).
22. Paulus is evidently convinced that he will be sentenced to death because of Hadrian's attitude toward the Alexandrians. Since the trial took place in Rome, the grave in Alexandria is the one in which Paulus will be placed after he has been executed.
23. The *genius* was the guardian deity of a person.

pressing circumstances and so many letters had been sent you saying that [the prefect] had ordered the impious Jews to transfer their residence[24] to a place from which they could easily attack and ravage our well-named city – if not a line on this matter fell into your beneficent hands, then the reason for your august words is clear. It is obvious that this has been perpetrated against you, to prevent you from having any evidence of the woes that have befallen us.'

Caesar: 'Let Paulus go; but have Antoninus bound. . . .'

Antoninus [?]: 'Emperor, Alexandrians did not ... many were condemned, sixty Alexandrians and their slaves, and the Alexandrians were exiled and their slaves beheaded, with no one ... or being sent forth with the lamentations that are permitted to all men, so that if some were to be exiled from Alexandria, they were none the less not seized by us, as they allege, but by them, and this occasioned a false accusation against us. Now all [the slaves] who had fled to their masters intending to secure complete safety were brought to justice by them and punished.'[25] (*CPJ*)

Commodus (Roman Emperor, 180–92 CE)

4.22 *CPJ*, no. 159 (first half of the third century CE)

In this fragmentary papyrus Appian, the Greek head of the gymnasium in Alexandria, presented here as a martyr, is sentenced to death (the charges are unclear) by the Emperor Commodus, whom Appian calls tyrannical, though there is some reason to think that the whole story is fictitious.

Appian: '. . . who sending the wheat [?] to the other cities, sell it at four times its price, so as to recover their expenses.'

The Emperor said: 'And who receives this money?'

Appian said: 'You do.'

The Emperor: 'Are you certain of this?'

Appian: 'No, but that is what we have heard.'

The Emperor: 'You ought not to have circulated the story without being certain of it. [I say,] executioner!'

As Appian was being taken off to execution he noticed a dead body and said: 'Ah, dead one, when I go to my country [i.e., Hades, the land of the dead], I shall tell [my father] Herakleianos. . . .'

'. . . my father and . . .' And while he was saying this, turning around he saw Heliodorus and said: 'Have you nothing to say, Heliodorus, at my being led to execution?'

Heliodorus[26] said: 'To whom can we speak, if we have no one who will listen? Go, my son, go to your death. Yours shall be the glory of dying for your dearest native city. Be not distressed. . . .'

---

24. Some have suggested that the intention of the governor was to erect a ghetto for the Jews of Alexandria. Others have suggested that the governor intended to expel the Jews from Alexandria.

25. The Alexandrian delegation insists that the Greeks were not guilty of rescuing the slaves who had been snatched away from custody and that those who fled were punished by their masters.

26. Apparently Heliodorus was an advocate for Appian.

Appian: 'Yes, I do; Appian speaks to a tyrant.'

The Emperor: 'No, to a king.'

Appian: 'Say not so! Your father, the divine Antoninus [i.e., the Emperor Marcus Aurelius], was fit to be emperor. For, look you, first of all he was a philosopher; secondly, he was not avaricious; thirdly, he was good. But you have precisely the opposite qualities: you are tyrannical, dishonest, crude!'

Caesar [then] ordered him to be led away to execution. As Appian was being taken, he said: 'Grant me but one thing, my Lord Caesar.'

The Emperor: 'What?'

Appian: 'Grant that I may be executed in my noble insignia.'

The Emperor: 'Granted.'

Appian [then] took his headband and put it on his head and, putting his white shoes on his feet, he cried out in the middle of Rome: 'Come up, Romans, and see a unique spectacle, an Alexandrian gymnasiarch and ambassador led to execution!'

The *evocatus*[27] immediately ran back and reported this to the emperor, saying: 'Do you sit idle, my Lord, while the Romans murmur in complaint?'

The Emperor: 'What are they complaining about?'

The consul: 'About the execution of the Alexandrian.'

The Emperor: 'Have him brought back.'

When Appian had come in, he said: 'Who is it this time that called me back as I was about to greet death again and those who died before me, Theon and Isidoros and Lampon?[28] Was it the Senate or you, you leader of gangsters?'

The Emperor: 'Appian, I am accustomed to chasten those who rave and have lost all sense of shame. You speak only so long as I permit you to.

Appian: 'By your *genius*, I am neither mad nor have I lost my sense of shame. I am making an appeal on behalf of my noble rank and my privileges.'

The Emperor: 'How so?'

Appian: 'As one of noble rank and a gymnasiarch.'

The Emperor: 'Do you suggest that I am not of noble rank?'

Appian: 'That I know not; I am merely appealing on behalf of my own nobility and privileges.'

The Emperor: 'Do you not know then that . . . ?'

Appian: 'If you are really not informed on this matter, I shall tell you. To begin with, Caesar saved Cleopatra [and then] he got control of the empire and, as some say, borrowed. . . .' (*CPJ*)

Elagabalus (Roman Emperor, 218–22 CE)

    4.23 *Scriptores Historiae Augustae* (end of the fourth century CE), *Antoninus Heliogabalus* 3.5

27. The *evocatus* was a veteran who served as a special officer of the emperor.

28. Isidoros and Lampon are the Alexandrian Greeks who were executed by the Emperor Claudius. Some identify Theon with the member of the embassy to Trajan, others with the Theon who was a friend of Claudius.

Elagabalus (Heliogabalus), priest of the sun god at Emesa in Syria, according to the passage below, sought to make the Syrian sun god, Elagabal, the chief god of the Roman pantheon, adding to this the religions of Judaism, Samaritanism, and Christianity.

He [Elagabalus] declared, furthermore, that the religions of the Jews and the Samaritans and the rites of the Christians must also be transferred to this place [Palatine Hill in Rome], in order that the priesthood of Elagabalus might include the mysteries of every form of worship. (LCL)

Alexander Severus (Roman Emperor, 222–35 CE)

4.24 *Scriptores Historiae Augustae* (end of the fourth century CE), *Alexander Severus* 22.4, 28.7, 29.2

So respectful of the Jewish privileges was the Emperor Alexander Severus that he was called "Syrian synagogue-chief" by his opponents. In his sanctuary he kept a statue of Abraham, according to one report.

He [the Emperor Alexander Severus] respected the privileges of the Jews and allowed the Christians to exist unmolested. . . .

He wished it to be thought that he derived his descent from the race of the Romans, for he felt shame at being called a Syrian, especially because, on the occasion of a certain festival, the people of Antioch and of Egypt and Alexandria had annoyed him with jibes, as is their custom, calling him a Syrian synagogue-chief and a high priest. . . .

His manner of living was as follows: First of all, if it were permissible, that is to say, if he had not lain with his wife, in the early morning hours he would worship in the sanctuary of his Lares,[29] in which he kept statues of the deified emperors – of whom, however, only the best had been selected – and also of certain holy souls, among them Apollonius,[30] and, according to a contemporary writer, Christ, Abraham, Orpheus and others of the same character and, besides, the portraits of his ancestors. (LCL)

4.25 *Scriptores Historiae Augustae* (end of the fourth century CE), *Alexander Severus* 45.7, 51.7–8

According to the passage below, the Emperor Alexander Severus was fond of quoting the Golden Rule.

For, he [the Emperor Alexander Severus] used to say, it was unjust that, when Christians and Jews observed this custom in announcing the names of those who were to be ordained priests, it should not be

29. The Lares were the spirits who were regarded as having special concern for the household and were worshipped at the hearth.
30. The reference is to Apollonius of Tyana (born *ca.* 4 BCE), a philosopher and mystic who became famous through the miracles which he is alleged to have performed. A biography of him by the third-century CE Philostratus is extant.

similarly observed in the case of governors of provinces, to whose keeping were committed the fortunes and lives of men. . . .

He used often to exclaim what he had heard from someone, either a Jew or a Christian, and always remembered, and he also had it announced by a herald whenever he was disciplining anyone, 'What you do not wish that a man should do to you, do not do to him.'[31] And so highly did he value this sentiment that he had it written up in the palace and in public buildings. (LCL)

Constantine the Great (Roman Emperor, 307–37 CE)

4.26 *Theodosian Code* 16.8.4 (330 CE)

It is notable that even after Constantine in 312 gave licit status to Christianity the tradition of imperial toleration of the Jews continued, inasmuch as the emperors were eager to maintain the appearance of continuity with the legislation of the emperors who had preceded them. Because the Christian emperors viewed Judaism as a religion rather than as a nation, its status as a *religio licita* was continued. Among privileges that the emperors continued was, as noted below, the exemption from liturgies [public services] enjoyed by holders of religious offices.

We order that the priests, archsynagogues, fathers of synagogues, and the others who serve in synagogues shall be free from all corporal liturgy. (A. L.)

Julian (Roman Emperor, 360–3 CE)

Despite the special status enjoyed by the Jews, taxes were apparently imposed upon them; and, in particular, heads of synagogues were held responsible for collecting the so-called "crown money" (*aurum coronarium*), which was then shipped to Palestine through "apostles," where it was used for the upkeep of the patriarch and the rabbis. The Emperor Julian, after he had reverted to paganism, took measures to abolish these taxes. Julian demonstrated goodwill to the Jews not merely as an anti-Christian gesture, but because he admired their integrity and exalted in general the performance of sacrifices to the gods. He abolished Hadrian's decree banishing the Jews from Jerusalem and proposed to go even further by restoring Jerusalem as a Jewish settlement at his own expense and even rebuilding the Temple, but he was discouraged by a fire which broke out in the ruins there.

31. This, the so-called Golden Rule, is ascribed in this negative formulation to Hillel in the Talmud (*Shabbath* 31a); but it is found earlier in the *Letter of Aristeas* (207), the Book of Tobit (4:15), Ben Sira (31:15), and in Philo (cited by Eusebius, *Preparation for the Gospel* 8.7), and is later attributed to Rabbi Aqiba (*Avoth de-Rabbi Nathan* B, 26 (ed. Schechter, p. 53). In the positive formulation, "Do unto others as you would have others do unto you," it is attributed to Jesus in Matt 7:12 and Luke 6:31.

4.27 Julian, To Theodore, no. 89a

Julian here expresses admiration for the willingness of Jews to die for their religion.

[I saw] that those applying themselves to the cult of the religion of the Jews are so ardent as to choose to die for it and endure all manner of want and starvation rather than taste pork or any animal that is strangled or squeezed to death. (LCL, adapted)

4.28 Julian, To the Community of the Jews, no. 204

The authenticity of the letter below by Julian, written to the Jews before he left for the Persian campaign, has been questioned by many scholars but affirmed by many others, notably, in recent years, by Menahem Stern. Julian's hope to glorify God in Jerusalem fits in well with his syncretistic outlook. Here Julian notes how unfairly the Jews had been treated by his predecessors and the measures that he had taken to correct this.

By far the most burdensome thing in the yoke of your slavery, even more than in times past, has been the fact that you were subjected to unauthorized ordinances and had to contribute an untold amount of money to the accounts of the treasury. Of this I used to see many instances with my own eyes, and I have learned of more, by finding the records which are preserved against you. Moreover, when a tax was about to be levied on you again I prevented it, and compelled the impiety of such obloquy to cease here; and I threw into the fire the records against you that were stored in my desks; so that it is no longer possible for anyone to aim at you such a reproach of impiety. My brother Constantius of honored memory was not so much responsible for these wrongs of yours as were the men who used to frequent his table, barbarians in mind, godless in soul. These I seized with my own hands and put them to death by thrusting them into the pit, that not even any memory of their destruction might still linger amongst us.

And since I wish that you should prosper yet more, I have admonished my brother Iulus,[32] your most venerable patriarch, that the levy which is said to exist among you should be prohibited, and that no one is any longer to have the power to oppress the masses of your people by such exactions, so that everywhere you may have security of mind, and in the enjoyment of my reign . . . may offer more fervid prayers for my reign to the Most High God, the Creator, who has deigned to crown me with his own immaculate right hand. For it is natural that the spirit of men who are afflicted by any anxiety should be distracted, and they would not have so much confidence in raising their hands to pray, but that those who are in all respects free from care should rejoice with their whole hearts and offer their suppliant prayers on behalf of my imperial office to Mighty God, even to him who is able to direct my reign to the noblest ends, according to my purpose. This you ought to do, in order that, when I have successfully concluded the

32. This is apparently the patriarch Hillel II, the son of the patriarch Judah III.

war with Persia,[33] I may rebuild by my own efforts the sacred city of Jerusalem, which for so many years you have longed to see inhabited, and may bring settlers there, and, together with you, may glorify the Most High God therein. (LCL)

4.29 Ammianus Marcellinus (*ca.* 330–95 CE), *History* 23.1.2–3

Ammianus Marcellinus (*ca.* 330–95 CE), the last important Roman historian, served with Julian in the Persian campaign. Here he tells of Julian's plan to rebuild the Temple in Jerusalem and of the fire which prevented the plan from being carried out.

And although he [Julian] weighed every possible variety of events with anxious thought, and pushed on with burning zeal the many preparations for his campaign, yet turning his activity to every part and eager to extend the memory of his reign by great works, he planned at vast cost to restore the once splendid temple at Jerusalem, which after many mortal combats during the siege by Vespasian and later by Titus had barely been stormed. He had entrusted the speedy performance of this work to Alypius of Antioch, who had once been vice-prefect of Britain. But, though this Alypius pushed the work on with vigor, aided by the governor of the province, terrifying balls of flame kept bursting forth near the foundations of the temple, and made the place inaccessible to the workmen, some of whom were burned to death, and since in this way the element[s] persistently repelled them, the enterprise halted. (LCL)

Valentinian I (Roman Emperor, 364–75 CE)

4.30 *Theodosian Code* 7.8.2 (Valentinian I [with Valens], 368 or 370 or 373 CE)

This law forbade intruders to invade synagogues while claiming the right of hospitality.

The two emperors and Augusti Valentinian and Valens to Remigius, master of the offices:
You shall order those that invade a synagogue of the Jewish law as though on right of hospitality to evacuate it, for they ought to occupy houses of private persons, not places of religion, on right of habitation. (A.L.)

Theodosius I (Roman Emperor, 379–95 CE)

4.31 *Theodosian Code* 16.8.8 (Theodosius I [with Arcadius and Honorius], 392 CE)

The following law, reaffirming the authority of the Jewish leaders in Palestine, as well as in the Diaspora, to excommunicate and to revoke excommunications, continued the Roman policy of, in effect, recognizing the Jewish religious leadership as autonomous in all religious matters.

33. In the year 363 Julian was killed during the course of this war.

In the complaints of the Jews it was affirmed that some people are received [i.e., reinstated] in their sect on the authority of the judges, against the opposition of the Primates of their Law, who had cast them out by their judgment and will. We order that this injury should be utterly removed, and that a tenacious group in their superstition shall not earn aid for their undue readmission through the authority of judges or of ill-gotten rescript, against the will of their Primates, who are manifestly authorized to pass judgment concerning their religion, under the authority of the most renowned and the illustrious patriarchs. (A.L.)

4.32 Theodosian Code 16.8.9 (393 CE)

In the year 388 the Emperor Theodosius ordered that those Christians responsible for the destruction of the synagogue in Callinicum on the Euphrates be punished and that the bishop pay for the rebuilding of the synagogue. Upon the protest of Bishop Ambrose of Milan the Emperor revised his instructions and ordered that the synagogue be rebuilt out of state funds. Acts of spoliation of synagogues apparently continued, and the following law reaffirmed the licit status of the Jewish religion, repealed the interdiction on assemblies of Jews, and directed the army to protect synagogues from destruction.

It is sufficiently established that the sect of the Jews is prohibited by no law. We are therefore gravely disturbed by the interdiction imposed in some places on their assemblies. Your Sublime Magnitude[34] shall, upon reception of this order, repress with due severity the excess of those who presume to commit illegal deeds under the name of the Christian religion and attempt to destroy and despoil synagogues. (A.L.)

Arcadius (Roman Emperor, 383–408 CE)

4.33 Code of Justinian 1.9.9 (Arcadius [with Honorius], 396 CE)

The following law reaffirms the Jewish autonomy in economic affairs, forbidding, as it does, non-Jews to establish prices for the merchandise of Jews.

No outsider to the religion of the Jews shall establish prices for the Jews when merchandise is offered for sale: for it is just to assign to each man what is his own. (A.L.)

4.34 Theodosian Code 9.45.2 (Arcadius [with Honorius], 397 CE)

The following law was directed against those missionaries who sought to convert Jews with the promise that once converted they would not have to pay their debts to Jews and would not be subjected to judicial proceedings.

34. The order is addressed to a certain Addeus, master of the soldiers in the East.

Jews who are oppressed by some legal charge or by debts and pretend that they wish to join the Christian Law in order to avoid their crimes or the burden of their debts by fleeing to churches shall be kept off and shall not be received before they have paid up all their debts or have been acquitted and proven innocent. (A.L.)

4.35 *Theodosian Code* 2.1.10 (Arcadius [with Honorius], 398 CE)

The following law reaffirms the jurisdiction of Jewish courts in matters of religious law.

If some [Jews] shall deem it necessary to litigate before the Jews or the patriarchs through mutual agreement, in the manner of arbitration, with the consent of both parties and in civil matters only, they shall not be prohibited by public law from accepting their verdict; the governors of the provinces shall even execute their sentences as if they were appointed arbiters through a judge's award. (A.L.)

Honorius (Roman Emperor, 393–423 CE)

4.36 *Theodosian Code* 16.8.20 (Honorius [with Theodosius II], 412 CE)

This law forbids damaging or seizing synagogues and reasserts the exemption of Jews from appearing in court on Sabbaths and holidays.

No one shall dare to violate or seize and occupy what are known by the names of synagogues and are assuredly frequented by the conventicles of the Jews, for all must retain what is theirs with unmolested right and without harm to religion and cult. Furthermore, since the ancient custom and usage preserved the day of Sabbath, sacred to the said people of the Jews, we decree that this too must be avoided, that no summons shall constrain a man of the said custom under pretext of public or private business, for it would seem that all the remaining time suffices for the public laws, and it would be most worthy of the government of our time that former privileges shall not be violated, although it would seem that enough had been legislated on this matter in general constitutions by past Emperors. (A.L.)

4.37 *Theodosian Code* 16.9.3 (Honorius [with Theodosius II], 415 CE)

This law is remarkable in that, in contradistinction to previous legislation, it permits Jews to own Christian slaves, although, to be sure, on condition that the slaves be permitted to adhere to their religion.

We order the Jews who are owners of Christian slaves that they shall have them without chicanery,[35] on this condition, however, that they shall permit them to keep their proper religion. (A.L.)

4.38 *Theodosian Code* 16.8.23 (Honorius [with Theodosius II], 416 CE)

This law permitted Jews who had been converted to Christianity to return to Judaism if the conversion was motivated by ulterior motives, notably material considerations or the desire to escape punishment.

35. I.e., without being disturbed by legal chicanery and persecution.

It had been ordained, in the old laws as well as in ours, that, since we have learned that adherents of the Jewish religion [i.e., previous adherents of Judaism] want to join the community of the Church in order to escape their crimes and out of various necessities, this is done not from devotion to the Faith, but as a false simulation. Let the judges of the provinces in which such crimes are said to have been committed know, therefore, that our laws are to be obeyed in such a way that those people whom they shall observe as not adhering to this cult in the constancy of their religious profession, nor to be imbued with the faith and mysteries of the venerable baptism, are to be allowed to return to their own law, for it is of greater benefit to Christianity. (A.L.)

Josephus as ecclesiastical writer, Latin manuscript of Antiquities, *late eleventh century.*

5

Pro-Jewish Attitudes by Intellectuals

The earliest references to the Jews, as noted above – Aristotle, Clearchus, Theophrastus, Hecataeus, and Megasthenes – are very complimentary. Favorable opinions continue to be expressed, often even in the midst of attacks upon the Jews, especially about Moses as a lawgiver.

BIBLIOGRAPHY

Robert H. Pfeiffer, "Hebrews and Greeks before Alexander," *JBL* 56 (1937), 91–101.

Werner Jaeger, "Greeks and Jews: the First Greek Records of Jewish Religion and Civilization," *JR* 18 (1938), 127–43.

Louis H. Feldman, "Philo-Semitism among Ancient Intellectuals," *Tradition* 1 (1958–9), 27–39.

Bilhah Wardy, "Tacitus on the Origin and Tradition of the Jewish People," in her "Jewish Religion in Pagan Literature during the Late Republic and Early Empire," *ANRW* 2.19.1 (1979), 613–31.

Doron Mendels, "Hecataeus of Abdera and a Jewish 'Patrios Politeia' of the Persian Period (Diodorus Siculus XL,3)," *ZAW* (1983), 96–110.

Frederick F. Bruce, "Tacitus on Jewish History," *JSS* 29 (1984), 33–44.

Louis H. Feldman, "Pro-Jewish Intimations in Anti-Jewish Remarks Cited in Josephus' *Against Apion*," *JQR* 78 (1987–8), 187–251.

Hans Lewy, "Tacitus on the Origin and Manners of the Jews," *Binah* 1 (1989), 15–46.

Louis H. Feldman, "Pro-Jewish Intimations in Tacitus' Account of Jewish Origins," *REJ* 150 (1991), 331–60.

Illustrious Origins of the Jews

5.1 Pompeius Trogus (end of the first century BCE to beginning of the first century CE), *Philippic Histories* 36, summarized by Justin (third or fourth century CE), *Epitome* 2.1–5

Pompeius Trogus traces the origin of the Jews to the famous city of Damascus. Abraham and Israel are said to have served as kings there.

The origin of the Jews was from Damascus, the most illustrious city of Syria, whence also the stock of the Assyrian kings through queen Semiramis had sprung.[1] The name of the city was given by King

1. Semiramis, who was said to be the daughter of the fish-goddess Atargatis, was reputed to have engaged in many successful wars and to have built great cities, notably Babylon.

Damascus, in honor of whom the Syrians consecrated the sepulcher of his wife Arathis as a temple, and regard her since then as a goddess worthy of the most sacred worship. After Damascus, Azelus, and then Adores, Abraham, and Israel were their kings. But a felicitous progeny of ten sons made Israel more famous than any of his ancestors.[2] Having divided his people, in consequence, into ten kingdoms, he committed them to his sons, and called them all Jews from Judas, who died soon after this division, and ordered his memory, whose portion was added to theirs, to be held in veneration by them all. (M.S.)

5.2 Tacitus (*ca.* 56–120 CE), *Histories* 5.2

In this passage Tacitus, who is otherwise vicious in denigrating the Jews, presents six theories of their origin, most of which are actually complimentary because they ascribe extreme antiquity to the Jews: (1) the Jews were exiled from Crete when the god Saturn was deposed by the god Jupiter; (2) they left Egypt during the reign of the goddess Isis; (3) they left their native Ethiopia during the reign of the mythological Cepheus; (4) they are refugees from Assyria; (5) they are the Solymi celebrated by Homer; (6) they were expelled from Egypt during a plague.

As I am about to describe the last days of a famous city, it seems proper for me to give some account of its origin. It is said that the Jews were originally exiles from the island of Crete who settled in the farthest parts of Libya at the time when Saturn had been deposed and expelled by Jove. An argument in favor of this is derived from the name; there is a famous mountain in Crete called Ida, and hence the inhabitants were called the Idaei, which was later lengthened into the barbarous form Iudaei.[3]

Some hold that in the reign of Isis the superfluous population of Egypt,[4] under the leadership of Hierosolymus and Iuda,[5] discharged itself on the neighboring lands.

Many others think that they were an Ethiopian stock, which in the reign of Cepheus[6] was forced to migrate by fear and hatred.

Still others report that they were Assyrian refugees, a landless people, who first got control of a part of Egypt, then later they had their

2. Trogus appears to conflate Jacob (Israel) with the ten tribes that much later constituted the kingdom of Israel.

3. The connection of the Jews with Crete may reflect the historical fact, as noted by Herodotus (7.171), that originally all Crete was inhabited by non-Greeks. Tacitus' theory may reflect a source which knew of the Phoenician contact with Crete, as indicated in the legend that Europa, a Phoenician princess, was carried off to Crete by Zeus.

4. Cf. Exod 1:7: "And the children of Israel were fruitful, and increased abundantly and multiplied and waxed exceedingly mighty, and the land was filled with them."

5. In Plutarch, *On Isis and Osiris* 31, Hierosolymus and Iudaeus are the sons of Tryphon, the wicked slayer of Osiris.

6. This view is clearly complimentary, inasmuch as Cepheus and his famed wife Cassiopeia were placed among the constellations after their deaths. Their daughter Andromeda was exposed at Joppa in Judaea, where she was rescued by the great hero Perseus. The connection with the Ethiopians may have been fostered by the fact that Ethiopic is a Semitic language.

own cities and lived in the Hebrew territory and the nearer parts of Syria.[7]

Still others say that the Jews are of illustrious origin, being the Solymi, a people celebrated in Homer's poems,[8] who founded a city and gave it the name Hierosolyma, formed from their own.

Most authors agree that once during a plague in Egypt, which caused bodily disfigurement, King Bocchoris approached the oracle of Ammon and asked for a remedy, whereupon he was told to purge his kingdom and to transport this race into other lands, since it was hateful to the gods. (LCL)

Praise of Moses

Bibliography

Gager (1972).

M. J. Edwards, "Atticizing Moses? Numenius, the Fathers, and the Jews," *VC* 44 (1990), 64–75.

5.3 Diodorus the Sicilian (latter part of the first century BCE), *Historical Library* 1.94.2

In the following passage Moses is mentioned with other famous ancient lawgivers. All of them claimed a divine origin for their laws.

Among the Arians Zathraustes[9] claimed that the Good Spirit gave him his laws, among the people known as the Getae who represent themselves to be immortal, Zalmoxis[10] asserted the same of their common goddess Hestia, and among the Jews Moyses referred his laws to the god who is invoked as Iao. They all did it either because they believed that a conception which would help humanity was marvelous and wholly divine, or because they held that the common crowd would be more likely to obey the laws if their gaze was directed towards the majesty and power of those to whom their laws were ascribed. (LCL)

5.4 Strabo (*ca*. 64 BCE–*ca*. 20 CE), *Geography* 16.2.36

Strabo remarks that Moses was able to institute an extraordinary political system because of his popularity with the people.

Now Moses enjoyed fair repute with these people, and organized no ordinary kind of government, since the people all round, one and all, came over to him, because of his dealings with them and of the prospects he held out to them. (LCL)

7. This version of the origin of the Jews is closest to the account in Genesis.

8. Homer (*Iliad* 6.184) describes the Solymi as the glorious people against whom the renowned Bellerophon fought. Bellerophon himself is said to have regarded this as his hardest battle.

9. Zarathustra (Zoroaster), founder of Zoroastrian religion in Persia in the sixth century BCE.

10. Zalmoxis was the semi-mythical religious lawgiver of the Getae, a people from Thrace in north-eastern Greece.

5.5 Numenius of Apamea (*ca.* 150–200 CE), cited by Clement of Alexandria, *Coverings* 1.22.150.4

Numenius, in an extraordinary compliment, remarks that Plato's views are identical with those of the Pentateuch.

Numenius the Pythagorean philosopher writes expressly: 'For what is Plato but Moses speaking in Attic?' (M.S.)

5.6 Numenius of Apamea (*ca.* 150–200 CE), *On the Good*, cited by Eusebius (265–340 CE), *Preparation for the Gospel* 9.8.1–2

Numenius here compares Moses' efficacy as a magician with that of the famous Egyptian magicians, Jannes and Jambres.

Also in his third book the same author [Numenius] makes mention of Moses speaking as follows: 'And next in order came Jannes and Jambres, Egyptian sacred scribes, men judged to have no superiors in the practice of magic at the time when the Jews were being driven out of Egypt. So then these were the men chosen by people of Egypt as fit to stand beside Musaeus[11] [i.e., Moses], who led forth the Jews, a man who was most powerful in prayer to God; and of the plagues which Musaeus brought upon Egypt, these men showed themselves able to disperse the most violent.'[12] (E.H.G.)

Praise of Jewish Theology

5.7 Varro (116–27 BCE), *Antiquities*, cited by Augustine (354–430 CE), *City of God* 4.31

Praise of the Jews coming from so influential a writer as Varro, who is alleged to have written no fewer than 490 books, who was encyclopedic in his knowledge, and whom the great literary critic Quintilian (10.1.95) termed "the most learned of the Romans," is noteworthy. That he, a pagan, should have praised their theological views and, in particular, their worship of an imageless God is particularly remarkable.

He [Varro] also says that for more than 170 years the ancient Romans worshipped the gods without an image. 'If this usage had continued to our own day,' he says, 'our worship of the gods would be more devout.' And in support of his opinion he adduces, among other things, the testimony of the Jewish race. And he ends with the forthright statement that those who first set up images of the gods for the people diminished reverence in their cities as they added to error, for he wisely judged that gods in the shape of senseless images might easily inspire contempt. (LCL)

---

11. Musaeus was actually the mythical son or disciple of the famed Orpheus. The Graeco-Jewish historian Artapanus, as cited by Eusebius, *Preparation for the Gospel* 9.27.1, identifies him with Moses and states that he became the teacher of Orpheus.

12. That Jannes and Jambres were capable of resisting Moses is implied in 2 Tim 3:8.

5.8 Varro (116–27 BCE), *Antiquities*, cited by Augustine (354–430 CE), *Concerning the Consensus of the Gospels* 1.22.30

Here Varro pays an extraordinary compliment to the Jews in comparing the Jewish view of God with that of the Roman Jupiter, the king of the gods.

Yet Varro, one of themselves [i.e., the Romans] – to a more learned man they cannot point – thought the God of the Jews to be the same as Jupiter, thinking that it makes no difference by which name he is called, so long as the same thing is understood. I believe that he did it being terrified by His sublimity. Since the Romans habitually worship nothing superior to Jupiter, a fact attested well and openly by their Capitol, and they consider him the king of all the gods, and as he perceived that the Jews worship the highest God, he could not but identify him with Jupiter. (M.S.)

5.9 Strabo (*ca.* 64 BCE–*ca.* 20 CE), *Geography* 16.2.35–6

Strabo praises Moses for conceiving of a God who embraces the entire universe and who should be worshipped without an image.

Moses, namely, was one of the Egyptian priests, and held a part of Lower Egypt, as it is called, but he went away from there to Judaea, since he was displeased with the state of affairs there, and was accompanied by many people who worshipped the Divine Being. For he said and taught that the Egyptians were mistaken in representing the Divine Being by the images of beasts and cattle, as were also the Libyans; and that the Greeks were also wrong in modeling gods in human form; for, according to him, God is the one thing alone that encompasses us all and encompasses land and sea – the thing which we call heaven, or universe, or the nature of all that exists. What man, then, if he has sense, could be bold enough to fabricate an image of God resembling any creature amongst us? Nay, people should leave off all image-carving, and, setting apart a sacred precinct and a worthy sanctuary, should worship God without an image; and people who have good dreams should sleep in the sanctuary, not only themselves on their own behalf, but also others for the rest of the people; and those who live self-restrained and righteous lives should always expect some blessing or gift or sign from God, but no other should expect them. Now Moses, saying things of this kind, persuaded not a few thoughtful men and led them away to this place where the settlement of Jerusalem now is. (LCL)

5.10 Plutarch (*ca.* 46–120 CE), *Festal Questions* 4.6

Plutarch presents a very sympathetic account of Jewish theology. The fact that he identifies the Jewish God with Adonis and with Dionysus is clearly complimentary in placing Him in immediate juxtaposition with the Greek mysteries. We may note that Plutarch has considerable knowledge of the way in which Jews celebrate the holiday of Tabernacles.

Who the god of the Jews is.

Symmachus, surprised at this last statement [asserting Adonis is identical with Dionysus], asked, 'Lamprias, are you enrolling your national god in the calendar of the Hebrews and insinuating into their secret rites "him of the orgiastic cry, exciter of women, Dionysus, glorified with mad honors?" Is there actually some tradition that demonstrates identity between him and Adonis?' Moeragenes interposed, 'Never mind him. I as an Athenian can answer you and say that the god is no other. Most of the relevant proofs can lawfully be pronounced or divulged only to those of us who have been initiated into the Perfect Mysteries celebrated every other year, but what I am going to speak of is not forbidden in conversation with friends, especially over after-dinner wine, while we are enjoying the god's own bounty. I am ready to speak if these gentlemen urge me.'

At this, all did urge him and beg him to go on. 'First,' he said, 'the time and character of the greatest, most sacred holiday of the Jews[13] clearly befit Dionysus. When they celebrate their so-called Fast,[14] at the height of the vintage, they set tables of all sorts of fruit under tents and huts plaited for the most part of vines and ivy. They call the first of the days of the feast Tabernacles. A few days later they celebrate another festival,[15] this time identified with Bacchus not through obscure hints but plainly called by his name, a festival that is a sort of "Procession of the Branches" or "Thyrsus Procession," in which they enter the temple each carrying a thyrsus.[16] What they do after entering we do not know, but it is probable that the rite is a Bacchic revelry, for in fact they use little trumpets to invoke their god as do the Argives at their Dionysia. Others of them advance playing harps; these players are called in their language *Levites*, either from *Lysios* ("Releaser") or, better, from *Evius* ("God of the Cry").

'I believe that even the feast of the Sabbath is not completely unrelated to Dionysus. Many even now call the Bacchants *Sabi* and utter that cry when celebrating the god. Testimony to this can be found in Demosthenes and Menander. You would not be far off the track if you attributed the use of this name *Sabi* to the strange excitement (*sobesis*) that possesses the celebrants. The Jews themselves testify to a connection with Dionysus when they keep the Sabbath by inviting each other to drink and to enjoy wine; when more important business interferes with this custom, they regularly take at least a sip of neat wine.

'Now thus far one might call the argument only probable; but the opposition is quite demolished, in the first place by the High Priest, who leads the procession at their festival wearing a mitre and clad in a gold-embroidered fawnskin, a robe reaching to the ankles and buskins,

13. The context would seem to indicate that the reference is to the festival of Tabernacles.

14. The reference is to the Day of Atonement.

15. The festival would seem to be Shemini Atzereth, which follows immediately after the conclusion of the festival of Tabernacles.

16. The reference is to the palm branches which are carried on the festival of Tabernacles.

with many bells attached to his clothes and ringing below him as he walks. All this corresponds to our custom. In the second place, they also have noise as an element in their nocturnal festivals, and call the nurses of the god "bronze rattlers." The carved thyrsus in the relief on the pediment of the Temple and the drums [provide other parallels]. All this surely befits [they might say] no divinity but Dionysus.

'Further, the Jews use no honey in their religious services because they believe that honey spoils the wine with which it is mixed; and they used honey as libation and in place of wine before the vine was discovered. Even up to the present time those of the barbarians who do not make wine drink mead, counteracting the sweetness somewhat by the use of winelike bitter roots. The Greeks, on the other hand, offer the same libations as "sober libations" and *meli-sponda*[17] on the principle that there is a particular opposition between honey and wine. To show that what I have said is the practice of the Jews we may find no slight confirmation in the fact that among many penalties employed among them the one most disliked is the exclusion of a convicted offender from the use of wine for such a period as the sentencing judge may prescribe.'[18] (LCL)

5.11 Tacitus (*ca.* 56–120 CE), *Histories* 5.5.4–5

Tacitus notes that the religion of the Jews is monotheistic and imageless. Like Plutarch, however, Tacitus notes that some have theorized that the Jews worshipped Dionysus because of the place of pipes, drums, ivy, and the vine in their worship.

The Egyptians worship many animals and monstrous images; the Jews conceive of one god only, and that with the mind only;[19] they regard as impious those who make from perishable materials representations of gods in man's image; that supreme and eternal being is to them incapable of representation and without end. Therefore they set up no statues in their cities, still less in their temples; this flattery is not paid their kings, nor this honor given to the Caesars.

But since their priests used to chant to the accompaniment of pipes and drums and to wear garlands of ivy, and because a golden vine was found in their temple, some have thought that they were devotees of Father Liber [i.e., Dionysus], the conqueror of the East, in spite of the incongruity of their customs. For Liber established festive ties of a joyous nature, while the ways of the Jews are preposterous and mean. (LCL)

5.12 Galen (*ca.* 129–200 CE), *On the Use of Parts* 11.14

Galen asserts that Moses' interpretation of nature is superior to that of Epicurus, though the best view is to add the material principle to Moses' principle of the demiurge.

17. I.e., drink-offerings of honey.
18. Stern suggests that this is a vague allusion to the institution of Naziriteship.
19. This would seem to contradict Tacitus' previous statement (*Histories* 5.4.2) that the Jews dedicated a statue of an ass in a shrine, since it was this animal that had enabled them to put an end to their wandering during the Exodus.

Did our demiurge[20] simply enjoin this hair [in eyelashes] to preserve its length always equal,[21] and does it strictly observe this order either from fear of its master's command, or from reverence for the god who gave this order, or is it because it itself believes it better to do this? Is not this Moses' way of treating Nature and is it not superior to that of Epicurus? The best way, of course, is to follow neither of these but to maintain like Moses the principle of the demiurge as the origin of every created thing, while adding the material principle to it. (R.W.)

> 5.13 Numenius of Apamea (*ca.* 150–200 CE), *On the Good*, cited by Origen (185–253 CE), *Against Celsus* 1.15

Numenius, in his eclectic philosophy, includes the Jews among those who regard God as incorporeal, cites the sayings of the prophets, and explains them allegorically.

How much better than Celsus is Numenius the Pythagorean, a man who showed himself in many works to be very learned and who by studying several doctrines made from many sources a synthesis of those which seemed to him to be true. In the first book on 'The Good,' where he speaks of the nations that believe God to be incorporeal, he also included the Jews among them, and did not hesitate to quote the sayings of the prophets in his book and to give them an allegorical interpretation. (H.C.)

> 5.14 Numenius of Apamea (*ca.* 150–200 CE), cited by Lydus (fifth century), *On Months* 4.53

Numenius notes that the Jewish God is incomparable.

In conformity with Livy Lucan[22] says that the Temple of Jerusalem belongs to an uncertain god, while Numenius says that the power of the god is not to be shared by any other, and that he is the father of all the gods, and that he deems any other god unworthy of having a share in his cult. (M.S.)

> 5.15 Porphyry (232–*ca.* 301 CE), *On the Philosophy to be Derived from Oracles*, cited by Augustine (354–430 CE), *City of God* 19.23

According to the pagan philosopher Porphyry, the Jewish God is so incomparable that even the other divinities shudder before him.

Let us come to plainer matters, and let us hear how great a god Porphyry says that the God of the Jews is. For example, Apollo, when asked which is the better, word (that is, reason) or law, replied, he says,

20. The demiurge is the name used by Plato in his dialogue, *Timaeus*, to designate the deity who fashions the material world.

21. In discussing the constant length of eyelashes, Galen asks whether this constant is to be attributed to the hair's fear of its master's command or to reverence for the god who ordered it or to the fact that the hair itself believes this to be best.

22. Livy is the great Roman historian (59 BCE–17 CE). Lucan (39–65 CE) is the author of the epic *Pharsalia* dealing with the civil war between Pompey and Julius Caesar.

in these verses, which he adds (and I select of them only the following, as sufficient): 'In one truly God, the creator and the king prior to all things, before whom tremble heaven and earth and the sea and the hidden places beneath, and the very divinities shudder; their law is the Father whom the holy Hebrews greatly honor.' In this oracle of his own god Apollo, Porphyry has cited the God of the Hebrews as being so great that the very divinities shudder before him. (LCL)

5.16 Iamblichus (*ca.* 250–330 CE), cited by Lydus (fifth century), *On Months* 4.53

The Neo-Platonist philosophers Iamblichus, Syrianus, and Proclus equated God with the demiurge, i.e., the creator, and regarded Him as the god of the four elements.

But the schools of Iamblichus, Syrianus and Proclus[23] consider him [i.e., the god worshipped by the Jews] to be the demiurge, calling him the god of the four elements. (M.S.)

Wisdom of the Jews

5.17 Pompeius Trogus (end of the first century BCE to beginning of the first century CE), *Philippic Histories* 36, summarized by Justin (third or fourth century CE), *Epitome* 2.6–10

Pompeius Trogus describes the biblical Joseph as a master magician and the founder of the science of interpreting dreams. It was his wise advice which enabled the Egyptians to survive the famine that afflicted them.

The youngest of the brothers [the sons of Jacob] was Joseph, whom the others, fearing his extraordinary abilities, secretly made prisoner and sold to some foreign merchants. Being carried by them into Egypt, and having there, by his shrewd nature, made himself master of the arts of magic, he found in a short time great favor with the king; for he was eminently skilled in prodigies, and was the first to establish the science of interpreting dreams; and nothing indeed of divine or human law seemed to have been unknown to him, so that he foretold a dearth in the land some years before it happened, and all Egypt would have perished by famine had not the king, by his advice, ordered the corn to be laid up for several years; such being the proofs of his knowledge that his admonitions seemed to proceed, not from a mortal, but a god. His son was Moyses,[24] whom, besides the inheritance of his father's knowledge, the comeliness of his person also recommended. (M.S.)

5.18 Diogenes Laertius (*ca.* 200–50 CE), *Lives of the Philosophers* 1.9

Diogenes Laertius presents the very complimentary view that the Jews are descended from the famed Magi.

23. Iamblichus was a renowned Neo-Platonist, a student of Porphyry. Syrianus and Proclus were Neo-Platonists who lived in the fifth century CE.

24. Pompeius Trogus is here mistaken, since, according to the Bible (Exod 2:1), Moses was the grandson of Levi, the brother of Joseph. Elsewhere Pompeius Trogus also speaks of Aaron as the son of Moses.

Clearchus of Soli in his tract *On Education* further makes the Gymnosophists to be descended from the Magi;[25] and some trace the Jews also to the same origin.[26] (LCL)

> 5.19 Porphyry (232–*ca*. 301 CE), *On the Philosophy to be Derived from Oracles*, cited by Eusebius (265–340 CE), *Preparation for the Gospel* 9.10.1, 4

Porphyry bears witness to the wisdom of the Jews, noting that the oracle of Apollo paid tribute to the Jews' wisdom in their pure theology.

Porphyry, in the first book of his *Philosophy from Oracles*, introduces his own god as himself bearing witness to the wisdom of the Hebrew race as well as of other nations renowned for intelligence. . . . In addition to this Apollo also says in another oracle: Only Chaldees and Hebrews found wisdom in the pure worship of a self-born God. (E.H.G.)

Knowledge of Astronomy

Astronomy was the most popular of the four branches of mathematics in Hellenistic times and was the one that aroused the most curiosity because of the practical importance of astrology. Hence, the fact that the Jews excelled in this field was a great compliment.

> 5.20 Hermippus of Smyrna (*ca*. 200 BCE), cited by Vettius Valens (second century CE), *Anthologies* 2.28

Hermippus, in a great compliment, refers to Abraham as most wonderful in his innovative astrological views.

On traveling, from the works of Hermippus. . . . The most wonderful Abramos [i.e., Abraham] has shown us about this [astrological] position in his books . . . and he himself on his part invented other things and tested them, especially on genitures [nativities] inclined to travelling. (M.S.)

> 5.21 Firmicus Maternus (first half of the fourth century CE), *Astrology* 4, Prooemium 5; 4.17.2, 5; 4.18.1

Firmicus Maternus refers to Abraham as an expert in the complex calculations of astrology.

All the things that Mercury and Chnubis [?] transmitted with difficulty to Aesculapius, and those that Petosiris and Nechepso[27] disentangled,

25. The Gymnosophists were a sect of philosophers found in India by Alexander the Great. They were famous for their asceticism. The Magi were priests in the Zoroastrian religion in Persia.

26. Inasmuch as the Indian Gymnosophists, known for their wisdom, had been traced back to the Magi, and since, as we see from the remarks of Aristotle, the Jews were said to be descended from Indian philosophers, it seemed reasonable to suppose that they, like the Indian Gymnosophists, were descended from the Magi.

27. Petosiris and Nechepso were well-known astrologers who were said to be the authors of an astrological handbook.

and those that Abram, Orfeus [Orpheus] and Critodemus and all others who are experts in this profession related, we have read through in equal degree, and collected them, and after comparing the opposing diversities of their views, we have written them down in books. . . .

All these things we shall set forth when we come to the exposition of the barbaric sphere. For that divine Abram and the very learned Achilles have attempted to find out all this by the truest calculations. . . .

From this position it is possible to disclose the quality of life, the richness of the patrimony and the progress of both happiness and unhappiness. Also from this position we learn about the nature of love and the fondness of men towards women, and from the essence of this position we inquire about the effects of all child-care and desires. By an easy calculation, this position [or the squared sides of this position] shows one's native country. It is called, as Abraham defines it, the Position of the Moon. . . .

The position of the daemon we deduce by this calculation; we inserted it into this book, because Abraham has shown by a similar calculation that this is the position of the Sun, and it seemed unfair for the position of the Sun to be separated from that of the Moon. (M.S.)

Knowledge of Medicine

There is ample indication in the Talmudic corpus of rabbinic knowledge of medicine on a high level. A celebrated Jewish physician in Alexandria was Adamantius, who flourished at the beginning of the fifth century CE (Socrates, *Ecclesiastical History* 7.13). Asaf Ha-Rofe in the sixth century CE composed the first book in Hebrew on medicine which shows a great knowledge of Greek medical writings.

5.22 Cornelius Celsus (the Encyclopedist) (early part of the first century CE), *On Medicine* 5.19.11, 5.22.4

The encyclopedic writer Celsus, whose work on medicine survives, refers to a remedy ascribed to a Jewish physician. There is a question whether Iudaeus is his real name or whether it simply indicates that he was a Jew. We have no means of dating him.

But among those [remedies] suitable for broken heads, some include the one which is ascribed to Iudaeus. It is composed of salt 16 grams, red copper scales and calcined copper, 48 grams each, ammoniacum for fumigation, frankincense soot and dried resin, 64 grams each, Colophon resin, wax, and prepared calf's suet, 80 grams each, vinegar 65 centimeters, less than 40 centimeters of oil. . . .

The compound of Iudaeus contains lime two parts; the reddest soda one part, mixed with the urine of a young boy to the consistency of strigil scrapings. But the place on which it is smeared should from time to time be moistened. (LCL)

5.23 Damascius (first half of the sixth century), *Life of Isidore*, cited by Suda (tenth century), s.v. *Gesios*

Damascius mentions a Jewish physician who had a student named Gesius who was even more distinguished than he was.

Gesius. Under Zeno[28] he distinguished himself in the art of medicine. He hailed from Petra.[29] He overthrew his teacher Domnus the Jew, and, transferring almost all his companions to himself, became known everywhere and attained great fame. (M.S.)

Magic

Jews in antiquity had a reputation for magic and the occult, and they are prominent in the magical papyri. Moses, in particular, was said to be the author of several magical books.

5.24 Pliny the Elder (23–79 CE), *Natural History* 30.11

Pliny, in his history of magic, pays tribute here to the role therein of Moses and the Jews.

There is yet another branch of magic, derived from Moses, Jannes,[30] Lotapes,[31] and the Jews, but dating from many thousand years after Zoroaster. (LCL, revised)

5.25 Apuleius (middle of the second century), *Apology* 90

It is significant that in listing famous magicians Apuleius, himself a well-known practitioner, refers to Moses as "of whom you have heard," clearly implying that his renown in the field was universal.

I am ready to be any magician you please – the great Carmendas himself or Damigeron or Moses of whom you have heard, or Iohannes or Apollobex or Dardanus[32] himself or any sorcerer of note from the time of Zoroaster and Ostanes till now. (LCL)

Rhetoric

BIBLIOGRAPHY

George P. Goold, "A Greek Professorial Circle at Rome," *TAPA* 92 (1961), 168–92.
Gager (1972), 56–63.
Stern, vol. 1 (1974), 361–5.

28. The Emperor Zeno reigned from 474 to 491 CE.
29. Petra was a city of major importance in Transjordan.
30. Other sources (e.g., Numenius, *ap.* Eusebius, *Preparation for the Gospel* 9.8.1–2) refer to Jannes as an Egyptian magician who was an opponent of Moses.
31. Lotapes is otherwise unknown.
32. The magicians mentioned here are otherwise unknown except for Damigeron, who wrote a well-known book on stones.

5.26 (Pseudo-)Longinus (first or second century CE), *On the Sublime* 9.9

The fact that the unknown author, (Pseudo-)Longinus, of the essay *On the Sublime*, the most important essay in ancient literary criticism after Aristotle's *Poetics*, cites the Pentateuch as an example of the most sublime style is a tremendous compliment. He is the only pagan writer to paraphrase the Bible so closely. The fact that he does not designate Moses by name but refers to him merely as the lawgiver of the Jews is an indication that he expected his readers to know to whom he was referring. (Pseudo-)Longinus includes this passage, together with four others from Homer and a verbal exchange between Alexander the Great and Parmenio, to illustrate his point that the basic ingredient of great writing is not literary style but rather a great mind. Because this is the last example cited, it would seem to be the climax, and the compliment is all the greater. Some scholars think that (Pseudo-)Longinus was a Jew, but the fact is that the author elsewhere (12.4) declares himself to be a Greek.

A similar effect was achieved by the lawgiver of the Jews – no mean genius, for he both understood and gave expression to the power of the divinity as it deserved – when he wrote at the very beginning of his laws, and I quote his words: 'God said' what? 'Let there be light. And there was. Let there be earth. And there was.'[33] (D.A.R.)

Military Prowess and Bravery

5.27 Cleodemus Malchus (before the middle of the first century BCE), cited by Josephus, *Jewish Antiquities* 1.238–41

BIBLIOGRAPHY
Wacholder (1974), 53–5.
Holladay, vol. 1 (1983), 245–59.

A certain Cleodèmus Malchus, who may have been a Samaritan, or a pagan, or a Jew, and who is designated by Josephus as "the prophet," is cited by Josephus, who, in turn, asserts that he has derived his information from Alexander Polyhistor, who wrote a treatise in Greek *Concerning Jews* in the first century BCE. The fact that he connects the sons of Abraham with Heracles, who was the most famous of all Greek mythical heroes, in his military campaign in Africa is clearly intended to be a compliment, though one wonders how a Jew (if Cleodemus was a Jew) could have been proud to be related to such a pagan figure.

Abraham afterwards married Katura,[34] by whom he had six sons, strong to labor and quick of understanding, viz., Zembran[es], Jazar[es], Madan[es], Madian[es], Lousoubak[os], Souos. These too had families: Souos begat Sabakin[es] and Dadan[es], from whom sprang Latousim[os], Assuris and Lououris; Madan begat Ephas, Eophren,

---

33. Gen 1:3, 9–10.
34. Cf. Gen 25:1–6.

Anochos, Ebidas and Eldas. All these sons and grandsons Abraham contrived to send out to found colonies, and they took possession of Troglodytis and that part of Arabia Felix which extends to the Red Sea. It is said moreover that this Eophren led an expedition against Libya and occupied it and that his grandsons settled there and called the land after his name Africa.

I have a witness to this statement in Alexander Polyhistor, whose words are as follows: 'Cleodemus the prophet, also called Malchus, in his history of the Jews, relates, in conformity with the narrative of their lawgiver Moses, that Abraham had several sons by Katura. He moreover gives their names, mentioning three – Apheras, Sures, Japhras – adding that Sures gave his name to Assyria, and the two others, Japhras and Apheras, gave their names to the city of Aphra and the country of Africa. In fact, he adds, these latter joined Heracles in his campaign against Libya and Antaeus;[35] and Heracles, marrying the daughter of Aphranes, had by her a son Didorus, who begat Sophon, from whom the barbarians take their name of Sophakes.' (LCL)

> 5.28 Claudius Iolaus (perhaps first century CE), cited by Stephanus of Byzantium (sixth century?), s.v. *Ioudaia*

It is clearly a compliment to the Jews that Claudius Iolaus derives the name Judaea from Udaeus, one of the military companions of the god Dionysus.

Alexander Polyhistor says that the name [Judaea] derives from that of the children of Semiramis,[36] Judas and Idumaea [?]. According, however, to Claudius Iolaus, it comes from Udaeus, one of the 'Sown-men' at Thebes,[37] who was among the military companions of Dionysus.[38] (M.S.)

> 5.29 Tacitus (*ca.* 56–120 CE), *Histories* 5.5.3, 5.13.3

Tacitus, who denigrates the Jews, here admits that the Jewish defenders, both men and women, were fearless in the war against the Romans.

They [the Jews] believe that the souls of those who are killed in battle or by the executioner are immortal; hence comes their passion for begetting children, and their scorn of death. . . .

We have heard that the total number of the besieged [by the Romans in Jerusalem in 70 CE] of every age and both sexes was 600,000; there were arms for all who could use them, and the number ready to fight

---

35. Antaeus was the giant son of Poseidon and Ge (Earth) with whom Heracles wrestled. The peculiar characteristic of Antaeus was that whenever he was thrown he rose up again stronger than before because of his contact with his mother Earth. Heracles was able to overcome him by lifting him up in the air and then crushing him.

36. Semiramis was the legendary Babylonian or Assyrian queen who was noted for her bravery in battle.

37. According to the myth, Cadmus the Phoenician, upon founding Thebes, killed a serpent. From its teeth, which he sowed, sprang armed men, who fought and killed each other, until only five were left. Udaeus was one of those who survived.

38. The connection of the Jews with Dionysus is noted by Plutarch and Tacitus.

was larger than could have been anticipated from the total population. Both men and women showed the same determination; and if they were to be forced to change their home, they feared life more than death. (LCL)

Justice

5.30 Pompeius Trogus (end of the first century BCE to the beginning of the first century CE), *Philippic Histories* 36, summarized by Justin (third or fourth century CE), *Epitome* 2.16

Pompeius Trogus compliments the Jews for combining justice with their religion.

After Moyses, his son Arruas[39] was made priest to supervise the Egyptian rites, and soon after created king; and ever afterwards it was a custom among the Jews to have the same persons both for kings and priests; and, by their justice combined with religion, it is incredible how powerful they became. (M.S.)

Piety

5.31 Strabo (*ca.* 64 BCE–*ca.* 20 ce), *Historical Memoranda*, cited by Josephus, *Jewish Antiquities* 14.66–8

Strabo, as well as Nicolaus of Damascus and Livy, marvels at the fact that even when the troops of Pompey were slaughtering Jews in the Temple, the priests bravely and resolutely continued with their sacrifices.

And, indeed, when the city [Jerusalem] was taken, in the third month [of the siege], on the Fast Day,[40] in the 179th Olympiad, in the consulship of Gaius Antonius and Marcus Tullius Cicero [63 BCE], and the enemy rushed in and were slaughtering the Jews in the Temple, those who were busied with the sacrifices none the less continued to perform the sacred ceremonies; nor were they compelled, either by fear for their lives or by the great number of those already slain, to run away, but thought it better to endure whatever they might have to suffer there beside the altars than to neglect any of the ordinances. And that this is not merely a story to set forth the praises of a fictitious piety, but the truth, is attested by all those who have narrated the exploits of Pompey, among them Strabo and Nicolaus and, in addition, Titus Livius, the author of a History of Rome. (LCL)

5.32 Strabo (*ca.* 64 BCE–*ca.* 20 CE), *Geography* 16.2.37

Strabo notes that Moses' successors acted piously.

39. Presumably Moses' brother Aaron is meant. Trogus has anachronistically read back into the biblical period the practice that prevailed under the Hasmonean monarchy of having the king serve also as high priest.
40. Apparently not the Day of Atonement but either the Fast of the Ninth of Ab or the Sabbath, which was regarded as a fast day by a number of pagan writers.

His [Moses'] successors for some time abided by the same course, acting righteously and being truly pious toward God. (LCL)

> 5.33 Seneca the Younger (*ca.* 4 BCE–65 CE), *Concerning Superstition*, cited by Augustine (354–430 CE), *City of God* 6.11

Seneca begrudgingly admits that Jews know the origin and significance of their practices, whereas most others do not.

He [Seneca] adds a statement that shows what he thought of their system of sacred institutions. 'The Jews, however, are aware of the origin and meaning of their rites. The greater part of the people go through a ritual not knowing why they do so.'[41] (LCL)

> 5.34 Julian (331–63 CE), *To Theodorus* 89a

Julian admires the Jews for their readiness to die for their religious beliefs, in contrast to non-Jews who are apathetic about them.

I saw that those whose minds were turned to the doctrines of the Jewish religion are so ardent in their belief that they would choose to die for it, and to endure utter want and starvation rather than taste pork or any animal that has not the life [i.e., the blood] squeezed out of it immediately; whereas we are in such a state of apathy about religious matters that we have forgotten the customs of our forefathers, and therefore we actually do not know whether any such rule has ever been prescribed. (LCL)

Charity

> 5.35 Julian (331–63 CE), *To Arsacius the High-priest of Galatia* 84a

Julian admires the Jews for their helpfulness to one another.

It is disgraceful that, when no Jew has to beg, and the impious Galileans [i.e., Christians] support not only their own poor but ours as well, all men see that our people lack aid from us. (LCL).

---

41. Some scholars interpret this as a contrast between full-fledged Jews and non-Jews who adopt Jewish customs. More likely Seneca is contrasting the Jews, who understand the reasons of their commandments, with non-Jews who do their religious acts by mere rote.

Joseph, Potiphar's wife, and Asenath, Vienna Genesis, Syria, sixth century.

6

❦

Conversion to Judaism

BIBLIOGRAPHY

Bernard J. Bamberger, *Proselytism in the Talmudic Period* (1939).

William G. Braude, *Jewish Proselyting in the First Five Centuries of the Common Era: the Age of the Tannaim and Amoraim* (1940).

Jacob S. Raisin, *Gentile Reactions to Jewish Ideals with Special Reference to Proselytes* (1953).

Karl G. Kuhn, "Proselutos," *TDNT*, vol. 6 (1968), 727–44.

Shaye J. D. Cohen, "Conversion to Judaism in Historical Perspective: From Biblical Israel to Postbiblical Judaism," *CJ* 36.4 (Summer, 1983), 31–45.

Shaye J. D. Cohen, "The Origins of the Matrilineal Principle in Rabbinic Law," *AJSR* 10 (1985), 19–53.

Dieter Georgi, *The Opponents of Paul in Second Corinthians*, rev. ed. (1985).

Fergus Millar, "Gentiles and Judaism: 'God-Fearers' and Proselytes," in Schürer, vol. 3.1 (1986), 150–76.

Shaye J. D. Cohen, "Crossing the Boundary and Becoming a Jew," *HTR* 82 (1989), 14–33.

Martin Goodman, "Proselytising in Rabbinic Judaism," *JJS* 40 (1989), 175–85.

Louis H. Feldman, "Proselytes and 'Sympathizers' in the Light of the New Inscriptions from Aphrodisias," *REJ* 148 (1989), 265–305.

Scot McKnight, *A Light among the Gentiles: Jewish Missionary Activity in the Second Temple Period* (1991).

Louis H. Feldman, "Jewish Proselytism," in Harold W. Attridge and Gohei Hata, eds, *Eusebius, Christianity, and Judaism* (1992), 372–408.

Shaye J. D. Cohen, "Was Judaism in Antiquity a Missionary Religion?" in Menahem Mor, ed., *Jewish Assimilation, Acculturation and Accommodation: Past Traditions, Current Issues, and Future Prospects* (1992), 14–23.

Louis H. Feldman, "Was Judaism a Missionary Religion in Ancient Times?" in Menahem Mor, ed., *Jewish Assimilation, Acculturation and Accommodation: Past Traditions, Current Issues, and Future Prospects* (1992), 24–37.

Louis H. Feldman, "The Contribution of Professor Salo W. Baron to the Study of Ancient Jewish History: His Appraisal of Anti-Judaism and Proselytism," *AJSR* 18 (1993), 1–27.

Feldman (1993), 288–341.

Martin Goodman, *Mission and Conversion: Proselytizing in the Religious History of the Roman Empire* (1994).

Gary G. Porton, *The Stranger within Your Gates: Converts and Conversion in Rabbinic Literature* (1994).

Conversion to Judaism in the Hellenistic–Roman period entailed, among other requirements, belief in God and denial of other gods. The Jewish attitude toward proselytism apparently changed from a passive to a more active approach during the Hellenistic period. The chief reason for presuming that there were massive conversions to Judaism during this period is the seemingly dramatic increase in Jewish population at this time. Pre-exilic Judaea (which contained the major part of the Jewish population at the time of the destruction of the First Temple in 586 BCE), according to Baron's calculations[1] based on biblical and archaeological data, had no more than 150,000 Jews. By the middle of the first century he estimates[2] that the total number of Jews in the world had risen to about eight million, and that the Jews constituted about one-eighth of the population of the Roman Empire. True, some of the increase can be accounted for by the Jews' superior hygiene (the incidental result of legislation both in the written and the oral Torah) and their refusal to practice birth control, abortion, or infanticide; but the figures demand further explanation. Only proselytism can account for this vast increase.

Forcible Conversion

In Palestine we hear of the forced (though some scholars argue that the conversions were voluntary) conversions, as a matter of national policy, of the Idumaeans in the south by John Hyrcanus and the Ituraeans in the north by Aristobulus I in the latter part of the second century BCE.

BIBLIOGRAPHY

Aryeh Kasher, *Jews, Idumaeans, and Ancient Arabs: Relations of the Jews in Eretz-Israel with the Nations of the Frontier and the Desert during the Hellenistic and Roman Era (332 BCE–70 CE)* (1988), 46–77, 79–85.
Feldman (1993), 324–6.

6.1 Strabo (*ca.* 64 BCE–*ca.* 20 CE), *Geography* 16.2.34

Strabo says that the Idumaeans joined the Jews and shared in their customs. This does not necessarily imply coercion, nor does it contradict it.

The Idumaeans are Nabateans,[3] but owing to a sedition they were banished from there, joined the Judaeans, and shared in the same customs with them. (LCL)

6.2 Josephus, *Jewish Antiquities* 13.257–8

The evidence of Josephus is conclusive, that the Jewish king John Hyrcanus permitted the Idumaeans to remain in the land only so long as they converted properly to Judaism.

1. Salo W. Baron, "Population," *Encyclopaedia Judaica* 13 (1971), 869.
2. Salo W. Baron, *A Social and Religious History of the Jews*, 2nd ed., vol. 1 (New York: Columbia University Press, 1952), 170, 370–2, note 7.
3. An Arab people who established a kingdom in the ancient territory of Edom in Transjordan.

Hyrcanus also captured the Idumaean cities of Adora and Marisa, and after subduing all the Idumaeans, permitted them to remain in their country so long as they had themselves circumcised and were willing to observe the laws of the Jews. And so, out of attachment to the land of their fathers, they submitted to circumcision and to making their manner of life conform in all other respects to that of the Jews. And from that time on they have continued to be Jews. (LCL)

6.3 Ptolemy the Historian (end of the first century BCE?), *History of Herod*, cited by Ammonius (first or second century CE), *Concerning the Difference of Related Words*, no. 243

Ptolemy the Historian says explicitly that the Idumaeans were forced to undergo circumcision.

Jews and Idumaeans differ, as Ptolemy states in the first book of the History of King Herod. Jews are those who are so by origin and nature. The Idumaeans, on the other hand, were not originally Jews, but Phoenicians and Syrians; having been subjugated by the Jews and having been forced to undergo circumcision, so as to be counted among the Jewish nation and keep the same customs, they were called Jews. (M.S.)

6.4 Josephus, *Jewish Antiquities* 13.318

Josephus says that when Aristobulus I conquered the Ituraeans, he forced them to convert if they wished to remain in the land.

In his reign of one year, with the title of Philhellene, he [Aristobulus I] conferred many benefits on his country, for he made war on the Ituraeans[4] and acquired a good part of their territory for Judaea and compelled their inhabitants, if they wished to remain in their country, to be circumcised and to live in accordance with the laws of the Jews. (LCL)

6.5 Timagenes (first century BCE), cited by Josephus, *Jewish Antiquities* 13.319

Timagenes, born in Alexandria, is noteworthy as the only Graeco-Alexandrian writer who is not hostile to Jews. He asserts that Aristobulus I brought over to Judaism a portion of the Ituraeans. Though he does not specifically say that he applied force, he does not contradict Josephus' clear statement.

He [Aristobulus I] had a kindly nature, and was wholly given to modesty, as Strabo also testifies on the authority of Timagenes, writing as follows: 'This man was a kindly[5] person and very serviceable to the Jews, for he acquired additional territory for them, and brought over to them a portion of the Ituraean nation, whom he joined to them by the bond of circumcision.' (LCL)

---

4. A nation located in Lebanon.

5. Nevertheless, Aristobulus was responsible for the murder of one brother, imprisoned the others, and starved his mother to death.

How Converts Were Won

The Conversion of the Royal Family of Adiabene

BIBLIOGRAPHY

Jacob Neusner, "The Conversion of Adiabene to Judaism," *JBL* 83 (1964), 60–6.
Lawrence H. Schiffman, "The Conversion of the Royal House of Adiabene in
    Josephus and Rabbinic Sources," *JJC* (1987), 293–312.
Feldman (1993), 328–30.

The most impressive achievement of the proselytizing movement
was the conversion of King Izates, his brother Monobazus, and their
mother Helena, of Adiabene in northern Mesopotamia. Our two
major accounts, Josephus and the Midrash, are in basic agreement
with regard to the conversion of the Adiabenians to Judaism. The
Adiabenian converts are highly praised for their sincerity by both
Josephus and the rabbis. According to Josephus (and, by implication, the
Midrash), when the mighty king of Parthia decided to attack Izates he
was saved by the providence of God.

> 6.6 Josephus, *Jewish Antiquities* 20.34–5, 38–9, 40, 41–6.

The role of a merchant in reaching out to the would-be converts in
Adiabene suggests an economic factor in winning them. The disagreement between two Jews as to whether circumcision is a *sine qua non*
indicates that for some "semi-conversion" to the role of "sympathizer"
was sufficient and, at any rate, safer. It is significant that in the first
instance it is women who are won over to Judaism, perhaps because they
did not have to undergo the operation of circumcision.

Now during the time when Izates resided at Charax Spasini [in
Mesopotamia], a certain Jewish merchant named Ananias visited the
king's wives and taught them to worship God after the manner of the
Jewish tradition. It was through their agency that he was brought to the
notice of Izates, whom he similarly won over with the co-operation of
the women. . . .
    When Izates had learned that his mother was very much pleased
with the Jewish religion, he was zealous to convert to it himself; and
since he considered that he would not be genuinely a Jew unless he
was circumcised, he was ready to act accordingly. When his mother
learned of his intention, however, she tried to stop him by telling him
that it was a dangerous move. For, she said, he was a king; and if his
subjects should discover that he was devoted to rites that were strange
and foreign to themselves, it would produce much disaffection, and
they would not tolerate the rule of a Jew over them. . . . He, in turn,
reported her arguments to Ananias. . . . The king could, he [Ananias]
said, worship God even without being circumcised if indeed he had
fully decided to be a devoted adherent of Judaism, for it was this that
counted more than circumcision. He told him, furthermore, that God
Himself would pardon him if, constrained thus by necessity and by fear
of his subjects, he failed to perform this rite. And so, for the time, the
king was convinced by his arguments.

Afterwards, however, since he had not completely given up his desire, another Jew, named Eleazar, who came from Galilee and who had a reputation for being extremely strict when it came to the ancestral laws, urged him to carry out the rite. For when he came to him to pay him his respects and found him reading the law of Moses, he said: 'In your ignorance, O king, you are guilty of the greatest offence against the law and thereby against God. For you ought not merely to read the law but also, and even more, to do what is commanded in it. How long will you continue to be uncircumcised? If you have not yet read the law concerning this matter, read it now, so that you may know what an impiety it is that you commit.' Upon hearing these words, the king postponed the deed no longer. (LCL)

6.7 *Midrash Genesis Rabbah* 46.11 (*ca.* fifth century CE)

Though citing a rabbi as late as the fourth century and though not codified until approximately the fifth century, the Midrash presents an account of the conversion of the brothers Monobazus and Izates that is consonant with the version of Josephus.

'You shall circumcise the flesh of your foreskin' [Gen 17:11]; like a sore it [the foreskin] is attached to the body. And it happened that Monobazus and Izates, the sons of Ptolemy the King, were sitting and reading the Book of Genesis when they came to this verse, 'You shall circumcise.' One turned his face to the wall and began to cry, and the other [also] turned his face to the wall and began to cry. One went and circumcised himself, and the other circumcised himself. After [a few] days, they were sitting and reading the Book of Genesis, and when they reached the verse, 'You shall circumcise,' one said to his companion, 'Woe to you, my brother.' He said, 'Woe to you, my brother, and not to me.' They revealed the matter one to another. When their mother became aware, she went and said to their father, 'A sore has developed on their flesh, and the physician has prescribed that they be circumcised.' He [their father] said that they should be circumcised. How did the Holy One, blessed be He, repay him? Said Rabbi Pinchas [Palestinian, fourth century]: When he went forth to war, an ambush was set for him, but an angel descended and saved him. (L.H.S.)

Positive Reactions to Proselytism

6.8 Philo, *On the Virtues* 20.102–4, 33.179

The passage below is particularly revealing, because the biblical verse on which Philo bases his point that proselytes should be accorded every consideration and true love, inasmuch as they have abandoned their families and their countries, clearly refers not to proselytes but to strangers in the land. It is especially effective, because the proselyte is compared, by implication, with the person who in Plato's parable of the Cave emerges from darkness into light.

He [Moses] holds that the incomers [proselytes] too should be accorded every favor and consideration as their due, because abandoning their kinsfolk by blood, their country, their customs and the temples and images of their gods, and the tributes and honors paid to them, they have taken the journey to a better home, from idle fables to the clear vision of truth and the worship of the one and truly existing God. He [Moses] commands all members of the nation to love the incomers, not only as friends and kinsfolk but as themselves both in body and soul; in bodily matters, by acting as far as may be for their common interest; in mental by having the same griefs and joys, so that they may seem to be the separate parts of a single living being which is compacted and unified by their fellowship in it. I will not go on to speak of the food and drink and raiment and all the rights concerning daily life and necessary needs, which the law assigns to incomers as due from the native born, for all these follow the statutes, which speak of the friendliness shown by him who loves the incomer even as himself.... All these who did not at the first acknowledge their duty to reverence the Founder and Father of all, yet afterwards embraced the creed of one instead of a multiplicity of sovereigns, must be held to be our dearest friends and closest kinsmen. They have shown the godliness of heart which above all leads up to friendship and affinity, and we must rejoice with them, as if though blind at the first they had recovered their sight and had come from the deepest darkness to behold the most radiant light. (LCL)

6.9 Josephus, *Against Apion* 2.123, 210

Josephus notes that Jews welcome as proselytes those who are sincere in seeking conversion. He notes that some proselytes have remained faithful, while others have not.

From the Greeks we are severed more by our geographical position than by our institutions, with the result that we neither hate nor envy them. On the contrary, many of them have agreed to adopt our laws; of whom some have remained faithful, while others, lacking the necessary endurance, have again seceded....

To all who desire to come and live under the same laws with us, he [Moses in the Pentateuch] gives a gracious welcome, holding that it is not family ties alone which constitute relationship, but agreement in principles of conduct. On the other hand, it was not his pleasure that casual visitors should be admitted to the intimacies of our daily life. (LCL)

Rabbinic Sources

In passages that appear in collections finally edited between the fifth and thirteenth centuries CE, but which some scholars contend reflect views dating back to a much earlier period, various rabbis, many of whom lived in the third, fourth, and fifth centuries CE, display the following range of attitudes about proselytes.

6.10 Mekilta Nezikin 18 on Exodus 22:20 (*ca.* fifth century CE)

The following passage stresses how dear converts are, noting, from the example of Abraham, that it is never too late to convert.

Dear are converts, for in every place the Torah warns against [abusing] them. Dear are converts, for every term that is applied to Israel [in the Bible] is applied also to converts. Dear are converts, for Abraham was not circumcised until the age of ninety-nine. Had he been circumcised at twenty or thirty, others would have converted only at less than twenty or thirty. Therefore the Holy One delayed in his case till he reached ninety-nine, in order not to shut the door in the face of converts who might come, to increase the reward of those who do His will. (B.J.B.)

6.11 Tanhuma B and *Nidpas, Lekh Lekha* 6 (*ca.* 800 CE)

The following passage insists that proselytes are actually dearer than those who stood at Sinai, because they accepted Judaism without witnessing the miracles there.

Said Resh Laqish [Palestinian, third century]: The proselyte who converts is dearer than Israel were when they stood before Mount Sinai. Why? Because, had they not seen the thunders and the lightning and the mountains quaking and the sound of the horns, they would not have accepted the Torah. But this one, who saw none of these things, came, surrendered himself to the Holy One, and accepted upon himself the Kingdom of Heaven. Could any be dearer than he? (B.J.B.)

6.12 Tanhuma Nidpas, Vayakhel 8 (*ca.* 800 CE)

According to the following passage, so highly regarded are proselytes that if they devote themselves to the study of Torah they are equal to the high priest himself.

Even proselytes, when they occupy themselves with the Torah, are accounted as equal to the High Priest, for it is said [Lev 18:5], 'Ye shall therefore keep My statutes and Mine ordinances, which, if a man do, he shall live by them' – Priest, Levite, or Israelite are not mentioned here, but man. Therefore [Num 15:16] 'one law and one ordinance shall be both for you and for the stranger that sojourneth with you.' (B.J.B.)

6.13 Babylonian Talmud, *Shabbath* 145b–6a (codified *ca.* 500 CE)

According to the following passage, although proselytes were actually not present at Sinai, their guiding stars were present.

Why are idolaters lustful? Because they did not stand at Mount Sinai. For when the serpent came upon Eve he injected a lust into her: [as for] the Israelites who stood at Mount Sinai, their lustfulness departed: the idolaters, who did not stand at Mount Sinai, their lustfulness did not depart. Rabbi Aha son of Raba [Babylonian, fourth and fifth centuries

CE] asked Rabbi Ashi [Babylonian, fourth and fifth centuries CE]: What about proselytes? – Though they were not present, their guiding stars [*mazzal*] were present, as it is written, ['Neither with you only do I make this covenant and this oath], but with him that standeth here with us this day before the Lord our God, and also with him that is not here with us this day.' [Deut 29:14–15]. (Soncino)

6.14 *Midrash Genesis Rabbah* 65.20 (*ca.* fifth century CE)

The following passage presents a scenario in which all the world's gentiles ask a non-Jewish philosopher whether it is possible to become converts to Judaism. To be sure, the answer is that they may not so long as Jewish children are engaged in their studies.

All the gentiles of the world met at his [Oenomaus of Gadara's, second century CE][6] house [and asked him, saying], 'Tell us, can we become one with this nation [Israel]?' He said to them: 'Go and tarry by their synagogues and schools, and as long as you hear the voices of the children piping there, you cannot join them, for their Father pledged them, saying: The voice is the voice of Jacob; so long as the voice of Jacob is heard in the synagogues, the hands are not the hands of Esau, but if the voice of Jacob is not heard there, the hands are those of Esau, and you may join them.' (Soncino)

6.15 *Midrash Exodus Rabbah* 30.12 (*ca.* tenth century CE)

In the following scenario Aquila tells his relative the Emperor Hadrian, who tries to deter him, that he wishes to convert to Judaism. Asked why he wishes to do so, he remarks that even Jewish children know the details of God's creation of the world.

Aquila [second century CE][7] said to the Emperor Hadrian: 'I wish to become a convert to Judaism.'

Hadrian: 'Is it this people which attracts you? How much have I humiliated it! How cruelly have I chastised it! You want to associate yourself with the lowest of nations? What draws you to them, and makes you want to become a convert?'

Aquila: 'Even their children know God created the world – what was created on the first and on the second day, and how much time has elapsed, and on what the world is founded. And their Torah is true.'

Hadrian: 'Well then, learn their Torah. But do not become circumcised.'

Aquila: 'Even the wisest and oldest in your empire cannot learn their Torah if he is not circumcised, for it is written [Ps 147:19], "He showeth his word unto Jacob, his statutes and his judgments unto Israel." He has not done so for any pagan.' (I.H.)

6. Oenomaus of Gadara (a town east of the Jordan River) was a Cynic philosopher who in this passage is cited (together with Balaam) by the rabbis as the greatest heathen philosopher of all time.

7. Aquila from Pontus in Asia Minor is said to have been a relative of Hadrian. A proselyte to Judaism, he translated the canonical Scriptures from Hebrew into literal Greek in the middle of the second century CE.

Negative Reactions to Conversion

6.16 Horace (65–8 BCE), *Satires* 1.4.139–43

From this passage in Horace, though since it comes from his *Satires* we may assume that it is exaggerated, we can see that Jewish zeal in seeking proselytes was apparently proverbial.

This is one of those lesser frailties I spoke of, and if you should make no allowance for it, then would a big band of poets come to my aid – for we are the big majority – and we, like the Jews, will compel you to make one of our throng. (LCL)

6.17 Seneca the Younger (*ca.* 4 BCE–65 CE), *Concerning Superstition*, cited by Augustine (354–430 CE), *City of God* 6.11

Seneca very bitterly remarks that the Jews, who politically are subject to the Romans, have actually triumphed over them through their success in winning converts.

When speaking of the Jews he [Seneca] says: 'Meanwhile the customs of this accursed race have gained such influence that they are now received throughout all the world. The vanquished have given laws to their victors.' He shows his surprise as he says this, not knowing what was being wrought by the providence of God. (LCL)

6.18 New Testament, Matt 23:15 [Jesus speaking]

The passage below, ascribed to Jesus, alludes to the zeal with which the Pharisees sought to win converts.

Woe to you, scribes and Pharisees, hypocrites! for you traverse sea and land to make a single proselyte, and when he becomes a proselyte, you make him twice as much a child of hell as yourselves. (RSV)

6.19 Tacitus (*ca.* 56–120 CE), *Histories* 5.5.1–2

Tacitus here refers to the success of the Jews in winning proselytes and bitterly laments that thus they gain more money for the Temple, since each Jew contributes annually to the Temple in Jerusalem. He likewise alludes to the degree to which proselytes cut themselves off from their previous family ties.

The other customs of the Jews are base and abominable, and owe their persistence to their depravity; for the worst rascals among other peoples, renouncing their ancestral religions, always kept sending tribute and contributing to Jerusalem, thereby increasing the wealth of the Jews.... Those who are converted to their ways follow the same practice [of cutting themselves off from other peoples], and the earliest lesson they receive is to despise the gods, to disown their country, and to regard their parents, children, and brothers as of little account. (LCL)

6.20 Scriptores Historiae Augustae (end of the fourth century CE), *Septimius Severus* 17.1

The passage below indicates that the Emperor Septimius Severus, who ruled from 193 to 211 CE, apparently disturbed by the success of the Jews in winning proselytes, forbade conversion to Judaism under severe penalties. This would seem to indicate that even after the terrible defeat of Bar Kochba in 135 and the ban on proselytism imposed thereafter, proselytism continued.

While on his way thither [to Alexandria] he [Emperor Septimius Severus] conferred numerous rights upon the communities of Palestine. He forbade conversion to Judaism under heavy penalties and enacted a similar law in regard to the Christians. (LCL)

6.21 Scriptores Historiae Augustae (end of the fourth century CE), *Antoninus Caracalla* 1.6

The revulsion against proselytism is indicated by this anecdote that one who had been converted was severely whipped. The Emperor Caracalla, however, who was favorably disposed toward the Jews, clearly opposed such a reaction. Indeed, some have identified him with the "Antoninus" who appears in several rabbinic texts as a close friend of Rabbi Judah the Prince.

Once, when a child of seven, hearing that a certain playmate of his had been severely scourged for adopting the religion of the Jews, he [the Emperor Caracalla, who ruled from 211 to 217 CE] long refused to look at either his own father or the boy's father, because he regarded them as responsible for the scourging. (LCL)

6.22 Babylonian Talmud, *Baba Metzia* 59 b (edited *ca.* 500 CE)

According to the famous Rabbi Eliezer, the reason why the Pentateuch warns against mistreating proselytes is that they have a strong inclination to do evil.

It has been taught: Rabbi Eliezer the Great [ben Hyrcanus, Palestinian, end of first and beginning of second century CE] said: Why did the Torah warn against [the wronging of] a proselyte in thirty-six, or, as others say, in forty-six places? Because he has a strong inclination to evil. (Soncino)

6.23 Babylonian Talmud, *Niddah* 13 b (edited *ca.* 500 CE)

Below is the most negative statement about proselytes that is found in the rabbinic literature, comparing them to a sore and asserting that they delay the coming of the Messiah. Rabbi Helbo's statement is also found in several other places in the Talmudic corpus (*Qiddushin* 70b and *Yevamoth* 47b, 109b).

Our Rabbis taught: 'Proselytes and those that play with children delay the advent of the Messiah.' The statement about proselytes may be understood on the lines of the view of Rabbi Ḥelbo [Babylonian and Palestinian, third and early fourth century CE]; for Rabbi Ḥelbo said, 'Proselytes are as hard for Israel to endure as a sore.' What, however, could be meant by 'those that play with children?' . . . The meaning . . . is: Those that marry minors who are not capable of bearing children. (Soncino)

Legal Reactions against Proselytism

The dismantling of bases of Jewish militancy, the staggering losses of the Jews in the revolts of 66–73/4, 115–17, and 132–5, their expulsion from Jerusalem, and a ban on (though certainly not an end to) proselytism led to a turning inward for survival. This entailed pacifism, pietism, study of the written and the oral Torah, life with the synagogue and the teaching of the rabbis as its center, and deferment of Messianic hopes. Resignation and withdrawal from the secular world preserved the identity of the Jews in a transcendent spiritual unity in a hostile world.

BIBLIOGRAPHY

Edith Mary Smallwood, "The Legislation of Hadrian and Antoninus Pius against Circumcision," *Latomus* 18 (1959), 334–47; 20 (1961), 93–6.

6.24 Modestinus (*ca.* 250 CE), *The Rules*, Book 6, cited in Justinian, *Digest* (sixth century CE) 48.8.11

The Emperor Antoninus Pius repealed Hadrian's prohibition of circumcision but only for sons of born Jews and not for proselytes.

Jews are permitted to circumcise only their sons on the authority of a rescript of the Divine [Emperor Antoninus] Pius [ruled 138–61 CE]: if anyone shall commit it on one who is not of the same religion, he shall suffer the punishment of a castrator. (A.L.)

6.25 Julius Paulus (first half of the third century CE), *Opinions* 5.22.3–4

Julius Paulus, distinguished Roman jurist of the early third century, was the author of over 300 books. The *Opinions* was probably an anthology of his writings. He indicates severe penalties for circumcision.

Roman citizens who suffer that they themselves or their slaves be circumcised in accordance with the Jewish custom are exiled perpetually to an island and their property confiscated; the doctors suffer capital punishment. If Jews shall circumcise purchased slaves of another nation, they shall be banished or suffer capital punishment. (A.L.)

6.26 *Theodosian Code* 16.8.1 (Constantine the Great, 329 CE)

Constantine indicates that proselytes are to be punished but does not specify the precise punishment.

If one of the people shall approach their [the Jews'] nefarious sect and join himself to their conventicles [synagogues], he shall suffer with them the deserved punishments.[8] (A.L.)

6.27 *Theodosian Code* 16.9.1 (Constantine the Great, 335 CE)

Constantine here specifies that if a Jew circumcises a non-Jewish slave that slave has the privilege of going free.

If one of the Jews shall buy and circumcise a Christian slave or a slave of any other sect, he shall on no account retain the circumcised in slavery, but he who suffered this shall acquire the privileges of liberty. (A.L.)

6.28 *Theodosian Code* 16.9.2 (Constantine II, 339 CE)

Below we see the penalty for circumcising a slave extended to include not merely freedom for the slave but also death for the Jewish owner.

If he [a Jew] shall circumcise the purchased slave, not only shall he suffer the loss of the slave, but he shall be punished, indeed, by capital punishment. (A.L.)

6.29 *Theodosian Code* 16.8.7 (Constantius II, 353 CE)

According to the following provision, if a Christian becomes a Jew his property is to be confiscated by the state.

If someone shall become Jew from Christian and shall be joined to sacrilegious assemblies [i.e., accepted by the Jewish community] after the venerable law had been established, we decreed that his property shall be vindicated to the fisc's dominion [i.e., confiscated by the government's treasury] once the accusation were proven. (A.L.)

6.30 *Theodosian Code* 16.7.3 (Gratian [with Valentinian II, Theodosius], 383 CE)

Both the Christian who becomes a Jew and the one who instigates this conversion are to be punished, but the penalty, though it is to be harsh, is left vague.

Those who despised the dignity of the Christian religion and name and polluted themselves with the Jewish contagions shall be punished for their disgraceful acts.... The instigators of this persuasion, who misled slipping minds to their peculiar fellowship, shall be visited by the same punishment as those guilty of such a deviation; moreover, we order that the nefarious perpetrators of this crime shall suffer generally harsher penalties than usual. (A.L.)

6.31 *Theodosian Code* 3.7.2 (Valentinian II, Theodosius [with Arcadius], 388 CE)

This law, forbidding marriage between Christians and Jews, seems to be a reaction to the apparently frequent conversion of the non-Jewish partner to Judaism. Hence, the severity of the penalty.

8. Apparently, the choice of punishment was left to the discretion of the judge.

No Jew shall take a Christian woman in marriage, neither shall a Christian marry a Jewess. Indeed, if anyone shall commit something of the kind, his crime shall be considered as an adultery[9] with the right to accuse allowed the general public. (A.L.)

9. The penalty, under the old Roman law, was exile, and confiscation of one-half of her dowry and a third of his property. Under the law passed by Constantius and Constans in 339, adulterers were to be drowned in a sack or put in a fire, like murderers.

Inscription from Aphrodisias, including God-fearers.

7

꧁꧂

"Sympathizers" ("God-Fearers")

BIBLIOGRAPHY

Kirsopp Lake, "Proselytes and God-fearers," in Frederick Foakes-Jackson and Kirsopp Lake, *The Beginnings of Christianity*, vol. 1: *The Acts of the Apostles* (1933), 74–96.

Louis H. Feldman, "Jewish 'Sympathizers' in Classical Literature and Inscriptions," *TAPA* 81 (1950), 200–8.

Ralph Marcus, "The Sebomenoi in Josephus," *JSoS* 14 (1952), 247–50.

Alf Thomas Kraabel, "The Disappearance of the God-Fearers," *Numen* 28 (1981), 113–26.

Thomas M. Finn, "The God-Fearers Reconsidered," *CBQ* 47 (1985), 75–84.

Fergus Millar, "Gentiles and Judaism: 'God-Fearers' and Proselytes," in Schürer, vol. 3.1 (1986), 150–76.

Louis H. Feldman, "The Omnipresence of the God-Fearers," *BAR* 12.5 (Sept–Oct 1986), 58–69.

Robert S. MacLennan and Alf Thomas Kraabel, "The God-Fearers – A Literary and Theological Invention," *BAR* 12.5 (Sept–Oct 1986), 46–53, 64.

Robert F. Tannenbaum, "Jews and God-Fearers in the Holy City of Aphrodite," *BAR* 12.5 (1986), 54–7.

Joyce M. Reynolds and Robert Tannenbaum, *Jews and God-Fearers at Aphrodisias: Greek Inscriptions with Commentary* (1987).

J. Andrew Overman, "The God-Fearers: Some Neglected Features," *JSNT* 32 (1988), 17–26.

Margaret H. Williams, "*Theosebes gar en* – The Jewish Tendencies of Poppaea Sabina," *JTS* 39 (1988), 97–111.

Louis H. Feldman, "Proselytes and 'Sympathizers' in the Light of the New Inscriptions from Aphrodisias," *REJ* 148 (1989), 265–305.

Pieter van der Horst, "Jews and Christians in Aphrodisias in the Light of their Relations in Other Cities of Asia Minor," *NTT* 43 (1989), 106–21.

Jerome Murphy-O'Connor, "Lots of God-Fearers? Theosebeis in the Aphrodisias Inscription," *RB* 99 (1992), 418–24.

Margaret H. Williams, "The Jews and Godfearers Inscription from Aphrodisias – a Case of Patriarchal Interference in Early 3rd Century Caria?" *Historia* 41 (1992), 297–310.

Feldman (1993), 342–82.

A number of passages in the New Testament Book of Acts refer to "fearers of God" or "worshippers of God." It is usually thought that these refer to those who, without converting to Judaism, adopted certain Jewish practices, notably the Sabbath. Some scholars, however, notably Kraabel, citing the fact that among the over 100 synagogue inscriptions that have been found, none mention the terms "fearers of God" or "worshippers of God" and that none suggest the presence of a Gentile "penumbra" around the synagogue communities or a reaching out by Jews toward their Gentile neighbors with some kind of religious message, have contended that the "God-fearers" are a figment of scholarly imagination, based on a literary and theological expansion of these passages in Acts. Moreover, it is not always clear from these selections whether people are becoming proselytes or "God-fearers" ("sympathizers").

Evidence from Pagan Writers

7.1 Petronius (died *ca.* 65 CE), fragment no. 37

Petronius draws a distinction between those who abstain from eating pork and adopt monotheism, thus presumably becoming "sympathizers," and those who actually undergo circumcision and become full-fledged Jews.

The Jew may worship his pig-god and clamor in the ears of high heaven, but unless he also cuts back his foreskin with the knife, he shall go forth from the people and emigrate to Greek cities, and shall not tremble at the fasts of Sabbath imposed by the law. (LCL)

7.2 Epictetus (*ca.* 60–140 CE), cited by Arrian (*ca.* 95–175 CE), *Discourses* 2.9.19–21

Epictetus here distinguishes between full-fledged proselytes who undergo baptism and those who merely act like Jews, i.e., "sympathizers."

For how much better is it to set forth these principles than those of other schools of thought? Sit down now and give a philosophical discourse upon the principles of Epicurus, and perhaps you will discourse more effectively than Epicurus himself. Why, then, do you call yourself a Stoic, why do you deceive the multitude, why do you act the part of a Jew, when you are a Greek? Do you not see in what sense men are severally called Jew, Syrian, or Egyptian? For example, whenever we see a man halting between two faiths, we are in the habit of saying, 'He is not a Jew, he is only acting the part.' But when he adopts the attitude of mind of the man who has been baptized and has made his choice, then he is both a Jew in fact and is also called one. So we also are counterfeit 'Baptists,' ostensibly Jews, but in reality something else, not in sympathy with our own reason, far from applying the principles that we profess, yet priding ourselves upon them as being men who know them.[1] (LCL)

---

1. Some have thought that the reference to baptism is an indication that Epictetus was referring to Christian baptism, but there is every reason to believe that in Epictetus' day immersion in a ritual pool was a prerequisite for admission to Judaism and that by his time he should have known the difference between Christians and Jews.

7.3 Juvenal (*ca.* 60–*ca.* 130 CE), *Satires* 14.96–106

In this famous passage Juvenal notes a progression from the "sympathizer" who observes the Sabbath to one who accepts monotheism and
abstains from pork to one who becomes a full-fledged Jew by undergoing
circumcision.

Some who have had a father who reveres the Sabbath worship nothing
but the clouds and the divinity of the heavens and see no difference
between eating swine's flesh, from which their father abstained, and
that of man; and in time they take to circumcision. Having been wont
to flout the laws of Rome, they learn and practice and revere the
Jewish law, and all that Moses handed down in his secret tome,
forbidding to point out the way to any not worshipping the same
rites, and conducting none but the circumcised to the desired
fountain. For all which the father was to blame, who gave up every
seventh day to idleness, keeping it apart from all the concerns of life.
(LCL)

Evidence from Jewish Writers

7.4 Philo, *Questions on Exodus* 2.2 (on Exodus 22:20 [21])

Philo speaks of those who have not actually but only figuratively undergone circumcision.

Why does [Scripture] in admonishing, 'Thou shalt not oppress a
sojourner,' add, 'For ye were sojourners in the land of the
Egyptians'?
[Scripture] first makes it clearly apparent and demonstrable that
in reality the sojourner is one who circumcises not his uncircumcision
but his desires and sensual pleasures and the other passions of the
soul. For in Egypt the Hebrew nation was not circumcised but being
mistreated with all [kinds of] mistreatment by the inhabitants in
their hatred of strangers, it lived with them in self-restraint and
endurance, not by necessity but rather of its own free choice, because
it took refuge in God the Savior, Who sent His beneficent power
and delivered from their difficult and hopeless situation those who
made supplication [to Him]. Therefore [Scripture] adds, 'Ye yourselves know the soul of the sojourner.' But what is the mind of the
sojourner if not alienation from belief in many gods and familiarity
with honoring the one God and Father of all?' (LCL)

7.5 Josephus, *Jewish Antiquities* 14.110

Josephus here distinguishes between those who are Jews and those who,
without actually becoming Jews, worshipped the God of the Jews.

But no one need wonder that there was so much wealth in our Temple,
for all the Jews throughout the habitable world, and those who
worshipped God, even those from Asia and Europe, had been contributing to it for a very long time. (LCL)

7.6 Josephus, *Jewish Antiquities* 20.195 (*ca.* 60 CE)

Here we have mention of Nero's wife Poppaea Sabina as a "worshipper of God," that is, a "God-fearer" or "sympathizer."

Nero, after a full hearing,[2] not only condoned what they had done, but also consented to leave the building as it was. In this he showed favor to his wife Poppaea, who was a worshipper of God and who pleaded on behalf of the Jews. (LCL)

7.7 Josephus, *Against Apion* 2.282

Josephus here mentions several Jewish practices, namely the Sabbath, fast days, lighting of lamps to usher in the Sabbath, and several (though not all) dietary laws that have spread among non-Jews, with the implication that they have not actually become Jews.

The masses have long since shown a keen desire to adopt our religious observances; and there is not one city, Greek or barbarian, nor a single nation, to which our custom of abstaining from work on the seventh day has not spread, and where the fasts and the lighting of lamps and many of our prohibitions in the matter of food are not observed. (LCL)

7.8 Jerusalem Talmud, *Megillah* 3.2.74d (codified *ca.* 400 CE)

In this passage the question is raised as to whether the Emperor Antoninus actually converted to Judaism. The fact that he wore cutaway sandals on the Day of Atonement is no proof, since "sympathizers" also do. Only when he circumcised himself did he become a Jew.

Antoninus[3] made a lampstand for the synagogue. Rabbi [Judah the Prince] [Palestine, end of the second century CE] heard of it and said: Blessed be God, who put into his heart to make a lampstand for the synagogue. Rabbi Samuel bar Rabbi Isaac [Palestinian, fourth century CE] inquired: Why did Rabbi say: Blessed be God? Why not: Blessed be our God? If he said: Blessed be God, this indicates that Antoninus was not converted. If he said: Blessed be our God, it indicates that Antoninus was converted. There are some things that indicate that he was converted and vice versa. They saw him going out on the Day of Atonement wearing a cutaway sandal [indicating that he was converted].[4] What can you deduce from that? Even fearers of heaven may go out wearing such a sandal. Antoninus asked Rabbi: Will you let

2. When King Agrippa II built a chamber of unusual size in the vicinity of the Temple in order to be able to gaze at everything that went on in the Temple, the eminent men of Jerusalem, deeming it contrary to tradition that the proceedings in the Temple should be spied on, erected a high wall to cut off the king's view. When the king and the procurator Festus expressed their indignation at this, the Jews successfully entreated Festus for permission to send an embassy to the Emperor Nero.

3. Attempts of scholars to identify this Antoninus, the royal friend of Rabbi Judah the Prince, have been inconclusive. Chronologically, the most likely candidate is the Roman Emperor Commodus.

4. Since on the Day of Atonement one is not permitted to wear leather shoes.

me eat of leviathan in the next world? He answered: Yes. But he objected: You will not let me eat of the paschal lamb; how then will you let me eat of leviathan? He replied: What can we do for thee, since it is written (Exod 12:48) 'no one that is uncircumcised may eat thereof.' When he heard this, he went and circumcised himself. ... This indicates that Antoninus was converted; the words of our Rabbis indicate the same, for said Rabbi Hezekiah [Palestinian, fourth century CE] [and] Rabbi Abbahu [Palestinian, fourth century CE] in the name of Rabbi Eleazar [ben Pedath, Palestinian, third century CE]: If righteous proselytes come into the future [life], Antoninus will come at the head of them. (B.J.B.)

7.9 Midrash Genesis Rabbah 28.6 (*ca.* fifth century CE)

According to the passage below, God has so much regard for the "sympathizers" that he declined to annihilate the nation of the Cherethites for the sake of merely a single "sympathizer."

Rabbi Huna [Babylonian, third century CE] said: What was perpetrated by the coastal cities was not perpetrated even by the generation of the Flood, for it is written, 'Woe unto the inhabitants of the sea-coast, the nation of the Cherethites'[5] (Zeph 2:5), which means that they deserved to be annihilated. Yet for whose sake do they stand? For the sake of one nation[6] and one God-fearing person whom the Holy One, blessed be He, receives from their hands. (Soncino)

7.10 Midrash Leviticus Rabbah 3.2 (*ca.* fifth century CE)

The following passage clearly distingishes between "God-fearers" ("sympathizers") and proselytes.

'And when one bringeth a meal-offering unto the Lord' (Lev 2:1). [Applicable to this is the passage], 'Ye that fear the Lord, praise Him; All ye the seed of Jacob, glorify Him; And stand in awe of Him, ye seed of Israel, for He hath not despised nor abhorred the lowliness of the poor; neither hath He hid face from him. But when he cried unto Him He heard' (Ps 22:24f.). 'Ye that fear the Lord,' said Rabbi Joshua ben Levi [Palestinian, third century CE], means those that fear heaven. Rabbi Samuel bar Naḥman [Palestinian, third century CE] said: It means the righteous proselytes. (Soncino)

7.11 Pesiqta Rabbati 43 (*ca.* ninth century CE)

The following passage distinguishes between those who accept conversion and those who fear God, i.e., "sympathizers."

At sight of Sarah's milk[7] the nations of the earth brought their children to Sarah to give them suck, thus confirming the truth of the statement

---

5. A Philistine people.

6. The variant reading here, "proselyte," indicates that there is a contrast between the convert and the "God-fearer" (or "sympathizer").

7. The reference is to the miraculous birth of Isaac in Sarah's old age.

that 'Sarah would give children suck.' Now some of them in all sincerity brought their children for Sarah to give them suck, some brought their children only to check up on her. Neither the former nor the latter suffered any loss. According to Rabbi Levi [Babylonian, third century CE], those who were brought in sincerity became proselytes. In regard to these Scripture says, 'Sarah would give children suck.' How is the expression 'give children suck' to be interpreted? That these children of the nations of the earth became children of Israel. And according to our Masters, those children who were brought to check up on Sarah achieved distinction in the world through promotion to great office. Accordingly, all Gentiles throughout the world who accept conversion and all Gentiles throughout the world who fear God[8] spring from the children who drank of the milk of Sarah. Hence Sarah is alluded to as 'a joyful mother of children.' (Soncino)

Evidence from Inscriptions

7.12 Joyce Reynolds and Robert Tannenbaum, Jews and God-Fearers at Aphrodisias: Greek Inscriptions with Commentary (1987), 5–7.

The chance discovery in 1976 of two inscriptions (the longest that have thus far been found in Greek pertaining to Jews) at Aphrodisias in Asia Minor, dating apparently from the third century CE, has shed dramatic light on the Jewish movement to win proselytes and especially "God-fearers" ("sympathizers"). There is important economic information, including the occupations of a number of the donors. The fact that nine of the "God-fearers" are city councillors indicates that the Jews attracted wealthy people, inasmuch as this office implied heavy financial obligations. The fact that one of the inscriptions lists a number of donors who are Jews, followed by the names of two proselytes and two "God-fearers," would seem to be conclusive evidence that proselytes are to be distinguished from "God-fearers."

Face a: God our help. Building [?] for the soup kitchen[?].[9] Below [are] listed the [members] of the decany[10] of the disciples of the law, also known as those who fervently praise God, [who] erected, for the relief of suffering for the community, at their personal expense, [this] memorial [building]:

Jael,[11] president, with son Joshua, magistrate; [in margin: Samuel, elder, from Perge];[12] Theodotos, employee of the [emperor's] court,

8. Note that the text distinguishes between proselytes and "God-fearers."
9. Apparently the reference is to a dish used for the daily collection of cooked food for the poor. The word *patella*, here translated "soup kitchen," may stand for the distribution station for charity food.
10. The decany is apparently ten men who ensure that a quorum will always be on hand for prayer and other ritual purposes. It may also refer to a benevolent society.
11. This may be a woman's name, in which case it is the only woman's name in the list. We know, from other inscriptions, that women were given titles of high synagogue office, though it is more likely that the reference is to a man.
12. A city in Pamphylia in Asia Minor.

with son Ilarianos; Samuel leader of the decany [?], a proselyte; Ioses [i.e., Joseph] son of Iesseos; Benjamin psalm-singer [?]; Judas good-tempered; Ioses [i.e., Joseph] a proselyte; Sabbatios son of Amachios; Emmonios 'God-fearer'; Antoninos 'God-fearer'; Samuel son of Politianos; Joseph a proselyte son of Eusebios; and Judas son of Theodoros; and Antipeos son of Hermes; and Sabathios fragrant;[13] and Samuel old priest. [L.H.F.]

Face b: ... son of Serapion; Joseph son of Zenon; Zenon Jacob; Manasseh Job [?]; Judas son of Eusebios; Eortasios son of Kallikarpos; Biotikos; Judas son of Amphianos; Eugenios goldsmith; Praoilios; Judas son of Praoilios; Rufus; Oxucholios an old man; Amantios son of Charinos; Murtilos Jacob shepherd [?]; Seberos; Euodos; Jason son of Euodos; Eusabbathios greengrocer [?]; Anusios Eusabbathios an immigrant; Milon Oxucholios the younger; Diogenes; Eusabbathios son of Diogenes; Judas son of Paulos; Theophilos; Jacob and Apellion; Zacharias retailer [?]; Leontios son of Leontios; Gemellos; Judas son of Acholios; Damonikos; Eutarkios son of Judas; Joseph son of Philer [?]; Eusabbathios son of Eugenios; Kurillos; Eutuchios bronze-smith [?]; Joseph confectioner [?]; Rouben confectioner [?]; Judas son of Ortasios; Eutuchios poulterer [?]; Judas and Zosi [?]; Zenon rag-dealer [?]; Ammianos dealer in horse-fodder[?];[14] Ailianos son of Ailianos; Ailianos and Samuel Philanthos; Gorgionos son of Oxucholios; Eortasios son of Achilleus; Eusabbathios son of Oxucholios; Paregorios; Eortasios son of Zotikos; Simon Zen [?] ... ; and as many as are God-fearers: Zenon councillor; Tertullos councillor; Diogenes councillor; Onesimos councillor; Zenon son of Longianos [?] councillor; Antipeos councillor; Antiochos councillor; Romanos councillor; Aponerios councillor; Eupithios purple-dyer; Strategios; Xanthos; Xanthos son of Xanthos; Aponerios son of Aponerios; Hupsikles ink-maker [?]; Poluchronios son of Xanthos; Athenion son of Ailianos [?]; Kallimorphos son of Kallimorphos [?]; Iounbalos; Tuchikos son of Tuchikos; Glegorios son of Tuchikos; Poluchronios missile-maker [?]; Chrusippos; Gorgonios bronze-smith [?]; Tatianos son of Oxucholios [?]; Apellas son of Hegemoneus [?]; Balerianos maker of wooden tablets [?]; Eusabbathios son of Heduchrous [?]; Manikios [?] son of Attalos [?]; Ortasios stone-cutter [?]; Brabeus; Klaudianos son of Kallimorphos [?]; Alexandros boxer [?]; Appianos marble-worker [?]; Adolios maker of mincemeat; Zotikos armlet-maker [?]; Zotikos Grullos [?]; Eupithios son of Eupithios; Patrikios bronze-smith; Elpidianos athlete [?]; Heduchrous; Eutropios son of Heduchrous [?]; Kallinikos; Balerianos treasurer [?]; Euretos son of Athenagoras; Paranomos image-painter [?]; Eutuchianos fuller; Prokopios money-changer [?]; Pounikios fuller; Stratonikos fuller; Athenagoras carpenter; Meliton son of Amazonios. ... [L.H.F.]

---

13. This may be a second name or a descriptive adjective.
14. Or perhaps stitcher, braider, plaiter.

The Sambathions

BIBLIOGRAPHY

Herbert Youtie, "Sambathis," *HTR* 37 (1944), 209–18.
Victor Tcherikover, "The Sambathions," *SH* 1 (1954), 79–98.
Victor Tcherikover, "The Sambathions," *CPJ*, vol. 3 (1964), 43–87.

In Egypt we have found twenty-nine papyri containing the name Sambathion (Sabbathaios, Sambathaios, etc.) (apparently given to male and female children born on the Sabbath) ranging in date from the early first century to the fifth century CE. They are apparently adherents of a sect of Sabbath-observers because their kinsfolk seem to be non-Jews; moreover, in one of the papyri a woman named Sambathion is recorded as paying a tax imposed on swine-owners, so that she is most likely not a Jew. Finally, the papyri are found in villages that are non-Jewish so far as we know. It is striking that no other Hebrew name was ever borrowed by non-Jews; and the most likely explanation for the choice of the name, consequently, is that the parents were Sabbath-observers. In fact, there is even one inscription referring to a Sabbatarian association, thus indicating that "sympathizers" were not merely individuals but were organized as a group. These people cannot be Jews because so far as we know Jews never refer to their God as "the God of the Sabbath"; and hence they are most likely "sympathizers." Moreover, there was a Hebrew Sibyl, a semi-mythological being, called Sambethe who appears to have been worshipped as a deity, presumably by people who were interested, to some degree at least, in Judaism.

7.13 *CPJ*, no. 481 (early first century CE)

... son of Ptollis and grandson of Sambathion (?).
Mysthas son of Dios. Sambathion his brother. (*CPJ*)

7.14 *CPJ*, no. 482 (27/8 CE)

To Chaireas the *strategos*, from Sambathaios son of Sambathaios. I declare, for the present thirteenth year of Tiberius Caesar Augustus, the thirty sheep, two goats in my possession, total thirty sheep ..., and the lambs (and) kids which follow them; they will be grazed around Pela in the Western toparchy [district] and throughout the nome by their shepherd, my brother ..., who is registered for the census around Satyros' Settlement in the Eastern toparchy; and I shall pay the proper dues for them. [second hand] Farewell. (*CPJ*)

7.15 *CPJ*, no. 488 (126 CE)

Year 10 of Traianus Hadrianus Caesar the lord, month Kaisareios 25. At Karanis. Tapetheus, daughter of Pasoknopaios and grand-daughter of Didymion, acknowledges to Sambathion daughter of Heras, under the guardianship of her husband Pekmeis son of Phaermis, a loan with interest of 382 silver drachmas; and in lieu of interest on this money she concedes that Sambathion should gather the fruits of a ¼ aroura of olive-grove around Psenarpsenesis until she [Tapetheus] returns the above-mentioned capital sum. (*CPJ*)

7.16 *CPJ*, no 489 (128/9 CE)

Sarapion, son of ... silos and grandson of Sarapion, mother Sambathion. Bank-payment. Phaophi ...: 8 drachmas, ... tax for prison-guards, for river patrol-boat tax ... for tower-guards, for guard-post ... pig-tax. (*CPJ*)

Reaction against "Sympathizers"

7.17 Dio Cassius (*ca.* 160–230 CE), *Roman History* 67.14.1–2 (95 CE).

Dio Cassius here mentions that many who had drifted into Jewish ways were condemned as atheists. The word *drifted* implies that they had not actually converted but merely had tendencies toward Judaism.

And the same year Domitian slew, along with many others, Flavius Clemens the consul, although he was a cousin and had to wife Flavia Domitilla, who was also a relative of the emperor. The charge brought against them both was that of atheism, a charge on which many others who drifted into Jewish ways were condemned. Some of these were put to death, and the rest were at least deprived of their property. (LCL)

7.18 *Theodosian Code* 16.5.43 (Honorius [with Arcadius, Theodosius I], 407 CE)

This law, directed against heretics, mentions a sect of "Heaven-Fearers," presumably identical with "God-fearers," referred to here as a new sect, and declares that the ownership of their buildings is to be transferred to the Church.

All that was decreed by us with the authority of general laws against the Donatists, who are also called Montenses, the Manichaeans, the Priscillianists[15] and the Gentiles, not only shall remain in force, but also brought into the fullest execution and effectuation, so that the edifices as well, which belong to them and also to the Heaven-Fearers, who have meetings of a new doctrine unknown to me, shall be vindicated to the churches. (A.L.)

---

15. These are various Christian heresies.

Josephus with monastic scribe, Latin manuscript of Jewish War,
ca. 1130.

8

❧

The Jews in Palestine

Establishment of an Independent Jewish State under the Hasmoneans (164–63 BCE)

BIBLIOGRAPHY

Tcherikover (1959), 117–265.

Solomon Zeitlin, *The Rise and Fall of the Judaean State: A Political, Social and Religious History of the Second Commonwealth*, 3 vols (1962–78).

Hengel, vol. 1 (1974), 255–314.

Fergus Millar, "The Background of the Maccabean Revolution: Reflections on Martin Hengel's 'Judaism and Hellenism,'" *JJS* 29 (1978), 1–21.

Elias Bickerman, *The God of the Maccabees: Studies in the Meaning and Origin of the Maccabean Revolt* (1979).

Joshua Efron, "The Hasmonean Revolt in Modern Historiography," in his *Studies on the Hasmonean Period* (1987), 1–32.

Bezalel Bar Kochva, *Judas Maccabaeus* (1989).

Joseph Sievers, *The Hasmoneans and Their Supporters* (1990).

Thomas Fischer, "Hasmoneans and Seleucids: Aspects of War and Policy in the Second and First Centuries BCE," in Aryeh Kasher, Uriel Rappaport, and Gideon Fuks, eds, *Greece and Rome in Eretz Israel: Collected Essays* (1990), 3–19.

Israel Shatzman, *The Armies of the Hasmonaeans and Herod* (1991).

Doron Mendels, "Jewish Kingship in the Hasmonean Period," in his *The Rise and Fall of Jewish Nationalism* (1992), 55–79.

When King Antiochus Epiphanes of Syria issued his decrees prohibiting the Jews of Palestine from observing the practices of the Jewish religion and forcing them to perform idolatrous rites and to eat food forbidden by the Torah, the revolt of the Jews was launched in 167 BCE by the head of a minor priestly clan, Mattathias of the Hashmon family, and was carried forward by his eldest son, Judah Makkabah (Maccabaeus). The rising was initially a religious rebellion, but it was gradually transformed into a war of national liberation, the leaders taking advantage of the instability of the Seleucid government. The Maccabees effectively saved Palestinian Judaism from extinction. In 163 BCE Antiochus V Eupator, the successor to Antiochus Epiphanes, in exchange for peace in Judaea, restored religious freedom to the Jews and dismantled the pagan trappings and the institutions of the Greek *polis* that had been introduced into Jerusalem.

After 163 BCE the Seleucid monarchy of Syria made no further attempts to interfere with the religion of the Jews. Upon the death of Judas

Maccabaeus in 160 BCE his brother Jonathan assumed authority. In the dynastic struggle for the throne of the Seleucid Empire that broke out in 152 BCE, King Demetrius I offered concessions to the Jews to win them over to his cause. The pretender to the throne, Alexander Balas, countered by appointing Jonathan high priest, and on his succession as king, Jonathan as his ally bore the title *"strategos* [general] and friend of the king."

It was, however, not until 142 BCE, shortly after Simon succeeded his brother Jonathan, that, under Demetrius II, payment of tribute was abolished. In this manner political independence was won by the Jews, the first time since the Babylonian exile that the Jews were free from foreign overlords. Thus began the Hasmonean dynasty (142–63 BCE), under which Judaea was transformed from a temple state into a Hellenistic kingdom.

8.1 Josephus, *Jewish Antiquities* 12.265–71 (167 BCE)

Josephus relates the story of how Mattathias defied the decrees of Antiochus Epiphanes and killed a Jew who obeyed them.

Now at this very time there was a man living in the village of Modein in Judaea whose name was Mattathias, son of Joannes, son of Simeon, son of Asmonaias, a priest of the line of Joarib and a native of Jerusalem. He had five sons: Joannes, who was called Gaddes; Simon, who was called Thatis; Judas, who was called Maccabaeus; Eleazar, who was called Auran; and Jonathan, who was called Apphus. Now this Mattathias lamented to his sons the state of affairs and the looting of the city and the plundering of the Temple and the calamities of the people. And he told them that it was better for them to die for their ancestral laws than to live so ingloriously.

When those who were appointed by the king came to the village of Modein to compel the Jews to do what had been commanded and to order the inhabitants to sacrifice as the king had directed, they invited Mattathias, a person of esteem, among other things because of his five sons, to begin the sacrifices, for his fellow citizens would follow his example and he himself would thus be held in honor by the king. But Mattathias said he would not do it; and that if all the other people obeyed the decrees of Antiochus, either out of fear or to please him, yet neither he nor his sons would ever be persuaded to abandon the ancestral cult. But as soon as he had ceased speaking, one of the Jews came forth into their midst and sacrificed as Antiochus had ordered. In a great rage Mattathias rushed upon him with his sons, who had knives with them, and killed both the man himself and Apelles, the king's officer who was compelling them to sacrifice, together with a few of his soldiers. Mattathias also pulled down the altar and cried out, 'Whoever is zealous for the ancestral laws and for the worship of God, let him follow me.' (M.R.)

8.2 Josephus, *Jewish Antiquities* 12.316–20, 323–5 (165 BCE)

Here Josephus describes how Judah Maccabee purified the Temple and rededicated it, reinstituted the sacrifices, and instituted the annual celebration of Hanukkah, the Festival of Lights, in commemoration of this rededication.

When, therefore, the generals of Antiochus' armies had been defeated many times, Judah assembled the people and said to them that after many victories which God had given them, they ought to go up to Jerusalem, purify the Temple, and offer the customary sacrifice. But when he came to Jerusalem with the whole multitude, and found the Temple deserted, and its gates burned down, and plants growing in the Temple of their own accord on account of its desertion, he and his men who were with him began to lament, dismayed at the sight of the Temple. So he chose some of his soldiers, and ordered them to fight against those guarding the citadel until he himself sanctified the Temple. When he had carefully purified it, and had brought in new equipment – the menorah, the table [of the shewbread], and the altar [for incense], all made of gold – he hung the curtains at the doors and replaced the doors themselves. He also pulled down the altar [for burnt offerings], and built a new one of various stones that were not hewn with iron tools. So on the twenty-fifth day of the month Kislev, which the Macedonians called Apellaeus, they kindled the lights on the menorah, and offered incense upon the altar and laid the loaves upon the table and offered burnt offerings upon the new altar. Now it so happened that these things were done on the very same day on which the holy service had been altered to an impure and profane form, three years before. For the Temple was made desolate by Antiochus and remained so for three years. . . .

Now Judah, together with his fellow citizens, celebrated the restoration of the sacrifices at the Temple for eight days, and omitted no kind of pleasure, but feasted them with very costly and splendid sacrifices, and he delighted them, honoring God, with hymns and psalms. They were so pleased at the restoration of their customs and at the unexpected regaining, after such a long time, of the freedom of their worship, that they made it a law for their posterity that they should have a festival for eight days in honor of the restoration of their Temple worship. And from that time to the present we observe this festival, and call it the Festival of Lights.[1] (M.R.)

8.3 *2 Maccabees* 11:27–33 (164 BCE)

King Antiochus V, the nine-year-old son of Antiochus Epiphanes, succeeded his father as king of Syria in 164. In the following letter he agrees to allow the Jews to follow their ancestral religious practices.

King Antiochus [V Eupator] to the Jewish senate and people, greeting. If you are well, I am pleased. We too are in good health. Menelaus [the high priest] has informed us of your desire to return to and dwell in your own homes. Therefore, we declare an assurance of amnesty to all who return before the thirtieth day of Xanthicus. The Jews may follow

---

1. The festival of Hanukkah ("rededication") was called *Enkainia* ("renewal") in Greek.

their own financial arrangements and laws as heretofore, and none of them shall in any manner be harassed with regard to any previous infringement. I have sent Menelaus to reassure you. Farewell. 15th of Xanthicus in the 148th Year [of the Seleucid Era = 164 BCE]. (M.R.)

8.4 1 Maccabees 10:22–47 (152 BCE)

After his rival for the throne, Alexander Balas, had appointed Jonathan the Hasmonean as high priest, Demetrius offered the Jews freedom from poll taxes and other imposts, freedom for Jewish captives, and many other gifts and privileges.

When Demetrius heard about this[2] he was distressed and said: 'What is this that we have done! Alexander has anticipated us in establishing friendship with the Jews to bolster his position. I too will write words of encouragement and flattery and offer gifts so that they may be my allies.'

With this in mind, he wrote to them, 'King Demetrius to the nation of the Jews, greetings! We were glad to hear that you have kept your agreements with us and have remained steadfast in friendship, and have not changed over to our enemies. Continue to be faithful to us, and we will requite you well for what you are doing in our behalf. We will grant you many exemptions and give you gifts. For the present, I free you and release all Jews from poll taxes,[3] from the custom on salt,[4] and from the crown tax.[5] Instead of one-third of the seed and half of the fruit of the trees which I receive as my share, from this day on I release for all time the right to take from the land of Judah and from the three districts which are added to it from Samaria and Galilee. Let Jerusalem and her borders, her tithes and taxes be holy and exempt. I give up, also, my authority over the citadel in Jerusalem. I give it to the high priest, that he may place there men whom he himself shall choose to guard it. Every Jewish person who has been carried into captivity from the land of Judah to any part of my kingdom, I release as a free gift. Let all officials remit the taxes upon their cattle also. All the feasts, the Sabbaths, new moons, public festivals (three days before a festival and three days after a festival), let them be days of exemption and release for all the Jews in my kingdom. No one shall have authority to exact payment or trouble any of them in any way.

Let about thirty thousand Jews be enrolled in the king's service. Maintenance and pay shall be given to them, as is proper for all the forces of the king. Some of them shall be stationed in the great strongholds of the king, and some of them shall be put in charge of the confidential affairs of the kingdom. Let those in charge of them, as well as their leaders, be from among their own. Let them obey their own laws, just as the king has commanded in the land of Judah.

---

2. Alexander Balas, the son of Antiochus Epiphanes, had appointed Jonathan high priest and had entitled him to be called "Friend of the King."
3. These taxes were proportionate to individual wealth.
4. The Jews obtained much salt from the marshes around the Dead Sea.
5. This was a fixed tribute to the Syrian government.

As for the three districts that were added to Judaea from the country of Samaria, let them be added to Judaea so that they may be considered under one man's authority, not obeying any other authority except that of the high priest. Ptolemais and the land contiguous with it I have given as a gift to the sanctuary in Jerusalem, for the expenses necessary for the sanctuary.

As for me, I shall give yearly fifteen thousand shekels of silver, from the revenues of the king, from suitable places. All the excess which the officials have not paid over from the revenues as in former years, from now on they shall contribute to the service of the Temple. In addition to this, the five thousand silver shekels which they were accustomed to take out of the dues of the sanctuary from the yearly revenue are released also, because they properly belong to the priests who perform the religious service. Whoever shall flee to the Temple in Jerusalem, or to any of its precincts, whether because they owe money to the king or for any other debt, shall be released, with all they possess in my kingdom. The expense of building and restoring the works of the sanctuary shall also be taken out of the king's revenue. Moreover, the expense of building the walls of Jerusalem, and fortifying it, and for building the walls in Judaea, shall be taken out of the revenue of the king.'

When Jonathan and the people heard these words, they did not believe nor accept them, because they were mindful of the great harm he had done to Israel, when he had greatly afflicted them. For that reason they favored Alexander [Balas],[6] because he had been the first to speak peaceful words to them, and they preserved their alliance with him always. (S.T.)

8.5 *1 Maccabees* 13:34–42 (142 BCE)

Demetrius II Nicator, the king of Syria from 142 to 125 BCE, was involved in a civil war with Tryphon, who had managed to win over the Syrian populace. Demetrius, thus weakened, offered Simon the Hasmonean ruler immunity from taxation and, finally, complete independence.

Simon selected men and sent them to King Demetrius to effect a release from taxation for the country, because the sole activities of Tryphon[7] were to plunder. King Demetrius sent a message to him in these words in answer, and wrote a letter to him in this manner:

'King Demetrius to Simon, the high priest and friend of kings, and to the elders and to the nation of the Jews, greetings! We have received the gold crown and the palm branch which you sent, and are ready to make a lasting peace with you, and to write to our officials to grant you immunities. Whatever favors we have guaranteed to you stand confirmed. The fortresses which you built, let them belong to you. We

---

6. Alexander Balas pretended to be the son of Antiochus Epiphanes and claimed the throne of his alleged father in opposition to Demetrius I Soter. His first act was to win Jonathan the Hasmonean to his side by appointing him high priest.

7. A usurping Syrian general. He had seized and executed Jonathan, previously his ally.

cancel in your favor any errors and omissions as of this day, as well as the crown tax which you owe. If there is any other tax collected in Jerusalem, let it be collected no longer. If any of you are eligible to be enrolled in our court, let them be enrolled, and let there be peace between us.'

In the 170th year [of the Seleucid era, i.e., 142 BCE] the yoke of the heathen was lifted from Israel. The people of Israel began to write in their documents and contracts, 'In the first year of Simon, the great high priest and general and ruler of the Jews.'[8] (S.T.)

8.6 1 Maccabees 14:25–32, 38–49 (140 BCE)

In the selection below we read that the leaders and people of Judaea, in their gratitude to Simon, confirmed him as high priest, general, and king. We may note that one of the factors that influenced King Demetrius of Syria to recognize the independence of Judaea was the warm reception that Simon's envoys had received from the Romans, the great rivals of the Syrian Greeks.

When the people heard this,[9] they said, 'How can we thank Simon and his sons? He and his brothers and his father's house have been steadfast. They fought off the enemies of Israel from them and assured its liberty.'

They engraved this on bronze tablets, and set it upon pillars on Mount Zion. This is a copy of the inscription:

On the 18th of Elul, the 172nd year [of the Seleucid era, i.e., 140 BCE] – this is the third year of the reign of Simon the high priest, prince of the people of Israel – in a Great Synagogue of priests and people and leaders of the nation and elders of the country, the following was decided: Often when wars have occurred in the country, Simon the son of Mattathias the priest, of the family of Joarib, and his brothers endangered their lives, and withstood their nation's adversaries, so that their sanctuary and the Law might be upheld, thus bringing great glory to their nation. Jonathan united their nation, and became their high priest and was gathered to his people. When the enemies planned to invade their country and to attack their sanctuary, Simon stood up and fought for his nation, and spent much of his own money in arming his nation's army and giving them wages. . . .

King Demetrius confirmed him in the high priesthood because of these things, and made him one of his Friends, treating him with great honor because he had heard that the Jews had been addressed by the Romans as friends and allies and brothers, and that they had received Simon's ambassadors with great honor, and because the Jews and the

---

8. The title "general" (*strategos*) was an administrative title of the Seleucid state; "ruler" (*sar-am* = prince of the people) is equivalent to the Greek *ethnarchos* (Latin *princeps*). It is noteworthy that the Hebrew title *melech* (king) was avoided at this time. It is interesting to compare the nomenclature of Augustus, the first Roman emperor, who also avoided the title king (Latin *rex*), using instead *imperator* ("commander"), *princeps* ("first citizen"), and *pontifex maximus* ("high priest").

9. That Simon, after the death of Jonathan, had renewed the treaties of friendship with Sparta and with Rome.

priests had agreed that Simon should be their leader and high priest forever, until a true prophet should arise, and had decided also that he should be their general, so that through him they might be assigned to their tasks, whether over the country, the arms, or the fortifications. They decided further that it was his responsibility to take care of the sanctuary, that all should obey him, and that all contracts in the country should be written in his name. It was also decided that he should be clothed in purple and wear gold. The record went further in saying that it should not be possible for any of the people or of the priests to set any of these things at naught nor to countermand whatever he should order, nor to convoke an assembly in the country without his permission nor to don purple nor to wear garments fastened with a gold clasp. 'Whoever shall act contrary to these things or set any of them at naught shall be liable to punishment.'

All the people agreed to make it a law that they should do all these things for Simon. Simon accepted and consented to serve as high priest, to be general and governor of the Jews and of the priests and to preside over all. They ordered that this decree be set upon bronze tablets, that they place them in a conspicuous place in the precinct of the sanctuary, and that copies of them be placed among the archives, so that Simon and his sons might have them. (S.T.)

8.7 A Setback: Diodorus the Sicilian (first century BCE), *Historical Library* 34.1.1, 3, 5

In 135/134 BCE, during the transition from the reign of Simon to that of Hyrcanus I, King Antiochus VII Sidetes of Syria succeeded in re-conquering Palestine. Despite his success, Antiochus Sidetes refused the advice of his friends to force the Jews to give up their religion. The following passage, from Diodorus, may have as its source the Stoic philosopher and historian Posidonius (*ca.* 135–*ca.* 51/50 BCE), who wrote Histories in fifty-two books, covering the period from about 146 to 78 BCE.

When King Antiochus [VII Sidetes], says Diodorus, was laying siege to Jerusalem, the Jews held out for a time, but when all their supplies were exhausted they found themselves compelled to make overtures for a cessation of hostilities. . . . His friends reminded Antiochus also of the enmity that in times past his ancestors had felt for this people. . . .

Rehearsing all these events, his friends strongly urged Antiochus to make an end of the race completely, or, failing that, to abolish their laws and force them to change their ways. But the king, being a magnanimous and mild-mannered person, took hostages but dismissed the charges against the Jews, once he had exacted the tribute that was due and had dismantled the walls of Jerusalem. (LCL)

The Hasmonean Rulers

BIBLIOGRAPHY

Saul Lieberman, "The Three Abrogations of Johanan the High Priest," in his *Hellenism in Jewish Palestine* (1950), 139–43.

Chaim Rabin, "Alexander Jannaeus and the Pharisees," *JJS* 7 (1956), 3–11.

Tcherikover (1959), 235–65.

Solomon Zeitlin, "Queen Salome and King Jannaeus Alexander: A Chapter in the History of the Second Jewish Commonwealth," *JQR* 51 (1960–1), 1–33.

Schürer (1973), 1.164–242.

Jonathan A. Goldstein, "The Hasmoneans: The Dynasty of God's Resisters," *HTR* 68 (1975), 53–8.

Bezalel Bar-Kochva, "Manpower, Economics, and Internal Strife in the Hasmonean State," in H. van Effenterre, ed., Colloques Nationaux du CNRS, no. 936, *Armées et Fiscalité dans le Monde Antique* (1977), 167–96.

M. J. Geller, "Alexander Jannaeus and the Pharisee Rift," *JJS* 30 (1979), 202–11.

Joshua Efron, *Studies on the Hasmonean Period* (1987).

Thomas Fischer, "Hasmoneans and Seleucids: Aspects of War and Policy in the Second and First Centuries BCE," in Aryeh Kasher, Uriel Rappaport, and Gideon Fuks, eds, *Greece and Rome in Eretz Israel: Collected Essays* (1990), 3–19.

Joseph Sievers, *The Hasmoneans and Their Supporters: From Mattathias to the Death of John Hyrcanus I* (1990).

James S. McLaren, *Power and Politics in Palestine: The Jews and the Governing of Their Land 100 BC–AD 70* (1991), 54–67.

Louis H. Feldman, "Josephus' Portrayal of the Hasmoneans Compared with 1 Maccabees," in Fausto Parente and Joseph Sievers, eds, *Josephus and the History of the Greco-Roman Period: Essays in Memory of Morton Smith* (1994), 41–68.

Clemens Thoma, "John Hyrcanus I as Seen by Josephus and Other Early Jewish Sources," in Fausto Parente and Joseph Sievers, eds, *Josephus and the History of the Greco-Roman Period: Essays in Memory of Morton Smith* (1994), 127–40.

Though Judah Maccabee (of the family of the Hasmoneans) had liberated Jerusalem and purified the Temple in the year 164 BCE, the struggle with Syria continued; and it was not until 141 BCE that the Acra fortress in Jerusalem was finally captured by Simon, Judah's brother. The Hasmonean state came into being at a propitious time, benefiting, as it did, from the disintegration of the Seleucid Empire. Simon, however, together with two of his sons, was murdered by his son-in-law Ptolemy in 134 BCE, but he was succeeded by his remaining son, John Hyrcanus, who expanded the kingdom considerably, in particular annexing Idumaea and converting its inhabitants to Judaism, and capturing the capital city of the Samaritans, Shechem, and destroying their temple. Significantly, he was the first of the dynasty to fight his wars not with a Jewish army but with one consisting of mercenaries. He was succeeded in 104 BCE by his son, Aristobulus I, who started his reign by starving his mother to death and imprisoning all his brothers except one, whom he loved deeply but later managed to murder. He completed the conquest of Galilee and forcibly converted the Ituraeans there. After a reign of only a year he died a natural death. The expansion of Judaea continued under his successor, Alexander Jannaeus, Aristobulus' younger brother, who ruled from 103 to 76 BCE. He was succeeded by his wife, Salome (Shelomziyyon) Alexandra, who ruled from 76 to 67 BCE, and whose reign was marked, on the whole, by peace and prosperity. Upon her death her two sons, Hyrcanus and Aristobulus, began a protracted civil war for the kingship, in which the younger brother Aristobulus was at first successful but which eventually led to the intervention by the Romans under Pompey.

8.8 Josephus, *Jewish Antiquities* 13.288–96: John Hyrcanus' (ruled 135–104 BCE) breach with the Pharisees

There is much dispute as to the origin of the Pharisees and their relationship to the Maccabean movement and to the party of Hasidim (the "Pious") who had originally joined the Maccabees in the war of independence. Though the original aim of the Maccabean movement was to preserve the ancestral religion, as time went on political goals became increasingly important. Though the Maccabees originally belonged neither to the Pharisees nor to the Sadducees, they were apparently at first closer to the former. Later the Hasmonean kings moved closer to the Sadducees, who were more worldly and more politically minded. The following excerpt describes the occasion of John Hyrcanus' breach with the Pharisees, namely the failure (in John Hyrcanus' view) of the Pharisees to punish properly one of the Pharisees who had told him to resign the position of high priest because as the son of a captive mother (the presumption being that she had been sexually defiled) he was not eligible – a report that actually proved to be false. Many scholars regard the whole story as a legend and postulate that the real grounds for the breach were Hyrcanus' desire to ally himself with the influential Saducean nobility.

As for Hyrcanus, the envy of the Jews was aroused against him by his own successes and those of his sons; particularly hostile to him were the Pharisees. . . . So great is their influence with the masses that even when they speak against a king or high priest, they immediately gain credence. Hyrcanus too was a disciple of theirs and was greatly loved by them. And once he invited them to a feast and entertained them hospitably, and when he saw that they were having a very good time, he began by saying that they knew he wished to be righteous and in everything he did tried to please God and them – for the Pharisees profess such beliefs; at the same time he begged them, if they observed him doing anything wrong or straying from the right path, to lead him back to it and correct him. But they testified to his being altogether virtuous, and he was delighted with their praise.

However, one of the guests, named Eleazar, who had an evil nature and took pleasure in dissension, said, 'Since you have asked to be told the truth, if you wish to be righteous, give up the high priesthood and be content with governing the people.' And when Hyrcanus asked him for what reason he should give up the high priesthood, he replied, 'Because we have heard from our elders that your mother was a captive in the reign of Antiochus Epiphanes.' But the story was false, and Hyrcanus was furious with the man, while all the Pharisees were very indignant.

Then a certain Jonathan, one of Hyrcanus' close friends, belonging to the school of the Sadducees, who hold opinions opposed to those of the Pharisees, said that it had been with the general approval of all the Pharisees that Eleazar had made his slanderous statement; and this, he added, would be clear to Hyrcanus if he inquired of them what punishment Eleazar deserved for what he had said. And so Hyrcanus asked the Pharisees what penalty they thought he deserved – for, he said, he would be convinced that the slanderous statement had not been made with their approval if they fixed a penalty commensurate with the crime – and they replied that Eleazar deserved stripes and chains; for they did not think it right to sentence a man to death for calumny, and anyway the Pharisees are naturally lenient in the matter of punishments. At this Hyrcanus became very angry and began to believe that the fellow had slandered him with their approval. And Jonathan in particular inflamed his anger, and so worked upon him that he brought him to join the Sadducean party and desert the Pharisees, and to abrogate the regulations which they had established for the people, and punish those who observed them. Out of this, of course, grew the hatred of the masses for him and his sons. (LCL)

8.9 Babylonian Talmud (codified ca. 500 CE), Qiddushin 66a: A Talmudic account of King Alexander Jannaeus' breach with the Sages

One of the very few instances where we see a direct parallel between an account in the Talmud with one in Josephus is in the following narrative concerning King Alexander Jannaeus' breach with the Sages, which bears a striking similarity to Josephus' account above of John Hyrcanus' breach with the Pharisees. The fact that the king in the Talmudic account is Alexander Jannaeus rather than John Hyrcanus may be explained by the fact that elsewhere in the Talmud (*Berakoth* 29a) the same rabbi, the fourth-century CE Abaye, in whose name the account here in *Qiddushin* is related, makes the statement that "Johanan [i.e., John Hyrcanus] is the same as Jannai [i.e., Alexander Jannaeus]." The Talmudic version here is presented as a *Baraitha*, that is a passage "outside" the Mishnah and often, perhaps usually, paralleling it in date (i.e., the second century CE). In both accounts one can see how sincere the king was originally in seeking to observe the Torah. In both narratives the Pharisees are mentioned by name. In both cases the objection is to the king's status as high priest and for the same reason, namely the fact that his mother had been taken captive. In Josephus the objector to his status is named Eleazar, whereas in the Talmud the objector is a man named Judah son of Gedidiah; and a man named Eleazar is responsible for advising the king to break with the Pharisees. In both cases the king is said to object to the fact that the penalty to be inflicted upon the slanderer is too mild.

Abaye [Babylonian, third and fourth centuries CE] also said: Whence do I know it [i.e., that in the case where a wife is charged with having committed adultery on the testimony of one witness and the husband is silent, he is believed]? Because it was taught,[10] it once happened that King Jannai [i.e., Alexander Jannaeus] went to Kohalith[11] in the

10. The word which is used indicates that this is a *Baraitha*, paralleling the Mishnah.
11. Apparently a town, otherwise unknown, perhaps in Transjordan, where King Alexander Jannaeus carried on one of his extensive military campaigns (*Ant.* 13.393–4), though there is no indication in Josephus as to the number of towns that he conquered (elsewhere Josephus, *Ant.* 14.18, lists twelve cities which Alexander had taken from the Arabs).

wilderness and conquered sixty towns there. On his return he rejoiced exceedingly and invited all the Sages of Israel. Said he to them, 'Our forefathers ate mallows[12] when they were engaged in the building of the [second] Temple; let us too eat mallows in memory of our forefathers.' So mallows were served on golden tables, and they ate.

Now, there was a man there, frivolous, evil-hearted, and worthless, named Eleazar son of Po'irah, who said to King Jannai, 'O King Jannai, the hearts of the Pharisees are against thee.' 'Then what shall I do?' 'Test them by the plate between thine eyes.'[13] So he tested them by the plate between his eyes. Now, an elder, named Judah son of Gedidiah, was present there. Said he to King Jannai, 'O King Jannai! Let the royal crown suffice thee, and leave the priestly crown to the seed of Aaron.' (For it was rumored that his mother had been taken captive in Modein.) Accordingly, the charge was investigated, but not sustained, and the Sages of Israel departed in anger.[14] Then said Eleazar ben Po'irah to King Jannai: 'O King Jannai! That is the law even for the most humble man in Israel, and thou, a King and a High Priest, shall that be thy law [too]!' 'Then what shall I do?' 'If thou wilt take my advice, trample them down.' 'But what shall happen with the Torah?' 'Behold, it is rolled up and lying in the corner; whoever wishes to study, let him go and study!' Said Rabbi Nahman ben Isaac [Babylonian, fourth century CE]: 'Immediately a spirit of heresy was instilled into him [Alexander Jannaeus], for he should have replied, "That is well for the Written Law, but what of Oral Law?"'[15] Straightway, the evil burst forth through Eleazar son of Po'irah, all the Sages of Israel were massacred,[16] and the world was desolate until Simeon ben Shetah [a contemporary of King Alexander Jannaeus and Queen Salome Alexandra in the early part of the first century BCE] came and restored the Torah to its pristine glory. (Soncino)

8.10 Josephus, *Jewish Antiquities* 13.348–55: Alexander Jannaeus and the Egyptian power struggle

The Hasmonean kings showed considerable skill in maneuvering amidst the constant dynastic wars of their powerful neighbors in Syria and Egypt, often taking advantage of the chaos to enlarge their realm.

---

12. Mallows are plants with soft, downy leaves which were apparently the food of the very poor.

13. The reference is to the gold plate which hung on a blue thread in front of the high priest's miter and which, according to the Pentateuch (Exod 28:36–38; 39:30–1) contained the words "Holy to the Lord." In other words, test the Pharisees by their reactions to your status as high priest.

14. Presumably, the Sages were angry at the false accusation.

15. Inasmuch as the Pharisees believed that in addition to the Written Law (the Pentateuch) Moses also received at Sinai an oral interpretation of that Law, they should, according to this view, have found in that oral interpretation a way to punish more severely the one who had slandered the king.

16. Josephus does not mention specifically any massacre of Sages by either John Hyrcanus or Alexander Jannaeus, but he does mention (*War* 1.97, *Ant.* 13.380) a massacre by Alexander Jannaeus of eight hundred Jewish rebels, whom he ordered to be crucified while slaughtering their wives and children before their very eyes while he feasted with his concubines.

Alexander Jannaeus spent most of his reign fighting wars. When he surrounded the seaport city of Ptolemais (Akko) north-west of Galilee, the people of Ptolemais sought help from King Ptolemy Lathyrus of Egypt, who had been dethroned by his mother Cleopatra III and who was then ruling in Cyprus. Alexander made peace with Ptolemy while secretly appealing to Cleopatra for help. When Ptolemy learned of this he broke the truce and defeated Alexander in a hard-fought battle. Cleopatra sent an army into Palestine under the leadership of two Jewish commanders-in-chief, Chelkias and Ananias. Ptolemy meanwhile hastened to Egypt seeking the kingship. Cleopatra succeeded in driving him out of Egypt. As the following excerpt indicates, some of her friends advised Cleopatra to occupy all of Judaea, since Alexander was clearly ambitious to extend his realm. Her commander Ananias succeeded in dissuading her, emphasizing that Alexander was an ally and that if she attacked him she would incur the enmity of the large Jewish community in Egypt.

When Cleopatra saw her son [Ptolemy Lathyrus] growing in power, and ravaging Judaea with impunity ..., she decided not to be idle while he, having grown greater, was at her gates and coveted the throne of Egypt; and so she at once set out against him with a sea and land force, appointing as leaders of her entire army the Jews Chelkias and Ananias.... Thereupon Ptolemy left Syria and hastened to Egypt, thinking to get possession of it suddenly while it was left without an army, but he was disappointed of his hope. It was just at this time that Chelkias, one of Cleopatra's two commanders, died in Coele-Syria [Palestine] while in pursuit of Ptolemy.

When Cleopatra heard of her son's attempt and learned that his plans concerning Egypt had not prospered as he had expected, she sent a portion of her army against him and drove him out of the country.... And when Alexander came to her with gifts and such marks of attention as were to be expected after the harsh treatment he had suffered at the hands of Ptolemy – for he had no other course of safety than this – some of her friends advised her to take these things and at the same time invade his country and occupy it, and not suffer such an abundance of resources to belong to one man, who was a Jew. Ananias, however, gave the opposite advice, saying that she would commit an injustice if she deprived an ally of his own possessions, 'especially one who is our kinsman. For I would have you know that an injustice done to this man will make all us Jews your enemies.' By this exhortation of Ananias Cleopatra was persuaded not to do Alexander any wrong, but instead she made an alliance with him at Scythopolis in Coele-Syria. (LCL)

8.11 Josephus, *Jewish War* 1.110–12: Queen Salome Alexandra dominated by the Pharisees

According to Josephus (*Ant.* 13.401–4), Alexander Jannaeus, on his deathbed in 76 BCE, advised his wife, Salome Alexandra, to make peace with the Pharisees. This she, in her deep religiosity, apparently did, according to the excerpt below, making the Pharisees, in effect, the rulers of the land.

Beside Alexandra, and growing as she grew, arose the Pharisees, a body of Jews with the reputation of excelling the rest of their nation in the observances of religion, and as exact exponents of the laws. To them, being herself intensely religious, she listened with too great deference; while they, gradually taking advantage of an ingenuous woman, became at length the real administrators of the state, at liberty to banish . . . whom they would. In short, the enjoyments of royal authority were theirs; its expenses and burdens fell to Alexandra. She proved, however, to be a wonderful administrator in larger affairs, and, by continually recruiting, doubled her army, besides collecting a considerable body of foreign troops; so that she not only strengthened her own nation, but became a formidable foe to foreign potentates. But if she ruled the nation, the Pharisees ruled her. (LCL)

8.12 Coins of the Hasmonean Dynasty

BIBLIOGRAPHY

Adolf Reifenberg, *Ancient Jewish Coins* (1940, 1947, 1965).

Baruch Kanael, "Ancient Jewish Coins and Their Historical Importance," *BA* 26 (1963), 38–62.

Josef Meyshan, "Jewish Coins in Ancient Historiography. The Importance of Numismatics for the History of Israel," *PEQ* 96 (1964), 46–52.

Arie Kindler, *Coins of Palestine* (1974).

Uriel Rappaport, "The Emergence of Hasmonean Coinage," *AJSR* 1 (1976), 171–86.

As rulers of an independent state, the Hasmoneans minted large issues of coins for circulation in their realm. The following coins are typical of the fusion of Jewish and Greek iconographic symbolism and languages found in their money. It is noteworthy that, whereas other Hellenistic monarchs displayed their portraits on their coinage, the Jewish kings did not, abiding by the religious injunction against "graven images."

John Hyrcanus I (135–104 BCE)

a. Obverse: Olive wreath. In Hebrew: YEHOHATHAN THE HIGH PRIEST AND THE CONGREGATION OF THE JEWS

   Reverse: Two cornucopias, pomegranate[17] (M.R.)

b. Obverse: In Hebrew: YEHONATHAN THE HIGH PRIEST AND THE CONGREGATION OF THE JEWS

   Reverse: Two cornucopias, pomegranate (M.R.)

Alexander Jannaeus (103–76 BCE)

b. Obverse: Star. In Hebrew: KING ALEXANDER;[18] YEAR 25

   Reverse: Anchor. In Greek: KING ALEXANDER (M.R.)

---

17. The pomegranate, a symbol of fertility, was embroidered on the high priest's robes.

18. I.e., King Alexander Jannaeus (ruled 103–76 BCE).

Antigonus Mattathias (40–37 BCE)

c. Obverse: Two cornucopias. In Hebrew: MATTATHIAS THE HIGH
   PRIEST AND THE CONGREGATION OF THE JEWS

   Reverse: Wreath. In Greek: KING ANTIGONUS (M.R.)

d. Obverse: Table of shewbread.[19] In Hebrew: MATTATHIAS THE
   HIGH PRIEST

   Reverse: Menorah. In Greek: KING ANTIGONUS (M.R.)

International Diplomacy of the Hasmonean Dynasty

Treaty with Rome (161 BCE)

BIBLIOGRAPHY

Wolf Wirgin, "Judah Maccabee's Embassy to Rome and the Jewish-Roman
   Treaty," *PEQ* 101 (1969), 15–20.
Wolf Wirgin, "Simon Maccabaeus' Embassy to Rome – Its Purpose and
   Outcome," *PEQ* 106 (1974), 141–6.

The Hasmoneans and the Romans had mutual interests in forging an
alliance, the former to achieve independence from Syria, the latter to
check Syrian dominance in the East. Though questions have been raised
as to the authenticity of the documents cited below, most scholars regard
them as genuine.

8.13 2 Maccabees 11:34–38 (164 BCE)

The following is the first known evidence of direct contact between Rome
and the Jews. The Roman envoys involved, en route to a diplomatic
conference in the Seleucid capital, may have met Jewish representatives
at a port of Seleucid Phoenicia.

The Romans sent them [the Jews] a letter as follows: Quintus
Memmius, Titus Manilius and Titus Manius Sergius, Roman envoys, to
the Jewish people, greetings. We concur with all that Lysias, the king's
relative, has granted to you. But consider carefully the questions which
he reserved for referral to the king. Then send someone immediately
so that we may make suitable proposals for you, for we are proceeding
to Antioch. Send people therefore without delay, so that we may also
know what your view is. Farewell. The 15th of Xanthicus, year 148 [of
the Seleucid Era, i.e., 164 BCE]. (M.R.)

8.14 1 Maccabees 8:1, 11–32 (161 BCE)

Judas Maccabaeus' embassy to Rome in 161/160 BCE was a rash step,
since the Jews were still subjects of the Seleucid king. But Judas was fully
aware of Rome's disposition to weaken the Seleucid Empire and of
Rome's overwhelming might. Jewish prophetic tradition, however, was

---

19. The priests placed twelve loaves of unleavened bread on a table in the sanctuary
of the Temple in Jerusalem.

suspicious of alliances with pagan states because of earlier disastrous relations with Assyria, Babylon, and Egypt. Hence the need of Judas (or the author of 1 Maccabees) to represent Rome as a paragon of a virtuous and mighty people, in a manner that would serve as propaganda for the Maccabean dynasty.

Judas had heard about the fame of the Romans: that they were a great power, who welcomed all who joined them, and established friendship with all who approached them. . . . The Romans had reduced to ruins and servitude whoever had opposed them. With their friends, however, and with those who relied on them, the Romans had maintained friendship, and had conquered the kings both near and far; and all those who heard of the fame of the Romans feared them. Those whom they chose to aid and to be client kings, those are kings; those whom they chose to, they deposed. Thus the Romans had risen to great heights. Nevertheless, among all of them not one had put on a diadem or clothed himself in purple for self-aggrandizement. They had established a senate house for themselves, in which every day[20] 320 sat deliberating continually how to maintain the good order of the people. They entrusted their government and the ruling of all their territory to one man each year,[21] everyone obeying him, without any envy or jealousy among themselves.

Judas chose Eupolemus son of Joannes, of the Hakkoz clan, and Jason son of Eleazar, and sent them to Rome to establish friendship and alliance with the Jews, and lift the yoke from them, for they saw that the Seleucid Empire was imposing slavery upon Israel. They journeyed to Rome – a very long journey – and came into the senate house and spoke as follows: 'Judas Maccabaeus and his brothers and the Jewish people have sent us to establish alliance and peace with you and to inscribe us as your allies and friends.' Their speech was approved on the spot.

The following is a copy of the letter the Romans engraved on bronze tablets and sent to Jerusalem for the Jews to keep there as a record of peace and alliance: 'Let there be good fortune for the Romans and the people of the Jews on sea and land forever! May sword and enmity be far from them! If war arises for Rome first or for any of their allies throughout their empire, the people of the Jews shall act as ally wholeheartedly, as circumstances present themselves. And to those at war with them the Jews shall not give or supply food, arms, money, or ships, as was agreed at Rome. The Jews shall carry out their obligations to the letter. Similarly, if war comes to the people of the Jews first, the Romans shall act as allies wholeheartedly, as circumstances present themselves. And to those at war with them there shall not be given food, arms, money, or ships, as was agreed at Rome. The Romans shall carry out their obligations without malice aforethought. On the

20. Daily sessions were held by the Sanhedrin in Jerusalem, but not by the Roman Senate.
21. This is an error: there were two annual consuls. This error may be due merely to misinformation or to the fact that in the East the Roman authority was represented in a province by one governor.

foregoing terms the Romans have made a treaty with the Jewish people. If after this covenant both sides shall consult for the purpose of adding or subtracting anything, they shall do so in accordance with their decisions, and any such addition or deletion shall be valid.'[22]

As for the misdeeds King Demetrius [of Syria] is perpetrating against you, we have written him as follows: 'Why have you made your yoke weigh heavily upon our friends, our allies, the Jews? If they make any further complaint against you, we shall judge in their favor and wage war upon you by sea and by land.' (M.R.)

8.15 1 Maccabees 14:24, 15:15–24 (139 BCE)

In this passage Simon, the Hasmonean king, renews his alliance with the Romans. The Romans write to the kings of Syria, Egypt, and various minor states to warn them not to harm the Judaeans.

After that Simon sent Numenius to Rome with a large gold shield weighing 1,000 minas to confirm the alliance with the Romans.... When Numenius and his staff returned from Rome, they had a letter to the kings and to the peoples, which read as follows:

'Lucius [Caecilius Metellus], consul of the Romans [142 BCE], to King Ptolemy [VIII], greeting. Ambassadors of our friends and allies the Jews sent by the high priest Simon and by the people of the Jews came to us to renew their long-standing friendship and alliance. They brought a shield of 1,000 minas. Accordingly, we resolved to write to the kings and peoples to refrain from harming them, and from making war upon them, their cities and their territory, and from acting in alliance with those at war with them. We have decided to accept the shield from them. Now, if any troublemakers have escaped from their territory to yours, deliver them up to the high priest Simon for him to punish in accordance with their law.'

He wrote the same letter to King Demetrius [II, of the Seleucid Empire], to Attalus [II, of Pergamum], to Ariarthes [V, of Cappadocia], and to Arsaces [of Parthia], and to all the following peoples: to Sampsaces and the Spartans, to Delos and to Myndos, to Sicyon and to Caria, and to Samos and Pamphylia, to Lycia and Halicarnassus, to Rhodes and Phaselis, to Cos and Side, to Aradus and Gortyn, and Cnidus and Cyprus and Cyrene. They sent a copy of the letter to the high priest Simon. (M.R.)

8.16 Josephus, *Jewish Antiquities* 13.259–65 (*ca.* 132 or 105 BCE)

In the following passage the Roman Senate confirms its alliance with King John Hyrcanus of Judaea. The Romans agree to deliberate the

---

22. Josephus, *Jewish Antiquities* 12.417–18, gives a similar version of the basic treaty between the Jews and the Romans, which has the standard form of the Roman "treaty on equal terms." "This decree," says Josephus, "was signed by Eupolemus son of Joannes and by Jason son of Eleazar, when Judas was high priest of the people and Simon his brother was commander of the army. And this is how the first treaty of friendship and alliance between the Romans and the Jews came about."

request to send envoys to the Syrians so that the territory seized from the Jews by Antiochus VII Sidetes be restored to them.

Now as the high priest [John] Hyrcanus wished to renew the friendship with the Romans, he sent an embassy to them. And the Senate received his letter and made an alliance of friendship with him in the following terms:

'Fannius, the son of Marcus, the praetor, convened the Senate on the eighth day before the Ides of February in the Comitium in the presence of Lucius Mallius, the son of Lucius, of the Menenian tribe, and of Gaius Sempronius, the son of Gaius, of the Falernian tribe, to discuss the matters presented by the envoys Simon, the son of Dositheus, and Apollonius, the son of Alexander, and Diodorus, the son of Jason, worthy and excellent men sent by the Jewish people, who also spoke of the friendship and alliance existing between their people and the Romans, and of public affairs such as their request that Joppa and its harbors and Gazara and Pegae and whatever other cities and territories Antiochus [VII Sidetes] took from them in war, contrary to the decree of the Senate, be restored to them, and that the soldiers of the king be not permitted to march through their country or those of their subjects, and that the laws made by Antiochus during this same war contrary to the decree of the Senate be annulled, and that the Romans send envoys to bring about the restitution of the places taken from the Jews by Antiochus and to estimate the value of the territory ruined during the war, and also that they give the Jewish envoys letters to the kings and free cities to assure their safe return homeward. Concerning these matters, therefore, it has been decreed that the alliance of friendship be renewed with the worthy men who have been sent by a worthy and friendly people.' Concerning the letters, however, they replied that they would deliberate when the Senate should have leisure from its own affairs, and that they would take care that no similar injustice should be done them in the future. (LCL)

Jewish Negotiations with Sparta (ca. 150 BCE)

BIBLIOGRAPHY

Michael S. Ginsburg, "Sparta and Judaea," *CP* 29 (1934), 117–22.

S. Schüller, "Some Problems Connected with the Supposed Common Ancestry of Jews and Spartans and their Relations during the Last Three Centuries BC," *JSS* 1 (1956), 257–68.

Ranon Katzoff, "Jonathan and Late Sparta," *AJP* 106 (1985), 485–9.

Documents preserved in Jewish sources concerning diplomatic relations between the Jews and Sparta are of doubtful authenticity. The ideal of Spartan culture seemed in many respects attractive to Jewish Hellenizers; they developed a number of simplistic analogies between Jews and Spartans. The claim of ancestral brotherhood, based on common descent from Abraham, was likely a product of Jewish apologetic literature, probably emanating from Alexandria.

8.17 Josephus, *Jewish Antiquities* 12.225–7 (*ca.* 300 BCE)

In the letter cited here the Spartan king Areios refers to a document asserting that the Jews and Spartans have a common ancestor in Abraham.

When he [the high priest Simon II] too died, his son Onias [III] became
his successor in office, and it was to him that the Lacedaemonian
[Spartan] king Areios sent an embassy with a letter, of which the
following is a copy. 'Areios,[23] king of the Lacedaemonians, to Onias,
greeting. We have come upon a certain document from which we have
learned that the Jews and Lacedaemonians are of one race and are
related by descent from Abraham. It is right, therefore, that you as our
brothers should send to us to make known whatever you may wish. We
also shall do this, and shall consider what is yours as our own, and
what is ours we shall also share with you. Demoteles, the courier, is
bringing this letter to you. The writing is square. The seal is an eagle
holding fast a serpent.' (LCL)

8.18 *1 Maccabees* 12:1–23 (143 BCE)

In the letter quoted below sent by Jonathan the Hasmonean to the
Spartans, he renews the friendship dating back to the time of King Areios,
noting that the Jews have remembered the Spartans in their prayers and
in connection with their sacrifices.

Jonathan, perceiving that time was working in his favor, appointed
men and sent them to Rome to confirm and renew friendship with
them. He also sent similar letters to the Spartans and other places. The
men journeyed to Rome. On entering the senate house they said: 'The
high priest Jonathan and the people of the Jews have sent us to renew
friendship and alliance with you as before.' The Romans gave them
letters to the authorities, place by place, with a view to their escorting
them peacefully to the land of Judaea. Here is a copy of the letter which
Jonathan wrote to the Spartans. 'The high priest Jonathan and the
Council of Elders of the people and the priests and the rest of the
people of the Jews to their brothers the Spartans, greeting. Previously a
letter was sent to our high priest Onias from Areios, your reigning king,
saying that you are our brothers, as in the copy subjoined. Onias
received your ambassador with honor and accepted the letter in which
details are given regarding alliance and friendship.

'Now, although we are not in need of such ties, since we have as our
consolation the Holy Books in our hands, we ventured to send word to
you to renew our brotherhood and friendship with you in order that we
may not become estranged from you. Indeed, a long time has passed
since you sent us your message. All this time we have un-failingly
made mention of you in our festivals and on the other appropriate days
on which we offer sacrifices, as well as in our prayer houses, inasmuch
as it is fitting and proper to make mention of brothers. We rejoice at

23. Inasmuch as there were only two Spartan kings by this name, Areios I, who
reigned from 309–265 BCE, and Areios II, who died as a child in 255 BCE, Josephus is
therefore mistaken in placing him in the time of Onias III instead of Onias I, who was
high priest *ca.* 300 BCE.

your reputation. As for us, many afflictions and many wars have beset us, as the kings in our vicinity waged war upon us. Now we do not wish to trouble you or our other allies and friends with these wars, for we have the help of Heaven aiding us, and we have been saved from our enemies, and our enemies have been humbled. Accordingly, we have appointed Numenius son of Antiochus, and Antipater son of Jason, and have sent them to the Romans to renew our previous friendship and alliance with them. And we have ordered them to journey to you, too, and greet you, and deliver to you our letter concerning the renewal of our brotherhood. Please be so good as to reply to us with regard to these matters.'

Here is a copy of the letter which they sent to Onias: 'To the high priest Onias, Areios King of the Spartans, greeting. In a work concerning the Spartans and the Jews there is found a statement that they are brothers and that they are descended from Abraham. And now that we have learned this, please be so good as to write concerning your peaceful conditions. We, too, reply to you, "Your cattle and property are ours, and ours are yours."[24] Accordingly, we have ordered that declaration be made to you along these lines.' (M.R.)

8.19 *1 Maccabees* 14:16–23 (143 BCE)

In the following letter the Spartans, upon hearing of the death of Jonathan the Hasmonean and the succession of his brother Simon as high priest, renew their friendship with the Judaeans.

The news of Jonathan's death was reported to Rome, and even as far as Sparta. And they were deeply grieved. And when they heard that his brother Simon had become high priest in his place and had won control of the land and of the cities in it, they wrote to him on bronze tablets to renew with him friendship and alliance which they had established with Judas and Jonathan, his brothers. The tablets were read in Jerusalem in the presence of the assembly. The following is a copy of the letter sent by the Spartans:

'The magistrates and the city of the Spartans to their brothers, the high priest Simon and the elders and the priests and the rest of the people of the Jews, greeting. The ambassadors sent by you to our people reported to us about your present fame and prestige, and we are delighted that they came. We have recorded their speeches in the proceedings of our people as follows:

"Numenius son of Antiochus and Antipater son of Jason, ambassadors of the Jews, came before us to renew their friendship with us. It pleased the people to receive the men with honor and to place a copy of their speeches in the volumes of the people's archives in order that the people might have a record." The people sent a copy of these proceedings to the high priest Simon.' (M.R.)

---

24. This is a standard formula for a military alliance in Semitic terminology. Josephus (*Jewish Antiquities* 14.255) states that the Pergamenes also claimed ancestral friendship with Abraham.

Jewish Negotiations with Pergamum (ca. 113 BCE)

The city (and kingdom) of Pergamum in north-western Asia Minor was in the third and second centuries BCE one of the greatest centers of Greek literature and sculpture. It was here that parchment, called after the city *charta Pergamena*, was invented, and here was the site of one of the greatest libraries of the ancient world. Upon his death in 133 BCE, the last king of Pergamum, Attalus III Philometor, bequeathed his kingdom to Rome.

8.20 Josephus, *Jewish Antiquities* 14.247–55 (*ca.* 113–112 BCE)

In the following document, apparently written during the reign of the Jewish king John Hyrcanus, the Pergamenes, like the Spartans, recall that the Jews and the people of Pergamum were friends during the time of Abraham and mention evidence in public records. Though at the time of this document an alliance with Pergamum meant little in practical terms, the prestige of the Pergamenes was so great that it clearly redounded to the credit of the Hasmoneans to have forged an alliance with them.

Decree of the people of Pergamum. 'In the presidency of Cratippus, on the first of the month Daisios, a decree of the magistrates. As the Romans in pursuance of the practices of their ancestors have accepted dangerous risks for the common safety of all mankind and strive emulously to place their allies and friends in a state of happiness and lasting peace, the Jewish nation and their high priest Hyrcanus have sent as envoys to them Straton, son of Theodotus, Apollonius, son of Alexander, Aeneas, son of Antipater, Aristobulus, son of Amyntas, and Sosipater, son of Philip, worthy and excellent men, and have made representations concerning certain particular matters, whereupon the Senate passed a decree concerning the matters on which they spoke, to the effect that King Antiochus, son of Antiochus,[25] shall do no injury to the Jews, the allies of the Romans; and that the fortresses, harbors, territory and whatever else he may have taken from them shall be restored to them;[26] and that it shall be lawful for them to export goods from their harbors and that no king or people exporting goods from the territory of the Jews or from their harbors shall be untaxed except only Ptolemy, king of Alexandria,[27] because he is our ally and friend; and that the garrison in Joppa shall be expelled, as they have requested.

'And one of our council, Lucius Pettius, a worthy and excellent man, has given orders that we shall take care that these things are done as the Senate has decreed, and that we shall see to the safe return of the envoys to their homes. We have also admitted Theodorus to the council and assembly, accepting from him the letter and the decree of the Senate; and after he had addressed us with great earnestness and pointed out the virtues and generosity of Hyrcanus and how he confers

---

25. It is usually assumed that the Syrian king Antiochus IX Cyzicenus, son of Antiochus VII Sidetes, is referred to here.

26. The reference is apparently to the harbors, notably Joppa, that had been seized from the Jews by Antiochus Sidetes.

27. Presumably the reference is to Ptolemy IX Alexander.

benefits upon all men generally, and in particular upon those who come to him, we deposited the documents in our public archives and passed a decree that we on our part, being allies of the Romans, would do everything possible on behalf of the Jews in accordance with the decree of the Senate.'

And when he delivered the letter to us, Theodorus also requested our magistrates to send a copy of the decree to Hyrcanus, as well as envoys who would inform him of the friendly interest of our people, and would urge him to preserve and increase his friendship with us and always be responsible for some act of good in the knowledge that he will receive a fitting recompense, and also remembering that in the time of Abraham, who was the father of all Hebrews, our ancestors were their friends, as we find in the public records.' (LCL)

Client State of Rome

BIBLIOGRAPHY

Baruch Kanael, "The Partition of Judaea by Gabinius," *IEJ* 7 (1957), 98–106.
Edith Mary Smallwood, "Gabinius' Organization of Palestine," *JJS* 18 (1967), 89–92.
Smallwood (1976).
Richard D. Sullivan, "The Dynasty of Judaea in the First Century," *ANRW* 2.8 (1977), 296–354.
Alfredo M. Rabello, "The Legal Condition of the Jews in the Roman Empire," *ANRW* 2.13 (1980), 662–766.
Daniel R. Schwartz, "Josephus on Hyrcanus II," in Fausto Parente and Joseph Sievers, eds, *Josephus and the History of the Greco-Roman Period: Essays in Memory of Morton Smith* (1994), 210–32.

Pompey's Capture of Jerusalem (63 BCE)

The Hasmonean alliance with Rome eventually turned Judaea into one of the many client states of Rome. The main terms and conditions on the basis of which Rome's client rulers served were the maintenance of stability in the country (especially important since Rome's two major rivals during the second and first centuries BCE were the Ptolemies of Egypt and the Seleucids of Syria, the immediate neighbors of Judaea) and supply of allied troops if Rome fought nearby. The death of Queen Salome Alexandra in 67 BCE resulted in a civil war between her elder son, Hyrcanus II, and her younger son, Aristobulus II. Rome, in the person of the Roman commander Pompey, in this as in later instances, became the arbiter in the internal Jewish dispute. In the year 63 BCE Pompey, having decided in favor of Hyrcanus II, defeated Aristobulus II's followers, captured the Temple in Jerusalem after a siege of three months, and, according to Josephus, killed no fewer than twelve thousand Jews in a general massacre. Pompey was careful to leave untouched the treasures of the Temple but he subjected the land, the extent of which was greatly reduced, to tribute. Hyrcanus himself was confirmed as high priest but not as king. Judaea was granted limited autonomy and was made dependent on the Roman governor of Syria.

8.21 Diodorus the Sicilian (first century BCE), *Historical Library* 40.2

During Pompey's stay in Damascus of Syria [64 BCE], Aristobulus, the king of the Jews, and Hyrcanus his brother came to him with their dispute over the kingship. Likewise, the leading men, more than two hundred in number, gathered to address the general and explain that their forefathers, having revolted from Demetrius, had sent an embassy to the senate, and received from them the leadership of the Jews, who were, moreover, to be free and autonomous, their ruler being called high priest, not king. Now, however, these men were lording it over them, having overthrown the ancient laws and enslaved the citizens in defiance of all justice; for it was by means of a horde of mercenaries, and by outrages and countless impious murders that they had established themselves as kings. Pompey put off till a later occasion the settlement of their rival claims, but as to the lawless behavior of the Jews and the wrongs committed against the Romans he bitterly upbraided the party of Hyrcanus. They deserved, he said, some graver and harsher visitation; nevertheless, in the spirit of Rome's traditional clemency, he could, if they were obedient henceforward, grant them pardon. (LCL)

8.22 Josephus, *Jewish Antiquities* 14.66–7, 70–3, 77–8

In the following passage Josephus describes Pompey's capture of Jerusalem, the slaughter of Jews (both by the Romans and by fellow Jews of the opposing faction) that accompanied it, and the suicide of Jews who could not bear their fate, while stressing Pompey's respect for the sanctity of the Temple.

When the city [Jerusalem] was taken [by Pompey], in the third month [of the siege] on the Fast Day [the ninth of Av], in the hundred and seventy-ninth Olympiad, in the consulship of Gaius Antonius and Marcus Tullius Cicero [63 BCE], and the enemy rushed in and were slaughtering the Jews in the Temple, those who were busied with the sacrifices none the less continued to perform the sacred ceremonies; nor were they compelled, either by fear for their lives or by the great number of those already slain, to run away, but thought it better to endure whatever they might have to suffer there beside the altars than to neglect any of the ordinances. . . . For some of the Jews were slain by the Romans, and others by their fellows [i.e., Jews of the opposing faction]; and there were some who hurled themselves down the precipices, and setting fire to their houses, burned themselves within them, for they could not bear to accept their fate. And so of the Jews there fell some twelve thousand, but of the Romans only a very few. . . .

And not light was the sin committed against the sanctuary, which before that time had never been entered or seen. For Pompey and not a few of his men went into it and saw what it was unlawful for any but the high priests to see. But though the golden table was there and the sacred lampstand and the libation vessels and a great quantity of spices, and beside these, in the treasury, the sacred moneys amounting to two thousand talents, he touched none of these because of piety, and in this respect also he acted in a manner worthy of his virtuous character. And on the morrow he instructed the temple servants to cleanse the Temple and to offer the customary sacrifice to God, and he restored the high priesthood to Hyrcanus because in various ways he had been useful to him and particularly because he had prevented the Jews throughout the country from fighting on Aristobulus' side; and those responsible for the war he executed by beheading. . . .

For this misfortune that befell Jerusalem Hyrcanus and Aristobulus were responsible because of their dissension. For we lost our freedom and became subject to the Romans, and the territory that we had gained by our arms and taken from the Syrians we were compelled to give back to them, and in addition the Romans exacted of us in a short space of time more than ten thousand talents; and the royal power that had formerly been bestowed on those who were high priests by birth became the privilege of commoners. (LCL)

The Aftermath of Pompey's Intervention

In the years that followed Pompey's intervention, until Herod was finally crowned as king in 40 BCE and managed to gain complete control of the land in 37 BCE, there were frequent revolts, and the situation changed several times. The Roman governor of Syria, Gabinius, crushed one of these revolts, led by Aristobulus II and his son Alexander, in the year 57 BCE, deprived Hyrcanus II of the title of ethnarch (vaguely "ruler" of the nation), left him merely with the title of high priest, and divided the country into five districts. Two years later Gabinius crushed another insurrection, this time led by Alexander, the son of Aristobulus II.

8.23 Josephus, *Jewish Antiquities* 14.127–30, 133–4, 136–7

A major change in the fortunes of the Jews occurred when Hyrcanus and his right-hand man Antipater (the father of Herod) aligned themselves with Julius Caesar after the latter's defeat of Pompey at Pharsalus (48 BCE). In particular, they gave crucial aid to Caesar in his war against King Ptolemy XII of Egypt. The passage below tells of Antipater's crucial role in enabling Mithridates of Pergamum to come to Caesar's aid. In the year 47 BCE Caesar appointed Antipater regent of Judaea and thereafter bestowed certain privileges upon him, namely citizenship and exemption from taxation. In addition, he bestowed privileges upon Judaea, notably that Roman troops should not winter in the country or raise levies; moreover, he restored the harbor of Joppa to the Jews. Antipater was, however, poisoned by one of his rivals in 43 BCE.

When Caesar, after his victory over Pompey and the latter's death, was fighting in Egypt, Antipater, the governor[28] of the Jews, under orders from Hyrcanus proved himself useful to Caesar in many ways. For when Mithridates of Pergamum, who was bringing an auxiliary force,

---

28. There is some doubt as to precisely what office this was. Apparently, it was a special office.

was unable to make his way through Pelusium,[29] and was delayed at Ascalon,[30] Antipater arrived with three thousand heavy-armed Jewish soldiers, and also managed to get the chiefs of Arabia to come to his aid; and it was owing to him that all the rulers of Syria furnished aid, not wishing to be outdone in their zeal for Caesar; among these were the prince Jamblichus and Ptolemy, the son of Soemus, who lived on Mount Lebanon, and almost all the cities. Mithridates then left Syria and came to Pelusium, and as its inhabitants would not admit him, besieged the city. Foremost in bravery was Antipater, who was the first to pull down part of the wall, and so opened a way for the others to pour into the city. This was how he took Pelusium. . . .

[In Egypt] Mithridates commanded the right wing, and Antipater the left. And when they met [the enemy] in battle, Mithridates' wing gave way and would have been in danger of suffering a very grave disaster, if Antipater, who had already defeated the enemy [opposite him], had not come running with his own soldiers along the bank of the river and rescued him, at the same time putting to flight the Egyptians who had defeated Mithridates. . . .

Mithridates thereupon wrote an account of this to Caesar, declaring that Antipater had been responsible for their victory and also for their safety; and as a result of this, Caesar commended Antipater on that occasion, and, what is more, made use of him for the most dangerous tasks throughout the entire war. The natural result was that Antipater was wounded in some of the battles.

Moreover, when Caesar in the course of time concluded the war and sailed to Syria, he honored him greatly; while confirming Hyrcanus in the highpriesthood, he gave Antipater Roman citizenship and exemption from taxation everywhere. (LCL)

Herod (King of Judaea 37–4 BCE)

BIBLIOGRAPHY

Frederic W. Farrar, *The Herods* (1898).

Arnaldo D. Momigliano, "Herod of Judaea," *Cambridge Ancient History*, vol. 10 (1934), 316–39.

Arnold H. M. Jones, *The Herods of Judaea* (1938).

Stewart Perowne, *The Life and Times of Herod the Great* (1956).

Samuel G. F. Brandon, "Herod the Great: Judaea's Most Able but Most Hated King," *HT* 12 (1962), 234–42; reprinted in his *Religion in Ancient History: Studies in Ideas, Men, and Events* (1969), 209–22.

William J. Gross, *Herod the Great* (1962).

Solomon Zeitlin, "Herod a Malevolent Maniac," *JQR* 54 (1963–4), 1–27; reprinted in his *Solomon Zeitlin's Studies in the Early History of Judaism*, vol. 1 (1973), 312–38.

Shimon Applebaum, "Herod I," *EJ*, vol. 8 (1971), 375–87.

Samuel Sandmel, *Herod: Profile of a Tyrant* (1967).

Michael Grant, *Herod the Great* (1971).

29. A city in Egypt.
30. A city in southern Palestine on the Mediterranean coast.

Schürer, vol. 1 (1973), 287–329.

Menahem Stern, "The Reign of Herod and the Herodian Dynasty," in Samuel Safrai and Menaham Stern, eds, in cooperation with David Flusser and Willem C. van Unnik, *The Jewish People in the First Century: Historical Geography, Political History, Social, Cultural and Religious Life and Institutions* (CRINT, vol. 1, 1974), 216–307.

Menahem Stern, "The Reign of Herod," in *World History of the Jewish People*, vol. 7 (1975), 71–123, 351–4, 388.

Menahem Stern, "Social and Political Realignments in Herodian Judaea," *JC* 2 (1982), 40–62.

Emilio Gabba, "The Finances of King Herod," in Aryeh Kasher, Uriel Rappaport, and Gideon Fuks, eds, *Greece and Rome in Eretz Israel: Collected Essays* (1990), 160–8.

James S. McLaren, *Power and Politics in Palestine: The Jews and the Governing of Their Land 100 BC–AD 70* (1991), 67–79.

Richard Fenn, *The Death of Herod* (1992).

The most colorful figure in the history of the Jews during this entire period was undoubtedly the infamous Herod, the son of the Idumaean Antipater. Though his personal problems would have required a team of psychiatrists (though perhaps, in the words of the historian Lewis Namier, psychologists should not be let loose on the dead), he managed to win the confidence of such diverse judges of responsible administration as Julius Caesar, Crassus, Cassius, Mark Antony, the Roman general Agrippa, and Augustus himself. His confidant, the non-Jew Nicolaus of Damascus, wrote voluminously, but clearly apologetically, about him (though his work is lost except for fragments). During the Parthian invasion in 40 BCE, Herod, Antipater's son, had escaped to Rome, where Antony and Octavian, who were then in control, concluding that he would be a faithful ally, proclaimed him king. Returning to Judaea in that year and with the massive help of Roman troops, Herod finally in 37 BCE defeated the then-ruling Antigonus, the Hasmonean son of Aristobulus II. Herod's position was different from that of his predecessors in that he did have a greater degree of independence, since the Romans saw in him a strong personality who preserved order in the country, whose loyalty to Rome was complete and without question, and whose military ability, as seen in his victory over the Nabateans and his success in holding his own against the feared Parthians, guaranteed secure borders. Inasmuch as there was a large non-Jewish population in the land, it was important that the ruler was not simultaneously high priest, as had been true under the Hasmoneans. Herod's own status was secure because he had cultivated personal relations with Augustus and with Agrippa, Augustus' commander, so that Josephus tells us (*War* 1.400), presumably based upon his source Nicolaus of Damascus, that what Herod valued more than all the privileges granted to him by Augustus was that in Augustus' affection he stood next after Agrippa. Herod had to contend with four hostile forces – the people (who, influenced by the Pharisees, resented the rule of an Idumaean), his family, the nobility in the Sanhedrin, and the Hasmoneans whom he had displaced. Though his secret police were everywhere and reported to Herod any murmurings of discontent, he was actually popular with many because the Hasmoneans had antagonized many; indeed, according to the Church Father Epiphanius, he was even recognized by some as the Messiah. He gave jobs to many through his ambitious building projects; and, in particular, he built a splendid Temple. He relieved a famine in 25 BCE, even selling the crown jewels. He reduced taxes by a third in 20 BCE and by a fourth in 13 BCE. It has been argued that because of his rule the Jewish state was preserved from extinction for a century.

8.24 Josephus, *Jewish War* 1.393–7 (30 BCE)

The following passage tells how Herod was crowned king by Octavian (Augustus) and how Augustus, impressed with Herod's pomp and splendor, substantially enlarged his kingdom, in particular granting him several port cities. The latter had considerable economic consequences in that these ports gave Herod an important position in the trade in luxury goods between the East and Asia Minor and Greece and must have enlarged his income greatly. In addition (*War* 1.399), after the Roman governor of Syria had cleared a portion of Syria that had been infested by bandits, Augustus gave this territory to Herod, confident that he would prevent it from being used as a base for raids upon Damascus, and even gave him the position of procurator of all Syria.

Thereupon, having embraced the king [Herod], he [Octavian (Augustus)] placed the diadem on his head, and the grant [of royal power] was announced by a decree in which he amply and generously expressed his praise of the man. Herod, after conciliating Octavian with presents, sought pardon for Alexas, one of Antony's friends, who was a suppliant; but Caesar's anger prevailed – he had many complaints against this petitioner and rejected the plea.

Afterwards [30 BCE], when Caesar [Augustus] passed through Syria on his way to Egypt, Herod entertained him for the first time with all the royal pomp. He accompanied the [future] emperor on horseback when he reviewed his forces at Ptolemais. He entertained him and all his friends at a banquet, and he also made all provision for the good cheer of the rest of the army. Then, for those marching to Pelusium across the desert, and likewise for their return, he made provision to furnish them with ample water; indeed, there were no necessities that the army lacked. The thought could not but occur both to Caesar himself and to his soldiers that Herod's kingdom was far too small considering the services he had rendered. Therefore, when Caesar came to Egypt after the death of Cleopatra and Antony, he not only heaped other honors upon Herod, but also added to his kingdom the territory that Cleopatra had cut off, and, in addition, not only Gadara and Hippus and Samaria, but also the maritime towns of Gaza, Anthedon, Joppa, and Strato's Tower [Caesarea]. He further presented to him, as a bodyguard, 400 Gauls, who had previously guarded Cleopatra. And nothing so much motivated Caesar in making these gifts as the generous spirit of the man who received them. (M.R.)

8.25 Josephus, Jewish War 1.422–5

Here Josephus notes Herod's lavish gifts, including gymnasia, temples, and theaters (which, if they had been in Palestine, would certainly have offended the Jews) to numerous cities outside his kingdom, namely in Greece, Asia Minor, and Syria. Apparently, he engaged in mutual gift-giving, in which he seems to have come out ahead overall. The best evidence is that he did not pay tribute.

After founding all these places he [Herod] displayed his magnanimity to numerous cities ouside his kingdom. He provided gymnasia for Tripolis, Damascus, and Ptolemais; a wall for Byblus; halls, stoas, temples, and agoras for Berytus and Tyre; theaters for Sidon and Damascus; an aqueduct and baths for Laodicea-on-the-Sea; and for Ascalon baths, too, sumptuous fountains, and colonnades, admirable for their architecture and their size; for others he dedicated groves and assigned meadow lands. Many cities, as though they were part of his kingdom, received from him grants of land; for others, like Cos, he set up sources of revenue to maintain the office of gymnasiarch[31] annually in perpetuity, to ensure that this office should never lapse. Wheat he bestowed on all who asked. To Rhodes he contributed money again and again for ship-building, and when their Pythian temple burned down, he rebuilt it on a grander scale at his own expense. Do I need to mention his gifts to the people of Lycia or Samos, or his liberality throughout all of Ionia, to meet all needs? The Athenians and Spartans, the people of Nicopolis and of Pergamum in Mysia, are they not laden with Herod's offerings? And that public square in Syrian Antioch, once shunned on account of the mud – did he not pave its twenty stades[32] with polished marble and adorn it with a stoa of equal size as a shelter from the rain? (M.R.)

8.26 Josephus, Jewish Antiquities 16.184–5 (ca. 10 BCE)

Herod, obsessed with suspicion that they were plotting against him, put to death his wife Mariamne and his two sons by her. His non-Jewish executive secretary, Nicolaus of Damascus, wrote a lengthy history (extant only in fragments) in the course of which he carefully defended his patron, though Josephus is critical of Nicolaus.

Since he [Nicolaus] lived in Herod's realm and was one of his associates, he wrote to please him and to be of service to him, dwelling only on those things that redounded to his glory, and transforming his obviously unjust acts into the opposite or concealing them with the greatest care. For example, in his desire to give a color of respectability to the putting to death of Mariamne [Herod's wife] and her sons, which had been so cruelly ordered by the king, Nicolaus makes false charges of licentiousness against her and of treachery against the youths. And throughout his work he has been consistent in excessively

31. The gymnasiarch was in charge of the games held on festivals.
32. A stade was approximately 600 feet.

praising the king for his just acts, and zealously apologizing for his unlawful ones. (LCL)

8.27 Josephus, *Jewish Antiquities* 15.267–9, 271, 272, 273, 274–6

Herod offended his Jewish subjects by adopting a number of pagan practices, notably the introduction of athletic contests, the practice of throwing men to wild beasts, and trophies with images upon them. On the other hand, we must, however, note that Herod carefully avoided erecting pagan temples in Jewish cities and did not build gymnasia (with their pagan connotations of exercise in the nude) in his entire realm, though he provided gifts of gymnasia, temples, market-places, theaters, baths, fountains, colonnades, and an aqueduct for various cities outside his realm, notably in Syria, Asia Minor, and Greece, and even endowed the Olympic Games in Greece.

Herod departed still further from the ancestral laws, and by foreign practices gradually corrupted their ancient institutions. Consequently, what had been inviolable was not a little impaired by us at a later time, for those observances that formerly led the multitude to piety were neglected.

For in the first place, he established athletic contests to be held every fifth year in honor of Caesar [Augustus], and he built a theater in Jerusalem and also a very large amphitheater in the plain. Both of these were conspicuously lavish, but foreign to Jewish custom, for the use of such buildings and the exhibition of such shows were not traditional. Nevertheless, he did celebrate this festival every five years in the most splendid manner, announcing it to the neighboring peoples, and summoning men from every people. Athletes and other types of contestants were attracted from every land, both by the hope of winning the prizes offered and by the glory of victory. . . .

He also offered no small rewards for four-horse chariots, two-horse chariots, and riding horses. . . . All around the theater were inscriptions also concerning Caesar [Augustus] and trophies of the peoples that he had conquered in war, all made for Herod of pure gold and silver. . . .

There also was a supply of wild beasts, a great number of lions having been assembled and other animals, extraordinary in strength or rare in species. . . .

To native Jews this was a conspicuous break with the customs venerated by them. For it appeared a glaring impiety to throw men to wild beasts for the pleasure of spectators, and impiety to change their customs for foreign practices; but above all it was the trophies that irked them most; for, thinking them to be images surrounded by weapons, they were highly displeased, because it was not their national custom to venerate such images. (M.R.)

8.28 Josephus, *Jewish Antiquities* 16.12–15

Herod knew how to win the favor of the Romans, notably through lavish receptions of their envoys, in this case through lavish entertainment of the Roman leader Marcus Agrippa, the right-hand man of the Emperor Augustus.

After disposing of these matters, when Herod learned that Marcus Agrippa had again sailed from Italy to Asia, he hastened to him and asked him to come to him into his kingdom and receive what he might expect from one who was a host and his friend. Agrippa, acquiescing in his earnest entreaties, yielded and came into Judaea [14 BCE]. Herod omitted nothing that might please him, received him in his newly built cities, and, showing him the buildings, entertained him and his friends with enjoyable food and luxuries. He did this at Sebaste and Caesarea, the harbor that he had built, and in the fortresses he had built at great expense – Alexandreion, Herodeion, and Hyrcania. He also brought him to the city of Jerusalem, where all the people met Agrippa in their holiday garments and welcomed him with acclamations. Agrippa offered a hecatomb to God and feasted the people, who were not second in numbers to those in the greatest of cities. Agrippa might have remained longer, so great was the pleasure, but the season of the year was pressing . . . and he returned again to Ionia. (M.R.)

8.29 Josephus, *Jewish Antiquities* 16.60–1

Herod's close connections with influential circles in Rome (notably Antony, Augustus, and the general Agrippa) were highly useful to the Jews of the Diaspora. Indeed, he turned out to be a champion of those Jews, as we see in the case of the Jews of Asia Minor, who had been prevented by the non-Jewish inhabitants from observing their ancestral customs. When Herod met the Roman general Agrippa in Asia Minor, the Jews appealed to Agrippa; and Herod assigned his right-hand man Nicolaus of Damascus to plead the case of the Jews. It was because of his personal friendship with Herod that Agrippa granted the petition of the Jews.

Thereupon Agrippa, who perceived that they [the Jews of Asia Minor] had been subjected to violence, replied that because of Herod's good-will and friendship for him he was ready to grant the Jews all they might ask for, and, he said, their requests seemed just in themselves, so that even if they were to ask for still more, he would not hesitate to give them this, provided, of course, that it did not cause the Roman government any trouble. And since they asked that the rights which they had formerly received should not be annulled, he would confirm their rights to continue to observe their own customs without suffering mistreatment.

Having spoken in this way, he dismissed the gathering, whereupon Herod went up to him and embraced him in grateful acknowledgment of his friendly attitude toward himself. To this too Agrippa responded in friendly fashion and behaved like an equal, putting his arms around Herod and embracing him in turn. (LCL)

8.30 Macrobius (first half of the fifth century CE), *Saturnalia* 2.4.11

Herod was particularly notorious for the executions that he ordered for members of his own family – his wife Mariamne, three of his fifteen children, three brothers-in-law, one mother-in-law, and one grandfather-in-law (though perhaps, to his credit, he twice resisted the charms of the famous Cleopatra). In this he was similar to the conduct of the Roman Emperor Caligula, who was responsible for the deaths of his grand-uncle, grandmother, nephew, father-in-law, and cousin; as well as to the conduct of Nero, who was responsible for the death of his mother, two wives, step-father, step-brother, and step-sister. Apparently, his conduct became proverbial, as we see in this quotation, which, to be sure, errs in stating that his sons were under the age of two when they were executed.

On hearing that in Syria boys under two years of age had been ordered killed by Herod, king of the Jews, among them even his own son, Augustus said: 'I would rather be Herod's swine than his son.'[33] (M.R.)

8.31 Coins of Herod

The legends of Herod's coinage are always in Greek. Like the Hasmonean kings, he did not place his portrait on Judaean coins, presumably because he was aware that to do so would arouse passions against him in view of the Jewish prohibition of sculpture. Indeed, no portrait statues of Herod are known.

a. Obverse: Tripod and bowl. KING HEROD; 3rd year.
    Reverse: Incense burner, star, palm branches. (M.R.)

b. Obverse: Winged caduceus. KING HEROD; Year 3.
    Reverse: Pomegranate. (M.R.)

c. Obverse: Cornucopia. KING HEROD.
    Reverse: Eagle. (M.R.)

Disorders after the Death of Herod

After the death of Herod in the year 4 BCE his kingdom was divided. His son Archelaus (by a Samaritan woman, Malthace) received the greater part of his kingdom, consisting of Judaea, Samaria (to the north), and Idumaea (to the south); another son, Herod Antipas, familiar from the Gospels, received Galilee and Peraea (east of the River Jordan); a third son, Philip, received a small region to the north and east.

8.32 Josephus, *Jewish Antiquities* 17.299–301, 304, 307, 314.

There was a popular demand in Judaea not only for relief from taxation but also for the actual abolition of the monarchy. Immediately disorders broke out. Augustus dispatched Quintilius Varus, his relative and governor of Syria, to restore order in Judaea. Meanwhile, a delegation of Jews came to Rome to ask the Emperor Augustus to abolish the Jewish kingship altogether. Augustus reaffirmed Herod's will but appointed

---

33. The remark is a pun based on the similarity of the words for swine (*hus*) and son (*huios*) in Greek.

Archelaus not as king but ethnarch, a lesser title for the ruler of the nation, and promised to elevate him to the higher title if he should prove worthy.

Having made these arrangements [for order in Judaea], Varus left, as a garrison for Jerusalem, the legion already there, and hastened to Antioch. Meanwhile, for Archelaus new troubles began in Rome, for the following reasons. There arrived at Rome an embassy of Jews – Varus had permitted the people to send it – concerning a request for autonomy. The envoys sent with the consent of the people were fifty in number, and there joined them more than 8,000 of the Jews in Rome. When Caesar [Augustus] had assembled a council of his friends and the leading Romans in the temple of Apollo, built by him at great expense, the envoys arrived together with the crowd of local Jews, as did Archelaus with his friends. . . .

When permission was given to the envoys of the Jews, who were waiting to speak for the abolition of the monarchy, they turned to accusing the lawless acts of Herod. They set forth that while he had been a king in name, he had assumed for himself the most ruthless practices of various tyrants, and had joined these together to use in the destruction of the Jews, and he had not been averse to inventing many new practices of his own natural bent. . . . He had reduced the people to helpless poverty after taking over Judaea in as prosperous a condition as few have ever been. . . .

The sum and substance of their petition was that they be delivered from monarchy and such kinds of rule, be added [to the province of] Syria, and be under the governors sent there. . . .[34] (M.R.)

The End of Archelaus' Rule

8.33 Josephus, Jewish Antiquities 17.342–4

The rule of Archelaus (4 BCE to 6 CE) was brutal and tyrannical. Eventually, a delegation of Jewish and Samaritan leaders came to Rome to bring charges before Augustus against him. Augustus summoned Archelaus, banished him to exile in Gaul, and placed his territory under direct Roman rule through procurators.

In the tenth year of Archelaus' rule, the leading men among the Jews and Samaritans, finding his cruelty and tyranny intolerable, brought charges against him before Caesar [Augustus] the moment they learned that Archelaus had disobeyed his instructions to show moderation in dealing with them. Accordingly, when Caesar heard the charges, he became angry, and summoning the man who looked after Archelaus' affairs at Rome – he was also named Archelaus – for he thought it beneath him to write to Archelaus (the ethnarch), he said to him, 'Go, sail at once and bring him here to us without delay.' So this

---

34. Augustus partitioned Herod's realm among his sons, Archelaus, Antipas, and Philip. Archelaus was appointed ethnarch of the southern part of Herod's kingdom, i.e., Judaea, Samaria, and Idumaea. In 6 CE Archelaus was deposed, and his realm was transformed into the Roman province of Judaea.

man immediately set sail, and on arriving in Judaea and finding Archelaus feasting with his friends, he revealed to him the will of Caesar and speeded his departure. And when Archelaus arrived, Caesar gave a hearing to some of his accusers, and also let him speak, and then sent him into exile, assigning him a residence in Vienna, a city in Gaul, and confiscating his property. (LCL)

Temporary Restoration of a Jewish King: Agrippa I, King of Judaea (ruled 41–4 CE)

BIBLIOGRAPHY

David C. Braund, *Rome and the Friendly King* (1984).
Daniel R. Schwartz, *Agrippa I: the Last King of Judaea* (1990).

8.34 Josephus, *Jewish Antiquities* 18.161–7

An outstanding example of Jewish power in the highest circles of the imperial Roman court may be seen in Agrippa I. Agrippa had been brought up in Rome side by side with the Roman imperial family. At one point he had managed to borrow huge sums of money which he used to win imperial favor and had even contemplated suicide. When evidence was brought that Agrippa had expressed the wish that Tiberius would relinquish his throne in favor of Gaius Caligula, Agrippa was imprisoned. When Tiberius died, Caligula named Agrippa as king of Herod Philip's tetrarchy.

When Agrippa had reached Puteoli, he sent a letter to the emperor Tiberius, who was then living at Capri, informing him that he had come to see and pay court to him and asking for permission to land at Capri. Tiberius without hesitation wrote him a courteous reply, expressing his particular pleasure upon his safe return to Capri. When Agrippa arrived there, Tiberius showed no less goodwill towards him than he had indicated in his letter and made him a welcome guest. On the following day the emperor received a letter from Herennius Capito stating that Agrippa, after borrowing 300,000 drachmas, had allowed the time stipulated for repayment to pass and that when he was asked to pay, he had gone off in flight from the territory under his jurisdiction, thus rendering him powerless to sue and recover the money. Upon reading this letter the emperor was hurt to the quick and ordered that Agrippa's visits should be barred until he had repaid the debt.

Undismayed by the emperor's anger, Agrippa asked Antonia, the mother of Germanicus and of the future emperor Claudius, to grant him a loan of 300,000 drachmas so that he might not lose the friendship of Tiberius. Antonia, both because she still remembered Berenice his mother – for the two ladies had been deeply attached to each other – and because Agrippa had been brought up with Claudius and his circle, provided the money. When he had discharged the debt, there was no longer any obstacle to his friendship with Tiberius.

Subsequently the emperor Tiberius recommended his grandson[35] to Agrippa and bade him always accompany him on his excursions. When

---

35. Tiberius Gemellus, the son of Drusus the Younger.

Agrippa was received as a friend by Antonia, he took to attendance upon her grandson Gaius [Caligula], who was held in the highest honor because of the popularity enjoyed by his father [Germanicus].

Now there was, in addition, a certain man of Samaritan origin who was a freedman of the emperor. Agrippa managed to borrow a million drachmas from him and repaid the money that he had borrowed from Antonia. The rest of the money he spent in paying court to Gaius, with whom he consequently rose to higher favor. (LCL)

8.35 Josephus, *Jewish Antiquities* 19.238–9, 242–6, 265–6, 274

The following passage indicates the key role played by Agrippa in advising Claudius how to deal with the Senate in order to become independent of them while attaining the imperial throne after the assassination of Gaius Caligula.

On hearing of the kidnapping of Claudius by the soldiers [who sought to proclaim him as emperor], Agrippa forced his way to him; and finding him perplexed and on the point of yielding to the senate [which sought to make him subordinate to themselves], he stirred him up and bade him make a bid for the empire. After these words to Claudius Agrippa returned home. On being summoned by the senate, ... [Agrippa said]: 'I must speak without shilly-shallying because my speech has a bearing on your security. You know, of course, that the army that will fight for Claudius has long trained to bear arms, while ours will be a motley rabble consisting of men who have unexpectedly been released from slavery and who are consequently hard to control. We shall fight against experts, having brought into play men who do not even know how to draw their swords. Therefore my judgment is to send a deputation to Claudius to persuade him to lay down his office; and I am ready to act as ambassador.'

So he spoke, and on their agreeing to his proposal he was dispatched with others. He thereupon recounted to Claudius in private the confusion of the senate and advised him to reply rather imperiously, speaking with the dignity of one in authority. Claudius accordingly replied that he did not wonder that the senate was not pleased at the prospect of submitting to authority because they had been oppressed by the brutality of those who had previously held the imperial office. But he promised to behave with such propriety that they would taste for themselves the savor of an era of fair dealing. . . .

King Agrippa then approached Claudius, and besought him to take a kinder attitude to the senators; for if any harm came to the senate, he would have no other subjects over whom to rule. Claudius agreed. . . .

Claudius speedily purged the army of all unreliable units. He then promulgated an edict whereby he both confirmed the rule of Agrippa, which Gaius had presented to him, and delivered a panegyric on the king. He also added to Agrippa's dominions all the other lands that had been ruled by King Herod, his grandfather, namely, Judaea and Samaria. (LCL)

8.36 Josephus, *Antiquities* 19.328–31: Agrippa Compared with Herod

When Agrippa returned to Judaea as king, he won the favor of the Jews by his pious behavior. In the following passage Josephus goes out of his way to compare his generous nature, particularly toward his Jewish subjects, with the meanspiritedness of Herod.

Now King Agrippa was by nature generous in his gifts and made it a point of honor to be highminded towards gentiles; and by expending massive sums he raised himself to high fame. He took pleasure in conferring favors and rejoiced in popularity, thus being in no way similar in character to Herod, who was king before him. The latter had an evil nature, relentless in punishment and unsparing in action against the objects of his hatred. It was generally admitted that he [Herod] was on more friendly terms with Greeks than with Jews. For instance, he adorned the cities of foreigners by giving them money, building baths and theaters, erecting temples in some and porticoes in others, whereas there was not a single city of the Jews on which he deigned to bestow even minor restoration or any gift worth mentioning.[36] Agrippa, on the contrary, had a gentle disposition and he was a benefactor to all alike. He was benevolent to those of other nations and exhibited his generosity to them also; but to his compatriots he was proportionately more generous and more compassionate. He enjoyed residing in Jerusalem and did so constantly; and he scrupulously observed the traditions of his people. He neglected no rite of purification, and no day passed for him without the prescribed sacrifice. (LCL)

Anti-Roman Sentiment among the Jews

BIBLIOGRAPHY

Moses Hadas, "Roman Allusions in Rabbinic Literture," *PQ* 8 (1929), 369–87.
Saul Lieberman, "Roman Legal Institutions in Early Rabbinics and in the Acta Martyrum," *JQR* 35 (1944–5), 1–55.
Geza Vermes, "Ancient Rome in Post-Biblical Jewish Literature," in his *Post-Biblical Jewish Studies* (1975), 215–24.
Isaac Herzog, "Rome in the Talmud and in the Midrash," in his *Judaism: Law and Ethics* (1976), 83–91.
Nicholas R. M. de Lange, "Jewish Attitudes to the Roman Empire," in Peter D. A. Garnsey and C. R. Whittaker, eds, *Imperialism in the Ancient World* (1978), 255–81.
Louis H. Feldman, "Abba Kolon and the Founding of Rome," *JQR* 81 (1990–1), 449–82.
Louis H. Feldman, "Some Observations on Rabbinic Reaction to Roman Rule in Third Century Palestine," HUCA 63 (1992), 1–43.

Despite constant protection of their privileges, to many Jews Rome, from the middle of the first century BCE, symbolized the grand oppressor. This

---

36. Though it is true that Herod gave money for the erection of monuments in Rhodes, Athens, Sparta, and many other cities outside Palestine, it is not true that he completely neglected buildings in Jewish cities, since, of course, his most magnificent work was the restoration of the Temple in Jerusalem.

sentiment had its origins not only in Rome's destruction of Jewish independence, but in increasing belief in a Messiah and in hopes that at times characteristically took the form of apocalyptic prophecy. In the case of the rabbinic passages, we should note that there are many scholars who do not accept the ascription to particular rabbis at face value but rather look at the date when the work was codified in which their opinions appear.

8.37 Anonymous, *Sibylline Oracles*, Book 3, verses 46–62, 350–80 (*ca.* 42 BCE)

The concept of a Jewish prophetess, a Sybil foretelling the doom of the oppressor, namely Rome, was apparently adapted by the Jews in the second century BCE in Egypt from the pagan Sibylline Oracles, the most famous of which was associated with the Cumaean Sibyl immortalized by Virgil in Book 6 of the *Aeneid*.

When Rome will rule over Egypt, then, delaying until then, the mighty kingdom of the immortal king will appear among men, and a holy lord will come who will rule over the whole world for all ages of future time. And then will inexorable wrath fall on the men of Latium. Three men[37] will ravage Rome with pitiable doom, and all men will perish in their own homes, when the fiery torrent will flow down from heaven. Ah, miserable me, when will that day come, and the judgment of immortal God, the mighty king? Yet still be built, you cities, and all be adorned with temples and stadia, with agoras and images of gold, silver and stone, that you may come thus to that bitter day. For it will come, when the smell of brimstone will come down upon all men. But I will tell of each one, in how many cities men will suffer ill. . . .

For all the wealth Rome took from tribute-paying Asia, three times as much will Asia get back from Rome, paying her back for her destructive arrogance. And for all the men taken out of Asia to dwell in Italy, twenty times as many men will serve as slaves in poverty in Asia, and a thousandfold will be the requital.

O daughter of Latin Rome, reveling in gold and luxury, often drunken with your weddings of many wooers, you will be a slave-bride in dishonor, and often will your mistress cut off your luxuriant hair, and in pursuit of justice cast you down from heaven to earth, and again raise you from earth to heaven, because men gave themselves over to evil and unjust living.

And Samos will become a sand, Delos will disappear, and Rome become a mere alley, and all that has been foretold will be accomplished, but no one will take account of the ruin of Smyrna. There will be an avenger, through evil counsels and the baseness of her leaders.

And calm peace will make its way to the land of Asia, and Europe be blessed then, the air fruitful year after year, healthy, without frost and hail, bearing everything – birds and beasts that move on the earth. Blessed shall be the man and woman who live to see that time, as are all who live on the Isles of the Blest. For all law and justice will come from the starry heaven upon men, and with them prudent harmony,

37. The triumvirate of Octavian, Antony, and Lepidus is meant.

best of all gifts for mortals, and love and faith and hospitable ways. But lawlessness, blame, envy, anger, madness, and poverty will depart from among men. Necessity will depart from men in those days, together with murder and destructive strife and pitiable wrangling, and theft by night and every ill. (M.R.)

8.38 *4 Ezra* 11:40–5.

The following bitter attack, the *Apocalypse of Ezra*, also known as *4 Ezra*, on the Roman Empire (symbolized by the eagle) was written in the aftermath of the destruction of the Temple. The work is a collection of visions ascribed to Ezra but written about 95 to 100 CE.

With your power you [the Romans] control the times with great terror and the whole world with vilest oppression, and you have inhabited the world for so long a time with fraud. And you have judged the world without righteousness. You have oppressed the gentle and injured the peaceful. You have hated those who speak the truth and have cherished the liars, and you have destroyed the homes of those who have prospered and razed the walls of those who did you no harm. And your insolence has ascended to the Most High, and your arrogance to the Mighty One. And the Most High looked upon your times, and, behold, they are finished, and its time is over. Therefore, you, O eagle, shall vanish and not be seen, and your horrible wings, and abominable feathers, and your evil head, and your wicked claws, and your whole worthless body. (M.R.)

8.39 *Sifre Deuteronomy* 43, p. 81a (edited *ca.* at the end of the fourth century CE)

The calamity of the destruction of the Temple and the burning of Jerusalem was compounded by the punishment visited by the Emperor Vespasian on Jews throughout the empire – the Jewish Tax. With the Temple lost, sacrifices were not resumed, the priesthood was eclipsed, and the Sadducees apparently, so far as we know, ceased to exist as a sect. Some of the rabbis, as would be expected, expressed bitter attitudes toward the Romans. In the anecdote below the great Rabbi Aqiba speaks of the Romans as those who anger God.

Once Rabban Gamaliel, Rabbi Joshua, Rabbi Eleazar ben Azariah, and Rabbi Aqiba [Palestinian rabbis who flourished at the end of the first century CE] were entering Rome. They heard the sound of the din [of Rome] from Puteoli, 120 miles away. They [the others] began to weep, but Rabbi Aqiba laughed. Rabbi Aqiba said to them, 'Why are you weeping?' They said to him, 'And why are you laughing?' He said to them, 'And why are you weeping?' They said to him, 'Shall we not weep, when Gentiles, idolaters, sacrifice to their idols and bow down to statues and dwell in security and peace, and the house of the footstool of our God will be food for fire and a lair for beasts of the field?' Said he to them, 'That is precisely why I laughed. If indeed he has dealt thus with those who anger him, how much the more will He do for those who do His will!' (L.H.F.)

8.40 Avoth de-Rabbi Nathan (ca. early third century CE) A.28

In this passage the patriarch Rabban Gamaliel II, who, by virtue of his position as the *de facto* head of the Jewish community in Palestine, would have been expected to be careful to be on good terms with the Romans, speaks bitterly of the way in which the Romans oppress and offend the Jews.

Rabban Gamaliel [II, Palestinian, end of the first century CE] said, 'With four things the [Roman] empire devours [us]: tolls, baths, theaters, and taxes from crops.'[38] (L.H.F.)

8.41 Babylonian Talmud, *Pesaḥim* 118b (edited *ca.* 500 CE.)

The rabbis were well aware of the tradition that the Romans were descended from Esau, Jacob's twin brother, and that therefore there was, paradoxically, a special relationship between the Jews and the Romans; but they also comment bitterly on this relationship as well, as seen in the passage below.

[Rabbi Ishmael (Palestinian, end of first and beginning of second century CE) said]: Egypt is destined to bring a gift to the Messiah. He will think not to accept it from them, but the Holy One, blessed be He, will instruct him, 'Accept it from them: they furnished hospitality to My children in Egypt. . . .'
     Then Ethiopia shall argue with herself: If those [the Egyptians] who enslaved them are thus [treated], how much the more we, who did not enslave them! At that the Holy One, blessed be He, shall bid him: 'Accept it from them.' . . .
     Then shall the wicked Roman state argue with herself: If those who are not their brethren are thus [accepted], how much the more we, their brethren. But the Holy One, blessed be He, will say to [the angel] Gabriel: 'Rebuke the wild beast of the reeds [*kaneh*]; the multitude ['*adath*] of the bulls' (Ps 68:31): rebuke the wild beast [Rome] and take thee possession [*keneh*] of the congregation ['*edah*]. Another interpretation: 'Rebuke the wild beast of the reeds,' i.e., that dwells among the reeds, as it is written, 'The boar out of the wood doth ravage it, that which moveth in the field feedeth on it.' (Ps 80:14).[39] Rabbi Ḥiyya bar Abba [Palestinian, third and fourth centuries CE] interpreted it in Rabbi Joḥanan's [Palestinian, third century CE] name: Rebuke the wild beast all of whose actions may be recorded with the same pen.[40] (Soncino)

38. The meaning may be that the Roman Empire enjoys its world through four things – tolls, baths, theaters, and taxes from crops.
39. The boar, according to this interpretation, represents Rome; the allusion is to the tradition (*Midrash Song of Songs Rabbah* 1.6) that when Solomon married the daughter of Pharaoh an angel planted a reed at the site where Rome was built.
40. The word *kaneh* is here connected with the word meaning "feather," "quill," "pen." In other words, all the activities of the Romans show the same hostility to the Jews.

8.42 Pesiqta Rabbati 21 (*ca.* ninth century CE)

In the passage below Rabbi Joshua ben Ḥananiah, who is said to have had more contacts with non-Jews than any other rabbi of his era, speaks of the Romans in the most disparaging terms.

Hadrian – may his bones rot! – [said] . . . to Rabbi Joshua ben Ḥananiah [Palestinian, first and centuries CE]: '. . . Come out and sport with me in the cities.' But in every place to which he brought him, he saw his statue brought in.

And he [Joshua] said to him, 'What is that?'

And Hadrian answered, 'My statue.'

Then he took him to a latrine. He [Joshua] said to him, 'My Lord, O King, I see that you are ruler in this whole city, since I see that your statue has been brought into every place, but in this place here it has not been brought.'

Hadrian answered, 'You want to be "the elder" of the Jews? Is it proper for the honor of a king that his statue should be brought into a contemptible, abominable, filthy place?'

So he answered him, 'Do your ears want to hear what your mouth says? Is it consonant with the exalted position of the Holy One – praised be He! – that his name should be mixed with murderers, adulterers, thieves?'

So he pushed him aside and went away from there. (L.H.F.)

8.43 Midrash Genesis Rabbah 67.8 (*ca.* fifth century CE)

In the passage below one of the rabbis gives an etymology of the Roman term "senator" as one who hates.

'And Esau hated' [Gen 27:41]. Rabbi Eleazar bar Yosi [Palestinian, second century CE]: 'He became a senator – one who hates, one who avenges, one who bears ill-will.[41] Until today senators from Rome are so called.' (L.H.F.)

8.44 Mishnah, Avoth 2:3 (edited *ca.* 220 CE)

The office of patriarch, said to go back to Jose ben Joezer (*ca.* 160 BCE) and said, according to the Talmud, to be that of the presiding officer of the Sanhedrin, was, in effect, that of the religious leader of the Jews in Palestine. Under the Romans the patriarch was in the very delicate position of standing up for Jewish interests while at the same time being careful not to antagonize the Roman administration. One detects a note of caution and suspicion toward the Romans in the advice given below by the patriarch Gamaliel III, the son of Rabbi Judah the Prince, who lived in the first half of the third century.

Be ye circumspect [in your dealings] with the ruling authorities [i.e., the Romans], for they suffer not a man to be near them except it be for

---

41. He derives the word *senator* from the first letters of the Hebrew words *sone* (one who hates), *noqem* (one who avenges), and *noter* (one who bears ill-will).

their own requirement; they show themselves as friends when it is to their own interest, but they do not stand by a man in the hour of his distress. (Soncino)

8.45 Midrash Genesis Rabbah 16.4 (*ca.* fifth century CE)

Here a third-century rabbi speaks of the Roman Empire as wicked and as being inferior to the Greeks not only in religion and athletics but even in language.

Rabbi Huna [Babylonian, third century CE] said: In three respects the Greek realm was superior to this wicked empire [Rome]: in temples,[42] in athletic contests involving boxing and wrestling,[43] and in language. (L.H.F.)

8.46 Babylonian Talmud, *Avodah Zarah* 2a–b (edited *ca.* 500 CE)

In this passage a third-century rabbi, while acknowledging the power of the Romans, bitterly declares that the Romans have acquired their wealth merely to satisfy their bodily desires.

Rabbi Ḥanina bar Papa [Palestinian, third and fourth centuries CE] – some say Rabbi Simlai [Palestinian, third century CE] – expounded thus: In times to come, the Holy One, blessed be He, will take a scroll of the Law in His embrace and proclaim: 'Let him who has occupied himself herewith, come and take his reward. . . .' Thereupon the kingdom of Edom [Rome] will enter first before Him. Why first? Because they are the most important.[44] Whence do we know they are so important? Because it is written: 'And he shall devour the whole earth and shall tread it down and break it in pieces' [Dan 7:23]; and Rabbi Joḥanan [ben Nappaḥa, Palestinian, third century CE] says that this refers to Rome, whose power is known to the whole world. . . . The Holy One, blessed be He, will then say to them: "Wherewith have you occupied yourselves?" They will reply: "O Lord of the Universe, we have established many market-places, we have erected many baths, we have accumulated much gold and silver, and all this we did only for the sake of Israel, that they might [have leisure] for occupying themselves with the study of the Torah."[45] The Holy One, blessed be He, will say in reply: "You foolish ones among peoples, all that which you have done, you have only done to satisfy your own desires. You have established market-places to place courtesans therein; baths, to

42. The word in the text (*naos*) perhaps should be *naus* ("ship-building") or *nomos* ("law").

43. The word *pankration* perhaps should be *pannukhos* ("all-night watches" or "camp vigils") or *portix* ("porticoes") or *pinakotheke* ("picture-gallery") or *pinax* ("painting").

44. The fact that the Romans are given first place among the nations despite the fact that the Babylonian Talmud was redacted in Persia *ca.* 500 under the Sassanian dynasty would seem to indicate that even though the Roman Empire was supposedly tottering, it was still regarded as mighty, at least in the eyes of some of the rabbis.

45. Presumably an allusion to the privileges which the Jews enjoyed under the Roman Empire and to their relative economic prosperity which enabled many Jewish students to pursue their studies without material worries.

revel in them; [as to the distribution of] silver and gold, that is mine, as it is written: 'Mine is the silver and Mine is the gold, saith the Lord of Hosts' [Hag 2:8]; are there any among you who have been declaring this?" And this is nought else than the Torah, as it is said: 'And this is the Law which Moses set before the children of Israel'" [Deut 4:44]. They will then depart crushed in spirit. (Soncino)

8.47 *Midrash Psalms* 80.6 (*ca.* tenth century CE)

In particular, as noted below, one of the rabbis attacks the hypocrisy of the Roman administrators and the injustice of their legal proceedings.

Just as the pig stretches out its hoofs and says, 'I am pure,' so also wicked Esau [i.e., Rome] displays himself so openly on the seats of justice that the legal tricks whereby he robs, steals, and plunders appear to be just proceedings. . . . So said Rabbi Phinehas [ben Hama, Palestinian, fourth century CE]. (L.H.F.)

Taxes Imposed by the Romans upon the Jews of Palestine

BIBLIOGRAPHY

Frederick C. Grant, *The Economic Background of the Gospels* (1926).
Shimon Applebaum, "Economic Life in Palestine," in Samuel Safrai and Menahem Stern, eds, *The Jewish People in the First Century* (CRINT 1.2) (1974), 631–700.
Sanders (1992), 161–9.

8.48 Babylonian Talmud, *Sanhedrin* 98b (codified *ca.* 500 CE)

Above all, the tax-collector was feared and despised, though the Romans varied taxes from time to time, particularly after each of the revolts of the Jews against the Romans.

Resh Laqish [Palestinian, third century CE] said . . . : When one goes out into the field and meets a bailiff, it is as though he had met a lion. When he enters the town, and is accosted by a tax-collector, it is as though he had met a bear. (Soncino)

8.49 *Pesiqta de Rav-Kahana* 2.2 (*ca.* sixth century CE)

The tax most often mentioned is the *arnona* [i.e., *annona*], the tax on grain. This was the most important source of revenue for maintaining the Roman army. During the third century CE it was extended to various food products, as well as to land, cattle, and clothing. In the following remark, the third-century CE Palestinian Rabbi Judah of Bet Gubrin is cited by Rabbi Jacob bar Judah (date unknown) as referring to Roman tax-collectors as a prickly hedge which, if one escapes from one side, pricks one from the other side, since they jab away with their demands.

Bring your head tax, bring your general tax, bring the levies upon your crops and herds. (L.H.F.)

8.50 Midrash Genesis Rabbah 76.6 (ca. fifth century CE)

Another objection of Jews to the Roman administration was to forced officeholding, though it must be noted that it was standard throughout the empire and was not a special penalty imposed on the Jews. We do not know when this practice began, though we do know that a great deal changed in Palestine after the Bar Kochba rebellion (132–5 CE), after which Roman troops occupied Palestine for the first time, the limited autonomy was reduced, and the country was Romanized more than it had been previously. As forced officeholders, Jews were then required to collect various oppressive taxes; and if they did not do so, they had to pay these imposts from their own pockets. In addition, they had to pay for their administrative expenses, in part, from their own resources. Hence the bitter complaint in the passage below.

Rabbi Johanan [ben Nappaḥa, Palestinian, third century CE] said: ... The wicked kingdom [i.e., Rome] ... casts an envious eye upon a man's wealth: 'yonder man is rich; we will make him *archon* [i.e., magistrate]; yonder man is rich, we will make him *bouleutes* [i.e., councilman].' (L.H.F.)

8.51 Jerusalem Talmud, Mo'ed Qatan 2.3.81b (codified ca. 400 CE)

As the following statement indicates, rather than serve as an officeholder, some preferred to escape to territory beyond Roman control.

Rabbi Johanan [Palestinian, third century CE] said: If they [i.e., the Romans] elect you to the *boule* [the Council], make the Jordan your boundary.[46] (L.H.F.)

8.52 Midrash Genesis Rabbah 80.1 (ca. fifth century CE)

Rabbi Jose of Ma'on [Palestinian, third century CE] said: ... The Lord will sit in judgment over them [the Roman governors], pronounce their sentence, and make them vanish from the earth. (L.H.F.)

8.53 Jerusalem Talmud, Rosh Hashanah 1.3.57a (edited ca. 500 CE)

Moreover, the Emperor himself was above the law.

Rabbi Eleazar [ben Pedath, Palestinian, third century CE] said, 'On the king the law is not binding.'[47] (L.H.F.)

8.54 Babylonian Talmud, Avodah Zarah 10a (edited ca. 500 CE)

The rabbis had contempt even for the Latin language, perhaps because they may have known that Rome was founded by emigrants from Asia Minor or that the Romans had borrowed their alphabet from the Greeks.

---

46. I.e., go beyond the Jordan, outside the boundary of the Roman province.
47. Rabbi Eleazar quotes this in the Greek, which was apparently proverbial.

Did not Rabbi Joseph [ben Ḥiyya, Babylonian, third century and early fourth century CE] apply [the following verse to Rome]: 'Behold I made thee small among the nations' [Obad 1:2] – in that they do not place the son of a king on the royal throne, – 'thou art greatly despised' [ibid.] – in that they do not possess a tongue or script?[48] (Soncino)

8.55 Babylonian Talmud, *Pesaḥim* 87b (edited *ca.* 500 CE)

During the first five centuries CE, and especially during the second and third centuries, many Jews left Palestine because of Roman oppression, heavy taxation, or lack of security and went to the Persian kingdom (the Parthians there were succeeded by the Sassanians in 226 CE). Hence, not surprisingly, the rabbis compare the Roman and Persian rule, and those who leave Palestine feel the need to justify their departure.

Rabbi Ḥiyya [Babylonian and Palestinian, end of second and beginning of third century CE] taught: What is meant by the verse, 'God understandeth the way thereof, and He knoweth the place thereof' [Job 28:23]? The Holy One, blessed be He, knoweth that Israel is unable to endure the cruel decrees of Edom [i.e., Rome]; therefore, He exiled them to Babylonia. Rabbi Eleazar [ben Pedath, Babylonian and Palestinian, third century CE], also said: The Holy One, blessed be He, exiled Israel to Babylonia only because it is as deep as *she'ol*, for it is said, 'I shall ransom them from the power of the nether-world [*she'ol*]; I shall redeem them from death' [Hos 13:14].[49] (Soncino)

8.56 Midrash Lamentations Rabbah 1.13.14–15 (*ca.* fifth century CE)

It is not surprising that some rabbis saw salvation only if the wicked empire of Rome should be overthrown; and since they saw that Persia was the one nation that the Romans had been unable to conquer they looked to Persia for the overthrow of the Roman Empire.

Said Rabbi Abba bar Kahana [Palestinian, third century CE], 'If you have seen benches filled with Babylonians in Palestine, expect the feet of the Messiah. What scriptural verse suggests so? "He spread a net for my feet." (Lam 1:13)

Said Rabbi Simeon bar Yoḥai [Palestinian, second century CE], 'If you have seen a Persian horse tied up at a grave in Palestine, look for the footsteps of the king Messiah. What scriptural verse suggests so? "And this shall be peace, when the Assyrian shall come into our land"' (Mic 5:4). (J.N.)

---

48. Greek, rather than Latin, was the spoken and written language throughout the eastern portion of the Roman Empire.

49. I.e., the fact that it is such a deep hell guarantees redemption.

Pro-Roman Sentiment among the Rabbis

8.57 Midrash Song of Songs Rabbah 1.6 (ca. sixth century CE)

BIBLIOGRAPHY

Louis H. Feldman, "Abba Kolon and the Founding of Rome," *JQR* 81 (1990–1),
449–82.

The fact that the rabbis synchronize the founding of Rome with the day
that King Solomon married the daughter of the Egyptian Pharaoh Necho,
the day when the king of Israel, Jeroboam the son of Nebat, made two
golden calves, and the day that the prophet Elijah was taken up to
heaven, indicates an attempt to link the destinies of the Jews and the
Romans. The fact that this chronology pushes back the founding of Rome
perhaps as many as two centuries before 753 BCE, the traditional date of
Rome's founding, is a distinct compliment to the Romans, since it adds to
the antiquity of Rome, which was self-conscious about its relatively
recent appearance on the scene of history. Similarly, the linkage with the
prophet Elijah, who is to usher in the Messiah, connects Rome with the
Messianic aspirations of the Jews.

Said Rabbi Levi [Babylonian, third century CE], 'On the day on which
Solomon was married to the daughter of Pharaoh Necho,[50] [the
archangel] Michael, the great prince, descended from heaven, and he
stuck a large reed into the sea, so that mud came up on either side, and
the place was like a marsh. And that was the site of Rome.

On the day on which Jeroboam ben Nebat set up two golden calves,
two huts[51] were built in Rome. And they would build them, but the huts
would fall down,[52] build and see the collapse. But there was a sage
there, by the name of Abba Qolon.[53] He said to them, "If you do not
bring water from the Euphrates River and mix it with the clay, the
building will not stand."'

They said to him, 'Who will do it?'

He said to them, 'I.'

50. Necho was actually king of Egypt from *ca.* 609–593 BCE, approximately three
and a half centuries after Solomon.

51. The two huts may refer to the fact that some magistracies in Rome were
collegial; for example, the consulship was dual. It may also reflect the period in the
third century CE (when Rabbi Levi lived), during which sometimes two emperors
shared the throne. The twin huts may also reflect the twin founders of Rome, Romulus
and Remus, and the two huts of Romulus that were still to be found in Rome.

52. The fact that the huts kept falling reflects the apparent chaos in the Roman
Empire in the middle of the third century, with no fewer than twenty-six emperors
(including colleagues in imperial power) being recognized in Rome within a span of
fifty years (235–84), only one of whom is definitely known to have died a natural
death.

53. Our passage, referring as it does to Abba Qolon ("father of a colony"), best fits a
date in the third century, since this was the golden age for the creation of colonies in
the Roman Empire, especially in the Fertile Crescent. The colony is perhaps best
identified as Palmyra, which had been raised to that status some time in the second or
early third century CE. The trip to the Euphrates to get water so as to enable the huts of
Rome to remain standing may reflect the achievement of the Palmyrene nobleman,
Odaenathus, who defeated the Persians on the banks of the Euphrates after the
Persians had defeated the Romans.

He dressed up like a wine-porter, going into a town and out of a town, into a province and out of a province, until he got there. When he reached there, he went and took water from the Euphrates. They kneaded it into mud and built with it, and the building stood.

From that time they would say, 'Any town that does not have an Abba Qolon cannot be called a town.' And they called it Rome Babylon.[54]

On the day on which Elijah, of blessed memory, was taken away, a king arose in Edom [Rome]. (J.N.)

8.58 Babylonian Talmud, *Sanhedrin* 98a–b (edited *ca.* 500 CE)

That Jewish destiny is bound up with Rome may be seen from the fact that the Messiah is said to sit at the entrance of the city of Rome, and that he will not make his entrance until the Roman Empire embraces the entire world.

Rabbi Joshua ben Levi [first half of the third century CE] met Elijah[55] standing by the entrance of Rabbi Simeon ben Yohai's [second century CE] tomb. . . . He then asked him, 'When will the Messiah come?' 'Go and ask him himself,' was his reply. 'Where is he sitting?' 'At the entrance of the town.'[56] . . .

Rab [Babylonian, second and third centuries CE] said: The son of David [i.e., the Messiah] will not come until the [Roman] power enfolds Israel for nine months,[57] as it is written, 'Therefore will he give them up, until the time that she which travaileth hath brought forth; then the remnant of his brethren shall return unto the children of Israel' [Mic 5:2].[58] (Soncino)

8.59 *Midrash Genesis Rabbah* 9.13 (*ca.* fifth century CE)

A supreme compliment is paid to the Roman fairness in their justice system in the following passage, ascribed to the Palestinian Rabbi Simeon ben Laqish, who lived in the third century CE, during the very period when the greatest Roman jurists flourished.

Rabbi Simeon ben Laqish said, 'Behold it was very good' [Gen 1:30]. This is the kingdom of heaven. 'And behold it was very good.' This is the kingdom of the Romans. Is then the kingdom of the Romans very good? Strange! But this is because it exacts justice for creatures, as it is said, 'I made earth and placed man upon it' [Isa 45:12]. (L.H.F.)

---

54. The equation of Babylon and Rome, which is also found in the New Testament (Rev 12:18; 14:8), may reflect the fact that the two temples of the Jews in Jerusalem had been destroyed respectively by the Babylonians and the Romans.

55. The traditional forerunner of the Messiah.

56. The Vilna Gaon deletes "of the town" and substitutes "of Rome."

57. I.e., until the Roman Empire embraces the entire world, throughout which the Jews are scattered.

58. The phrase "therefore will he give them up" is here understood as referring to a foreign, i.e., Roman, power. "Until the time that she which travaileth" is understood to mean nine months, the period of pregnancy.

8.60 Midrash Song of Songs Rabbah 6.11 (ca. sixth century CE)

In view of the general prevalence of highwaymen and terrorists, the Jews were particularly grateful, as we see in the passage below, for the concern taken by the Roman administration to guard the security of the inhabitants.

Said Rabbi Levi [Babylonian, third century CE], [The matter may be compared to the case of] a lonely spot, which is infested with terrorists. What does the king do? He assigns there brigades to guard the place so that the terrorists will not attack travellers on the way. (J.N.)

8.61 Babylonian Talmud, Giṭṭin 55b (edited ca. 500 CE)

In the following passage the Romans are said to have gone so far in enforcing security for Jews that they eventually sentenced to death anyone who killed a Jew.

Rabbi Assi [Babylonian, third and fourth centuries CE] has stated: They [the Roman government] issued three successive decrees [dates not given]. The first was that whoever did not kill [a Jew on finding him] should himself be put to death. The second was that whoever killed [a Jew] should pay four *zuz*[59] [as a fine]. The last was that whoever killed a Jew should himself be put to death. Hence in the first two [periods] [the Jew], being in danger of his life, would determine to transfer his property [to the *sicaricon*],[60] but in the last [period] he would say to himself, Let him take it today, tomorrow I will sue him for it. (Soncino)

Populousness of the Jews

BIBLIOGRAPHY

Chester C. McCown, "The Density of Population in Ancient Palestine," *JBL* 66 (1947), 425–36.

Joseph Klausner, "How Many Jews Will Be Able to Live in Palestine? Based on an Analysis of the Jewish Population in Palestine in the Days of the Second Temple," *JSoS* 11 (1949), 119–28.

Salo W. Baron, *A Social and Religious History of the Jews*, 2nd ed., vol. 1 (1952), 370–2.

Anthony Byatt, "Josephus and Population Numbers in First Century Palestine," *PEQ* 105 (1973), 51–60.

John Wilkinson, "Ancient Jerusalem: Its Water Supply and Population," *PEQ* 196 (1974), 33–51.

Magen Broshi, "Estimating the Population of Ancient Jerusalem." *BAR* 4.2 (June, 1978), 10–15.

Magen Broshi, "The Population of Western Palestine in the Roman-Byzantine Period," *BASOR* 236 (1979), 1–10.

Feldman (1993), 555–6.

59. A *zuz* was a denarius, approximately a penny.
60. A *sicaricon* was a terrorist who threatened to kill a Jew but let him go on being given some of his property.

That the Jews in the Roman Empire were very numerous, numbering in the millions, seems clear from various references below. In view of the evidence in Josephus, a Jewish population in Palestine in the first century CE of from two to four million is, according to Baron, well within the range of possibility. Moreover, there is reason to believe that there were a million Jews each in Egypt, Syria and Asia Minor. Inasmuch as there may well have been a million more Jews living in Babylonia and other countries of the world at that time, Baron concludes that a Jewish world population of more than eight million is fully within the range of probability.

> *8.62* Strabo (*ca.* 64 BCE–*ca.* 20 CE), *Historical Memoranda*, cited by Josephus, *Jewish Antiquities* 14.114–18

Here Josephus cites Strabo, who had traveled very widely in the world of his day, as stating that Jews are to be found everywhere in the world. He notes that the rulers of Egypt had encouraged settlement by Jews in Egypt and Cyrene.

And this same Strabo in another passage testifies that at the time when Sulla crossed over to Greece to make war on Mithridates and sent Lucullus to put down the revolt of our nation in Cyrene [86 BCE] the habitable world was filled with Jews, for he writes as follows: 'There were four classes in the state of Cyrene; the first consisted of citizens, the second of farmers, the third of resident aliens [metics], and the fourth of Jews. This people has already made its way into every city, and it is not easy to find any place in the habitable world that has not received this nation and in which it has not made its power felt. And it has come about that Cyrene, which had the same rulers as Egypt, has imitated it in many respects, particularly in notably encouraging and aiding the expansion of the organized groups of Jews that observe the national Jewish laws. In Egypt, for example, territory has been set apart for a Jewish settlement, and in Alexandria a great part of the city has been allocated to this nation. And an ethnarch of their own has been installed, who governs the people and adjudicates suits and supervises contracts and ordinances, just as if he were the head of a sovereign state. And so this nation has flourished in Egypt because the Jews were originally Egyptians and because those who left that country made their homes nearby; and they migrated to Cyrene because this country bordered on the kingdom of Egypt, as did Judaea – or rather, it formerly belonged to that kingdom.' (LCL)

> *8.63* Philo, *Embassy to Gaius* 36.281–4 (40 CE)

The following extract from a letter sent by King Agrippa I of Judaea to the Emperor Gaius Caligula indicates how widespread Jewish settlements were in Egypt, Syria, Greece, Cyprus, Crete, and Babylonia, among other lands.

As for the holy city [Jerusalem], I must say what befits me to say. While she, as I have said, is my native city, she is also the mother city not of one country, Judaea, but of most of the others in virtue of the colonies sent out at divers times to the neighboring lands – Egypt, Phoenicia, the part of Syria called the Hollow [Coele Syria][61] and the rest as well and the lands lying far apart, Pamphylia, Cilicia, most of Asia up to Bithynia and the corners of Pontus, similarly also into Europe, Thessaly, Boeotia, Macedonia, Aetolia, Attica, Argos, Corinth and most of the best parts of Peloponnese. And not only are the mainlands full of Jewish colonies but also the most highly esteemed of the islands – Euboea, Cyprus, Crete. I say nothing of the countries beyond the Euphrates, for except for a small part they all, Babylon and of the other satrapies those where the land within their confines is highly fertile, have Jewish inhabitants. So that if my own home-city is granted a share of your goodwill the benefit extends not to one city but to myriads of the others situated in every region of the inhabited world, whether in Europe or in Asia or in Libya, whether in the mainlands or on the islands, whether it be seaboard or inland. It well befits the magnitude of your great good fortune that by benefiting one city you should benefit myriads of others also so that through every part of the world your glory should be celebrated and your praises mingled with thanksgiving resound. (LCL)

8.64 Philo, *Against Flaccus* 6.43

Here Philo, who, as the head of the Jewish community of Alexandria, should have been well informed, states that there were no fewer than a million Jews in Egypt in his day.

He [Flaccus, the Roman governor of Egypt in 38 CE] knew that both Alexandria and the whole of Egypt had two kinds of inhabitants, us and them, and that there were no less than a million Jews resident in Alexandria and the country from the slope into Libya into the boundaries of Ethiopia. (LCL)

8.65 Josephus, *Jewish Antiquities* 11.133

Here Josephus tells us that the number of Jews in Babylonia in his day consists of so many thousands that it cannot be ascertained.

The Israelite nation as a whole remained in the country [Babylonia, despite the Persian king Xerxes' decree permitting the Jews to return to Jerusalem]. In this way has it come about that there are two tribes in Asia and Europe subject to the Romans, while until now there have been ten tribes beyond the Euphrates – countless myriads whose number cannot be ascertained. (LCL)

8.66 Josephus, *Jewish War* 3.43 (66 CE)

Here Josephus refers to the populousness of the Jews in Galilee.

---

61. Philo probably refers here to the area south of Damascus and east of the Jordan River.

The towns [of Galilee], too, are thickly distributed, and even the villages, thanks to the fertility of the soil, are all so densely populated that the smallest of them contains above 15,000 inhabitants. (LCL)

8.67 Josephus, *Life* 235 (66 CE)

If the passage below is combined with the passage above, there was a population of a minimum of 3,060,000 Jews in Galilee alone. Most scholars regard this as a gross exaggeration; but Josephus, who is the source for this information, was commander in Galilee at the beginning of the war against the Romans in the year 66, and he should have had sound information as to the area of his command.

I [Josephus] then wrote to them [the embassy sent from Jerusalem to depose him] as follows: 'If you seriously desire me to come to you, there are 204 cities and villages in Galilee.' (LCL)

8.68 Josephus, *Jewish War* 6.423–7 (66 CE)

One way of estimating the number of Jews in Jerusalem at the season of Passover was through the number of lambs slaughtered for the occasion. Estimating that at least ten persons joined in eating a lamb, he concludes that there were 2,700,000 people. In addition, since menstruous women or those who were defiled were not permitted to partake of the pascal lamb, the number must have been even greater.

Accordingly, on the occasion of the feast called Passover, at which they sacrifice from the ninth to the eleventh hour, and a little fraternity, as it were, gathers round each sacrifice, of not fewer than ten persons (feasting alone not being permitted), while the companies often include as many as twenty, the victims were counted and amounted to 255,600; allowing an average of ten diners to each victim, we obtain a total of 2,700,000,[62] all pure and holy. For those afflicted with leprosy or gonorrhoea, or menstruous women, or persons otherwise defiled were not permitted to partake of this sacrifice, nor yet any foreigners present for worship, and a large number of these assemble from abroad. (LCL)

8.69 Tacitus (*ca.* 56–120 CE), *Histories* 5.5.3

Tacitus makes note of the fact that the Jews do not practice infanticide, as so many others in antiquity did.

They [the Jews] take thought to increase their numbers; for they regard it as a crime to kill any late-born child. (LCL)

8.70 Dio Cassius (*ca.* 160–230 CE), *Roman History* 37.17.1

Dio Cassius notes how greatly the number of Jews has increased, despite repression.

62. The actual total is 2,556,000.

This class [the Jews] exists even among the Romans, and though often repressed has increased to a very great extent and has won its way to the right of freedom in its observances. (LCL)

8.71 Menander of Laodicea (end of the third century CE), *Declamations* (in Leonardus Spengel, *Rhetores Graeci*, vol. 3, p. 366)

Menander notes the tremendous number of Jews who gather from other countries in Palestine on the occasion of the pilgrimage festivals.

The largest multitudes are to be found at the festival of the Hebrews living in Syria Palaestina, as they are gathered in very large numbers from most nations. (M.S.)

Wealth of the Jews

BIBLIOGRAPHY
Feldman (1993), 110–13.

The several references in Greek and Latin literature to the wealth of the Jews or, at any rate, of Jewish rulers, are a clue that envy of this wealth was a source of hostility to the Jews through much of the classical period. Particular sources of wealth were balsam, palm groves, and flax. The increasing wealth of the Temple was a major source of hostility felt by the Romans toward the Jews.

8.72 Josephus, *Jewish Antiquities* 5.77: The natural wealth of Palestine

Upon entering Palestine Joshua, according to the Bible (Josh 18:8) sent out a delegation to go throughout the land and write a description of it. Josephus here adds a number of details, emphasizing the richness of the soil, especially the regions of Jericho and Jerusalem.

The nature of the land of Canaan is such that one may see plains, of great area, fully fitted for bearing crops, and which compared with another district might be deemed altogether blest, yet when set beside the regions of the people of Jericho and Jerusalem would appear as naught. Aye, though the territory of these folk happens to be quite diminutive and for the most part mountainous, yet for its extraordinary productiveness of crops and for beauty it yields to no other. (LCL)

8.73 Pompeius Trogus, *Philippic Histories* 36, summarized by Justin (third or fourth century CE), *Epitome* 3.1–2

No fewer than six ancient authors – Theophrastus in the fourth century BCE, Diodorus in the first century BCE, Strabo in the first century BCE, Pompeius Trogus in the first century CE, Dioscorides in the first century CE, and Pliny the Elder in the first century CE – mention that balsam is produced nowhere else in the whole world except in Judaea. According to Strabo (17.1.15.800), the value of the balsam was increased through the deliberate limiting of its growth by the Jews to only a few places. The demand was particularly great from its use as a medicinal substance and its employment in elaborate funeral pyres.

The wealth of the nation [Judaea] was increased by the income from balsam, which is produced only in that country; for there is a valley, encircled with an unbroken ridge of hills, as if it were a wall, in the form of a camp, the space enclosed being about two hundred iugera[63] and called Aricus. (M.S.)

8.74 Pliny the Elder (23–79 CE), *Natural History* 12.111, 113, 118

So precious is the balsam grown in Judaea, according to Pliny the Elder, that battles have been fought over it.

But every other scent ranks below balsam. The only country to which this plant has been vouchsafed is Judaea, where formerly it grew in only two gardens, both belonging to the king; one of them was not more than twenty iugera in extent and the other less. . . . The Jews vented their wrath upon this plant as they also did upon their own lives, but the Romans protected it against them, and there have been pitched battles in defence of a shrub. . . . There is a market even for the twigs too; within five years of the conquest of Judaea the actual loppings and the shoots fetched 800,000 sesterces. . . . Even the bark fetches a price for drugs. (LCL)

8.75 Josephus, *Jewish War* 3.41–3

In the passage below Josephus mentions the agricultural wealth of Galilee, a region with which he must have been well acquainted since at the beginning of the war with the Romans in 66 he was appointed to be general there. So rich is the soil that even the laziest devote themselves to farming.

With this limited area, and although surrounded by such powerful foreign nations, the two Galilees have always resisted any hostile invasion, for the inhabitants are from infancy inured to war, and have at all times been numerous; never did the men lack courage nor the country men. For the land is everywhere so rich in soil and pasturage and produces such variety of trees that even the most indolent are tempted by these facilities to devote themselves to agriculture. In fact, every inch of the soil has been cultivated by the inhabitants; there is not a parcel of waste land. The towns, too, are thickly distributed, and even the villages, thanks to the fertility of the soil, are all so densely populated that the smallest of them contains above fifteen thousand inhabitants. (LCL)

8.76 Tacitus (*ca.* 56–120 CE), *Histories* 5.8.1

Tacitus notes the particular wealth of the Temple in Jerusalem, owing, primarily, to the fact that each year every adult male Jew in the world was obliged to contribute a half shekel to it.

63. A *iugerum* is approximately two-thirds of an acre.

Jerusalem is the capital of the Jews. In it was a temple possessing enormous riches. (LCL)

Economic Inequalities

8.77 Ecclesiasticus (Wisdom of Ben-Sira) 13:15–23 (*ca.* 175 BCE)

The Book of Ecclesiasticus by Ben-Sira in the Apocrypha, in its prophetic-like concern for social justice and giving of aid to the poor, sheds light on the sharp division between rich and poor in his time in Palestine.

> All flesh loveth its kind,
>> And every man his like.
> All flesh consorteth according to its kind,
>> And with his kind man associateth.
> What association can wolf have with lamb?
>> Even so is the ungodly that consorteth with the righteous.
> What peace can the hyena have with the dog?
>> Or what peace rich with poor?
> Food for the lion are the wild asses of the desert:
>> Even so the pasture of the rich are the poor.
> An abomination to pride is humility;
>> Even so an abomination to the rich are the poor.
> A rich man when he is shaken is supported by a friend,
>> But the poor man when he is shaken is thrust away by a friend.
> A rich man speaketh and his helpers are many;
>> And though his words be unseemly, they are pronounced lovely.
> A poor man speaketh, and they jeer at him;
>> Yea, though he speak with wisdom, there is no place for him.
> When the rich man speaketh, all keep silence,
>> And they extol his intelligence to the clouds.
> When the poor man speaketh: 'Who is this?' they say;
>> And if he stumble they will assist his overthrow. (R.H.C.)

Social Life of Palestinian Jews

The Status of Women

BIBLIOGRAPHY

Raphael Loewe, *The Position of Women in Judaism* (1966).

Saul J. Berman, "The Status of Women in Halakhic Judaism," *Tradition* 14, no. 2 (Feb, 1973), 5–28.

Rosemary R. Reuther, ed., *Religion and Sexism: Images of Women in the Jewish and Christian Tradition* (1974).

Leonard Swidler, *Women in Judaism: The Status of Women in Formative Judaism* (1976).

Moshe Meiselman, *Jewish Woman in Jewish Law* (1978).

Evelyn and Frank Stagg, *Women in the World of Jesus* (1978).

Solomon Appleman, *The Jewish Woman in Judaism: The Significance of Woman's Status in Religious Culture* (1980).

Rosalyn Lacks, *Women and Judaism: Myth, History, and Struggle* (1980).

Warren C. Trenchard, *Ben Sira's View of Women: A Literary Analysis* (1982).

Leonie J. Archer, "The Role of Jewish Women in the Religion, Ritual and Cult of Graeco-Roman Palestine," in Averil Cameron and Amelie Kuhrt, eds, *Images of Women in Antiquity* (1983), 273–87.

Rachel Biale, *Women and Jewish Law: An Exploration of Women's Issues in Halachic Sources* (1984).

Ross S. Kraemer, "A New Inscription from Malta and the Question of Women Elders in the Diaspora Jewish Communities," *HTR* 78 (1985), 431–8.

Ross S. Kraemer, "Non-literary Evidence for Jewish Women in Rome and Egypt," in Mary Skinner, ed., "Rescuing Creusa: New Methodological Approaches to Women in Antiquity," *Helios* 13.2 (1986), 85–101.

Betsy H. Amaru, "Portraits of Biblical Women in Josephus' *Antiquities*," *JJS* 39 (1988), 143–70.

Judith R. Wegner, *Chattel or Person? The Status of Women in the Mishnah* (1988).

Amy-Jill Levine, ed., "*Women like This*": *New Perspectives on Jewish Women in the Greco-Roman World* (1991).

Susan Grossman and Rivka Haut, eds, *Daughters of the King: Women and the Synagogue* (1992).

8.78 Testaments of the Twelve Patriarchs, Testament of Reuben 5 (ca. 100 BCE)

The following passage, written in Greek in Palestine, looks upon all women as scheming covertly and treacherously by adorning themselves in their effort to entice men and even angels. According to the passage, women are said to be more easily overcome by promiscuity than men. In it Jacob's son Reuben warns his descendants not to be ensnared by them.

For women are evil, my children, and by reason of their lacking authority or power over man, they scheme treacherously how they might entice him to themselves by means of their looks. And whomever they cannot entice by their appearance they conquer by a stratagem. Indeed, the angel of the Lord told me and instructed me that women are more easily overcome by the spirit of promiscuity than are men. They contrive in their hearts against men, then by decking themselves out they lead men's minds astray, by a look they implant their poison, and finally in the act itself they take them captive. For a woman is not able to coerce a man overtly, but by a harlot's manner she accomplishes her villainy. Accordingly, my children, flee from sexual promiscuity, and order your wives and your daughters not to adorn their heads and their appearances so as to deceive men's sound minds. For every woman who schemes in these ways is destined for eternal punishment. For it was thus that they charmed the Watchers,[64] who were before the Flood. As they continued looking at the women, they were filled with desire for them and perpetrated the act in their minds. Then they were transformed into human males, and while the women were cohabiting with their husbands they appeared to them. Since the

---

64. Angels forming some kind of heavenly council who are said to have had relations with women. They are mentioned in the Book of Daniel and in the Dead Sea Scrolls and play an important role in later mystical literature.

women's minds were filled with lust for their apparitions, they gave birth to giants. For the Watchers were disclosed to them as being as high as the heavens. (H.C.K.)

8.79 *Ecclesiasticus* 25:15–26 (*ca.* 175 BCE)

The following outburst against women is extreme, but it should be noted that the author, Ben Sira, elsewhere stresses that the mutual love of husband and wife is pleasing to God and to humans.

> There is no venom worse than a snake's venom,
>   and no anger worse than a woman's wrath.
> I would rather live with a lion and a dragon
>   than live with an evil woman.
> A woman's wickedness changes her appearance,
>   and darkens her face like that of a bear.
> Her husband sits among the neighbors,
>   and he cannot help sighing bitterly.
> Any iniquity is small compared to a woman's iniquity;
>   may a sinner's lot befall her!
> A sandy ascent for the feet of the aged –
>   such is a garrulous wife to a quiet husband.
> Do not be ensnared by a woman's beauty,
>   and do not desire a woman for her possessions.
> There is wrath and impudence and great disgrace
>   when a wife supports her husband.
> Dejected mind, gloomy face,
>   and wounded heart come from an evil wife.
> Drooping hands and weak knees
>   come from the wife who does not make her husband happy.
> From a woman sin had its beginning,
>   and because of her we all die.
> Allow no outlet to water,
>   and no boldness of speech to an evil wife.
> If she does not go as you direct,
>   separate her from yourself. (RSV)

8.80 Babylonian Talmud, *Soṭah* 11b (edited *ca.* 500 CE)

In view of the fact that rabbinic literature places a premium upon debate, we should not be surprised to find divergent opinions with regard to women, ranging from great respect for their piety, intelligence, and compassionate nature to disdain for their talkativeness, lightmindedness, and witchcraft. Surely a central event in the emergence of the Jewish people is the Exodus from Egypt; and no greater compliment could be paid to women than to say what we find in the passage below, namely that this deliverance was due to the righteous women who lived at that time and who withstood the cruel decrees of the Pharaoh.

Rabbi ʿAviva [Babylonian, fourth century CE] expounded: As the reward for the righteous women who lived in that generation were the

Israelites delivered from Egypt. When they went to draw water, the Holy One, blessed be He, arranged that small fishes should enter their pitchers, which they drew up half full of water and half full of fishes. They then set two pots on the fire, one for hot water and the other for the fish, which they carried to their husbands in the field, and washed, anointed, fed, gave them to drink, and had intercourse with them among the sheepfolds. (Soncino)

8.81 Babylonian Talmud, *Qiddushin* 31b (edited *ca.* 500 CE)

In the following passage we see how great was the respect for their mothers on the part of two of the greatest rabbis.

Rabbi Tarfon [Palestinian, end of the first and beginning of the second century] had a mother for whom, whenever she wished to mount into bed, he would bend down to let her ascend [by stepping upon him], (and when she wished to descend, she stepped down upon him). He went and boasted thereof in the school. Said they to him, 'You have not yet reached half the honor [due]: has she then thrown a purse before you into the sea without your shaming her?'

When Rabbi Joseph [Babylonian, third century CE] heard his mother's footsteps he would say, 'I will arise before the approaching *Shechinah.'*[65] (Soncino)

8.82 Babylonian Talmud, *Niddah* 45b (edited *ca.* 500 CE)

Rabbi Ḥisda [Babylonian, third century CE] stated: What is Rabbi's [Rabbi Judah the Prince's] [Palestinian, end of second century CE] reason [for stating that girls mature earlier than boys]? Because it is written in Scripture, 'And the Lord God built the rib' which teaches that the Holy One, blessed be He, endowed the woman with more understanding than the man.[66] (Soncino)

8.83 Babylonian Talmud, *Gittin* 6b (edited *ca.* 500 CE)

Here the great Rabbi Ḥisda warns of the terrible results of the mistreatment by a husband of a wife.

Rabbi Ḥisda [Babylonian, third century CE] said: A man should never terrorize his household. The concubine of Gibea was terrorized by her husband and she was the cause of many thousands being slaughtered in Israel. Rab Judah [ben Ezekiel, Babylonian, third century CE] said in the name of Rab [Babylonian, second and third centuries CE]: If a man terrorizes his household, he will eventually commit the three sins of unchastity,[67] blood-shedding,[68] and desecration of the Sabbath.[69] (Soncino)

65. The *Shechinah* is the Divine Presence.
66. The word for understanding, *binah*, is here understood to be analogous to the verb *vayiben*, "built."
67. He will have relations with his wife when she is menstruating because she will be afraid to tell him.
68. She will have fatal accidents while running away from him.
69. She will light the Sabbath lamp after dark because of fear of him.

8.84 Babylonian Talmud, *Megillah* 14b (edited *ca.* 500 CE)

Here one of the rabbis explains how a woman prophetess may be superior to a male prophet, namely because she is more tender-hearted.

If [the prophet] Jeremiah was there, how could she [Huldah] prophesy? It was said in the school of Rab in the name of Rab [Babylonian, second and third centuries CE], Hulda was a near relative of Jeremiah, and he did not object to her doing so.

But how could [King] Josiah himself pass over Jeremiah and send to her? The members of the school of Rabbi Shila [Babylonian, third century CE] replied, 'Because women are tender-hearted.' (Soncino)

8.85 Mishnah, *Soṭah* 3:4 (edited *ca.* 200 CE)

Here we have a dispute between two great rabbis, Ben Azzai and Eliezer, as to whether one should teach one's daughter Torah. By Torah, however, Rabbi Eliezer may mean not the study of the basic principles of Judaism, but, as the context seems to imply, the study of Torah as an academic discipline with all its technicalities, with the implication that a smattering of such knowledge is undesirable. In any case, we may note that Rabbi Eliezer's wife, Imma Shalom, is presented (*Shabbath* 116a–b) as extremely intelligent and learned.

Declared [Simeon] Ben Azzai [Palestinian, second century CE]: A man is under the obligation to teach his daughter Torah, so that if she has to drink [the water of bitterness],[70] she may know that the merit suspends its effect. Rabbi Eliezer [ben Hyrcanus, Palestinian, end of first century, beginning of second century] says: Whoever teaches his daughter Torah teachers her obscenity.[71] (Soncino)

8.86 Babylonian Talmud, *Shabbath* 152a (edited *ca.* 500 CE)

This is the most negative statement about women in rabbinic literature. It represents the view of a single rabbi rather than of rabbis in general. The author is anonymous, perhaps because his followers and editors did not have the nerve to put his name to such a statement; but since it is ascribed to a Tanna, this is indication that its author comes from the first two centuries CE. The immediate context is a statement by Rabbi Kahana [Palestinian, third century CE] to the effect that it is God's decree that man should desire woman.

A Tanna taught: Though a woman be as a pitcher full of filth and her mouth be full of blood, yet all speed after her. (Soncino)

70. This is the ordeal of jealousy outlined in Num 5:11–31, whereby a woman suspected of adultery is given bitter water to drink by a priest. She is told that if she is innocent she will be immune to harm, but if she is guilty her "belly shall distend."
71. This word may also mean "lasciviousness" or "silliness." In the Gemara (*Sotah* 21b) Rabbi Abbahu (Palestinian, third and fourth centuries CE) explains that Rabbi Eliezer's reason is that "when wisdom enters a man subtlety enters with it."

8.87 Mishnah, *Sotah* 3:4 (edited *ca.* 200 CE)

In the following statement Rabbi Joshua generalizes that women prefer sex even if they must starve. He groups a learned woman with a foolish pietist and a rogue.

Rabbi Joshua [ben Hananiah, first and second century CE] says: A woman prefers one *kab*[72] [of food] and sexual indulgence to nine *kab*[73] and continence. He used to say: a foolish pietist, a cunning rogue, a female Pharisee, and the plague of Pharisees bring destruction upon the world. (Soncino)

8.88 Babylonian Talmud, *Shabbath* 33b (edited *ca.* 500 CE)

The famous rabbi Simeon bar Yoḥai remarks that women are light-minded; but in the context the meaning may be not that they are lacking in intelligence but rather that they may be more easily overcome by torture.

He [Simeon bar Yohai] [Palestinian, second century CE] and his son went and hid themselves in the Beth Hamidrash,[74] [and] his wife brought him bread and a jug of water and they dined. [But] when the decree became more severe he said to his son, 'Women are light-minded: she [his wife] may be put to the torture and expose us.' So they went and hid in a cave. (Soncino)

8.89 Babylonian Talmud, *Megillah* 14b (edited *ca.* 500 CE)

In the passage below one of the rabbis mentions a popular saying that indicates that a woman has her wits about her and prosecutes her schemes even when she does not appear to do so.

Rabbi Naḥman [ben Jacob, Babylonian, fourth century CE] said: This[75] bears out the popular saying: While a woman talks she spins. Some adduce the saying: The goose stoops as it goes along, but its eyes peer afar. (Soncino)

8.90 Babylonian Talmud, *Soṭah* 22a (edited *ca.* 500 CE)

Here we see a debate as to whether a woman who gives herself up to prayer and a gadabout widow are to be viewed positively or negatively.

Our Rabbis have taught: A maiden who gives herself up to prayer [and] a gadabout widow . . . – behold these bring destruction upon the world. But it is not so, for Rabbi Joḥanan [Palestinian, second and third centuries CE] has said: We learnt fear of sin from a maiden [who gave

72. A measure of volume equal to approximately 1.2 liters.
73. A luxurious style of living.
74. The House of Study. This occurred during the period when the Romans forbade study of the Torah and observance of the other commandments.
75. The reference is to Abigail who, when speaking about her husband Nabal, put in a word for herself, proposing that David should marry her, as he later did, if Nabal should die.

herself up to prayer] and [confidence in] the bestowal of reward from a [gadabout] widow! Fear of sin from a maiden – for Rabbi Johanan heard a maiden fall upon her face and exclaim, 'Lord of the Universe! Thou hast created Paradise and Gehinnom; Thou hast created righteous and wicked. May it be Thy will that men should not stumble through me.' [Confidence in] the bestowal of reward from a widow – a certain widow had a synagogue in her neighborhood; yet she used to come daily to the school of Rabbi Johanan and pray there. He said to her, 'My daughter, is there not a synagogue in your neighborhood? She answered him, "Rabbi, but have I not the reward for the steps!"[76] When it is said "that they bring destruction upon the world" the reference is to such a person as Johani the daughter of Retibi.'[77] (Soncino)

Children

8.91 Babylonian Talmud, *Kethuboth* 50a (edited *ca.* 500 CE)

The following excerpt emphasizes how praiseworthy it is to maintain children, especially orphans.

'Happy are they that keep justice, that do righteousness at all times.' (Ps 106:3). Is it possible to do righteousness at all times? This, explained our Rabbis of Jabneh [Palestinian, end of the first century CE] (or, as others say, Rabbi Eliezer [ben Hyrcanus, Palestinian, end of the first and beginning of the second century CE]), refers to a man who maintains his sons and daughters while they are young.[78] Rabbi Samuel bar Nahmani [Palestinian, third century CE] said: This refers to a man who brings up an orphan boy or orphan girl in his house and enables them to marry. (Soncino)

8.92 Babylonian Talmud, *Semahoth* 2:6 (*ca.* eighth century CE)

The passage below advises parents on how to discipline children. Punishment should be prompt but not excessive.

A man should never threaten his child but punish him at once or say nothing. Rabbi Simeon ben Eleazar [Babylonian, end of second and beginning of third century CE] says: The proper course with a child and with a woman is to push away with the left hand and draw near with the right hand. (A.C.)

Education

8.93 Babylonian Talmud, *Baba Bathra* 21a (edited *ca.* 500 CE)

Below is an account of the establishment by the community of schools for young boys, as well as advice by various rabbis as to the age when such

---

76. I.e., for walking the extra distance.
77. Johani is said to have been a widow who through witchcraft made childbirth difficult for a woman but who later prayed in her behalf.
78. Legally children have no claim upon a father for maintenance after the age of six.

an education should begin, how the pupils should be taught and disciplined, what the maximum number of pupils in a class should be, and what qualifications are to be sought in a teacher.

Verily the name of that man is to be blessed, to wit Joshua ben Gamala [Palestinian, first century CE],[79] for but for him the Torah would have been forgotten from Israel. For at first if a child had a father, his father taught him, and if he had no father he did not learn at all. . . . They then made an ordinance that teachers of children should be appointed in Jerusalem. . . . Even so, however, if a child had a father, the father would take him up to Jerusalem and have him taught there, and if not, he would not go up to learn there. They therefore ordained that teachers should be appointed in each prefecture, and that boys should enter school at the age of sixteen or seventeen. [They did so] and if the teacher punished them they used to rebel and leave the school. At length Joshua ben Gamala came and ordained that teachers of young children should be appointed in each district and each town, and that children should enter school at the age of six or seven.

Rab [Babylonian, second and third centuries CE] said to Rabbi Samuel ben Shilath [Babylonian, first half of the third century CE]: Before the age of six do not accept pupils; from that age you may accept them, and stuff them with Torah like an ox. Rab also said to Rabbi Samuel ben Shilath: When you punish a pupil, only hit him with a shoe latchet.[80] The attentive one will read [of himself], and if one is inattentive, put him next to a diligent one. . . .

Raba [Babylonian, third and fourth centuries CE] said: Under the ordinance of Joshua ben Gamala, children are not to be sent [every day to school] from one town to another,[81] but they can be compelled to go from one synagogue to another [in the same town]. If, however, there is a river in between, we cannot compel them. . . .

Raba further said: The number of pupils to be assigned to each teacher is twenty-five. If there are fifty, we appoint two teachers. If there are forty, we appoint an assistant, at the expense of the town.

Raba also said: If we have a teacher who gets on with the children and there is another who can get on better, we do not replace the first by the second, for fear that the second when appointed will become indolent.[82] Rabbi Dimi from Nehardea [Babylonian, fourth century CE], however, held that he would exert himself still more if appointed: 'the jealousy of scribes increaseth wisdom.'

Raba further said: If there are two teachers of whom one gets on fast but with mistakes and the other slowly but without mistakes, we appoint the one who gets on fast and makes mistakes, since the mistakes correct themselves in time. Rabbi Dimi from Nehardea, on the other hand, said that we appoint the one who goes slowly but makes no mistakes, for once a mistake is implanted it cannot be eradicated. (Soncino)

79. Joshua ben Gamala was a high priest who died in 69 or 70 CE.
80. Hence, do not hurt him excessively.
81. There is fear that the child may be assaulted along the way.
82. Inasmuch as he will have no competitor.

Moral Life: Charity

8.94 Babylonian Talmud, *Baba Bathra* 9a (edited *ca.* 500 CE)

Here we see the importance attached to the precept of giving charity (literally, "righteousness").

Rabbi Assi [Babylonian, third and fourth centuries CE] . . . said: Charity is equivalent to all the other religious precepts combined. (Soncino)

8.95 Babylonian Talmud, *Baba Bathra* 10a (edited *ca.* 500 CE)

Here we see the greatest rabbis of their day, Rabbis Aqiba and Meir, and their answer to the charge that God was guilty of neglecting the poor.

It has been taught: Rabbi Meir [Palestinian, second century CE] used to say: The critic [of Judaism] may bring against you the argument, 'If your God loves the poor, why does He not support them?' If so, answer him, 'So that through them we may be saved from the punishment of Gehinnom.'[83] This question was actually put by Turnus Rufus[84] to Rabbi Aqiba [Palestinian, first and second centuries CE]: 'If your God loves the poor, why does He not support them?' He replied, 'So that we may be saved through them from the punishment of Gehinnom.' 'On the contrary,' said the other, 'it is this which condemns you to Gehinnom. I will illustrate by a parable. Suppose an earthly king was angry with his servant and put him in prison and ordered that he should be given no food or drink, and a man went and gave him food and drink. If the king heard, would he not be angry with him? And you are called "servants," as it is written, "For unto me the children of Israel are servants"' (Lev 25:55). Rabbi Aqiba answered him: 'I will illustrate by another parable. Suppose an earthly king was angry with his son, and put him in prison and ordered that no food and drink should be given to him, and someone went and gave him food and drink. If the king heard of it, would he not send him a present?' (Soncino)

Religious Life of Jews in Palestine

The Temple and the Priesthood

BIBLIOGRAPHY

Edith Mary Smallwood, "High Priests and Politics in Roman Palestine," *JTS* 13 (1962), 14–34.

Jacob Liver, "The Half Sheqel Offering in Biblical and Post-Biblical Literature," *HTR* 56 (1963), 173–98.

Joachim Jeremias, *Jerusalem in the Time of Jesus: An Investigation into Economic and Social Conditions during the New Testament Period* (trans. of *Jerusalem zur Zeit Jesu: Kulturgeschichtliche Untersuchung zur neutestamentlichen Zeitgeschichte* by F. H. and C. H. Cave, 1969), 147–221.

---

83. I.e., through the performance of a *mitzvah*.
84. Roman governor of Judaea in the first half of the second century CE.

John Bowker, *Jesus and the Pharisees* (1973).

Shmuel Safrai, "The Temple and the Divine Service," in Michael Avi-Yonah and Zvi Baras, eds, *World History of the Jewish People*, vol. 7 (1973), 282–337.

Joseph Blenkinsopp, "Prophecy and Priesthood in Josephus," *JJS* 25 (1974), 239–62.

Menahem Stern, "Aspects of Jewish Society: The Priesthood and Other Classes," in Shmuel Safrai and Menahem Stern, eds, *The Jewish People in the First Century*, vol. 2 (1976), 561–630.

Shmuel Safrai, "The Temple," in Shmuel Safrai and Menahem Stern, eds, *The Jewish People in the First Century*, vol. 2 (1976), 865–907.

Richard A. Horsley, "High Priests and the Politics of Roman Palestine," *JSJ* 17 (1986), 23–55.

Steve Mason, "Priesthood in Josephus and the 'Pharisaic Revolution,'" *JBL* 106 (1987), 657–61.

Clemens Thoma, "The High Priesthood in the Judgment of Josephus," *JBH* (1989), 196–215.

Seth Schwartz, "The Priesthood," in his *Josephus and Judaean Politics* (1990), 58–109.

Doron Mendels, "Jerusalem: Capital, Temple, and Cult (200–63 BCE)" and "Jerusalem and the Temple, 63 BCE–66 CE," in his *The Rise and Fall of Jewish Nationalism* (1992), 107–59, 277–331.

E. P. Sanders, *Judaism: Practice and Belief 63 BCE–66 CE* (1992), 45–189.

8.96 Hecataeus of Abdera (*ca.* 300 BCE), cited by Diodorus the Sicilian, *Historical Library* 40.3.4–6

The earliest extra-biblical description of the priests and their duties and of the reverence which the Jews show to the high priest is to be found in Hecataeus, who is quite clearly impressed with the entire arrangement.

He [Moses] picked out the men of most refinement and with the greatest ability to head the entire nation, and appointed them priests; and he ordained that they should occupy themselves with the Temple and the honors and sacrifices offered to their God. These same men he appointed to be judges in all major disputes, and entrusted to them the guardianship of the laws and customs. For this reason the Jews never have a king,[85] and authority over the people is regularly vested in whichever priest is regarded as superior to his colleagues in wisdom and virtue.[86] They call this man the high priest, and believe that he acts as a messenger to them of God's commandments. It is he, we are told, who in their assemblies and other gatherings announces what is ordained; and the Jews are so docile in such matters that straightway they fall to the ground and do reverence to the high priest when he expounds the commandments to them. (LCL)

---

85. Presumably Hecataeus is misled by the fact that in his own day the Jews did not have a king and, for that matter, did not have an independent state.

86. Hecataeus is mistaken, since, in general, the high priesthood passed from father to son and, in any case, was restricted to a particular family, the Zadokite, from the time of the Exile to Hecataeus' own day.

8.97 Josephus, *Life* 1 (first century CE)

So long as the Temple stood it was the central focus of religious life of the Jews of Palestine. Inasmuch as Josephus himself was a priest and was particularly proud of that fact, he has much to say about the priesthood, notably about the care that the priests took to ensure that their lineage should be pure.

My family is no ignoble one, tracing its descent far back to priestly ancestors. Different races base their claim to nobility on various grounds; with us a connection with the priesthood is the hallmark of an illustrious line. Not only, however, were my ancestors priests, but they belonged to the first of the twenty-four courses – a peculiar distinction – and to the most eminent of its constituent clans. (LCL)

8.98 Josephus, *Against Apion* 1.30–6

Josephus here sets forth the attention given by priests, both in Palestine and in the Diaspora, to investigating the genealogy of their brides. In particular, they were heedful to disqualify for marriage with priests women who had been taken captive. When Josephus himself (*Life* 414) states that he married a woman who had been taken captive at Caesarea, he is careful to add that she was a virgin.

Not only did our ancestors in the first instance set over this business [the care bestowed upon the Scriptures] men of the highest character, devoted to the service of God, but they took precautions to ensure that the priests' lineage should be kept unadulterated and pure. A member of the priestly order must, to beget a family, marry a woman of his own race, without regard to her wealth or other distinctions; but he must investigate her pedigree, obtaining the genealogy from the archives and producing a number of witnesses. And this practice of ours is not confined to the home country of Judaea, but wherever there is a Jewish colony, there too a strict account is kept by the priests of their marriages; I allude to the Jews in Egypt and Babylon and other parts of the world in which any of the priestly order are living in dispersion. A statement is drawn up by them and sent to Jerusalem, showing the names of the bride and her father and more remote ancestors, together with the names of the witnesses.

In the not infrequent event of war, for instance when our country was invaded by Antiochus Epiphanes, by Pompey the Great, by Quintilius Varus, and above all in our own times, the surviving priests compile fresh records from the archives; they also pass scrutiny upon the remaining women, and disallow marriage with any who have been taken captive, suspecting them of having had frequent intercourse with foreigners.

But the most convincing proof of our accuracy in this matter is that our records contain the names of our high priests, with the succession from father to son for the last two thousand years. And whoever violates any of the above rules is forbidden to minister at the altars or to take any other part in divine worship. (LCL)

8.99 Josephus, *Against Apion* 1.284

Josephus here notes that even the slightest mutilation was sufficient to disqualify a person from exercising the duties of a priest.

The very slightest mutilation of the person was a disqualification for the priesthood, and a priest who in the course of his ministry met with such an accident was deprived of his office. (LCL)

8.100 Josephus, *Against Apion* 2.102–9

Josephus comments on the design of the Temple and the precision of the Temple ritual, including the hours when the priests were permitted to enter the Temple. He is careful to add that unlike the procedure in many pagan cults there were no mysteries in the Temple.

All who ever saw our Temple are aware of the general design of the building, and the inviolable barriers which preserved its sanctity. It had four surrounding courts, each with its special statutory restrictions. The outer court was open to all, foreigners included; women during their impurity were alone refused admission. To the second court all Jews were admitted and, when uncontaminated by any defilement, their wives; to the third male Jews, if clean and purified; to the fourth the priests robed in their priestly vestments.

The sanctuary was entered only by the high priests, clad in the raiment peculiar to themselves. So careful is the provision for all the details of the service that the priests' entry is timed to certain hours. Their duty was to enter in the morning, when the Temple was opened, and to offer the customary sacrifices, and again at mid-day, until the Temple was closed.

One further point: no vessel whatever might be carried into the Temple, the only objects in which were an altar, a table, a censer, and a lampstand, all mentioned in the Law. There was nothing more; no unmentionable mysteries took place, no repast was served within the building.

The foregoing statements are attested by the whole community and conclusively proved by the order of procedure. For although there are four priestly tribes,[87] each comprising upwards of five thousand members, these officiate by rotation for a fixed period of days; when the term of one party ends, others come to offer the sacrifices in their place, and assembling at mid-day in the Temple, take over from the outgoing ministers the keys of the building and all its vessels, duly numbered. Nothing of the nature of food or drink is brought within the Temple; objects of this kind may not even be offered on the altar, save those which are prepared for the sacrifices. (LCL)

---

87. The reference here is to the four priestly tribes which returned from Babylonia to Palestine with Zerubbabel (Ezra 2:36 and Neh 7:39). Elsewhere Josephus (*Life* 2) follows 1 Chron 24:7–18 in speaking of twenty-four courses of priests.

8.101 Josephus, *Against Apion* 2.185–9

Those who were entrusted with the arrangement of divine worship had to be priests who were especially gifted with eloquence. Their duties included a strict superintendence of the Law and the activities of daily life.

Could there be a finer or more equitable polity than one which sets God at the head of the universe, which assigns the administration of its highest affairs to the whole body of priests, and entrusts to the supreme high priest the direction of the other priests? These men, moreover, owed their original promotion by the legislator to their high office, not to any superiority in wealth or other accidental advantages. No; of all his companions, the men to whom he entrusted the ordering of divine worship as their first charge were those who were pre-eminently gifted with persuasive eloquence and discretion. But this charge further embraced a strict superintendence of the Law and of the pursuits of everyday life; for the appointed duties of the priests included general supervision, the trial of cases of litigation, and the punishment of condemned persons. (LCL)

8.102 Josephus, *Jewish Antiquities* 3.184–7

We may see how significant the high priest is for Josephus, in universal and not merely national, terms, in his elaborate allegorical explanation of the meaning of his garments.

The high priest's tunic likewise signifies the earth, being of linen, and its blue the arch of heaven, while it recalls the lightnings by its pomegranates, the thunder by the sound of its bells. His upper garment, too, denotes universal nature, which it pleased God to make of four elements, being further interwoven with gold in token, I imagine, of the all-pervading sunlight. The *essen* [breast-plate], again, he set in the midst of this garment, after the manner of the earth, which occupies the midmost place [in the universe]; and by the girdle wherewith he encompassed it he signified the ocean, which holds the whole in its embrace. Sun and moon are indicated by the two sardonyxes wherewith he pinned the high priest's robe.
    As for the twelve stones, whether one would prefer to read in them the months or the constellations of like number, which the Greeks call the circle of the zodiac, he will not mistake the lawgiver's intention. Furthermore, the headdress appears to me to symbolize heaven, being blue; else it would not have borne upon it the name of God, blazoned upon the crown – a crown, moreover, of gold by reason of that sheen in which the Deity most delights. (LCL)

8.103 Josephus, *Jewish Antiquities* 20.179–81 (59 CE)

The passage below illustrates the factional strife within the aristocracy. Chief priests fought against one another, as well as against ordinary priests and leaders of the populace. In particular, the populace opposed the iniquity of some of the chief priests, who stole from the ordinary priests.

At this time King Agrippa [II] conferred the high priesthood upon Ishmael, the son of Phabi. There now was enkindled enmity among the chief priests against one another, and strife between the chief priests and the [ordinary] priests and the prominent members of the populace of Jerusalem. Each of the factions formed and collected for itself a band of the most reckless revolutionaries and acted as their leader. And when they clashed, they used abusive language and pelted each other with stones. And there was not even one person to rebuke them. No, it was as if there was no one in charge of the city, so that they acted as they did with full license. Such was the shamelessness and effrontery which possessed the chief priests that they actually were so brazen as to send slaves to the threshing floors to receive the tithes that were due to the priests, with the result that the poorer priests starved to death. Thus did the violence of the contending factions suppress all justice. (LCL [amended])

8.104 Babylonian Talmud, *Pesaḥim* 57a (edited *ca.* 500 CE)

The strife between the family of the high priest Ishmael ben Phabi and the ordinary priests that is mentioned by Josephus in the passage above is likewise cited by the Talmud in the passage below.

Abba Saul ben Bathnith [Palestinian, first century CE] said in the name of Abba Joseph ben Ḥanin [Palestinian, first century CE]: . . . 'Woe is me because of the house of Ishmael the son of Phabi, woe is me because of their fists! For they are high priests and their sons are [Temple] treasurers and their sons-in-law are trustees and their servants beat the people with staves.' (Soncino)

8.105 Josephus, *Jewish Antiquities* 20.206–7 (*ca.* 62–4 CE)

Josephus here relates the actions of the servants of the high priest Ananias in actually beating those who refused to give them tithes, with the result that some ordinary priests even starved to death.

Ananias [the high priest] had servants who were utter rascals and who, combining operations with the most reckless men, would go to the threshing floors and take by force the tithes of the priests; nor did they refrain from beating those who refused to give. The chief priests were guilty of the same practices as their slaves, and no one could stop them. So it happened at that time that those of the priests who in olden days were maintained by the tithes now starved to death. (LCL)

8.106 Josephus, *Jewish Antiquities* 20.216–18 (*ca.* 64 CE)

Josephus here relates the successful attempt of the Levites to wear robes on a par with the priests.

Those of the Levites – this is one of our tribes – who were singers of hymns urged the king [Agrippa II] to convene the Sanhedrin and get them permission to wear linen robes on equal terms with the priests, maintaining that it was fitting that he should introduce, to mark his reign, some innovation by which he would be remembered. Nor did they fail to obtain their request; for the king, with the consent of those who attended the Sanhedrin, allowed the singers of hymns to discard their former robes and to wear linen ones such as they wished. A part of the tribe that served in the Temple were also permitted to learn the hymns by heart, as they had requested. All this was contrary to the ancestral laws, and such transgression was bound to make us liable to punishment. (LCL)

The Sanhedrin

BIBLIOGRAPHY

Sidney B. Hoenig, *The Great Sanhedrin: A Study of the Origin, Development, Composition, and Functions of the Bet Din ha-Gadol during the Second Jewish Commonwealth* (1953).

Hugo Mantel, *Studies in the History of the Sanhedrin* (1961).

Joseph S. Kennard, "The Jewish Provincial Assembly," *ZNW* 53 (1962), 25–51.

Ellis Rivkin, "Beth Din, Boulé, Sanhedrin: A Tragedy of Errors," *HUCA* 46 (1975), 181–99.

Alon (1980), 185–252.

Joshua Efron, "The Great Sanhedrin in Vision and Reality," in his *Studies on the Hasmonean Period* (1987), 287–338.

James McLaren, *Power and Politics in Palestine: The Jews and the Governing of Their Land. 100 BC–AD 70* (1991).

Anthony J. Saldarini, "Sanhedrin," *ABD*, vol. 5 (1992), 975–80.

Sanders (1992), 472–88.

There is a wide range of opinion among scholars with regard to the nature of the Sanhedrin [Synhedrion], largely occasioned by the debate with regard to the nature, composition, and powers of the Sanhedrin mentioned in the Gospels. Part of the confusion is due to the failure to realize that the Greek word *synedrion*, which passed over into Hebrew as *sanhedrin*, is simply a gathering for consultation and not necessarily for purposes of a trial, whereas the Sanhedrin (capitalized) always refers to the supreme Jewish court of seventy-one members.

8.107 Mishnah, *Sanhedrin* 1:6, 4:5 (codified *ca.* 220 CE]

In the passage which follows we have the account in the Mishnah, as codified by Rabbi Judah the Prince, of the make-up of the Sanhedrin and of their procedure in trials, and, in particular, their method of interrogating witnesses.

The great Sanhedrin was [made up of] of seventy-one members, and the small one was [made up of] twenty-three.... Your verdict of acquittal is not equivalent to your verdict of guilt. Your verdict of acquittal may be on the vote of a majority of one, but your vote for guilt must be by a majority of two....

How do they admonish witnesses in capital cases? They would bring them in and admonish them [as follows]: 'Perhaps it is your intention to give testimony (1) on the basis of supposition, (2) hearsay, or (3) of what one witness has told another; or you may think, "We heard it from a reliable person." Or, you may not know that in the end we are going to interrogate you with appropriate interrogation and examination. You should know that the laws governing a trial for property cases are different from the laws governing a trial for capital cases. In the case of a trial for property cases, a person pays money and achieves atonement for himself. In capital cases [the accused's] blood and the blood of all those who were destined to be born from him [who was wrongfully convicted] are held against him [who testifies falsely] to the end of time.' (J.N.)

8.108 Josephus, *Jewish Antiquities* 14.165, 167–8, 170–2, 174–5 (*ca.* 47 BCE)

Herod had been accused of taking the law into his own hands in putting to death a certain Ezekias, a brigand-chief, and many of his men. In the passage below we see that Josephus believed that a court, the Synhedrion, rather than the ruler of the state, should try capital cases; but there is no indication in this passage that the Synhedrion was a standing body, with a fixed number of members and of a given composition. In the end, as the passage indicates, in practice the Synhedrion was circumvented by power politics and, in particular, the intervention of the Roman governor of Syria and the appearance of Herod with his troops.

The chief Jews were in great fear when they saw how powerful and reckless Herod was and how much he desired to be a dictator. And so they came to Hyrcanus [the king and high priest] and now openly accused Antipater [Herod's father], saying, 'How long will you keep quiet in the face of what is happening? . . . Thus Herod, his son, has killed Ezekias and many of his men in violation of our Law, which forbids us to slay a man, even an evildoer, unless he has first been condemned by the Synhedrion to suffer this fate. He, however, has dared to do this without authority from you.'

Having heard these arguments, Hyrcanus was persuaded. And his anger was further kindled by the mothers of the men who had been murdered by Herod, for every day in the Temple they kept begging the king and the people to have Herod brought to judgment in the Synhedrion for what he had done. . . .

However, Sextus, the governor of Syria, wrote to urge Hyrcanus to acquit Herod of the charge, and added threats as to what would happen if he disobeyed. The letter from Sextus gave Hyrcanus a pretext for letting Herod go without suffering any harm from the Synhedrion; for he loved him as a son. But when Herod stood in the Synhedrion with his troops, he overawed them all, and no one of those who had denounced him before his arrival dared to accuse him thereafter; instead there was silence and doubt about what was to be done. While they were in this state, someone named Samaias,[88] an upright man and for that reason superior to fear, arose and said, . . . 'Be assured, . . . this man, whom you now wish to release for Hyrcanus' sake, will one day punish you and the king as well.' And he was not mistaken in either

---

88. Elsewhere (Josephus, *Antiquities* 15.3) Samaias is referred to as a disciple of the Pharisee Pollion (who is identified by some scholars with Abtalion).

part of his prediction. For when Herod assumed royal power, he killed Hyrcanus and all the other members of the Synhedrion with the exception of Samaias. (LCL)

8.109 Josephus, *Jewish Antiquities* 15.166, 167, 168, 170, 171, 172, 173–4 (*ca.* 31 BCE)

In the following passage we see how the Synhedrion functioned in practice. Herod himself, at least according to his Memoirs, as the passage indicates, thought that there should have been a Synhedrion for the case of Hyrcanus, the high priest; but the Synhedrion did not act on its own but merely went along with what the ruler had decided. In fact, Josephus himself, as we see below, follows the account taken from Herod's Memoirs with another version, according to which Herod tricked Hyrcanus into admitting that he had received from Malchus, the Arab ruler, four beasts for riding, which Herod construed as evidence that Hyrcanus was guilty of accepting a bribe and consequently ordered him to be put to death, clearly without a trial before the Synhedrion.

Alexandra[89] . . . kept telling her father [Hyrcanus] that he ought not forever to put up with Herod's lawless treatment of their family. . . . She begged him to write of this matter to Malchus, who was ruler of the Arabs, and ask him to receive them and lead them to safety. . . . Hyrcanus rejected her arguments. Since, however, she had an aggressive and very womanly nature and did not leave off either night or day but always kept speaking to him about this matter and about Herod's treacherous designs against them, he finally let himself be persuaded to give to Dositheus, one of his friends, a letter in which it was arranged that the Arab should send him some horsemen who were to take them and escort them to Lake Asphaltitis [the Dead Sea]. . . . Since he [Dositheus] counted on hopes of greater reward from the king than from Hyrcanus, he handed the letter over to Herod. The king . . . urged him to do him the further service of . . . taking it to Malchus. . . . The Arab ruler wrote in reply that he would receive both Hyrcanus himself and all his party. . . . When Herod received this letter, he immediately sent for Hyrcanus and questioned him about the agreements which he had made with Malchus. When the other denied having made any, Herod showed the letters to the Synhedrion and had the man put to death.

We have written about these matters as they are found in the Memoirs of King Herod. But other sources do not agree with this account, for they hold that it was not for such reasons that Herod killed Hyrcanus but rather that he did so after bringing charges against him which were invented with characteristic trickery. Their account is as follows. Once, while they were at a banquet, Herod, without giving Hyrcanus any ground for suspicion, put the question to him whether he had received any letters from Malchus, and when Hyrcanus admitted having received greeting-cards from him, he asked also

---

89. Alexandra was the daughter of the high priest Hyrcanus and the mother of Mariamne, Herod's wife.

whether he had taken any gift from him, and the other replied that he had received nothing more than four beasts for riding, which Malchus had sent him. This act Herod construed as evidence of bribe-taking and treason, and ordered the man to be strangled. (LCL)

8.110 Josephus, *Jewish Antiquities* 16.356–7, 360, 362, 363, 365, 367

In some instances, noted by Josephus, a ruler assembled a *synhedrion* (that is, a council) as a court on a particular case, as, for example, when Herod assembled a *synhedrion*, upon the suggestion of the Emperor Augustus, to try two of his sons for treason. In this case the *synhedrion*, as we see, consisted of 150 men, whom Herod himself had chosen, and included Roman officials.

And so, being reconciled with Herod, Caesar [Augustus] wrote to him, saying that he was distressed because of his sons, and that if they had been so reckless as to attempt an unnatural crime, he ought to punish them as parricides – for this power was granted him – but if they had planned to flee, he should merely admonish them and not inflict irreparable punishment upon them. He also advised him to appoint and convene a *synhedrion* at Berytus, where Romans were settled as colonists, and to take along the governors [of Syria], Archelaus, the king of Cappadocia, and as many others as he thought conspicuously friendly or important, and with their advice to determine what should be done. . . .
   He [Herod] therefore sent letters around and invited to the council those whom he thought suitable, with the exception of Archelaus. Him he did not choose to have present either because of his hatred of him or because he thought that he would interfere with his plans. . . .
   All alone, therefore, and by himself he [Herod] went before the [*synedrion* of a] hundred and fifty men seated there, and made the accusation. . . . He did not permit the members of the council to examine the proofs but offered arguments in advocacy of these that were a disgrace for a father to use against his sons. . . . He said that both by nature and by Caesar's grant he himelf had authority to act. . . . After the king had spoken in this manner, without letting the youths be produced even long enough to defend themselves, the members of the council, being agreed that they were in no position to soften him or effect a reconciliation, confirmed his authority. (LCL)

8.111 New Testament, *Mark* 14:53–64 (29 CE)

There are a number of differences between the portrayal of the trial of Jesus before the Sanhedrin in the Gospels and that in the Talmud in the tractate *Sanhedrin*: the presiding officer is the high priest, not a Pharisaic scholar; the place is the house of the high priest, not the Hall of Gazit; the trial takes place at night or on a festival morning, whereas it is prohibited then according to the Talmud; the verdict is rendered on the same day, whereas it must be delayed for at least one day according to the Talmud; the witnesses are not warned, as they must be according to the Talmud;

the defendant accuses himself, whereas self-incrimination is not permitted according to the Talmud; a unanimous vote for conviction by the Sanhedrin acquits the defendant, according to the Talmud. These discrepancies are sometimes explained as due to the fact that the Mishnah is a Pharisaic work dating from about 200 CE, whereas the trial took place in 29 CE, or that the emergency justified departure from the usual procedure. Yet, if one claims that Jesus' trial does not reflect the procedure found in the Mishnah, one must declare that the procedure changed very drastically within a short period of time. In point of fact, however, as we see in the pages of Josephus, rulers routinely managed in various ways to execute people who were deemed troublesome or dangerous. If that is the case, Jesus was the rule rather than the exception.

And they led Jesus to the high priest; and all the chief priests and the elders and the scribes were assembled. And Peter had followed him at a distance, right into the courtyard of the high priest; and he was sitting with the guards, and warming himself at the fire. Now the chief priests and whole council [Sanhedrin] sought testimony against Jesus to put him to death; but they found none. For many bore false witness against him, and their witness did not agree. And some stood up and bore false witness against him, saying, 'We heard him say, "I will destroy this temple that is made with hands, and in three days I will build another, not made with hands."' Yet not even so did their testimony agree. And the high priest stood up in the midst, and asked Jesus, 'Have you no answer to make? What is it that these men testify against you?' But he was silent and made no answer. Again the high priest asked him, 'Are you the Christ, the Son of the Blessed?' And Jesus said, 'I am; and you will see the Son of man sitting at the right hand of Power, and coming with the clouds of heaven.' And the high priest tore his mantle, and said, 'Why do we still need witnesses? You have heard his blasphemy. What is your decision?' And they all condemned him as deserving death. (RSV)

8.112 Josephus, *Jewish Antiquities*, 20.200–3 (62 CE)

In the passage which follows, as in the Gospels, it is the high priest who convenes the Synhedrion for the trial of James, the brother of Jesus, but he is criticized for doing so, because he had not received the prior consent of the Roman procurator.

He [the high priest Ananus] convened the judges of the Synhedrion and brought before them a man named James, the brother of Jesus who was called the Christ, and certain others. He accused them of having transgressed the law and delivered them up to be stoned. Those of the inhabitants of the city who were considered the most fair-minded and who were strict in observance of the law were offended at this. They therefore secretly sent to King Agrippa [II] urging him, for Ananus had not even been correct in his first step,[90] to order him to desist from any further such actions.

90. I.e., in convening the Sanhedrin without the procurator's consent.

Certain of them even went to meet [the procurator] Albinus, who was on his way from Alexandria, and informed him that Ananus had no authority to convene the Synhedrion without his consent. Convinced by these words, Albinus angrily wrote to Ananus threatening to take vengeance upon him. King Agrippa, because of Ananus' action, deposed him from the high priesthood which he had held for three months and replaced him with Jesus the son of Damnaeus. (LCL)

8.113 Josephus, Jewish Antiquities 20.216–17 (64 CE)

In the passage which follows it is the king who convenes the Synhedrion. The occasion is not a trial but rather a request to grant the Levites the right to wear garments on a par with the priests.

Those of the Levites ... who were singers of hymns urged the king [Agrippa II] to convene the Synhedrion and get them permission to wear linen robes on equal terms with the priests.... Nor did they fail to obtain their request; for the king, with the consent of those who attended the Synhedrion, allowed the singers of hymns to discard their former robes and to wear linen ones such as they wished. (LCL)

8.114 Josephus, Life 62 (66 CE)

In the passage which follows we see still another function of the Synhedrion, namely to give political and military advice, in this case to Josephus, who had just been appointed general in Galilee in the war that had just broken out against the Romans.

When, on my arrival in Galilee, I was informed of the above position of affairs,[91] I wrote to the Synhedrion at Jerusalem and asked for instructions how I should proceed. They advised me to remain at my post and take precautions for Galilee, retaining my colleagues, if willing to stay. (LCL)

The 'Amme Ha-aretz

BIBLIOGRAPHY

Aharon Oppenheimer, *The 'Am Ha-Aretz. A Study in the Social History of the Jewish People in the Hellenistic-Roman Period* (1977).

8.115 Babylonian Talmud, Pesaḥim 49a–b (edited ca. 500 CE)

During the Second Temple period the *'amme ha-aretz* were presumed to be lax in the observance of the laws pertaining to tithing and to ritual impurity, in contrast to the Pharisees and the *ḥaverim*,[92] who were very careful about these laws. Hence, the Pharisees and *ḥaverim* had to create a barrier between themselves and the *'amme ha-aretz* so as not to eat untithed produce or become unclean. The *'amme ha-aretz* belonged mainly, though not exclusively, to the lower classes; but the gap between

---

91. That Varus, the Jewish king Agrippa II's viceroy, who intended to massacre in one day the Jewish population of Caesarea, was recalled by King Agrippa II.

92. The *ḥaverim* were a group that undertook to observe with the greatest care the laws of *terumah* ("heave-offering"), *ma'aser*, purity, and impurity.

them and the Pharisees was not unbridgeable; and there were economic, cultural, and family links between them. Some have connected them with the beginnings of Christianity. After the destruction of the Temple in 70 the term took on the meaning of "unlearned," and the animosity between them and the learned class grew in intensity, as the passage below indicates.

Our Rabbis taught: Let a man always sell all he has and marry the daughter of a scholar, for if he dies or goes into exile, he is assured that his children will be scholars. But let him not marry the daughter of an *'am ha-aretz*, for if he dies or goes into exile, his children will be *'amme ha-aretz*.

Our Rabbis taught: Let a man always sell all he has and marry the daughter of a scholar, and marry his daughter to a scholar. This may be compared to [the grafting of] grapes of a vine with grapes of a vine, [which is] a seemly and acceptable thing. But let him not marry the daughter of an *'am ha-aretz*. This may be compared to [the grafting of] grapes of a vine with berries of a thorn bush, [which is] a repulsive and unacceptable thing.

Our Rabbis taught: Let a man always sell all he has and marry the daughter of a scholar. If he does not find the daughter of a scholar, let him marry the daughter of [one of] the great men of the generation.[93] If he does not find the daughter of [one of] the great men of the generation, let him marry the daughter of the head of synagogues. If he does not find the daughter of the head of synagogues, let him marry the daughter of a charity treasurer. If he does not find the daughter of a charity treasurer, let him marry the daughter of an elementary school-teacher, but let him not marry the daughter of an *'am ha-aretz*, because they are detestable and their wives are vermin, and of their daughters it is said, 'Cursed be he that lieth with any manner of beast' [Deut 27:21]. . . .

Rabbi Eleazar [ben Azariah, Palestinian, end of first century and beginning of second century CE] said: 'An *'am ha-aretz*, it is permitted to stab him [even] on the Day of Atonement that falls on the Sabbath.' Said his disciples to him, 'Master, say to slaughter him [ritually]?' He replied: 'This [ritual slaughter] requires a benediction, whereas that [stabbing] does not require a benediction.'

Rabbi Eleazar said: 'One must not join company with an *'am ha-aretz* on the road, because it is said, "for that [the Torah] is thy life, and the length of thy days" [Deut 30:20], [seeing that] he has no care [pity] for his own life,[94] how much the more for the life of his companions!' Rabbi Samuel bar Naḥmani [Palestinian, third century CE] said in Rabbi Joḥanan's [Palestinian, third century CE] name: 'One may tear an *'am ha-aretz* like a fish!' Said Rabbi Samuel bar Isaac [Palestinian, fourth century CE]: 'And [this means] along his back.'

It was taught: Rabbi Aqiba [Palestinian, end of first century and beginning of second century CE] said: 'When I was an *'am ha-aretz*[95] I

93. Presumably the reference is to the civic leaders of the community.
94. Since he does not observe the Torah fully.
95. Before he became a great scholar Rabbi Aqiba was an illiterate shepherd.

said: "I would that I had a scholar [before me], and I would maul him like an ass."' Said his disciples to him, 'Rabbi, say like a dog!' 'The former bites and breaks the bones, while the latter bites but does not break the bones,' he answered them.

It was taught, Rabbi Meir [Palestinian, second century CE] used to say: Whoever marries his daughter to an *'am ha-aretz* is as though he bound and laid her before a lion: just as a lion tears [his prey] and devours it and has no shame, so an *'am ha-aretz* strikes and cohabits and has no shame.

It was taught, Rabbi Eliezer [ben Hyrcanus, Palestinian, end of the first century, beginning of second century] said: But that we are necessary to them for trade, they would kill us. Rabbi Ḥiyya [Palestinian and Babylonian, end of second century CE] taught: Whoever studies the Torah in front of an *'am ha-aretz* is as though he cohabited with his betrothed in his presence, for it is said, 'Moses commanded us a law, an inheritance [*morashah*] of the congregation of Jacob' [Deut 33:4]: read not *morashah* but *me'orasah* [the betrothed].[96] Greater is the hatred wherewith the *'amme ha-aretz* hate the scholar than the hatred wherewith the heathens hate Israel, and their wives [hate even] more than they. It was taught: He who has studied and then abandoned [the Torah] [hates the scholar] more than all of them.

Our Rabbis taught: Six things were said of the *'amme ha-aretz*: We do not commit testimony to them; we do not accept testimony from them; we do not reveal a secret to them; we do not appoint them as guardians for orphans; we do not appoint them stewards over charity funds; and we must not join their company on the road. Some say, We do not proclaim their losses too.[97] And the first Tanna?[98] Virtuous seed may sometimes issue from him, and they will enjoy it, as it is said, 'He will prepare it, and the just shall put it on.' [Job 27:17] (Soncino)

8.116 Mishnah, Ṭebul-Yom 4:5 (codified ca. 220 CE)

Lest one think that the *'amme ha-aretz* were completely untrustworthy when it came to ritual laws, we see in the passage below that they were actually trusted when it came to exchanging the second tithe for their produce. Apparently, there was fluctuation in the attitude toward the *'amme ha-aretz*. Toward the end of the second century the hatred diminished, and it was even said that an *'am ha-aretz* might be virtuous.

Formerly they used to say: one may redeem for the produce of an *'am ha-aretz*.[99] Later they reconsidered and said: Also for money of his. (Soncino)

96. The Torah is regarded as being betrothed to the Jewish people.
97. I.e., if one finds lost property one is required to announce it; but if the owner is an *'am ha-aretz* the finder is not bound to announce it.
98. I.e., why does he omit this last statement?
99. According to the Bible (Lev 27:30–31, Deut 14:22–26), one had to take the second tithe to Jerusalem and eat it there, or to redeem it and take the money to Jerusalem and spend it there. According to this passage in the Mishnah, we are not afraid that the produce which we purchase with the money we have acquired through the exchange of the second tithe for money is itself second-tithe produce.

Belief in a Messiah

BIBLIOGRAPHY

George Foot Moore, " Messianic Expectations," in his *Judaism in the First Centuries of the Christian Era: The Age of the Tannaim,* vol. 2 (1927), 323–76.

Abba Hillel Silver, *A History of Messianic Speculations in Israel* (1927).

William D. Davies, *Torah in the Messianic Age* (1952), 50–85.

Joseph Klausner, *The Messianic Idea in Israel from Its Beginning to the Completion of the Mishnah* (1955).

Sigmund Mowinckel, *He That Cometh* (trans. George W. Anderson, 1956).

Marinus de Jonge, "The Use of the Word 'Anointed' in the Time of Jesus," *NT* 8 (1966), 132–48.

Marinus de Jonge and Adam S. van der Woude, "Messianic Ideas in Late Judaism," *TDNT* 9 (1974), 509–27.

Samson H. Levey, *The Messiah: An Aramaic Interpretation; the Messianic Exegesis of the Targum* (1974).

Jacob Neusner, *Messiah in Context: Israel's History and Destiny in Formative Judaism* (1984).

Richard A. Horsley and John S. Hanson, *Bandits, Prophets and Messiahs* (1985).

Jacob Neusner, William S. Green, and Ernest Frerichs, eds, *Judaisms and Their Messiahs at the Turn of the Christian Era* (1987).

Ithamar Gruenwald, Shaul Shaked, and Gedaliahu G. Stroumsa, eds, *Messiah and Christos: Studies in the Jewish Origins of Christianity: Presented to David Flusser on the Occasion of His Seventy-fifth Birthday* (1992).

Richard A. Horsley, "Messianic Movements in Judaism," *ABD*, vol. 4 (1992), 791–7.

Marinus de Jonge, "Messiah," *ABD*, vol. 4 (1992), 777–88.

The title "Messiah" ["anointed," in Greek *Christos*] to designate an eschatological descendant of King David who would overcome the heathen and reign over a restored Kingdom of Israel to which all Jews from the Diaspora would return is not found explicitly in the Bible, though some Talmudic rabbis insisted that the idea is implicit in a number of biblical passages. In the period of the Second Temple we find a number of messianic figures. In particular, the figures of the high priest, the messianic king, and the prophet of the Last Days play important roles in the Dead Sea Scrolls. The expectation of a Davidic Messiah is apparent in the New Testament, where Jesus' genealogy is traced back to David. That the first revolt of the Jews in 66 CE against the Romans had a messianic element may be surmised from the fact that Menahem, the leader of the Sicarii, appears in the Temple dressed in royal robes (Josephus, *Jewish War* 2.444). The leader of the revolt in 115 CE, Lukuas-Andreas, is likewise hailed as a king (Eusebius, *Ecclesiastical History* 4.2) and is thus a messianic-like figure. Bar Kochba, the leader of the revolt in 132 CE, was hailed as Messiah by none other than the leading rabbi of the day, Aqiva (Jerusalem Talmud, *Ta'anith* 68d). There was much speculation among the rabbis, as the passages below indicate, as to what conditions would bring the Messiah.

8.117 *Psalms of Solomon* 17: 21–5 (first century BCE)

In the passage below we see that the messianic king will defeat the enemies of the Jews and restore the sanctity of Jerusalem.

Behold, O Lord, and raise up unto them their king, the son of
David,
At the time in which Thou seest, O God, that he may reign
over Israel Thy servant.
And gird him with strength, that he may shatter unrighteous
rulers,
And that he may purge Jerusalem from nations that trample
[her] down to destruction.
Wisely, righteously he shall thrust out sinners from [the]
inheritance,
He shall destroy the pride of the sinner as a potter's
vessel.
With a rod of iron he shall break in pieces all their substance,
He shall destroy the godless nations with the word of his
mouth;
At his rebuke nations shall flee before him,
And he shall reprove sinners for the thoughts of their heart.
(G.B.G.)

8.118 1 Enoch 48:8–10 (first or second century BCE)

The passage below describes in graphic terms how utterly the enemies of
the Jews will be overcome by the Messiah.

In these days downcast in countenance shall the kings of the
earth have become,
And the strong who possess the land because of the works of
their hands,
For on the day of their anguish and affliction they shall not [be
able to] save themselves.
And I will give them over into the hands of Mine elect:
As straw in the fire so shall they burn before the face of the
holy:
As lead in the water shall they sink before the face of the
righteous,
And no trace of them shall any more be found.
And on the day of their affliction there shall be rest on the
earth,
And before them they shall fall and not rise again:
And there shall be no one to take them with his hands and
raise them:
For they have denied the Lord of Spirits and His anointed.
The name of the Lord of Spirits be blessed. (R.H.C.)

8.119 Babylonian Talmud, Sanhedrin 98a–99a (edited ca. 500 CE)

There is a striking variety of opinions expressed by rabbis through the
first four centuries CE as to what will bring about the coming of the
Messiah and how long he will rule. Of particular interest is the statement
of the patriarch Hillel II that the Messiah has already come in the person
of King Hezekiah of Judah.

Rabbi Ḥama ben Ḥanina [Palestinian, second century CE] said: The son of David will not come until even the pettiest kingdom ceases [to have power] over Israel. . . . Rabbi Joḥanan [bar Nappaḥa, Palestinian, third century CE] . . . said: The son of David will come only in a generation that is either altogether righteous or altogether wicked. . . . Rab [Babylonian, third century CE] said: The son of David will not come until the [Roman] power enfolds Israel[100] for nine months. . . . Ulla [Palestinian, third century CE] said: Let him [the Messiah] come, but let me not see him.[101] . . . Rabbi Hillel [II] [patriarch in Palestine, fourth century CE] said: There shall be no Messiah for Israel because they have already enjoyed him in the days of Hezekiah. Rabbi Joseph [Babylonian, fourth century CE] said: May God forgive him [for saying so.] . . .

Another [Baraitha] taught: Rabbi Eliezer [ben Hyrcanus, Palestinian, first and second centuries CE] said: The days of the Messiah will be forty years.[102] . . . Rabbi Dosa [Palestinian, second century CE] said: Four hundred years.[103] . . . Rabbi [Judah the Prince, Palestinian, end of second century CE] said: Three hundred and sixty-five years.[104] . . . Abimi the son of Rabbi Abbahu [Palestinian, fourth century CE] learned: The days of Israel's Messiah shall be seven thousand years.[105] . . . Rab Judah [bar Ilai, Palestinian, second century CE] said in Samuel's [Babylonian, end of second century to mid third century CE] name: The days of the Messiah shall endure as long as from the Creation until now. . . .

Samuel . . . said: This world differs from [that of] the days of the Messiah only in respect of servitude to [foreign] powers. (Soncino)

8.120 *Manual of Discipline* 9.11 (*ca*. second century BCE)

The Dead Sea sect expected that just as Israel had been led by prophets and teachers, so at the end of days a prophet and teacher (perhaps the same person) would usher in a golden age. At that time there would be two Messiahs, a priest and a king.

Until the coming of the Prophet[106] and of both the priestly and the lay Messiah,[107] these men [i.e., the members of the Dead Sea sect] are not to depart from the clear intent of the Law to walk in any way in the stubbornness of their own hearts. They shall judge by the original laws

---

100. I.e., the entire world, wherein Jews are scattered.

101. The reference is to the fact that the coming of the Messiah will be preceded by terrible troubles, which are denominated birth pangs.

102. Corresponding to the number of years that the Israelites spent in their sojourn in the desert after the Exodus from Egypt.

103. Corresponding to the number of the years that the Israelites were in Egypt.

104. Corresponding to the number of days in the solar year.

105. Corresponding, according to the Talmudic comment at this point, to the number of days that a bridegroom rejoices over his bride, God's day being equivalent to a thousand years, as may be deduced from Ps 90:4.

106. The reference is to the prophet foretold in Deut 18:18: "I will raise up for them a prophet like you from among their brethren; and I will put my words in his mouth, and he shall speak to them all that I command him."

107. Literally, "the Messiahs [i.e., anointed] of Aaron and Israel."

in which the members of the community were schooled from the beginning. (T.H.G.)

8.121 The War Scroll 17.6 (ca. end of the first century BCE or early first century CE)

One of the Dead Sea Scrolls, *The War Scroll*, also known as *The War of the Sons of Light against the Sons of Darkness*, describes a battle at the end of days, conducted by priests and led by the chief priest, that is to take place against the Kittim.[108] While there is no mention of a messianic figure as such in this scroll, his place seems to be taken by an angelic host or an individual angel, namely Michael, or God Himself. In the description below of the eschatological victory the key role is played by the angel Michael, who is the angel who guards Israel (cf. Dan 12:1–4) and brings about Israel's triumph over all the nations of the world.

This is the day which He hath appointed for abasing and humbling the [Prince] of the Dominion of Wickedness. But He will send perpetual help to those who have a share in His redemption through the power of Michael, the mighty, ministering angel; and He will send also an eternal light to light up the children of Israel with joy. They that have cast their lot with God will enjoy peace and blessing. In this way, the rule of Michael will be exalted among the angels, and the dominion of Israel among all flesh. Righteousness shall flourish in heaven, and all who espouse God's truth shall rejoice in the knowledge of eternal things. And ye, the sons of the covenant, be of good courage in the trial which God visits upon you, until He gives the sign that He has completed His test. His secret powers will always support you. (T.H.G.)

8.122 Philo, On Rewards and Punishments 28.164–29.165

While Philo, in the selection below, does not mention a Messiah as such, he describes a sudden, unexpected messianic age in which, as a reward for repentance of the Jews, they will be freed from their current masters and, guided by a divine vision, they will be gathered from the ends of the earth to their home in Palestine.

For even though they dwell in the uttermost parts of the earth, in slavery to those who led them away captive, one signal, as it were, one day will bring liberty to all. This conversion in a body to virtue will strike awe into their masters, who will set them free, ashamed to rule over men better than themselves.

When they have gained this unexpected liberty, those who but now were scattered in Greece and the outside world over islands and continents will arise and post from every side with one impulse to the one appointed place, guided in their pilgrimage by a vision divine and superhuman unseen by others but manifest to them as they pass from exile to their home. (LCL)

108. In the Table of Nations (Gen 10:4) the Kittim are the descendants of Javan, the grandson of Noah through Japheth, and hence associated with the Greeks of the Aegean and the Eastern Mediterranean. In the Dead Sea Scrolls the term has usually been thought to refer to the Romans.

Belief in a Last Judgment and an Afterlife

BIBLIOGRAPHY

Moore, vol. 2 (1927), 279–322, 377–95.

George W. E. Nickelsburg, *Resurrection, Immortality, and Eternal Life in Intertestamental Judaism* (1972).

Hans C. C. Cavallin, *Life after Death* (1974).

George W. E. Nickelsburg, "Resurrection: Early Judaism and Christianity," *ABD*, vol. 5 (1992), 684–91.

Although direct references to divine judgment and a meaningful existence after death do not appear in the Torah, the Talmudic rabbis insisted that they were implicit there. Such references are explicit in such works of the Apocrypha as 2 Maccabees and Wisdom of Solomon; in such works of the Pseudepigrapha as *4 Maccabees, 1 Enoch, Jubilees, Psalms of Solomon, 2 Baruch, 4 Ezra*; and in the Dead Sea Scrolls.

8.123 *1 Enoch* 22:1–7 (first or second century BCE)

Below we have a description of the place, seen by Enoch in a vision, where the dead assemble before their judgment.

And thence I went to another place,[109] and he [an angel] showed me in the west another great and high mountain [and] of hard rock. And there were four hollow places in it, deep and very smooth: three of them were dark and one bright, and there was a fountain of water in its midst. And I said: 'How smooth are these hollow places, and deep and dark to view.' Then Raphael answered, one of the holy angels who was with me, and said unto me: 'These hollow places have been created for this very purpose, that the spirits of the dead should assemble therein, yea that all the souls of the children of men should assemble here. And these places have been made to receive them till the day of their judgment and till their appointed period, till the great judgment [comes] upon them.' I saw [the spirit of] a dead man making suit, and his voice went forth to heaven and made suit. And I asked Raphael the angel who was with me, and I said unto him: 'This spirit which maketh suit, whose is it, whose voice goeth forth and maketh suit to heaven?' And he answered me saying: 'This is the spirit which went forth from Abel, whom his brother Cain slew, and he makes his suit against him till his seed is destroyed from the face of the earth, and his seed is annihilated from amongst the seed of men.' (R.H.C.)

8.124 *4 Ezra* 7:31–9 (*ca.* end of the first century CE)

Here we have a description of the resurrection which will take place at the end of days, when the good will be rewarded and the evil will be punished.

> And it shall be after seven days that the Age which is not yet awake shall be roused, and that which is corruptible shall perish.

---

109. Sheol or the Underworld.

And the earth shall restore those that sleep in her,
and the dust those that are at rest therein,
[and the chambers shall restore those that were committed
  unto them].
And the Most High shall be revealed upon the throne of
  judgment:
[and then cometh the End]
and compassion shall pass away,
[and pity be far off],
and longsuffering withdrawn;
But judgment alone shall remain,
truth shall stand,
and faithfulness triumph.
And recompense shall follow,
and the reward be made manifest;
Deeds of righteousness shall awake,
and deeds of iniquity shall not sleep.
And then shall the pit of torment appear,
and over against it the place of refreshment;
The furnace of Gehenna shall be made manifest,
and over against it the Paradise of delight.
And then shall the Most High say to the nations that have been
  raised [from the dead]:
Look now and consider whom ye have denied, whom ye have
  not served, whose commandments ye have despised.
Look now, before [you]:
here delight and refreshment,
there fire and torments!
For thus shall the Day of Judgment be. (G.H.B.)

8.125 *Avoth de-Rabbi Nathan* 28 (*ca.* 220 CE)

Here we have a classic formulation of theodicy, namely that those who suffer in this life are rewarded in the world to come and vice versa.

Rabbi Judah the Prince [Palestinian, end of second, beginning of third century CE] said: Whoever accepts the delights of this world will be deprived of the delights of the World to Come, and whoever declines the delights of this world will receive the delights of the World to Come. (A.C.)

8.126 Babylonian Talmud, *Berakoth* 17a (edited *ca.* 500 CE)

Here we have a description of what the future world is like, namely that it is not at all corporeal.

A favorite saying of Rab [Babylonian, end of second, beginning of third century CE] was: [The future world is not like this world.] In the future world there is no eating nor drinking nor propagation nor business nor jealousy nor hatred nor competition, but the righteous sit with their crowns on their heads feasting on the brightness of the divine presence, as it says, 'And they beheld God, and did eat and drink' (Exod 24:11). (Soncino)

Folklore, Astrology, and Magic

8.127 Babylonian Talmud, *Berakoth* 6a (edited *ca*. 500 CE)

The world of demons was very real for some of the rabbis, as we see in the selection below.

It has been taught: Abba Benjamin [Palestinian, second century CE] says, If the eye had the power to see them, no creature could endure the demons. Abaye [Babylonian, end of third, beginning of fourth century CE] says: They are more numerous than we are and they surround us like the ridge round a field. Rabbi Huna [Babylonian, third century CE] says: Everyone among us has a thousand on his left hand and ten thousand on his right hand. Raba [Babylonian, end of third, beginning of fourth century CE] says: The crushing in the *Kallah*[110] lectures comes from them.[111] Fatigue in the knees comes from them. The wearing out of the clothes of the scholars is due to their rubbing against them. The bruising of the feet comes from them. If one wants to discover them, let him take sifted ashes and sprinkle around his bed, and in the morning he will see something like the footprints of a cock. If one wishes to see them, let him take the after-birth of a black she-cat, the offspring of a black she-cat, the first-born of a first-born, let him roast it in fire and grind it to powder, and then let him put some into his eye, and he will see them. Let him also pour it into an iron tube and seal it with an iron signet that they should not steal it from him. Let him also close his mouth, lest he come to harm. Rabbi Bibi ben Abaye [Babylonian, fourth century CE] did so, saw them and came to harm. The scholars, however, prayed for him and he recovered. (Soncino)

8.128 Babylonian Talmud, *Shabbath* 156a–b (edited *ca*. 500 CE)

Here we find a debate among the rabbis as to whether or not Israel is immune from planetary influence.

It was stated, Rabbi Ḥanina [Babylonian, third century CE] said: The planetary influence gives wisdom, the planetary influence gives wealth, and Israel stands under planetary influence. Rabbi Joḥanan [ben Nappaḥa, Palestinian, end of second, beginning of third century CE] maintained: Israel is immune from planetary influence. Now, Rabbi Joḥanan is consistent with his view, for Rabbi Joḥanan said: How do we know that Israel is immune from planetary influence? Because it is said: 'Thus saith the Lord, Learn not the way of the nations, and be not dismayed at the signs of heaven, for the nations are dismayed at them' (Jer 10:2): they are dismayed but not Israel. Rab [Babylonian, end of second, beginning of third century CE] too holds that Israel is

110. These were assemblies of students held during the months preceding Passover and Rosh Hashanah.

111. Actually, the lectures are not overcrowded, but the presence of demons makes them appear overcrowded.

immune from planetary influence. For Rab Judah [Babylonian, third century CE] said in Rab's name: How do we know that Israel is immune from planetary influence? Because it is said, 'and he brought him forth from abroad' (Gen 15:5). Abraham pleaded before the Holy One, blessed be He, 'Sovereign of the Universe! one born in mine house is mine heir' (Gen 15:3). 'Not so,' He replied, 'but he that shall come forth out of thine own bowels' (Gen 15:4). 'Sovereign of the Universe!' cried he, 'I have looked at my constellation and find that I am not fated to beget a child.' 'Go forth from [i.e., cease] thy planet [gazing], for Israel is free from planetary influence. What is thy calculation? Because Zedek [Jupiter] stands in the West?[112] I will turn it back and place it in the East.' And thus it is written, 'Who hath raised Zedek from the East? He hath summoned it for his sake' (Isa 41:2). (Soncino)

Hellenization in Palestine

BIBLIOGRAPHY

Saul Lieberman, *Greek in Jewish Palestine* (1942).

David Daube, "Rabbinic Methods of Interpretation and Hellenistic Rhetoric," *HUCA* 22 (1949), 239–64.

Saul Lieberman, *Hellenism in Jewish Palestine* (1950).

David Daube, "Alexandrian Methods of Interpretation and the Rabbis," *Festchrift Hans Lewald* (1953), 21–44.

Siegfried Stein, "The Influence of Symposia Literature and the Literary Form of the Pesach Haggadah," *JJS* 8 (1957), 33–44.

Geza Vermes, *Scripture and Tradition in Judaism: Haggadic Studies* (1961).

Saul Lieberman, "How Much Greek in Jewish Palestine?" in Philip W. Lown Institute of Advanced Judaic Studies, Brandeis University: *Studies and Texts*, vol. 1: *Biblical and Other Studies*, ed. Alexander Altmann (1963), 123–41.

Henry Fischel, *Rabbinic Literature and Greco-Roman Philosophy* (1973).

Martin Hengel, *Judaism and Hellenism*, 2 vols. (1974).

Louis H. Feldman, "Hengel's *Judaism and Hellenism* in Retrospect," *JBL* 96 (1977), 371–82.

Henry Fischel, *Essays in Greco-Roman and Related Talmudic Literature* (1977).

Shaye J. D. Cohen, "Patriarchs and Scholarchs," *PAAJR* 48 (1981), 57–85.

Shaye J. D. Cohen, "Epigraphical Rabbis," *JQR* 72 (1981–2), 1–17.

Jonathan A. Goldstein, "Jewish Acceptance and Rejection of Hellenism," in E. P. Sanders *et al.*, eds, *Jewish and Christian Self-Definition*, vol. 2: *Aspects of Judaism in the Greco-Roman Period* (1981), 64–87, 318–26.

Louis H. Feldman, "How Much Hellenism in Jewish Palestine?" *HUCA* 57 (1985), 83–111.

Louis H. Feldman, "Torah and Secular Culture: Challenge and Response in the Hellenistic Period," *Tradition* 23.2 (Summer, 1987), 1–15.

Eric M. Meyers, "The Challenge of Hellenism for Early Judaism and Christianity," *BA* 55 (1992), 84–91.

Feldman (1993), 3–44.

Few Jews in Palestine seem to have mastered Greek literature. Herod, Josephus, and Justus of Tiberias are clearly exceptional; and even

---

112. This would be an unfavorable time to beget a child.

Josephus admits that he needed assistants to help him with the Greek when he was writing his *Jewish War*. Of the rabbis, Elisha ben Abuyah apparently was well acquainted with Greek poetry, but he is held up as an example of apostasy. Nevertheless, there is reason to think that Hellenization increased after the failure of the Bar Kochba rebellion (135 CE).

Graeco-Jewish Writers

EUPOLEMUS

> *8.129* Eupolemus (middle of the second century BCE), quoted by Eusebius (265–340 CE), *Preparation for the Gospel* 9.34.4

BIBLIOGRAPHY

Wacholder (1974).
Holladay, vol. 1 (1983), 93–156.
John R. Bartlett, *Jews in the Hellenistic World* (1985), 56–71.
Francis T. Fallon, "Eupolemus," OTP, vol. 2 (1985), 861–72.
Robert Doran, "The Jewish Hellenistic Historians before Josephus," *ANRW* 2.20.1 (1987), 263–70.
Arthur J. Droge, *Homer or Moses? Early Christian Interpretations of the History of Culture* (1989), 13–19.
Sterling (1992), 207–22.

Josephus (*Against Apion* 1.218) mentions a certain Eupolemus as a pagan writer who was exceptional in his approximation to the truth. Most scholars, however, follow Eusebius in identifying him as a Palestinian Jewish writer and, indeed, with the Eupolemus whom Judah Maccabee sent to negotiate an alliance with Rome in 161 BCE. Fragments of his work, *Concerning the Kings in Judaea*, have been preserved by the pagan Alexander Polyhistor, who lived in the first century BCE and who, in turn, is quoted by Eusebius. His work contains a number of non-biblical traditions, especially about Solomon and the building of the Temple.

Solomon, accompanied by his father's advisors, journeyed to the mountain of Lebanon with the Sidonians and Tyrians.[113] The trees which had been cut previously by his father he transported by sea to Joppa and from there by land to Jerusalem.[114] He began to build the temple of God when he was thirteen years old.[115] The aforementioned nations supplied the labor[116] and the twelve tribes of the Jews also supplied the 160,000 men with all the necessary provisions – one tribe each month.[117] He laid the foundations of the Temple of God sixty

---

113. The Bible has no mention of a trip by Solomon to Lebanon.

114. The statement that Solomon transported the lumber by sea to Joppa and from there by land to Jerusalem is extra-biblical.

115. Here Eupolemus is contradicting the Bible (1 Kgs 6:1), which indicates that the work on the Temple was begun in the fourth year of Solomon's reign, whereas Eupolemus elsewhere (in Eusebius 9.30.8) declares that he began to build the Temple a year after his accession.

116. According to one account in the Bible (1 Kgs 5:13–18), the workers were Israelites; 2 Chr (2:17–18) states that the workers were aliens living in Palestine.

117. This is an extra-biblical detail.

cubits long and sixty cubits wide;[118] the width of the building and its foundations was ten cubits, for this is what Nathan,[119] the prophet of God, had commanded him. (C.R.H.)

PSEUDO-EUPOLEMUS

8.130 Pseudo-Eupolemus (first half of the second century BCE), cited by Eusebius (265–340 CE), *Preparation for the Gospel* 9.17.3–5

BIBLIOGRAPHY

Ben Zion Wacholder, "Pseudo-Eupolemos' Two Greek Fragments on the Life of Abraham," *HUCA* 34 (1963), 83–113.
Holladay, vol. 1 (1983), 157–87.
Robert Doran, "Pseudo-Eupolemus," OTP, vol. 2 (1985), 873–82.
Robert Doran, "The Jewish Hellenistic Historians before Josephus," ANRW 2.20.1 (1987), 270–4.
Sterling (1992), 187–206.

Two fragments, the first ascribed to Eupolemus and the second to "some anonymous writings," are quoted by Alexander Polyhistor and, in turn, by Eusebius. Most scholars have concluded that the fragments, despite their syncretistic flavor, are too biblical to have been composed by a pagan and have ascribed them to a Palestinian Jewish or, more usually, a Samaritan author. The ascription to a Samaritan author rests largely on the centrality accorded to Mount Gerizim. He is usually regarded as coming from Palestine and as having lived in the first half of the second century BCE. In the passage below he extols the achievements of Abraham in science and in war.

He [Abraham] excelled all men in nobility of birth and wisdom. In fact, he discovered both astrology and Chaldean science.... By teaching the Phoenicians the movements of the sun and moon, and everything else as well, he found favor with their king. Later, the Armenians[120] waged war against the Phoenicians. After the Armenians won a victory and had taken Abraham's nephew as prisoner, Abraham, accompanied by his household servants, came to the assistance of the Phoenicians, gained mastery of the captors, and captured the enemies' children and women....[121] He was also received as a guest by the city at the temple Argarizin,[122] which is interpreted 'mountain of the Most High.' (C.R.H.)

118. These dimensions are at variance with the biblical figures. The dimensions in the Hebrew text of 1 Kgs 6:2 are 60 cubits long and 2 cubits wide; in the Septuagint for this passage they are 40 cubits long and 20 cubits wide; in the Hebrew and Greek text of 2 Chr 3:4 they are 60 cubits long and 20 cubits wide.

119. Nathan is not mentioned by name in the Bible in this connection.

120. In the Bible (Gen 14:1–12) the Armenians are not mentioned among those against whom the Canaanite kings waged war.

121. The Bible (Gen 14:16) does not state that Abraham captured the enemies' children and women.

122. This mention of the sacred mountain of the Samaritans has no basis in the Masoretic text of the Bible (Gen 14:17), which indicates that negotiations took place in Shaveh.

CLEODEMUS MALCHUS

> *8.131* Cleodemus Malchus (before the middle of the first century BCE), quoted by Alexander Polyhistor (first century BCE), cited by Josephus, *Jewish Antiquities* 1.240–1

BIBLIOGRAPHY

Holladay, vol. 1 (1983), 245–59.

Nothing is known of the writer Cleodemus, who has the curious surname Malchus and is also called "the prophet." Most scholars have assumed that he came from Palestine and that he was either a Jew or a Samaritan, but it is also possible that he was a pagan, especially in view of the obvious pride that he takes in the fact that the most famous Greek hero, Heracles, married Abraham's granddaughter. His date is somewhere between 200 BCE and 50 BCE.

Cleodemus the prophet,[123] also called Malchus,[124] in his history of the Jews, relates . . . that Abraham had several sons by Katura. . . . These latter joined Heracles in his campaign against Libya and Antaeus;[125] and Heracles, marrying the daughter of [Abraham's son] Aphranes,[126] had by her a son Didorus. (LCL)

THEODOTUS

> *8.132* Theodotus (second century BCE), *On the Jews*, cited by Eusebius (265–340 CE), *Preparation for the Gospel* 9.22.1

BIBLIOGRAPHY

Robert J. Bull, "A Note on Theodotus' Description of Shechem," *HTR* 60 (1967), 221–7.
John J. Collins, "The Epic of Theodotus and the Hellenism of the Hasmoneans," *HTR* 73 (1980), 91–104.
Holladay, vol. 2 (1989), 51–204.

Eusebius quotes, from the pagan Alexander Polyhistor, eight fragments, totaling forty-seven lines of hexameter verse, of a poet named Theodotus. Because Shechem seems to be the central focus of Theodotus' poem and, indeed, is designated as a "sacred city," most scholars have identified the author as a Samaritan from Palestine. Likewise, the statement that

123. Elsewhere Josephus (*Against Apion* 1.41) speaks of the failure of the exact succession of the prophets in the reign of Artaxerxes, whom he identifies with the biblical Ahasuerus. The reference to Cleodemus as a prophet may, however, be due to the fact that Josephus is here quoting Alexander Polyhistor, who did not have Josephus' qualms about applying the term "prophet" to a more recent figure.

124. The name "Malchus" may refer to Cleodemus as a *malakh*, that is, a messenger, which is another name for a prophet.

125. Antaeus, the son of the divinities Poseidon and Ge (Earth), was a giant with whom Heracles wrestled. Whenever he was thrown he rose stronger than ever because of his contact with his mother Earth. According to Greek mythology Heracles overcame him singlehanded by lifting him in the air so that he lost contact with the earth.

126. This would appear to be identical with Iaphras and is thus equated in the text of Eusebius when he quotes this passage.

Shechem was founded by Sikimios the son of Hermes would seem to reflect a syncretistic tendency which is characteristic of Samaritan Hellenism. Others, however, arguing that the reference to Shechem as a sacred city does not necessarily imply a Samaritan author and that the reference to Hermes is due to Alexander Polyhistor rather than to Theodotus, suggest that he was a Jew. Various dates have been suggested for the poem, ranging from 200 BCE to 107 BCE. Most scholars, especially those who regard the author as a Samaritan, have postulated that the poem was composed in Palestine. Others, noting the existence of a Samaritan group in Alexandria, have suggested an Alexandrian provenance.

Now Theodotus says in his work *On the Jews*[127] that Shechem received its name from Sikimius, son of Hermes,[128] for this one also founded the city. In his work *On the Jews* he says that it is situated as follows:

> 'Now thus the land was indeed fertile, browsed by goats and well-watered,
> Neither was it a long way to enter the city
> From the country. Nor were there ever dense thickets for laborers.
> And out of it very near two mountains appear quite steep.
> Full of grass and trees. And between them
> Is cut a path, a narrow hollow; and on the other side
> The living [city of] Shechem appears, a holy city,
> Built below at the base [of the mountain], and around [the city] a smooth wall
> Running [in] under the foot of the mountain, on high, a defense enclosure.' (C.R.H.)

HEROD

> 8.133 Nicolaus of Damascus (64 BCE–beginning of the first century CE), *Autobiography*, cited by Constantine Porphyrogenitus, *Excerpts Concerning Virtues and Vices* 1

Here we have a picture of Herod's interest in rhetoric, history, and philosophy. In this he was encouraged by his executive secretary, Nicolaus of Damascus, whom he, in turn, successfully urged to write a universal history.

Herod, having given up his enthusiasm for philosophy, as it commonly happens with people in authority because of the abundance of goods that distract them, was eager again for rhetoric and pressed Nicolaus to practice rhetoric together with him. . . . Again, he was seized by a love of history, since Nicolaus praised the subject and said that it was proper for a statesman, and useful also for a king, to know the works and achievements of the former generations. Herod, becoming eager to study this subject, also influenced Nicolaus to busy himself with

127. Inasmuch as Alexander Polyhistor assigns the same title to works by various authors whom he cites, some have regarded this as a descriptive phrase rather than the actual title.

128. If the reference is indeed due to Theodotus and is not a textual corruption, this would be the one instance of syncreticism in the fragments of his poem. Some, however, have regarded this as merely a euhemeristic identification of Hermes with a human being.

history. Nicolaus applied himself vigorously to that undertaking, collecting material for the whole of history, and working incomparably harder than other people, completed the project after a long toil. He used to say that if Eurystheus[129] had suggested this task to Heracles, he would have very much worn him out. Then Herod, when sailing to Rome to meet Caesar, took Nicolaus with him on the same ship, and they discussed philosophy together. (M.S.)

JOSEPHUS

8.134 Josephus, *Jewish Antiquities* 20.263–5

Though Josephus worked hard at mastering the Greek language and literature, he apparently did not really feel completely at home in the language. He notes the negative attitude of Jews toward linguists and rhetoricians, preferring instead those who have mastered the law.

I [Josephus] have also labored strenuously to partake of the realm of Greek prose and poetry, after having gained a knowledge of Greek grammar, although the habitual use of my native tongue has prevented my attaining precision in the pronunciation. For our people do not favor those persons who have mastered the speech of many nations, or who adorn their style with smoothness of diction, because they consider that not only is such skill common to ordinary freemen but that even slaves who so choose may acquire it. But they give credit for wisdom to those alone who have an exact knowledge of the law and who are capable of interpreting the meaning of the Holy Scriptures. Consequently, though many have laboriously undertaken this training, scarcely two or three have succeeded, and have forthwith reaped the fruit of their labors. (LCL)

8.135 Josephus, *Against Apion* 1.50

Here Josephus says that when he translated his account of the *Jewish War* he required the aid of some assistants to help him with the Greek.

Then, in the leisure that Rome afforded me, with all my materials in readiness, and with the aid of some assistants for the sake of the Greek, at last I committed to writing my narrative of the events.[130] (LCL)

8.136 Josephus, *Life* 64–5

In the passage below we see that Josephus, despite his liberal attitude toward the study of the Greek language and literature, was very stringent, upon his arrival in Galilee as general against the Romans, on the matter of decorative art prohibited by the law of the Pentateuch. Apparently, Herod Antipas, the tetrarch of Galilee, had disregarded the Pentateuchal law (and presumably the view of the sages) on this matter.

129. Eurystheus was the king of Tiryns in Greece whom Heracles served for twelve years. Heracles gained immortality by performing the labors which Eurystheus imposed.
130. Josephus is here referring to his composition of the Greek version of his *Jewish War*, originally composed in his vernacular language (*War* 1.3).

I [Josephus] ... sent to the council and principal men of that city [Tiberias in Galilee], requesting them to come to me. On their arrival, Justus [of Tiberias, the historian] being among them, I told them that I and my associates had been commissioned by the Jerusalem assembly [which had appointed Josephus as general] to press for the demolition of the palace erected by Herod the tetrarch, which contained representations of animals – such a style of architecture being forbidden by the laws [Exod 20:4] – and I requested their permission to proceed at once with the work. (LCL)

The Rabbinic Attitude: Prohibition of the Study of Greek Wisdom (63 BCE)

8.137 Babylonian Talmud, *Soṭah* 49b (edited *ca.* 500 CE)

BIBLIOGRAPHY

Saul Lieberman, "The Alleged Ban on Greek Wisdom," in his *Hellenism in Jewish Palestine: Studies in the Literary Transmission Beliefs and Manners of Palestine in the I Century BCE – IV Century CE* (1950), 100–14.
Ernest Wiesenberg, "Related Prohibitions: Swine Breeding and the Study of Greek," *HUCA* 27 (1956), 213–33.

In the civil war between Hyrcanus II and Aristobulus II, according to this anecdote, an old man, conversant in Greek culture, was responsible for the interruption of the Temple sacrifices, whereupon it was declared that whoever teaches his son Greek wisdom is accursed.

Our Rabbis taught: When the kings of the Hasmonean house fought one another [in 63 BCE], Hyrcanus [II] was outside and Aristobulus [II] within [Jerusalem].[131] Each day they used to let down denarii [coins] in a basket, and haul up for them [animals for] the continual offerings. An old man there, who was learned in Greek wisdom, spoke with them in Greek, saying, 'As long as they carry on the Temple-service, they will never surrender to you.' On the morrow they let down denarii in a basket and hauled up a pig. . . . At that time they declared, 'Cursed be a man who rears pigs and cursed be a man who teaches his son Greek wisdom!' (Soncino)

8.138 Babylonian Talmud, *Ḥagigah* 15b (edited *ca.* 500 CE)

Here it is suggested that what led Elisha ben Abuyah to become a heretic was his preoccupation with pagan Greek poetry.

But what of Aḥer [i.e., Elisha ben Abuyah, second century CE]?[132] Greek song[133] did not cease from his mouth. It is told of Aḥer that when he

131. According to the parallel passage, *Baba Qamma* 82b, Hyrcanus was within and Aristobulus was without the city wall. According to Josephus (*Ant.* 14.58) Aristobulus was being held prisoner by Pompey, and his adherents were within the city.
132. The context asks why the study of the Torah did not save Elisha ben Abuyah from apostasy.
133. The reference is to Greek poetry. The only Greek poet who is mentioned by name in rabbinic literature is Homer (Mishnah, *Yadaim* 4:6), whose poems, of course, celebrate Greek polytheism.

used to rise [to go] from the schoolhouse [i.e., before his apostasy] many heretical books used to fall from his lap. (Soncino)

Rabbinic Attitude toward Attendance at Sporting Events and Theaters

8.139 Babylonian Talmud, *Avodah Zarah* 18b (edited *ca.* 500 CE)

The rabbinic attitude toward attendance at sporting events and theaters was negative because they felt that the time spent there should have been spent in studying the Torah; but they found a justification for attending stadia if they might thus save the victims through shouting in their behalf or if they might thus be able to give evidence of the death of the victim so that his widow might be free to remarry.

Our Rabbis taught: Those who visit stadiums or a camp and witness there [the performance] of sorcerers and enchanters, or of *bukion* and *mukion*, *lulion* and *mulion*, *blurin* or *salgurin*[134] – lo, this is 'the seat of the scornful,' and against those [who visit them] Scripture says, 'Happy is the man that hath not walked in the counsel of the wicked . . . nor sat in the seat of the scornful, but his delight is in the law of the Lord.' (Ps 1.1–2). From here you can infer that those things cause one to neglect the Torah.

The following was cited as contradicting the foregoing: It is permitted to go to stadiums, because by shouting one may save [the victim].[135] One is also permitted to go to a camp for the purpose of maintaining order in the country, providing he does not conspire [with the Romans]; but for the purpose of conspiring it is forbidden.

There is thus a contradiction between [the laws relating to] stadiums as well as between [those relating to] camps! There may indeed be no contradiction between those relating to camps, because the one may refer to where he conspires with them, and the other to where he does not, but the laws relating to stadiums are surely contradictory! They represent the differing opinions of [two] Tannaim.[136] For it has been taught: One should not go to stadiums because [they are] 'the seat of the scornful,' but Rabbi Nathan [Palestinian, second century CE] permits it for two reasons: first, because by shouting one may save [the victim], secondly, because one might be able to give evidence [of death] for the wife [of a victim] and so enable her to remarry. (Soncino)

8.140 Babylonian Talmud, *Baba Qamma* 82b–83a (edited *ca.* 500 CE)

The following passage from the Talmud indicates that the prohibition of the study of Greek wisdom was relaxed in the case of certain students of the patriarch Rabban Gamaliel in the first century since they had to know Greek in order to carry on negotiations with the Roman government.

---

134. The Latin equivalents are *bucco, maccus, ludio, morio, burrae,* and *scurrae* and refer to various kinds of clowns and clownish performances.

135. Presumably the reference is to the practice of calling upon the spectators to turn thumbs either up or down when the victim was on the verge of being killed.

136. Rabbis who lived before the codification of the Mishnah *ca.* 200 CE.

But was Greek wisdom[137] proscribed [in 63 BCE, during the civil war between Hyrcanus II and Aristobulus II]? ... It may, however, be said that the Greek language is one thing and Greek wisdom is another. But was Greek wisdom proscribed? Did not Rab Judah [Babylonian, third century CE] say that Samuel [Babylonian, end of second and beginning of third century CE] stated in the name of Rabban Simeon ben Gamaliel [Palestinian, second century CE]: '[The words] "Mine eye affected my soul because of all the daughters of my city" [Lam 3:51] [could very well be applied to the] thousand youths who were in my father's house, five hundred of them learned Torah and the other five hundred learned Greek wisdom, and out of all of them there remain only I here and the son of my father's brother in Asia'? It may, however, be said that the family of Rabban Gamaliel [Palestinian, end of first and beginning of second century CE] was an exception, as they had associations with the Government. (Soncino)

8.141 Babylonian Talmud, *Soṭah* 49b (edited *ca.* 500 CE)

The following passage indicates that, in the eyes of the extremely influential patriarch, Rabbi Judah the Prince, the redactor of the Mishnah (*ca.* 220 CE) and the close friend of the Roman emperor "Antoninus," Greek was to be preferred to Aramaic in Palestine.

Rabbi [Judah the Prince] said: Why use the Syrian [i.e. Aramaic] language in Palestine? Either use the holy tongue or Greek! ... The Greek language and Greek wisdom are distinct.[138] (Soncino)

Hellenization in Tombstone Inscriptions

After Alexander the Greek language, especially if we are to judge from tombstone inscriptions, made increasing headway in Palestine, though there were few religious defections and the study and practice of Judaism in its traditional form remained strong. The enormous Jewish necropolis at Beth She'arim contains numerous inscriptions, mostly brief and mostly in Greek, which was the spoken language of many people.

8.142 Catacomb 18, Hall B (third century CE)

Eulogy to a pious woman (in Greek).

This tomb contains the mortal remains of the gentlewoman Carteria, preserving her immortal illustrious memory. Zenobia buried her here, accomplishing the behest of her mother. O most blessed one, for you your offspring whom you bore from your gentle womb, your pious daughter, erected this, for she ever does deeds famed among mortals, so that both of you may after the end of life have once more new, indestructible riches. (M.R.)

---

137. There is considerable debate as to what is meant by Greek wisdom in this passage. It may refer to Greek culture, science, philosophy, literature, or rhetoric.

138. The reference is to the fact that the rabbis forbade the study of Greek wisdom but not the Greek language.

Hellenization in Letters

That Greek was widely prevalent in Palestine in the second century may be seen from one of the Bar Kochba letters (*ca.* 134 CE). The sender, whose name is unfortunately not well preserved, informs Yehonathan and Masabala that he is sending a certain Agrippa in order that they may send back with him palm branches and citrons for the festival of Tabernacles. What is significant is that, requesting these religious articles, no one could be found to write the letter in Hebrew or Aramaic.

> *8.143 Sammelbuch griechischer Urkunden aus Ägypten*, vol. 8, no. 9843 (from a grotto in the Judaean desert)

[In Greek] Soumaios[139] to Ionathes son of Baianus, and to Masabala, greeting. Since I sent Agrippa to you, hurry and send me stalks[140] and citrons, and get them to me for the Jewish Feast of Tabernacles, and don't do otherwise. This is written in Greek because no one had been found to write it in Hebrew. Send him back quickly because of the holiday, and don't do otherwise. Soumaios. Goodbye. (Y.Y.)

Hellenization in Legal Documents

BIBLIOGRAPHY

Naphtali Lewis, Ranon Katzoff, Jonas C. Greenfield, "Papyrus Yadin 18: I. Text, Translation, Notes; II. Legal Commentary; III. The Aramaic Subscription," *IEJ* 37 (1987), 229–50.

Abraham Wasserstein, "A Marriage Contract from the Province of Arabia Nova: Notes on Papyrus Yadin 18," *JQR* 80 (1989–90), 93–130.

> *8.144 Papyrus Yadin 18 (128 CE)*

Among the papyri discovered by the expedition led by the late Yigael Yadin in the "Cave of Letters" in Naḥal Ḥever in Israel is a marriage contract in Greek dating from the year 128. The document is a blend of Greek (notably the opening statement and the very term, *proix*, for dowry), Roman (notably the dating and the clause at the end: "in good faith the formal question was asked and it was acknowledged in reply that this is thus rightly done"), and Jewish elements (notably that the husband adds to his wife's dowry). What is particularly remarkable is not merely that the document is written in Greek but that there is in it a specific, unmistakable, and unambiguous statement that the husband obligates himself to provide for his wife and future children in accordance with Greek custom.

In the consulship of Publius Metilius Nepos for the second time and Marcus Annius Libo on the nones of April, and by the compute of the new province of Arabia year twenty-third, month of Xandikos fifteenth, in Maoza, Zoara district, Judah son of Eleazar, also known as Khthousion, has given over Shelamzion, his very own daughter, a virgin, to Judah, surnamed Cimber, son of Ananias son of Somalas,

---

139. Greek for Shimon (or Shimeon).
140. The word may mean "wood slats."

both of the village of 'En Gedi in Judaea residing here, for Shelamzion to be a wedded wife to Judah Cimber for the partnership of marriage according to the laws, she bringing to him on account of bridal gift feminine adornment in silver and gold and clothing appraised by mutual agreement, as they both say, to be worth two hundred denarii of silver, which appraised value the bridegroom Judah called Cimber acknowledged that he has received from her by hand forthwith from Judah her father and owes to the said Shelamzion his wife together with another three hundred denarii which he promised to give her in addition to the sum of her aforestated bridal gift, all accounted toward her dowry, pursuant to his undertaking of feeding and clothing both her and the children to come in accordance with Greek custom upon the said Judah Cimber's good faith and peril and [the security of] all his possessions, both those which he now possesses in his said home village and here and all those which he may in addition validly acquire everywhere, in whatever manner his wife Shelamzion may choose, or whoever acts through her or for her may choose, to pursue the execution. Judah called Cimber shall redeem this contract for his wife Shelamzion, whenever she may demand it of him, in silver secured in due form, at his own expense interposing no objection. If not, he shall pay to her all the aforestated denarii twofold, she having the right of execution both from Judah Cimber her husband and upon the possessions lawfully his in whatever manner Shelamzion or whoever acts through her or for her may choose to pursue the execution. In good faith the formal question was asked and it was agreed in reply that this is thus rightly done.

[2nd hand, Aramaic] Judah son of Eleazar Khthousion: I have given my daughter Shelamzion, a virgin, in marriage to Judah Cimber son of Hanania son of Somala, according to what is written above. Judah wrote it.

[3rd hand, Aramaic] Judah Cimber son of Hanania son of Somala: I acknowledge the debt of silver denarii five hundred, the dowry of Shelamzion, according to what they wrote above. Judah wrote it.

[1st hand] I, Theenas, son of Simon, *librarius*, wrote [this]. (N.L.)

Sectarianism among Jews

BIBLIOGRAPHY

John W. Lightley, *Jewish Sects and Parties in the Time of Christ* (1925).

Marcel Simon, *Jewish Sects at the Time of Jesus* (1967).

Kurt Schubert, "A Divided Faith: Jewish Religious Parties and Sects," in Arnold J. Toynbee, ed., *The Crucible of Christianity: Judaism, Hellenism and the Historical Background to the Christian Faith* (1969), 77–98.

Hugo Mantel, "The Dichotomy of Judaism during the Second Temple," *HUCA* 44 (1973), 55–87.

Michael E. Stone, *Scriptures, Sects and Visions* (1980).

Joseph Blenkinsopp, "Interpretation and the Tendency to Sectarianism," in E. P. Sanders *et al.*, *Jewish and Christian Self-Definition*, vol. 2: *Aspects of Judaism in the Graeco-Roman Period* (1981), 1–26.

Lawrence H. Schiffman, "Jewish Sectarianism in Second Temple Times," in Raphael Jospe and Stanley Wagner, eds, *Great Schisms in Jewish History* (1981), 1–46.

Gary Porton, "Diversity in Postbiblical Judaism," in Robert A. Kraft and George W. E. Nickelsburg, eds, *Early Judaism and Its Modern Interpreters* (1986), 57–80.

Shaye J. D. Cohen, *From the Maccabees to the Mishnah* (1987), 60–173.

Lawrence H. Schiffman, *From Text to Tradition: A History of Second Temple and Rabbinic Judaism* (1991), 98–119.

The Jerusalem Talmud (*Sanhedrin* 10.6.29c) tells us that there were twenty-four sects of heretics at the time of the destruction of the Temple in 70 CE. Josephus (*Antiquities* 13.171–3) tells us about three schools of thought (the Greek word that he uses, *hairesis*, has given rise to our word "heresy," although it had no such connotation in the original). The movements that were active in first-century Palestine may perhaps be divided into two groups: those that attempted to make a mass, egalitarian appeal (the Samaritans, Pharisees, Sadducees, and the Fourth Philosophy) and those that were separatist, monastic, utopian, ascetic, esoteric, and preoccupied with ethics (the Essenes and/or the Dead Sea sect, and [in Egypt] the Therapeutae). The *Haverim* have some but not all of these latter qualities; Christianity would seem to have elements of both. All of these groups, with the exception of the Samaritans, the Pharisees, and the Christians, apparently disappeared with the destruction of the Temple in Jerusalem.

Samaritans

BIBLIOGRAPHY

Moses Gaster, *The Samaritans: Their History, Doctrines and Literature* (1925).

Theodor H. Gaster, "Samaritans," in George H. Buttrick, ed., *Interpreter's Dictionary of the Bible*, vol. 4 (1962), 190–7.

John MacDonald, *Memar Marqah*, vol. 1 (1963).

John MacDonald, *Theology of the Samaritans* (1964).

Frank M. Cross, "Aspects of Samaritan and Jewish History in the Late Persian and Hellenistic Times," *HTR* 9 (1966), 201–11.

James A. Montgomery, *The Samaritans: The Earliest Jewish Sect (Their History, Theology and Literature)* (reprint ed. with an introduction by Abraham S. Halkin, 1968).

James D. Purvis, *The Samaritan Pentateuch and the Origin of the Samaritan Sect* (1968).

John MacDonald, *The Samaritan Chronicle II* (1969).

R. J. Coggins, *Samaritans and Jews: The Origins of Samaritanism Reconsidered* (1975).

Jeffrey M. Cohen, *A Samaritan Chronicle* (1981).

James Purvis, "The Samaritans and Judaism," in Robert A. Kraft and George W. E. Nicklesburg, eds, *Early Judaism and Its Modern Interpreters* (1986).

R. J. Coggins, "The Samaritans in Josephus," *JJC* (1987), 257–73.

Reinhard Plummer, *The Samaritans* (1987).

Alan D. Crown, ed., *The Samaritans* (1989).

Robert T. Anderson, "Samaritans," *ABD*, vol. 5 (1992), 940–7.

Louis H. Feldman, "Josephus' Attitude toward the Samaritans: A Study in Ambivalence," in Menachem Mor, ed., *Jewish Sects, Religious Movements, and Political Parties* (1992), 23–45.

The Jews were in constant conflict with the Samaritans, though the rabbis themselves disagreed whether the Samaritans were to be treated as Jews. The Samaritans not only had a different text of the Torah, but they did not accept the books of the Prophets or the third segment of the Hebrew Bible, the Writings. The Samaritans also refused to recognize the Oral Torah (the rules that ultimately came to be codified in writing in the Talmud), and they had a different calendar. Finally, the sacred mountain that the Samaritans recognized was Mount Gerizim, not the Temple Mount in Jerusalem.

8.145 Josephus, *Jewish Antiquities* 9.288–91 (722/721 BCE)

Below is Josephus' account of the origin of the Samaritans, namely from the Chutaioi of Persia who were transported by the Assyrians to Samaria when they conquered the Kingdom of Israel and who, when beset by a plague, were instructed by Israelite priests. According to Josephus they claim to be Jews only when it is to their advantage to say so.

As for the Chutaioi [Samaritans] who were transported to Samaria – this is the name by which they have been called to this day because of having been brought over from the region called Chutha, which is in Persia, as is a river by the same name – each of their tribes – there were five – brought along its own god, and, as they reverenced them in accordance with the custom of their country, they provoked the Most High God to anger and wrath. For He visited upon them a pestilence by which they were destroyed; and, as they could devise no remedy for their sufferings, they learned from an oracle that they should worship the Most High God, for this would bring them deliverance. And so they sent envoys to the king of Assyria, asking him to send them some priests from the captives he had taken in his war with the Israelites. Accordingly, he sent some priests, and they, after being instructed in the ordinances and religion of this God, worshipped Him with great zeal, and were at once freed of the pestilence. These same rites have continued in use even to this day among those who are called *Chuthaioi* (*Cuthim*) in the Hebrew tongue, and *Samareitai* (Samaritans) by the Greeks; but they alter their attitude according to circumstance and, when they see the Jews prospering, call them their kinsmen, on the ground that they are descended from Joseph and are related to them through their origin from him; but, when they see the Jews in trouble, they say that they have nothing whatever in common with them nor do these have any claim of friendship or race, and they declare themselves to be aliens of another race. (LCL)

8.146 Josephus, *Jewish Antiquities* 12.257–60 (168 BCE)

According to Josephus, the Samaritans wrote to King Antiochus Epiphanes of Syria commending him for his punishment of the Jews and asserting that they were not Jews but were actually from the city of Sidon in Phoenicia.

When the Samaritans saw the Jews suffering these misfortunes [at the hands of Antiochus Epiphanes], they would no longer admit that they were their kin or that the temple on Garizein was that of the Most Great God, thereby acting in accordance with their nature, as we have shown. . . .

Accordingly, they sent envoys to Antiochus with a letter in which they made the following statements. 'To King Antiochus Theos Epiphanes, a memorial from the Sidonians in Shechem.[141] Our forefathers because of certain droughts in their country, and follow-ing a certain ancient superstition, made it a custom to observe the day which is called the Sabbath by the Jews, and they erected a temple without a name on the mountain called Garizein, and there offered the appropriate sacrifices. Now you have dealt with the Jews as their wickedness deserves; but the king's officers, in the belief that we follow the same practices as they through kinship with them, are involving us in similar charges, whereas we are Sidonians by origin, as is evident from our state documents.' (LCL)

8.147 Babylonian Talmud, *Qiddushin* 75b–76a (edited *ca.* 500 CE)

The Rabbis were quite clearly divided on the issue of the status of the Samaritans. As the selection below indicates, as late as the second century there was a three-way dispute, particularly with regard to the laws of marriage and the unleavened bread on Passover: the great Rabbi Aqiba regarded them as true proselytes, Rabbi Ishmael felt that they were not legitimate proselytes, and others viewed their observance of certain commandments as acceptable.

There are three opposing views in this matter [the status of the Samaritans]. Rabbi Ishmael [Palestinian, first half of the second century CE] holds: Cutheans [Samaritans] are proselytes [through fear] of lions,[142] and the priests who became mixed up with them were unfit priests, as it is said, 'and they made unto them from among themselves priests of the high places' [2 Kgs 17:32], whereon Rabbah bar Bar Ḥanah [Palestinian, third century CE] commented: From the most unworthy of the people [i.e., priests], and on that account they were disqualified.

Rabbi Aqiba [second half of first century and first half of second century CE] holds: Cutheans are true proselytes, and the priests who became mixed up in them were fit priests, as it is said, 'and they made unto them from among themselves priests of the high places,' which Rabbi bar Bar Ḥanah interpreted from the choicest of the people. Yet why did they interdict them? Because they subjected *arusoth* [betrothed maidens] to *yibum* [levirate marriage] but exempted married women.[143] What was their interpretation? 'The wife of the dead shall not marry without [*ha-ḥuzah*] unto a stranger':

141. The Samaritans, whose sacred city was Shechem in Samaria, apparently wished to be known as being of Phoenician (Sidonian) origin.

142. Hence, they did not convert to Judaism out of conviction.

143. Exempted altogether, even from *ḥalizah*, the ceremony of drawing off the shoe of the brother of a husband who has died childless (Deut 25:5–9).

she who sat 'without' shall not marry a stranger, but she who did not sit 'without' may marry a stranger.". . .[144]

Some state, because they are not thoroughly versed in the [minute] details of precepts. Who is meant by 'some state?' Said Rabbi Idi bar Abin [Babylonian, fourth century CE]: It is Rabbi Eliezer [ben Hyrcanus, Palestinian, end of first and beginning of second century CE]. For it was taught: The unleavened bread of a Cuthean is permitted [to be eaten on Passover], and one fulfills his obligation therewith on Passover; but Rabbi Eliezer forbids it, because they are not thoroughly versed in the [minute] details of precepts.

Rabbi Simeon ben Gamaliel [Palestinian, first half of second century CE] said: Every precept which Cutheans have adopted, they observe it with minute care, [even] more than the Israelites. But here [in respect to marriage], wherein are they not well-versed? Because they are not well-versed in the law of betrothal and divorce. (Soncino)

Pharisees

BIBLIOGRAPHY

Robert Travers Herford, *The Pharisees* (1924).

Moore, 3 vols (1927–30).

Jacob Z. Lauterbach, "The Pharisees and Their Teachings," *HUCA* 6 (1929), 69–139.

Louis Finkelstein, *The Pharisees: The Sociological Background of Their Faith*, 2 vols (1938).

Leo Baeck, *The Pharisees and Other Essays* (1947).

Louis Finkelstein, *The Pharisees and the Men of the Great Synagogue* (1950).

Ralph Marcus, "Pharisaism in the Light of Modern Scholarship," *JR* 32 (1952), 154–64.

Morton Smith, "Palestinian Judaism in the First Century," in Moshe Davis, *Israel: Its Role in Civilization* (1956).

Cecil Roth, "The Pharisees in the Jewish Revolution of 66–73," *JSS* 7 (1962), 62–80.

Asher Finkel, *The Pharisees and the Teacher of Nazareth: A Study of Their Background, Their Halakhic and Midrashic Teachings, the Similarities and Differences* (1964).

Ellis Rivkin, Henry Fischel, Louis Feldman, Ben Zion Wacholder, Allan Cutler, "A Symposium on the Pharisees," *CCARJ* 14.3 (1967), 32–47.

Henry A. Fischel, "Story and History: Observations on Greco-Roman Historiography and Pharisaism," in Denis Sinor, ed., *American Oriental Society – Middle West Branch: Semi-Centennial Volume* (Asian Studies Research Institute Oriental Series, 3, 1969), 59–83.

Wilfred L. Knox, "Pharisaism and Hellenism," in William O. E. Oesterley, Herbert M. J. Loewe, and Erwin I. J. Rosenthal, eds, *Judaism and Christianity: Three Volumes in One* (1969 [1937–8]), 61–111.

Herbert M. J. Loewe, "The Ideas of Pharisaism," in William O. E. Oesterley, Herbert M. J. Loewe, and Erwin I. J. Rosenthal, eds, *Judaism and Christianity: Three Volumes in One* (1969 [1937–8]), 3–58.

Ellis Rivkin, "Defining the Pharisees: The Tannaitic Sources," *HUCA* 40–1 (1969–70), 205–49.

---

144. Apparently, the Samaritans take the word *ha-ḥuẓah* as an adjective. The wife who is characterized as "without" is a betrothed maiden, since she may not have relations with her husband-to-be until the actual marriage occurs.

Jacob Neusner, *The Rabbinic Traditions about the Pharisees before 70*, 3 vols (1971).

Louis Finkelstein, *Pharisaism in the Making: Selected Essays* (1972).

Jacob Neusner, "The Rabbinic Traditions about the Pharisees in Modern Historiography," *CCARJ* 19 (1972), 78–108.

Jacob Neusner, *From Politics to Piety: The Emergence of Pharisaic Judaism* (1973).

Solomon Zeitlin, "Spurious Interpretations of Rabbinic Sources in the Studies of Pharisees and Pharisaism," *JQR* 65 (1974–5), 122–35.

Michael J. Cook, "Jesus and the Pharisees – the Problem as It Stands Today," *JES* 15 (1978), 441–60.

Ellis Rivkin, *The Hidden Revolution: The Pharisees' Search for the Kingdom Within* (1978).

Joseph M. Baumgarten, "The Pharisaic–Sadducean Controversies about Purity and the Qumran Texts," *JJS* 31 (1980), 157–70.

Albert I. Baumgarten, "The Name of the Pharisees," *JBL* 102 (1983), 411–28.

Daniel R. Schwartz, "Josephus and Nicolaus on the Pharisees," *JSJ* 14 (1983), 157–71.

Albert I. Baumgarten, "Josephus and Hippolytus on the Pharisees," *HUCA* 55 (1984), 1–25.

Jacob Neusner, "Josephus' Pharisees: A Complete Repertoire," *JJC* (1987), 274–92.

David Goodblatt, "The Place of the Pharisees in First-Century Judaism: The State of the Debate," *JSJ* 20 (1989), 12–30.

Seth Schwartz, "AJ, the Pharisees, and Early Rabbinic Judaism," in his *Josephus and Judaean Politics* (1990), 170–208.

Steve Mason, *Flavius Josephus on the Pharisees: A Composition-Critical Study* (1991).

Anthony J. Saldarini, "Pharisees," *ABD*, vol. 5 (1992), 289–303.

Though Josephus, in distinguishing between the Pharisees and the Sadducees, places the emphasis on their respective attitudes toward fate and free will, the distinctive feature of the views of the Pharisees, according to the rabbinic tradition, is their insistence on the validity of the Oral Law and not merely of the written law, which was the only part of the law accepted by the Sadducees. In point of fact, this meant that the Pharisees were generally considerably more liberal in their interpretation of the law. Moreover, whereas in the eyes of the Sadducees God was essentially a national God, to the Pharisees He was a universal God. Apparently, the Pharisees had much more of a popular following than the Sadducees.

8.148 Josephus, *Jewish War* 2.162–3, 166

Josephus, who, after making trial of the Pharisees, Sadducees, and Essenes, allied himself with the party of the Pharisees (*Life* 12), asserts that the Pharisees are the leading sect, are most accurate in interpreting the laws, and believe in the immortality of the soul. In their view fate plays a role in every human action.

The Pharisees, who are considered the most accurate interpreters of the laws, and hold the position of the leading sect, attribute everything to Fate and to God; they hold that to act rightly or otherwise rests, indeed, for the most part with men, but that in each action Fate cooperates. Every soul, they maintain, is imperishable, but the soul of the good alone passes into another body, while the souls of the wicked suffer eternal punishment. . . .

The Pharisees are affectionate to each other and cultivate harmonious relations with the community. (LCL)

8.149 Josephus, *Jewish Antiquities* 13.297–8

Here Josephus refers to the Pharisaic belief in the validity of the oral law in contrast to the Sadducean view accepting only the written law. According to him the Sadducees are identified with the wealthy, while the masses favor the Pharisees.

For the present I wish merely to explain that the Pharisees had passed on to the people certain regulations handed down by former generations and not recorded in the Laws of Moses, for which reason they are rejected by the Sadducean group, who hold that only those regulations should be considered valid that were written down [in Scripture], and that those that had been handed down by former generations need not be observed. And concerning these matters the two parties came to have controversies and serious differences, the Sadducees having the confidence of the wealthy alone but no following among the populace, while the Pharisees have the support of the masses. (LCL)

8.150 Josephus, *Jewish Antiquities* 18.12–15

Josephus here notes the Pharisees' simple style of living, and their belief in a modified view of the power of fate, the immortality of the soul, and reward and punishment after death. He notes their great influence among the masses.

The Pharisees simplify their standard of living, making no concession to luxury. They follow the guidance of that which their doctrine has selected and transmitted as good, attaching the chief importance to the observance of those commandments that it has seen fit to dictate to them. They show respect and deference to their elders, nor do they rashly presume to contradict their proposals.

Though they postulate that everything is brought about by fate, still they do not deprive the human will of the pursuit of what is in man's power, since it was God's good pleasure that there should be a fusion and that the will of man with his virtue and vice should be admitted to the council-chamber of fate.

They believe that souls have power to survive death and that there are rewards and punishments under the earth for those who have led lives of virtue or vice: eternal imprisonment is the lot of evil souls, while the good souls receive an easy passage to a new life.

Because of these views they are, as a matter of fact, extremely influential among the masses; and all prayers and sacred rites of divine worship are performed according to their exposition. This is the great tribute that the inhabitants of the cities, by practicing the highest ideals both in their way of living and in their discourse, have paid to the excellence of the Pharisees. (LCL)

Sadducees

BIBLIOGRAPHY

Jacob Z. Lauterbach, "The Sadducees and the Pharisees: A Study of Their Respective Attitudes toward the Law," in *Studies in Jewish Literature Issued in Honor of Professor Kaufmann Kohler . . . on the Occasion of His Seventieth Birthday* (1913), 176–98.

Moses H. Segal, "Pharisees and Sadducees," *The Expositor* 8 (1917), 81–108.

Moore, vol. 1 (1927), 56–71.

Thomas W. Manson, "Sadducee and Pharisee: The Origin and Significance of Their Names," *BJRL* 22 (1938), 144–59.

Bernard J. Bamberger, "The Sadducees and the Belief in Angels," *JBL* 82 (1963), 433–5.

Victor Eppstein, "When and How the Sadducees Were Excommunicated," *JBL* 85 (1966), 213–23.

Jack Lightstone, "Sadducees *versus* Pharisees: The Tannaitic Sources," in Jacob Neusner, ed., *Christianity, Judaism and Other Greco-Roman Cults: Studies for Morton Smith at Sixty* (1975), 206–17.

Samuel T. Lachs, "The Pharisees and Sadducees on Angels: A Reexamination of Acts XXIII.8," *GCAJS* 6 (1977), 35–42.

Hugo Mantel, "The Sadducees and the Pharisees," in Michael Avi-Yonah and Zvi Baras, eds, *The World History of the Jewish People*, First Series: *Ancient Times*, vol. 8: *Society and Religion in the Second Temple Period* (1977), 99–123.

Lee I. Levine, "The Political Struggle between Pharisees and Sadducees in the Hasmonean Period," in Aharon Oppenheimer *et al.*, eds, *Abraham Schalit Memorial Volume: Jerusalem in the Second Temple Period* (1980), 61–83.

Anthony J. Saldarini, *Pharisees, Scribes and Sadducees in Palestinian Society* (1988).

Günther Baumbach, "The Sadducees in Josephus," *JBH* (1989), 173–95.

Gary G. Porton, "Sadducees," *ABD*, vol. 5 (1992), 892–5.

8.151 Josephus, *Jewish War* 2.164–6

According to Josephus, the Sadducees deny the power of fate, the belief in immortality of the soul, and reward and punishment after death.

The Sadducees, the second of the orders, do away with Fate altogether, and remove God beyond, not merely the commission, but the very sight of evil. They maintain that man has the free choice of good or evil, and that it rests with each man's will whether he follows the one or the other. As for the persistence of the soul after death, penalties in the underworld, and rewards, they will have none of them. . . .

The Sadducees . . . are, even among themselves, rather boorish in their behavior, and in their intercourse with their peers are as rude as to aliens. (LCL)

8.152 Josephus, *Jewish Antiquities* 18.16–17

According to Josephus, few identify with the Sadducean point of view, but they are of the highest standing. The masses would not tolerate them if they did not follow the Pharisaic formulas.

The Sadducees hold that the soul perishes along with the body. They own no observance of any sort apart from the laws; in fact, they reckon it a virtue to dispute with the teachers of the path of wisdom that they pursue. There are but few men to whom this doctrine has been made known, but these are men of the highest standing. They accomplish practically nothing, however. For whenever they assume some office, though they submit unwillingly and perforce, yet submit they do to the formulas of the Pharisees, since otherwise the masses would not tolerate them. (LCL)

> 8.153 Tosefta, *Yadaim* 2.20 (edited *ca.* end of fourth century CE)

In this passage the Boethusians, whose views closely resemble those of the Sadducees, argue on the basis of logic that in inheritance a daughter should take precedence over a grand-daughter who happens to be the daughter of the deceased's son, whereas the Pharisees say that in that case the grand-daughter takes precedence.

Say the Boethusians,[145] 'We cry out against you Pharisees! If the daughter of my son who came from the strength of my son who [in turn] came from my strength, lo, inherits me, then [is it not the case that] my daughter who came [directly] from my strength should, all the more so, inherit me?'

Say the Pharisees, 'No! If you say [thus] in the case of a daughter of a son who shares with the brothers [of her father in the inheritance of her grandfather], then will you say [thus] in the case of a daughter who does not share with the [i.e., her] brothers [in the inheritance of her father]?'[146] (J.L.)

Essenes

BIBLIOGRAPHY

Matthew Black, "The Account of the Essenes in Hippolytus and Josephus," in William D. Davies and David Daube, eds, *The Background of the New Testament and Its Eschatology* (1956), 172–5.

Morton Smith, "The Description of the Essenes in Josephus and the Philosophoumena," *HUCA* 29 (1958), 273–313.

John Strugnell, "Flavius Josephus and the Essenes: *Antiquities* XVIII.18–22," *JBL* 87 (1958), 106–15.

Solomon Zeitlin, "The Account of the Essenes in Josephus and the Philosophumena," *JQR* 49 (1958–9), 292–300.

Horst R. Moehring, "Josephus on the Marriage Customs of the Essenes. Jewish War II: 119–66 and Antiquities XVIII: 11–25," in Allen Wikgren, ed., *Early Christian Origins: Studies in Honor of H. R. Willoughby* (1961), 120–7.

Jerome Murphy-O'Connor, "The Essenes and Their History," *RB* 81 (1974), 215–44.

145. The Boethusians in their theological views closely resembled the Sadducees and are always mentioned together with them, so that some scholars view them as a branch of the Sadducees.

146. The Boethusian argues, *a fortiori*, that if the daughter of a deceased son inherits, then surely the daughter of the deceased should take precedence. The Pharisee replies by noting that if a man has several sons, one of whom has predeceased him, a daughter, and a grand-daughter who is the only child of the deceased son, the grand-daughter inherits the deceased son's portion, whereas the daughter inherits nothing.

Jerome Murphy-O'Connor, "The Essenes in Palestine," *BA* 40 (1977), 100–24.

Allen H. Jones, *Essenes* (1985).

John Kampen, "A Reconsideration of the Name 'Essene' in Greco-Jewish Literature in Light of Recent Perceptions of the Qumran Sect," *HUCA* 57 (1986), 61–81.

Todd S. Beall, *Josephus' Description of the Essenes Illustrated by the Dead Sea Scrolls* (1988).

Geza Vermes and Martin Goodman, *The Essenes according to the Classical Sources* (1989).

John J. Collins, "Essenes," *ABD*, vol. 2 (1992), 619–26.

Rebecca Gray, "The Essenes," in her *Prophetic Figures in Late Second Temple Jewish Palestine: The Evidence from Josephus* (1993), 80–111.

The Essenes, though apparently few in number, receive much more attention in Josephus, at least in his *Jewish War*, than do the Pharisees or the Sadducees, although they are not mentioned at all in the Talmud or the New Testament or the Dead Sea Scrolls (though most scholars have identified them with the Dead Sea sect). They were an ascetic, monastic-like sect with elaborate rules for initiates. Except for a small offshoot they were in principle opposed to marriage. Because they insisted on using a different ritual of purification when performing their sacrifices, they were barred from the Temple in Jerusalem. They shared their property and had common meals. They excelled in divination and practiced faith-healing.

8.154 Philo, *Every Good Man Is Free* 12.75–82, 86–7, 13.89, 91

The Essenes, according to Philo, avoid living in cities, money, commerce, implements of war, slaves, and logic-chopping. They observe the law strictly, study it industriously, share all their goods, and refuse to succumb to persecution.

Palestinian Syria, too, has not failed to produce high moral excellence. In this country live a considerable part of the very populous nation of the Jews, including, as it is said, certain persons, more than four thousand in number, called Essenes. Their name which is, I think, a variation, though the form of the Greek is inexact, of *hosiotes* (holiness), is given them, because they have shown themselves especially devout in the service of God, not by offering sacrifices of animals but by resolving to sanctify their minds.

    The first thing about these people is that they live in villages and avoid the cities because of the iniquities which have become inveterate among city dwellers, for they know that their company would have a deadly effect upon their own souls, like a disease brought by a pestilential atmosphere. Some of them labor on the land and others pursue such crafts as cooperate with peace and so benefit themselves and their neighbors. They do not hoard gold and silver or acquire great slices of land because they desire the revenues therefrom, but provide what is needed for the necessary requirements of life. For while they stand almost alone in the whole of mankind in that they have become moneyless and landless by deliberate action rather than by lack of good fortune, they are esteemed exceedingly rich, because they judge frugality with contentment to be, as indeed it is, an abundance of wealth.

As for darts, javelins, daggers, or the helmet, breastplate or shield, you could not find a single manufacturer of them, nor, in general, any person making weapons or engines or plying any industry concerned with war, nor, indeed, any of the peaceful kind, which easily lapse into vice, for they have not the vaguest idea of commerce either wholesale or retail or marine, but pack the inducements to covetousness off in disgrace.

Not a single slave is to be found among them, but all are free, exchanging services with each other, and they denounce the owners of slaves, not merely for their injustice in outraging the law of equality, but also for their impiety in annulling the statute of Nature, who mother-like has borne and reared all men alike, and created them genuine brothers, not in mere name, but in very reality, though this kinship has been put to confusion by the triumph of malignant covetousness, which has wrought estrangement instead of affinity and enmity instead of friendship.

As for philosophy, they abandon the logical part to quibbling verbalists as unnecessary for the acquisition of virtue, and the physical to visionary praters as beyond the grasp of human nature, only retaining that part which treats philosophically of the existence of God and the creation of the universe. But the ethical part they study very industriously, taking for their trainers the laws of their fathers, which could not possibly have been conceived by the human soul without divine inspiration.

In these they are instructed at all other times, but particularly on the seventh days. For that day has been set apart to be kept holy and on it they abstain from all other work and proceed to sacred spots which they call synagogues. There, arranged in rows according to their ages, the younger below the elder, they sit decorously as befits the occasion with attentive ears. Then one takes the books and reads aloud and another of especial proficiency comes forward and expounds what is not understood. For most of their philosophical study takes the form of allegory, and in this they emulate the tradition of the past. . . .

They all have a single treasury and common disbursements; their clothes are held in common and also their food through the institution of public meals. In no other community can we find the custom of sharing roof, life and board more firmly established in actual practice. And that is no more than one would expect. For all the wages which they earn in the day's work they do not keep as their private property, but throw them into the common stock and allow the benefit thus accruing to be shared by those who wish to use it.

The sick are not neglected because they cannot provide anything, but have the cost of their treatment lying ready in the common stock, so that they can meet expenses out of the greater wealth in full security. To the elder men too is given the respect and care which real children give to their parents, and they receive from countless hands and minds a full and generous maintenance for their latter years. . . .

Many are the potentates who at various occasions have raised themselves in power over the country.... They left no form of cruelty untried.... Yet none of these, neither the extremely ferocious nor the deep-dyed treacherous dissemblers, were able to lay a charge against this congregation of Essenes or holy ones here described. Unable to resist the high excellence of these people, they all treated them as self-governing and freemen by nature and extolled their communal meals and that ineffable sense of fellowship which is the clearest evidence of a perfect and supremely happy life.[147] (LCL)

8.155 Philo, *Hypothetica* 11.1–2, 14–18

According to Philo, the Essenes refuse to marry because marriage endangers communal life and because they view women as jealous and seductive.

Multitudes of his disciples has the lawgiver trained for the life of fellowship. These people are called Essenes, a name awarded to them doubtless in recognition of their holiness. They live in many cities of Judaea and in many villages and grouped in great societies of many members. Their persuasion is not based on birth, for birth is not a descriptive mark of voluntary associations, but on their zeal for virtue and desire to promote brotherly love....

Furthermore, they eschew marriage because they clearly discern it to be the sole or the principal danger to the maintenance of the communal life, as well as because they particularly practice continence. For no Essene takes a wife, because a wife is a selfish creature, excessively jealous and an adept at beguiling the morals of her husband and seducing him by her continued impostures. For by the fawning talk which she practices and the other ways in which she plays her part like an actress on the stage she first ensnares the sight and hearing, and when these subjects as it were have been duped she cajoles the sovereign mind. And if children come, filled with the spirit of arrogance and bold speaking she gives utterance with more audacious hardihood to things which before she hinted covertly and under disguise, and casting off all shame she compels him to commit actions which are all hostile to the life of fellowship. For he who is either fast bound in the love lures of his wife or under the stress of nature makes his children his first care ceases to be the same to others and unconsciously has become a different man and has passed from freedom into slavery.

Such then is the life of the Essenes, a life so highly to be prized that not only commoners but also great kings look upon them with admiration and amazement, and the approbation and honors which they give add further veneration to their venerable name. (LCL)

---

147. We do not know about the persecutions to which Philo is referring. Perhaps Antiochus Epiphanes is the persecutor to whom reference is made here.

8.156 Josephus, *Jewish War* 2.119–55, 159–61

According to Josephus, the Essenes shun marriage and riches. They do not believe in private ownership. They strictly obey their superiors. Initiates must go through a probationary period. They swear tremendous oaths. Anyone expelled from the community suffers dreadfully. They are particularly strict in their observance of the Sabbath. They refuse to yield to their persecutors. Some of them are gifted with prophetic insight and seldom err. One branch of the sect do marry but put their wives on three years' probation.

The Essenes have a reputation for cultivating peculiar sanctity. Of Jewish birth, they show a greater attachment to each other than do the other sects. They shun pleasures as a vice and regard temperance and the control of the passions as a special virtue. Marriage they disdain, but they adopt other men's children, while yet pliable and docile, and regard them as their kin and mould them in accordance with their own principles. They do not, indeed, on principle, condemn wedlock and the propagation thereby of the race, but they wish to protect themselves against women's wantonness, being persuaded that none of the sex keeps her plighted troth to one man.

Riches they despise, and their community of goods is truly admirable; you will not find one among them distinguished by greater opulence than another. They have a law that new members on admission to the sect shall confiscate their property to the order, with the result that you will nowhere see either abject poverty or inordinate wealth; the individual's possessions join the common stock and all, like brothers, enjoy a single patrimony. Oil they consider defiling, and anyone who accidentally comes in contact with it scours his person; for they make a point of keeping a dry skin and of always being dressed in white. They elect officers to attend to the interests of the community, the special services of each officer being determined by the whole body.

They occupy no one city, but settle in large numbers in every town. On the arrival of any of the sect from elsewhere, all the resources of the community are put at their disposal, just as if they were their own; and they enter the houses of men whom they have never seen before as though they were their most intimate friends. Consequently, they carry nothing whatever with them on their journeys, except arms as a protection against brigands. In every city there is one of the order expressly appointed to attend to strangers, who provides them with raiment and other necessaries. In their dress and deportment they resemble children under rigorous discipline. They do not change their garments or shoes until they are torn to shreds or worn threadbare with age. There is no buying or selling among themselves, but each gives what he has to any in need and receives from him in exchange something useful to himself; they are, moreover, freely permitted to take anything from any of their brothers without making any return.

Their piety towards the Deity takes a peculiar form. Before the sun is up they utter no word on mundane matters, but offer to him certain prayers, which have been handed down from their forefathers, as though entreating him to rise. They are then dismissed by their superiors to the various crafts in which they are severally proficient and are strenuously employed until the fifth hour, when they again assemble in one place and, after girding their loins with linen cloths, bathe their bodies in cold water.

After this purification, they assemble in a private apartment which none of the uninitiated is permitted to enter; pure now themselves, they repair to the refectory, as to some sacred shrine. When they have taken their seats in silence, the baker serves out the loaves to them in order, and the cook sets before each one plate with a single course. Before meat the priest says a grace, and none may partake until after the prayer. When breakfast is ended, he pronounces a further grace; thus at the beginning and at the close they do homage to God as the bountiful giver of life. Then laying aside their raiment, as holy vestments, they again betake themselves to their labors until the evening. On their return they sup in like manner, and any guests who may have arrived sit down with them.

No clamor or disturbance ever pollutes their dwelling; they speak in turn, each making way for his neighbor. To persons outside the silence of those within appears like some awful mystery; it is in fact due to their invariable sobriety and to the limitation of their allotted portions of meat and drink to the demands of nature.

In all other matters they do nothing without orders from their superiors; two things only are left to individual discretion, the rendering of assistance and compassion. Members may of their own motion help the deserving, when in need, and supply food to the destitute; but presents to relatives are prohibited, without leave from the managers. Holding righteous indignation in reserve, they are masters of their temper, champions of fidelity, very ministers of peace.

Any word of theirs has more force than an oath; swearing they avoid, regarding it as worse than perjury, for they say that one who is not believed without an appeal to God stands condemned already.

They display an extraordinary interest in the writings of the ancients, singling out in particular those which make for the welfare of soul and body; with the help of these, and with a view to the treatment of diseases, they make investigations into medicinal roots and the properties of stones.

A candidate anxious to join their sect is not immediately admitted. For one year, during which he remains outside the fraternity, they prescribe for him their own rule of life, presenting him with a small hatchet,[148] the loin-cloth already mentioned, and white raiment. Having given proof of his temperance during this probationary period, he is brought into closer touch with the rule and is allowed to share the purer kind of holy water, but is not yet received into the meetings of the community. For after this exhibition of endurance, his character is tested for two years more, and only then, if found worthy, is he enrolled in the society.

---

148. The hatchet, as indicated below, is used to create a receptacle when they relieve themselves.

But before he may touch the common food he is made to swear tremendous oaths: first that he will practice piety towards the Deity, next that he will observe justice towards men: that he will wrong none, whether of his own mind or under another's orders; that he will forever hate the unjust and fight the battle of the just; that he will forever keep faith with all men, especially with the powers that be, since no ruler attains his office save by the will of God; that, should he himself bear rule, he will never abuse his authority nor, either in dress or by other outward marks of superiority, outshine his subjects; to be forever a lover of truth and to expose liars; to keep his hands from stealing and his soul pure from unholy gain; to conceal nothing from the members of the sect and to report none of their secrets to others, even though tortured to death. He swears, moreover, to transmit their rules exactly as he himself received them; to abstain from robbery; and in like manner carefully to preserve the books of the sect and the names of the angels. Such are the oaths by which they secure their proselytes.

Those who are convicted of serious crimes they expel from the order; and the ejected individual often comes to a most miserable end. For, being bound by their oaths and usages, he is not at liberty to partake of other men's food, and so falls to eating grass and wastes away and dies of starvation. This has led them in compassion to receive many back in the last stage of exhaustion, deeming that torments which have brought them to the verge of death are a sufficient penalty for their misdoings.

They are just and scrupulously careful in their trial of cases, never passing sentence in a court of less than a hundred members; the decision thus reached is irrevocable. After God they hold most in awe the name of their lawgiver, any blasphemer of whom is punished with death. It is a point of honor with them to obey their elders, and a majority; for instance, if ten sit together, one will not speak if the nine desire silence.

They are careful not to spit into the midst of the company or to the right, and are stricter than all Jews in abstaining from work on the seventh day; for not only do they prepare their food on the day before, to avoid kindling a fire on that one, but they do not venture to remove any vessel or even to go to stool. On other days they dig a trench a foot deep with a mattock – such is the nature of the hatchet which they present to the neophytes – and wrapping their mantle about them, that they may not offend the rays of the Deity, sit above it. They then replace the excavated soil in the trench. For this purpose they select the more retired spots. And though this discharge of the excrements is a natural function, they make it a rule to wash themselves after it, as if defiled.

They are divided, according to the duration of their discipline, into four grades; and so far are the junior members inferior to the seniors, that a senior if but touched by a junior, must take a bath, as after contact with an alien. They live to a great age – most of them to upwards of a century – in consequence, I imagine, of the simplicity and regularity of their mode of life. They make light of danger, and triumph over pain by their resolute will; death, if it come with honor, they consider better than immortality.

The war with the Romans tried their souls through and through by every variety of test. Racked and twisted, burnt and broken, and made to pass through every instrument of torture, in order to induce them to blaspheme their lawgiver or to eat some forbidden thing, they refused to yield to either demand, nor ever once did they cringe to their persecutors or shed a tear. Smiling in their agonies and mildly deriding their tormentors, they cheerfully resigned their souls, confident that they would receive them back again.

For it is a fixed belief of theirs that the body is corruptible and its constituent matter impermanent, but that the soul is immortal and imperishable. Emanating from the finest ether, these souls become entangled, as it were, in the prison-house of the body, to which they are dragged down by a sort of natural spell; but when once they are released from the bonds of the flesh, then, as though liberated from a long servitude, they rejoice and are borne aloft. . . .

There are some among them who profess to foretell the future, being versed from their early years in holy books, various forms of purification and apophthegms of prophets; and seldom, if ever, do they err in their predictions.

There is yet another order of Essenes, which, while at one with the rest in its mode of life, customs, and regulations, differs from them in its views on marriage. They think that those who decline to marry cut off the chief function of life, the propagation of the race, and, what is more, that were all to adopt the same view, the whole race would very quickly die out. They give their wives, however, a three years' probation, and only marry them after they have by three periods of purification given proof of fecundity. They have no intercourse with them during pregnancy, thus showing that their motive in marrying is not self-indulgence but the procreation of children. (LCL)

8.157 Josephus, *Jewish Antiquities* 18.18–20

The Essenes do send sacrificial offerings to the Temple, but they believe in a different ritual and consequently are barred from the Temple. Their virtue, says Josephus, is beyond compare.

The doctrine of the Essenes is wont to leave everything in the hands of God. They regard the soul as immortal and believe that they ought to strive especially to draw near to righteousness. They send votive offerings to the Temple, but perform their sacrifices employing a different ritual of purification.[149] For this reason they are barred from those precincts of the Temple that are frequented by all the people and perform their rites by themselves.

Otherwise they are of the highest character, devoting themselves solely to agricultural labor. They deserve admiration in contrast to all others who claim their share of virtue because such qualities as

---

149. An alternative translation is: "Although the Essenes send offerings to the Temple, they do not sacrifice there because of a difference about the purifications that should be used."

theirs were never found before among any Greek or barbarian people, nay, not even briefly, but have been among them in constant practice and never interrupted since they adopted them from of old. (LCL)

8.158 Pliny the Elder (23–79 CE), *Natural History* 5.73

Pliny comments on the Essenes' avoidance of marriage and of money. The fact that he notes that they live on the west side of the Dead Sea has been a major factor leading most scholars to identify them with the Dead Sea sect. They have existed through thousands of ages.

On the west side of the Dead Sea, but out of range of the noxious exhalations of the coast, is the solitary tribe of the Essenes, which is remarkable beyond all the other tribes in the whole world, as it has no women and has renounced all sexual desire, has no money, and has only palm-trees for company. Day by day the throng of refugees is recruited to an equal number by numerous accessions of persons tired of life and driven thither by the waves of fortune to adopt their manners. Thus through thousands of ages (incredible to relate) a race in which no one is born lives on forever: so prolific for their advantage is other men's weariness of life! (LCL)

8.159 Dio Chrysostom (*ca.* 40–*ca.* after 113 CE), cited by Synesius (*ca.* 373–414 CE), *Life of Dio*

Dio Chrysostom, like Pliny, places the Essenes near the Dead Sea.

Moreover, he [Dio Chrysostom] praises the Essenes, a very blessed city situated near the Dead Water in the interior of Palestine, in the very vicinity of Sodoma. (M.S.)

8.160 Solinus (third century?), Collection of *Memorable Matters* 35.9–11

Solinus marvels at their self-discipline, notes their renunciation of marriage and money and the difficulty in gaining admittance to the order.

The interior of Judaea that gazes at the west is occupied by the Essenes. These, provided with a memorable discipline, seceded from the customs of all other nations, having been destined for this way of life by divine providence. No woman is to be found among them, and they have renounced sex completely. They ignore money and live on palms. Nobody is born among them, yet their members do not decrease. The place is dedicated to chastity. There many people flock from every nation; however, nobody is admitted who has not a reputation for chastity and innocence. For one who is responsible even for the smallest fault, although he may make the greatest effort in order to obtain entrance, is kept away by divine command. Thus through innumerable ages (incredible to relate), a race in which no childbirths occur lives on forever. (M.S.)

Therapeutae

BIBLIOGRAPHY

Alfred G. Langley, "Philo and the Therapeutae," *The Baptist Quarterly Review* 4 (1882), 36–56.

James Moffatt, "Therapeutae," in James Hastings, ed., *Encyclopaedia of Religion and Ethics* 2 (1922), 315–19.

Geza Vermes, "Essenes–Therapeutae–Qumran," *RQ* 2 (1960–1), 97–115.

The Therapeutae ("Healers") were an ascetic sect who lived on the shores of Lake Mareotis near Alexandria in Egypt during the first century CE; but unlike the mainstream of the Essenes they consisted of both men and women. Some scholars have thought that they were a radical off-shoot of the Essenes. They apparently left no trace on Jewish life, but they may have influenced the later development of Christian monasticism.

> 8.161 Philo, *On the Contemplative Life* 1.2, 2.13, 2.18, 8.65–8, 9.70, 9.73, 10.75, 11.83–4, 11.90

Philo refers to the Therapeutae as excelling in the art of healing body and soul. They abandon all ties with blood relations and give up all property. They revere the numbers seven, and especially fifty, as most sacred. Women, too, are members of the order. They are vegetarians and serve no wine in their sacred banquets. In principle they are opposed to slavery. The men and the women sing hymns antiphonally.

The vocation of these philosophers is at once made clear from their title of Therapeutae and Therapeutrides, a name derived from *therapeuo*, either in the sense of 'cure' because they profess an art of healing better than that current in the cities which cures only the bodies, while theirs treats also souls oppressed with grievous and well-nigh incurable diseases, inflicted by pleasures and desires and griefs and fears, by acts of covetousness, folly and injustice and the countless host of the other passions and vices: or else in the sense of 'worship' because nature and the sacred laws have schooled them to worship the Self-existent who is better than the good, purer than the One and more primordial than the Monad. . . .

Then such is their longing for the deathless and blessed life that thinking their mortal life already ended they abandon their property to their sons or daughters or to other kinsfolk, thus voluntarily advancing the time of their inheritance, while those who have no kinsfolk give them to comrades and friends. . . .

So when they have divested themselves of their possessions and have no longer aught to ensnare them they flee without a backward glance and leave their brothers, their children, their wives, their parents, the wide circle of their kinsfolk, the groups of friends around them, the fatherlands in which they were born and reared, since strong is the attraction of familiarity and very great its power to ensnare. . . .

First of all, these people assemble after seven sets of seven days[150] have passed, for they revere not only the simple seven but its square also, since they know its chastity and perpetual virginity. This is the

---

150. Presumably the reference is to Shavuoth (Pentecost).

eve of the chief feast which Fifty takes for its own, Fifty the most sacred of numbers and the most deeply rooted in nature, being formed from the square of the right-angled triangle which is the source from which the universe springs.[151] So then they assemble, white-robed and with faces in which cheerfulness is combined with the utmost seriousness; but before they recline, at a signal from a member of the Rota, which is the name commonly given to those who perform these services, they take their stand in a regular line in an orderly way, their eyes and hands lifted up to Heaven, eyes because they have been trained to fix their gaze on things worthy of contemplation, hands in token that they are clean from gain-taking and not defiled through any cause of the profit-making kind. So standing they pray to God that their feasting may be acceptable and proceed as He would have it.

After the prayers the seniors recline according to the order of their admission, since by senior they do not understand the aged and grey-headed who are regarded as still mere children if they have only in late years come to love this rule of life, but those who from their earliest years have grown to manhood and spent their prime in pursuing the contemplative branch of philosophy, which indeed is the noblest and most God-like part.

The feast is shared by women also, most of them aged virgins, who have kept their chastity not under compulsion, like some of the Greek priestesses, but of their own free will in their ardent yearning for wisdom. . . .

They do not have slaves to wait upon them, as they consider that the ownership of servants is entirely against nature. For nature has borne all men to be free, but the wrongful and covetous acts of some who pursued that source of evil, inequality, have imposed their yoke and invested the stronger with power over the weaker. . . .

In this [sacred] banquet – I know that some will laugh at this, but only those whose actions call for tears and lamentation – no wine is brought during those days but only water of the brightest and clearest, cold for most of the guests but warm for such of the older men as live delicately. The table too is kept pure from the flesh of animals; the food laid on it is loaves of bread with salt as a seasoning, sometimes also flavored with hyssop as a relish for the daintier appetites. . . .

Such are the preliminaries. But when the guests have lain themselves down arranged in rows, as I have described, and the attendants have taken their stand with everything in order ready for their ministry, the President of the company, when a general silence is established – here it may be asked when is there no silence – well, at this point there is silence even more than before so that no one ventures to make a sound or breathe with more force than usual – amid this silence, I say, he discusses some question arising in the Holy Scriptures or solves one that has been propounded by someone else. In doing this he has no thought of making a display, for he has no ambition to get a reputation for clever oratory but desires to gain a closer insight into some

---

151. In a right-angled triangle whose sides are 3, 4, and 5, the squares of those sides, when added together, amount to 50.

particular matters and having gained it not to withhold it selfishly from those who, if not so clear-sighted as he, have at least a similar desire to learn. . . .

After the supper they hold the sacred vigil which is conducted in the following way. They rise up all together and standing in the middle of the refectory form themselves first into two choirs, one of men and one of women, the leader and precentor chosen for each being the most honored amongst them and also the most musical. Then they sing hymns to God composed of many measures and set to many melodies, sometimes chanting together, sometimes taking up the harmony antiphonally, hands and feet keeping time in accompaniment, and rapt with enthusiasm reproduce sometimes the lyrics of the procession, sometimes of the halt and of the wheeling and counter-wheeling of a choric dance. . . .

So much then for the Therapeutae, who have taken to their hearts the contemplation of nature and what it has to teach, and have lived in the soul alone, citizens of Heaven and the world, presented to the Father and Maker of all by their faithful sponsor Virtue, who has procured for them God's friendship and added a gift going hand in hand with it, true excellence of life, a boon better than all good fortune and rising to the very summit of felicity. (LCL)

Dead Sea Sect

BIBLIOGRAPHY

Moshe H. Gottstein, "Anti-Essene Traits in the Dead Sea Scrolls," *VT* 4 (1954), 141–7.

Chaim Rabin, *Qumran Studies* (1957).

George J. Brooke, *Exegesis at Qumran: 4Q Florilegium in Its Jewish Context* (1959).

Frederick F. Bruce, *Biblical Exegesis in the Qumran Texts* (1959).

Kurt Schubert, *The Dead Sea Community: Its Origin and Teachings* (1959).

Menahem Mansoor, *The Dead Sea Scrolls: A College Textbook and a Study Guide* (1964).

Godfrey R. Driver, *The Judaean Scrolls: The Problem and a Solution* (1965).

Cecil Roth, *The Dead Sea Scrolls: A New Historical Approach* (1965).

Alfred R. C. Leaney, *The Rule of Qumran and Its Meaning* (1966).

Charles F. Pfeiffer, *The Dead Sea Scrolls and the Bible* (1969).

Edmund Wilson, *The Dead Sea Scrolls 1947–1969* (1969).

Roland de Vaux, *Archaeology and the Dead Sea Scrolls* (1973).

Lawrence H. Schiffman, *The Halakhah at Qumran* (1975).

Geza Vermes, *The Dead Sea Scrolls: Qumran in Perspective* (1977).

James H. Charlesworth, "The Origin and Subsequent History of the Authors of the Dead Sea Scrolls: Four Transitional Phases among the Qumran Essenes," *RQ* 10 (1980), 213–33.

Frank M. Cross, *The Ancient Library at Qumran and Modern Biblical Studies*, rev. ed. (1980).

Philip R. Davies, *The Damascus Covenant: An Interpretation of the "Damascus Document"* (1983).

Lawrence H. Schiffman, *Sectarian Law in the Dead Sea Scrolls* (1983).

Ben Zion Wacholder, *The Dawn of Qumran: The Sectarian Torah and the Teacher of Righteousness* (1983).

Yigael Yadin, *The Temple Scroll: The Hidden Law of the Dead Sea Sect* (1985).

Moshe Weinfeld, *The Organizational Pattern and the Penal Code of the Qumran Sect: A Comparison with Guilds and Religious Associations of the Hellenistic–Roman Period* (1986).

Michael A. Knibb, *The Qumran Community* (1987).

Phillip R. Callaway, *The History of the Qumran Community: An Investigation* (1988).

Michael Fishbane, "Use, Authority and Interpretation of Mikra at Qumran," *Mikra* (1988), 339–77.

George J. Brooke, ed., *Temple Scroll Studies: Papers Presented at the International Symposium on the Temple Scroll. Manchester, December 1987* (1989).

John J. Collins, "The Origin of the Qumran Community: A Review of the Evidence," in Maury P. Horgan and Paul J. Kobelski, eds, *To Touch the Text: Biblical and Related Studies in Honor of Joseph A. Fitzmyer, S.J.* (1989).

Shemaryahu Talmon, *The World of Qumran from Within: Collected Essays* (1989).

Joseph A. Fitzmyer, *The Dead Sea Scrolls: Major Publications and Tools for Study*, rev. ed. (1990).

Lawrence H. Schiffman, ed., *Archeology and History in the Dead Sea Scrolls: The New York University Conference in Memory of Yigael Yadin* (1990).

Hershel Shanks et al., *The Dead Sea Scrolls after Forty Years: Symposium at the Smithsonian Institution October 27, 1990. Sponsored by the Resident Associate Program* (1991).

John J. Collins, "Dead Sea Scrolls," *ABD*, vol. 2 (1992), 85–101.

Devorah Dimant and Uriel Rappaport, eds, *The Dead Sea Scrolls: Forty Years of Research* (1992).

Joseph A. Fitzmyer, *Responses to 101 Questions on the Dead Sea Scrolls* (1992).

Norman Golb, *Who Wrote the Dead Sea Scrolls?* (1994).

Lawrence H. Schiffman, *Reclaiming the Dead Sea Scrolls* (1994).

Florentino Garcia Martinez, *The Dead Sea Scrolls Translated* (1994).

James C. VanderKam, *The Dead Sea Scrolls Today* (1994).

No discovery in the field of Second Temple studies has been more dramatic or has occasioned more discussion and controversy than the Dead Sea Scrolls which have been found in Qumran and vicinity. Much of this discussion has centered around the identification of the sect itself. Originally, there was near unanimity that the sect was the Essenes. The similarities were striking: the location near the Dead Sea, the monastic-like separatist organization with a graded novitiate, the language of the initiates' oaths, a strict rule of discipline demanding absolute obedience to superior officers, frequent ablutions, a strongly negative attitude toward sex, absolutely meticulous observance of the Sabbath, emphasis on divination, faith-healing, prohibition against spitting in the midst of the assembly or to the right. But there are also important differences: they have diametrically opposed conceptions of purity and purification; among the Essenes the maximum punishment was death, whereas in the sect it was expulsion; the Essenes possessed no private property, whereas members of the sect did; the sect had a solar calendar, whereas, so far as we can tell, the Essenes agreed with other Jews in having a lunar–solar calendar; the sect believed that sacrifices should be made in the Temple, whereas the Essenes disagreed; there is nothing to indicate that the Essenes were sons of Zadok or that they had a new covenant in Damascus or that they claimed to be the true Israel; the priests are more prominent in the Dead Sea sect; there is no mention in Josephus of the key figure of the sect, the Teacher of Righteousness; the Essenes prohibited slavery, whereas the sect permitted it; there are some differences in procedure for admitting new members, with the probation among the Essenes being both longer (three years as against two years) and stricter; there is nothing in Qumran to indicate that the group prayed in the direction of the sun, as the Essenes apparently did; there is no indication that the Essenes' meals had a sacred character as did those at Qumran; the main Essene community avoided marriage in principle, whereas women and children are named in the description of the Qumran congregation; Josephus emphasizes the peaceful character of the Essenes, whereas the sect had a militaristic flavor; to judge from one of the most recently published documents, *Miqsat Ma'aseh ha-Torah*, the sect agreed with the Sadducees in a number of important legal interpretations.

8.162 *The Manual of Discipline* 1.1–15, 2.19–25, 5.1–7, 5.20–24, 6.8, 6.13–24, 7.4–5, 7.9–10, 7.14–15, 7.25, 9.7, 9.21–2 (second century BCE)

Here are set forth the requirements for those wishing to join the order. After a year in the novitiate his case is carefully reviewed; after a second year his case is further reviewed before he gains membership. Specific and severe penalties are prescribed for various lapses, particularly in ethics and manners. One may not associate in any way with one who leaves the order.

Everyone who wishes to join the community must pledge himself to respect God and man; to live according to the communal rule; ... to love all the children of light, each according to his stake in the formal community of God; and to hate all the children of darkness, each according to the measure of his guilt, which God will ultimately requite.

All who declare their willingness to serve God's truth must bring all of their mind, all of their strength, and all of their wealth into the community of God, so that their minds may be purified by the truth of His precepts, their strength controlled by His perfect ways, and their wealth disposed in accordance with His just design. They must not deviate by a single step from carrying out the orders of God at the times appointed for them; they must neither advance the statutory times nor postpone the prescribed seasons. They must not turn aside from the ordinances of God's truth either to the right or to the left....

The following procedure is to be followed year by year so long as Belial [Satan] continues to hold sway. The priests are first to be reviewed in due order, one after another, in respect of the state of their spirits. After them, the Levites shall be similarly reviewed, and in the third place all the laity one after another, in their thousands, hundreds, fifties and tens. The object is that every man in Israel may be made aware of his status in the community of God in the sense of the ideal, eternal society, and that none may be abased below his status nor exalted above his allotted place. All of them will thus be members of a community founded at once upon true values and upon a becoming sense of humility, upon charity and mutual fairness – members of a society truly hallowed, partners in an everlasting communion....

This is the rule for all the members of the community.... They are to abide by the decisions of the sons of Zadok, the same being priests that still keep the Covenant, and of the majority of the community that stand firm in it. It is by the vote of such that all matters doctrinal, economic and judicial are to be determined.... They are to regard as felons all that transgress the law....

When a man enters the covenant, minded to act in accordance with all the foregoing ordinances and formally to ally himself to the holy congregation, inquiry is to be made concerning his temper in human relations and his understanding and performance in matters of doctrine. This inquiry is to be conducted jointly by the priests who have undertaken concertedly to uphold God's Covenant and to supervise the execution of all the ordinances which He has commanded, and by a majority of the laity who have likewise undertaken concertedly to return to that Covenant. Every man is then to be registered in a particular rank, one after the other, by the standard of his understanding and performance. The object is that each person will be rendered subject to his superior. Their spiritual attitudes and their performances are to be reviewed, however, year by year, some being then promoted by virtue of their [improved] understanding and the integrity of their conduct, and others demoted for their waywardness....

The general members of the community are to keep awake for a third of all the nights of the year reading books, studying the Law and worshiping together....

After he [a novice] has spent a full year in the midst of the community, the members are jointly to review his case, as to his understanding and performance in matters of doctrine. If it then be voted by the opinion of the priests and of a majority of their co-covenanters to admit him to the sodality, they are to have him bring with him all his property and the tools of his profession. These are to be committed to the custody of the community's 'minister of works.' They are to be entered by that officer into an account, but he is not to disburse them for the general benefit.

Not until the completion of a second year among the members of the community is the candidate to be admitted to the common board. When, however, that second year has been completed, he is to be subjected to a further review by the general membership, and if then it be voted to admit him to the community, he is to be registered in the due order of rank that he is to occupy among his brethren in all matters pertaining to doctrine, judicial procedure, degree of purity and share in the common funds....

If there be found in the community a man who consciously lies in the matter of [his] wealth, he is to be regarded as outside the state of purity entailed by membership, and he is to be deprived of one fourth of his food ration.

If a man dissemble about what he really knows, he is to do penance for six months.

If a man defames his neighbor unjustly, and does so deliberately, he is to do penance for one year and regarded as 'outside'....

Anyone who interrupts his neighbor in a public session is to do penance for ten days.

Anyone who lies down and goes to sleep at a public session is to do penance for thirty days. . . .

If a man indulge in raucous, inane laughter, he shall do penance for thirty days.

If a man put forth his left hand to gesticulate with it in conversation, he shall do penance for ten days. . . .

If a man has been a formal member of the community for a full ten years, but then, through a spiritual relapse, betrays the principles of the community and quits the general body in order to walk in the stubbornness of his own heart, he is never to return to formal membership in the community. No member of the community is to associate with him either by recognizing him as of the same state of purity or by sharing property with him. Any of the members who does so shall be liable to the same sentence: he too shall be expelled. . . .

The priests alone are to have authority in all judicial and economic matters, and it is by their vote that the ranks of the various members of the community are to be determined. . . .

And these are the regulations of conduct for every man that would seek the inner vision in these times, touching what he is to love and what he is to hate.

He is to bear unremitting hatred towards all men of ill repute, and to be minded to keep in seclusion from them. He is to leave it to them to pursue wealth and mercenary gain, like servants at the mercy of their masters or wretches truckling to a despot. (T.H.G., slightly amended)

The Fourth Philosophy and Other Revolutionary Groups

BIBLIOGRAPHY

William R. Farmer, *Maccabees, Zealots, and Josephus: An Inquiry into Jewish Nationalism in the Greco-Roman Period* (1956).

Borge Salomonsen, "Some Remarks on the Zealots with Special Regard to the Term 'Qannaim' in Rabbinic Literature," *NTS* 12 (1965–6), 164–76.

Solomon Zeitlin, "The Sicarii and Masada," *JQR* 57 (1966–7), 251–70.

Morton Smith, "Zealots and Sicarii: Their Origin and Relation," *HTR* 64 (1971), 1–19.

H. Paul Kingdon, "The Origin of the Zealots," *NTS* 19 (1972–3), 74–81.

Menahem Stern, "Zealots," *Encyclopaedia Judaica Year Book 1973* (1973), 135–52.

Francis Loftus, "The Anti-Roman Revolts of the Jews and the Galileans," *JQR* 68 (1977), 78–98.

Menahem Stern, "Sicarii and Zealots," in Michael Avi-Yonah and Zvi Baras, eds, *The World History of the Jewish People*, vol. 8: *Society and Religion in the Second Temple Period* (1977), 263–301.

Richard A. Horsley, "Sicarii: Ancient Jewish Terrorists," *JR* 59 (1979), 435–58.

Paul W. Barnett, "The Jewish Sign Prophets – A.D. 40–70 – Their Intentions and Origins," *NTS* 27 (1981), 679–97.

Richard A. Horsley, "Ancient Jewish Banditry and the Revolt against Rome, AD 66–70," *CBQ* 43 (1981), 409–32.

Richard A. Horsley and John S. Hanson, *Bandits, Prophets, and Messiahs: Popular Movements at the Time of Jesus* (1985).

Richard A. Horsley, "Popular Prophetic Movements at the Time of Jesus: Their Principal Features and Social Origins," *JSNT* 26 (1986), 3–27.

Richard A. Horsley, "The Zealots. Their Origin, Relationships and Importance in the Jewish Revolt," *NT* 2 (1986), 159–92.

Martin Goodman, *The Ruling Class of Judaea: The Origins of the Jewish Revolt against Rome AD 66–70* (1987).

Martin Hengel, *The Zealots: Investigations into the Jewish Freedom Movement in the Period from Herod I until 70 AD* (trans. David Smith, 1989).

Valentin Nikiprowetzky, "Josephus and the Revolutionary Parties," *JBH* (1989), 216–36.

Doron Mendels, *The Rise and Fall of Jewish Nationalism* (1992).

Jonathan J. Price, *Jerusalem under Siege: The Collapse of the Jewish State 66–70 CE* (1992).

Rebecca Gray, "The Sign Prophets," in her *Prophetic Figures in Late Second Temple Jewish Palestine: The Evidence from Josephus* (1993), 112–44.

8.163 Josephus, *Jewish Antiquities* 18.4–6, 8, 9–10, 23–4 (6 CE)

As the selection below indicates, Josephus finds in the Fourth Philosophy the source of the tragedy endured by the Jews in the revolt against the Romans. Though in agreement with the Pharisees in all else, they had as the central feature of their platform the idea that independence is a *sine qua non* for Judaism and that Jews can accept the overlordship of God alone. They did not hesitate to slaughter fellow-Jews who disagreed with them. They gladly submitted to death for their cause. Most scholars identify the Fourth Philosophy with the Sicarii, but Josephus himself does not explicitly make this identification.

A certain Judas, a Gaulanite from a city named Gamala, who had enlisted the aid of Saddok, a Pharisee, threw himself into the cause of rebellion.[152] They [Judas' followers] said that the assessment[153] carried with it a status amounting to downright slavery, no less, and appealed to the nation to make a bid for independence. They urged that in case of success the Jews would have laid the foundation of prosperity, while if they failed to obtain any such boon, they would win honor and renown for their lofty aim; and that Heaven would be their zealous helper to no lesser end than the furthering of their enterprise until it succeeded – all the more if with high devotion in their hearts they stood firm and did not shrink from the bloodshed that might be necessary.

Since the populace, when they heard their appeals, responded gladly, the plot to strike boldly made serious progress; and so these men sowed the seed of every kind of misery, which so afflicted the nation that words are inadequate. . . . They sowed the seed from which sprang strife between factions and the slaughter of fellow citizens. Some were slain in civil strife, for these men madly had recourse to butchery of each other and of themselves from a longing not to be outdone by their opponents; others were slain by the enemy in war. . . .

152. In protest against the census of Quirinius (6 CE).
153. This was the census of Quirinius, which required assessment of property.

Here is a lesson that an innovation and reform in ancestral traditions weighs heavily in the scale in leading to the destruction of the congregation of the people. In this case certainly, Judas and Saddok started among us an intrusive fourth school of philosophy; and when they had won an abundance of devotees, they filled the body politic immediately with tumult, also planting the seeds of those troubles which subsequently overtook it, all because of the novelty of this hitherto unknown philosophy that I shall now describe. My reason for giving this brief account of it is chiefly that the zeal which Judas and Saddok inspired in the younger element meant the ruin of our cause. . . .

As for the fourth of the philosophies, Judas the Galilean set himself up as leader of it. This school agrees in all other respects with the opinions of the Pharisees, except that they have a passion for liberty that is almost unconquerable, since they are convinced that God alone is their leader and master. They think little of submitting to death in unusual forms and permitting vengeance to fall on kinsmen and friends if only they may avoid calling any man master.

Inasmuch as most people have seen the steadfastness of their resolution amid such circumstances, I may forego any further account. For I have no fear that anything reported of them will be considered incredible. The danger is, rather, that report may minimize the indifference with which they accept the grinding misery of pain. (LCL)

8.164 Josephus, *Jewish War* 7.262–70 (66–70 CE)

In the following passage Josephus comments on five revolutionary leaders or groups of revolutionaries – Sicarii, John of Gischala, Simon son of Gioras, the Idumaeans, and the Zealots. Clearly, he is, to say the least, very unsympathetic to all of them, and stresses the cruelty with which they dealt with their own fellow-Jews.

The Sicarii were the first to set the example of this lawlessness and cruelty to their kinsmen, leaving no word unspoken to insult, no deed untried to ruin, the victims of their conspiracy.

Yet even they were shown by John [of Gischala] to be more moderate than himself. For not only did he put to death all who proposed just and salutary measures, treating such persons as his bitterest enemies among all the citizens, but he also in his public capacity loaded his country with evils innumerable, such as one might expect would be inflicted upon men by one who had already dared to practice impiety even towards God. For he had unlawful food served at his table and abandoned the established rules of purity of our forefathers;[154] so that it could no longer excite surprise that one guilty of such mad impiety towards God failed to observe towards men the offices of gentleness and charity.

Again, there was Simon, son of Gioras: what crime did he not commit? Or what outrage did he refrain from inflicting upon the persons of

---

154. Josephus seems to be claiming here that John of Gischala, in his disregard of the laws of purity, was an *'am ha-aretz*.

those very freemen who had created him a despot? What ties of friendship or of kindred but rendered these men more audacious in their daily murders? For to do injury to a foreigner they considered an act of petty malice, but thought they cut a splendid figure by maltreating their nearest relations.

Yet even their infatuation was outdone by the madness of the Idumaeans. For those most abominable wretches, after butchering the chief priests, so that no particle of religious worship might continue, proceeded to extirpate whatever relics were left of our civil polity, introducing into every department perfect lawlessness.

In this the so-called Zealots excelled, a class which justified their name by their actions; for they copied every deed of ill, nor was there any previous villainy recorded in history that they failed zealously to emulate. And yet they took their title from their professed zeal for virtue, either in mockery of those they wronged, so brutal was their nature, or reckoning the greatest of evils good. (LCL)

Battles within besieged Jerusalem, woodcut, Paris, 1492.

9

꧁꧂

Revolts of the Jews against the Roman Empire

The First Jewish Revolt (66–73/4)

BIBLIOGRAPHY

Leo Kadman, *The Coins of the Jewish War of 66–73 CE* (1960).

Cecil Roth, "The Historical Implications of the Jewish Coinage of the First Revolt," *IEJ* 12 (1962), 33–46.

Cecil Roth, "The Constitution of the Jewish Republic of 66–70," *JSS* 9 (1964), 295–319.

Moses Aberbach, *The Roman-Jewish War (66–70 AD): Its Origin and Consequences* (1966).

David M. Rhoads, *Israel in Revolution: 6–74 CE: A Political History Based on the Writings of Josephus* (1976).

Francis Loftus, "The Anti-Roman Revolts of the Jews and the Galileans," *JQR* 68 (1977), 78–98.

Per Bilde, "The Causes of the Jewish War according to Josephus," *JSJ* 10 (1979), 179–202.

Shaye J. D. Cohen, *Josephus in Galilee and Rome: His Vita and Development as a Historian* (1979).

Mordecai Gichon, "Cestius Gallus' Campaign in Judaea," *PEQ* 113 (1981), 39–62.

Robert Goldenberg, "Early Rabbinic Explanations of the Destruction of Jerusalem," *JJS* 33 (1982), 517–25.

Uriel Rappaport, "John of Gischala: From Galilee to Jerusalem," *JJS* 33 (1982), 479–93.

Uriel Rappaport, "John of Gischala in Galilee," in Lee I. Levine, ed., *JC* 3 (1983), 46–57.

Martin Goodman, *The Ruling Class of Judaea: The Origins of the Jewish Revolt against Rome AD 66–70* (1987).

Shaye J. D. Cohen, "Roman Domination: The Jewish Revolt and the Destruction of the Second Temple," in Hershel Shanks, ed., *Ancient Israel: A Short History from Abraham to the Roman Destruction of the Temple* (1988), 205–35, 257–9.

Shimon Applebaum, "Josephus and the Economic Causes of the Jewish War," *JBH* (1989), 237–64.

Heinz Kreissig, "A Marxist View of Josephus' Account of the Jewish War," *JBH* (1989), 265–77.

Valentin Nikiprowetzky, "Josephus and the Revolutionary Parties," *JBH* (1989), 216–36.

Martin Goodman, "The Origins of the Great Revolt: A Conflict of Status Criteria," in Aryeh Kasher, Uriel Rappaport, and Gideon Fuks, eds, *Greece and Rome in Eretz Israel: Collected Essays* (1990), 39–53.

James S. McLaren, *Power and Politics in Palestine: The Jews and the Governing of Their Land 100 BC–AD 70* (1991), 158–87.

Doron Mendels, *The Rise and Fall of Jewish Nationalism* (1992), 355–83.

Jonathan J. Price, *Jerusalem under Siege: The Collapse of the Jewish State 66–70 CE* (1992).

Millar (1993), 70–9, 359–66.

The fact that the Jews revolted against the mighty Roman Empire three times within a span of less than seventy years and the degree to which each of these revolts had popular support indicates how oppressive the Jews found Roman rule to be and how crucial many of them deemed independence. To a considerable degree these revolts were civil wars, brought about through vast social, economic, and religious divisions within the Jewish population and furthered by growing tensions between the Jewish and non-Jewish populations. Indeed, one of the major causes of the revolt of 66 was the favoritism shown by the Roman procurators for the non-Jewish population of Judaea and the lack of order and security which they allowed. A further precipitating cause was the fact that the Roman soldiers in Judaea were recruited almost entirely from the local Hellenized cities, especially Sebaste (Samaria) and Caesarea. And we must not forget that the Jewish king of Judaea, Agrippa II, actually fought on the side of the Romans during the Great Revolt of 66–73/4.

Most students join Josephus in looking upon the first revolt as foolhardy, but that is largely due to the fact that our chief source of information about this revolt is Josephus, who played an ignominious role in it and who devotes a great deal of attention to defending his actions. In point of fact, the revolt, which broke out in 66 CE, had at least some chance of success. In the first place, Rome was ruled by Nero, who, by any medical standard, would have to be regarded as insane. In the second place, there was a sharp division within Rome between the senate and the emperor and between various military cliques which ultimately led to civil war, in the years 68–9, when there were no fewer than four emperors within a single year in the very midst of the Jewish revolt. In the third place, the Jews of Judaea could reasonably have hoped for support from the numerous Jews – constituting, at least a tenth of the population of the Roman Empire – throughout the Empire; and indeed the severity with which the troops of the Roman governor of Egypt, Tiberius Julius Alexander, dealt with the Jews of Alexandria on the eve of the revolution may have been occasioned by his fear that they would send aid to their co-religionists in Judaea. Fourthly, the revolt came in the midst of the climax of successes by the Jews in proselytizing, the greatest achievement being the conversion of the royal family of Adiabene in Mesopotamia; and the rebels could have hoped – as, indeed, materialized – that they would get military aid from the kingdom of Adiabene. Fifthly, the fact that Agrippa I was able to arrange a meeting not many years before this of a number of rulers of petty kingdoms would give hope that some of them might again be attracted to join a coalition against Rome. Sixthly, there had been numerous revolts against the

Romans in areas such as Britain, Gaul, Batavia, Germany, and Pannonia; and if these revolts could be coordinated the Romans hardly had sufficient troops to deal with them all. Seventhly, the great enemy of Rome at this time, as it had been for at least a century before this and was to remain for several centuries thereafter was Parthia; if the Parthians (and the large Jewish population within the Parthian kingdom might well have been able to induce the Parthians to co-ordinate their activities) would attack the Romans while the Jews in Judaea were revolting, the Romans would have to fight major battles on two fronts. The chief disadvantages for the Jews were their disunity, the inexperience of their generals, and their poor strategy in choosing to bottle themselves up within walled cities, notably Jerusalem, thus playing to the advantage of the Romans, who were particularly skilled in attacking such walls with their catapults and other machinery; if they had chosen to fight a guerrilla-type war, such as the Maccabees had, to a considerable degree, fought two centuries earlier, they would probably have given the Romans a more difficult time, since one needs a tremendous superiority in manpower, food, water, and supplies to be able to overcome guerrillas.

Prophecies of the Revolt

One major cause of the revolt was the ideological conflict between the Jewish conception of Israel as the elect and the reality of the powerful Roman Empire. One of the factors bringing on the revolt was the plethora of Messianic or Messianic-like movements, though Josephus does not actually use the word "Messiah" in connection with the revolt. Many Jews, it appears, were indeed awaiting a mighty leader who would bring them independence from the Romans or, as in the case of the Qumran sect, direct intervention by God.

9.1 Josephus, *Jewish War* 6.312–13

Josephus here cites an ambiguous prediction found in the Bible which led Jews to believe that they would rule the world. Josephus, however, interprets this to refer to Vespasian.

But what more than all else incited them [the Jews] to the war [against the Romans in 66 CE] was an ambiguous oracle, likewise found in their sacred scriptures,[1] to the effect that at that time one from their country would become ruler of the world. This they understood to mean someone of their own race, and many of their wise men went astray in their interpretation of it. The oracle, however, in reality signified the sovereignty of Vespasian, who was proclaimed Emperor on Jewish soil. (LCL)

9.2 Tacitus (*ca.* 56–120 CE), *Histories* 5.13.1–2

Tacitus, like Josephus, mentions a prophecy in the ancient writings of the Jews that men starting from Judaea would conquer the world, though

1. Presumably the allusion is to the prophecy in Dan 2:44–45.

various prodigies in Jerusalem should have warned the Jews that the end was near. He, too, like Josephus, interprets the prophecy as referring to Vespasian.

Prodigies had indeed occurred [in Jerusalem, 70 CE], but to avert them either by victims or by vows is held unlawful by a people that, though prone to supersitition, is opposed to all propitiatory rites. Contending hosts were seen meeting in the skies, arms flashed, and suddenly the Temple was illuminated with fire from the clouds. Of a sudden the doors of the shrine opened and a superhuman voice cried: 'The gods are departing;' at the same moment the mighty stir of their going was heard. Few interpreted these omens as fearful; the majority firmly believed that their ancient priestly writings contained the prophecy that this was the very time when the East should grow strong and that men starting from Judaea should possess the world. This mysterious prophecy had in reality pointed to Vespasian and Titus, but the common people, as is the way of human ambition, interpreted these great destinies in their own favor and could not be turned to the truth even by adversity. (LCL)

9.3 Suetonius (*ca. 69–ca. 150 CE*), *Life of Vespasian* 4.5

Suetonius, like Josephus and Tacitus, mentions a prophecy that men from Judaea were destined to rule the world. Though the Jews understood it to refer to themselves, he, too, refers it to Vespasian.

There had spread over all the Orient an old and established belief, that it was fated at that time for men coming from Judaea to rule the world. This prediction, referring to the emperor of Rome, as afterwards appeared from the event, the people of Judaea took to themselves; accordingly they revolted and after killing their governor they routed the consular ruler of Syria as well, when he came to the rescue, and took one of his eagles. (LCL)

The Proposed Plan of Resistance

The following passage presents a plan for resistance against the Romans, as found in the *War Scroll*, one of the scrolls in the library of the sect at Qumran near the Dead Sea. The scroll is a kind of military manual for war with the Romans (here called Kittim). The sect apparently believed that a military confrontation with the Romans was inevitable. Qumran became a resistance center, and the sect apparently joined the anti-Roman revolt. The sect's fate was sealed by the Romans, who dispersed the community in 68/9 CE.

9.4 *The War Scroll* 16.24, 18, 19.31 (end of the first century BCE or early first century CE)

In this passage we have a description of the military array and the call to battle led by the priests against the enemy, who will be totally destroyed.

All this disposition they shall carry out on that day in the place where they stand over against the camp of the Kittim.[2] Afterwards the priests shall blow for them the trumpets of remembrance. They shall open the battle intervals, and the skirmishers shall go forth and take up positions in columns between the lines. The priests shall blow for them a fanfare for the array, and the columns shall keep fanning out at the sound of the trumpets until each man has fallen in at his proper position. Then the priests shall blow for them another fanfare, signals for engaging. When they stand near the line of the Kittim within throwing range, they shall each man raise his hand with his weapon. Then the six priests shall blow on the trumpets of assault a high-pitched intermittent note to direct the fighting, and the Levites and the whole band of horn-blowers shall sound a battle fanfare, a great noise. As soon as the sound goes forth, the skirmishers shall attack to fell the slain of the Kittim, and all the people shall cease from the sound of the fanfare, while the priests keep blowing a fanfare on the trumpets of assault, and the battle is waged victoriously against the Kittim. . . .

The Kittim shall be smashed without remnant and survivor, and there shall be an uprising of the hand of the God of Israel against the whole multitude of Belial.[3] At that time the priests shall sound a fanfare on the six trumpets of remembrance, and all battle formations shall follow their call and spread out against the entire army of the Kittim to destroy them utterly. . . .

And there shall come forward in that place the chief priest and his deputy and his brother-priests and the Levites and all the elders . . . and the mighty men of war, and all chiefs of the formations and their subordinates, and they shall bless the God of Israel. (Y.Y.)

The Course of the Revolt

9.5 Josephus, *Jewish War* 1.1–3, 7–8.

Our chief source for the account of the war is the Jewish historian Josephus. The very title of his work, *The Jewish War*, betrays the fact that he is writing about it from the point of view of the Romans, inasmuch as, if he were writing about it from the point of view of the Jews, he should have entitled it *The Roman War*. In the passage below Josephus notes the inadequacy of previous accounts of the war and remarks that his Greek version is a translation from the Aramaic account which he had written for the barbarians of the interior, namely those of Mesopotamia. The long duration of the war and the fact that it took a huge Roman army and the most gifted generals to defeat the Jews lends some support to Josephus' view that this was the greatest of all wars and that one ought not to disparage the efforts of the Jews.

The war of the Jews against the Romans – the greatest not only of the wars of our own time, but, so far as accounts have reached us, well nigh

2. The fact that in the Dead Sea Pesher of Habakkuk the Kittim are said to come from far by sea, that they will afflict atrocities on all peoples, and will dominate Israel, has led many scholars to identify them as the Romans.
3. A satanic personification of wickedness.

of all that ever broke out between cities or nations – has not lacked its historians. Of these, however, some, having taken no part in the action, have collected from hearsay casual and contradictory stories which they have then edited in a rhetorical style; while others, who witnessed the events, have either from flattery of the Romans or from hatred of the Jews, misrepresented the facts, their writings exhibiting alternatively invective and encomium, but nowhere historical accuracy. In these circumstances, I – Josephus, son of Matthias, a Hebrew by race, a native of Jerusalem and a priest, who at the opening of the war myself fought against the Romans and in the sequel was perforce an onlooker – propose to provide the subjects of the Roman Empire with a narrative of the facts, by translating into Greek the account that I previously composed in my vernacular tongue [presumably Aramaic] and sent to the barbarians in the interior. . . .

Though the writers in question presume to give their works the title of histories, yet throughout them, apart from the utter lack of sound information, they seem, in my opinion, to miss their own mark. They desire to represent the Romans as a great nation, and yet they continually depreciate and disparage the actions of the Jews. But I fail to see how the conquerors of a puny people deserve to be accounted great. Again, these writers have respect neither for the long duration of the war, nor for the vast numbers of the Roman army that it engaged, nor for the prestige of the generals, who, after such herculean labors under the walls of Jerusalem, are, I suppose, of no repute in these writers' eyes, if their achievement is to be underestimated. (LCL)

9.6 Josephus, *Jewish War* 2.409–16

The following passage comments on the decision of the revolutionaries in the year 66 not to accept sacrifices offered on behalf of the Romans and their emperor and the vain attempt of the Pharisaic leaders to convince the revolutionaries of the serious consequences of their decision and to induce them to repeal it.

Eleazar, son of Ananias the high priest, a very bold youth then holding the position of captain [of the Temple],[4] persuaded those who officiated in the cult to accept no gift or sacrifice from a foreigner. This action laid the beginning of the war against the Romans; for the sacrifices offered on behalf of that people and of the emperor were thus terminated. The chief priests and the notables over and over again urged them not to discontinue the customary offerings on behalf of their rulers, but the priests did not accede. They had great confidence in their numbers, and they were, moreover, supported by the stalwarts among the revolutionaries. But above all they relied on the captain Eleazar.

Thereupon the powerful men met in the same place with the chief priests and the most notable of the Pharisees for a comprehensive deliberation with regard to the desperate situation. Deciding to try a direct appeal to the revolutionaries, they assembled the people before

---

4. The position of captain of the Temple was second in rank to that of the high priest.

the bronze gate – that of the inner Temple facing east. And first they expressed great indignation at the audacity of the revolt and the serious war threatening the country. Then they exposed the absurdity of the pretext. Their forefathers, they said, had adorned the Temple mostly with the aid of foreigners, and had always accepted the gifts of foreign peoples; not only had they not forbidden anyone to offer sacrifices – for this would be most sacrilegious – but they had set up around the Temple the dedicatory offerings which were still to be seen and had remained there for a long time. But now Eleazar and his men were provoking the arms of the Romans and courting war with them, introducing a strange innovation into the cult, and, besides the danger to the city, laying open the city to the charge of impiety if Jews were to be the only people to allow no aliens the right of sacrifice or worship. If someone introduced such a law in the case of a single private individual they would be indignant at this as being an inhumane decision, yet they made light of it when all the Romans and the emperors were excluded. It was to be feared, however, that if the sacrifices for these were rejected, they might be prevented from offering sacrifices even for themselves; and that the city would be placed outside the pale of the empire, unless they quickly returned to discretion and restored the sacrifices and corrected the insult before the report came to the ears of those whom they had insulted. (M.R.)

9.7 Josephus, *Jewish War* 2.562–9

Josephus' role in the war has been the subject of much scholarly debate, fueled, in particular, by the fact that he seems to contradict himself. After the Roman governor of Syria, Cestius Gallus, had been defeated by the rebels in the opening skirmish of the war in 66, Josephus, according to the *Jewish War*, which was apparently written between 79 and 81 CE, was appointed to conduct the war in Galilee, whereas in his autobiography, written toward the end of his life (*ca.* 100 CE), he indicates that he was dispatched to induce the rebels to lay down their arms. There is no indication as to what military qualifications he possessed for this task.

The Jews who had pursued Cestius, on their return to Jerusalem, partly by force, partly by persuasion, brought over to their side such pro-Romans as still remained; and, assembling in the Temple, appointed additional generals to conduct the war. Joseph, son of Gorion, and Ananus the high priest were elected to the supreme control of affairs in the city, with a special charge to raise the height of the walls. As for Eleazar, son of Simon, notwithstanding that he had in his hands the Roman spoils, the money taken from Cestius, and a great part of the public treasure, they did not entrust him with office, because they observed his despotic nature and that his subservient admirers conducted themselves like his bodyguard. Gradually, however, financial needs and the intrigues of Eleazar had such influence with the people that they ended by yielding the supreme command to him.

Other generals were selected. . . . Josephus son of Matthias [the historian] was given the two Galilees [upper and lower], with the addition of Gamala [in the Golan region], the strongest city in that region. Each of these generals executed his commission to the best of his zeal or ability. (LCL)

9.8 Josephus, *Life* 28–9

In this account Josephus seems to say that he was appointed as general not to fight against the Romans but rather to induce those bent on revolution to lay down their arms. Perhaps this account may be reconciled with the account above in the *War* if we suggest that originally it was Josephus' hope that he could defuse the revolution but that when he realized that he could not he organized an army to fight against the Romans.

After the defeat of Cestius, . . . the leading men of Jerusalem, observing that the brigands and revolutionaries were well provided with arms, feared that, being without weapons themselves, they might be left at the mercy of their adversaries, as in fact eventually happened. Being informed, moreover, that the whole of Galilee had not yet revolted from Rome, and that a portion of it was still tranquil, they dispatched me with two other priests, Joazar and Judas, men of excellent character, to induce the disaffected to lay down their arms and to impress upon them the desirability of reserving these for the picked men of the nation. The latter, such was the policy determined on, were to have their weapons constantly in readiness for future contingencies, but should wait and see what action the Romans would take. (LCL)

9.9 Josephus, *Jewish War* 4.128–9, 131–2, 133–5, 143–6

Josephus describes in graphic detail the factional strife both in Jerusalem and indeed throughout Judaea. Especially fierce was the contention between those who favored the continuation of the war and those who were for peace.

By these harangues[5] most of the youth were corrupted and incited to war. But of the sober and elder men everyone foresaw what was to come and mourned for the city as already lost. Such confusion reigned among the people. But even before sedition broke out in Jerusalem there was party strife in the country. . . .

In every city tumult and civil war were stirred up, and as soon as they had a breathing spell from the Romans they turned their hands against one another. Between the enthusiasts for war and those desiring peace there was fierce strife. At the start this party strife in the homes assailed those who had long been friends. . . .

Faction reigned everywhere, and the revolutionary and war party overpowered by its youth and recklessness the old and prudent. Each side turned first to pillaging of their neighbors, then organizing themselves in companies for brigandage throughout the country, so

---

5. Of John of Gischala (in Galilee), one of the acknowledged leaders of the revolt against the Romans. Josephus regarded him as an extremist. He was eventually taken prisoner and exhibited by Titus in his triumph in Rome.

much so that in cruelty and lawlessness the victims found no difference between compatriots and Romans. Indeed, capture by the Romans seemed a far lighter fate to those who were being plundered.

The [Roman] garrisons of the cities, partly from reluctance to expose themselves to risk, partly from their hatred of the people, provided little or no protection to the victims. At length, satiated with their pillage of the country, the brigand chiefs of all these bands everywhere joined forces and, becoming one pack of villainy, stole into wretched Jerusalem. . . .

[The brigands arrested and murdered eminent people in Jerusalem.] The brigands, however, were not satisfied with having put their captives in irons, and did not consider it safe to keep influential persons in custody for a long time, with large families quite capable of avenging them. Moreover, they feared that the people might be stirred by their lawlessness to rise against them. They accordingly decided to kill the captives, and sent for this purpose the most expert in murdering, a certain John, called in their native tongue 'son of Dorcas.'[6] Accompanied by ten others, he entered the jail with drawn sword, and they butchered the prisoners. For such a crime they invented a monstrous excuse: they declared that they had conferred with the Romans concerning the surrender of Jerusalem, and that they had them killed as traitors to the freedom of the state. In short, they boasted of their iniquitous acts as though they had been the benefactors and saviors of the city. (M.R.)

9.10 Babylonian Talmud, *Giṭṭin* 55b–56a (edited *ca*. 500 CE)

The Talmud, which stresses the point that the destruction of the Temple was due to groundless hatred, has a similar picture of factional strife and of pressure exerted by the revolutionaries upon the moderates. As in Josephus, we find the beginning of the war ascribed to the refusal to accept the offering of the emperor.

Rabbi Joḥanan [ben Nappaḥa, third century CE] said: . . . The destruction of Jerusalem came through a Kamza and a Bar Kamza[7] in this way. A certain man had a friend Kamza and an enemy Bar Kamza. He once made a party and said to his servant, 'Go and bring Kamza.' The man went and brought Bar Kamza. When the man [who gave the party] found him there he said, 'See, you tell tales about me, what are you doing here? Get out.' Said the other: 'Since I am here, let me stay, and I will pay you for whatever I eat and drink.' He said, 'I won't.' 'Then let me give you half the cost of the party.' 'No,' said the other. 'Then let me pay for the whole party.' He still said, 'No,' and he took him by the hand and put him out. Said the other, 'Since the Rabbis were sitting there and did not stop him, this shows that they agreed with him. I will

6. In Aramaic Bar Tabitha, i.e., "son of a gazelle."

7. These two men are otherwise unknown. Josephus (*Life* 33) does mention a Compsus son of Compsus as one of the respectable citizens in Tiberias who in the year 66 recommended that the city continue its allegiance to the Romans and King Agrippa II. Rabbi Joḥanan, the source of this account, taught in Tiberias, and may reflect a local tradition.

go and inform against them to the Government.' He went and said to the Emperor, 'The Jews are rebelling against you.' He [the Emperor] said, 'How can I tell?' He said to him: 'Send them an offering and see whether they will offer it [on the altar].' So he sent with him a fine calf. While on the way he made a blemish on its upper lip, or as some say on the white of its eye, in a place where we [Jews] count it a blemish but they do not. The Rabbis were inclined to offer it in order not to offend the Government. Said Rabbi Zechariah ben Abkulas [Palestinian, first century CE] to them: 'People will say that blemished animals are offered on the altar.' They then proposed to kill Bar Kamza so that he should not go and inform against them, but Rabbi Zechairah ben Abkulas said to them, 'Is one who makes a blemish on consecrated animals to be put to death?' Rabbi Johanan thereupon remarked: 'Through the scrupulousness of Rabbi Zechariah ben Abkulas our House has been destroyed, our Temple burnt, and we ourselves exiled from our land. . . .' (Soncino)

9.11 Josephus, *Jewish War* 4.401–9

Josephus places the chief blame for the debacle upon the various revolutionary groups, particularly the Sicarii, gangs of whom made raids everywhere.

When they [the Sicarii] learnt that the Roman army was inactive and that in Jerusalem the Jews were distracted by sedition and domestic tyranny, they embarked on more ambitious enterprises. Thus, during the feast of unleavened bread – a feast which has been kept by the Jews in thanksgiving for deliverance ever since their return to their native land on their release from bondage in Egypt[8] – these assassins, eluding under cover of night those who might have obstructed them, made a raiding descent upon a small town called Engaddi.[9] Those of the inhabitants who were capable of resistance were, before they could seize their arms and assemble, dispersed and driven out of the town; those unable to flee, women and children numbering upwards of seven hundred, were massacred. They then rifled the houses, seized the ripest of the crops, and carried off their spoil to Masada.[10]

They made similar raids on all the villages around the fortress, and laid waste the whole district, being joined daily by numerous dissolute recruits from every quarter.

Throughout the other parts of Judaea, moreover, the predatory bands, hitherto quiescent, now began to bestir themselves. And as in the body when inflammation attacks the principal member all the members catch the infection, so the sedition and disorder in the capital gave the scoundrels in the country free license to plunder; and each gang after pillaging their own village made off into the wilderness.

8. Consequently, most of the people would be in Jerusalem, where Jews congregated during the three pilgrimage festivals each year.

9. Engaddi [Engedi] is an oasis on the western shore of the Dead Sea.

10. The Sicarii had previously occupied Masada, near the Dead Sea, where they were to make their last stand against the Romans in the year 73/4 prior to committing mass suicide.

Then joining forces and swearing mutual allegiance, they would proceed by companies – smaller than an army but larger than a mere band of robbers – to fall upon temples[11] and cities. The unfortunate victims of their attacks suffered the miseries of captives of war, but were deprived of the chance of retaliation, because their foes in robber fashion at once decamped with their prey. There was, in fact, no portion of Judaea which did not share in the ruin of the capital. (LCL)

9.12 Babylonian Talmud, *Giṭṭin* 56a–b (edited *ca*. 500 CE)

The terror which the Sicarii exercised over the population, including their own members, is indicated by the following passage, in the course of which the head of the Sicarii secretly advises Rabban Joḥanan ben Zakkai, the greatest of the rabbinic leaders of the day, how he might escape from Jerusalem, namely by pretending to be dead and being carried out of the city. Joḥanan ben Zakkai then proceeds prophetically (in a manner similar to Josephus' prediction to Vespasian) to greet the general Vespasian as king.

Abba Sikra,[12] the head of the *biryoni* [revolutionaries] in Jerusalem was the son of the sister of Rabban Joḥanan ben Zakkai [Palestinian, first century CE]. [The latter, during the siege of Jerusalem by the Romans] sent to him saying, 'Come to visit me privately.' When he came he said to him, 'How long are you going to carry on in this way and kill all the people with starvation? He replied: 'What can I do? If I say a word to them, they will kill me.' He said: 'Devise some plan for me to escape. Perhaps I shall be able to save a little.' He said to him: 'Pretend to be ill, and let everyone come to inquire about you. Bring something evil smelling and put it by you so that they will say you are dead. Let then your disciples get under your bed, but no others, so that they shall not notice that you are still light, since they know that a living being is lighter than a corpse.' He did so, and Rabbi Eliezer [ben Hyrcanus, Palestinian, end of first and beginning of second century CE] went under the bier from one side and Rabbi Joshua [ben Ḥananiah, Palestinian, end of first and beginning of second century CE] from the other. When they reached the door, some men wanted to put a lance through the bier. He said to them: 'Shall [the Romans] say, They have pierced their Master?' . . .

When he reached the Romans he said, 'Peace to you, O king, peace to you, O king.' He [Vespasian] said: 'Your life is forfeit on two counts, one because I am not a king and you call me king, and again, if I am a king, why did you not come to me before now?' He replied: 'As for your saying that you are not a king, in truth you are a king, since if you were not a king Jerusalem would not be delivered into your hand. . . . As for your question, why if you are a king, I did not come to you till now, the answer is that the *biryoni* among us did not let me. . . .'

At this point a messenger came to him from Rome saying, 'Up, for the Emperor is dead, and the notables of Rome have decided to make you head [of the State].' (Soncino)

11. Presumably the reference is to synagogues.
12. I.e., Father of the Sicarii.

9.13 Josephus, *Jewish War* 5.442–5, 449, 450–1

Josephus gives graphic pictures of the terrible suffering endured by the Jews while they were besieged in Jerusalem in the year 70. Josephus puts the chief blame upon the Jews themselves. He attempts to exonerate the Roman general Titus, who, he says, hoped by continuing the crucifixions of Jews to induce them to surrender.

No other city ever endured such suffering, nor from the beginning of time has there been a generation more productive of crime. Indeed, in the end they actually disparaged the Hebrew people, in order to seem less impious toward foreigners, and confessed themselves what indeed they were – slaves, the dregs, and the bastard scum of the nation. It was they who overthrew the city, and compelled the reluctant Romans to record such a melancholy triumph, and all but drew to the Temple the tardy flames. Indeed, when from the upper town they beheld the city burning, they neither grieved nor wept, though among the Romans these emotions were detected. . . .

[When Jews sought to escape from the burning city] they defended themselves of necessity when caught [by the Romans], and after a conflict it seemed too late to ask for mercy. They were indeed scourged and subjected to torture of every description before death, and then crucified opposite the walls. . . . The main reason [on Titus' part] for not stopping [the crucifixions] was the hope that at the sight the Jews might surrender in fear that if they did not surrender they would suffer a similar fate. The soldiers out of anger and hatred amused themselves by nailing their prisoners in different postures; and so great was their number that space could not be found for the crosses nor crosses for the bodies. (M.R.)

9.14 Josephus, *Jewish War* 6.201–13, 317–22

The Jews besieged in Jerusalem were beset by incredible hunger and thirst. The account of Mary, the mother who devoured her own son, is perhaps the most horrifying of all the episodes of the war.

Among the residents of the region beyond Jordan was a woman named Mary, daughter of Eleazar, of the village of Bethezuba . . . , eminent by reason of her family and fortune, who had fled with the rest of the people to Jerusalem and there become involved in the siege. The bulk of her property, which she had packed up and brought with her from Peraea[13] to the city, had been plundered by the tyrants; while the relics of her treasures, with whatever food she had contrived to procure, were being carried off by their satellites in their daily raids. With deep indignation in her heart, the poor woman constantly abused and cursed these extortioners and so incensed them against her.

But when no one either out of exasperation or pity put her to death, weary of finding for others food, which indeed it was now impossible from any quarter to procure, while famine coursed through her intestines and marrow and the fire of rage was more consuming even

13. A region to the east of the Jordan.

than the famine, impelled by the promptings alike of fury and necessity, she proceeded to an act of outrage upon nature. Seizing her child, an infant at the breast, 'Poor babe,' she cried, 'amidst war, famine, and sedition, to what end should I preserve thee? With the Romans slavery awaits us, should we live till they come; but famine is forestalling slavery, and more cruel than both are the rebels. Come, be thou food for me, to the rebels an avenging fury, and to the world a tale such as alone is wanting to the calamities of the Jews.' With these words she slew her son, and then, having roasted the body and devoured half of it, she covered up and stored the remainder.

At once the rebels were upon her and, scenting the unholy odor, threatened her with instant death unless she produced what she had prepared. Replying that she had reserved a goodly portion for them also, she disclosed the remnants of her child. Seized with instant horror and stupefaction, they stood paralyzed by the sight. She, however, said, 'This is my own child, and this my handiwork. Eat, for I too have eaten. Show not yourselves weaker than a woman, or more compassionate than a mother. But if you have pious scruples and shrink from my sacrifice, then let what I have eaten be your portion and the remainder also be left for me.' At that they departed trembling, in this one instance cowards, though scarcely yielding even this food to the mother. The whole city instantly rang with the abomination, and each, picturing the horror of it, shuddered as though it had been perpetrated by himself. The starving folk longed for death, and felicitated those who had gone to their rest ere they had heard or beheld such evils. . . .

So glutted with plunder were the troops, one and all, that throughout Syria the standard of gold was depreciated to half its former value.

Among the priests still holding out on the wall of the sanctuary a lad, who was parched with thirst, confessed his condition to the Roman guards and besought them to pledge him security. Taking pity on his youth and distress, they promised him protection; whereupon he came down and drank, and then, after filling with water a vessel which he had brought with him, raced back to his comrades above. The guards all failing to catch him and cursing his perfidy, he replied that he had broken no covenant; for the accepted pledge did not bind him to remain with them, but merely permitted him to descend and procure water; both these actions he had done, and therefore considered that he had been true to his word.

Such cunning, especially in so young a boy, astonished the Romans whom he had outwitted; however, on the fifth day, the priests, now famishing, came down and, being conducted by the guards to Titus, implored him to spare their lives. But he told them that the time for pardon had for them gone by, that the one thing for whose sake he might with propriety have spared them was gone, and that it behoved priests to perish with their temple, and so ordered them to execution. (LCL)

9.15 Josephus, *Jewish War* 6.403–8

Josephus describes in vivid detail the gruesome stages of the final massacre of the Jews.

The Romans, now in control of the walls, planted their standards on the towers, and with clapping of hands and rejoicing raised a paean for their victory. They had found the end of the war much lighter than the beginning. Indeed, they could not believe that they had climbed the last wall without bloodshed, and, seeing no one opposing them, were really perplexed. Pouring into the narrow streets, sword in hand, they massacred indiscriminately those whom they met, and burned the houses of people who fled into them, people and all.

Often in their raids, on entering the houses for loot they would find whole families dead and the rooms filled with the victims of the famine, and then, shuddering at the sight, they would depart empty-handed. Yet, while they pitied those who had perished, they did not feel the same for the living, but running everyone through who fell in their way, they choked the narrow streets with corpses and deluged the whole city with blood, so that many of the fires were extinguished by the slaughter. Towards evening they ceased slaughtering, but during the night the fire gained the mastery, and the dawn of the eighth day of the month Gorpiaeus rose upon Jerusalem in flames – a city which suffered such calamities in the siege that, had she from her foundation enjoyed as many blessings, she would have been thought completely enviable, a city undeserving, moreover, of such great misfortunes on any other ground, except that she produced a generation by which she was overthrown. (M.R.)

9.16 Babylonian Talmud, *Giṭṭin* 56a (edited *ca.* 500 CE)

The Talmud, like Josephus, paints a picture of incredible famine besetting the Jews besieged in Jerusalem.

The *biryoni* [revolutionaries] were then in the city [Jerusalem]. The Rabbis said to them: 'Let us go out and make peace with them [the Romans].' They would not let them, but on the contrary said, 'Let us go out and fight them.' The Rabbis said: 'You will not succeed.' They then rose up and burnt the stores of wheat and barley so that a famine ensued. Martha the daughter of Boethius was one of the richest women in Jerusalem. She sent her man-servant out saying, 'Go and bring me some fine flour.' By the time he went it was sold out. He came and told her, 'There is no fine flour, but there is white [flour].' She then said to him, 'Go and bring me some.' By the time he went he found the white flour sold out. He came and told her: 'There is no white flour but there is dark flour.' She said to him, 'Go and bring me some.' By the time he went it was sold out. He returned and said to her, 'There is no dark flour, but there is barley flour.' She said, 'Go and bring me some.' By the time he went this was also sold out. She had taken off her shoes, but she said, 'I will go out and see if I can find anything to eat.' Some dung stuck to her foot and she died [from the shock].

Rabban Joḥanan ben Zakkai [Palestinian, first century CE] applied to her the verse, 'The tender and delicate woman among you which would not adventure to set the sole of her foot upon the ground' [Deut 28:57]. Some report that she ate a fig left by Rabbi Zadok [Palestinian, first century CE], and became sick and died. For Rabbi Zadok observed fasts for forty years in order that Jerusalem might not be destroyed, [and he became so thin that] when he ate anything the food could be seen [as it passed through his throat]. When he wanted to restore himself, they used to bring him a fig, and he used to suck the juice and throw the rest away.

When Martha was about to die, she brought out all her gold and silver and threw it in the street, saying, 'What is the good of this to me?' thus giving effect to the verse, 'They shall cast their silver in the streets.' (Soncino)

9.17 The Coins of the Revolutionaries

BIBLIOGRAPHY

Baruch Kanael, "The Historical Background of the Coins 'Year Four . . . of the Redemption of Zion,'" *BASOR* 129 (Feb., 1953), 18–20.
Leo Kadman, *The Coins of the Jewish War of 66–73* CE (1960).
Ya'akov Meshorer, *Jewish Coins of the Second Temple Period* (1967), 154–8.
Ya'akov Meshorer, *Ancient Jewish Coinage*, 2 (1982).
Leo Mildenberg, "Rebel Coinage in the Roman Empire," in Aryeh Kasher, Uriel Rappaport, and Gideon Fuks, eds, *Greece and Rome in Eretz Israel: Collected Essays* (1990), 362–74.

The revolutionary authorities coined silver and bronze money with archaic Hebrew script.

(1) Obverse: Chalice: SHEKEL OF ISRAEL YEAR 1.
    Reverse: JERUSALEM THE HOLY CITY

(2) Obverse: Amphora: YEAR 2.
    Reverse: Vine leaf. FREEDOM OF ZION

(3) Obverse: Citron, palm branch YEAR FOUR-AND-A-HALF.
    Reverse: Palm tree, baskets THE REDEMPTION OF ISRAEL (M.R.)

The Destruction of the Temple

BIBLIOGRAPHY

Hugh Montefiore, "Sulpicius Severus and Titus' Council of War," *Historia* 11 (1962), 156–70.
G. K. van Andel, *The Christian Concept of History in the Chronicle of Sulpicius Severus* (1976).
Gedaliah Allon, "The Burning of the Temple," in his *Jews, Judaism and the Classical World: Studies in Jewish History in the Times of the Second Temple and Talmud* (1977), 252–68.
Timothy D. Barnes, "The Fragments of Tacitus' *Histories*," *CP* 72 (1977), 224–31.

9.18 Josephus, *Jewish War* 6.236–43, 249–53.

According to Josephus, as indicated in the passage below, Titus, in the council that he held with his staff prior to the attack on Jerusalem, showed so much clemency that he declared that the Temple should be spared even if the Jews should fight from it. Nevertheless, one of the Roman soldiers, contrary to orders, set fire to the Temple.

On the following day [after setting on fire the gates and porticoes of the Temple] Titus, after giving orders to a division of his army to extinguish the fire and make a road to the gates to facilitate the ascent of the legions, called together his generals. Six of his chief staff-officers were assembled, namely Tiberius Alexander, the prefect of all the forces,[14] Sextus Cerealius, Larcius Lepidus, and Titus Phrygius, the respective commanders of the fifth, tenth, and fifteenth legions; Fronto Haterius, prefect of the two legions from Alexandria, and Marcus Antonius Julianus, procurator of Judaea; and the procurators and tribunes being next collected, Titus brought forward for debate the subject of the Temple.

Some were of opinion that the law of war should be enforced, since the Jews would never cease from rebellion while the Temple remained as the focus for concourse from every quarter. Others advised that if the Jews abandoned it and placed no weapons whatever upon it, it should be saved, but that if they mounted it for purposes of warfare, it should be burnt, as it would then be no longer a temple, but a fortress, and thenceforward the impiety would be chargeable, not to the Romans but to those who forced them to take such measures.

Titus, however, declared that even were the Jews to mount it and fight therefrom, he would not wreak vengeance on inanimate objects instead of men, nor under any circumstances burn down so magnificent a work, for the loss would affect the Romans, inasmuch as it would be an ornament to the empire if it stood.

Fortified by this pronouncement, Fronto, Alexander, and Cerealis now came over to his view. He then dissolved the council, and, directing the officers to allow the other troops an interval of repose, that he might find them reinvigorated in action, he gave orders to the picked men from the cohorts to open a road through the ruins and extinguish the fire. . . .

Titus then withdrew to Antonia,[15] determined on the following day, at dawn, to attack with his whole force, and invest the Temple. That building, however, God, indeed long since, had sentenced to the flames; but now in the revolution of the years had arrived the fated day, the tenth of the month Lous, the day on which of old it had been burnt by the king of Babylon.[16] The flames, however, owed their origin and cause to God's own people. For, on the withdrawal of Titus, the insurgents, after a brief respite, again attacked the Romans, and an engagement ensued between the guards of the sanctuary and the troops who were endeavoring to extinguish the fire in the inner court; the latter routing the Jews and pursuing them right up to the sanctuary.

At this moment, one of the soldiers, awaiting no orders and with no horror of so dread a deed, but moved by some supernatural impulse, snatched a brand from the burning timber and, hoisted up by one of his comrades, flung the fiery missile through a low golden door, which gave access on the north side to the chambers surrounding the

14. This is the apostate nephew of Philo who had been procurator of Judaea and governor of Egypt and who was now, in effect, quartermaster general.

15. The Antonia was the fortified portion of the Temple in Jerusalem.

16. The traditional date, still observed as a fast day by Jews, is the ninth of Ab.

sanctuary. As the flame shot up, a cry, as poignant as the tragedy, arose from the Jews, who flocked to the rescue, lost to all thought of self-preservation, all husbanding of strength, now that the object of all their past vigilance was vanishing. (LCL)

9.19 Sulpicius Severus (*ca.* 363–*ca.* 425 CE), *Chronica* 2.30.6–7

The Christian historian, Sulpicius Severus, in a passage which some have thought was derived from a lost portion of Tacitus?, *Histories*, asserts (in obvious contradiction to Josephus) that Titus, in the council which he held with his officers, demanded the destruction of the Temple in order to crush Judaism as well as Christianity.

It is said that Titus summoned his council, and before taking action consulted it whether he should overthrow a sanctuary of such work-manship, since it seemed to many that a sacred building, one more remarkable than any other human work, should not be destroyed. For if preserved it would testify to the moderation of the Romans, while if demolished it would be a perpetual sign of cruelty.

On the other hand, others, and Titus himself, expressed their opinion that the Temple should be destroyed without delay, in order that the religion of the Jews and Christians should be more completely exterminated. For those religions, though opposed to one another, derive from the same founders; the Christians stemmed from the Jews and the extirpation of the root would easily cause the offspring to perish. (M.S.)

9.20 Babylonian Talmud, *Giṭṭin* 56b (edited *ca.* 500 CE)

The rabbis were particularly hostile to Titus, inasmuch as he was held responsible for the desecration and destruction of the Temple; and they note his inglorious end, presumably a divinely-inflicted punishment. On the ninth day of Ab, when the two Temples were said to have been destroyed and when, according to tradition, it is not permitted for Jews to have the enjoyment of study except for accounts of Jewish catas-trophes, the Talmudic passage in *Giṭṭin* 55b–57a describing this catastrophe is permitted to be read.

Vespasian sent Titus, who said, 'Where is their God, the rock in whom they trusted [Deut 32:17]?' This was the wicked Titus who blasphemed and insulted Heaven. What did he do? He took a harlot by the hand and entered the Holy of Holies and spread out a scroll of the Law and committed a sin on it. . . . A gnat came and entered his nose, and it knocked against his brain for seven years. . . . It has been taught: Rabbi Phineas ben Aruba [Palestinian, first century CE] said: 'I was in company with the notables of Rome, and when he died they split open his skull and found there something like a sparrow two *selas* in weight.' A Tanna[17] taught: Like a young dove two pounds in weight. Abaye [Babylonian, end of third and beginning of fourth century CE] said: We have it on record that its beak was of brass and its claws of iron. When

---

17. One of the rabbis of the first two centuries CE.

he died he said: 'Burn me and scatter my ashes over the seven seas so that the God of the Jews should not find me and bring me to trial.' (Soncino)

The Fall of Masada

BIBLIOGRAPHY

Yigael Yadin, *Masada: Herod's Fortress and the Zealots' Last Stand* (1966).

Trude Weiss-Rosmarin, "Masada, Josephus and Yadin," *Jewish Spectator* 32.8 (Oct, 1967), 2–8, 30–2.

Zalman Dimitrovsky, "Masada," *CJ* 22.2 (Winter, 1968), 36–47.

Trude Weiss-Rosmarin, "Masada Revisited," *JS* 34 (Dec, 1969), 3–5, 29–32.

Sidney B. Hoenig, "The Sicarii in Masada – Glory or Infamy?" *Tradition* 11 (1970), 5–30.

Louis I. Rabinowitz, "The Masada Martyrs according to the Halakah," *Tradition* 11 (1970), 31–7.

Shubert Spero, "In Defense of the Defenders of Masada," *Tradition* 11 (1970), 31–43.

Dov I. Frimer, "Masada – in the Light of Halakah," *Tradition* 12.1 (Summer, 1971), 27–43.

Zvi Kolitz, "Masada: Suicide or Murder?" *Tradition* 12.1 (Summer, 1971), 5–26.

Sidney B. Hoenig, "Historic Masada and the Halakhah," *Tradition* 13.2 (Fall, 1972), 100–15.

Louis H. Feldman, "Masada: A Critique of Recent Scholarship," in Jacob Neusner, ed., *Christianity, Judaism and Other Graeco-Roman Cults* (1975), 218–48.

Virginia L. Trimble, "Masada, Suicide, and Halakhah," *CJ* 31 (1977), 45–55.

David J. Ladouceur, "Masada: A Consideration of the Literary Evidence," *GRBS* 21 (1980), 245–60.

Shaye J. D. Cohen, "Masada: Literary Tradition, Archaeological Remains, and the Credibility of Josephus," *JJS* 33 (1982), 385–405.

Louis H. Feldman, *Josephus and Modern Scholarship (1937–1980)* (1984), 763–90, 964–6.

David J. Ladouceur, "Josephus and Masada," *JJC* (1987), 95–113.

Hannah M. Cotton, "The Date of the Fall of Masada: The Evidence of the Masada Papyri," *ZPE* 78 (1989), 157–62.

Yigael Yadin and Joseph Naveh, *Masada I: The Aramaic and Hebrew Ostraca and Jar Inscriptions*; Yaacov Meshorer, *The Coins of Masada* (1989).

Hannah M. Cotton and Joseph Geiger, *Masada II: The Yigael Yadin Excavations 1963–1965, Final Reports. The Latin and Greek Documents* (1989).

Ehud Netzer, *Masada III: The Yigael Yadin Excavations 1963–1965. Final Reports. The Buildings, Stratigraphy and Architecture* (1991).

Herod's fortress palace at Masada, on the western shore of the Dead Sea in Idumaean country, was captured by Jewish extremists, the Sicarii, who massacred its Roman garrison. Reinforced by new arrivals, the partisans held out until 73 or 74, when the most spectacular event of the whole war occurred, namely the mass mutual suicide of the defenders. The excavations of Masada by Yigael Yadin in 1963–5 have disclosed Herod's palace complex, as well as relics of the partisans and their families.

Our only version of the episode comes from Josephus, who was not present but who presumably had access to an account that may have been written by the Roman general Flavius Silva, who directed the operations at Masada. Josephus mentions that one of the seven survivors was a woman who recounted the grisly tale to the Romans when they arrived.

The accuracy of Josephus' account has been much debated: it is said that since the defenders were pious Jews they would have known how strongly forbidden suicide is in Jewish law, and they should have fought to the last man, especially since they had an abundance of food and water and plenty of stones to hurl down upon the Romans. Moreover, whereas Josephus says that all the possessions of the defenders were gathered together in one large pile and set on fire, archaeology shows that there were many piles and many fires. Furthermore, Josephus says that Eleazar ben Jair, the leader of the Sicarii, ordered his men to destroy everything except the foodstuffs, but archaeology shows that many storerooms containing food provisions were burnt. In addition, Josephus says that 960 committed suicide, whereas Yadin, in his extremely comprehensive excavations, found only twenty-five skeletons. Finally, the long speeches put into the mouth of Eleazar hardly seem authentic, since it would be unlikely that the ultra-pious Sicarii would use arguments clearly taken from Plato's *Phaedo*.

But inasmuch as there were many Romans and Jews (who were forced to help the Romans during the siege) still alive at the time when Josephus issued his book who could have contradicted him, it would seem likely that Josephus was careful with his details. In any case, the fact that the Romans, upon entering Masada, are said by Josephus to have marveled at the bravery of the defenders would further tend to verify the authenticity of the account, inasmuch as Josephus would hardly have been expected to say anything positive about the Sicarii, whom he elsewhere denigrates to such a degree.

9.21 Josephus, *Jewish War* 7.320–6, 328, 331, 333–40, 386–7, 389, 391–2, 395–406

However, neither did Eleazar [ben Jair, the leader of the Sicarii at Masada] himself contemplate flight,[18] nor did he intend to permit any other to do so. Seeing the wall consuming in the flames, unable to devise any further means of deliverance or gallant endeavor, and setting before his eyes what the Romans, if victorious, would inflict on them, their children and their wives, he deliberated on the death of all. And judging, as matters stood, this course the best, he assembled the most doughty of his comrades and incited them to the deed by such words as these:

'Long since, my brave men, we determined neither to serve the Romans nor any other save God, for He alone is man's true and righteous Lord; and now the time is come which bids us verify that resolution by our actions. At this crisis let us not disgrace ourselves; we who in the past refused to submit even to a slavery involving no peril, let us not now, along with slavery, deliberately accept the irreparable penalties awaiting us if we are to fall alive into Roman hands. For as we

18. The wall around the fortress at Masada had, in part, been breached, and the defenders' second wooden wall had been destroyed by fire.

were the first of all to revolt, so are we the last in arms against them. Moreover, I believe that it is God who has granted us this favor, that we have it in our power to die nobly and in freedom – a privilege denied to others who have met with unexpected defeat. Our fate at break of day is certain capture, but there is still the free choice of a noble death, with those we hold most dear.... For had He [God] continued to be gracious, or but lightly incensed, He would never have overlooked such wholesale destruction or have abandoned His most holy city to be burnt and razed to the ground by our enemies.... For not even the impregnable nature of this fortress has availed to save us; nay, though ample provisions are ours, piles of arms, and a superabundance of every other requisite, yet we have been deprived, manifestly by God Himself, of all hope of deliverance....

'The penalty for those crimes let us pay not to our bitterest foes, the Romans, but to God through the act of our own hands. It will be more tolerable than the other. Let our wives thus die undishonored, our children unacquainted with slavery; and when they are gone, let us render a generous service to each other, preserving our liberty as a noble winding-sheet. But first let us destroy our chattels and the fortress by fire; for the Romans, well I know, will be grieved to lose at once our persons and the lucre. Our provisions only let us spare; for they will testify, when we are dead, that it was not want which subdued us, but that, in keeping with our initial resolve, we preferred death to slavery.'

Thus spoke Eleazar; but his words did not touch the hearts of all hearers alike. Some, indeed, were eager to respond and all but filled with delight at the thought of a death so noble; but others, softer-hearted, were moved with compassion for their wives and families, and doubtless also by the vivid prospect of their own end, and their tears as they looked upon one another revealed their unwillingness of heart.

Eleazar, seeing them flinching and their courage breaking down in face of so vast a scheme, feared that their whimpers and tears might unman even those who had listened to his speech with fortitude. Far, therefore, from slackening in his exhortation, he roused himself and, fired with mighty fervor, essayed a higher flight of oratory on the immortality of the soul....

'Unenslaved by the foe let us die, as free men with our children and wives let us quit this life together! This our laws enjoin,[19] this our wives and children implore of us....'

He would have pursued his exhortation but was cut short by his hearers, who, overpowered by some uncontrollable impulse, were all in haste to do the deed. Like men possessed they went their way, each eager to outstrip his neighbor and deeming it a signal proof of courage and sound judgment not to be seen among the last; so ardent the passion that had seized them to slaughter their wives, their little ones and themselves....

---

19. There is no such law in the Bible, nor is there any such law in the Oral Torah as codified in the Talmud. Perhaps it was in accordance with the law as understood by the sect of the Sicarii.

While they caressed and embraced their wives and took their children in their arms, clinging in tears to those parting kisses, at that same instant, as though served by hands other than their own, they accomplished their purpose, having the thought of the ills they would endure under the enemy's hands to console them for their constraint in killing them. . . .

Then, having chosen by lot ten of their number to dispatch the rest, they laid themselves down each beside his prostrate wife and children, and, flinging their arms around them, offered their throats in readiness for the executants of the melancholy office. These, having unswervingly slaughtered all, ordained the same rule of the lot for one another, that he on whom it fell should slay first the nine and then himself last of all; such mutual confidence had they all that neither in acting nor in suffering would one differ from another.

Finally, then, the nine bared their throats, and the last solitary survivor, after surveying the prostrate multitude, to see whether haply amid the shambles there was yet one left who needed his hand, and finding that all were slain, set the palace ablaze, and then collecting his strength drove his sword clean through his body and fell beside his family.

They had died in the belief that they had left not a soul of them alive to fall into Roman hands; but an old woman and another, a relative of Eleazar, superior in sagacity and training to most of her sex, with five children, escaped by concealing themselves in the subterranean aqueducts, while the rest were absorbed in the slaughter.

The victims numbered 960, including women and children; and the tragedy occurred on the fifteenth of the month Xanthicus.

The Romans, expecting further opposition, were by daybreak under arms and, having with gangways formed bridges of approach from the earthworks, advanced to the assault. Seeing none of the enemy but on all sides an awful solitude, and flames within and silence, they were at a loss to conjecture what had happened.

At length, as if for a signal to shoot, they shouted, to call forth haply any of those within. The shout was heard by the women-folk, who, emerging from the caverns, informed the Romans how matters stood, one of the two lucidly reporting both the speech and how the deed was done. But it was with difficulty that they listened to her, incredulous of such amazing fortitude; meanwhile they endeavored to extinguish the flames and soon cutting a passage through them entered the palace. Here encountering the mass of slain, instead of exulting as over enemies, they admired the nobility of their resolve and the contempt of death displayed by so many in carrying it, unwavering, into execution. (LCL)

The Aftermath of the Revolt

9.22 Josephus, *Jewish War* 7.409–19

Some of the Sicarii had apparently managed to flee to Alexandria, where they embarked on revolutionary activities, murdering those Jews who opposed them. The leaders of the Jewish community were successful in convincing the Jewish populace to hand over these Sicarii to the Roman authorities. And thus we have the spectacle of Jews handing over other Jews to the government for certain torture and death. Even Josephus marvels at the tremendous courage which the Sicarii showed while being tortured.

Moreover, at Alexandria in Egypt, after this date[20] many Jews met with destruction. For certain of the faction of the Sicarii who had succeeded in fleeing to that country, not content with their escape, again embarked on revolutionary schemes, and sought to induce many of their hosts to assert their independence, to look upon the Romans as no better than themselves and to esteem God alone as their lord. Meeting with opposition from certain Jews of rank, they murdered these; the rest they continued to press with solicitations to revolt.

Observing their infatuation, the leaders of the council of elders, thinking it no longer safe for them to overlook their proceedings, convened a general assembly of the Jews and exposed the madness of the Sicarii, proving them to have been responsible for all their troubles.

'And now,' they said, 'these men, finding that even their flight has brought them no sure hope of safety – for if recognized by the Romans they would instantly be put to death, are seeking to involve in the calamity which is their due persons wholly innocent of their crimes.'

They, accordingly, advised the assembly to beware of the ruin with which they were menaced by these men and, by delivering them up, to make their peace with the Romans. Realizing the gravity of the danger, the people complied with this advice, and rushed furiously upon the Sicarii to seize them. Six hundred of them were caught on the spot; and all who escaped into Egypt and the Egyptian Thebes were ere long arrested and brought back.

Nor was there a person who was not amazed at the endurance and – call it what you will – desperation or strength of purpose displayed by these victims. For under every form of torture and laceration of body, devised for the sole object of making them acknowledge Caesar as lord, not one submitted nor was brought to the verge of utterance; but all kept their resolve, triumphant over constraint, meeting the tortures and the fire with bodies that seemed insensible of pain and souls that wellnigh exulted in it. But most of all were the spectators struck by the children of tender age, not one of whom could be prevailed upon to call Caesar lord. So far did the strength of courage rise superior to the weakness of their frames. (LCL)

9.23 Josephus, *Jewish War* 7.421, 433–6 (73/4 CE)

Apparently, the Emperor Vespasian was afraid that the temple of Onias in Egypt, like the Temple in Jerusalem, would be used as a rallying point for revolutionaries, and so after the fall of Masada he ordered that it be demolished.

The emperor [Vespasian], suspicious of the unceasing revolutionary activity of the Jews, and fearing that they might again assemble in force

---

20. I.e., after the capture of Masada in 73 or 74.

and draw away others along with them, ordered Lupus [governor of Egypt] to demolish the temple of the Jews in the so-called district of Onias. . . .

Lupus, the governor of Alexandria, on receipt of Caesar's letter, came to the sanctuary, and, having carried out some of the votive offerings, shut up the temple. When Lupus died soon after, Paulinus, his successor in the office, completely stripped the place of its offerings, threatening the priests severely if they failed to produce them all, and prohibited those who worshipped there to approach the precinct. Instead, closing the gates, he debarred all access, so as to leave no trace of the cult of God in the place. The duration of the Temple, from its erection to its closing, was 343 years.[21] (M.R.)

9.24 Josephus, *Jewish War* 7.132–3, 142–57

Josephus describes the triumphal procession in Rome accorded to Vespasian and Titus (in effect reviewing the whole war) and, in particular, the spoils taken from the Temple. The procession ended with the execution of one of the leaders of the revolutionaries, Simon bar Giora.

It is impossible adequately to describe the multitude of those spectacles and their magnificence under every conceivable aspect, whether in works of art or diversity of riches or natural rarities; for almost all the objects which men who have ever been blessed by fortune have acquired one by one – the wonderful and precious productions of various nations – by their collective exhibition on that day displayed the majesty of the Roman empire. . . .

The war was shown by numerous representations, in separate sections, affording a very vivid picture of its episodes. Here was to be seen a prosperous country devastated, there whole battalions of the enemy slaughtered; here a party in flight, there others led into captivity; walls of surpassing compass demolished by engines, strong fortresses overpowered, cities with well-manned defences completely mastered and an army pouring within the ramparts, an area all deluged with blood, the hands of those incapable of resistance raised in supplication, temples set on fire, houses pulled down over their owners' heads, and, after general desolation and woe, rivers flowing, not over a cultivated land, nor supplying drink to man and beast, but across a country still on every side in flames. For to such sufferings were the Jews destined when they plunged into the war; and the art and magnificent workmanship of these structures now portrayed the incidents to those who had not witnessed them, as though they were happening before their eyes. On each of the stages was stationed the general of one of the captured cities in the attitude in which he was taken. A number of ships also followed.[22]

---

21. The correct figure would be approximately 243 years, from *ca.* 170 BCE to 73/4 CE.

22. Among other battles during the war there was a naval battle in the Sea of Galilee.

The spoils in general were borne in promiscuous heaps; but conspicuous above all stood out those captured in the Temple at Jerusalem.[23] These consisted of a golden table, many talents in weight, and a lampstand, likewise made of gold, but constructed on a different pattern from those which we use in ordinary life. Affixed to a pedestal was a central shaft, from which there extended slender branches, arranged trident-fashion, a wrought lamp being attached to the extremity of each branch; of these there were seven, indicating the honor paid to that number among the Jews. After these, and last of all the spoils, was carried a copy of the Jewish Law. Then followed a large party carrying images of victory, all made of ivory and gold. Behind them drove Vespasian, followed by Titus; while Domitian rode beside them, in magnificent apparel and mounted on a steed that was itself a sight.

The triumphal procession ended at the temple of Jupiter Capitolinus, on reaching which they halted; for it was a time-honored custom to wait there until the execution of the enemy's general was announced. This was Simon, son of Gioras, who had just figured in the pageant among the prisoners, and then, with a halter thrown over him and scourged meanwhile by his conductors, had been hauled to the spot abutting on the Forum, where Roman law required that malefactors condemned to death should be executed.[24] After the announcement that Simon was no more and the shouts of universal applause which greeted it, the princes began the sacrifices, which having been duly offered with the customary prayers, they withdrew to the palace. Some they entertained at a feast at their own table: for all the rest provision had already been made for banquets in their several homes. For the city of Rome kept festival that day for her victory in the campaign against her enemies, for the termination of her civil dissensions, and for her dawning hopes of felicity. (LCL)

9.25 *Corpus Inscriptionum Latinarum* 6.944 (= Emilio Gabba, *Iscrizioni greche e latine per lo studio della Bibbia* [1958], 27)

The inscription on the Arch of Titus records his victory over the Jewish people and his destruction of the city of Jerusalem.

The Senate and the Roman people to Imperator Titus Caesar Vespasian Augustus, son of the deified Vespasian, *pontifex maximus* [high priest], possessor of the tribunician power for the tenth year, hailed *imperator* [general] seventeen times, consul eight times, father of his country, their *princeps* [first citizen], because under the direction and plans and auspices of his father he subdued the Jewish people, destroyed the city of Jerusalem, previously either attacked in vain by generals, kings, peoples, or completely unassailed.[25] (M.R.)

---

23. Visitors to Rome may still see on the Arch of Titus above the Forum the spoils from the Temple that were borne in the procession.

24. This was the Mamertine prison at the north-eastern end of the Forum.

25. This is unhistorical. Jerusalem had been captured, e.g., by Nebuchadnezzar, Antiochus Epiphanes, and Pompey.

9.26 Roman Coins Commemorating the Capture of Judaea

The victory over the Jews was treated by the Flavian emperors, Vespasian and Titus, as the most important event of their dynasty. An enormous number of coins commemorating the capture of Judaea were minted all over the empire.

(1) Obverse: Portrait of Vespasian. IMPERATOR CAESAR VESPASIAN AUGUSTUS
Reverse: Goddess Victory, trophies, palm tree, captive Jewess weeping. VICTORY OF AUGUSTUS (M.R.)

(2) Obverse: Portrait of Vespasian. IMPERATOR CAESAR VESPASIAN AUGUSTUS, CONSUL SEVEN TIMES, FATHER OF HIS COUNTRY
Reverse: Captive Jewess weeping, trophies, palm tree. JUDAEA CAPTURED (M.R.)

The Fiscus Judaicus

Among the penalties visited on the Jews by Vespasian was a most extraordinary tax imposed by the Roman government: it was its only tax on a religion, and the only one for the support of a specific Roman temple. In 71/2 CE a special treasury was established, the *Fiscus Judaicus*, into which was paid the Jewish tax for the support of the temple of Jupiter Optimus Maximus Capitolinus in Rome. Whereas the age-old Temple tax, in the amount of one-half shekel, had been paid to the Temple in Jerusalem by males over the age of twenty, the Jewish tax of two denarii (two drachmas) was imposed annually on all Jews of both sexes, from the age of three, as well as on slaves of Jewish households. The tax was, in effect, a license to practice Judaism.

9.27 *CPJ*, nos 160, 192, 207, 321

These are receipts on ostraca [potsherds] from the Jewish Quarter of Apollinopolis Magna [modern Edfu, Egypt] for payment of the Jewish tax.

Herenius son of Didymus, receipt for the two-denarius tax on the Jews, for the fourth year of our lord Vespasian Caesar [71–2 CE]. (M.R.)

Paid by Thedetus son of Alexion, for the Jewish tax for the fourteenth year of Domitian, four drachmas; by Philip his son, 4. Total, 8. Year 14, Mesore 25 [August 18, 95 CE]. (M.R.)

Paid by Copreus, slave of Antipater, for the Jewish tax for the ninth year of our lord Trajan, 4 obols. Year 10, Choiak 13 [December 9, 106 CE]. (M.R.)

Sambathion, also known as Jesous, son of Papius, for tax of the seventh year of our lord Trajan, 4 drachmas. Year 7, Pachon 6 [May 1, 104 CE]. (M.R.)

9.28 CPJ, no. 421 (May 16, 73 CE)

This is a long schedule of various tax payments due from Jews living in Arsinoe in the Fayum, Egypt. Here we have evidence that the Jewish tax was exacted from men, women, and children from the age of three. The fact that there are so few children is surprising. It has been suggested that this may have been due to the fact that peasant women were eager to prolong the period of suckling their children so as to prevent a new pregnancy.

From Heraclides in charge of the district of the quarter of Apollonius' Camp. Liability for the Jewish tax of the fifth year of our Emperor Caesar Vespasian Augustus, summarized according to the fourth year. The total of the Jews taken up by previous accounts: five adult males, six adult females, one of whom is over-age . . . and so adjudicated in the fourth year as being 59 years of age; one minor, four years old in the fourth year. Total names: twelve. And those taken up through transcript of the preceding revision of lists shown to be three years old in the fourth year, being one year old in the second year. Males: Philiscus son of Ptollas, grandson of Philiscus, mother Erotion. Females: Protous daughter of Simon, son of Ptolemaeus, mother Dosarion; total two. Making fourteen. Of these adult males five, one minor male four years old in the fifth year. Adult females six, one minor female who in the fifth year was five years old. Likewise one minor female four years old. Total names, fourteen. (M.R.)

9.29 Suetonius (*ca.* 69–*ca.* 150 CE), *Life of Domitian* 12.2

Under Domitian (81–96) the *Fiscus Judaicus* was collected most rigorously.

The Jewish tax was exacted most assiduously. To the *Fiscus Judaicus* were reported those who lived as Jews without declaring this, or who by concealing their origin did not pay the tribute imposed on their people. I recall when I was a young man being present when an old man in his nineties was examined by a procurator and a very large number of advisors to see whether he was circumcised. (M.R.)

9.30 Babylonian Talmud, *Baba Bathra* 9a (edited *ca.* 500 CE)

The following seems to be a reference to the *Fiscus Judaicus*.

Rabbi Eleazar [ben Pedath, Babylonian and Palestinian, third century CE] . . . said: When the Temple stood, a man used to bring his shekel and so make atonement. Now that the Temple no longer stands, if they give for charity, well and good, and if not, the heathens will come and take from them forcibly. (Soncino)

The Lukuas-Andreas Rebellion (War of Quietus) (115–17 CE)

BIBLIOGRAPHY

Shimon Applebaum, "The Jewish Revolt in Cyrene in 115–117, and the Subsequent Recolonisation," *JJS* 2 (1951), 177–86.

Alexander Fuks, "The Jewish Revolt in Egypt (AD 115–17) in the Light of the Papyri," *Aegyptus* 33 (1953), 151–8.

Alexander Fuks, "The Jewish Revolt in Egypt (AD 115–17)," in Victor A. Tcherikover and Alexander Fuks, eds, *Corpus Papyrorum Judaicarum*, vol. 2 (1960), 225–60.

Alexander Fuks, "Aspects of the Jewish Revolt in AD 115–17," *JRS* 51 (1961), 98–104.

Edith Mary Smallwood, "Palestine *c*. AD 115–18," *Historia* 11 (1962), 500–10.

Schürer (1973), 1.529–34.

Shimon Applebaum, *Greeks and Jews in Ancient Cyrene* (1979).

Alon (1980), 413–29.

Timothy D. Barnes, "Trajan and the Jews," *JJS* 40 (1989), 145–62.

David Frankfurter, "Lest Egypt's City Be Deserted: Religion and Ideology in the Egyptian Response to the Jewish Revolt (116–17 CE)," *JJS* 48 (1992), 203–20.

Modrzejewski (1995), 198–205.

During the reign of Trajan a second revolt of the Jews against the Romans occurred. Unlike the revolt of 66–73/4, which was confined to Judaea, this one engulfed large areas of the Roman Empire, from Cyrenaica to Mesopotamia, and indeed was apparently primarily centered in lands outside Judaea, notably Libya, Egypt, and Cyprus. Whereas we have a Josephus to give us an account in the utmost detail of the revolt of 66–73/4, our information about this revolt (known in the Mishnah as the War of Quietus) is extremely scanty. The immediate causes are obscure; but the uprising, which lasted from 115 to 117, took on the aspects of a Messianic movement led by a certain Libyan Jew named Lukuas-Andreas.[26] The Jews, as we see from the papyri, were accused of terrible atrocities; and such accusations brought about a war of annihilation against them, so much so that when order was finally restored, the Jewish community in Alexandria and throughout the rest of Egypt became virtually extinct.

9.31 Arrian (*ca.* 95–175 CE), *Parthian Affairs*, cited by Suda (tenth century CE), s.v. *atasthala* and *pareikoi*

So successful was the revolt at first that Trajan, in his frustration, resolved to destroy the Jewish people completely.

Trajan [116 CE] was determined above all, if it were possible, to destroy the nation utterly, but if not, at least to crush it and stop its presumptuous wickedness.[27] (M.S.)

9.32 Dio Cassius (*ca.* 160–230 CE), *Roman History* 68.32.1–3, 5.

Dio Cassius here describes the massacre by Jews of Romans and Greeks in Cyrene and Egypt. Here the name of the Jewish leader is given as Andreas.

---

26. Eusebius (*Ecclesiastical History* 4.2.4) refers to him as Lukuas; Dio Cassius (68.32) calls him Andreas.

27. The Jews had joined in the general revolt of the lands formerly part of the Parthian kingdom that had been conquered by the Romans.

Meanwhile, the Jews in Cyrene, putting a certain Andreas at their head, massacred the Romans and the Greeks, ate their flesh, tied their entrails around themselves, smeared themselves with their blood, and put on their skins. Many they virtually sawed down the middle; others they turned over to wild beasts, and compelled others to fight as gladiators. As a result, they destroyed in all 220,000 people. In Egypt, likewise, they committed atrocities; similarly in Cyprus, under the leadership of a certain Artemion, there perished 240,000 persons. It was for this reason that no Jew is permitted to debark on Cyprus; even if one is driven there by the wind and lands on the island, he is put to death. The Jews were crushed by various generals, notably by Lusius [Lucius Quietus], sent by Trajan. . . . (M.R.)

Being honored for this he [Lucius Quietus] performed far greater and more numerous exploits in the second war, and finally advanced so far in bravery and good fortune during this present war that he was enrolled among the ex-praetors, became consul, and then governor of Palestine. (LCL)

9.33 Eusebius (265–340 CE), *Ecclesiastical History* 4.2

Eusebius here describes the spread of the rebellion and the tremendous loss of life. He gives the name of the Jewish leader as Lukuas.

In the course of the eighteenth year [115 CE] of the reign of the Emperor [Trajan] a rebellion of the Jews again broke out and destroyed a great multitude of them. For both in Alexandria and in the rest of Egypt and especially in Cyrene, as though they had been seized by some terrible spirit of rebellion, they rushed into sedition against their Greek fellow citizens, and increasing the scope of the rebellion in the following year started a great war while Lupus was governor of all Egypt.

In the first engagement they happened to overcome the Greeks, who fled to Alexandria and captured and killed the Jews in the city; but though thus losing the help of the townsmen, the Jews of Cyrene continued to plunder the country of Egypt and to ravage the districts in it under their leader Lukuas. The Emperor sent against them Marcius Turbo with land and sea forces including cavalry. He waged war vigorously against them in many battles for a considerable time and killed many thousands of Jews, not only those of Cyrene but also those of Egypt who had rallied to Lukuas, their king.

The Emperor suspected that the Jews in Mesopotamia would also attack the inhabitants and ordered Lucius Quietus to clean them out of the province. He organized a force and murdered a great multitude of the Jews there, and for this reform was appointed governor of Judaea by the Emperor. The Greek authors who chronicle the same period have related this narrative in these very words. (LCL)

9.34 Artemidorus (second half of the second century CE), *Interpretation of Dreams* 4.24

An indication of the tremendous impact of the rebellion may be seen in the fact that Artemidorus, in his handbook on the interpretation of dreams, alludes to it.

There are some dreams that cannot be solved before the events come to pass. If you solve those dreams you will be lucky in my opinion, but if you fail you will not be reckoned unskilful. Of that kind was one in which a *praefectus castrorum* [commander of the camp] saw written upon his sword: *iota, kappa, theta*. Then there came the Jewish war in Cyrene, and the fellow who had seen the dream distinguished himself in the war, and this was what the above-mentioned dream had signified: by the *iota* were meant the Jews [Greek *Ioudaioi*], by the *kappa* the C[K]yrenaeans, by the *theta* [Greek *thanatos* = 'death']. However, before it came to pass, this dream was unresolvable, but when the event happened, it was very manifest. (M.S.)

9.35 *CPJ*, no. 435 (115 CE)

Just before the date of the papyrus below, a battle between the Romans and the Jews had taken place in Alexandria, the outcome of which apparently was a Roman victory. The speaker in the papyrus is apparently the governor of Egypt. The papyrus indicates that the emperor sent a special judge to investigate the case.

They [the Alexandrian Greeks] are preparing fire and weapons against us. I know that they are few, but many more abet them, and the powerful support them, paying up not to be mistreated, not to be plundered. The evil-doing among the few is not unjustly an indictment of the whole city. I know that among them most are slaves; therefore, the masters are abused. Therefore, I enjoin upon all not to simulate anger because of lust for gain. Let them know that we no longer are in ignorance of who they are. Let them not rely on my[28] indulgence. . . . If anyone wants to make a charge, there is available a judge sent by the emperor for this purpose. Not even governors have the power to execute persons without a trial, but there is a proper time for a trial, and a proper place, and proper types of punishment. Let those stop who say, some truthfully, some falsely, that they have been wounded and that they demand justice with violence and outside the law. For there was no need to be wounded. Some of the mistakes might possibly have been excused before the battle of the Romans against the Jews. But now they are idle judgments, which were not even previously permissible. Year 19 of Trajan, 16 Phaophi. (M.R.)

9.36 *CPJ*, no. 436 (115 CE)

In the papyrus below, an Egyptian Greek woman writes to her brother and husband telling of her great anxiety for his safety during this revolt.

Aline to Apollonios her brotherly greetings. I am terribly anxious about you because of what they say about what is happening, and because of your sudden departure. I take no pleasure in food or drink, but stay awake continually night and day with one worry, your safety. (*CPJ*)

---

28. The writer would appear to be the governor of Egypt.

9.37 CPJ, no. 437 (116 or 117 CE)

In the papyrus below, an Egyptian Greek woman prays to the gods, particularly Hermes, to save her son from being roasted by the Jews.

With the goodwill of the gods, above all Hermes the invincible, may they not roast you. For the rest, may all be well with you and all your men. Heraidous, your daughter, who is free from harm, greets you. Epeiph 6. (*CPJ*)

9.38 CPJ, no. 438 (116 CE)

In this papyrus, from Hermopolis in Egypt, we get a picture of the fierce fighting that marked the uprising and of the successes of the Jews. The only hope of the Egyptian Greeks is to be rescued by the Roman armies.

There was one hope and expectation left – to drive the villagers from our district in a body against the impious Jews. But now the opposite has happened. For on the . . . day our men attacked and were defeated, and many of them were killed. . . . We have received the news that another legion of Rutilius[29] came to Memphis on the twenty-second and is awaited. (M.R.)

9.39 CPJ, no. 439 (117 CE)

In this papyrus we learn that the Roman forces have defeated the Jews in a battle in the vicinity of Memphis in Egypt.

Aphrodisios to his dearest Herakleios, greeting. I have learnt from men who arrived today from Ibion [an Egyptian village] that they had traveled with a slave of our lord Apollonios; the slave was coming from Memphis to bring the good news of his victory and success. I have therefore sent to you specially, that I may know with certainty and make festival and pay the due offerings to the gods. (*CPJ*)

9.40 CPJ, no. 445 (117/18 CE)

In this papyrus, dating from a period shortly after the end of the fighting, we hear of property confiscated from the Jews. The fact that the administrator of one district sends copies of his decree concerning confiscated Jewish property to colleagues in other districts would indicate that similar measures either had been or were about to be taken in those districts.

Aquillius Pollio, *strategos*[30] of the Herakleopolite nome [district], to his dearest Apollonius, *strategos* of the Oxyrhynchite nome, greeting.
  Please receive two letters which I have written, one to you, one to Sabinus, *strategos* of the Cynopolite nome, about the schedule of the property belonging to the Jews. Retain the one addressed to you and transmit the other to the Cynopolite nome. (M.R.)

29. Marcus Rutilius Lupus, governor of Egypt from 113 to 117 CE.
30. Military and civil governor.

9.41 *Supplementum Epigraphicum Graecum*, vol. 17, no. 804 (118 CE)

The following inscription, in Greek and Latin, from Cyrene, mentions the temple of the emperor destroyed in the Jewish uprising.

Imperator Caesar Trajan Hadrian Augustus, son of the deified Trajan Parthicus, grandson of the deified Nerva, *pontifex maximus* **[high priest], possessor of the tribunician power for the second year, consul twice, ordered the city of Cyrene to restore the Caesareum [temple of the emperor], destroyed and burned in the Jewish uprising. (M.R.)**

9.42 *CPJ*, no. 450 (199/200 CE)

The following papyrus refers to a petition by an Alexandrian Greek to the Roman emperors Septimius Severus (reigned 193–211) and Caracalla (reigned 211–17) reminding them of the help which the people of Oxyrhynchus, a small town in Egypt, gave to the Romans during the war of 115–17. Though it dates from more than eighty years after the uprising, it indicates that the uprising was so memorable that the people of Oxyrhynchus were still celebrating an annual festival commemorating their victory over the Jews.

Most humane emperors, . . . to a great city . . . and still preserving . . . Titus Titianus . . . and more which I pass over, but they also possess the goodwill, faithfulness, and friendship to the Romans which they exhibited in the war against the Jews, giving aid then and even now keeping the day of victory as a festival every year. (CPJ)

The Bar Kochba Rebellion (132–5 CE)

BIBLIOGRAPHY

William D. Gray, "The Founding of Aelia Capitolina and the Chronology of the Jewish War under Hadrian," *AJSL* 39 (1923), 248–56.
James Rendel Harris, "Hadrian's Decree of Expulsion of the Jews from Jerusalem," *HTR* 19 (1926), 199–206.
Fritz Heichelheim, "New Light on the End of the Bar Kokba's War," *JQR* 34 (1943–4), 61–3.
Solomon Zeitlin, "The Assumption of Moses and the Revolt of Bar-Kokba," *JQR* 38 (1947–8), 1–45.
Solomon Zeitlin, "Bar Kokba and Bar Kozeba," *JQR* 43 (1952–3), 77–82.
Lawrence E. Toombs, "Barcosiba and Qumran," *NTS* 4 (1957), 65–71.
Joseph Meyshan, "The Legion which Reconquered Jerusalem in the War of Bar Kochba (AD 132–5)," *PEQ* 90 (1958), 19–26.
Edith Mary Smallwood, "The Legislation of Hadrian and Antoninus Pius against Circumcision," *Latomus* 18 (1959), 334–47; 20 (1961), 93–6.
Joseph A. Fitzmyer, "The Bar Kochba Period," in John L. McKenzie, ed., *The Bible in Current Catholic Thought* (Saint Mary's Theology Studies, 1) (1962), 133–68.
Shimon Applebaum, "The Agrarian Question and the Revolt of Bar Kokhba," *E-I 8* (1967), 283–7.
Hugo Mantel, "The Causes of the Bar Kokba Revolt," *JQR* 58 (1967–8), 224–42, 274–96; 59 (1968–9), 341–2.
Leslie W. Barnard, "Hadrian and Judaism," *JRH* 5 (1969), 285–98.

Yigael Yadin, *Bar-Kokhba: The Rediscovery of the Legendary Hero of the Second Jewish Revolt against Rome* (1971).

Moshe D. Herr, "Persecution and Martyrdom in Hadrian's Days," *SH* 23 (1972), 93–102.

Schürer (1973), 1.534–57.

Shimon Applebaum, *Prolegomena to the Study of the Second Jewish Revolt* (AD 132–35) (1976).

Benjamin Isaac, "Judaea in the Early Years of Hadrian's Reign," *Latomus* 38 (1979), 54–66.

Alon (1980), 592–637.

Glen W. Bowersock, "A Roman Perspective on the Bar Kochba War," in William S. Green, ed., *Approaches to Ancient Judaism*, vol. 2 (1980), 131–41.

Peter Schäfer, "Rabbi Aqiva and Bar Kokhba," in William S. Green, ed., *Approaches to Ancient Judaism*, vol. 2 (1980), 113–30.

Yehoshafat Harkabi, *The Bar Kokhba Syndrome: Risk and Realism in International Politics* (trans. by Max D. Ticktin) (1983).

Shimon Applebaum, "Points of View on the Second Jewish Revolt," *SCI* 7 (1983–84), 77–87.

Benjamin Isaac, "Cassius Dio on the Revolt of Bar-Kokhba," *SCI* 7 (1983–4), 68–76.

Shimon Applebaum, "The Second Jewish Revolt (AD 131–5)," *PEQ* 160 (1984), 35–41.

Aharon Oppenheimer and Benjamin Isaac, "The Revolt of Bar Kokhba: Ideology and Modern Scholarship," *JJS* 36 (1985), 33–60.

Menahem Mor, "The Bar-Kokhba Revolt and Non-Jewish Participants," *JJS* 36 (1985), 200–9.

Mordecai Gichon, "New Insight into the Bar-Kokhba War and a Reappraisal of Dio Cassius 69:12–13," *JQR* 77 (1986–7), 15–43.

Naphtali Lewis, *The Documents from the Bar Kochba Period in the Cave of Letters: Greek Papyri* (1989)

Doron Mendels, "The 'Polemus Quietus' and the Revolt of Bar Kokhba, 132–5 CE," in his *The Rise and Fall of Jewish Nationalism* (1992), 385–93.

Millar (1993), 372–4, 545–52.

In 130/1 the emperor Hadrian visited Judaea, which was simmering with explosive forces: intense economic suffering, Jewish nationalist aspirations still fervent, and fanatical Messianism. The immediate cause of the rebellion, according to the *Historia Augusta* (a work which, to be sure, has been called an historical novel rather than a history), was the decree of Hadrian forbidding circumcision, which he regarded as a barbaric practice and which he ruled to be a capital offense. While the ban was not directed solely against the Jews, it constituted a death blow for the Jewish people. The view of Dio Cassius is that the rebellion was occasioned by Hadrian's decision to establish a city of his own, which he named Aelia Capitolina, on the site of the ruins of the old one and to build a temple to Jupiter on the site of the old one. Both decisions may have triggered the revolt.

The leader of the revolt, which resisted Roman power for three years (132–5 CE), was Simon bar Kosiba, whose Messianic title was Bar Kochba ("Son of a Star"; enemies called him Bar Koziba – "Son of Lies"). The revolt might have had some chance for success if (1) the rebels had received the help of the Parthians, but Hadrian relinquished Trajan's conquests there and restored to the Parthian king his daughter who had been captured by Trajan and even invited the king to visit Rome; (2) the rebels had coordinated their rebellion with rebellions in Scotland and Antioch, since the Roman forces in other provinces were thinned out; (3) the rebels had managed to secure the backing of the Jews of Galilee (by far the most populous Jewish area of the land); and (4) the rebels had secured help from the Jews of the Diaspora. In any case, Bar Kochba apparently had no prior military experience, whereas the Romans were led by their most experienced general, Julius Severus. Moreover, 18 per cent of the entire Roman army (four out of twenty-two legions) were in the tiny state of Judaea; and their soldiers were professional, serving from twenty to twenty-five years. The rebellion was suppressed with enormous losses to the Jews in lives and property. So many Jews were taken captive that, according to Jerome, a Jewish slave fetched no more than a horse.

9.43 *Scriptores Historiae Augustae* (end of fourth century), *Hadrian* 14.2

Here the reason for the rebellion is given as Hadrian's decree forbidding circumcision.

At this time [in the course of Hadrian's travels] the Jews began war, because they were forbidden to practice circumcision. (LCL)

9.44 Dio Cassius (*ca.* 160–230 CE), *Roman History* 69.12–15

Dio Cassius here indicates that the Jews revolted because Hadrian erected a temple to Jupiter on the site of the Temple. At first Hadrian ignored the revolt, but when the revolt spread throughout Judaea and even beyond, he sent his best general, Julius Severus, against them. Though the losses of the Jews were huge, many Romans also were killed.

When he [Hadrian] founded at Jerusalem his own city [*ca.* 130 CE] in place of the one destroyed, a city which he named Aelia Capitolina,[31] and erected on the site of the Temple of their god another temple, to Jupiter, a war broke out that was neither small nor of short duration. The Jews, though incensed that another people should be settled in their city and that alien rites should be installed in it, as long as Hadrian was in Egypt and again in Syria, remained quiet. . . . But once he was at a distance, they openly revolted. They did not dare to risk battle with the Romans in regular formation [and resorted to guerrilla warfare].

At first the Romans took no account of them. But when all of Judaea was stirred up, and Jews from all parts of the earth were agitated and assembling and inflicting much trouble on the Romans, some secretly, some openly, and many others also from other peoples were joining them in hope of advantage, and seeing that virtually the whole world was stirred up because of this, then at last Hadrian sent the best of his

---

31. The city was so named after the emperor Hadrian (Aelius Hadrianus) and the chief god Jupiter Capitolinus.

generals against them, first among them Julius Severus, sent against the Jews from Britain, of which he was governor. (M.R.)

Severus did not venture to attack his opponents in the open at any one point, in view of their numbers and their desperation, but by intercepting small groups, thanks to the number of his soldiers and his under-officers, and by depriving them of food and shutting them up, he was able, rather slowly, to be sure, but with comparatively little danger, to crush, exhaust and exterminate them. (LCL)

Very few of them, in fact, survived. Fifty of their most notable fortresses, and 985 of their most important villages were razed; 580,000 people perished in the raids and battles. As for those who succumbed to thirst and disease and fire – the number of these cannot be determined. As a result, almost all of Judaea became a desert, just as had been predicted before the war. Indeed, the tomb of Solomon, which they hold in veneration, was accidentally weakened and collapsed.... (M.R.)

Many Romans, moreover, perished in this war. Therefore Hadrian in writing to the senate did not employ the opening phrase commonly affected by the emperors, 'If you and your children are in health, it is well; I and the legions are in health.' This, then, was the end of the war with the Jews. (LCL)

9.45 Eusebius (265–340 CE), *Ecclesiastical History* 4.6.1

The account of Eusebius is based on a lost work of Ariston of Pella, a Christian apologist who lived in the middle of the second century CE. Unlike the accounts of Dio Cassius and the *Historia Augusta*, Eusebius gives the name of the Jewish leader of the revolt, Bar Kochba, states that he claimed to perform miracles, and mentions that the city where he was finally besieged was Betar. When the revolt was finally suppressed, Hadrian decreed that Jews should be prohibited from setting foot in Jerusalem.

As the revolt of the Jews again expanded in size and extent, Rufus, procurator of Judaea, after military reinforcements had been sent by the emperor, taking advantage of their madness, proceeded against them without mercy. He destroyed a great many thousands of men, as well as women and children, and, following the law of war, reduced their land to slavery. The leader of the Jews at this time was a man called Bar Chochebas (which means 'star'), a man who was a robber and a murderer, but who, exploiting his name, as if dealing with slaves, claimed that he was a radiance that had come down to them from heaven to shine on those in misery by working miracles.

The war reached its height in the eighteenth year of the reign of Hadrian, at Beththera [Betar], which was a very powerful fortress situated not far distant from Jerusalem. The siege lasted a long time, until the rebels were driven to the last extremity by hunger and thirst. After the instigator of their madness had paid the just penalty, the whole people was prohibited from this time on, by a legal enactment and the decrees of Hadrian, from ever setting foot in the district around Jerusalem. He enjoined that they should not see the land of their fathers even from a distance. Ariston of Pella wrote this account. And thus, when the city had been emptied of the Jewish people and had suffered the total destruction of its ancient inhabitants, it was colonized by a foreign people, and the Roman city which then was established changed its name and was called Aelia, in honor of the emperor Aelius Hadrian. (M.R.)

9.46 Midrash Lamentations Rabbah 2 on Lamentations 2:2 (ca. fifth century CE)

The greatest rabbi of that era, Rabbi Aqiva, recognized Bar Kochba as the Messiah, but this was disputed by other rabbis.

When Rabbi Aqiva [second half of the first and first half of the second century CE] saw Bar Koziba, he said, 'This is the royal messiah.' Rabbi Johanan ben Torta [Palestinian, first half of the second century CE] said to him, 'Aqiva, grass will grow from under your cheeks and he will still not have come.' (L.H.F.)

9.47 Midrash Lamentations Rabbah 2 on Lamentations 2:2 (ca. fifth century CE)

The Rabbis, while painting a glowing picture of Bar Kochba's bravery in withstanding the mighty Roman forces for over three years, are also critical of him for initiating, clearly in opposition to the Torah's prohibition of disfigurement, an acceptance test for his soldiers, namely their willingness to cut off one of their fingers.

Rabbi Johanan [ben Nappaha, Palestinian, third century CE] interpreted the verse, 'The voice is the voice of Jacob' [Gen 27:22] in this way: 'The voice is the voice of Caesar Hadrian, who killed 80,000 myriads [i.e., 800,000,000] of people at Betar.'

Eighty thousand trumpeters besieged Betar. There Bar Koziba was encamped, with 200,000 men with an amputated finger. Sages sent word to him, saying, 'How long are you going to produce blemished men in Israel?' He said to them, 'And what shall I do to examine them [to see whether or not they are brave]?' They said to him, 'Whoever cannot uproot a cedar of Lebanon do not enroll in your army.'

He had 200,000 men of each sort [half with an amputated finger, half proved by uprooting a cedar]. When they went out to battle, he would say, 'Lord of all ages, don't help us and don't hinder us!' . . .

What did Bar Koziba do? He could catch a missile from the enemy's catapult on one of his knees and throw it back, killing many of the enemy. That is why Rabbi Aqiva said what he said [about Bar Koziba's being the royal Messiah]. (J.N.)

9.48 Midrash Lamentations Rabbah 2 on Lamentations 2:2 (ca. fifth century CE)

Some of the rabbis are also critical of Bar Kochba's hot temper and, in particular, of his unwarranted decision to put to death his own uncle, Rabbi Eleazar the Modiite, on grounds that the latter was a traitor. Consequently they speak of him as a worthless shepherd.

For three and a half years Hadrian besieged Betar. Rabbi Eleazar the Modiite [Palestinian, end of the first and beginning of the second century CE] was sitting in sackcloth and ashes, praying, and saying, 'Lord of all the ages, do not sit in judgment today, do not sit in judgment today.' Since [Hadrian] could not conquer the place, he considered going home.

There was with him [Hadrian] a Samaritan, who said to him ,'My lord, as long as that old cock [Rabbi Eleazar] wallows in ashes, you will not conquer the city. But be patient, and I shall do something so you can conquer it today.'

He went into the gate of the city and found Rabbi Eleazar standing in prayer. He pretended to whisper something into his ear, but the other paid no attention to him.

People went and told Bar Koziba, 'Your friend wants to betray the city.' He sent and summoned the Samaritan and said to him, 'What did you say to him?' He said to him, 'If I say, Caesar will kill me, and if not, you will kill me. Best that I kill myself and not betray state secrets.'

Nonetheless, Bar Koziba reached the conclusion that he [Rabbi Eleazar] wanted to betray the city. When Rabbi Eleazar had finished his prayer, he sent and summoned him, saying to him, 'What did this one say to you.' He said to him, 'I never saw that man.' He kicked and killed him.

At that moment an echo proclaimed, 'Woe to the worthless shepherd who leaves the flock; the sword shall be upon his arm and upon his right eye' [Zech 11:17]. Said the Holy One, blessed be He, 'You have broken the right arm of Israel and blinded their right eye. Therefore, your arm will wither and your eye grow dark.' Forthwith Betar was conquered and Bar Koziba was killed. (J.N.)

9.49 Babylonian Talmud, *Giṭṭin* 57a, 58a (edited *ca.* 500 CE)

The rabbis note the tremendous loss of life during the rebellion.

'He hath cut off in fierce anger all the horn of Israel.' Rabbi Zera [Babylonian and Palestinian, fourth century CE] said in the name of Rabbi Abbahu [Palestinian, end of third and beginning of fourth century CE], who quoted Rabbi Joḥanan [ben Nappaḥa, Palestinian, third century CE]: These are the eighty (thousand)[32] battle trumpets which assembled in the city of Betar when it was taken and men, women, and children were slain in it until their blood ran into the great sea. Do you think this was near? It was a whole *mil*[33] away. It has been taught: Rabbi Eliezer the Great [Palestinian, end of the first, beginning of the second century CE] said: There are two streams in the valley of Yadaim, one running in one direction and one in another, and the Sages estimated that [at that time] they ran with two parts water to one of blood. In a Baraitha it has been taught: For seven years the Gentiles fertilized their vineyards with the blood of Israel without using manure. . . .

32. This word is bracketed in the text.
33. A *mil* was a Roman mile (about 1,620 yards, somewhat smaller than the mile, equivalent to 1,760 yards, in use in the United States today).

Rab Judah [ben Ezekiel, Babylonian, third century CE] reported Samuel [end of second to mid-third century CE] as saying in the name of Rabban Simeon ben Gamaliel [Palestinian, second century CE]: What is signified by the verse, 'Mine eye affecteth my soul because of all the daughters of my city?' [Lam 3:51]. There were four hundred synagogues in the city of Betar, and in every one were four hundred teachers of children, and each one had under him four hundred pupils, and when the enemy entered there they pierced them with their staves, and when the enemy prevailed and captured them, they wrapped them in their scrolls and burnt them with fire. (Soncino)

9.50 Appian of Alexandria (*ca.* 160 CE), *Syrian Book* 50.253

Appian here states that the poll tax was imposed upon the Jews as a response to three rebellions.

On account of those rebellions [i.e., against Pompey, Vespasian, and Hadrian] the poll tax imposed upon all Jews is heavier than that imposed upon the surrounding peoples. (LCL)

Bar Kochba Letters

One of the most exciting discoveries in modern times has been an archive found by Yigael Yadin at Wadi Murabba'at, in the Judaean desert, in a cave that served as the headquarters of Simon Bar Kochba. These letters were communications between Bar Kochba and his followers. One can readily see the stern authoritarian character of these communications, ordering confiscations, reprimanding those who are not sufficiently concerned with their fellows, and threatening punishments. We may also note the concern with observing Jewish law, notably with regard to tithing and with regard to the four species for the festival of Tabernacles. Significantly, there are letters in all three languages current among the Jews, namely Hebrew, Aramaic, and Greek.

9.51

[In Aramaic] Shimeon bar Kosiba, prince over Israel, to Yehonathan and Masabala, peace. [He orders confiscation of a supply of wheat, and warns against giving shelter to anyone from Tekoa]. (Y.Y.)

9.52

[In Aramaic] Shimeon bar Kosiba to Yehonathan son of Be'ayan and to Masabala . . . Get hold of young men and come with them; if not – a punishment. And I shall deal with the Romans. (Y.Y.)

9.53

[In Aramaic] Shimeon to Yehudah bar Menashe at Qiryath 'Arab(v)aya. I have sent to you two donkeys that you shall send with them two men to Yehonathan bar Be'ayan and to Masabala in order that they shall pack and send to the camp, toward you, palm branches and citrons.[34] And you, from your place, send others who will bring you

34. For the festival of Tabernacles.

myrtles and willows.[35] See that they are tithed . . . and send them to the camp. [The request is made] since the army is big. Be well. (Y.Y.)

9.54

[In Greek] Aelianus to Yonathes the brother, greetings. Simon Kosiba has written to me that you must send the . . . needs of the brothers. . . . Aelianus. Be well, my brother! (Y.Y.)

9.55

[In Hebrew] From Shimeon bar Kosiba to the men of En-gadi. To Masabala and to Yehonathan bar Be'ayan, peace. In comfort you sit, eat and drink from the property of the House of Israel, and care nothing for your brothers. (Y.Y.)

9.56 Coins of Bar Kochba

BIBLIOGRAPHY

Leo Mildenberg, "The Eleazar Coins of the Bar-Kochba Rebellion," *HJ* 11 (1949), 77–108.

Leo Kadman, *The Coins of Aelia Capitolina* (1956).

Aryeh Kindler, "The Coinage of the Bar-Kokhba War," in *Numismatic Studies and Researches*, vol. 2: *The Dating and Meaning of Ancient Jewish Coins and Symbols. Six Essays in Jewish Numismatics* (1958), 62–80.

Baruch Kanael, "Notes on the Dates used during the Bar Kokhba Revolt," *IEJ* 21 (1971), 39–46.

Arie Kindler, *Coins of Palestine* (1974).

Leo Mildenberg, "Bar Kochva Coins and Documents," *HSCP* 84 (1980), 311–35.

Leo Mildenberg, *The Coinage of the Bar Kochba War* (ed. Patricia E. Mottahedeh, 1984).

The fact that the coins mention Jerusalem would seem to indicate that Bar Kochba's forces captured Jerusalem. On one of the coins there is a four-columned building surmounted by a star, probably symbolizing the Temple.

a. Obverse: Temple (?) façade. JERUSALEM
   Reverse: Palm branch, citron. YEAR ONE OF THE REDEMPTION OF ISRAEL (M.R.)

b. Obverse: Wreath. SHIMON PRINCE OF ISRAEL
   Reverse: Lyre. YEAR ONE OF THE REDEMPTION OF ISRAEL (M.R.)

c. Obverse: Palm tree and dates. ELEAZAR THE PRIEST
   Reverse: YEAR ONE OF THE REDEMPTION OF ISRAEL (M.R.)

d. Obverse: Temple façade. JERUSALEM
   Reverse: YEAR TWO OF THE FREEDOM OF ISRAEL (M.R.)

e. Obverse: Wreath. SHIMON
   Reverse: Two trumpets. FOR THE FREEDOM OF JERUSALEM (M.R.)

---

35. Likewise needed for the festival of Tabernacles.

Josephus presents his work to Titus and Vespasian. Latin manuscript of Jewish War, late eleventh century.

10

꧁꧂

Criticism and Hostility towards Jews

BIBLIOGRAPHY

Isaak Heinemann, "The Attitude of the Ancient World toward Judaism," *RR* 4 (1939–40), 385–400.

Ralph Marcus, "Antisemitism in the Hellenistic–Roman World," in Koppel S. Pinson, ed., *Essays in Antisemitism*, 2nd edn (1946), 61–78.

Tcherikover (1959), 357–77.

Jan N. Sevenster, *The Roots of Pagan Anti-Semitism in the Ancient World* (1975).

Menahem Stern, "The Jews in Greek and Latin Literature," in Samuel Safrai and Menahem Stern, eds, *The Jewish People in the First Century* (*CRINT*, sect. 1, vol. 2) (1976), 1101–59.

John P. V. D. Balsdon, *Romans and Aliens* (1979).

Jerry L. Daniel, "Anti-Semitism in the Hellenistic–Roman Period," *JBL* 98 (1979), 45–65.

John G. Gager, *The Origins of Anti-Semitism: Attitudes toward Judaism in Pagan and Christian Antiquity* (1983).

Shaye J. D. Cohen, "'Anti-Semitism' in Antiquity: The Problem of Definition," in David Berger, *History and Hate: The Dimensions of Anti-Semitism* (1986), 43–7.

Louis H. Feldman, "Anti-Semitism in the Ancient World," in David Berger, *History and Hate: The Dimensions of Anti-Semitism* (1986), 15–42.

Robert Littman, "Anti-Semitism in the Greco-Roman Pagan World," in Yehuda Bauer *et al.*, *Remembering for the Future: Working Papers and Addenda*, vol. 1: *Jews and Christians during and after the Holocaust* (1989), 825–35.

Nicholas de Lange, "The Origins of Anti-Semitism: Ancient Evidence and Modern Interpretations," in S. L. Gilman and S. T. Katz, eds, *Anti-Semitism in Times of Crisis* (1991), 21–7.

Gavin I. Langmuir, *History, Religion and Antisemitism* (1990).

Feldman (1993), 84–176.

Zvi Yavetz, "Judaeophobia in Classical Antiquity: A Different Approach," *JJS* 44 (1993), 1–22.

Modrzejewski (1995), 135–57.

It is important to stress that there is a crucial difference between criticism and hostility toward Jews in pagan antiquity and modern "anti-Semitism." A natural corollary to their polytheism, which allowed for many divinities of all sorts, was a tolerance by the pagans toward various religious points of view. They felt that people should be permitted to keep their ancestral traditions but that they should respect or worship the local gods and the gods of the empire, since there was no separation of religion and state. The Jews were given special privileges, notably by Julius Caesar and regularly reaffirmed by his successors, exempting them from this worship. The term "anti-Semitism," which is actually a mis-nomer since "Semitic" refers to a system of languages rather than to religious or other points of view, was coined in 1879 by the German agitator Wilhelm Marr to denote hatred toward Jews as a race regardless of their religious adherence or observance. The Greeks and Romans, on the other hand, did not have a conception of "race." The Greeks divided the world into Greeks and barbarians; and we find, for example, that the requirement for initiation into the Eleusinian Mysteries was merely that the person speak Greek, regardless of his racial or other origin. The Greeks and Romans recognized that there were differences among various peoples, but they ascribed these differences to climate and other such natural phenomena.

As the selections below indicate, there was certainly criticism of and hostility toward Jews, but this was, in general, not deep-seated or utterly irrational, even if we may surely condemn it, especially its excesses. Sometimes it was based on criticism of Jews for attempting to gain citizenship while being exempted from the requirement of all other citizens to worship the pagan gods. Sometimes it was based on aggressive attempts to convert non-Jews to Judaism and thus, from the point of view of the pagans, to undermine the state, since it was the pagan gods, they felt, who had enabled the state to triumph. Sometimes it was based on revolts of Jews against the state. Sometimes it was the very intolerance of the Jews who asserted, at least in theory, that all religious points of view other than their own were utterly false. And, we must not forget, side by side with hatred of Jews there was admiration for Jews and even a good deal of conversion to Judaism. The love–hate syndrome is surely complex, and there were considerable variations and gradations through the centuries of pagan antiquity.

Persecution by Governments and by the Masses

Ptolemy IV Philopator (reigned 221–203 BCE)

BIBLIOGRAPHY

Tcherikover (1959), 72–5, 274–5.
Victor Tcherikover, "The Third Book of Maccabees as a Historical Source," *SH* 7 (1961), 1–26.
Kasher (1985), 212–32.
Modrzejewski (1995), 141–6.

10.1 3 Maccabees 2:25–30

The growth of tensions between Egyptians and Jews is documented in *3 Maccabees*, written in Alexandria *ca.* 100 BCE. Ptolemy IV Philopator's victory over Antiochus III at Raphia (near Gaza) in 217 BCE was possible only because of the aid of native Egyptian troops. As a revenge for not being permitted to enter the Temple, he is said, as we see in the passage below, to have reduced the Jews to the status of slaves. He even ordered, upon his return to Egypt, that the Jews be massacred in the Alexandrian arena by a horde of elephants; but the animals turned instead upon the king's troops.

[Ptolemy Philopator was prevented from entering the sanctuary of God in Jerusalem.] So, increasing his wickedness, . . . he proposed upon his return to Egypt to inflict publicly a disgrace upon the Jewish people there. He erected a stele on the tower of the palace and had inscribed on it that none of those who did not sacrifice should be allowed to enter their temples; and that all Jews should be degraded to the payment of poll tax and the condition of slaves; that those who spoke against it should be seized by force and put to death; and that those who were registered should even be branded on their bodies with an ivy leaf, the sign of Dionysus. . . . But that he might not appear hostile to all, he added: 'But if any of them choose to join those who are initiated into the mysteries, they shall have equal rights with the citizens of Alexandria.' (M.R.)

Antiochus Epiphanes (reigned 175–164 BCE)

BIBLIOGRAPHY

Tcherikover (1959), 152–234.

Otto Mørkholm, *Antiochus IV of Syria* (1966).

Hengel, vol. 1 (1974), 277–309.

Martin A. Cohen, "The Hasmonean Revolution Politically Considered: Outline of a New Interpretation," in Saul Lieberman and Arthur Hyman, eds, *Salo Wittmayer Baron Jubilee Volume*, vol. 1 (1974), 263–85.

Fergus Millar, "The Background to the Maccabean Revolution: Reflections on Martin Hengel's 'Judaism and Hellenism,'" *JJS* 29 (1978), 1–21.

Elias Bickerman, *The God of the Maccabees: Studies on the Meaning and Origin of the Maccabean Revolt* (1979).

Joshua Efron, "The Hasmonean Revolt in Modern Historiography," in his *Studies on the Hasmonean Period* (1987), 1–32.

The Jews lived at the crossroads of large empires, in a small country, Judaea, which after the death of Alexander the Great in 323 BCE became a political football for Ptolemaic Egypt, Seleucid Syria, Parthia, and later Rome. For the Seleucids, who managed to conquer Judaea from the Ptolemies in 198 BCE, Judaea was a buffer state of strategic importance on the Egyptian border. Threatened by court intrigues, dynastic struggles, a huge indemnity owed to Rome, instability in his empire, and the hostility of Egypt and Parthia, the flamboyant King Antiochus IV Epiphanes (175–164 BCE), was driven to desperate measures. He was an Athenian citizen and admired Greek culture, which he sought to make the common denominator of his empire, in which the Greeks and Macedonians were actually in the minority. The steady inroads of Hellenization among the Jews in the 170s had fragmented them into partisan groups. At one extreme were the assimilationist pro-Seleucid Jews (particularly among the upper classes, including a portion of the priesthood), who were attracted to the glittering Hellenistic culture because of their aspirations for secular status and wealth. At the other extreme were those Jewish conservatives who were repelled by Hellenism because of their fear of impurity in the cult and in their own way of life. In 169 BCE, as civil strife threatened in the wake of struggles over control of the lucrative high priesthood, Antiochus plundered the treasury of the Temple. Supported by the Hellenizers, who were themselves divided between those who were extreme Hellenizers and those who were even more extreme Hellenizers, he decided to bring Jerusalem into the mainstream of the Hellenic world by transforming the Jews from a people living in a theocratic temple-state to the people of a Greek city-state with the name Antioch-at-Jerusalem. This entailed abrogation of the age-old Mosaic Law and the end of the traditional way of life, as well as the requirement of living according to the customs of the Greeks. It was to be the end of the worship of God, which would be transformed into a pagan cult merged with that of Olympian Zeus. Some Jews, led by Judas Maccabaeus, revolted, and there followed a massive organized religious persecution by King Antiochus Epiphanes.

10.2 Josephus, *Jewish Antiquities* 12.237–41

The passage below illustrates the infighting between two Hellenizers, Jason and Menelaus, both of whom sought the high priesthood. Menelaus actually indicated to King Antiochus Epiphanes that he and his followers were ready to give up the Jewish way of life altogether.

About this same time, when Onias the high priest died, Antiochus gave the high priesthood to his brother Jesus, for the son that Onias had left was still an infant. . . . But Jesus . . . was deprived of the high priesthood when the king became angry with him and gave it to his youngest brother, whose name was also Onias. . . . Now Jesus changed his name to [the Greek name] Jason, while Onias was called Menelaus. Now when the former high priest Jesus raised sedition against Menelaus, who was appointed after him, the multitude was divided between them both. The Tobiads were on the side of Menelaus, while the majority of the people supported Jason. Being harassed by him, Menelaus and the Tobiads went to Antiochus and informed him that they wished to leave their ancestral laws and the Jewish way of life in accordance with them, and to follow the king's laws and the Greek way of life. Therefore, they petitioned him to permit them to build a gymnasium in Jerusalem. When he had granted this, they also concealed the circumcision of their genitals,[1] that even when they were unclothed they might be Greeks; and they abandoned all their ancestral customs, and imitated the practices of foreign peoples. (M.R.)

10.3 2 Maccabees 4:7–17

The passage below indicates how, to obtain the high priesthood, Jason promised to give a huge sum to King Antiochus Epiphanes and agreed to adopt the Greek way of life. It also indicates the measures undertaken by Antiochus to abolish totally the traditional Jewish way of life.

Jason, Onias' brother, usurped the high priesthood by corrupt means. He promised the king through a petition 360 talents of silver and 80 talents from other revenue. In addition, he agreed to pay another 150 talents for the authority to establish a gymnasium and the institution of

---

1. By a plastic surgical operation called epispasm.

ephebes,[2] and to enroll them in Jerusalem as Antiochenes.[3] The king agreed, and, as soon as he had seized the high priesthood, Jason made his fellow Jews conform to the Greek way of life.

[Antiochus] set aside the royal privileges previously established for the Jews. . . . He abolished the customary way of life and introduced practices which were against the Law. He delighted in establishing a gymnasium at the foot of the citadel itself, and assigned the most outstanding of the youth to assume the Greek ephebic hat. Thus Hellenism reached a high point with the introduction of foreign customs through the overweening wickedness of the impious Jason, no true high priest. As a result, the priests no longer had any enthusiasm for their duties at the altar, but scorned the Temple and neglected the sacrifices. They eagerly contributed to the expenses of maintaining the wrestling school, which is contrary to the Law. . . . They considered of no value their hereditary dignities, but regarded the Greek honors as the most prestigious. (M.R.)

10.4 1 Maccabees 1:41–63

Below is another version of the measures instituted by King Antiochus Epiphanes to force Jews to give up their ancestral ways and the penalties inflicted upon those who disobeyed them.

The king [Antiochus Epiphanes] wrote to all his kingdom, for all to become one people, and for each to abandon his own customs.[4] All the gentiles accepted the terms of the king's proclamation. Many Israelites, too, accepted worship of him, and sacrificed to idols, and violated the Sabbath.

The king sent documents by messengers to Jerusalem and the cities of Judaea containing orders to follow customs alien to the land, namely to put a stop to burnt offerings and sacrifices and libation in the sanctuary, to violate the Sabbath and festivals, to defile the Temple and holy things, to build altars and sanctuaries[5] and make idols, to sacrifice swine and ritually unfit animals, to cease circumcising their sons, and to make themselves abominable by all kinds of uncleanliness and profanation, so as to forget the Law and violate all the commandments. And whoever did not carry out the word of the king was to be put to death. He wrote to the same effect to his entire kingdom, and he appointed officials to watch over all the people, and sent orders to the cities of Judaea to offer sacrifices in every town. Many from among the people gathered round the officials, every forsaker of the Law, and they committed wicked deeds in the land, and drove Israel into hiding places in every place of refuge.

On the fifteenth day of Kislev in the 145th year [of the Seleucid Era, i.e., December 6, 167 BCE] the king had an abomination of desolation[6]

2. Youths in Greek cities who, after a standard education, were enrolled as citizens.
3. I.e., they were to be called citizens of Antioch-at-Jerusalem.
4. Actually Antiochus' decree was limited to Judaea and did not extend throughout his empire.
5. I.e., temples and altars elsewhere than in Jerusalem.
6. It is not known precisely what was involved in this profanation.

built upon the altar; and in the outlying cities of Judaea they built altars, and at the doors of houses and in the squares they offered sacrifices. Whatever scrolls of the Law they found they tore up and burned. And whoever was found with a scroll of the Covenant in his possession or showed his love for the Law, the king's decree put him to death. Through their power they acted against the Israelites who were found in the cities each month, as on the twenty-fifth day of the month they would offer sacrifices upon the altar which they had built upon the Temple altar. The women who had their sons circumcised they put to death according to the decree, hanging the babies from their mothers' necks, and executing also their households and the men who performed the circumcision. Many Israelites vigorously and steadfastly refused to eat forbidden food. They accepted death in order not to be defiled by foods, and in order not to violate the Holy Covenant, and they died. (M.R.)

10.5 Josephus, *Jewish Antiquities* 12.248–56

Below is an account of how Antiochus Epiphanes plundered the wealth of the Temple in Jerusalem and desecrated the altar there, as well as the cruel punishments inflicted upon those who disobeyed the king's orders.

It happened that in the 145th year [167 BCE], on the twenty-fifth day[7] of the month which by us is called Kislev, and by the Macedonians Apellaeus, in the 153rd Olympiad, the king [Antiochus Epiphanes] came to Jerusalem, and pretending peace got possession of the city by treachery. At this time he spared not even those who admitted him, on account of the riches of the Temple. But because of his greed (for he saw that there was a great deal of gold in the Temple and an array of other very costly dedications), and in order to plunder this wealth, he went so far as to break the treaty he had made with the Jews. He stripped the Temple bare, taking away the appurtenances, the golden menorah, the golden altar [for incense], and the table [of the shewbread], and the altar [of burnt offerings], and he did not even refrain from taking the curtains, which were made of fine linen and were scarlet. He also emptied it of its hidden treasures and left nothing at all, as a result throwing the Jews into great mourning. For he forbade them to offer the daily sacrifices which they used to offer to God, according to the Law. And when he had plundered the whole city, of the inhabitants he killed some and some he took captive together with their wives and children, so that the number of those taken alive amounted to about 10,000. He also burned down the finest parts of the city. And when he had pulled down the walls, he built a citadel in the lower city, at a place that was high and overlooked the Temple. This is why he fortified it with high walls and towers, and stationed in it a garrison of Macedonians. Moreover, in the citadel there remained those of the people who were impious and wicked in character, people from whom the citizens came to suffer many terrible calamities.

---

7. Josephus is in error; the day was the 15th day of the month of Kislev. The 25th of Kislev would produce a dramatic coincidence with the date of the rededication of the Temple.

And when the king had built an altar upon the Temple altar, he slaughtered swine upon it and thereby offered a sacrifice according to neither the Law nor the tradition of Jewish cult. He also compelled them to abandon the worship of their own God, and to venerate those whom he considered to be gods; to build sanctuaries and set up altars in every city and village, and to sacrifice swine upon them daily. He also ordered them not to circumcise their sons, and threatened to punish anyone found doing this. He also appointed overseers, who would assist in compelling them to carry out his orders. And there were many Jews who complied with the king's orders, some voluntarily, some out of fear of the penalty announced. But the most worthy people and those of noble soul disregarded him, considering the ancestral customs of greater importance than the punishment which he threatened against the disobedient. Therefore, every day they were tormented and underwent bitter torture, and died, for they were whipped, and their bodies were mutilated; and they were crucified while still alive and breathing. They also strangled women and their sons whom they had circumcised contrary to the king's policy, hanging the children from the necks of the crucified parents. And if any sacred book or copy of the Law was found, it was destroyed; and those in whose possession they were found, they too, poor wretches, died miserably. (M.R.)

10.6 Josephus, *Against Apion* 2.83–4

Here Josephus cites various pagan historians who assert that Antiochus' motive in plundering the Temple was his need for money.

That the raid of Antiochus on the Temple was iniquitous, that it was impecuniosity which drove him to invade it, when he was not an open enemy, that he attacked us, his allies and friends, and that he found there nothing to deserve ridicule; these facts are attested by many sober historians: Polybius of Megalopolis, Strabo the Cappadocian, Nicolaus of Damascus, Timagenes, Castor the chronicler, and Apollodorus all assert that it was impecuniosity that induced Antiochus, in violation of his treaties with the Jews, to plunder the Temple with its stores of gold and silver. (LCL)

10.7 2 Maccabees 5:27–6:11

Below we have an account of how Judas Maccabaeus and his few followers fled into the desert to escape the terrible measures – particularly to force the Jews to violate the Sabbath and dietary laws, to forego circumcision, and to worship the Greek gods – instituted by Antiochus Epiphanes.

Judas Maccabaeus with about nine others fled into the desert, the lair of wild animals, where he and his companions lived in the mountains after the fashion of wild animals. They remained there living on what vegetation they found, so as not to share in the pollution [i.e., by eating ritually unclean animals].

Shortly afterwards, King Antiochus sent an elderly Athenian to compel the Jews to abandon their ancestral customs and no longer regulate their lives according to the laws of God; also to pollute the Temple at Jerusalem and dedicate it to Olympian Zeus; and to dedicate the sanctuary on Mount Gerizim to Zeus Xenios, god of hospitality, following the practice of the local inhabitants.[8] The intensity of the evil was grievous and a severe trial. The gentiles filled the Temple with licentiousness and revelry; they took their pleasure with prostitutes and had intercourse with women in the sacred precincts, after bringing forbidden things inside and heaping the altar with impure offerings contrary to the Law. It was not permitted either to observe the Sabbath nor to keep the traditional festivals, nor simply to admit being a Jew. On the monthly celebration of the king's birthday the Jews were compelled by brute force to eat the entrails of the sacrificial animals; and on the feast of Dionysus they were forced to wear ivy wreaths and join the procession in honor of Dionysus. At the instigation of the inhabitants of Ptolemais, a decree was promulgated in the neighboring Greek cities to the effect that they should adopt the same policy of compelling the Jews to eat the entrails, and should kill those who refused to change over to Greek ways.

Their wretched fate was there for all to see. For instance, two women were brought to trial for having had their children circumcised. They were paraded in public, with their babies hanging at their breasts, and then flung down from the walls. Other Jews had assembled in caves near Jerusalem to keep the Sabbath in secret; they were denounced to Philip[9] and were burned alive, since they refused to defend themselves out of regard for the holiness of the day. (M.R.)

Ptolemy VIII Physcon (Euergetes II) (reigned 145–116 BCE)

BIBLIOGRAPHY

Modrzejewski (1995), 146–53.

10.8 Josephus, *Against Apion* 2.51–5

Ptolemy Philometor (180–146 BCE) and his consort Cleopatra III had, according to Josephus (*Against Apion* 2.49), entrusted their entire realm to Jews and placed their entire army under the command of two Jewish generals, Onias[10] and Dositheos. Upon Philometor's death Ptolemy Physcon usurped the crown from Philometor's sons and widow. The incident that follows, telling how the Jews of Alexandria were rounded up to be trampled upon by elephants, only to have the elephants turn around and trample upon the adherents of Ptolemy Physcon, whereupon Ptolemy repented of his ways, is very similar to one which is described in 3 Maccabees 5–6 as occurring during the reign of Ptolemy IV Philopator

---

8. Samaritans, who accepted a Greek appellation for God, whom they worshipped in their sanctuary on Mount Gerizim in Samaria.

9. A friend of Antiochus Epiphanes and guardian of the heir to the throne.

10. Some identify this Onias as the founder of the temple at Leontopolis, but the name is not uncommon.

(221–203 BCE). Most scholars conclude that there was only one such incident and that the account of Josephus is the less improbable.

On the death of his brother Ptolemy Philometor, Ptolemy surnamed Physcon left Cyrene with the intention of dethroning Cleopatra [III] and the deceased king's sons, and iniquitously usurping the crown himself. That was why, on Cleopatra's behalf, Onias took up arms against him, refusing to abandon at a crisis his allegiance to the throne. Moreover, the justice of his action was signally attested by God. For Ptolemy Physcon, though [not] daring to face the army of Onias, had arrested all the Jews in the city with their wives and children, and exposed them, naked and in chains, to be trampled to death by elephants, the beasts being actually made drunk for the purpose. However, the outcome was the reverse of his intentions. The elephants, without touching the Jews at their feet, rushed at Physcon's friends, and killed a large number of them.

Afterwards Ptolemy saw a terrible apparition, that forbade him to injure these people. His favorite concubine (some call her Ithaca, others Irene) adding her entreaty to him not to perpetrate such an enormity, he gave way and repented of his past actions and further designs. That is the origin of the well-known feast that the Jews of Alexandria keep, with good reason, on this day, because of the deliverance so manifestly vouchsafed to them by God. (LCL)

Expulsion of the Jews from Rome (139 BCE)

BIBLIOGRAPHY

Stern, vol. 1 (1974), 357–60.
Eugene N. Lane, "Sabazius and the Jews in Valerius Maximus: A Re-examination," *JRS* 69 (1979), 35–8.

The two (or possibly three) expulsions of the Jews from Rome seem to be connected with the fear that the Romans had of the Jews' expansion in number through proselytizing. Some scholars have connected the expulsion in 139 BCE with the alleged missionary zeal shown by Simon the Hasmonean's delegation to Rome at about this time (140 BCE). The account by Valerius Maximus of this expulsion has been preserved only in the summaries of Nepotianus and Paris. The expulsion could not have lasted very long, inasmuch as we find Jews once again in Rome soon after this event.

10.9 Valerius Maximus (beginning of the first century CE), *Memorable Deeds and Words* 1.3.3, in the epitome of Julius Paris (fourth century CE)

According to this account, in the epitome by Julius Paris, the charge against the Jews is that they had tried to infiltrate the Roman way of life with the worship of the Jewish God.

Cnaeus Cornelius Hispalus, *praetor peregrinus*[11] in the year of the consulate of Publius Popilius Laenas and Lucius Calpurnius, ordered

11. The *praetor peregrinus* was the Roman magistrate in charge of administering justice in cases involving citizens vs. non-citizens.

the astrologers by an edict to leave Rome and Italy within ten days, since by a fallacious interpretation of the stars they perturbed fickle and silly minds, thereby making profit out of their lies. The same praetor compelled the Jews, who attempted to infect the Roman customs with the cult of Jupiter Sabazius,[12] to return to their homes. (M.S.)

> 10.10 Valerius Maximus, *Memorable Deeds and Words* 1.3.3, in the epitome of Januarius Nepotianus (fourth or fifth century CE)

According to the epitome of Januarius Nepotianus the charge against the Jews is that the Jews had not only attempted to get the Romans to adopt Judaism but that they had aggressively destroyed the Roman religious altars.

Cornelius Hispalus expelled from Rome the astrologers and ordered them to leave Italy within ten days and thus not offer for sale their foreign science. The same Hispalus banished the Jews from Rome, because they attempted to transmit their sacred rites to the Romans, and he cast down their private altars from public places. (M.S.)

Ptolemy IX Lathyrus (reigned 116–80 BCE)

In the civil war between the Egyptian Queen Cleopatra III and Ptolemy IX Lathyrus, the Jews, following the lead of two Jews named Chelkias and Ananias, whom Cleopatra had appointed as her generals, remained loyal to her.

> 10.11 Strabo (*ca.* 64 BCE–*ca.* 20 CE), *Historical Memoranda*, cited by Josephus, *Jewish Antiquities* 13.345–7

The passage below describes the victorious campaign of Ptolemy Lathyrus against King Alexander Jannaeus of Judaea and the brutal vengeance which he took upon the Jews.

After this victory [*ca.* 107 BCE] Ptolemy [Lathyrus] overran other territory, and when evening fell, halted in some villages of Judaea, which he found full of women and infants; he thereupon commanded his soldiers to cut their throats and chop them up and then to fling the pieces into boiling cauldrons and to taste of them. This order he gave that those who had escaped from the battle and had returned to their homes might get the notion that the enemy were eaters of human flesh, and so might be the more terrified by this sight. And both Strabo and Nicolaus [of Damascus] say that they treated the Jews in the manner which I have just mentioned. (LCL)

---

12. Sabazius was actually a Phrygian god identified with Dionysus. The confusion with the Jewish God probably arises from the similarity of Sabazius and *Sabaoth* ("Hosts"), an epithet of God as Lord of Hosts. Another possibility connecting Dionysus with God is noted by Plutarch, *Festal Questions* 4.6.2.

Popular Hatred (first half of the first century BCE)

10.12 CPJ, no. 141

This fragmentary papyrus is the earliest example of popular hatred of Jews that has come down to us. The sense seems to be that when dealing with Egyptian priests Jews should remember that they hate Jews.

Herakles to Ptolemaios . . . many greetings and wishes of good health. I have asked Hippalos [?] in Memphis about the priest of Tebtynis. Write to him a letter in order that I may know what is the matter. I ask you that, so that he [?] will not be detained. Manage . . . in what he may need. You know that they loathe the Jews. Greet . . . Epimene and Tryphona . . . take care. . . . (*CPJ*)

Cleopatra VII (reigned 51–30 BCE)

Apparently, by not distributing grain to the Jews during a time of famine the famous Cleopatra indicated that she did not regard them as citizens. But that she was not consistently anti-Jewish seems clear from the support that she gave to Alexandra the Hasmonean (the daughter of King Hyrcanus II of Judaea) and her children (Josephus, *Jewish Antiquities* 15.23–4, 42–9). She apparently spoke Hebrew (or Aramaic) and even attempted, unsuccessfully to be sure, according to Josephus (*Jewish Antiquities* 15.96–103), to seduce the infamous Herod.

10.13 Apion (first half of the first century CE), *History of Egypt*, cited by Josephus, *Against Apion* 2.56, 60

Here Josephus notes that Queen Cleopatra refused to give food to the Jews during a famine.

He [Apion] further alludes to Cleopatra, the last queen of Alexandria, apparently reproaching us for her ungracious treatment of us. He ought instead to have set himself to rebuke that woman. . . . If, as Apion asserts, this woman in time of famine refused to give the Jews any rations of wheat, is not that, pray, a fact of which we should be proud? (LCL)

10.14 Plutarch (*ca.* 46–120 CE), *Life of Antony* 27.4

As the passage below indicates, Cleopatra spoke a number of languages, including Hebrew. So far as we know, she is the only non-Jew in the Hellenistic–Roman period who could speak Hebrew.

And her tongue, like an instrument of many strings, she [Cleopatra] could readily turn to whatever language she pleased, so that in her interviews with barbarians she very seldom had need of an interpreter, but made her replies to most of them herself and unassisted, whether they were Ethiopians, Troglodytes,[13] Hebrews, Arabians, Syrians, Medes or Parthians. (LCL)

---

13. A race of African cave-dwellers who inhabited the coast of the Red Sea.

The Reign of the Roman Emperor Tiberius (14–37 CE)

Expulsion of the Jews from Rome (19 CE)

Bibliography

Elmer T. Merrill, "The Expulsion of Jews from Rome under Tiberius," *CP* 14 (1919), 365–72.

William A. Heidel, "Why Were the Jews Banished from Italy in 19 AD?", *AJP* 41 (1920), 38–47.

Horst R. Moehring, "The Persecution of the Jews and the Adherents of the Isis Cult at Rome AD 19," *NT* 3 (1954), 293–304.

Ernest L. Abel, "Were the Jews Banished from Rome in 19 AD?", *REJ* 127 (1968), 383–6.

Margaret H. Williams, "The Expulsion of the Jews from Rome in AD 19," *Latomus* 48 (1989), 765–84.

The expulsion of the Jews from Rome in 19 CE, like that in 139 BCE, seems to be connected with alleged proselytizing activities, though proselytism is explicitly mentioned in only one of the four (possibly five, if Seneca is referring to this expulsion) accounts of this expulsion, and so it is of interest to compare them. Again, the expulsion could not have lasted very long, inasmuch as we find the Jews once again in Rome very shortly after this event.

10.15 Josephus, *Jewish Antiquities* 18.81–4

According to this account, the Jews were expelled because a Jew and his confederates had appropriated for themselves the gifts which a certain noble Jewish proselyte had directed to be sent to the Temple in Jerusalem. In particular, four thousand Jews were drafted for military service in Sardinia.

There was a certain Jew, a complete scoundrel, who had fled his own country because he was accused of transgressing certain laws and feared punishment on this account. Just at this time he was resident in Rome and played the part of an interpreter of the Mosaic law and its wisdom. He enlisted three confederates not a whit better in character than himself; and when Fulvia, a woman of high rank who had become a Jewish proselyte, began to meet with them regularly, they urged her to send purple and gold to the Temple in Jerusalem. They, however, took the gifts and used them for their own personal expenses, for it was this that had been their intention in asking for gifts from the start. Saturninus, the husband of Fulvia, at the instigation of his wife, duly reported this to [the Roman Emperor] Tiberius, whose friend he was, whereupon the latter ordered the whole Jewish community to leave Rome. The consuls drafted four thousand of these Jews for military service and sent them to the island of Sardinia; but they penalized a good many of them, who refused to serve for fear of breaking the Jewish laws. And so because of the wickedness of four men the Jews were banished from the city. (LCL)

10.16 Tacitus (*ca.* 56–120 CE), *Annals* 2.85

Tacitus, in the passage below, does not give the reason for the expulsion but states merely that they were forced to leave Italy unless they renounced their Judaism. He, like Josephus, mentions that four thousand were to be shipped to Sardinia, where, presumably, many of them would die because of the pestilential climate.

Another debate dealt with the proscription of the Egyptian and Jewish rites, and a senatorial edict directed that four thousand descendants of enfranchised slaves, tainted with that superstition and suitable in point of age, were to be shipped to Sardinia and there employed in suppressing brigandage: 'if they succumbed to the pestilential climate, it was a cheap loss.' The rest had orders to leave Italy, unless they had renounced their impious ceremonial by a given date. (LCL)

10.17 Suetonius (*ca.* 69–150 CE), *Life of Tiberius* 36

Suetonius mentions but likewise does not give the reason for the expulsion; he notes that Jews were assigned to army service in provinces with a less healthy climate (presumably including Sardinia but others as well).

He [Tiberius] abolished foreign cults, especially the Egyptian and the Jewish rites, compelling all who were addicted to such superstitions to burn their religious vestments and all their paraphernalia. Those of the Jews who were of military age he assigned to provinces of less healthy climate, ostensibly to serve in the army; the others of the same race or of similar beliefs he banished from the city, on pain of slavery for life if they did not obey. (LCL)

10.18 Dio Cassius (*ca.* 160–230 CE), *Roman History* 57.18.5a

Dio Cassius is the only writer who explicitly states that the reason for the expulsion is that the Jews were converting many non-Jews in Rome to Judaism.

As the Jews flocked to Rome in great numbers and were converting many of the natives to their ways, he [i.e., Tiberius] banished most of them. (LCL)

10.19 Seneca the Younger (*ca.* 4 BCE–65 CE), *Moral Epistles* 108.22

The passage below does not mention Jews by name, but the fact that it does mention foreign rites being inaugurated in the early part of the reign of Tiberius (emperor from 14 to 37; the expulsion occurred in the year 19) would appear to indicate that efforts were being made to get others to embrace these rites. The fact that the rites included, in particular, abstention from certain kinds of animal foods may well refer to the Jewish dietary laws.

I was imbued with this teaching,[14] and began to abstain from animal food; at the end of a year the habit was as pleasant as it was easy. I was

14. The reference is presumably to the Pythagoreans' abstention from animal food.

beginning to feel that my mind was more active; though I would not today positively state whether it really was or not. Do you ask how I came to abandon the practice? It was this way: The days of my youth coincided with the early part of the reign of Tiberius Caesar. Some foreign rites were at that time being inaugurated, and abstinence from certain kinds of animal food was set down as a proof of interest in the strange cult. So at the request of my father, who did not fear prosecution, but who detested philosophy, I returned to my previous habits; and it was no very hard matter to induce me to dine more comfortably. (LCL)

Judaea as a Roman Province during the Reign of Tiberius: Pontius Pilate (Procurator, 26–36 CE)

Bibliography

Carl H. Kraeling, "The Episode of the Roman Standards at Jerusalem," *HTR* 35 (1942), 263–89.

Paul L. Maier, *Pontius Pilate* (1968).

Ian H. Eybers, "The Roman Administration of Judaea between AD 6 and 41," *TE* 2 (1969), 131–46.

Paul L. Maier, "The Episode of the Golden Roman Shields at Jerusalem," *HTR* 62 (1969), 109–21.

Shimon Applebaum, "Judaea as a Roman Province: the Countryside as a Political and Economic Factor," *ANRW* 2.8 (1977), 355–96.

Gideon Fuks, "Again on the Episode of the Gilded Roman Shields at Jerusalem," *HTR* 75 (1982), 503–7.

Daniel R. Schwartz, "Josephus and Philo on Pontius Pilate," *JC* 3 (1983), 26–45.

Philip R. Davies, "The Meaning of Philo's Text about the Gilded Shields," *JTS* 37 (1986), 109–14.

Of all the procurators of Judaea Pontius Pilate served longer, a period of ten years, than any other, with the exception of his immediate predecessor, Valerius Gratus, who served eleven years. It was during Pilate's rule that Jesus of Nazareth was put to death in the year 29. Josephus portrays Pilate as deliberately offending the religious sensibilities of the Jews.

10.20 Josephus, Jewish Antiquities 18.55–9

According to Josephus, in the year 36, Pilate, as we see in the passage below, went to Jerusalem with a military unit bearing standards with portraits of the emperor. Not unexpectedly the Jews *en masse* protested most vigorously; and though at first he refused to yield, eventually Pilate withdrew.

Now [Pontius] Pilate,[15] prefect of Judaea, when he brought his army from Caesarea and removed it to winter quarters in Jerusalem, was inclined to violate the Jewish customs by introducing into the city the busts of the emperor [Tiberius] that were attached to the military

---

15. An inscription discovered in Caesarea in 1961 refers to Pilate as prefect (a term with connotations more military than administrative). The later term "procurator" is apparently anachronistic.

standards. Our Law forbids us to make images. It was for this reason that the previous governors when they entered the city used standards that had no such ornaments. Pilate was the first to bring the images into Jerusalem, and he set them up without the knowledge of the people, for his entrance took place at night. But when the people discovered it, they went in a throng to Caesarea, and for many days entreated him to remove the images. He refused to yield, since that would be an insult to the emperor. Since they did not cease entreating him, on the sixth day, after secretly equipping and placing his troops in position, he himself came to the speaker's stand. This had been set up in the stadium, which concealed the army lying in wait. When the Jews again engaged in entreaties, as prearranged he surrounded them with his soldiers and threatened to punish them with immediate death if they did not stop their tumult and return to their homes. But throwing themselves prostrate and baring their throats, they declared that they gladly welcomed death rather than dare to transgress the wisdom of their laws. Pilate, astonished at the strength of their devotion to the laws, at once removed the images from Jerusalem and took them back to Caesarea. (M. R.)

10.21 Philo, *Embassy to Gaius* 38.299–305

According to Philo, Pilate offended the Jews by setting up votive shields with inscriptions honoring Tiberius on the walls of his residence in Jerusalem. When Pilate refused the appeal of a delegation of high-ranking Jews they wrote to the emperor, who ordered Pilate to remove the shields. There are clear differences between Josephus' and Philo's accounts, and most scholars regard them as separate incidents.

I [Agrippa I] can quote in addition one act showing a fine spirit [on the part of the Emperor Tiberius]. For though I experienced many ills when he was alive, truth is dear and is held in honor by you [the Emperor Gaius Caligula]. One of his lieutenants was Pilate, who was appointed to govern Judaea. He, not so much to honor Tiberius as to annoy the multitude, dedicated in Herod's palace in the holy city some shields coated with gold. They had no image work traced on them nor anything else forbidden by the law apart from the barest inscription stating two facts, the name of the person who made the dedication and of him in whose honor it was made. But when the multitude understood the matter which had by now become a subject of common talk, having put at their head the king's four sons, who in dignity and good fortune were not inferior to a king, and his other descendants and the persons of authority in their own body, they appealed to Pilate to redress the infringement of their traditions caused by the shields and not to disturb the customs which throughout all the preceding ages had been safeguarded without disturbance by kings and by emperors. When he, naturally inflexible, a blend of self-will and relentlessness, stubbornly refused they clamored, 'Do not arouse sedition, do not make war, do not destroy the peace; you do not honor the emperor by dishonoring ancient laws. Do not take Tiberius as your pretext for outraging the nation; he does not wish any of our customs to be overthrown. If you say that he does, produce yourself an order or a letter or something of the kind so that we may cease to pester you, and having chosen our envoys may petition our lord.'

It was this final point which particularly exasperated him, for he feared that if they actually sent an embassy they would also expose the rest of his conduct as governor by stating in full the briberies, the insults, the robberies, the outrages and wanton injuries, the executions without trial constantly repeated, the ceaseless and supremely grievous cruelty. So with all his vindictiveness and furious temper, he was in a difficult position. He had not the courage to take down what had been dedicated nor did he wish to do anything that would please his subjects. At the same time he knew full well the constant policy of Tiberius in these matters. The magnates saw this and understanding that he had repented of his action but did not wish to appear penitent sent letters of very earnest supplication to Tiberius. When he had read them through, what language he used about Pilate, what threats he made! The violence of his anger, though he was not easily roused to anger, it is needless to describe since the facts speak for themselves. For at once without even postponing it to the morrow he wrote to Pilate with a host of reproaches and rebukes for his audacious violation of precedent and bade him at once take down the shields and have them transferred from the capital to Caesarea on the coast surnamed Augusta after your great-grandfather, to be set up in the temple of Augustus, and so they were. So both objects were safeguarded, the honor paid to the emperor and the policy observed from of old in dealing with the city. (LCL)

10.22 Josephus, *Jewish Antiquities* 18.60–2

As indicated in the passage below, Pilate took money from the Temple treasury and sought to use it to construct an aqueduct to bring water to Jerusalem. When the Jews protested vehemently this misuse of sacred money, Pilate ordered his soldiers to disperse the Jews; in the process many Jews were slain.

He [Pontius Pilate] spent money from the sacred treasury[16] in the construction of an aqueduct to bring water into Jerusalem, intercepting the source of the stream at a distance of two hundred furlongs.[17] The Jews did not acquiesce in the operations that this involved; and tens of thousands of men assembled and cried out against him, bidding him relinquish his promotion of such designs. Some too even hurled insults and abuse of the sort that a throng will commonly engage in. He thereupon ordered a large number of soldiers to be dressed in Jewish garments, under which they carried clubs, and he sent them off this way and that, thus surrounding the Jews, whom he ordered to withdraw. When the Jews were in full torrent of abuse he gave his soldiers

16. The Jews were outraged because Pilate was appropriating for his own secular purposes the money that had been contributed by Jews everywhere for the purchase of animals to be sacrificed in the Temple in Jerusalem.
17. About 23 miles.

the prearranged signal. They, however, inflicted much harder blows than Pilate had ordered, punishing alike both those who were rioting and those who were not. But the Jews showed no faintheartedness; and so, caught unarmed, as they were, by men delivering a prepared attack, many of them actually were slain on the spot, while some withdrew disabled by blows. Thus ended the uprising. (LCL)

The Reign of Caligula (37–41 CE)

THE RIOT OF 38 CE IN ALEXANDRIA

BIBLIOGRAPHY

Edith Mary Smallwood, ed., *Philonis Alexandrini Legatio ad Gaium* (1961), 14–23.
Feldman (1993), 113–17.
Modrzejewski (1995), 165–73.

As a result of Augustus' social policy in the province of Egypt, which created an elite hierarchy of Romans and Greeks, Jews were excluded from the military and the civil service and apparently from entry into Alexandrian citizenship. Yet it was only through Alexandrian citizenship that residents of Egypt could aspire to Roman citizenship. Moreover, the Jews, having been accorded the same status as Egyptians, had to pay the resented poll tax. Though their religious and communal privileges were protected by the Roman government, many Jews sought to break out of the social and political restrictions imposed by Rome. Their ancestors had lived in Alexandria for centuries, but they were now virtually in the status of resident aliens. Their numbers were large, and their religious and social exclusiveness, their dutiful sending of sacred money to Jerusalem, and their exemption from supporting the religious and municipal expenses of the city stirred resentment among the Greeks. There were, it seems, agitators on both sides, and tensions mounted between Greeks and Jews in the early first century.

When Gaius Caligula succeeded Tiberius as emperor in 37 CE, the Jews deemed it politic to send a delegation to Rome to congratulate him. The governor of Egypt, Aulus Avilius Flaccus, thwarted this out of favor for anti-Jewish activists among the Greeks.

10.23 Philo, *Against Flaccus* 5.29–30, 33–34, 35

On August 1, 38, Marcus Julius Agrippa, grandson of Herod and close friend of Caligula, who had just been named king of Judaea by Caligula in Rome, arrived in Alexandria en route to his realm. His ostentatious display of his bodyguard of spearmen decked in armor overlaid with gold and silver led the Alexandrian mob to respond by dressing up a lunatic named Carabas in mock-royal apparel with a crown and bodyguards and by saluting him as Marin, the Aramaic word for 'lord.' The implied charge clearly was that the Alexandrian Jews, in giving homage to Agrippa as king, were guilty of dual loyalty and of constituting themselves, in effect, as a state within a state. When the Alexandrian mob continuously vilified Agrippa, the Roman governor, Flaccus, was silent.

The people of Egypt were bursting with envy – jealousy is characteristically Egyptian – and they assumed that any good fortune of others was their misfortune. In their ancient and one might say inbred hostility to the Jews, they resented that a Jew had been made a king, just as if each of them had been deprived of an ancestral throne. And the unhappy Flaccus was again egged on by his companions, inciting him and appealing to him so as to make him equally envious....

The lazy and shiftless mob of the city, who devote themselves to idle chatter and pass their time in slander and defamation, was permitted by him to vilify the king, whether he himself began the abuse or was incited and provoked by those who were his customary minions in such matters. Thus impelled they spent their days in the gymnasium, jeering at the king and uttering gibe upon gibe against him....

Why was Flaccus not indignant? Why did he not arrest them? Why did he not punish them for their incorrigible evil-speaking? Even if Agrippa had not been king, yet as a member of Caesar's household should not he have had some privilege and respect?...

And if an undisciplined mob should get a starting point for their misconduct in any matters, they do not stop there but pass on from one thing to another, always engaging in some new form of violence. (M.R.)

10.24 Philo, *Against Flaccus* 6.41–2, 43; 8.53–7; 10.73–5

Aulus Avilius Flaccus, who had been appointed governor of Egypt in 32 and had shown efficiency and fairness during his first five years in office, found his position endangered by the accession of Caligula, since he had favored a rival for the succession and was particularly friendly with a certain Macro, who had fallen into disfavor with Caligula. Those who were hostile to the Jews in Alexandria offered Flaccus their support if he would favor them. Flaccus did not intervene with his troops. Now assured that they might proceed as they pleased, the Alexandrians desecrated the synagogues by setting up images of Caligula, thus emphasizing their charge that the Jews were unpatriotic. Flaccus then issued a proclamation declaring the Jews to be aliens and evicting them from four of the five sections of the city, thus, in effect, creating a Jewish ghetto. The anti-Jewish bigots then proceeded to pillage Jewish homes and shops with abandon and to massacre the Jews. To underscore the lack of patriotism of the Jews, the mob desecrated synagogues by introducing into them busts of the emperor. As the passage below shows, Flaccus then permitted the mob to plunder the homes of the Jews. The economic losses of the Jews were tremendous. There ensued the first pogrom in world history. Even Jewish leaders were arrested and cruelly flogged. But in the end Flaccus was recalled by Caligula in that year, condemned, exiled, and later executed. Philo recounts the events in two of his essays, *Against Flaccus* and *Embassy to Gaius*.

[The mob of Alexandria] called out with one accord to install images in the synagogues, thereby proposing a breach of the Law entirely novel and never before done. And knowing this, quite shrewd as they are in villainy, they whitewashed it by using the name of Caesar as a screen. . . .

What then did the governor of the country do? He knew that both Alexandria and the whole of Egypt had two kinds of inhabitants, us and them, and that there were no less than a million Jews resident in Alexandria and the country from the descent into Libya up to the boundaries of Ethiopia; he knew also that this was an attack against them all, and that it is disadvantageous to disturb ancestral customs. Yet he permitted the mob to install the images, though he could have set before them numerous considerations, all cautionary, either as orders from a ruler or as advice from a friend. . . .

When Flaccus' attack against our laws by ravaging the synagogues without even leaving them their names appeared to be going well, he turned to another scheme, namely the destruction of civic rights. When our ancestral customs and our participation in political rights, the sole anchor on which our life was secured, had been rescinded, he envisioned that we would undergo the most extreme misfortunes, with no cable left for safety. For a few days later he issued a proclamation in which he stigmatized us as foreigners and aliens and gave us no opportunity for pleading our case, but condemned us without a trial. What stronger profession of tyranny could there be than this? He became everything himself, accuser, enemy, witness, judge, and punisher, and then to the two previous wrongs he added a third, by permitting those who wished to pillage the Jews, as in the sacking of a city, to do so.

Having secured this immunity, what did they do? There are five quarters in the city, named after the first letters of the alphabet; two of these are called Jewish because most of the Jews live in them, though in the rest also there are not a few Jews scattered about. What then did they do? From four of the districts they ejected the Jews and drove them together into a very small part of one. The Jews, on account of their numbers, poured out over beaches, dunghills and tombs, robbed of all their belongings. Their enemies overran the empty houses and turned to looting, distributing the contents like spoils of war; and as no one prevented them, they broke into the workshops of the Jews, which had been closed as a sign of mourning for Drusilla,[18] carried out all the articles they found, which were very numerous, and took them to the middle of the agora, dealing with other people's property as if it was their own. A still more grievous evil than the looting was the unemployment caused. The tradespeople had lost their stock, and no one – farmer, ship captain, merchant, artisan – was allowed to practice his usual business. Thus poverty was caused in two ways: first, looting, by which in the course of a single day they had become penniless, completely stripped of all they had; and, secondly, their inability to make a living from their usual employment. . . .

Having broken into and burglarized everything and left no part of Jewish life untouched by enmity carried to the highest pitch, Flaccus

---

18. Caligula's favorite sister, who died in 38. He ordered public mourning for her throughout the empire.

devised another monstrous and unprecedented line of attack, worthy of this worker of enormities, the inventor of novel crimes. After the death of the ethnarch,[19] our senate had been established to take charge of Jewish affairs by our savior and benefactor Augustus, in orders to that effect given by him to Magius Maximus when he was about to take office for the second time as governor of Alexandria and the province. The members of this senate who were found in their houses, thirty-eight in number, were arrested by Flaccus, who, having ordered them to be at once put into chains, organized a splendid procession through the middle of the agora of these elderly men chained and pinioned, some with leather thongs, others with iron chains. Then he brought them into the theater, a spectacle most pitiable and excessive even for the occasion. Then as they stood in front, with their enemies seated to underscore their disgrace, he ordered all of them to be stripped and tortured with whips, which it is the practice to use for the degradation of the most vicious criminals. In consequence of the flogging, some were carried out in stretchers and died at once, while others lay sick for a long time despairing of recovery. (M.R.)

10.25 Philo, *Embassy to Gaius* 18.120, 18.121–2, 124; 19.127, 19.131–20.133, 20.134

In the following passage Philo gives another view of the devastation, human and material, wrought in the attack by the Alexandrian mob upon the Jews. In particular, he highlights the failure of the Roman governor to act.

[In the reign of Caligula] the motley and volatile Alexandrian mob assumed ... that a most opportune moment had come its way and attacked us. It revealed the hatred which had for a long time been smoldering, and threw everything into disorder and confusion....

They assaulted us with insane and bestial fury. They overran our homes and drove the owners out with their wives and children, so as to leave the houses empty. No longer waiting for darkness of night in fear of arrest like burglars, they looted our furniture and valuables, they carried them off openly in broad daylight, and showed them to those they met....

The Greeks herded together many thousands of men, with their wives and children, from the whole city into a very small part of it, like cattle and sheep. They expected that within a few days they would find piles of bodies of Jews who had died either of starvation through lack of necessities (since they had had no intimation of this sudden disaster to enable them to store up supplies in advance) or of overcrowding and suffocation....

So, no longer able to endure the lack of space, the Jews poured onto the desert, the shores and the cemeteries, longing to breathe pure, untainted air. Any who had already been caught in other parts of the city or who were visiting the country in ignorance of the calamities

---

19. The ethnarch was the official who was the general administrator and judge of the Jews.

that had fallen on us experienced sufferings of every kind. They were stoned, or wounded with tiles, or battered to death. . . .

They bound many Jews, still alive, with straps and ropes, tied their ankles together, and dragged them through the middle of the agora, jumping on them and not sparing even their dead bodies. More cruel and savage than wild animals, they tore them limb from limb, trampled on them, and utterly destroyed their entire appearance, so that there were no remains left which could be given decent burial. . . .

The prefect [governor] of the province, who alone could have checked the mob rule in an hour had he wished, pretended not to see and hear what he did see and hear and allowed the Greeks to make war without restraint. Thus he shattered the peace, and they consequently were still more stirred up and rushed headlong into outrageous and bolder plots. Organizing numerous groups, they attacked the synagogues, of which there were many in each section of the city. Some they knocked down, some they razed to the ground, and others they set on fire and burned, giving no thought even to the adjacent houses in their fury and groundless insanity. . . .

I say nothing about the destruction and burning, at the same time, of dedications in honor of the emperors – gilded shields and crowns, monuments and inscriptions. . . .

Those synagogues which they could not destroy either by fire or demolition, because large numbers of Jews lived crowded together close by, they defiled in a different way, by overturning our lives and customs; they placed portraits of Caligula in all of them, and in the largest and most distinguished they also placed a bronze statue of him riding in a four-horse chariot. (M.R.)

The Embassy of the Alexandrian Jews to Caligula (39/40 ce)

Bibliography

Edith Mary Smallwood, ed., *Philonis Alexandrini Legatio ad Gaium* (1961), especially 3–27.

Pieter J. Sijpesteijn, "The Legationes ad Gaium," *JJS* 15 (1964), 87–96.

Smallwood (1976), 235–50.

In the wake of the popular attack upon the Jews in 38 ce, the Jews of Alexandria sent an embassy to the Emperor Caligula in 39/40 to gain recognition of their claim to citizenship. It was led by Philo, the distinguished Hellenistic–Jewish philosopher, who was the head of the Jewish community of Alexandria. The Alexandrian Greeks sent a delegation which included Isidorus, the head of the gymnasium, and the infamous Jew-baiter Apion. Caligula was prejudicially antagonistic to the Jews because of their refusal to acknowledge his godship and was deluded by the adoration of the Alexandrian Greeks. While waiting to see the emperor the Jewish delegation heard the news that Caligula was preparing to introduce busts of himself into the Temple in Jerusalem. When the delegation finally met with the emperor they were treated with contempt.

10.26 Philo, *Embassy to Gaius* 44.349, 353–45.362

In the passage below Philo records the contemptuous way in which the Emperor Gaius Caligula dealt with the delegation of Jews from Alexandria.

It is right that I [Philo] should record also both what we saw and what we heard when we were summoned to take a part in the contention about our citizenship. The moment we entered we knew from his look and movements that we had come into the presence not of a judge but of an accuser more hostile than those arrayed against us. . . .

In a sneering, snarling way he said, 'Are you the god-haters who do not believe me to be a god, a god acknowledged among all the other nations but not to be named by you?' And stretching out his hands toward heaven he gave utterance to an invocatory address which it was a sin even to listen to, much more to reproduce in the actual words. How vast was the delight which at once filled the envoys on the other side! They thought that Gaius' first utterance had secured the success of their mission. They gesticulated, they danced about and invoked blessings on him under the names of all the gods.

Seeing that he was delighted at being addressed as of more than human nature the virulent sycophant Isidorus said, 'My lord, you will hate still more these people here present, and those of whose nation they are, if you understand their malevolence and impiety towards you. For when all men were offering sacrifices of thanksgiving for your preservation they alone could not bear the thought of sacrificing. And when I say "they" I include also the other Jews.'

We cried out with one accord, 'Lord Gaius, we are slandered; we did sacrifice and sacrifice hecatombs too, and we did not just pour the blood upon the altar and take the flesh home to feast and regale ourselves with it as some do, but we gave the victims to the sacred fire to be entirely consumed, and we have done this not once but thrice already, the first time at your accession to the sovereignty, the second when you escaped the severe sickness which all the habitable world suffered with you, the third as a prayer of hope for victory in Germany.'

'All right,' he replied, 'that is true, you have sacrificed, but to another, even if it was for me; what good is it then? For you have not sacrificed to me.' When we heard these words following on his first remark we were seized by a profound terror which spread till it became visible in the countenance.

While he was saying this he was going on with his survey of the houses, the different chambers, men's or women's, the ground floors, the upper floors, all of them, and some he censured as defective in structure, and for others he made his own plans and gave orders that they should be more magnificent. Then driven along we followed him up and down mocked and reviled by our adversaries, as they do in the mimes at the theaters. For indeed the business was a sort of mime; the judge had taken on the role of accuser, the accusers the role of a bad judge who had eyes only for his enmity and not for the actual truth. But when the person on trial is accused by a judge and that one of such eminence, he must needs hold his peace. For silence too may in a way serve as a defence, particularly to us who could not answer any of the points which he was investigating and wished to press, because our customs and laws muzzled the tongue and closed and stitched up the mouth. But after giving some of his orders about the buildings he put to us this grave and momentous question, 'Why do you refuse to eat pork?' The question was greeted by another outburst of laughter from some of our opponents because they were delighted, while with others it was a studied attempt to flatter him, intended to make the remark seem witty and sprightly. The laughter was so great that some of the servants following him were annoyed at it as showing disrespect for the emperor, with whom even a tempered smile is unsafe except for quite intimate friends. We answered, 'Different people have different customs and the use of some things is forbidden to us as others are to our opponents.' Then someone said, 'Yes, just as many don't eat lamb, which is so easily obtainable,' whereupon Gaius laughed and said, 'Quite right too, for it's not nice.' Under such befooling and reviling we were helpless. (LCL)

THE ATTEMPT TO SET UP CALIGULA'S STATUE IN THE TEMPLE (40 CE)

BIBLIOGRAPHY

John P. V. D. Balsdon, "The Chronology of Gaius' Dealings with the Jews," *JRS* 24 (1934), 13–24.
Edith Mary Smallwood, "The Chronology of Gaius' Attempt to Desecrate the Temple," *Latomus* 16 (1957), 3–17.
Solomon Zeitlin, "Did Agrippa Write a Letter to Gaius Caligula?" *JQR* 56 (1965–6), 22–31.
Per Bilde, "The Roman Emperor Gaius (Caligula)'s Attempt to Erect His Statue in the Temple of Jerusalem," *ST* 32 (1978), 67–93.
Edith Mary Smallwood, "Philo and Josephus as Historians of the Same Events," *JJC* (1987), 120–5.
Daniel R. Schwartz, "Gaius' Attempt to Erect His Statue in the Temple of Jerusalem," in his *Agrippa I: The Last King of Judaea* (1990), 77–89.
James S. McLaren, *Power and Politics in Palestine: The Jews and the Governing of their Land 100 BC–AD 70* (1991), 114–26.

10.27 Philo, *Embassy to Gaius* 30.199–203

The Emperor Gaius Caligula, afflicted with egomania, was particularly indignant because the Jews refused to honor him with statues and to swear by his name. When the non-Jewish inhabitants of Jamnia in Judaea set up an altar which the Jewish inhabitants proceeded to tear down, this was reported to Capito, the tax-collector for Judaea, who wrote an exaggerated version of the event to the Emperor Gaius Caligula. Caligula then, in his anger, ordered Petronius, the Roman governor of Syria, to set up a colossal statue of himself in the Temple in Jerusalem.

But now his [Caligula's] eagerness [to be deified] has become keener than ever before owing to a letter sent to him by Capito. Capito is the tax-collector for Judaea and cherishes a spite against the population. When he came there he was a poor man, but by his rapacity and

peculation he has amassed much wealth in various forms. Then fearing
that some accusation might be brought against him he devised a
scheme to elude the charges by slandering those whom he had
wronged. It chanced that an opportunity for obtaining his object was
given by the following incident. Jamnia, one of the most populous cities
of Judaea, is inhabited by a mixture of people, the majority being Jews,
with some others of alien races, intruders for mischief from the
dwellers in adjacent countries. These people being new settlers have
made themselves a pest and a nuisance to those who are in a sense
indigenous by perpetually subverting some part of the institutions of
the Jews. Hearing from travelers visiting them how earnestly Gaius
was pressing his deification and the extreme hostility which he felt
towards the whole Jewish race, they thought that a fit opportunity of
attacking them had fallen in their way. Accordingly they erected an
extemporized altar of the commonest material with the clay moulded
into bricks, merely as a plan to injure their neighbors, for they knew
that they would not allow their customs to be subverted, as indeed it
turned out. For, when they saw it and felt it intolerable that the sanctity
which truly belongs to the Holy Land should be destroyed, they met
together and pulled it down. The others at once went off to Capito, who
was the author of the whole episode, and he, thinking that he had
found a piece of luck which he had long been seeking, wrote to Gaius a
highly exaggerated account of the facts.

Gaius after reading it gave orders that, in place of the altar of bricks
erected in wanton spite in Jamnia, something richer and more
magnificent, namely a colossal statue coated with gold, should be set
up in the Temple of the mother city. In this he followed the advice of
those excellent and sapient advisers, that member of the aristocracy
Helicon, slave, scrap retailer, piece of riff-raff, and one Apelles, a tragic
actor, who, they say, in the flower of his prime had trafficked his youth-
ful charms, but when the bloom was passed went on to the stage. (LCL)

10.28 Josephus, *Jewish Antiquities* 18.263–9, 270–2, 276, 277–8, 289–90, 291–
9, 300, 302, 303–5

The passage below describes the mass protest by the Jews urging
Petronius, the Roman governor of Syria, not to set up the image
which the emperor had ordered him to erect in the Temple. At first
Petronius insisted that he could do nothing since he was merely the
emissary of the emperor; but when he saw that the Jews were ready to
die rather than to violate their ancestral laws, he wrote to the emperor
asking that he rescind the order. Meanwhile, King Agrippa I arrived in
Rome and succeeded in persuading Caligula to give up his plan. Shortly
thereafter, however, Caligula, upon receiving Petronius' letter and
wrongly concluding that the Jews were intending to revolt, apparently
changed his mind; and it was only his death that finally scuttled the
scheme.

Meanwhile, many tens of thousands of Jews came to Petronius at
Ptolemais with petitions not to use force to make them transgress and
violate their ancestral code. 'If,' they said, 'you propose at all costs to

bring in and set up the image, slay us first before you carry out these resolutions. For it is not possible for us to survive and to behold actions that are forbidden us by the decision both of our lawgiver and of our forefathers who cast their votes enacting these measures as moral laws.' To this Petronius indignantly replied: 'If I were the emperor and intended to take this action of my own choice, you would have a right to speak as you do. As it is, I am Caesar's emissary and bound to carry out the decision he has already made, since to disregard it would bring on me irretrievable punishment.'

'Equal to this determination of yours, O Petronius,' replied the Jews, 'not to transgress the orders of Gaius, is our determination not to transgress the declaration of the law. We have put our trust in the goodness of God and in the labors of our forefathers and have hitherto remained innocent of transgression. Nor could we ever bring ourselves to go so far in wickedness as by our own act to transgress, for any fear of death, the law bidding us abstain, where He thought it conducive to our good to do so. In order to preserve our ancestral code, we shall patiently endure what may be in store for us, with the assurance that for those who are determined to take the risk there is hope even of prevailing; for God will stand by us if we welcome danger for His glory. Fortune, moreover, is wont to veer now toward one side, now toward the other in human affairs. To obey you, on the other hand, would bring on us the grave reproach of cowardice, because that would be the explanation of our transgressing the law, and at the same time we should incur God's severe wrath – and He even in your eyes must be accounted a higher power than Gaius.'

Now Petronius saw from their words that their spirit was not easily to be put down and that it would be impossible for him without a battle to carry out Gaius' behest and set up his image. Indeed there would be great slaughter. . . .

As before, many tens of thousands faced Petronius on his arrival at Tiberias. They besought him by no means to put them under such constraint nor to pollute the city by setting up a statue. 'Will you then go to war with Caesar,' said Petronius, 'regardless of his resources and of your own weakness?' 'On no account would we fight,' they said, 'but we will die sooner than violate our laws.' And falling on their faces and baring their throats, they declared that they were ready to be slain. They continued to make these supplications for forty days. Furthermore, they neglected their fields, and that, too, though it was time to sow the seed. For they showed a stubborn determination and readiness to die rather than to see the image erected. . . . When Aristobulus[20] and the rest appealed to Petronius along such lines, he was influenced by them. . . . He considered it far better to send a letter to Gaius and to endure the latter's inexorable wrath aroused by his not carrying out the orders at once. Perhaps, moreover, he might even convince him. Nevertheless, if Gaius persisted in his original lunacy, he would undertake war against them [the Jews]. But if, after all, Gaius should turn some of his wrath against him, a man who made virtue his

20. The brother of King Agrippa I.

goal might well die on behalf of such a multitude of men. And so he decided to recognize the cogency of the plea of the petitioners....

Meanwhile, King Agrippa, who, as it happened, was living in Rome, advanced greatly in friendship with Gaius. Once he made a banquet for him with the intention of surpassing everyone both in the expenditure on the banquet and in provision for the pleasure of the guests. He was so successful that, to say nothing of the others, even Gaius himself despaired of equalling, much less surpassing it, if he should desire to do so....

Hence while he [Gaius] was relaxed with wine and while his mood was unusually genial, he said during the banquet when Agrippa invited him to drink: 'Agrippa, I have known in my heart before how highly you regarded me and how you have proved your great loyalty even amidst the dangers with which, because of it, you were encircled by Tiberius. And now you never fail to show kindness to us, going even beyond your means. Consequently, inasmuch as it would be a stain on my honor to let you outdo me in zeal, I wish to make amends for past deficiencies. Indeed, all the gifts that I have allotted to you are but slight in amount; any service that can add its weight in the scale of prosperity shall be performed for you with all my heart and power.'

He spoke these words thinking that Agrippa would ask for a large accession of territory adjoining his own or for the revenues of certain cities. As for Agrippa, although he was quite ready to make his request, he did not reveal his intention. On the contrary, he at once replied to Gaius that it was not in expectation of any benefit from him that he had in the past paid court to him in spite of Tiberius' orders; nor were any of his present activities in giving him pleasure designed as a road to personal gain. He said that the gifts that Gaius had already presented to him were great and went beyond any expectations that he would dare to cherish. 'For even if they have been inferior to your capacity, they exceed my thoughts and my claims as a recipient.'

Gaius, amazed at his character, insisted all the more on his telling what he might grant to please him. Agrippa replied: 'Since, my lord, in your kindness you declare me worthy of gifts, I shall ask for nothing that would make me richer inasmuch as I am already extremely conspicuous because of the gifts that you have hitherto bestowed upon me. But I shall ask for something that will bring you a reputation for piety and will induce the Deity to help you in everything that you wish; and it will bring me the renown, among those who hear of it, of never having known failure in anything that I desired your authority to obtain for me. Well, I ask you to abandon all further thought of erecting the statue that Petronius has your orders to set up in the Temple of the Jews.'

Hazardous as he considered this petition – for if Gaius did not regard it with favor, it would bring him certain death – yet, because he thought the issue important, as it truly was, he chose to make the gamble on this occasion. Gaius was bound by Agrippa's attentions to him.... So he yielded and wrote to Petronius ... before reading the latter's message from which he wrongly concluded that the Jews were bent on revolt and that their attitude indicated no other intent than a threat of downright war against the Romans. Upon receiving this letter, ... he wrote to Petronius as follows: 'Since you have held the gifts that the Jews have bestowed upon you in higher regard than my orders and have presumed to minister in everything to their pleasure in violation of my orders, I bid you act as your own judge and consider what course it is your duty to take, since you have brought my displeasure upon yourself. For I assure you that you shall be cited as an example by all men now and all that will come hereafter to point the moral that an emperor's commands are never to be flouted.'

Such was the letter that he wrote to Petronius. But Petronius did not receive it while Gaius was alive since the voyage of those who brought the message was so delayed that before it arrived Petronius had received a letter with news of the death of Gaius. (LCL)

The Reign of Claudius (41–54 CE)

TENSION IN EGYPT

10.29 CPJ, no. 152 (41 CE)

This papyrus, referring to Jewish money-lenders in Alexandria, with its statement to "beware of the Jews," illustrates the high tension between Jews and non-Jews generally, since it contains the phrase "like everyone else."

Serapion to our Herakleides, greeting. I have sent you two other letters, one by Nedymos, one by Kronios the policeman. Well, then, I received the letter from the Arab. I read it and I was upset. Keep close to Ptollarion the whole time. He can perhaps put you straight. Tell him 'It is one thing for everyone else and another for me. I am a slave. I sold you my goods for a talent too little. I don't know what my master will do to me. We have many creditors. Don't put us out of business.' Ask him every day. Perhaps he may take pity on you. If not, like everyone else, do you too beware of the Jews. It is better to keep close to him and make friends with him, if you can. Or you may, through Diodoros, get the document signed by the wife of the Commander. If you do your part, you are not to blame. My best greetings to Diodoros. Farewell. My greetings to Harpokration. In the first year of Tiberius Claudius Caesar Augustus Germanicus, the Emperor. The eleventh of the month Kaisareios. (CPJ)

EXPULSION OF THE JEWS FROM ROME

BIBLIOGRAPHY

Stephen Benko, "The Edict of Claudius of AD 49 and the Instigator Chrestus," *TZ* 25 (1969), 406–18.

Dixon Slingerland, "Suetonius, *Claudius* 25.4 and the Account in Dio Cassius," *JQR* 79 (1988–9), 305–22.

Dixon Slingerland, "Chrestus, Christus?," in Alan J. Avery-Peck, ed., *New Perspectives on Ancient Judaism*, vol. 4: *The Literature of Early Rabbinic Judaism* (1989), 133–44.

Dixon Slingerland, "Suetonius, *Claudius* 25.4, Acts 18, and Paulus Orosius' *Historiarum Adversum Paganos Libri VII* Dating the Claudian Expulsion(s) of Roman Jews," *JQR* 83 (1992–3), 127–44.

There is considerable dispute as to whether the expulsion of the Jews during the reign of Claudius in the middle of the first century actually affected only the Christians, though both Suetonius and the Book of Acts speak of the expulsion of the Jews as such, and Cassius Dio actually denies that an expulsion took place.

10.30 Suetonius (*ca.* 69–*ca.* 150 CE), *Life of Claudius* 25.4

There has been a tremendous amount of discussion as to who Chrestus is in the passage below. Most scholars assume that Jesus is meant and that the reference is to the disturbances created by the spread of Christianity in Rome.

Since the Jews constantly made disturbances at the instigation of Chrestus, he [Claudius] expelled them from Rome. (LCL)

10.31 New Testament, Acts 18:2

The passage below seems to be explicit in stating that Claudius expelled all the Jews from Rome.

And he [Paul] found a Jew named Aquila, a native of Pontus, lately come from Italy with his wife Priscilla, because Claudius had commanded all the Jews to leave Rome. (RSV)

10.32 Dio Cassius (*ca.* 160–230 CE), *Roman History* 60.6.6

The passage below alludes to the great increase in the Jewish population of Rome, at least in part by winning proselytes. Instead of stating that the Jews were expelled because of the tumult that they had caused, it asserts that Claudius refrained from expelling them because he realized that this would have caused a tumult. His order that the Jews not hold meetings was presumably intended to stop them from proselytizing activities.

As for the Jews, who had again increased so greatly that by reason of their multitude it would have been hard without raising a tumult to bar them from the city, he [Claudius] did not drive them out, but ordered them, while continuing their traditional mode of life, not to hold meetings. (LCL)

ROMAN OBJECTION TO THE GROWTH OF AGRIPPA I'S POPULARITY WITH OTHER STATES (*ca.* 44 CE)

BIBLIOGRAPHY

Daniel R. Schwartz, *Agrippa I: The Last King of Judaea* (1990), 137–40.

10.33 Josephus, *Jewish Antiquities* 19.338–42

Even though Agrippa I was the king of a minuscule country, the Romans constantly feared lest petty rulers such as he might form alliances with other petty rulers and even revolt against the Romans. Hence, as we see in the passage below, despite Agrippa's close relationship with the imperial family and the Emperor Claudius in particular, his meeting with several of his fellow petty rulers, especially since some of them were related by blood or marriage with Agrippa, was summarily broken up by the Roman governor of Syria, Marsus, who was particularly apprehensive because of the proximity of these kingdoms to the Parthian frontier, where the Romans felt constant tension. Marsus may also have regarded Agrippa's spectacular rise to power as a threat to his own supremacy as the most powerful Roman leader in the East.

Now he [Agrippa I] was evidently admired by the other kings. At any rate, he was visited by Antiochus king of Commagene,[21] Sampsigermaus[22] king of Emesa,[23] and Cotys king of Armenia Minor,[24] as well as by Polemo, who held sway over Pontus,[25] and Herod his brother, who was ruler of Chalcis.[26] His converse with all of them when he entertained and showed them courtesies was such as to demonstrate an elevation of sentiment that justified the honor done him by a visit of royalty.

It so happened, however, that while he was still entertaining them, Marsus, the governor of Syria, arrived. The king, therefore, to do honor to the Romans, advanced seven furlongs outside the city to meet him. Now this action, as events proved, was destined to be the beginning of a quarrel with Marsus; for Agrippa brought the other kings along with him and sat with them in his carriage; but Marsus was suspicious of such concord and intimate friendship among them. He took it for granted that a meeting of minds among so many chiefs of state was prejudicial to Roman interests. He therefore at once sent some of his associates with an order to each of the kings bidding him set off without delay to his own territory. Agrippa felt very much hurt by this and henceforth was at odds with Marsus. (LCL)

POPULAR OUTBREAK AFTER THE DEATH OF AGRIPPA I

10.34 Josephus, *Jewish Antiquities* 19.356–9 (44 CE)

The following passage shows how virulent the popular sentiment of the non-Jews was against Agrippa I, as seen in their behavior after his death, and this despite his benefactions toward them.

When it became known that Agrippa had departed this life, the people of Caesarea and of Sebaste [Samaria], forgetting his benefactions, behaved in the most hostile fashion. They hurled insults, too foul to be mentioned, at the deceased; and all who were then on military service – and they were a considerable number – went off to their homes, and

21. A petty kingdom between Cilicia (in Asia Minor) and Armenia.
22. His daughter Jotape was married to Agrippa's brother Aristobulus.
23. A petty kingdom in Syria just north-east of the Lebanese border.
24. A small district west of Armenia proper.
25. A country in north-eastern Asia Minor.
26. A kingdom at the foot of Mount Lebanon.

seizing the images of the king's daughters[27] carried them with one accord to the brothels, where they set them up on the roofs and offered them every possible sort of insult, doing things too indecent to be reported. Moreover, they reclined in the public places and celebrated feasts for all the people, wearing garlands and using scented unguents; they poured libations to Charon,[28] and exchanged toasts in celebration of the king's death. In this they were unmindful not only of Agrippa, who had treated them with much generosity, but also of his grandfather Herod, who had built their cities and had erected harbors and temples at lavish expense. (LCL)

Cuspius Fadus, Procurator of Judaea (44–6 CE)

10.35 Josephus, *Jewish Antiquities* 20.2–4 (44 CE)

In the passage below we see one of the recurring problems of the Jews in Judaea, namely the infestation by bandits, the self-defense measures taken by the Jews, and the consequent measures taken by the new Roman procurator, Fadus, to punish the Jewish hotheads for taking up arms without waiting for him to pass judgment.

Fadus, on his arrival in Judaea as procurator, found that the Jewish inhabitants of Peraea[29] had fallen out with the [non-Jewish] people of Philadelphia[30] over the boundaries of a village called Zia, which was infested with warlike men. Moreover, the [Jewish] Peraeans, who had taken up arms without the sanction of their leaders, inflicted much loss of life on the Philadelphians.

Fadus, on being informed of this, was greatly incensed that the Peraeans, granted that they thought themselves wronged by the Philadelphians, had not waited for him to give judgment but had instead resorted to arms. He therefore seized three of their leaders, who were in fact responsible for the revolt and ordered them to be held prisoner. Next he put one of them, named Annibas, to death, and imposed exile on the other two, Amaramus and Eleazar. (LCL)

The Rise of Messianic-like Figures

Bibliography

Morton Smith, "Messiahs: Robbers, Jurists, Prophets, and Magicians," *PAAJR* 44 (1977), 185–95.

Richard A. Horsley and John S. Hanson, *Bandits, Prophets, and Messiahs* (1985).

27. Elsewhere (*Ant.* 19.331) Josephus says that Agrippa scrupulously observed the traditions of his people. It seems, therefore, remarkable that such a pious person should have erected images of his daughters. But on Agrippa's coins there is the same inconsistency, since those minted in Jerusalem have no image, while those from other cities often have the image of Agrippa or the emperor.

28. The mythical ferryman of the dead.

29. Peraea was a Transjordanian region extending in length from Machaerus to Pella and in breadth from Philadelphia to the Jordan.

30. Philadelphia is the biblical Rabbah of Ammon, modern Amman, present-day capital of the kingdom of Jordan. It was called Philadelphia after Ptolemy II Philadelphus of Egypt.

Steve Mason, *Josephus and the New Testament* (1992), 208–25

Rebecca Gray, *Prophetic Figures in Late Second Temple Jewish Palestine: The Evidence from Josephus* (1993), 112–44.

The Romans were particularly sensitive to the numerous Messianic-like figures that arose during this period, especially if they attracted large crowds and claimed to perform miraculous deeds, inasmuch as one of the common denominators of Messiahs was their goal of establishing an independent Jewish state, hence, in this case, requiring revolt against the Roman Empire. In the following passages we have vignettes of several representative Messianic-like figures, though none of them is actually referred to as a Messiah.

10.36 Josephus, *Jewish Antiquities* 20.97–8

In the passage below we see the miracle prophesied by the charismatic leader Theudas and the speedy and brutal response of the Roman procurator, Fadus.

During the period when Fadus was procurator of Judaea, a certain impostor named Theudas persuaded the majority of the masses to take up their possessions and to follow him to the Jordan River. He stated that he was a prophet and that at his command the river would be parted and would provide them an easy passage. With this talk he deceived many. Fadus, however, did not permit them to reap the fruit of their folly, but sent against them a squadron of cavalry. These fell upon them unexpectedly, slew many of them, and took many prisoners. Theudas himself was captured, whereupon they cut off his head and brought it to Jerusalem. (LCL)

10.37 Acts 5:36.

It is significant that in the Book of Acts in the New Testament we likewise have reference to a Messianic-like figure named Theudas, though there is a discrepancy between Josephus and Acts, since the reference to Theudas in Acts is found in a speech which Gamaliel must have made before 37, whereas the revolt mentioned in Josephus occurred in 45 or 46. Moreover, Gamaliel (Acts 5:37) says that after Theudas Judas the Galilean arose in the days of the census, presumably that of Quirinius in the year 6. Consequently, some have contended that the Theudas referred to in Acts is not the same as the Theudas mentioned by Josephus.

For before these days Theudas arose, giving himself out to be somebody, and a number of men, about four hundred, joined him; but he was slain, and all who followed him were dispersed and came to nothing. (RSV)

VENTIDIUS CUMANUS, PROCURATOR OF JUDAEA (48–52 CE)

After the death of Agrippa I in 44 Judaea reverted to the status of a Roman procuratorship. During the procuratorship of Cumanus tension increased, especially because of the Romans' uneasiness at the rise of revolutionary groups, as well as the provocative behavior of Roman soldiers, the continuing quarrels between Jews and Samaritans, and the readiness of Cumanus himself to accept bribes. In the end, however, thanks to the influence of Agrippa II (Agrippa I's son), the Emperor Claudius ruled in favor of the Jewish cause against the Samaritans and condemned Cumanus to exile.

10.38 Josephus, *Jewish Antiquities* 20.105–6, 108–22, 125, 129, 132, 135–6

In the passage below we see how passions were provoked by the indecent and sacrilegious behavior of Roman soldiers, robbery by some Jewish revolutionaries, and tension between the Jews of Galilee and the Samaritans, and how Cumanus responded with a massive show of force. In the last case we see how the justice system of the day worked: first the Roman governor of Syria, Quadratus, after a full hearing condemned the Samaritans; then he referred the issue to the imperial court in Rome, where the Jews, through the influence of Agrippa II (the Younger) with the wife of the Roman Emperor Claudius, managed to get the emperor to condemn the Samaritans.

While Cumanus was administering affairs in Judaea, an uprising occurred in the city of Jerusalem as a result of which many of the Jews lost their lives. I shall first narrate the cause that brought about this uprising. When the festival called Passover was at hand ... a large multitude from all quarters assembled for it. Cumanus, fearing that their presence might afford occasion for an uprising, ordered one company of soldiers to take up arms and stand guard on the porticoes of the Temple so as to quell any uprising that might occur. . . .

On the fourth day of the festival, one of the soldiers uncovered his genitals and exhibited them to the multitude – an action which created anger and rage in the onlookers, who said that it was not they who had been insulted, but that it was a blasphemy against God. Some of the bolder ones also reviled Cumanus, asserting that the soldier had been prompted by him. Cumanus, when informed, was himself not a little provoked at the insulting remarks, but still merely admonished them to put an end to this lust for revolution and not to set disorders ablaze during the festival. Failing, however, to persuade them, for they only attacked him with more scurrilities, he ordered the whole army to take full armor and come to Antonia; this was, as I have said before, a fortress overlooking the Temple. The crowd, seeing the arrival of the soldiers, was frightened and started to flee. But since the exits were narrow, they, supposing that they were being pursued by the enemy, pushed together in their flight and crushed to death many of their number who were caught in the narrow passages. Indeed, the number of those who perished in that disturbance was computed at twenty thousand. So there was mourning henceforth instead of feasting; and all, utterly oblivious of prayers and sacrifices, turned to lamentation and weeping. Such were the calamities produced by the indecent behavior of a single soldier.

Their first mourning had not yet ceased when another calamity befell them. For some of the seditious revolutionaries robbed Stephen, a slave of Caesar, as he was traveling on the public highway at a distance of about one hundred furlongs from the city, and despoiled him of all his belongings. When Cumanus heard of this, he at once dispatched soldiers with orders to plunder the neighboring villages and to bring before him their most eminent men in chains so that he might exact vengeance for their effrontery.

After the sacking of the villages, one of the soldiers, who had found a copy of the laws of Moses that was kept in one of the villages, fetched it out where all could see and tore it in two while he uttered blasphemies and railed violently. The Jews, on learning of this, collected in large numbers, went down to Caesarea, where Cumanus happened to be, and besought him to avenge not them but God, whose laws had been subjected to outrage. For, they said, they could not endure to live, since their ancestral code was thus wantonly insulted. Cumanus, alarmed at the thought of a fresh revolution of the masses, after taking counsel with his friends, beheaded the soldier who had outraged the laws and thus prevented the uprising when it was on the verge of breaking out a second time.

Hatred also arose between the Samaritans and the Jews for the following reason. It was the custom of the [Jewish] Galileans at the time of a festival to pass through the Samaritan territory on their way to the Holy City. On one occasion, while they were passing through, certain of the inhabitants of a village called Ginae, which was situated on the border between Samaria and the Great Plain, joined battle with the Galileans and slew a great number of them. The leaders of the Galileans, hearing of the occurrence, came to Cumanus and besought him to seek out the murderers of those who had been slain. He, however, having been bribed by the Samaritans, neglected to avenge them. The Galileans, indignant at this, urged the Jewish masses to resort to arms and to assert their liberty; for, they said, slavery was in itself bitter, but when it involved insolent treatment, it was quite intolerable. Those in authority tried to mollify them and reduce the disorder, and offered to induce Cumanus to punish the murderers. The masses, however, paid no heed to them, but taking up arms and inviting the assistance of Eleazar son of Deinaeus – he was a brigand who for many years had had his home in the mountains – they fired and sacked certain villages of the Samaritans. When the affair came to Cumanus' ears, he took over the squadron of the Sebastenians[31] and four units of infantry and armed the Samaritans. He then marched out against the Jews and, in an encounter, slew many, but took more alive. . . .

The leaders of the Samaritans met with Ummidius Quadratus, the governor of Syria, who at that time was at Tyre, and accused the Jews of firing and sacking their villages. . . . Not long afterwards Quadratus reached Samaria, where, after a full hearing, he came to the conclusion that the Samaritans had been responsible for the disorder. He then crucified those of the Samaritans and of the Jews who, he had learned, had taken part in the rebellion and whom Cumanus had taken prisoner. . . .

---

31. These were troops who had been drafted by the Romans in the region of Sebaste (Samaria).

He further ordered the leaders of the Samaritans, those of the Jews, Cumanus the procurator, and Celer, a military tribune, to set off to Italy to get a decision in the imperial court concerning the matters in dispute between them.... Caesar's freedmen and friends displayed the greatest partiality for Cumanus and the Samaritans, and they would have got the better of the Jews, had not Agrippa the Younger, who was in Rome and saw that the Jewish leaders were losing the race for influence, urgently entreated Agrippina, the wife of the emperor [Claudius], to persuade her husband to give the case a thorough hearing in a manner befitting his respect for law and to punish the instigators of the revolt. Claudius was favorably impressed by this petition. He then heard the case through, and, on discovering that the Samaritans were the first to move in stirring up trouble, he ordered those of them who had come before him to be put to death, condemned Cumanus to exile, and ordered Celer the tribune to be taken to Jerusalem, where he was to be dragged around the whole city in a public spectacle and then put to death. (LCL)

Antonius Felix, Procurator of Judaea (52–60 ce)

Bibliography

Moses Aberbach, "The Conflicting Accounts of Josephus and Tacitus concerning Cumanus' and Felix' Terms of Office," *JQR* 40 (1949–50), 1–14.

10.39 Josephus, *Jewish Antiquities* 20.162–5

The procurator Felix, as the passage below indicates, even went to the extent of arranging to have the high priest Jonathan himself murdered by the revolutionary group known as the Sicarii, because Jonathan constantly kept warning him to improve his administration. Thereafter the Sicarii, according to Josephus, felt free to murder their enemies even in the Temple itself.

Felix ... bore a grudge against Jonathan the high priest because of his frequent admonition to improve the administration of the affairs of Judaea. For Jonathan feared that he himself might incur the censure of the multitude in that he had requested Caesar to dispatch Felix as procurator of Judaea. Felix accordingly devised a pretext that would remove from his presence one who was a constant nuisance to him; for incessant rebukes are annoying to those who choose to do wrong. It was such reasons that moved Felix to bribe Jonathan's most trusted friend, a native of Jerusalem named Doras, with a promise to pay a great sum, to bring in brigands to attack Jonathan and kill him. Doras agreed and contrived to get him murdered by the brigands in the following way. Certain of these brigands went up to the city as if they intended to worship God. With daggers concealed under their clothes, they mingled with the people about Jonathan and assassinated him.

As the murder remained unpunished, from that time forth the brigands with perfect impunity used to go to the city during the festivals and, with their weapons similarly concealed, mingle with the crowds. In this way they slew some because they were private enemies, and others because they were paid to do so by someone else. They committed these murders not only in other parts of the city but even in some cases in the Temple; for there too they made bold to slaughter their victims, for they did not regard even this as a desecration. (LCL)

10.40 Josephus, *Jewish Antiquities* 20.167–72

According to the passage below, an unnamed prophet from Egypt promised that at his word the walls of Jerusalem would fall down, presumably an indication that he would capture the city without a struggle. The Roman procurator, Felix, regarded this as incitement to insurrection and proceeded to slay four hundred of his followers (in the parallel account in *War* 2.261 the prophet is said to have collected thirty thousand followers and to have led them from the desert to the Mount of Olives).

Moreover, impostors and deceivers called upon the mob to follow them into the desert. For they said that they would show them unmistakable marvels and signs that would be wrought in harmony with God's design. Many were, in fact, persuaded and paid the penalty of their folly; for they were brought before Felix and he punished them.
　At this time there came to Jerusalem from Egypt a man who declared that he was a prophet and advised the masses of the common people to go out with him to the mountain called the Mount of Olives, which lies opposite the city at a distance of five furlongs. For he asserted that he wished to demonstrate from there that at his command Jerusalem's walls would fall down, through which he promised to provide them an entrance into the city. When Felix heard of this he ordered his soldiers to take up arms. Setting out from Jerusalem with a large force of cavalry and infantry, he fell upon the Egyptian and his followers, slaying four hundred of them and taking two hundred prisoners. The Egyptian himself escaped from the battle and disappeared. (LCL)

10.41 Acts 21:37–8

In the passage below the unnamed Egyptian is identified as a leader of the Sicarii, whereas in Josephus there is no such identification. Nothing is said in Acts of an attempt to seize Jerusalem; rather he leads his followers into the Judaean desert.

As Paul was about to be brought into the barracks, he said to the tribune, 'May I say something to you?' And he said, 'Do you know Greek? Are you not the Egyptian then who recently stirred up a revolt and led the four thousand men of the Assassins [Sicarii] out into the wilderness?' (RSV)

10.42 Josephus, *Jewish Antiquities* 20.173–8

The following passage describes the dispute between the Jewish and non-Jewish inhabitants of Caesarea, the resulting violence and triumph of the Jews, and the consequent slaughter of the Jews by the procurator Felix.

There arose also a dispute between the Jewish and Syrian inhabitants of Caesarea on the subject of equal civic rights. The Jews claimed that they had the precedence because the founder of Caesarea, their king Herod, had been of Jewish descent; the Syrians admitted what they said about Herod, but asserted that Caesarea had before that been called Strato's Tower, and that before Herod's time there had not been a single Jewish inhabitant in the city.

When the magistrates of the district heard of this quarrel they arrested those on both sides who were responsible for it and gave them a sound beating. Thus they calmed the disturbance for a time but not for long. For the Jews in the city, drawing confidence from their wealth and consequently despising the Syrians, again started reviling them, expecting thereby to provoke the Syrians against the Jews. The Syrians, though inferior in wealth, yet taking great pride in the fact that most of those in military service there under the Romans were from Caesarea and Sebaste, for a while retaliated by using insulting language to the Jews.

Next the Jews and Syrians took to casting stones at each other, until it came about that many on both sides were wounded and fell. Nevertheless, it was the Jews who carried the day.

When [the procurator] Felix saw that their rivalry had taken on the shape of war, he rushed ahead and summoned the Jews to desist. When they did not obey, he armed his soldiers, let them loose upon them, and thus slew many of the Jews and took more alive. He also allowed his men to plunder certain houses of the inhabitants that were laden with very large sums of money. The more moderate Jews and those who were of eminent rank, alarmed for themselves, besought Felix to sound the trumpet so as to recall the soldiers, and to show mercy from then on, thus giving them a chance to repent for what they had done. And Felix was prevailed upon to do so. (LCL)

The Reign of Nero (54–68 CE)

PORCIUS FESTUS, PROCURATOR OF JUDAEA (60–2 CE)

10.43 Josephus, *Jewish Antiquities* 20.188

In the following passage we read of an unnamed figure who promised salvation to his followers. Here also, as with the Egyptian prophet, he leads them into the desert, presumably where they could hide from the Romans. Again, the Roman procurator, Festus, responded with a massacre.

[The procurator] Festus also sent a force of cavalry and infantry against the dupes of a certain impostor who had promised them salvation and rest from troubles if they chose to follow him into the wilderness. The force which Festus dispatched destroyed both the deceiver himself and those who had followed him. (LCL)

LUCCEIUS ALBINUS, PROCURATOR OF JUDAEA (62–4 CE)

10.44 Josephus, *Jewish Antiquities* 20.215 (64 CE)

One of the chief causes of the increased tension between Jews and the Roman procurators was the propensity of the latter to accept bribes, whether it was to favor the non-Jewish opponents of the Jews or to release bandits and revolutionaries. According to the passage below, the procurator Albinus, in return for a personal consideration, released prisoners, thus infesting the land with brigands.

When [the procurator] Albinus heard that Gessius Florus was coming to succeed him, he sought to gain a name as one who had done some service to the inhabitants of Jerusalem. He therefore brought out those prisoners who clearly deserved to be put to death and sentenced them to execution, but released for a personal consideration those who had been cast into prison for a trifling and commonplace offence. Thus the prison was cleared of inmates and the land was infested with brigands. (LCL)

GESSIUS FLORUS, PROCURATOR OF JUDAEA (64–6 CE)

10.45 Josephus, *Jewish Antiquities* 20.252–7

The climax in maladministration by the procurators came with the last of them, Florus, who openly displayed his wickedness. The devotion to law and order, for which the Romans were so famous, he wantonly abandoned and permitted brigandage to flourish so that people no longer felt safe and in many cases felt compelled to desert the land.

Gessius Florus, who had been sent by Nero as successor to Albinus, filled the cup of the Jews with many misfortunes. He was a native of Clazomenae[32] and brought with him a wife Cleopatra, who was not a whit behind him in wickedness. It was through her influence that he obtained the post, she being a friend of Poppaea, Nero's consort.

So wicked and lawless was Florus in the exercise of his authority that the Jews, owing to the extremity of their misery, praised Albinus as a benefactor. For the latter used to conceal his villainy and took precautions not to be altogether detected; but Gessius Florus, as if he had been sent to give an exhibition of wickedness, ostentatiously paraded his lawless treatment of our nation and omitted no form of pillage or unjust punishment. Pity could not soften him, nor any amount of gain sate him; he was one who saw no difference between the greatest gains and the smallest, so that he even joined in partnership with brigands. In fact, the majority of people practiced this occupation with no inhibitions, since they had no doubt that their lives would be insured by him in return for his quota of the spoils. There was no limit in sight. The ill-fated Jews, unable to endure the devastation by brigands that went on, were one and all forced to abandon their own country and flee, for they thought that it would be

---

32. On the central coast of Asia Minor.

better to settle among gentiles, no matter where. What more need be
said? It was Florus who constrained us to take up war with the Romans,
for we preferred to perish together rather than by degrees. (LCL)

10.46 Tacitus (*ca.* 56–120 CE), *Histories* 5.10.1

Even Tacitus, no great lover of the Jews, here admits that Florus
exhausted the Jews' patience.

Still the Jews' patience lasted until Gessius Florus became procurator:
in his time war began. (LCL)

QUARRELS BETWEEN JEWS AND NON-JEWS IN PALESTINE AND IN THE DIASPORA IN
66 CE

BIBLIOGRAPHY

Lee I. Levine, "The Jewish-Greek Conflict in First Century Caesarea," *JJS* 25
    (1974), 381–97.
Aryeh Kasher, "The Isopoliteia Question in Caesarea Maritima," *JQR* 68 (1978),
    16–27.
Uriel Rappaport, "Jewish–Pagan Relations and the Revolt against Rome in 66–70
    CE," *JC* 1 (1981), 81–95.
Feldman (1993), 117–20.
Modrzejewski (1995), 185–90.

While it is true that the majority of inhabitants in what is today called
Israel were Jews during the Hellenistic and Roman periods, there were
apparently sizable numbers of Samaritans (though some would class
them as a sect of Jews) and other non-Jews (parallel, as some have
suggested, to today's "Palestinians"). The Roman administrators often
found themselves in the uneasy position of mediating these disputes; and
one major cause of the outbreak of the revolt against the Romans was
their favoring non-Jews from time to time. In particular, the city of
Caesarea, the second largest city in the country in population and the
seat of Roman rule, was the focus of dispute over civic rights.
The fact that most of those stationed in the Roman army in the land
at that time were from the non-Jewish population of the area contributed
to the tension and increased violence. The degree of the fury may
be seen from Josephus' report, which is reminiscent in its concentrated
violence of the massacre that began on St. Bartholemew's Day in France
in 1572. In instance after instance the Jews fought back.

10.47 Josephus, *Jewish War* 2.457–68

The following passage describes the massacre of the Jews of Caesarea
and the furious response of Jews in attacking other cities and villages. In
Syria non-Jews, instigated by greed, massacred Jews and plundered their
property; though they did not actually kill the "Judaizers," those who
sympathized with the Jews without actually converting to Judaism, they
were equally afraid of them. In Scythopolis some Jews, concerned about
their security, joined with the non-Jews against their fellow rebellious

Jews, but in the end even those who did not attack the non-Jews were massacred.

The same day [as the capitulation and massacre of the Roman garrison in Jerusalem][33] and at the same hour, as it were by the hand of Providence, the [non-Jewish] inhabitants of Caesarea massacred the Jews who resided in their city; within one hour more than twenty thousand were slaughtered, and Caesarea was completely emptied of Jews, for the fugitives were arrested by orders of [the procurator] Florus and conducted, in chains, to the dockyards. The news of the disaster at Caesarea infuriated the whole nation; and parties of Jews sacked the Syrian villages and the neighboring cities, Philadelphia, Heshbon and its district, Gerasa, Pella, and Scythopolis. Next they fell upon Gadara, Hippos, and Gaulanitis, destroying or setting fire to all in their path, and advanced to Kedasa, a Tyrian village, Ptolemais, Gaba, and Caesarea. Neither Sebaste nor Ascalon withstood their fury: these they burnt to the ground and then razed Anthedon and Gaza. In the vicinity of each of these cities many villages were pillaged and immense numbers of the inhabitants captured and slaughtered.

The Syrians [i.e., the non-Jews] on their side killed no less a number of Jews; they, too, slaughtered those whom they caught in the towns, not merely now, as before, from hatred, but to forestall the peril which menaced themselves. The whole of Syria was a scene of frightful disorder; every city was divided into two camps, and the safety of one party lay in anticipating the other. They passed their days in blood, their nights, yet more dreadful, in terror. For, though believing that they had rid themselves of the Jews, still each city had its Judaizers, who aroused suspicion; and while they shrank from killing offhand this equivocal element in their midst, they feared these neutrals as much as pronounced aliens. Even those who had long been reputed the very mildest of men were instigated by avarice to murder their adversaries; for they would then with impunity plunder the property of their victims and transfer to their own homes, as from a battlefield, the spoils of the slain, and he who gained the most covered himself with glory as the most successful murderer. One saw cities choked with unburied corpses, dead bodies of old men and infants exposed side by side, poor women stripped of the last covering of modesty, the whole province full of indescribable horrors; and even worse than the tale of atrocities committed was the suspense caused by the menace of evils in store.

Thus far the Jews had been faced with aliens only, but when they invaded Scythopolis [biblical Bethshan] they found their own nation in arms against them; for the Jews in this district ranged themselves on the side of the Scythopolitans, and, regarding their own security as more important than the ties of blood, met their own countrymen in battle. However, this excess of ardor brought them under suspicion: the people of Scythopolis feared that the Jews might attack the city by

---

33. The reference is to the massacre of the Roman garrison in the royal towers in Jerusalem by the Jewish rebels just before the onset of the actual war against the Romans.

night and inflict upon them some grave disaster, in order to make amends to their brethren for their defection. They, therefore, ordered them if they wished to confirm their allegiance and demonstrate their fidelity to their foreign allies, to betake themselves and their families to the adjoining grove. The Jews obeyed these orders, suspecting nothing. For two days the Scythopolitans made no move, in order to lull them into security, but on the third night, watching their opportunity when some were off their guard, and others asleep, they slaughtered them all to the number of upward of thirteen thousand and pillaged all their possessions. (LCL)

10.48 Josephus, *Jewish War* 2.490–8

The intensity of hate felt by the Alexandrian masses may be seen in the following incident which took place in the year 66 CE on the eve of the rebellion of the Jews in Judaea. This time, the Roman governor, the apostate Jew Tiberius Julius Alexander, Philo's nephew, in ordering his troops to end the riot, is reported to have brought about the death of some fifty thousand Jews.

On one occasion, when the Alexandrians were holding a public meeting on the subject of an embassy which they proposed to send to Nero, a large number of Jews flocked into the amphitheater along with the Greeks; their adversaries, the instant they caught sight of them, raised shouts of 'enemies' and 'spies,' and then rushed forward to lay hands on them. The majority of the Jews took flight and scattered, but three of them were caught by the Alexandrians and dragged off to be burnt alive. Thereupon the whole Jewish colony rose to the rescue; first they hurled stones at the Greeks, and then snatching up torches rushed to the amphitheater, threatening to consume the assembled citizens in the flames to the last man. And this they would actually have done, had not Tiberius Alexander, the governor of the city, curbed their fury. He first, however, attempted to recall them to reason without recourse to arms, quietly sending the principal citizens to them and entreating them to desist and not to provoke the Roman army to take action. But the rioters only ridiculed this exhortation and used abusive language of Tiberius.

Understanding then that nothing but the infliction of a severe lesson would quell the rebels, he let loose upon them the two Roman legions stationed in the city, together with two thousand soldiers who by chance had just arrived from Libya, to complete the ruin of the Jews; permission was given them not merely to kill the rioters but to plunder their property and burn down their houses. The troops, thereupon, rushed to the quarter of the city called 'Delta,' where the Jews were concentrated, and executed their orders, but not without bloodshed on their own side; for the Jews, closing their ranks and putting the best armed among their number in the front, offered a prolonged resistance; but when once they gave way, wholesale carnage ensued. Death in every form was theirs; some were caught in the plain, others driven into their houses, to which the Romans set fire after stripping them of their contents; there was no pity for infancy, no respect for years: all ages fell before their murderous career, until the whole district was deluged with blood and the heaps of corpses numbered fifty thousand; even the remnant would not have escaped, had they not sued for quarter. Alexander, now moved to compassion, ordered the Romans to retire. They, broken to obedience, ceased massacring at the first signal; but the Alexandrian populace in the intensity of their hate were not so easily called off and were with difficulty torn from the corpses. (LCL)

The Reign of Domitian (81–96 CE)

BIBLIOGRAPHY

Shirley Jackson Case, "Josephus' Anticipation of a Domitianic Persecution," *JBL* 44 (1925), 10–20.
Edith Mary Smallwood, "Domitian's Attitude toward the Jews and Judaism," *CP* 51 (1956), 1–13.
Lloyd A. Thompson, "Domitian and the Jewish Tax," *Historia* 31 (1982), 329–42.

The rule of Domitian (81–96) was a veritable reign of terror. He banished philosophers from Italy and executed many prominent persons on charges of treason or "atheism." His own wife Domitia was one of the conspirators who succeeded in assassinating him.

10.49 Suetonius (*ca.* 69–*ca.* 150 CE), *Life of Domitian* 12.2

The *Fiscus Judaicus* took the place of the annual contribution which had formerly been paid by Jews to the Temple in Jerusalem and which now had to be paid to Jupiter Capitolinus. Domitian enforced this tax with the utmost vigor.

The Jewish tax was exacted most assiduously. To the *Fiscus Judaicus* were reported those who lived as Jews without declaring this or who by concealing their origin did not pay the tribute imposed on their people. I recall when I was a young man being present when an old man in his nineties was examined by a procurator and a very large number of advisers to see whether he was circumcised. (M.R.)

10.50 *Midrash Psalms* 10.6 (*ca.* tenth century CE)

The following passage, undated as to its rabbinic source, reflects the bitter response of the Jews of Palestine to the poll-tax.

When the wicked empire says to Israel, 'Bring your poll-tax,' and it [Israel] says, 'I have orphans to feed!' And it [the empire] says to it [Israel], 'Do you ask me to feed your orphans? Go to the God of Jacob, about whom it is said, "Father of orphans and judge of widows" – he will be the one to feed your orphans. He will provide you with a Remus and Romulus, whom their mother did [not] want to bring up, and so He provided them with a wolf to suckle them, and she suckled them. So then they girded themselves and built two wicker-work huts in Rome. So you were an aid to the orphan.' (L.H.F.)

10.51 Dio Cassius (*ca.* 160–230 CE), *Roman History* 67.14.1–2

Among those whom Domitian executed were some prominent converts to Judaism or Christianity, notably his cousin Flavius Clemens and the latter's wife Domitilla. As to those who observed certain practices of Judaism without actually being converted, he executed some and deprived others of their property.

The same year [95 CE] Domitian executed many persons, among them a consul, Flavius Clemens, although he was his cousin, and Flavia Domitilla, the latter's wife, who was also a relative of the emperor. Both were charged with atheism, an accusation by which many others were convicted for veering toward the practices of the Jews.[34] Some were put to death, others were deprived of their property. As for Domitilla, she was only exiled, to Pandateria.[35] (M.R.)

Pescennius Niger (end of second century CE)

10.52 Scriptores Historiae Augustae (end of fourth century CE), *Pescennius Niger* 7.9

The Romans had to maintain a large army because they had such a long frontier, because they were frequently engaged in fighting the Parthians, and because they were confronted with frequent revolts in their huge empire. The fact that many in the empire avoided paying taxes meant that those who remained had to pay still higher taxes. The passage below cites the reply of the Roman governor of Judaea to entreaties by the Jews to lower the taxes.

Likewise, when the people of Palestine besought him [Pescennius Niger, governor of Judaea, *ca.* 192 CE] to lessen their tribute, saying that it bore heavily on them, he replied: 'So you wish me to lighten the tax on your lands; verily, if I had my way, I would tax the air.' (LCL)

The Reign of Julian (360–3 CE)

10.53 Julian, *To the Community of the Jews* 204

In the following passage the Emperor Julian, who ruled from 360 to 363, recognizes the huge burden of taxation which the Jews of Palestine bore.

By far the most burdensome thing in the yoke of your slavery, even more than in times past, has been the fact that you were subjected to unauthorized ordinances and had to contribute an untold amount of money to the accounts of the treasury. Of this I used to see many instances with my own eyes, and I have learned of more, by finding the records which are preserved against you. (LCL)

---

34. The reference is presumably to "sympathizers," those non-Jews who adopted certain practices of Judaism without actually becoming Jews.
35. An island (also known as Ventotene) 70 miles west of Naples.

Roman Christian Imperial Legislation Pertaining to Jews (fourth century through sixth century CE)

BIBLIOGRAPHY

Solomon Grayzel, "The Jews and Roman Law," *JQR* 59 (1968–9), 93–117.

Alfredo Mordecai Rabello, "The First Law of Theodosius II and Celebrations of Purim," *Christian News from Israel* 24.4 (16) (Spring, 1974), 159–66.

Alfredo Mordecai Rabello, "The Legal Condition of the Jews in the Roman Empire," *ANRW* 2.13 (1980), 662–762.

Linder (1987).

Feldman (1993), 385–97.

There is evidence that in the third century CE Jews in the Diaspora in the eastern part of the Roman Empire were not excluded from the civic life of the Greek cities. With the triumph of Christianity in the fourth century, however, the privileges that the Jews had enjoyed for centuries under Roman rule were gradually altered or abolished. Beginning with the reign of Constantine, although they were free to practice their religion, Jews throughout the Roman Empire experienced increasing restrictions as anti-Jewish measures made inroads on their traditional rights in civil matters. Toleration was gradually replaced by anti-Jewish propaganda, repression, and persecution.

10.54 *Theodosian Code* 16.8.1 (Constantine the Great, 329 CE)

This law punished with death those Jews who attacked fellow-Jews who had converted to Christianity.

We want the Jews, their principals [senior communal officials], and their patriarchs informed that if anyone – once this law has been given – dare attack by stoning or by other kind of fury one escaping from their deadly sect and raising his eyes to God's cult [i.e., Christianity], which, as we have learned, is being done now, he shall be delivered immediately to the flames and burnt with all his associates. (A.L.)

10.55 *Theodosian Code* 16.9.2 (Constantine II, 339 CE)

This law deprived Jews of the possession of Christian slaves whom they had purchased.

If a Jew shall not hesitate to purchase slaves who are associates in the venerable faith [Christianity], all those found with him shall be immediately taken away, and he shall be deprived, in no time at all, of the possession of those men who are Christians. (A.L.)

10.56 *Theodosian Code* 12.1.100 (Gratian [with Valentinian II, Theodosius I], 383 CE)

By the end of the fourth century CE we find that the Christian emperors, who had earlier in the century reaffirmed Jewish privileges, gradually start to repeal them. Among these privileges, which had been reaffirmed by Constantine the Great earlier in the century, was the exemption from serving in municipal offices enjoyed by holders of religious offices.

All those of curial origin who inserted themselves into the different grades of the state administration should be returned to their own curias, except those who are succored by the authority of the ancient law, which established a certain number of service years to people serving in the armed service or in the palatine administration. (A.L.)

10.57 *Theodosian Code* 16.8.18 (Theodosius II [with Honorius], 408 CE)

The following law, directed against burning Haman in effigy during the celebration of Purim since it was regarded by Christians as a mockery of the crucifixion of Jesus, reminds the Jews of the privileges that have been traditionally granted to them.

The governors of the provinces shall prohibit the Jews from setting fire to Aman [i.e., Haman] in memory of his past punishment, in a certain ceremony of their festival, and from burning with sacrilegious intent a form made to resemble the sacred cross in contempt of the Christian faith, lest they mingle the sign of our faith with their jests, and they shall restrain their rites from ridiculing the Christian Law, for they are bound to lose what had been permitted them till now unless they abstain from those matters that are forbidden. (A.L.)

10.58 *Theodosian Code* 16.8.22 (Honorius [with Theodosius II], 415 CE)

This law placed a number of restrictions upon Jews, notably forbidding the establishment of new synagogues, and especially upon the patriarch, the leader of the Palestinian Jewish community, notably forbidding him to judge Christians.

Since [the patriarch] Gamaliel [VI] supposed that he could transgress the law with impunity all the more because he was elevated to the pinnacle of dignities, Your Illustrious Authority shall know that Our Serenity has directed orders to the Illustrious Master of the Offices that the appointment documents to the honorary prefecture shall be taken from him, so that he shall remain in the honor that was his before he was granted the prefecture; and henceforth he shall cause no synagogues to be founded, and if there are any in deserted places, he shall see to it that they are destroyed, if it can be done without sedition. He shall have no power to judge Christians; if any contention shall arise between them and Jews it shall be settled by the governors of the province. (A.L.)

10.59 *Theodosian Code* 16.8.24 (Honorius [with Theodosius II], 418 CE)

This law forbade hiring of Jews for public service, though it still permitted Jews to practice as attorneys and to hold municipal offices.

The entrance to the State Service shall be closed from now on to those living in the Jewish superstition who attempt to enter it. We concede therefore to all those who took the oath of the Service, either among the Executive Agents or among the Palatins[36] the opportunity to

36. The Palatins were employees of the financial department of the imperial court.

terminate their service on its statutory term, suffering the deed rather than encouraging it, though what we wish to be alleviated at present to a few shall not be permitted in the future. As for those, however, who are subject to the perversity of this nation and are proven to have entered the military service, we decree that their military belt shall be undone without any hesitation, and that they shall not derive any help or protection from their former merits. Nevertheless, we do not exclude Jews educated in the liberal studies from the freedom of practicing as advocates, and we permit them to enjoy the honor of the curial liturgies, which they possess by right of their birth's prerogative and their family's splendor. Since they ought to be satisfied with these, they should not consider the interdiction concerning the State Service as a mark of infamy. (A.L.)

10.60 *Theodosian Code* 15.5.5 (Theodosius II [with Valentinian III], 425 CE)

This law forbade public entertainment, including celebrations in honor of the emperor, by anyone, including Jews and heretics, on Sundays and Christian holidays.

All entertainment of theaters and circuses in all the cities shall be denied to their population, so that the minds of the Christians and the faithful should be devoted entirely to God's cults on the Lord's day, which is the first day of the whole week, on Christ's Nativity and Epiphany, also on the days of Easter and of Pentecost, when the vestments testify to the new light of the sacred baptism by their imitation of the light on the heavenly baptismal font, in the time also, when the commemoration of the Apostolic Passion[37] – the teacher of the entire Christendom – is rightfully celebrated by all. If some are even now detained either by the madness of the Jewish impiety or by the error and insanity of the senseless paganism, they should know that there is time for supplications and time for entertainments. And lest anyone consider that he is obliged to the honor of our divinity as if by a greater duty towards the imperial office, and that perhaps he is bound to suffer if he offends our serenity unless he offers entertainments even to the contempt of the divine religion, if he exhibits towards us a devotion smaller than he was wont to, let no one be in doubt, that our clemency is honored by humankind to the greatest degree when the entire world serves God's miracles and merits. (A.L.)

10.61 *Theodosian Code* 16.8.28 (Theodosius II [with Valentinian III], 426 CE)

This law forbade Jews and Samaritans from disinheriting converts to Christianity.

If a son, daughter, or grandchild, one or more, of a Jew or a Samaritan should with better counsel be converted to the light of the Christian religion from the darkness of their own superstition, their relatives, that is, father, mother, grandfather, or grandmother, shall not be permitted to disinherit them or pass over them in silence in their

---

37. The Passions of Peter and Paul, celebrated on June 29.

testaments, or leave them less than they could obtain if they were called to the inheritance on intestacy. But if such a contingency should occur, we order that the will shall be rescinded, and that the aforementioned persons shall succeed as though on intestacy.... (M.R.)

10.62 *Code of Justinian* 1.5.21 (Justinian, 521 CE)

This law disqualified Jews from giving evidence in trials against Orthodox Christians.

Since many judges in course of determining litigation addressed us, needing our oracle in order that it will be revealed to them what must be decided about heretic witnesses, whether their testimonies should be accepted or rejected, we determine that there should be no participation of a heretic, or even of those who practice the Jewish superstition, in testimonies against Orthodox litigants, whether one party to the trial is Orthodox or the other.... (A.L.)

10.63 *Novellae of Justinian* 146 (Justinian, 553 CE)

This law prohibited the study of the Mishnah, as well as the denial of resurrection, the last judgment, and the creation of angels.

What they call the Mishnah, ... we prohibit entirely, for it is not included among the Holy Books, nor was it handed down from above by the prophets, but it is an invention of men in their chatter, exclusively of earthly origin and having in it nothing of the divine.... And if there are some people among them who shall attempt to introduce ungodly nonsense, denying either the resurrection or the last judgment or that the angels exist as God's work and creation, we want these people expelled from all places, and that no word of blasphemy of this kind and absolutely erring from that knowledge of God shall be spoken. (A.L.)

Criticism by Intellectuals: The Charges

The Egyptian Version of the Exodus

MANETHO (THIRD CENTURY BCE)

BIBLIOGRAPHY

William G. Waddell, ed., *Manetho* (1940, LCL), vii–xiv.
Tcherikover (1959), 361–4.
John Van Seeters, *The Hyksos: A New Investigation* (1966), 121–6.
Gager (1972), 113–18.
Stern, vol. 1 (1974), 62–86.
Doron Mendels, "The Polemical Character of Manetho's *Aegyptiaca*," in Herman Verdin, Guido Schepens, Eugenie de Keyser, eds, *Purposes of History. Studies in Greek Historiography from the 4th to the 2nd Centuries* BC (*Proceedings of the International Colloquium Leuven 24–26 May 1988*), (1990), 91–110.
Sterling (1992), 117–35.

Manetho, an Egyptian priest who lived in the third century BCE, in effect presents an answer to the biblical account of the Exodus. Fragments of his Egyptian history, the first such systematic history to be written in Greek, have been preserved by Josephus (though some scholars deny that these are really by Manetho), who replies to it in his essay *Against Apion*.

10.64 Manetho, *History of Egypt*, cited by Josephus, *Against Apion* 1.75–6, 82, 85–90

In the fragment cited below, Manetho seems to identify the Hyksos, who had conquered Egypt, with the Hebrews, since he makes them the founders of Jerusalem.

Tutimaeus. In his reign, I know not why, a blast of God's displeasure broke upon us. A people of ignoble origin from the east, whose coming was unforeseen, had the audacity to invade the country, which they mastered by main force without difficulty or even a battle. Having overpowered the chiefs, they then savagely burnt the cities, razed the temples of the gods to the ground, and treated the whole native population with the utmost cruelty, massacring some, and carrying off the wives and children of others into slavery.... Their race bore the generic name of Hyksos, which means 'king-shepherds.'...

Then the kings of the Thebaid and of the rest of Egypt rose in revolt against the shepherds, and a great war broke out, which was of long duration. Under a king named Misphragmouthosis, the shepherds, he says, were defeated, driven out of all the rest of Egypt, and confined to a place called Auaris, containing ten thousand *arourae*. The shepherds, according to Manetho, enclosed the whole of this area with a great strong wall, in order to secure all their possessions and spoils. Thoummosis, the son of Misphragmouthosis [he continues], invested the walls with an army of 480,000 men, and endeavored to reduce them to submission by siege. Despairing of achieving his object, he concluded a treaty under which they were all to evacuate Egypt and go whither they would unmolested. Under these terms no fewer than two hundred and forty thousand, entire households with their possessions, left Egypt and traversed the desert to Syria. Then, terrified by the might of the Assyrians, who at that time were masters of Asia, they built a city in the country now called Judaea, capable of accommodating their vast company, and gave it the name of Jerusalem. (LCL)

10.65 Manetho, *History of Egypt*, cited by Josephus, *Against Apion* 1.232–43, 248–50

In this fragment Manetho asserts that the Hebrews were actually expelled from Egypt by the pharaoh in order to purge the country of lepers and other polluted persons, and that under the leadership of a certain Osarsiph, whom he identifes with Moses, they subdued the Egyptians with the utmost cruelty. Osarsiph is said to have deliberately promulgated a code of laws and customs in direct contradiction to those of the Egyptians and to have joined with the Hyksos in an attack upon the Egyptians.

This king [Amenophis], he [Manetho] states, wishing to be granted, like Or, one of his predecessors on the throne, a vision of the gods, communicated his desire to his namesake, Amenophis, son of Paapis, whose wisdom and knowledge of the future were regarded as marks of divinity. This namesake replied that he would be able to see the gods if he purged the entire country of lepers and other polluted persons. Delighted at hearing this, the king collected all the maimed people in Egypt, numbering 80,000, and sent them to work in the stone-quarries on the east of the Nile, segregated from the rest of the Egyptians. They included, he adds, some of the learned priests, who were afflicted with leprosy. Then this wise seer Amenophis was seized with a fear that he would draw down the wrath of the gods on himself and the king if the violence done to these men were detected; and he added a prediction that the polluted people would find certain allies who would become masters of Egypt for thirteen years. He did not venture to tell this himself to the king, but left a complete statement in writing, and then put an end to himself. The king was greatly disheartened.

Then Manetho proceeds (I quote his actual words):

When the men in the stone-quarries had continued long in misery, the king acceded to their request to assign them for habitation and protection the abandoned city of the shepherds, called Auaris, and according to an ancient theological tradition dedicated to Typhon.[38] Thither they went; and, having now a place to serve as a base for revolt, they appointed as their leader one of the priests of Heliopolis called Osarsiph,[39] and swore to obey all his orders.

By his first law he ordained that they should not worship the gods nor abstain from the flesh of any of the animals held in special reverence in Egypt, but should kill and consume them all, and that they should have no connection with any save members of their own confederacy. After laying down these and a multitude of other laws, absolutely opposed to Egyptian custom, he ordered all hands to repair the city walls and make ready for war with King Amenophis. Then, in concert with other priests and polluted persons like himself, he sent an embassy to the shepherds, who had been expelled by Tethmosis, in the city called Jerusalem, setting out the position of himself and his outraged companions, and inviting them to join in a united expedition against Egypt. He undertook to escort them first to their ancestral home at Auaris, to provide abundant supplies for their multitudes, to fight for them when the moment came, and without difficulty to reduce the country to submission. The shepherds, delighted with the idea, all eagerly set off in a body numbering 200,000 men, and soon reached Auaris. . . .

The Solymites [i.e., the Hyksos] came down with the polluted Egyptians and treated the inhabitants in so sacrilegious a manner that the regime of the shepherds seemed like a golden age to those who

38. Typhon is the Egyptian god Set who is said to have murdered his brother Osiris and who is regarded as the author of all evil.

39. Though Osarsiph is later identified by Manetho with Moses, the name looks like an Egyptian version of Joseph, with the name Osiris being substituted for Io, which was taken to be the name of the Jewish God.

now beheld the impieties of their present enemies. Not only did they set cities and villages on fire, not only did they pillage the temples and mutilate the images of the gods, but, not content with that, they habitually used the very sanctuaries as kitchens for roasting the venerated sacred animals, and forced the priests and prophets to slaughter them and cut their throats, and then turned them out naked. It is said that the priest who gave them a constitution and code of laws was a native of Heliopolis, named Osarsiph after the Heliopolitan god Osiris, and that when he went over to this people he changed his name and was called Moses. (LCL)

LYSIMACHUS (PERHAPS SECOND OR FIRST CENTURY BCE)

BIBLIOGRAPHY

Gager (1972), 118–20.
Stern, vol. 1 (1974), 382–8.

> *10.66* Lysimachus, *History of Egypt*, cited by Josephus, *Against Apion* 1.305–11

Lysimachus, whose dates are unknown (perhaps second or first century BCE), is an Egyptian who, like Manetho, wrote in Greek what was, in effect, a viciously anti-Jewish Egyptian version of the Exodus, namely that those Jews who had been afflicted with leprosy and scurvy were drowned, while the others were exposed in the desert to perish. Under the leadership of Moses, who taught them to maltreat others, they crossed the desert and founded Jerusalem.

In the reign of Bocchoris,[40] king of Egypt, the Jewish people, afflicted with leprosy, scurvy, and other diseases, took refuge in the sanctuaries and lived as beggars. Since very many people had succumbed to illness, a dearth occurred in Egypt. Bocchoris, king of the Egyptians, then sent men to consult the oracle of Ammon about the dearth. The god responded with instructions to cleanse the temples of impure and impious persons, to expel them from the sanctuaries into the desert, to drown those afflicted with leprosy and scurvy, as the sun was displeased that such persons should live, and to purify the sanctuaries; then the land would yield crops.

On receiving these oracular responses, Bocchoris summoned the priests and sacrificial attendants, and ordered them to round up the unclean persons and hand them over to soldiers to be conducted into the desert, and to wrap the lepers in rolls of lead and cast them into the sea. When the lepers and those afflicted with scurvy were drowned, the others were assembled and exposed in the desert to perish.

When they had assembled, they deliberated about themselves. At nightfall, lighting a bonfire and torches, they mounted guard, and on the following night fasted and begged the gods to save them. The next day a certain Moses counseled them to take a risk and follow a straight road until they reached inhabited places. And he instructed them to

---

40. A pharaoh of the late eighth century BCE.

show goodwill to no man, to give not the best counsel but the worst, and to destroy temples and altars of the gods that they came upon. The others agreeing, they proceeded to do what had been decided. They crossed the desert, and after great suffering reached inhabited country. They maltreated the people, and plundered and set fire to the temples, until they came to the country now called Judaea, where they founded a city and dwelled. This town was called Hierosyla[41] because of their disposition. Later, when they had risen to power, they changed the name, to avoid the reproachful imputation, and called the city Hierosolyma (Jerusalem) and themselves Hierosolymites. (M.R.)

APION (FIRST HALF OF THE FIRST CENTURY CE)

BIBLIOGRAPHY

Gager (1972), 122–4.
Stern, vol. 1 (1974), 389–416.
Louis H. Feldman, "Pro-Jewish Intimations in Anti-Jewish Remarks Cited in Josephus' *Against Apion*," *JQR* 78 (1987–8), 187–251.

Apion was an Egyptian who wrote a history of Egypt in Greek. He was noted as a scholar, particularly as a commentator on Homer. He represented the Greeks of Alexandria in the charges that they brought against the Jews before the Emperor Gaius Caligula.

10.67 Apion, *History of Egypt*, cited by Josephus, *Against Apion* 2.10, 15, 17, 20–1, 25

Like Manetho and Lysimachus, Apion presents an Egyptian version of the Exodus, namely that the Jews were expelled because they were diseased. He gives an anti-Jewish etymology of the word *sabbath*. He says that Moses, after ascending a mountain called Sinai and remaining there concealed for forty days, gave the Jews their laws.

In the third book of his *History of Egypt* he [Apion] makes the following statement: 'Moses, as I have heard from old people in Egypt, was a native of Heliopolis, who, being pledged to the customs of his country, erected prayer-houses, open to the air, in the various precincts of the city, all facing eastwards, such being the orientation also of Heliopolis. . . .'

On the question of the date which he assigns to the exodus of the lepers, the blind and the lame under Moses' leadership, we shall find, I imagine, this accurate grammarian in perfect agreement with previous writers. . . .

Apion, however, the surest authority of all, precisely dates the exodus in the seventh Olympiad, and in the first year of that Olympiad [752 BCE], the year in which, according to him, the Phoenicians founded Carthage. . . .

After stating that the fugitives numbered 110,000, in which imaginary figure he agrees with Lysimachus, he [Apion] gives an astonishing and plausible explanation of the etymology of the word 'sabbath'!

41. I.e., (town of) temple-robbers.

After a six days' march, he says, they developed tumors in the groin, and that was why after safely reaching the country now called Judaea, they rested on the seventh day, and called that day *sabbaton*, preserving the Egyptian terminology; for disease of the groin in Egypt is called *sabbatosis*. . . .

This astonishing Apion, after stating that they reached Judaea in six days tells us elsewhere that Moses went up into the mountain called Sinai, which lies between Egypt and Arabia, remained in concealment there for forty days, and then descended and gave the Jews their laws. (LCL)

> *10.68* Apion, *History of Egypt*, cited by Eusebius, *Preparation for the Gospel* 10.10.16

In the fragment cited below Apion concedes antiquity to the Jews, noting, as he does, that they left Egypt in the time of Inachus, who is contemporary with the Titans, the second generation of the gods.

Apion, the son of Poseidonius, the most inquisitive of grammarians, in his book *Against the Jews*, which constitutes the fourth book of his *History*, writes that the Jews under the leadership of Moses left in the time of Inachus, the king of Argos, who was a contemporary of Amosis, king of Egypt.[42] (M.S.)

CHAEREMON (FIRST CENTURY CE)

BIBLIOGRAPHY

Gager (1972), 120–2.
Stern, vol. 1 (1974), 417–21.

Chaeremon, an Egyptian priest, is also said to have been a Stoic. He is reported to have been a teacher of Nero and a member of the delegation of Alexandrian Greeks who appeared before the Roman Emperor Claudius.

> *10.69* Chaeremon, *History of Egypt*, cited by Josephus, *Against Apion* 1.288–92

Like Manetho, Lysimachus, and Apion, Chaeremon asserts that the Jews were expelled from Egypt because they were contaminated. Their leaders are said to have been Moses and Joseph. Upon being reinforced they marched upon Egypt; but they were later driven into Syria by the pharaoh's son.

42. This would actually concede tremendous antiquity to the Jews, inasmuch as Inachus was the son of Oceanus and Tethys, both of whom were Titans, and hence of the second generation of the Greek gods. Inachus' daughter, Io, who was impregnated by Zeus, became the ancestress of Cadmus and through him of the god Dionysus and of the hero Oedipus, as well as the ancestress of Europa and through her of the legendary Cretan lawgiver Minos and finally, in the thirteenth generation, through her descendants Aegyptus and Danaus, of the great hero Heracles.

This writer [Chaeremon] likewise professes to write the history of Egypt, and agrees with Manetho in giving the names of Amenophis and Ramesses to the king and his son. He then proceeds to state that Isis[43] appeared to Amenophis in his sleep, and reproached him for the destruction of her temple in war-time. The sacred scribe Phritobautes told him that, if he purged Egypt of its contaminated population, he might cease to be alarmed. The king thereupon collected 250,000 afflicted persons and banished them from the country. Their leaders were scribes, Moses and another sacred scribe – Joseph! Their Egyptian names were Tisithen (for Moses) and Peteseph (Joseph). The exiles on reaching Pelusium fell in with a body of 380,000 persons, left there by Amenophis, who had refused them permission to cross the Egyptian frontier. With these the exiles concluded an alliance and marched upon Egypt. Amenophis, without waiting for their attack, fled to Ethiopia, leaving his wife pregnant. Concealing herself in some caverns she gave birth to a son named Ramesses, who, on reaching manhood, drove the Jews, to the number of about 200,000, into Syria, and brought home his father Amenophis from Ethiopia. (LCL)

POMPEIUS TROGUS (END OF THE FIRST CENTURY BCE TO THE BEGINNING OF THE FIRST CENTURY CE)

BIBLIOGRAPHY

Gager (1972), 48–56.
Stern, vol. 1 (1974), 332–43.

Pompeius Trogus, who wrote in Latin, composed, as a companion to Livy's *History of Rome*, a history dealing with the peoples outside of Italy. The work is lost except for an epitome by a certain Justin, who lived in the third or fourth century CE. Trogus was apparently dependent solely upon Greek authors, including a Jewish source, a Damascene source, and a pagan source, the last of which included the traditional account of the expulsion of the diseased Israelites under the leadership of Moses.

> 10.70 Pompeius Trogus, *Philippic Histories* 36, summarized by Justin (third or fourth century CE), *Epitome* 2.12–13

Trogus here presents the traditional account of the expulsion of the diseased Jews under the leadership of Moses, who stole the sacred utensils of the Egyptians.

The Egyptians, being troubled with scabies and leprosy and warned by an oracle, expelled him [Moses], with those who had the disease, out of Egypt, that the distemper might not spread among a greater number. Becoming leader, accordingly, of the exiles, he carried off by stealth the sacred utensils of the Egyptians, who, trying to recover them by force of arms, were compelled by tempests to return home. (M.S.)

43. Isis was the most important Egyptian goddess, sister and wife of Osiris.

TACITUS (*ca.* 56–120 CE)

BIBLIOGRAPHY

Gager (1972), 127–8.

Stern, vol. 2 (1980), 1–93.

Bilhah Wardy, "Tacitus on the Origin and Tradition of the Jewish People," in her "Jewish Religion in Pagan Literature during the Late Republic and Early Empire," *ANRW* 2.19.1 (1979), 613–31.

Frederick F. Bruce, "Tacitus on Jewish History," *JSS* 29 (1984), 33–44.

Johanan [Hans] Lewy, "Tacitus on the Origin and Manners of the Jews" (trans. and adapted from the Hebrew original by A. Rubinstein), *Binah* 1 (1989), 15–46.

Louis H. Feldman, "Pro-Jewish Intimations in Tacitus' Account of Jewish Origins," *REJ* 150 (1991), 331–60.

Tacitus, the celebrated Roman historian, has the most detailed account of the history and religion of the Jews to be found in all of pagan classical literature. Though claiming to write without prejudice, he writes with venom about the Jews, basing himself, presumably, upon Alexandrian Greek writers such as Lysimachus.

10.71 Tacitus, *Histories* 5.3.1

According to Tacitus, there is general agreement that the Jews were expelled from Egypt into the desert, since they were said to be responsible for a plague. Their leader, Moses, convinced them to trust only to themselves.

Most authors agree that once during a plague in Egypt, which caused bodily disfigurement, King Bocchoris approached the oracle of Ammon and asked for a remedy, whereupon he was told to purge his kingdom and to transport this race into other lands, since it was hateful to the gods. So the crowd was searched out and gathered together; then, being abandoned in the desert, while all others lay idle and weeping, one only of the exiles, Moses by name, warned them not to hope for help from gods or men; for they were deserted by both; but to trust to themselves, regarding as a guide sent from heaven the one whose assistance should first give them escape from their present distress. They agreed, and then set out on their journey in utter ignorance, but trusting to chance. (LCL)

Political Charges

LACK OF PATRIOTISM

10.72 Apion (first half of the first century CE), *History of Egypt*, cited by Josephus, *Against Apion* 2.65–73, 75–7

Apion (there being no separation of religion and state) argues that the Jews cannot be citizens inasmuch as they do not set up statues of the emperors and do not worship the same gods as the Alexandrians do. He also accuses the Jews of promoting sedition.

Apion says, 'Why then, if they are citizens, do they not worship the same gods as the Alexandrians do?' My reply is: Why do you, too, though you are Egyptians, wage with one another bitter and irreconcilable battles regarding religion? Indeed, is this not why we do not call you all Egyptians, or even collectively men, since you breed with so much care animals that are hostile to humans, and worship them? We, on the other hand, can be seen to be one and the same people. Since, however, among you Egyptians there are such wide differences of opinion, why should you be surprised at us, a people who came to Alexandria from another country, if we abide by the laws established from the beginning concerning this matter?

He accuses us also of causing sedition. But, if he is correct in bringing this accusation against the Jews of Alexandria, why does he blame all of us living everywhere because we are known to be a harmonious people? Moreover, these 'promoters of sedition,' as anyone can discover, have been citizens of Alexandria like Apion. The Greeks and Macedonians, so long as they possessed citizenship, never fomented sedition against us, but granted us our ancient worship. But when, owing to the disorders of the times, their numbers were increased by a host of Egyptians, sedition also became chronic. Our people, however, remained unmixed. It is Alexandrians, then, who originated this disturbance, because the people, possessing neither the Macedonians' strength of character, nor the Greeks' intelligence, universally adopted the evil habits of the Egyptians, and indulged their hostility toward us. . . .

The majority of them [being Egyptians] hold the rights of that citizenship improperly. . . . We, on the contrary, were brought into the city by Alexander, our privileges were extended by the kings, and the Romans deemed it proper to safeguard them.

And so Apion has attempted to denounce us on the ground that we do not set up statues of the emperors – as if they were ignorant of this, or needed Apion to defend them! . . . Our legislator . . . forbade the making of images of any living creature, and much more so of God. . . . He did not, however, prohibit the payment of other types of honors, secondary to that paid to God, in honoring worthy men, honors which we do confer upon the emperors and the people of Rome. For them we offer sacrifices continually, and we perform these ceremonies daily, at the common expense of all the Jews. (M.R.)

ALLEGED UNDUE INFLUENCE OF THE JEWS

BIBLIOGRAPHY

Anthony J. Marshall, "Flaccus and the Jews of Asia – Cicero *Pro Flacco* 28:67–9," *Phoenix* 29 (1975), 139–54.

10.73 Cicero, *Defense of Flaccus* 28.66 (59 BCE)

Flaccus, the Roman governor of the province of Asia (Minor), was accused of confiscating the money which the Jews had collected to be sent to the Temple in Jerusalem. Laelius was the prosecutor, acting on behalf of the cities of the province. Cicero was the lawyer for Flaccus.

Cicero here alludes to the alleged Jewish influence in informal assemblies.

There follows the odium that is attached to Jewish gold.[44] This is no doubt the reason why this case is being tried not far from the Aurelian Steps.[45] You procured this place and that crowd, Laelius, for this trial. You know what a big crowd it is, how they stick together, how influential they are in informal assemblies. So I will speak in a low voice so that only the jurors may hear; for those are not wanting who would incite them against me and against every respectable man. I shall not help them to do this more easily. (LCL)

ACTS OF THE ALEXANDRIAN MARTYRS

BIBLIOGRAPHY

Ernst von Dobschütz, "Jews and Antisemites in Ancient Alexandria," *AJT* 8 (1904), 728–55.
Herbert A. Musurillo, "The Pagan Acts of the Martyrs," *TS* 10 (1949), 555–64.
Harold Idris Bell, "The Acts of the Alexandrines," *JJP* 4 (1950), 19–42.
Herbert A. Musurillo, ed., *The Acts of the Pagan Martyrs – Acta Alexandrinorum* (1954).
Victor A. Tcherikover, "'The Jewish Question' in Alexandria," in *CPJ*, vol. 2 (1960), 25–107.
Kasher (1985), 342–5.
Modrzejewski (1995), 175–83.

10.74 *CPJ*, no. 156 (middle of the second or early third century CE)

A number of papyrus fragments found in Egypt purport to be the accounts of trials of Alexandrian non-Jews before the Roman emperors, from the time of Caligula (37–41 CE) to that of Commodus (180–92 CE). Actually, the form is a literary disguise, and the main goal of the work is to ridicule the Roman emperors. The fragmentary papyrus below deals with a lawsuit by Isidoros, the head of the gymnasium of Alexandria, and his friend Lampon against Agrippa I, king of Judaea, brought before the Emperor Claudius *ca.* 41 CE. They also accuse the Jews generally of sedition. In the end Jewish 'influence' prevailed, and the prosecutors Isidoros and Lampon not only failed but were found guilty and put to death.

Tarquinius a senator ... to the Emperor ... for the native city ... Aviola a senator ... therefore I ask ... the Council. ... The Alexandrian envoys were summoned and the Emperor postponed their hearing until the following day. The fifth day of Pachon, in the [first?] year of Claudius Caesar Augustus. ... The sixth day of Pachon: the second day. Claudius Caesar Augustus hears the case of Isidoros, gymnasiarch of Alexandria versus King Agrippa in the ... gardens. With him sat twenty senators

---

44. Flaccus, the Roman governor of Asia Minor, had been charged with seizing the gold which the Jews had collected to be sent to the Temple in Jerusalem.
45. The meetings of the popular Roman assemblies, in which the Jews also participated, took place near the Aurelian Steps.

[and in addition to these] sixteen men of consular rank, the women of the court also attending ... Isidoros' trial.

Isidoros was the first to speak: 'My Lord Caesar, I beseech you to listen to my account of my native city's sufferings.'

The emperor: 'I shall grant you this day.'

All the senators who were sitting as assessors agreed with this, knowing the kind of man Isidoros was.

Claudius Caesar: 'Say nothing [God forbid it!][?] against my friend. You have already done away with two of my friends, Theon the exegete and Naevius, prefect of Egypt and prefect of the praetorian guard at Rome; and now you prosecute this man.'

Isidoros: 'My Lord Caesar, what do you care for a twopenny-halfpenny Jew like Agrippa?'

Claudius Caesar: 'What? You are the most insolent of men to speak. . . .'

Isidoros: '. . . I will not deny . . . be quiet . . . beaten. Olympian Caesar . . .' . . . about Augustus . . . I am brought here, a gymnasiarch of Alexandria, fifty-six years old, a Greek . . . an orator, with right hand . . . he threw off his cloak . . . and said: 'One must not. . . .'

Claudius Caesar: '. . . Isidoros, against Theon . . . neither Rome nor Alexandria. . . .'

Isidoros: '. . . a gymnasiarch of Alexandria . . . by nature . . . seven temples of Augustus . . . not allow me . . . being taken away in the robes of a gymnasiarch.'

Claudius Caesar: 'Do not say anything, Isidoros, Isidoros, – God forbid! – anything against my friend. . . .'

Isidoros: 'My Lord Augustus, with regard to your interests, Balbillos indeed speaks well. But to you, Agrippa, I wish to retort in connection with the points you bring up about the Jews. I accuse them of wishing to stir up the entire world. . . . We must consider every detail in order to judge the whole people. They are not of the same nature as the Alexandrians, but live rather after the fashion of the Egyptians. Are they not on a level with those who pay the poll-tax?'

Agrippa: 'The Egyptians have had taxes levied on them by their rulers. . . . But no one has imposed tributes on the Jews.'

Balbillos: 'Look to what extremes of insolence either his god or. . . . .'

Lampon to Isidoros: 'I have looked upon death. . . .'

Claudius Caesar: 'Isidoros, you have killed many friends of mine.'

Isidoros: 'I merely fulfilled the wish of the king then ruling. So too I should be willing to denounce anyone you wish.'

Claudius Caesar: 'Isidoros, you are really the son of a girl-musician.'

Isidoros: 'I am neither a slave nor a girl-musician's son but gymnasiarch of the glorious city of Alexandria. But you are the cast-off son of the Jewess Salome! And therefore. . . .'

Lampon said to Isidoros: 'We might as well give in to a crazy emperor.'

Claudius Caesar: 'Those whom I told [to carry out] the execution of Isidoros and Lampon. . . .' (*CPJ*)

Religious Charges

THEOLOGY

BIBLIOGRAPHY

Feldman (1993), 149–53.

10.75 Celsus the Philosopher (second century CE), *The True Doctrine*, cited by Origen, *Against Celsus* 6.28, 42

Celsus, an eclectic philosopher of whom little is known, here attacks the Jewish view of God, asserting that a God that cursed the serpent for imparting the knowledge of good and evil Himself deserves to be cursed. He likewise attacks the Jewish concept of Satan as God's opponent.

That he [Celsus] is confusing the issue is shown when he gives the reason why the God of the Mosaic cosmogony is said to be accursed. For he says that 'such a God even deserves to be cursed in the opinion of those who hold this view of him, because he cursed the serpent which imparted to the first men knowledge of good and evil. . . .'

'That they make some quite blasphemous errors is also shown by his example of their utter ignorance, which has similarly led them to depart from the true meaning of the divine enigmas, when they make a being opposed to God; devil and, in the Hebrews' tongue, Satanas are the names which they give to this same being. At all events these notions are entirely of mortal origin, and it is blasphemy to say that when the greatest God indeed wishes to confer some benefit upon men, he has a power which is opposed to Him, and so is unable to do it.' (H.C.)

10.76 Julian (331–63 CE), *Against the Galileans* 155C–E, 161B, 168B–C

The Emperor Julian, though raised as a Christian, became an adherent of paganism. He is particularly bitter in his attack on Christianity but, while criticizing Judaism for its hostility to other religions, he praises the Jews' loyalty to their ancestral ways and, in particular, for their view of the importance of sacrificial worship. In the passage below he criticizes the Jewish view of a jealous God, regarding it as inappropriate to ascribe such a quality to God. Moreover, he contrasts the anger of God with the mildness of the Greek lawgivers Lycurgus and Solon.

But as for the commandment 'Thou shalt not worship other gods,' to this surely he adds a terrible libel upon God. 'For I am a jealous God' [Exod 20:5], he says, and in another place again [Deut 4:24], 'Our God is a consuming fire.' Then if a man is jealous and envious you think him blameworthy, whereas if God is called jealous you think it a divine quality? And yet, how is it reasonable to speak falsely of God in a matter that is so evident? For if he is indeed jealous, then against his will are all other gods worshipped, and against his will do all the remaining nations worship their gods. Then how is it that he did not himself restrain them, if he is so jealous and does not wish that the others should be worshipped, but only himself? Can it be that he was not able to do so, or did he not wish even from the beginning to prevent the other gods also from being worshipped? However, the first explanation is impious, to say, I mean, that he was unable; and the second is in accordance with what we do ourselves. Lay aside this nonsense, and do not draw down on yourselves such terrible blasphemy. . . .

For if the anger of even one hero or unimportant demon is hard to bear for whole countries and cities, who could have endured the wrath of so mighty a God, whether it were directed against demons or angels or mankind? . . . It is worthwhile to compare his behavior with the mildness of Lycurgus and the forbearance of Solon, or the kindness and benevolence of the Romans towards transgressors. (LCL)

> *10.77* Rutilius Namatianus (beginning of the fifth century CE), *On His Return* 1.393–4

Rutulius Namatianus, a Roman poet, born in Gaul, because of an unpleasant experience with a Jew in charge of fish-ponds, rails against the Jews, charging that the Jewish religion is utterly irrational.

The other wild ravings from their lying bazaar methinks not even a child in his sleep could believe. (LCL)

IMPIETY

> *10.78* Aelius Aristides (second century CE), *Orations* 46: *On the Quattuorviri* 309

The charge of impiety, like the charge of atheism that is leveled against the Jews, arises from their failure to worship the gods of the state, just as it arose against Socrates in the fifth century BCE for the same reason.

The sign of their [the people who live in Palestine] impiety consists in that they do not recognize their betters [i.e., believe in gods], and these also have in some way seceded from the Greeks or rather from all the better people. (M.S.)

WORSHIP OF AN ASS

> *10.79* Mnaseas of Patara (*ca.* 200 BCE), cited by Josephus, *Against Apion* 2.112–14

Mnaseas of Patara (in Asia Minor), said to have been a pupil of the great polymath Eratosthenes, in a lost work, from which the following fragment comes, refers to the ass-worship of the Jews and to their excessive credulity. This charge of ass-worship was later attached to the Christians. If, as seems likely, the charge arose in Egypt, it shows the great hostility toward the Jews, inasmuch as the ass was connected with Typhon-Seth, who was said to have murdered Osiris.

[Mnaseas], according to Apion, relates that in the course of a long war between the Jews and the Idumaeans, an inhabitant of an Idumaean city, called Dorii,[46] who worshipped Apollo and bore (so we are told)

---

46. On the coast of Palestine, 10 miles north of Caesarea.

the name of Zabidus, came out to the Jews and promised to deliver into their hands Apollo, the god of his city, who would visit our Temple if they all took their departure. The Jews all believed him; whereupon Zabidus constructed an apparatus of wood, inserted in it three rows of lamps, and put it over his person. Thus arrayed he walked about, presenting the appearance to distant onlookers of stars perambulating the earth. Astounded at this amazing spectacle, the Jews kept their distance, in perfect silence. Meanwhile, Zabidus stealthily passed into the sanctuary, snatched up the golden head of the pack-ass (as he facetiously calls it), and made off post-haste to Dora.[47] (LCL)

> 10.80 Apion (first half of the first century CE), *History of Egypt*, cited by Josephus, *Against Apion* 2.80

Apion, like Mnaseas, asserts that the Jews kept an ass's head in the Temple and worshipped it. He claims that Antiochus Epiphanes discovered it when he despoiled the Temple.

Within this sanctuary [the Temple] Apion has the effrontery to assert that the Jews kept an ass's head, worshipping that animal and deeming it worthy of the deepest reverence; the fact was disclosed, he maintains, on the occasion of the spoliation of the Temple by Antiochus Epiphanes, when the head, made of gold and worth a high price, was discovered. (LCL)

> 10.81 Plutarch (*ca.* 46–120 CE), *On Isis and Osiris* 31

In the following passage Plutarch, though he does not say explicitly that the Jews worshipped an ass, does connect them with Typhon, the Egyptian god who is the author of all evil, who is said to have escaped on the back of an ass.

But those who relate that Typhon's flight from the battle was made on the back of an ass and lasted for seven days, and that after he had made his escape, he became the father of sons, Hierosolymus and Judaeus, are manifestly, as the very names show, attempting to draw Jewish traditions into legend.[48] (LCL)

> 10.82 Tacitus (*ca.* 56–120 CE), *Histories* 5.4.2

Though elsewhere (*Histories* 5.5.4), and indeed very shortly after the passage below, Tacitus explicitly states that the Jews conceive of one god only, and that with the mind alone, he here states that the Jews worship the ass because it was under that animal's guidance that they managed to end their wandering in the desert during the Exodus from Egypt.

They [the Jews] dedicated, in a shrine, a statue of that creature [the ass] whose guidance enabled them to put an end to their wandering [in the desert after the Exodus from Egypt] and thirst. (LCL)

---

47. A city in Phoenicia on the Mediterranean Sea.
48. This account, which attempts to explain the Jewish reverence for the ass, is clearly anti-Jewish, inasmuch as Typhon was the Egyptian god Set who had murdered Osiris.

THE BIBLE

> *10.83* Celsus the Philosopher (second century CE), *The True Doctrine*, cited by Origen, *Against Celsus* 4.36, 41, 51, 71; 6.60, 61

In the passage below the pagan philosopher Celsus ridicules the biblical accounts of the six days of creation, the creation of Adam and Eve, the role of the serpent, the Flood, and divine anthropomorphisms.

'They [the Jews] composed a most improbable and crude history that a man was formed by the hands of God and given breath, that a woman was formed out of his side, that God gave commands, and that a serpent opposed them and even proved superior to the ordinances of God – a legend which they expound to old women, most impiously making God into a weakling right from the beginning, and incapable of persuading even one man whom He had formed. . . .

'They then tell of a flood and a prodigious ark holding everything inside it, and that a dove and a crow were messengers. This is a debased and unscrupulous version of the story of Deucalion.[49] I suppose they did not expect that this would come to light, but simply recounted the myth to small children. . . .'

He [Celsus] seems to me [Origen] to have heard also that there are treatises containing allegories of the law. But if he had read them he would not have said: 'At any rate, the allegories that seem to have been written about them are far more shameful and preposterous than the myths, since they connect with some amazing and utterly senseless folly ideas that cannot by any means be made to fit. . . .'

He [Celsus] ridicules passages in the Bible which speak of God as though he were subject to human passions, in which angry utterances are spoken against the impious and threats against people who have sinned . . . . 'But far more silly is to have allotted certain days to the making of the world before days existed. For when the heaven had not yet been made or the earth yet fixed, or the sun borne round it, how could days exist? . . . 'After this [creation of the world], indeed, God, exactly like a bad workman, was worn out and needed a holiday to have a rest.' (H.C.)

> *10.84* Julian (331–63 CE), *Against the Galileans* 75A–B, 86A, 89A–B, 93D–E, 135A–B

In the passage below the Emperor Julian attacks improbabilities in the story of Adam and Eve and the serpent, claiming that the story hardly differs from the Greek myths. He regards it as foolish to suppose that God deprived the original humans of the power to distinguish between good and evil. He ridicules the account of building of the Tower of Babel, which he compares with the Greek myth of the giants piling three mountains one upon another.

Compare with them [the Greek myths] the Jewish doctrine, how the garden was planted by God and Adam was fashioned by Him, and

---

49. Because of his piety, according to Greek mythology, Deucalion, together with his wife Pyrrha, survived the flood sent by Zeus.

next, for Adam, woman came to be. For God said [Gen 2:18], 'It is not good that the man should be alone. Let us make him an help-mate like him.' Yet so far was she from helping him at all that she deceived him and was in part the cause of his and her own fall from their life of ease in the garden. This is wholly fabulous. For is it probable that God did not know that the being He was creating as a help-mate would prove to be not so much a blessing as a misfortune to him who received her? . . . Again, what sort of language are we to say that the serpent used when he talked with Eve? Was it the language of human beings? And in what do such legends as these differ from the myths that were invented by the Hellenes? . . .

Moreover, is it not excessively strange that God should deny to the human beings whom he had fashioned the power to distinguish between good and evil? What could be more foolish than a being unable to distinguish good from bad? For it is evident that he would not avoid the latter. I mean things evil, nor would he strive after the former, I mean things good. And in short, God refused to let man taste of wisdom, than which there could be nothing of more value for him. For that the power to distinguish between good and less good is the property of wisdom is evident surely even to the witless; . . . so that the serpent was a benefactor rather than a destroyer of the human race. Furthermore, their God must be called envious. For when he saw that man had attained to a share of wisdom, that he might not, God said, taste of the tree of life, he cast him out of the garden, saying in so many words [Gen 3:22], 'Behold, Adam has become one of us, because he knows good from bad; and now let him not put forth his hand and take also of the tree of life and eat and then live forever. . . .'

And then you demand that we should believe this account [the building of the Tower of Babel], while you yourselves disbelieve Homer's narrative of the Aloadae,[50] namely that they planned to set three mountains one on another, 'that so the heavens might be scaled' [*Odyssey* 11.316]. For my part, I say that this tale is almost as fabulous as the other. But if you accept the former, why in the name of the gods do you discredit Homer's fable? For I suppose that to men so ignorant as you I must say nothing about the fact that even if all men throughout the inhabited world ever employ one speech and one language, they will not be able to build a tower that will reach to the heavens, even though they should turn the whole earth into bricks. (LCL)

THE SYNAGOGUE

10.85 Artemidorus (second half of the second century CE), *Interpretation of Dreams* 3.53

Artemidorus of Ephesus wrote a work in five books, all of them extant, on the interpretation of dreams. In the passage below he associates dreams about synagogues with beggars.

50. The Aloadae are the mythical Otus and Ephialtes, who, according to Homer, were 9 fathoms (approximately 54 feet) tall and 9 cubits (approximately 13½ feet) broad. They threatened the Olympian gods with war and tried to pile Mount Pelion upon Mount Ossa upon Mount Olympus. However, Apollo destroyed them before their beards began to grow.

[In dreams] A synagogue and beggars and all people who ask for gifts, and such as arouse pity, and mendicants, foretell grief, anxiety and heartache to both men and women. For on the one hand, no one departs for a synagogue without a care, and, on the other, beggars who are very odious-looking and without resources and have nothing wholesome about them are an obstacle to every plan. (M.S.)

SUPERSTITIOUS OBSERVANCE OF THE SABBATH

BIBLIOGRAPHY

Hugh J. Michael, "The Jewish Sabbath in the Latin Classical Writers," *AJSL* 40 (1923–4), 117–24.

Robert Goldenberg, "The Jewish Sabbath in the Roman World up to the Time of Constantine the Great," *ANRW* 19.1 (1979), 414–47.

Louis H. Feldman, "The Enigma of Horace's Thirtieth Sabbath," *SCI* 10 (1989–90), 87–112.

Feldman (1993), 158–67.

Heather A. McKay, *Sabbath and Synagogue: The Question of Sabbath Worship in Ancient Judaism* (1994), 89–131.

The idea of a seven-day week and consequently of a seventh-day Sabbath on which work was prohibited seems to have been restricted to the Jews and must have seemed strange to non-Jews.[51] Meleager of Gadara, a town just east of the River Jordan, ridicules in one of his poems the prohibition of lighting fires on the Sabbath; in this he is followed by the poet Rutilius Namatianus. Strabo, together with several other writers, notably the historian Pompeius Trogus, the epigrammist Martial, and the biographer Suetonius, mistakenly views the Sabbath as a fast day, presumably confusing the fact that it was a day of abstention from work with the conception of a day of abstention from food. Seneca, followed by the poet Rutilius Namatianus, introduces the idea that the Jews are a lazy people inasmuch as they waste one seventh of their lives in idleness. The historian Tacitus and the biographer Suetonius are also aware of and ridicule the observance by Jews of the sabbatical year. The pagans, notably Tacitus, speculate as to the origin of the Sabbath, suggesting that it was the seventh day after they began the Exodus from Egypt or that it is in honor of Saturn, with whom the Jews are particularly identified. The picture that emerges, notably from such writers as the satirist Horace, the poet Ovid, the philosopher Seneca the Younger, the satirist Persius, the essayist Plutarch, and the philosopher Synesius, is of Jews universally and devotedly observing the laws of the Sabbath in all its particulars, especially abstention from work, and ushering in the Sabbath by the lighting of lamps and the drinking of wine.

---

51. The idea of a seven-day week was eventually, and gradually, adopted, apparently during the period of the early Roman Empire in the first century. See Francis H. Colson, *The Week: An Essay on the Origin and Development of the Seven-Day Cycle* (Cambridge University Press, 1926); John P. V. D. Balsdon, *Life and Leisure in Ancient Rome* (London: Bodley Head, 1969); John P. V. D. Balsdon, *Romans and Aliens* (London: Duckworth, 1979), 232–4.

10.86 Agatharchides (second century BCE), cited by Josephus, *Against Apion* 1.205, 208–11

The historian Agatharchides of Cnidus, who lived in Alexandria for some time, ridicules, in particular, the prohibition of bearing arms on the Sabbath. Because of this "superstition" King Ptolemy I of Egypt was able to capture Jerusalem. In this criticism Agatharchides is echoed by the military strategist Frontinus, by the antiquarian Plutarch, and by the historian Dio Cassius.

There is another writer whom I shall name without hesitation, although he mentions us only to ridicule our folly, as he regards it – I mean Agatharchides. . . . The following are his words: 'The people known as Jews, who inhabit the most strongly fortified of cities, called by the natives Jerusalem, have a custom of abstaining from work every seventh day; on those occasions they neither bear arms nor take any agricultural operations in hand, nor engage in any other form of public service, but pray with outstretched hands in the temples until the evening. Consequently, because the inhabitants, instead of protecting their city, persevered in their folly, Ptolemy, son of Lagus,[52] was allowed to enter with his army; the country was thus given over to a cruel master, and the defect of a practice enjoined by law was exposed. That experience has taught the whole world, except that nation, the lesson not to resort to dreams and traditional fancies about the law, until its difficulties are such as to baffle human reason.'[53] (LCL)

10.87 Meleager of Gadara (end of the second century BCE to the beginning of the first century BCE?), *Greek Anthology* 5.160

In this passage Meleager refers to the Sabbath as a time when the Jew is not permitted to ignite fires.

White-cheeked Demo, someone hath thee naked next him and is taking his delight, but my heart groans within me. If thy lover is some Sabbath-keeper no great wonder! Love burns hot even on cold Sabbaths. (LCL)

10.88 Horace (65–8 BCE), *Satires* 1.9.60–78

The poet is beset by a bore and hopes to be saved by the poet Aristius Fuscus, whom he happens to meet. He pretends to have something to discuss with him privately, but Fuscus does not get the hint and instead declares obscurely that he cannot discuss the matter since it is the thirtieth, a Sabbath of the Jews.

While he is thus running on, lo! there comes up Aristius Fuscus, a dear friend of mine, who knew the fellow right well. We halt. 'Whence come you? Whither go you?' he asks and answers. I begin to twitch his cloak

52. Ptolemy I Soter conquered Palestine four times – 320, 312, 302, 301 BCE. It is not clear to which of these conquests the passage refers; the most likely date is 302 BCE.
53. It was not until 167 BC that Mattathias the Hasmonean (1 Macc 2:41) issued his decree permitting self-defense on the Sabbath.

and squeeze his arms – they were quite unfeeling – nodding and winking hard for him to save me. The cruel joker laughed, pretending not to understand. I grew hot with anger. 'Surely you said that there was something you wanted to tell me in private.'

'I mind it well, but I'll tell you at a better time. Today is the thirtieth, a Sabbath.[54] Would you affront the circumcised Jews?'

'I have no scruples,' say I.

'But I have. I am a somewhat weaker brother, one of the many. You will pardon me; I'll talk another day.'

To think so black a sun as this has shone for me! The rascal runs away and leaves me under the knife.

It now chanced that the plaintiff came face to face with his opponent. 'Where go you, you scoundrel?' he loudly shouts, and to me 'May I call you as witness?' I offer my ear to touch. He hurries the man to court. There is shouting here and there, and on all sides a running to and fro. Thus was I saved by Apollo. (LCL)

10.89 Strabo (*ca.* 64 BCE–*ca.* 20 CE), *Geography* 16.2.40

In this passage Strabo notes that the Romans were able to capture Jerusalem on the Sabbath, since the Jews abstained from all work on that day.

Pompey seized the city [Jerusalem], it is said, after watching for the day of fasting,[55] when the Judaeans were abstaining from all work; he filled up the trench and threw ladders across it; moreover, he gave orders to raze all the walls and, so far as he could, destroyed the haunts of robbers and the treasure-holds of the tyrants. (LCL)

10.90 Pompeius Trogus (end of first century BCE to the beginning of the first century CE), *Philippic Histories* 36, summarized by Justin (third or fourth century), *Epitome* 2.14

Pompeius Trogus explains the origin of the celebration of the Sabbath as a fast-day as due to the fact that on that day the Jews' hunger and wanderings in the desert during the Exodus ended.

Moses, having reached Damascus, his ancestral home, took possession of Mount Sinai, on his arrival at which, after having suffered together

---

54. A number of theories have been presented to explain the reference to the thirtieth Sabbath: (1) the "Great Sabbath" (the Sabbath before Passover); (2) the first day of Passover itself; (3) the last day of Passover; (4) the special Sabbath known as Shabbath Parashath Ha-hodesh (the Sabbath preceding or falling on the first day of the month of Nisan); (5) the Festival of Pentecost; (6) the Day of Atonement; (7) the Feast of Tabernacles; (8) Parashath Tokhahah, the thirtieth in the weekly reading of the Pentateuch according to the set weekly cycle; (9) the last day of a period of fasting and penitence; (10) an oblique reference to the thirtieth year after the conquest of Judaea by Pompey in 63 BCE; (11) the thirtieth Sabbath after the assault on Jerusalem by Gaius Sosius, the Roman legate of Mark Antony in Syria in 37 BCE; (12) the thirtieth, a Sabbath, that is, the New Moon; (13) the reference is pure nonsense and this is the basis of the humor of the situation.

55. Strabo, like many other ancient writers, thought that the Sabbath was a fast day. The origin of this error, perhaps, lies in the word "abstention," referring to the prohibition of work on the Sabbath; but it may also mean "not working."

with his followers from a seven days' fast in the deserts of Arabia, he, for all time, consecrated the seventh day, which used to be called Sabbath by the custom of the nation, for a fast-day, because that day had ended at once their hunger and their wanderings. (M.S.)

10.91 Ovid (43 BCE–18 CE), *Art of Love* 1.75–6

Ovid here refers to the sacredness of the Sabbath to the Jews. His mention of Adonis in juxtaposition with this statement may have been influenced by the fact that the name Adonis is probably of Semitic origin, being derived from the word *Adon*, "lord."

Nor let Adonis, bewailed of Venus,[56] escape you, nor the seventh day that the Syrian Jew holds sacred. (LCL)

10.92 Ovid (43 BCE–18 CE), *Art of Love* 1.413–16

Ovid here suggests that the Sabbath, being a day when business is prohibited, is a fitting time to make love.

You may begin [to make love] on the day on which woeful Allia[57] flows stained with the blood of Latin wounds, or on that day, less fit for business, whereon returns the seventh-day feast that the Syrian of Palestine observes. (LCL)

10.93 Ovid (43 BCE–18 CE), *Remedies of Love* 217–20

Ovid, in giving advice as to how to fall out of love, urges escape to the country. He tells the lover not to let the Sabbath stop him from going.

Yet the less you wish to go, the more be sure of going; persist, and compel your unwilling feet to run. Hope not for rain, nor let foreign sabbath stay you, nor Allia well-known for its ill-luck. (LCL)

10.94 Seneca the Younger (*ca.* 4 BCE–65 CE), *Concerning Superstition*, cited by Augustine, *City of God* 6.11

Seneca here criticizes the Jewish observance of the Sabbath on two counts: (1) the loss of time through idleness; (2) the losses suffered because of failure to act.

Along with other superstitions of the civil theology Seneca also censures the sacred institutions of the Jews, especially the Sabbath. He declares that their practice is inexpedient, because by introducing one day of rest in every seven they lose in idleness almost a seventh of their life, and by failing to act in times of urgency they often suffer loss. (LCL)

---

56. The reference is to the youth Adonis with whom Aphrodite (Venus) fell in love and who was killed by a boar while hunting. Both Aphrodite and Persephone claimed him, whereupon Zeus decided that he should spend part of the year with each.

57. The Allia is a small river flowing into the Tiber about eleven miles from Rome. Inasmuch as the Romans were defeated there by the Gauls in 390 BCE, it became a symbol of bad luck.

10.95 Seneca the Younger (*ca.* 4 BCE–65 CE), *Moral Epistles* 95.47

Seneca here ridicules the Jewish practice of lighting lamps to usher in the Sabbath.

Precepts are commonly given as to how the gods should be worshipped. But let us forbid lamps to be lighted on the Sabbath, since the gods do not need light, neither do men take pleasure in soot. (LCL)

10.96 Persius (34–62 CE), *Satires* 5.179–84

Persius here alludes to the lighting of lamps and the drinking of wine to usher in the Sabbath, as well as to the customs of having flowers and eating fish.

But when the day of Herod[58] comes round, when the lamps wreathed with violets and ranged round the greasy window-sills have spat forth their thick clouds of smoke, when the floppy tunnies' tails are curled round the dishes of red ware,[59] and the white jars are swollen out with wine, you silently twitch your lips, turning pale at the sabbath of the circumcised. (LCL)

10.97 Frontinus (*ca.* 40–104 CE), *Stratagems* 2.1.17

Frontinus here refers to the Jews' abstention from work on the Sabbath and to the fact that Vespasian was able to take advantage of this in attacking Jerusalem.

The deified Augustus Vespasian attacked the Jews on the day of Saturn, a day on which it is sinful for them to do any business, and defeated them.[60] (M.S.)

10.98 Plutarch (*ca.* 46–120 CE), *On Superstition* 3

Plutarch regards the observance of the Sabbath as a superstitious practice.

'Greeks from barbarians finding evil ways!' [Euripides, *The Trojan Women* 764], because of superstition, such as smearing with mud, wallowing in filth, keeping of the Sabbath, casting oneself down with face to the ground, disgraceful besieging of the gods, and uncouth prostrations. (LCL)

10.99 Plutarch (*ca.* 46–120 CE), *On Superstition* 8

Plutarch criticizes the Jews for being so superstitious as to allow the enemy to capture their city due to their observance of the Sabbath as a day of rest from labor.

58. Most scholars interpret the day of Herod to refer to the Sabbath, owing to the fame of Herod and his descendants. Others view it as a reference to the day of Herod's accession or his birthday.

59. The allusion here is apparently to the Jewish custom of having fish at the Sabbath evening meal.

60. This statement contradicts the fact that the Jews apparently did fight on the Sabbath during the revolt against the Romans.

But the Jews, because it was the Sabbath day, sat in their places immovable, while the enemy were planting ladders against the walls and capturing the defenses, and they did not get up, but remained there, fast bound in the toils of superstition as in one great net.[61] (LCL)

10.100 Martial (*ca.* 40–104 CE), *Epigrams* 4.4

Here Martial alludes to the view, so often repeated by pagan writers, that Jews fast on the Sabbath.

The stench of the bed of a drained marsh, of the raw vapors of sulphur springs, . . . of the breath of fasting Sabbatarian women . . . – all these stenches would I prefer to your stench, Bassa! (LCL)

10.101 Tacitus (*ca.* 56–120 CE), *Histories* 5.4.3–4

Tacitus here ascribes the Jews' choice of the Sabbath as a day of rest to the fact that it was on that day that their toils ended during their Exodus from Egypt or, alternatively, to their honoring of Saturn. He ascribes their continuation of this practice as due to their laziness.

They [the Jews] say that they first chose to rest on the seventh day because that day ended their toils [during the sojourn in the desert after the Exodus from Egypt]; but after a time they were led by the charms of indolence to give over the seventh year as well to inactivity. Others say that this is done in honor of Saturn, whether it be that the primitive elements of their religion were given by the Idaeans, who, according to tradition, were expelled with Saturn and became the founders of the Jewish race, or is due to the fact that, of the seven planets that rule the fortunes of mankind, Saturn moves in the highest orbit and has the greatest potency; and that many of the heavenly bodies traverse their paths and courses in multiples of seven. (LCL)

10.102 Suetonius (*ca.* 69–*ca.* 150 CE), *Life of Augustus* 76.2

The faithfulness of Jews in observing the Sabbath was apparently proverbial, to judge from this passage in Suetonius. Like many other pagans, he thinks that the Sabbath is a day of fasting.

Not even a Jew, my dear Tiberius, fasts so scrupulously on his sabbaths as I [Augustus] have today; for it was not until after the first hour of the night that I ate two mouthfuls of bread in the bath before I began to be anointed.[62] (LCL)

10.103 Suetonius (*ca.* 69–*ca.* 150 CE), *Life of Tiberius* 32.2

Suetonius here alludes to the scrupulousness of the Jews in observing the Sabbath. He is also aware of the observance of the Sabbatical year.

---

61. Perhaps Plutarch is referring to the incident noted by Agatharchides when Ptolemy I was able to capture Jerusalem on the Sabbath because the Jews refused to do any work on that day even in self-protection.
62. This comes from a letter written by Augustus to Tiberius.

The grammarian Diogenes,[63] who used to lecture every Sabbath at Rhodes, would not admit Tiberius when he came to hear him on a different day, but sent a message by a common slave of his, putting him off to the seventh day. When this man waited before the Emperor's door at Rome to pay his respects, Tiberius took no further revenge than to bid him return seven years later.[64] (LCL)

10.104 Dio Cassius (*ca..* 160–230 CE), *Roman History* 37.16.2–4

It was the Jews' refusal to work on the Sabbath, even in self-defense, according to Dio Cassius, that permitted Pompey in the year 63 BCE to capture Jerusalem.

If they [the Jews] had continued defending it [the Temple] on all days alike, he [Pompey] could not have got possession of it. As it was, they made an exception of what are called the days of Saturn, and by doing no work at all on those days afforded the Romans an opportunity in this interval to batter down the wall. The latter, on learning of this superstitious awe of theirs, made no serious attempts the rest of the time, but on those days, when they came round in succession, assaulted most vigorously. Thus the defenders were captured on the day of Saturn, without making any defense, and all the wealth was plundered. (LCL)

10.105 Synesius (*ca.* 373–414 CE), *Letters* 5

Synesius, here describing a voyage of his from Alexandria to Cyrene, notes that the captain of the ship, together with at least six of the twelve members of the crew, were Jews. He is particularly angry because the captain, despite the fact that the ship was in serious trouble, let go of the rudder of the ship at the onset of the eve of the Sabbath. When, however, the danger reached the life-threatening stage, the captain returned to the helm.

Now it so happened that this [the day before the Sabbath] was the day on which the Jews make what they term the 'preparation'; and they reckon the night, together with the day following this, as a time during which it is not lawful to work with one's hands. They keep this day holy and apart from the others, and they pass it in rest from labor of all kinds. Our skipper accordingly let go the rudder from his hands the moment he guessed that the sun's rays had left the earth, and throwing himself prostrate [Sophocles, *Ajax* 1146] 'Allowed to trample on him what sailor so desired.' We, who at first could not understand why he was thus lying down, imagined that despair was the cause of it all. We rushed to his assistance and implored him not to give up the last hope yet. Indeed, the greatest waves were actually menacing the vessel, and the very deep was at war with itself. . . .

To people who are at sea in such a crisis, life may be said to hang by a thread only, for if our skipper proved at such a moment to be an

---

63. Apparently, this Diogenes was a Jew.
64. Apparently, an allusion to the Sabbatical year.

orthodox observer of the Mosaic law, what was life worth in the future? Indeed, we soon understood why he had abandoned the helm, for when we begged him to do his best to save the ship, he stolidly continued reading his roll. Despairing of persuasion, we finally attempted force, and one staunch soldier – for many Arabs of the cavalry were of our company – one staunch soldier, I say, drew his sword and threatened to behead the fellow on the spot if he did not resume control of the vessel. But the Maccabean in very deed was determined to persist in his observances. However, in the middle of the night he voluntarily returned to the helm. 'For now,' he said, 'we are clearly in danger of death, and the law commands.' (A.F.)

10.106 Rutilius Namatianus (beginning of the fifth century CE), *On His Return* 1.389–92

Rutilius Namatianus ridicules the Jews' observance of the Sabbath as a day of rest. The reference to the chill Sabbaths is an allusion to the fact that the Pentateuch forbids lighting of fires on that day.

Chill Sabbaths are after their own heart, yet their heart is chillier than their creed. Each seventh day is condemned to ignoble sloth, as 'twere an effeminate picture of the god fatigued. (LCL)

SUPERSTITION: DIETARY LAWS

BIBLIOGRAPHY

Robert M. Grant, "Dietary Laws among Pythagoreans, Jews and Christians," *HTR* 73 (1980), 299–310.
Feldman (1993), 167–70.

10.107 Strabo (*ca.* 64 BCE–*ca.* 20 CE), *Geography* 16.2.37

The historian and geographer Strabo seems to imply that the dietary laws date not from the time of Moses but from a later period.

[After Moses] superstitious men were appointed to the priesthood and then tyrannical people; and from superstition arose abstinence from flesh, from which it is their custom to abstain even today. (LCL)

10.108 Petronius (died *ca.* 65 CE), *Satyricon*, fragment 37

Petronius here refers to the abstention from pork as an important tenet of the Jews.

Even if a Jew should worship the divinity of pork and invoke the ears of the sky above, if, however, he did not submit to circumcision and removal of the foreskin skillfully, driven out by his own people he will emigrate from a Greek city and not be able to observe the law of fasting on the Sabbath. (M.R.)

10.109 Plutarch (46–120 CE), *Festal Questions* 4.4–5.3

Of the ancient writers who mention the Jews few refer to them more often than does Plutarch. The very fact that there is little that is new in his works and that he is a teacher rather than an innovator, makes them valuable as a restatement of the thinking that was current among intellectuals in the early Roman imperial period. His speculation about the reasons for the dietary laws, notably the abstention from pork (a practice that was particularly startling to the ancients, since pork was such a favorite food), is particularly interesting, especially since he suggests medical reasons and is not disrespectful, noting, as he does, that others have peculiar dietary laws as well. He also speculates that abstention from pork may be due to the Jews' honoring of the pig for having taught them how to plow or to the fact that it was a boar that killed Adonis, who is said to be identified with Dionysus, whom the Jews are said to worship.

'You are right,' said Lamprias, 'but let us add a little to our speculations. My grandfather used to say on every occasion, in derision of the Jews, that what they abstained from was precisely the most legitimate meat. But we shall say that of all delicacies the most legitimate kind is that from the sea.'

Question 5: Whether the Jews abstain from pork because of reverence or aversion for the pig.

When he had finished, and some of those present would have made an extended reply to his arguments, Callistratus headed them off by saying, 'What do you think of the assertion that it is precisely the most proper type of meat that the Jews avoid eating?' 'I heartily agree with it,' replied Polycrates, 'but I have another question: do they abstain from eating pork by reason of some special respect for hogs or from abhorrence of the creature? Their own accounts sound like pure myth, but perhaps they have some serious reasons which they do not publish.'

'My impression,' said Callistratus, 'is that the beast enjoys a certain respect among that folk; granted that he is ugly and dirty, still he is no more absurd in appearance or crude in disposition than dung-beetle, crocodile, or cat, each of which is treated as sacred by a different group of Egyptian priests. They say, however, that the pig is honored for a good reason: according to the story, it was the first to cut the soil with its projecting snout, thus producing a furrow and teaching man the function of a ploughshare. Incidentally, this is the origin, they say, of the word *hynis* [from *hys*, "swine"] for that implement. The Egyptians who cultivate the soft soil of their low-lying areas have no use for ploughing at all. After the Nile overflows and soaks their acres, they follow the receding water and unload the pigs, which by trampling and rooting quickly turn over the deep soil and cover the seed. We need not be surprised if some people do not eat pork for this reason.'

'Other animals receive even greater honors among the barbarians for slight and in some cases utterly ridiculous reasons. The field-mouse is said to have been deified among the Egyptians because of its blindness, since they regarded darkness as superior to light; and they thought that the field-mouse was born of ordinary mice every fifth generation at the new moon, and also that its liver was reduced in size at the dark of the moon. . . . How could anyone blame the Egyptians for such irrationality when it is recorded that the Pythagoreans respect even a white cock, and that they abstain particularly from the red mullet and the sea anemone among marine animals? Or when we remember that the Magi, followers of Zoroaster, especially esteem the hedgehog and abominate water mice, regarding the person who kills the greatest number of the latter as blest and dear to the gods? So I think the Jews would kill pigs if they hated them, as the Magi kill water mice; but in fact it is just as unlawful for Jews to destroy pigs as to eat them.[65] Perhaps it is consistent that they should revere the pig which taught them sowing and plowing, inasmuch as they honor the ass which first led them to a spring of water.[66] Otherwise, so help me, someone will say that the Jews abstain from the hare because they can't stomach anything so filthy and unclean.'

'No indeed,' countered Lamprias.... 'The Jews apparently abominate pork because barbarians especially abhor skin diseases like lepra and white scale, and believe that human beings are ravaged by such maladies through contagion. Now we observe that every pig is covered on the under side by lepra and scaly eruptions, which, if there is general weakness and emaciation, are thought to spread rapidly over the body. What is more, the very filthiness of their habits produces an inferior quality of meat. We observe no other creature so fond of mud and of dirty, unclean places, if we leave out of account those animals that have their origin and natural habitat there. People say that the eyes of swine are so twisted and drawn down that they can never catch sight of anything above them or see the sky unless they are carried upside down so that their eyes are given an unnatural tilt upward. Wherefore the animal, which usually squeals immoderately, holds still when it is carried in this position, and remains silent because it is astonished at the unfamiliar sight of the heavenly expanse and restrained from squealing by an overpowering fear.'

'If it is legitimate to bring in mythology too, Adonis is said to have been slain by the boar. People hold Adonis[67] to be none other than Dionysus, a belief supported by many of the rites at the festivals of both; though others have it that he was the favorite of Dionysus. Phanocles, an erotic poet, surely knew whereof he spoke when he wrote the following lines: "And how the mountain-coursing Dionysus seized the divine Adonis, as the god did visit holy Cyprus."' (LCL)

10.110 Plutarch (*ca.* 46–120 CE), *Life of Cicero* 7.6

Plutarch here cites Cicero's pun on the name of Verres ("porker"), whom he prosecuted and who was defended by a certain Caecilius, who was

---

65. The reference presumably is the prohibition of causing pain to animals. Cf., e.g., *Hullin* 7b. Indeed, many acts, otherwise forbidden on the Sabbath, are permitted when their purpose is to relieve the animal's pain, on the ground that cruelty to animals is prohibited by the Bible (*Shabbath* 128b; cf. Exod 23:5).

66. So also Tacitus, *Histories* 5.3.2, who declares that the Israelites, while wandering, exhausted by thirst in the desert after their Exodus from Egypt, were led by Moses, who followed a herd of wild asses and thereby discovered abundant streams of water.

67. Presumably Plutarch is aware of a connection between the name of Adonis and the Hebrew word *Adon*, meaning "lord."

suspected of being a Jew (though apparently this was only a rumor – one which Cicero, in his oration against Caecilius, does not mention).

Nevertheless, many witty sayings of his [Cicero] in connection with this trial[68] are on record. For instance, *verres* is the Roman word for a castrated porker; when, accordingly, a freedman named Caecilius, who was suspected of Jewish practices, wanted to thrust aside the Sicilian accusers and denounce Verres himself,[69] Cicero said: 'What has a Jew to do with Verres?' (LCL)

> 10.111 Epictetus (*ca.* 60–140 *ce*), cited by Arrian (second century CE), *Discourses* 1.11.12–13

Epictetus, the well-known Stoic philosopher who was originally a slave, seems actually to be neutral in his views on the Jewish dietary laws.

Come, tell me, are all things that certain persons regard as good and fitting, rightly so regarded? And is it possible at this present time that all the opinions which Jews and Syrians and Egyptians and Romans hold on the subject of food are rightly held? And how can it be possible? But, I fancy, it is absolutely necessary, if the views of the Egyptians are right, that those of the others are not right; if those of the Jews are well founded, that those of the others are not. (LCL)

> 10.112 Epictetus (*ca.* 60–140 CE), cited by Arrian (second century CE), *Discourses* 1.22.4

Epictetus does not take sides on the difference of opinion between Jews and Syrians and Egyptians and Romans on the attitude toward the eating of pork.

This is the conflict between Jews and Syrians and Egyptians and Romans, not over the question whether holiness should be put before everything else and should be pursued in all circumstances, but whether the particular act of eating swine's flesh is holy or unholy. (LCL)

> 10.113 Tacitus (*ca.* 56–120 CE), *Histories* 5.4.2–3

Tacitus explains that the reason why Jews abstain from eating pork is that the pig is subject to the leprosy. He also explains that the reason why Jews eat unleavened bread on Passover is to memorialize their speedily gathered grain.

They [the Jews] abstain from pork in memory of the disaster of the leprosy which had once defiled them, a disease to which that animal is subject. They commemorate still a long famine that once happened by frequent fasting, and as a testimonial of speedily gathered grain Jewish bread is prepared without yeast.[70] (M.R.)

---

68. Cicero successfully prosecuted Verres, the governor of Sicily, in 70 BCE for extortion.
69. Caecilius tried to be put in charge of the prosecution of Verres so as to get him acquitted by presenting a weak case against him.
70. Unleavened bread (*matzah*), eaten on the Jewish festival of Passover.

10.114 Juvenal (*ca.* 60–*ca.*130 CE), *Satires* 6.160

Juvenal implies that the reason why Jews abstain from eating pork is that they feel merciful toward pigs.

In that country ... where a long-established clemency suffers pigs to attain old age. (LCL)

10.115 Sextus Empiricus (latter part of the second century CE), *Outlines* 3.222–3

From Sextus Empiricus we may see that the Jews' abstention from pork is so strong, even to the point of dying rather than eat it, that it is proverbial.

A similar behavior may be found in respect of food in people's worship of their gods. A Jew or an Egyptian priest would prefer to die instantly rather than eat pork, while to taste mutton is reckoned an abomination in the eyes of a Libyan, and Syrians think the same about pigeons, and others about cattle. (M.S.)

10.116 Macrobius (flourished *ca.* 400 CE), *Saturnalia* 2.4.11

The proverbial nature of the Jews' strictness in abstaining from eating pork may be seen in this quip ascribed to the Emperor Augustus.

When he [Augustus] heard that among the boys under the age of two years whom in Syria Herod the king of the Jews had ordered to be put to death was the king's own son, he exclaimed: 'I'd rather be Herod's pig than Herod's son.' (M.S.)

10.117 Damascius (first half of the sixth century CE), *Life of Isidore*, cited by Suda, s.v. *Domninos* and *diagkōnisámenos*

From the following remark of Damascius, a Neoplatonic philosopher, we can see the apparently general view that Jews, even when pork is prescribed for health reasons, are not expected to eat it.

Plutarch,[71] ... gazing at the statue of Asclepius,[72] ... exclaimed: 'Lord, what would you have ordered a Jew if he had got this disease? Surely you would have urged him to be filled with pork!' That is what he said; and Asclepius, immediately sending forth from the statue some harmonious sound, suggested another cure for the illness. (M.S.)

SUPERSTITION: CIRCUMCISION

BIBLIOGRAPHY

Feldman (1993), 153–8.

Circumcision was regarded by the Greeks and Romans as a physical deformity and hence, like others who had various deformities, circumcised men were not permitted to participate in the Olympic Games.

71. The reference is to Plutarch the Athenian Neo-Platonist philosopher who lived at the beginning of the fifth century.
72. The reference is to the god of medicine, the son of Apollo.

10.118 Herodotus (*ca.* 480–*ca.*425 BCE), *Histories* 2.104.1–3

Significantly, the first reference to the Jews (though, admittedly, some scholars have questioned whether the reference to the "Syrians of Palestine" is indeed to the Jews) in classical literature, namely in Herodotus, is to their practice of circumcision, which obviously set the Jews apart from most other peoples. According to Herodotus the "Syrians of Palestine" acknowledge that they learned the practice from the Egyptians.

For it is plain to see that the Colchians[73] are Egyptians; and this that I say I myself noted before I heard it from others. When I began to think on this matter, I inquired of both peoples; and the Colchians remembered the Egyptians better than the Egyptians remembered the Colchians; the Egyptians said that they held the Colchians to be part of Sesostris'[74] army. I myself guessed it to be so, partly because they are dark-skinned and woolly-haired; though that indeed goes for nothing, seeing that other peoples, too, are such; but my better proof was that the Colchians and Egyptians and Ethiopians are the only nations that have from the first practiced circumcision. The Phoenicians and the Syrians of Palestine[75] acknowledge of themselves that they learned the custom from the Egyptians; and the Syrians of the valleys of the Thermodon and the Parthenius, as well as their neighbors the Macrones, say that they learned it lately from the Colchians. (LCL)

10.119 Strabo (*ca.* 64 BCE–*ca.* 20 CE), *Geography* 16.2.37

It is of interest that Strabo, who knew a fair amount about Judaism, says that the practice of circumcision was introduced after the time of Moses. It is also of interest that he refers to excisions of the clitoris in females as a Jewish practice, though it is actually not found among Jews.

[After Moses] from superstition arose . . . circumcisions and excisions [i.e., of the females] and other observances of the kind. (LCL)

10.120 Apion (first half of the first century), cited by Josephus, *Against Apion* 2.137, 140–2

In answer to the Egyptian Apion's derision of the Jewish practices of abstaining from eating pork and circumcision Josephus replies that even the Egyptian priests follow these same practices.

73. Colchis was a country to the east of the Black Sea and south of the Caucasus Mountains. Though this area is far from Egypt, it seems that Egypt received immigrants from this district at the close of the Old Kingdom.

74. Sesostris was the name borne by the Pharaohs of the twelfth dynasty; it was also the name of a legendary king of Egypt who, according to Herodotus, Diodorus Siculus, and Strabo, is said to have conquered the whole world, including Scythia and Ethiopia.

75. There is some question as to whether the Syrians of Palestine are the Jews. Josephus (*Antiquities* 8.262 and *Against Apion* 1.168–71), who cites Herodotus' passage, remarks that the reference must be to the Jews, inasmuch as the only inhabitants of Palestine who practice circumcision are the Jews. Despite Herodotus, however, there were other peoples in the region who apparently did practice circumcision.

He [Apion] denounces us for sacrificing domestic animals and for not eating pork, and he derides the practice of circumcision. . . . Had Apion been asked who, in his opinion, were the wisest and most God-fearing of all the Egyptians, he would undoubtedly have made the admission, 'the priests'; for they, as is said, originally received two commissions from royalty: divine worship and the charge of learning. But all those priests are circumcised, and all abstain from swine's flesh. Even among the rest of the Egyptians there is not a man who sacrifices a pig to the gods. Was, then, Apion's mind blinded when, in the interest of the Egyptians, he undertook to revile us and actually condemned them? For not only do they practice the customs which he abuses, but, as Herodotus [2.104] has informed us, they have taught others to adopt circumcision. (LCL)

10.121 Petronius (died *ca.* 65 CE), *Satyricon* 68.8

Petronius jokes about circumcision as a practice which prevents one from being perfect.

He [a slave] has only two faults, and if he were rid of them he would be simply perfect. He is circumcised and he snores. (LCL)

10.122 Martial (*ca.* 40–104 CE), *Epigrams* 7.35.3–4

Martial, the epigrammist, jokes about the circumcision of a slave.

But my slave – to be silent about myself, Laecania – has a Jewish weight beneath his naked skin. (L.H.F.)

10.123 Martial (*ca.* 40–104 CE), *Epigrams* 7.82

Martial jokes about someone who was trying to hide the fact that he was circumcised.

Menophilus' person a sheath covers so enormous that it alone would be sufficient for the whole tribe of comic actors. This fellow I had imagined – for we often bathe together – was solicitous to spare his voice, Flaccus; but while he was exercising himself in the view of the people in the middle of the exercise ground, the sheath unluckily fell off; lo, he was circumcised! (LCL)

10.124 Martial (*ca.* 40–104 CE), *Epigrams* 11.94

Your overflowing malice, and your detraction everywhere of my books, I pardon; circumcised poet,[76] you are wise! This, too, I disregard, that when you carp at my poems you plunder them: so, too, circumcised poet, you are wise! What tortures me is this, that you, circumcised poet, although born in the very midst of Solyma,[77] outrage my boy. There!

---

76. Martial is complaining about a Jewish poet who has, he claims, not only stolen from his works but has also stolen his favorite boy.
77. That is, Jerusalem.

you deny it, and swear to me by the Thunderer's Temple.[78] I don't believe you: swear, circumcised one, by Anchialus.[79] (LCL)

10.125 Tacitus (*ca.* 56–120 CE), *Histories* 5.5.2

They [the Jews] adopted circumcision to distinguish themselves from other peoples by this difference. (LCL)

10.126 Pseudo-Acro (date unknown *ca.* 400 CE), *Scholia on Horace, Satires* 1.9.70

Pseudo-Acro, a commentator on Horace, explains the origin of the practice of circumcision as due to the fact that Moses became circumcised because of a physician's negligence, whereupon he ordained the practice so that he should not be the only one thus circumcised.

The circumcised Jews: Therefore circumcised because Moyses the king of the Jews, by whose laws they are ruled, became so by the negligence of the physician, and in order not to be the only person conspicuous by this he wanted all to be circumcised. (M.S.)

HEALING THROUGH EXORCISMS AND SPELLS

The reputation of the Jews for healing may have arisen because so many of the 613 commandments are concerned, in one way or another, with hygiene and health. Moreover, in the oral tradition as embodied in the Talmudic literature, there are many remedies based, presumably, upon actual experience. What added to the standing of the Jews in this area was their reputation in astrology and the interpretation of dreams, allegedly going back to biblical days.

10.127 Lucian (*ca.* 115–200 CE), *Lovers of Lies* 16

Lucian here describes how a Jew practices exorcism of evil spirits from those who are possessed.

For my part, I should like to ask you what you say to those who free possessed men from their terrors by exorcising the spirits so manifestly? I need not discuss this; everyone knows about the Syrian from Palestine, the adept in it [i.e. exorcism], how many he takes in hand who fall down in the light of the moon and roll their eyes and fill their mouths with foam; nevertheless, he restores them to health and sends them away normal in mind, delivering them from their straits for a large fee. When he stands beside them as they lie there and asks: 'Whence came you into his body?' the patient himself is silent, but the spirit answers in Greek or in the language of whatever foreign country he comes from, telling how and whence he entered into the man; whereupon, by adjuring the spirit and if he does not obey threatening him, he drives him out. (LCL)

78. That is, Jupiter.
79. The reference is obscure. Perhaps it was suggested to Martial because of its phonetic similarity to the names of foreign deities.

10.128 Lucian (*ca.* 115–200 CE), *Tragic Gout* 171–3

Lucian derides those who think that the spells of Jews can cure them.

Some purge themselves with sacred medicine, others are mocked by chants impostors sell, and other fools fall for the spells of Jews. (LCL)

> *10.129* Damascius (first half of the sixth century CE), *Life of Isidore*, cited by Photius, *Library* 242, p. 339a–b

Damascius here mentions the invocation of "the God of the Hebrews" in expelling an evil spirit.

Hierocles married a child-bearing woman. As the evil could not be persuaded to leave the woman by gentle words, Theosebius compelled it to do so by an oath, although he was not versed in magic, nor practiced any theurgy. He adjured it by invoking the rays of the sun and the God of the Hebrews. The bad spirit was expelled while crying out that he both reverenced the gods and felt shame before Him. (M.S.)

SOOTHSAYING

> *10.130* *Scriptores Historiae Augustae* (end of the fourth century CE), *Four-horse Chariot of Tyrants* 8.1, 3

The author of this portion of the *Scriptores Historiae Augustae* claims that all the heads of the Jewish communities, without exception, are adept in astrology and foretelling the future through inspection of entrails.

From [the emperor] Hadrian Augustus to Servianus the consul, greeting. . . .[In Egypt] there is no chief of the Jewish synagogue,[80] no Samaritan, no Christian presbyter, who is not an astrologer, a soothsayer, or an anointer. (LCL)

UNJUST LAWS

> *10.131* Apion (first half of the first century CE), cited by Josephus, *Against Apion* 2.125

Apion offers as proof that the Jewish laws are unjust and their religion erroneous the fact that the Jews are subject to other nations and that many calamities have befallen them.

A clear proof, according to him [Apion], that our laws are unjust and our religious ceremonies erroneous is that we are not masters of an empire, but rather the slaves, first of one nation, then of another, and that calamity has more than once befallen our city. (LCL)

---

80. The *archisynagogus* (chief of the synagogue) had the most important function in a Jewish community. He is presumably equivalent to the *rosh ha-knesset*, the functionary cited in the Mishnah (*Yoma* 7:1, *Sotah* 7:7–8).

10.132 Julian (331–63 CE), *Against the Galileans* 202A

The Emperor Julian regards the laws of the Jews as harsh and barbarous and consequently inferior to the laws of the pagans, but nonetheless as superior to those of the Christians, which are less pure.

[If you had remained Jews instead of becoming Christians], though you would be following a law that is harsh and stern and contains much that is savage and barbarous, instead of our mild and humane laws, and would in other respects be inferior to us [pagans], yet you would be more holy and purer than now in your forms of worship. But now it has come to pass that like leeches you have sucked the worst blood from that source and left the purer. (LCL)

ATTACKS ON MOSES

10.133 Apollonius Molon (first century BCE), *On the Jews*, cited by Josephus, *Against Apion* 2.145

Apollonius Molon and Lysimachus, among others, look upon Moses as an impostor.

Seeing, however, that Apollonius Molon, Lysimachus, and others, partly from ignorance, mainly from ill will, have made reflections, which are neither just nor true, upon our lawgiver Moses and his code, maligning the one as charlatan and impostor, and asserting that from the other we receive lessons in vice and none in virtue, I desire to give, to the best of my ability, a brief account of our constitution as a whole and of its details. (LCL)

10.134 Alexander Polyhistor (first century BCE), *On Rome*, cited by Suda (tenth century CE), s.v. "Alexander of Miletus"

One of the most peculiar statements about Moses is Alexander Polyhistor's remark, found uniquely there, that Moses was a woman. This idea may have originated with the history of the prophetic Sibyls. Whether this is to be viewed as mockery of the Jews has been debated by scholars.

And about Rome [Alexander wrote] five books, in which he states that there lived a Hebrew woman Moso, who composed the Law of the Hebrews. (M.S.)

10.135 Nicarchus (first century CE?), *On the Jews*, cited by Photius (ninth century CE), *Lexicon*, s.v. *alpha*

BIBLIOGRAPHY

John G. Gager, "Moses and Alpha," *JTS* 20 (1969), 245–8.

Nicarchus, apparently an Egyptian Greek, wrote a special monograph on the Jews. His statement, connecting Moses with leprosy, which is in line with the Alexandrian tradition that the Jews were driven out of Egypt because they were lepers, is quite clearly a perversion of the meaning that Moses was foremost (hence *alpha*) among the Jews.

Alpha. – A cow-head was thus called by the Phoenicians, and also Moyses the legislator by the Jews was so called because he had much dull-white leprosy on his body. That sort of nonsense is told by Nicarchus, the son of Ammonius, in his work on Jews. (M.S.)

10.136 Tacitus (*ca.* 56–120 CE), *Histories* 5.4.1

According to Tacitus, it was Moses who, in order to establish his influence over the Jews forever, introduced new religious practices among them. These were deliberately completely different from those of other peoples.

To establish his influence over this people for all time, Moses introduced new religious practices, quite opposed to those of all other religions. (LCL)

10.137 Celsus the Philosopher (second century CE), *The True Doctrine*, cited by Origen, *Against Celsus* 1.16

Celsus the philosopher deliberately rejects Moses from his list of ancient wise men.

When he [Celsus] makes a list of ancient and wise men who were of service to their contemporaries and to posterity by their writings, he rejects Moses from the list of wise men. . . . For he says that Linus,[81] Musaeus, Orpheus, Pherecydes,[82] Zoroaster the Persian, and Pythagoras understood these doctrines, and their opinions were put down in books and are preserved to this day. (H.C.)

10.138 Celsus the Philosopher (second century CE), *The True Doctrine*, cited by Origen, *Against Celsus* 1.23

According to the philosopher Celsus, Moses used deception in order to get his ignorant followers to believe in monotheism.

Celsus next says: 'The goatherds and shepherds who followed Moses as their leader were deluded by clumsy deceits into thinking that there was only one God.' (H.C.)

10.139 Galen (*ca.* 129–200 CE), *On Hippocrates' Anatomy* (fragment extant in Arabic translation)

According to Galen, Moses is the paradigm of those who make assertions without proof.

81. Linus was a Greek mythical hero, who, according to one version, was slain by his father Apollo because he dared to enter upon a musical contest with him. According to another version, he instructed Heracles in music but was killed by the latter when Linus attempted to punish him.

82. Pherecydes, who apparently lived in the sixth century BCE, is said to have been a teacher of the philosopher Pythagoras and to have taught him the doctrine of the transmigration of souls.

They compare those who practice medicine without scientific knowledge to Moses, who framed laws for the tribe of the Jews, since it is his method in his books to write without offering proofs, saying 'God commanded, God spake.' (R.W.)

Social Charges

HATRED OF NON-JEWS

> 10.140 Apollonius Molon (first century BCE), *On the Jews*, cited by Josephus, *Against Apion* 2.258

Apollonius Molon condemns the Jews for their illiberalism in refusing to admit to their fold those who have different views of God or to have dealings with those who follow a different life style.

Of these facts[83] Apollonius Molon took no account when he condemned us for refusing admission to persons with other preconceived ideas about God, and for declining to associate with those who have chosen to adopt a different mode of life. (LCL)

> 10.141 Diodorus the Sicilian (latter part of the first century BCE), *Historical Library* 34.1.1–4

Diodorus tells how the Syrian king Antiochus VII was advised to wipe out the Jews completely on the ground that they look upon all non-Jews as their enemies. It was Moses, they claimed, who ordained their misanthropic ways.

When King Antiochus [VII Sidetes], says Diodorus, was laying siege to Jerusalem, the Jews held out for a time, but when all their supplies were exhausted they found themselves compelled to make overtures for a cessation of hostilities. Now the majority of his friends advised the king to take the city by storm and to wipe out completely the race of Jews, since they alone of all nations avoided dealings with any other people and looked upon all men as their enemies. They pointed out, too, that the ancestors of the Jews had been driven out of all Egypt as men who were impious and detested by the gods. For by way of purging the country all persons who had white or leprous marks on their bodies had been assembled and driven across the border, as being under a curse; the refugees had occupied the territory round about Jerusalem, and having organized the nation of the Jews had made their hatred of mankind into a tradition, and on this account had introduced utterly outlandish laws: not to break bread with any other race, nor to show them any goodwill at all.

His friends reminded Antiochus also of the enmity that in times past his ancestors had felt for this people. Antiochus, called Epiphanes, on defeating the Jews had entered the innermost sanctuary of the god's temple, where it was lawful for the priest alone to enter. Finding there

---

83. Josephus has just noted that Moses took precautions to prevent foreigners from mixing with the Jews at random and to keep the state pure and confined to law-abiding citizens.

a marble statue of a heavily bearded man seated on an ass, with a book in his hands, he supposed it to be an image of Moses, the founder of Jerusalem and organizer of the nation, the man, moreover, who had ordained for the Jews their misanthropic and lawless customs. And since Epiphanes was shocked by such hatred directed against all mankind, he had set himself to break down their traditional practices.

Accordingly, he sacrificed before the image of the founder and the open-air altar of the god a great sow, and poured its blood over them. Then, having prepared its flesh, he ordered that their holy books, containing the xenophobic laws, should be sprinkled with the broth of the meat; that the lamp, which they call undying and which burns continually in the temple, should be extinguished; and that the high priest and the rest of the Jews should be compelled to partake of the meat. (LCL)

10.142 Pompeius Trogus (end of the first century BCE to the beginning of the first century CE), *Philippic Histories* 36, summarized by Justin (third or fourth century CE), *Epitome* 2.15

Pompeius Trogus explains that the reason why the Jews refuse to have anything to do with non-Jews is that they remembered that it was because they did have contact with the Egyptians that they had been driven from Egypt as having spread infection.

As they [the Israelites in the Exodus] remembered that they had been driven from Egypt for fear of spreading infection, they took care, in order that they might not become odious, from the same cause, to their neighbors, to have no communication with strangers; a rule which, from having been adopted on that particular occasion, gradually became a religious institution. (M.S.)

10.143 Apion (first half of the first century CE), cited by Josephus, *Against Apion* 2.121

Apion asserts that the Jews take a solemn oath to show no goodwill to non-Jews.

Then he [Apion] attributes to us an imaginary oath, and would have it appear that we swear by the God who made heaven and earth and sea to show no goodwill to a single alien, above all to Greeks. (LCL)

10.144 Tacitus (*ca.* 56–120 CE), *Histories* 5.4.1

Tacitus says that the Jews, in their perversity, regard as profane those things which are sacred to non-Jews.

Among them all things are profane which are sacred with us, and again things are allowed among them which are impure for us. (M.R.)

10.145 Tacitus (*ca.* 56–120 CE), *Histories* 5.5.1

According to Tacitus, the Jews show compassion but only to one another, whereas they hate non-Jews.

The Jews are extremely loyal toward one another, and always ready to show compassion, but toward every other people they feel only hate and enmity. (LCL)

> *10.146* Philostratus (second half of second century to the forties of the third century CE), *Life of Apollonius* 5.33

According to Philostratus, the Jews have for a long time been completely sundered from non-Jews.

The Jews have long been in revolt not only against the Romans but against humanity; and a race that has made its own a life apart and irreconcilable, that cannot share with the rest of mankind in the pleasures of the table nor join in their libations or prayers or sacrifices, are separated from ourselves by a greater gulf than divides us from Susa or Bactra or the more distant Indies. What sense then or reason was there in chastising them for revolting from us, whom we had better have never annexed? (LCL)

> *10.147* Synesius (*ca.* 373–414 CE), *Letters* 5

According to Synesius, Jews consider it pious to kill as many Greeks as possible.

More than half of them [the sailors on the ship taken by the author], including the skipper, were Jews – a graceless race and fully convinced of the piety of sending to Hades as many Greeks as possible. (A.F.)

Annual Murder of a Greek

> *10.148* Apion (first half of the first century CE), *History of Egypt*, cited by Josephus, *Against Apion* 2.91–6

According to Apion, when King Antiochus Epiphanes of Syria entered the Temple he found a Greek who told him that it was a law of the Jews to kidnap a Greek every year, fatten him up, sacrifice him, partake of his flesh, and swear an oath of hostility to the Greeks.

Antiochus [Epiphanes] found in the temple a couch, on which a man was reclining, with a table before him laden with a banquet of fish of the sea, beasts of the earth, and birds of the air, at which the poor fellow was gazing in stupefaction. The king's entry was instantly hailed by him with adoration, as about to procure him profound relief; falling at the king's knees, he stretched out his right hand and implored him to set him free. The king reassured him and bade him tell him who he was, why he was living there, what was the meaning of his abundant fare. Thereupon, with sighs and tears, the man, in a pitiful tone, told the tale of his distress. He said that he was a Greek and that, while traveling about the province for his livelihood, he was suddenly kidnapped by men of a foreign race and conveyed to the Temple; there he was shut up and seen by nobody, but was fattened on feasts of the most lavish description. At first these unlooked for attentions deceived him and caused him pleasure; suspicion followed, then consternation.

Finally, on consulting the attendants who waited upon him, he heard of the unutterable law of the Jews, for the sake of which he was being fed. The practice was repeated annually at a fixed season. They would kidnap a Greek foreigner, fatten him up for a year, and then convey him to a wood, where they slew him, sacrificed his body with their customary ritual, partook of his flesh, and, while immolating the Greek, swore an oath of hostility to the Greeks. The remains of their victim were then thrown into a pit. The man (Apion continues) stated that he had now but a few days to live, and implored the king, out of respect for the gods of Greece, to defeat this Jewish plot upon his life-blood and to deliver him from his miserable predicament. (LCL)

10.149 Damocritus (first century CE?), *On Jews*, cited by Suda (tenth century CE), s.v. "Damokritos"

Damocritus has an account similar to that of Apion, but according to him, the foreigner is sacrificed not every year but every seven years.

Damocritus, an historian. He wrote a work about tactics in two volumes and a work *On Jews*. In the latter he states that they used to worship an asinine golden head and that every seventh year[84] they caught a foreigner and sacrificed him. They used to kill him by carding his flesh into small pieces. (M.S.)

LECHERY

The charge of lechery may have arisen as a result of the fecundity of the Jews, and their shunning of intermarriage, promiscuous sexual relations, birth control, abortion, and infanticide.

10.150 Martial (*ca.* 40–104 CE), *Epigrams* 7.30

Martial regards the Jews as the paradigm of lechery.

You grant your favors to Parthians, you grant them to Germans . . . ; nor do you shun the lecheries of circumcised Jews. . . . What is your reason that, although you are a Roman girl, no Roman lewdness has attraction for you? (LCL)

10.151 Tacitus (*ca.* 56–120 CE), *Histories* 5.5.2

Tacitus remarks that, on the one hand, the Jews are lustful among themselves, but they refuse to have relations with non-Jews.

They [the Jews] sit apart [from non-Jews] at meals and they sleep apart, and although as a race, they are prone to lust, they abstain from intercourse with foreign women; yet among themselves nothing is unlawful. (LCL)

---

84. Note that in Damocritus it is a foreigner and not specifically a Greek who is caught by the Jews.

Cultural Charges

LACK OF EDUCATION

> *10.152* Celsus the Philosopher (second century CE), *The True Doctrine*, cited by Origen (third century), *Against Celsus* 4.36

The Jews, says Celsus, are obscurantists who know nothing of the great poetry of the Greeks.

He [Celsus] says that the Jews, being bowed down in some corner of Palestine, were totally uneducated and had not heard of these things which were sung in poetry long before by Hesiod and thousands of other inspired men. (H. C.)

LACK OF GENIUS

> *10.153* Apion (first half of the first century CE), cited by Josephus, *Against Apion* 2.135

Jews, says Apion, have not produced inventors or wise men.

But [urges Apion] we have not produced any geniuses, for example, inventors in arts and crafts or eminent sages. He enumerates Socrates, Zeno, Cleanthes,[85] and others of that caliber; and then – most astounding master-stroke – adds his own name to the list, and felicitates Alexandria on possessing such a citizen! (LCL)

> *10.154* Apollonius Molon (first century BCE), *On the Jews*, cited by Josephus, *Against Apion* 2.148

The famous rhetorician Apollonius Molon disdainfully asserts that the Jews are the most untalented of people and that they have contributed nothing useful to mankind.

He [Apollonius Molon] adds that we are the most witless of all barbarians, and are consequently the only people who have contributed no useful invention to civilization. (LCL)

> *10.155* Julian (331–63 CE), *Against the Galileans* 176A–B, 178A–C, 184B–C, 224C–D

The Emperor Julian remarks that Jews are undistinguished in philosophy or science. Even Solomon is no match for the Greek wise men.

Furthermore, observe from what follows that God did not take thought for the Hebrews alone, but though he cared for all nations, he bestowed on the Hebrews nothing considerable or of great value, whereas on us he bestowed gifts far higher and surpassing theirs. For instance, the Egyptians, as they reckon up the names of not a few wise men among themselves, can boast that they possess many successors of Hermes, I mean of Hermes who in his third manifestation visited Egypt, while

---

85. Zeno was the founder of the Stoic school of philosophy *ca.* 300 BCE and was succeeded by Cleanthes as head of the school.

the Chaldeans and Assyrians can boast of Oannes[86] and Belos,[87] the Hellenes can boast of countless successors of Cheiron.[88] ...

But has God granted to you to originate any science or any philosophical study? Why, what is it? For the theory of the heavenly bodies was perfected among the Hellenes, after the first observations had been made among the barbarians in Babylon. And the study of geometry took its rise in the measurement of the land in Egypt, and from this grew to its present importance. Arithmetic began with the Phoenician merchants and among the Hellenes in course of time acquired the aspect of a regular science. These three the Hellenes combined with music into one science, for they connected astronomy with geometry and adapted arithmetic to both, and perceived the principle of harmony in it. Hence they laid down the rules for their music, since they had discovered for the laws of harmony with reference to the sense of hearing an agreement that was infallible, or something very near to it. ...

Need I tell over their names man by man or under their professions? I mean, either the individual men, as for instance Plato, Socrates, Aristides, Cimon, Thales, Lycurgus, Agesilaus, Archidamus,[89] – or should I rather speak of the class of philosophers, of generals, of artificers, of lawgivers? For it will be found that even the most wicked and most brutal of the generals behaved more mildly to the greatest offenders than Moses did to those who had done no wrong. ...

Is their [the Jews'] 'wisest' man Solomon at all comparable with Phocylides or Theognis or Isocrates[90] among the Hellenes? Certainly

---

86. Oannes is a Babylonian mythical figure, described by Berossus in his history of Babylonia as being partly human and partly fish. He is said to have given mankind instruction in writing and to have taught human beings the arts and the sciences.

87. Belos was erroneously believed to be the founder of Babylon.

88. Ch(e)iron, a mythical Centaur, was said to have been particularly skilled in music and medicine and to have educated such renowned Greek heroes as Asclepius, Achilles, and Jason.

89. Aristides was the fifth-century Athenian leader who was particularly famous for his sense of justice. He led the Athenians at the Battle of Plataea (479 BCE) against the Persians. His greatest achievement was the organization of the Delian Confederacy.

Cimon was the great Athenian leader immediately after the defeat of the Persians in 479 BCE.

Thales of Miletus, who flourished in the latter part of the seventh century BCE, was the first of the pre-Socratic philosophers. He reduced all things essentially to a single substance, water.

Lycurgus was the legendary lawgiver of Sparta.

Agesilaus was a Spartan king at the beginning of the fourth century BCE who defeated the Persians but was eventually defeated by the Thebans.

Archidamus was the Spartan king who invaded Attica at the beginning of the Peloponnesian War in 431 BCE.

90. Phocylides of Miletus, who apparently lived in the sixth century BCE, is famous for his gnomic verse couplets which contain moral precepts.

Theognis of Megara, who flourished in the sixth century BCE, wrote elegiac verse enjoining the traditional virtues and passionately attacking the popular movement that had displaced the old oligarchs.

Isocrates, the great Athenian orator of the fourth century BCE, urged Athens and Sparta to unite against Persia and later turned to Philip of Macedon for leadership in this struggle.

not. At least, if one were to compare the exhortations of Isocrates with Solomon's proverbs, you would, I am sure, find that the son of Theodorus [Isocrates] is superior to their 'wisest' king. 'But,' they answer, 'Solomon was proficient in the secret cult of God.' What then? Did not this Solomon serve our gods also, deluded by his wife, as they assert [1 Kgs 11:4]? (LCL)

POVERTY OF LANGUAGE

BIBLIOGRAPHY

Saul Lieberman, *Greek in Jewish Palestine* (1942), 29–30.

   10.156 Cleomedes (first or second century CE), *On Circular Motion* 2.1.91

Cleomedes says that Epicurus' corrupt, debased language is due, in part, to Jewish influence.

Since, in addition to other things, his [Epicurus'] style is also a corrupt motley, making use of expressions like 'stable states of the flesh' and 'hopeful hopes' concerning it, and calling tears 'glistenings of the eyes' and having recourse to phrases like 'holy screechings' and 'ticklings of the body' and 'wenchings' and other bad mischief of this kind, one may say that these expressions derive in part from brothels, in part they are similar to those spoken by women celebrating the Thesmophoria at the festivals of Demeter, and in part they issue from the midst of the synagogue and the beggars in its courtyards. These are Jewish and debased and much lower than reptiles. (M.S.)

POLITICS AND LAW

   10.157 Julian (331–63 CE), *Against the Galileans* 221E

According to the Emperor Julian, in their political and legal institutions and in their cultural achievements the Jews were barbarous.

Further, as regards the constitution of the state and the fashion of the law courts, the administration of cities and the excellence of the laws, progress in learning and the cultivation of the liberal arts, were not all these things in a miserable and barbarous state among the Hebrews? (LCL)

POOR LEVEL OF MEDICAL PRACTICE

   10.158 Julian (331–63 CE), *Against the Galileans* 222A

The practice of medicine among the Jews, according to Julian, was on a lower level than that among the Greeks.

What kind of healing art has ever appeared among the Hebrews, like that of Hippocrates among the Hellenes, and of certain other schools that came after him? (LCL)

CREDULITY

The charge of credulity may have arisen from the tradition (Exod 19:8) that the Israelites had been ready and eager to accept the laws transmitted by Moses from God even before they had heard their full contents or from the tradition that the Israelites were so ready to obey their high priests.

10.159 Horace (65–8 BCE), *Satires* 1.5.96–104

Horace, while on a voyage to Brundisium in southern Italy, comes to a town, Gratia, famous for its supposed miracle. Horace, refusing to accept the account of this miracle, says that Jews may believe it, but not a man as sophisticated as himself.

Next day's weather was better, but the road worse, right up to the walls of Barium, a fishing town. Then Gratia,[91] built under the wrath of the water-nymphs, brought up laughter and mirth in its effort to convince us that frankincense melts without fire at the temple's threshold. Apella, the Jew, may believe it, not I; for I 'have learned that the gods lead a care-free life,'[92] and if Nature works any marvel, the gods do not send it down from their heavenly home aloft when in surly mood! Brundisium is the end of a long story and a long journey. (LCL)

10.160 Galen (*ca.* 129–200 CE), *Against the Theology of Aristotle* (fragment extant in Arabic translation)

Galen says that Jews and Christians accept everything on faith rather than through reason.

If I had in mind people who taught their pupils in the same way as the followers of Moses and Christ teach theirs – for they order them to accept everything on faith – I should not have given you a definition. (R.W.)

Character Charges

COWARDICE

10.161 Apollonius Molon (first century BCE), *On the Jews*, cited by Josephus, *Against Apion* 2.148

Apollonius Molon contradicts himself, on the one hand accusing the Jews of being cowards and, on the other hand, accusing them of being reckless.

Apollonius, unlike Apion, has not grouped his accusations together, but scattered them here and there all over his work, reviling us in one place as atheists and misanthropes, in another reproaching us as cowards, whereas elsewhere, on the contrary, he accuses us of temerity and reckless madness. (LCL)

10.162 Julian (331–63 CE), *Against the Galileans* 218B–C

The Jews have produced not a single general of the caliber of Alexander or Caesar or even anyone much inferior to them.

91. Gratia is a town in Italy which the poet reaches on his voyage to Brundisium. The town was proud of its miracle whereby frankincense melted of itself.
92. This is an Epicurean belief, as we see in Lucretius (5.82).

Will anyone think that victory in war is less desirable than defeat?
Who is so stupid? But if this that I assert is the truth, point out to me
among the Hebrews a single general like Alexander or Caesar! You
have no such man. And indeed, by the gods, I am well aware that I am
insulting these heroes by the question, but I mentioned them because
they are well known. For the generals who are inferior to them are
unknown to the multitude, and yet every one of them deserves more
admiration than all the generals put together whom the Jews have had.
(LCL)

Economic Charges

EXPORT OF GOLD TO THE TEMPLE IN JERUSALEM

BIBLIOGRAPHY

Feldman (1993), 107–13.

> 10.163 Cicero (106–43 BCE), *Defense of Flaccus* 28.67, 68–9 (59 BCE)

In 59 BCE Cicero defended Lucius Valerius Flaccus, the Roman governor
of Asia Minor, who had been charged with seizing gold in 62 BCE that the
Jews had gathered to be sent to the Temple in Jerusalem. Cicero's attack
on the Jews in his defense of Flaccus is to be understood in the light of the
fact that the Roman Senate had on several occasions forbidden the export
of gold on account of the shortage of gold in Italy.

When every year it was customary to send gold to Jerusalem on the
order of the Jews from Italy and from all our provinces, Flaccus forbade
by an edict its exportation from Asia. Who is there, gentlemen, who
could not honestly praise this action? The senate often earlier and also
in my consulship [63 BCE] most urgently forbade the export of gold. . . .
At Apamea a little less than a hundred pounds of gold was openly
seized and weighed before the seat of the praetor in the forum through
the agency of Sextius Caesius, a Roman knight, an upright and
honorable man; at Laodicea a little more than twenty pounds by Lucius
Peducaeus, our juror. At Adramytium a hundred pounds by Gnaeus
Domitius, the commissioner, at Pergamum[93] a small amount. The
accounting for the gold is correct. The gold is in the treasury, no
embezzlement is charged; it is just an attempt to fix odium on him.
(LCL)

GREED

> 10.164 Ptolemy the Astronomer (Claudius Ptolemaeus) (second century
> CE), *Influences* 2.3.65–6 (29–31)

Ptolemy, the famous astronomer and astrologer, believed that the
characteristics of a given nation were determined by their geography and
by their astrological situation. In particular, he asserts that the Near East,
including Judaea, is consequently an area where the peoples are gifted in
trade and are unscrupulous.

---

93. Apamea, Laodicea, Adramytium, and Pergamum are cities in Asia Minor.

The remaining parts of the quarter, situated about the center of the inhabited world, Idumaea, Coele-Syria, Judaea, Phoenicia, Chaldea, Orchinia,[94] and Arabia Felix, which are situated toward the north-west of the whole quarter, have additional familiarity with the north-western triangle, Aries, Leo, and Sagittarius, and, furthermore, have as co-rulers Jupiter, Mars, and Mercury. Therefore, these peoples are, in comparison with the others, more gifted in trade and exchange; they are more unscrupulous, despicable cowards, treacherous, servile, and in general fickle, on account of the stars mentioned. Of these, again the inhabitants of Coele-Syria, Idumaea, and Judaea are more closely familiar to Aries and Mars, and therefore these peoples are in general bold, godless, and scheming. The Phoenicians, Chaldeans, and Orchinians have familiarity with Leo and the sun, so that they are simpler, kindly, addicted to astrology, and beyond all men worshippers of the sun. (LCL)

10.165 Scriptores Historiae Augustae (end of fourth century CE), *Four-horse Chariot of Tyrants* 8.5–7

In this letter to Servianus the consul the Emperor Hadrian (ruled 117–38 CE), in speaking of the prosperity of Alexandria, remarks that the Jews among others adore money.

They [the people of Egypt] are a folk most seditious, most deceitful, most given to injury; but their city [Alexandria] is prosperous, rich and fruitful, and in it no one is idle. Some are blowers of glass, others makers of paper, all are at least weavers of linen or seem to belong to one craft or another; the lame have their occupations, the wounded have theirs, the blind have theirs, and not even those whose hands are crippled are idle. Their only god is money, and this the Christians, the Jews, and, in fact, all nations adore. And would that this city had a better character, for indeed it is worthy by reason of its richness and by reason of its size to hold the chief place in the whole of Egypt. (LCL)

10.166 Rutilius Namatianus (beginning of the fifth century CE), *On His Return* 1.381–9

On a trip in Italy, Rutilius Namatianus is angry with a Jew, the host of a place where he had stopped, who had charged him for losses he had caused, and accuses him of greed.

We were made to pay dear for the repose of the delightful halting-place by a lessee who was harsher than Antiphates[95] as a host! For a crabbed Jew was in charge of the spot – a creature that quarrels with sound human food. He charges in our bill for damaging his bushes and hitting the sea-weed, and bawls about his enormous loss in water we had sipped. We pay the abuse due to the filthy race that infamously practices circumcision, a root of silliness they are. (LCL)

94. A land in the Near East which is apparently unidentifiable.
95. Antiphates was the cruel king of the Laestrygonians (*Odyssey* 10.114ff.).

BEGGING

The depiction of Jews as beggars may have arisen from the emphasis which Jews placed upon charity. Or there may here be a sarcastic allusion to the economic power of the Jews.

10.167 Martial (*ca.* 40–104 CE), *Epigrams* 12.57

The Jewish beggar is apparently proverbial, to judge from this epigram of Martial.

Do you ask why I often resort to my small fields in arid Nomentum,[96] and the unkempt household of my villa? Neither for thought, Sparsus, nor for quiet is there any place in the city for a poor man. Schoolmasters in the morning do not let you live . . . nor the Jew taught by his mother to beg, nor the blear-eyed huckster of sulphur-wares. (LCL)

10.168 Juvenal (*ca.* 60–*ca.* 130 CE), *Satires* 3.10–16

The satirist Juvenal bitterly laments the fact that uncultured Jewish beggars now inhabit the area of Rome formerly associated with the revered king Numa Pompilius.

But while all his goods and chattels were being packed upon a single wagon, my friend halted at the dripping archway of the old Porta Capena.[97] Here Numa[98] held his nightly assignations with his mistress; but now the holy fount and grove and shrine are let out to Jews, who possess a basket and a truss of hay for all their belongings.[99] For as every tree nowadays has to pay toll to the people, the Muses have been ejected, and the wood has to go a-begging. (LCL)

10.169 Juvenal (*ca.* 60–*ca.*130 CE), *Satires* 3.290–6

The implication in this satire is that Rome is full of Jewish beggars.

The fellow stands up against me, and bids me halt; obey I must. What else can you do when attacked by a madman stronger than yourself? 'Where are you from?' shouts he; 'whose vinegar, whose beans have blown you out? With what cobbler have you been munching cut leeks and boiled wether's chaps? What sirrah, no answer? Speak out, or take that upon your shins! Say, where is your stand?[100] In what prayer-house[101] shall I find you?' (LCL)

10.170 Juvenal (*ca.* 60–*ca.*130 CE), *Satires* 6.542–7

Poverty-stricken and begging Jewesses who are interpreters of dreams are common in Rome, according to Juvenal.

96. A rustic town in Italy.
97. The Porta Capena was a gate in the wall around Rome.
98. Numa Pompilius, revered second king of Rome, is said to have communed with the goddess Egeria, who loved him.
99. The ancient anonymous commentator on Juvenal explains that the basket and the hay refer to the Jewish practice of keeping food warm in this way on the Sabbath.
100. I.e., where is your stand for begging?
101. The word which is used, *proseucha*, refers to a Jewish synagogue.

No sooner has that fellow departed than a palsied Jewess, leaving her basket and her truss of hay, comes begging to her secret ear; she is an interpreter of the laws of Jerusalem, a high priestess of the tree, a trusty go-between of highest heaven. She, too, fills her palm, but more sparingly, for a Jew will tell you dreams of any kind you please for the minutest of coins. (LCL)

Glossary of Recurring Terms

Agoranomos. Clerk of the market who regulated buying and selling.

Amme ha-aretz. Literally "people of the land." In the Talmud those who are lax in religious observance, especially with regard to tithes and ritual purity; in later parlance, an ignoramus.

Amoraim (Hebrew "speakers"). The name given to the rabbis of Palestine and Babylonia of the period of the Gemara (200–500 CE) who explained the Mishnah.

Aramaic. Semitic language, a dialect of which was the customary tongue of the Jews in south-west Asia after the Babylonian exile (586 BCE) until approximately the eighth century CE.

Archon. High elected official of Greek cities and of Greek communal and social organizations.

Aroura. Measure of land in Egypt, approximately half an acre.

Artaba. Dry measure in Egypt, varying from about 3 to 6 pecks.

Coele-Syria. (Greek "Hollow Syria," probably a corruption of the Semitic for "All Syria"), the region west of the River Euphrates, between the Lebanon and Anti-Lebanon Mountains.

Consul. Highest Roman magistrate. Two were elected annually during the Roman Republic. During the Roman Empire there were also "substitute" consuls for parts of the year.

Cubit. A unit of length equal to approximately 18 inches.

Demiurge. The name used by Plato to designate the deity who created the material world.

Denarius. Roman silver coin, approximately the same value as the Greek drachma.

Diaspora (Greek "dispersion"). Jewish communities outside of Palestine.

Drachma. Greek silver coin, approximately the same value as the Roman denarius; but in the Roman province of Egypt 1 denarius was worth 4 drachmas.

Ephebe. A Greek youth entering manhood who received gymnastic and military training.

Epigone. Descendants of foreign military settlers in Egypt.

Ethnarch. The general administrator of the autonomous Jewish community but without the title of king.

Evocatus. A veteran who served as a special officer of the emperor.

Gemara. Rabbinic commentary on the Mishnah, compiled in two versions, one in the Land of Israel *ca.* 400 and one in Babylonia *ca.* 500.

Genius. The guardian deity of a Roman man.

Gerousia. The council of elders which was the chief Jewish legislative and judicial body, corresponding to the later Sanhedrin.

God-fearer. One who accepted certain of the practices of Judaism but without actually converting.

Gymnasiarch. The head of the gymnasium (a secondary school) who was in charge of providing funds and who, in the case of the Alexandrian gymnasiarch, represented the city. He was also in charge of the games held on festivals.

Gymnosophists. A sect of philosophers found in India.

Halakah (Hebrew "law," "practice"). The legal system of Judaism.

Ḥaliẓah. A rite freeing one from the obligation of levirate marriage.

Hipparchy. A squadron of cavalry.

Imperator (Latin "Commander"). The title bestowed by soldiers on a victorious general during the Roman Republic; later an official title of all Roman emperors.

Iugerum. Approximately two-thirds of an acre.

Kab. A unit of volume equal to approximately 2 quarts.

Kanephoros (Greek "Basket-bearer"). The title of maidens who carried baskets in religious processions.

Kosmetes. Magistrate in charge of the ephebes.

Medimnus. Greek dry measure, equivalent to about 1½ bushels.

Mekilta. Rabbinic midrash on the biblical book of Exodus.

Menorah. Sacred candelabrum, with seven branches, kept in the Tabernacle of the Temple in Jerusalem; later a principal Jewish symbol.

Midrash. Homiletic commentary on the Bible by the rabbis in the first centuries CE, codified in the period from the fourth to the twelfth centuries.

Mina. Greek monetary unit equal to 100 drachmas.

Mishnah. The codification by Rabbi Judah the Prince *ca.* 220 CE of the Oral Law which is traditionally said to have been transmitted by God to Moses at Sinai. It is the core of the Talmud, which consists of the Mishnah and the Gemara.

Mitzvah. A divine commandment, the number of which in the Pentateuch is traditionally counted as 613.

Municipium. A free town, the inhabitants of which had Roman citizenship but were governed by their own magistrates and laws.

Nome (Greek "portion"). Administrative division of Egypt, headed by a *strategos.*

Pancratium. An athletic contest involving both boxing and wrestling.

Papyrus. Egyptian plant which was formed into sheets and became the principal writing material in antiquity.

Patriarch. The leader of the Jewish community in Palestine who, from the first to the fifth century CE, in effect controlled Jewish religious life.

Pesiqta Rabbati. A collection of rabbinic homilies on the festivals of the Jewish calendar.

Plethron. A measure of length of approximately 100 feet.

Politeuma. Corporate body of immigrants of a given ethnic origin who had some autonomy but not citizenship in a city.

Pontifex Maximus (Latin "Supreme Pontiff"). Head of the Roman state religion. During the period of the empire every emperor held this post.

Praetor. Roman official, primarily in charge of the administration of justice.

Praetor peregrinus. The Roman magistrate in charge of administering justice in cases involving citizens vs. non-citizens.

Prefect. Administrator; in Egypt the title of the Roman governor.

Proconsul. Ex-consul, governor of certain provinces.

Propraetor. Ex-praetor, governor of certain provinces.

Proquaestor. Ex-quaestor, adjutant of the governor of a province.

Quaestor. Roman official, primarily responsible for finance.

Quartodecimans. Christians who insisted on observing Easter on the fourteenth day of the Jewish month of Nisan.

Sanhedrin. Judaized form of Greek *synedrion* ("council"). The highest political, judicial and religious council of the Jewish people in Palestine during the Roman period, both before and after the destruction of the Temple until 425 CE, consisting of seventy-one members.

Seleucid Era. The Jewish basis for reckoning years during the Hellenistic, Roman, and medieval periods, beginning with the year 311 BCE.

Shewbread. The twelve loaves of unleavened bread displayed every Sabbath in the inner sanctum of the Temple by the priests.

Shemittah. Every seventh year, during which, according to the Bible, land in Palestine must lie fallow.

Sheol. The biblical term for the Underworld.

Sifra. A Midrash on the Book of Leviticus dealing with religious legal matters.

Sifre. A Midrash on the Books of Numbers and Deuteronomy dealing with religious legal matters.

Stade. Approximately one-eighth of a mile.

Strategos. Greek title of a military commander, as well as of various categories of civil officials.

Talent. Greek monetary unit equal to 6,000 drachmas.

Talmud. The collection of rabbinic writings (the "Oral Torah" according to tradition) consisting of the Mishnah in sixty-three tractates and the Gamara commenting upon it. It exists in two versions – the Jerusalem Talmud, codified *ca.* 400, and the Babylonian Talmud, approximately three times as long, codified *ca.* 500.

Tanhuma. A midrash on the Pentateuch.

Tannaim. The name given to the rabbis of the first two centuries CE.

Torah (Hebrew "teaching"). The Pentateuch (Genesis, Exodus, Leviticus, Numbers, and Deuteronomy).

Tosefta. Rabbinic work parallel to the Mishnah and supplementing it.

Tribunician power. Supreme power of Roman emperors over civil affairs.

Zuz. A coin in use among Jews in the Land of Israel equivalent to a *denarius*, i.e., worth about a penny.

Suggested Topics for Further Research

1. A comparison of Josephus with Tacitus where they deal with the same material, e.g., the Jewish war.
2. A critical analysis of the sources of the military tactics employed by Josephus while he was commander in Galilee.
3. A comparison of Josephus with Suetonius and Dio Cassius where they deal with the same material, e.g., the assassination of Caligula and the accession of Claudius.
4. A comparison of Josephus and rabbinic sources where they deal with the same material, e.g., the Maccabean revolt; the reign of Salome Alexandra; the reign of Agrippa I; the conversion of the royal family of Adiabene; the burning of the Temple.
5. A comparison of Josephus' *Jewish War* and *Antiquities* where they deal with the same person or incident, e.g., Antiochus Epiphanes; Judah Maccabee; John Hyrcanus; Alexander Jannaeus; Salome Alexandra; some aspect of Herod's reign.
6. A comparison of Josephus' account of the Pharisees, the Sadducees or the Essenes in the *Jewish War* with his account in the *Antiquities*.
7. A comparison of Josephus' account of a given person or incident in the *Jewish War* with the corresponding account in *Sefer Yosippon* or the Slavonic Josephus.
8. A comparison of Josephus and papyrological evidence as to whether the Jews were citizens of Alexandria.
9. A comparison of Josephus and Philo where they deal with the same incident or person, e.g., Pontius Pilate or the Essenes or Caligula's order to set up a statue in the Temple.
10. A comparison of Josephus' and Sulpicius Severus' accounts of the burning of the Temple.
11. A comparison and critical analysis of Josephus' account and the Gospels' accounts of John the Baptist (*Antiquities* 18.116–19).
12. A critique of recent treatments of the question of the authenticity of the *Testimonium Flavianum* (*Antiquities* 18.63–4) dealing with Jesus.
13. A critical discussion of the value of the passages pertaining to John the Baptist and Jesus in the Slavonic version of Josephus' *Jewish War*.
14. The authenticity of the account of James the brother of Jesus in Josephus (*Antiquities* 20.197–203).

15. A comparison of a biblical figure or incident as treated by Josephus with the treatment in Philo or Pseudo-Philo's *Biblical Antiquities* or the Midrash.

16. A critical analysis of the various theories to explain what Josephus means by saying that he has not added to or subtracted from the biblical narrative (Josephus, *Antiquities* 1.17).

17. A comparison of Josephus' treatment of some aspect of Jewish law that has not been treated by David Goldenberg in his doctoral dissertation, *The Halakah in Josephus and in Tannaitic Literature: A Comparative Study* (Dropsie University, 1978), with the treatment in Philo, the Dead Sea documents, and rabbinic literature: the sanctuary (*Ant.* 3.102–50, 179–83); the garments of the priests (3.151–78, 184–7); the sacrifices (3.224–57, 4.206, *Against Apion* 2.195–8); purity laws (3.258–69); the woman accused of adultery (3.270–3); forbidden marriages (3.274–5); laws pertaining to priests (3.276–9, *Against Apion* 2.193–4); the sabbatical year and the jubilee year (3.280–5); laws pertaining to Levites (4.67–9); priestly and levitical dues (4.69–75, 205, 242), cities of refuge (4.172–3); inheritance (4.174–5); festival laws (4.203–4); idolatry (4.207 and *passim*); mixture of wool and linen in a garment (4.208); convocation at the close of the Sabbatical year (4.209–11); laws concerning prayers (4.212–13); administration of justice (4.214–18); witnesses (4.219); undetected murderer (4.220–2); laws pertaining to the king (4.223–4); non-removal of landmarks (4.225); fruits of the fourth year (4.226); hybridization (4.228–30); rights of the poor, widows, and orphans (4.231–41); marriage and divorce (4.244–59, *Against Apion* 2.199–203); slavery and the emancipation of slaves (4.273); "an eye for an eye" (4.280); the vicious ox (4.281–2); safeguards for wells and roofs (4.283–4); receivers of deposits (4.285–7, *Against Apion* 2.208, 216); eunuchs (4.290–1); laws pertaining to waging war (4.292–300 and *passim*); transvesticism (4.301); education of children (*Against Apion* 2.204); attitude toward aliens (*Against Apion* 2.209–10 and *passim*).

18. A critical analysis of theories to explain the disappearance of the Greek original of part of Josephus' essay *Against Apion*.

19. A critical discussion of the degree to which Josephus follows the criteria for historiography mentioned by Dionysius of Halicarnassus in his treatises on rhetoric and historiography.

20. A comparison of Josephus, Tacitus, Suetonius, and Dio Cassius in their treatment of Parthian affairs.

21. An examination of the degree to which Josephus was acquainted with Latin sources, notably Sallust and Cicero.

22. A critique of recent books and articles dealing with the question of the reliability of Josephus' account of the Masada episode, particularly in the light of the recent publication of the final report of Yigael Yadin's excavations.

23. A comparison of Josephus' defense of Judaism in his essay *Against Apion* with Philo's *Hypothetica*.

24. A critique of a recent book on Josephus and related subjects, e.g., Christopher Begg, *Josephus' Account of the Early Divided Monarchy (AJ 8,212–420): Rewriting the Bible* (Leuven University Press, 1993); Per

Bilde, *Flavius Josephus between Jerusalem and Rome: His Life, His Works, and Their Importance* (Sheffield Academic Press, 1988); Louis H. Feldman, *Jew and Gentile in the Ancient World: Attitudes and Interactions from Alexander to Justinian* (Princeton University Press, 1993); Rebecca Gray, *Prophetic Figures in Late Second Temple Jewish Palestine: The Evidence from Josephus* (New York: Oxford University Press, 1993); Dennis R. Lindsay, *Josephus and Faith: "Pistis" and "Pisteuein" as Faith Terminology in the Writings of Flavius Josephus and the New Testament* (Leiden: Brill, 1993); Steve Mason, *Flavius Josephus on the Pharisees* (Leiden: Brill, 1991); Steve Mason, *Josephus and the New Testament* (Peabody: Hendrickson, 1992); Doron Mendels, *The Rise and Fall of Jewish Nationalism* (New York: Doubleday, 1992); Joseph Mélèze Modrzejewski, *The Jews of Egypt from Rameses II to Emperor Hadrian* (trans. by Robert Cornman; Philadelphia: Jewish Publication Society, 1995); Maren Niehoff, *The Figure of Joseph in Post-Biblical Jewish Literature* (Leiden: Brill, 1992); Jonathan J. Price, *Jerusalem under Siege: The Collapse of the Jewish State 66–70* CE (Leiden: Brill, 1992); Tessa Rajak, *Josephus: The Historian and His Society* (Philadelphia: Fortress, 1983); Leonard V. Rutgers, *The Jews in Late Ancient Rome: Evidence of Cultural Interaction in the Roman Diaspora* (Leiden: Brill, 1995); Heinz Schreckenberg, "Josephus in Early Christian Literature and Medieval Christian Art," in Heinz Schreckenberg and Kurt Schubert, *Jewish Historiography and Iconography in Early and Medieval Christianity* (Assen: Van Gorcum, 1992), 1–138; Seth Schwartz, *Josephus and Judaean Politics* (Leiden: Brill, 1990); Gregory E. Sterling, *Historiography and Self-definition: Josephos, Luke–Acts and Apologetic Historiography* (Leiden: Brill, 1992); Pere Villalba I Varneda, *The Historical Method of Flavius Josephus* (Leiden: Brill, 1986); David S. Williams, *Stylometric Authorship Studies in Flavius Josephus and Related Literature* (Lewiston: Mellen, 1992).

25. An analysis of Josephus' influence on a Greek Church Father (e.g., Origen, Eusebius, Pseudo-Eustathius, John Chrysostom, Theodore of Mopsuestia, Isidore of Pelusium); a Latin Church Father (e.g., Tertullian, Lactantius, Ambrose, Jerome, Augustine, Cassiodorus); Syriac literature (e.g., Ephraem Syrus, Aphraates); Armenian literature; medieval Latin literature (e.g., Isidore of Seville, Adamnan, Bede, Alchrine, Notker, Angelomus, Albarus of Cordova, Lupus, Remigius, Frechulph, Widukind, Odo of Cluny, Adalger, Lanthert of Deutz, Marianus Scotus, Gerhoh of Reichersburg, Peter Comestor, Peter Cantor, Lambert of St. Omer, Peter of Blois, Frutolf, Otto of Freising, Rahewin, Gotfrid of Viterbo, Baudri of Bourgeuil, Wilhelm of Tyre, Galfred of Monmouth, Oderic, Radulf de Diceto, Walter of Chatillon, Acardus of Arroasia); Josephus' influence on the Crusades; on Byzantine Greek writers (e.g., Syncellus, Photius, Nikephoros Kallistos Xanthopoulos); on Karaite writers; on Renaissance Hebrew literature (e.g., Isaac Abravanel, Azariah dei Rossi); the use of the *Testimonium Flavianum* in Christian–Jewish polemics and disputations; on Czech, Dutch, English, American, French, German, Hungarian, Italian, Polish, and Spanish literature;

on modern historiography (e.g., Heinrich Graetz, Isaac Halevi, Joseph Klausner); on art and music; the influence of Hegesippus, of the Slavonic version, and of Arabic and Ethiopic versions of Josephus.

26. An analysis of the Greek and Jewish elements in Ezekiel the Dramatist's tragedy, *Exodus,* and a comparison of it with Euripides.
27. An analysis of the Greek and Jewish elements in Philo the Elder's epic poem, *On Jerusalem,* and Theodotus' *On Shechem,* and a comparison with Homer.
28. An analysis pro, and con, as to whether one of the following was a Jew or a non-Jew: Eupolemus, Pseudo-Eupolemus, Artapanus, Pseudo-Hecataeus.
29. A comparison of the Greek and Jewish elements in the political theory of Philo.
30. A comparison of Philo and Gnosticism.
31. A comparison of two views of Platonism (limited to a single aspect) in the Hellenistic–Roman Age: Philo vs. Plutarch.
32. Wolfson vs. Goodenough: a comparison and critique of their analyses of a given aspect of Philo.
33. A critique of a recent book on Philo, Pseudo-Philo, and related subjects, e.g., David M. Hay, ed., *Both Literal and Allegorical: Studies in Philo of Alexandria's Questions and Answers on Genesis and Exodus* (Atlanta: Scholars Press, 1991); Alan Mendelson, *Philo's Jewish Identity* (Atlanta: Scholars Press, 1988); Frederick J. Murphy, *Pseudo-Philo: Rewriting the Bible* (New York: Oxford University Press, 1993); David T. Runia, *Exegesis and Philosophy: Studies on Philo of Alexandria* (Aldershot: Variorum, 1990); David T. Runia, *Philo in Early Christian Literature* (Assen: Van Gorcum, 1993); Dorothy Sly, *Philo's Perception of Women* (Atlanta: Scholars Press, 1990); Howard Jacobson, *A Commentary on Pseudo-Philo's Liber Antiquitatum Biblicarum,* 2 vols (Leiden: Brill, 1996); Torrey Seland, *Establishment Violence in Philo and Luke: A Study of Non-Conformity to the Torah and Jewish Vigilante Reaction* (Leiden: Brill, 1995).
34. A critique of a recent book dealing with anti-Judaism, e.g., Hans Conzelmann, *Gentiles–Jews–Christians: Polemics and Apologetics in the Greco-Roman Era,* trans. from the German by M. Eugene Boring (Minneapolis: Fortress, 1992); Judith Lieu, John North, Tessa Rajak, eds, *The Jews among Pagans and Christians* (London, Routledge, 1992); Arnaldo D. Momigliano, *On Pagans, Jews, and Christians* (Middletown, Conn.: Wesleyan University, 1987).
35. A critique of theories on the sources of the blood libel as found in Apion and Damocritus.
36. A critique of a recent book dealing with proselytism by Jews in antiquity, e.g., Scot McKnight, *A Light among the Gentiles: Jewish Missionary Activity in the Second Temple Period* (Minneapolis: Fortress, 1991); Gary G. Porton, *The Stranger within Your Gates: Converts and Conversion in Rabbinic Literature* (University of Chicago Press, 1994); Martin Goodman, *Mission and Conversion: Proselytizing in the Religious History of the Roman Empire* (Cambridge University Press, 1994).

37. A critique of a recent book dealing with Judaism in the Second Temple period, e.g., Jacob Neusner, *The Philosophical Mishnah*, 4 vols. (Atlanta: Scholars Press, 1988–9); E. P. Sanders, *Jewish Law from Jesus to the Mishnah* (London: SCM, 1990); E. P. Sanders, *Judaism: Practice and Belief, 63 BCE–66 CE* (London: SCM, 1992); Jacob Neusner, ed., *Judaism in Late Antiquity*, 2 vols (Leiden: Brill, 1995).

38. A critique of a recent book dealing with women in the ancient world, e.g., Leila L. Bronner, *From Eve to Esther: Rabbinic Reconstructions of Biblical Women* (Louisville: Westminster/Knox, 1994); Cheryl Anne Brown, *No Longer Be Silent: First Century Jewish Portraits of Biblical Women* (Louisville: Westminster, 1992); Averil Cameron and Amelie Kuhrt, *Images of Women in Antiquity* (Detroit: Wayne State University Press, 1983); Amy-J. Levine, ed., *"Women like This": New Perspectives on Jewish Women in the Greco-Roman World* (Atlanta: Scholars Press, 1991).

39. A critique of a recent book dealing with the Jewish background of Christianity, e.g., David Flusser, *Judaism and the Origins of Christianity* (Jerusalem: Magnes, 1988); John P. Meier, *A Marginal Jew: Rethinking the Historical Jesus*, 2 vols (New York: Doubleday, 1991–4); Daniel R. Schwartz, *Studies on the Jewish Background of Christianity* (Tübingen: Mohr, 1992); Hershel Shanks, ed., *Christianity and Rabbinic Judaism: A Parallel History of Their Origins and Early Development* (Washington: Biblical Archaeology Society, 1992).

40. A critical analysis of Robert Tannenbaum's discussion of the Jewish institutions and the historical significance of the recently discovered inscriptions at Aphrodisias (in Joyce Reynolds and Robert Tannenbaum, *Jews and God-fearers at Aphrodisias* [Cambridge Philological Society, Supplementary Vol. 12, 1987]).

41. A critical analysis of Erwin R. Goodenough's thesis in his *Jewish Symbols in the Greco-Roman Period*, 13 vols (Princeton University Press, 1953–68) that Rabbinic teachings had little influence on the practices of the Hellenistic Jewish community and/or the Palestinian Jewish community, especially with respect to the laws pertaining to art and art objects.

42. A critique of Horace M. Kallen's *The Book of Job as a Greek Tragedy* (New York: Moffat, Yard, 1918).

43. A critique of Rozelaar's attempt (in *Eshkolot* I [1954], pp. 33–48) to view the Song of Songs as a Hellenistic work.

44. A critique of Henry A. Fischel's *Rabbinic Literature and Greco-Roman Philosophy* (Leiden: Brill, 1973).

45. A critique of Yitzchak Baer's *Yisrael Ba-amim* [Hebrew] (Jerusalem: Mosad Bialik, 1955).

46. A critique of a chapter of Saul Lieberman's *Greek in Jewish Palestine* (New York: Jewish Theological Seminary, 1942) or his *Hellenism in Jewish Palestine* (New York: Jewish Theological Seminary, 1950).

47. A critique of a recent book dealing with the great Jewish revolt against the Romans, e.g., Martin Goodman, *The Ruling Class of Judaea: The Origins of the Jewish Revolt against Rome AD 66–70* (Cambridge University Press, 1987); Martin Hengel, *The Zealots*

(Edinburgh: T&T Clark, 1989); Richard A. Horsley, *Jesus and the Spread of Violence: Popular Jewish Resistance in Roman Palestine* (San Francisco: Harper, 1987).

48. A critique of a Marxist interpretation of Josephus' account of the great Jewish revolt against the Romans, e.g., Heinz Kreissig, "A Marxist View of Josephus' Account of the Jewish War," in Louis H. Feldman and Gohei Hata, eds., *Josephus, the Bible, and History* (Detroit: Wayne State University, 1989), 265–77.

49. A comparison of one category of the legal documents (e.g., loans, divorce) found in Egyptian Jewish papyri with the format of such documents as discussed in Talmudic literature, and conclusions as to the relevance of such evidence in evaluating the degree to which Alexandrian Jewry was "Orthodox."

50. A critique of the evidence as to the political status of the Jews in Alexandria, with particular attention to Aryeh Kasher's *The Jews in Hellenistic and Roman Egypt* (Tübingen: Mohr, 1985) and Constantine Zuckerman's "Hellenistic politeumata and the Jews: A Reconsideration," *Scripta Classica Israelica* 8–9 (1985–8), 171–85.

51. A critical analysis of the treatment in Greek and Roman pagan writers (e.g., Hecataeus of Abdera, Alexander Polyhistor, Pompeius Trogus) of a particular portion of the Bible or a particular portion of Jewish history.

52. A critique of the views of Elias J. Bickerman, *The God of the Maccabees: Studies on the Meaning and Origin of the Maccabean Revolt* (Leiden: Brill, 1979), Victor Tcherikover, *Hellenistic Civilization and the Jews* (Philadelphia: Jewish Publication Society, 1959), 152–203, Martin Hengel, *Judaism and Hellenism*, vol. 1 (Philadelphia: Fortress, 1974), 267–303, and Fergus Millar, "The Background of the Maccabean Revolution: Reflections on Martin Hengel's 'Judaism and Hellenism,'" *Journal of Jewish Studies* 29 (1978), 1–21, with regard to the role of Antiochus Epiphanes in the Maccabean revolt.

53. An analysis and critique of Plutarch's views on one aspect of Judaism: the dietary laws, Jewish theology, or the celebration of Tabernacles.

54. A critical analysis of the various theories concerning the meaning of *ḥochmah yevanit* (Babylonian Talmud, *Menaḥoth* 64b, 99b, *Sotah* 49b, *Baba Qamma* 82b).

55. A critical analysis of the meaning of *Sifrei Homiros* (Mishnah, *Yadaim* 4:6).

56. A critical analysis of the theory that the Septuagint contains Greek philosophical elements.

57. A comparison and analysis of the differences between pagan anti-Judaism and the anti-Judaism of a given Church Father, e.g., John Chrysostom.

General Bibliography

ALON, GEDALIAH. *Jews, Judaism and the Classical World: Studies in Jewish History in the Times of the Second Temple and Talmud,* trans. by Israel Abrahams (1977).

——. *The Jews in Their Land in the Talmudic Age (70–640 CE)* (1980).

APPLEBAUM, SHIMON. *Prolegomena to the Study of the Second Jewish Revolt (132–135)* (1976).

——. *Jews and Greeks in Ancient Greece* (1978).

——. *Jews and Greeks in Ancient Cyrene* (1979).

ATTRIDGE, HAROLD W. *The Interpretation of Biblical History in the Antiquitates Judaicae of Flavius Josephus* (1976).

AVI-YONAH, MICHAEL. *The Holy Land from the Persian to the Arab Conquests (536 BC to AD 640): A Historical Geography* (1966).

——. *The Jews of Palestine: A Political History from the Bar Kochba War to the Arab Conquest* (1976).

——. *Hellenism and the East: Contacts and Interactions from Alexander to the Roman Conquest* (1978).

—— and BARAS, ZVI, eds. *The World History of the Jewish People,* First Series: Ancient Times, vol. 7: *The Herodian Period* (1975).

—— and BARAS, ZVI, eds. *The World History of the Jewish People,* First Series: Ancient Times, vol. 8: *Society and Religion in the Second Temple Period* (1977).

BALSDON, JOHN P. V. D. *Romans and Aliens* (1979).

BAMBERGER, BERNARD J. *Proselytism in the Talmudic Period* (1939).

BAR-KOCHVA, BEZALEL. *Judas Maccabaeus: The Jewish Struggle against the Seleucids* (1989).

BARON, SALO W. *A Social and Religious History of the Jews,* 2nd edn, vols 1 and 2 (1952).

—— and BLAU, JOSEPH L., eds. *Judaism: Postbiblical and Talmudic Period* (1954).

BARTLETT, JOHN R. *Jews in the Hellenistic World* (1985).

BELL, HAROLD IDRIS. *Cults and Creeds in Greco-Roman Egypt* (1952).

BICKERMAN, ELIAS J. *From Ezra to the Last of the Maccabees: Foundations of Postbiblical Judaism,* 7th edn (1962).

——. *The God of the Maccabees: Studies in the Meaning and the Origin of the Maccabean Revolt* (1979).

——. *The Jews in the Greek Age* (1988).

BILDE, PER. *Flavius Josephus between Jerusalem and Rome: His Life, His Works, and Their Importance* (1988).

BOKSER, BARUCH M. "Recent Developments in the Study of Judaism 70–200 CE," *Second Century* 3 (1983), 1–68.

BOWERSOCK, GLEN W. *Hellenism in Late Antiquity* (1990).

BOX, GEORGE H. *Judaism in the Greek Period from the Rise of Alexander the Great to the Intervention of Rome (333–63 BC)* (1932).

BRAUDE, WILLIAM G. *Jewish Proselyting in the First Five Centuries of the Common Era: The Age of the Tannaim and Amoraim* (1940).

BRAUN, MARTIN. *History and Romance in Graeco-Oriental Literature* (1938).

BROWN, PETER. *The Making of Late Antiquity* (1978).

CHARLESWORTH, JAMES H. *The Pseudepigrapha and Modern Research*, 2nd edn (1981).

——. *The Old Testament Pseudepigrapha*. 2 vols (1985).

COGGINS, R. J. *Samaritans and Jews* (1975).

COHEN, SHAYE J. D. *Josephus in Galilee and Rome: His Vita and Development as a Historian* (1979).

——. *From the Maccabees to the Mishnah* (1987).

——. "Roman Domination: The Jewish Revolt and the Destruction of the Second Temple," in Hershel Shanks, ed., *Ancient Israel: A Short History from Abraham to the Roman Destruction of the Temple* (1988), 205–35, 257–9.

—— and FRERICHS, ERNEST S., eds. *Diasporas in Antiquity* (1993).

COLLINS, JOHN J. *Between Athens and Jerusalem: Jewish Identity in the Hellenistic Diaspora* (1983).

——. "Dead Sea Scrolls," *ABD* 6 (1992), 85–101.

CROWN, ALAN D., ed. *The Samaritans* (1988).

——; PUMMER, REINHARD; and TAL, ABRAHAM, eds. *A Companion to Samaritan Studies* (1993).

DANIEL, JERRY L. "Anti-Semitism in the Hellenistic–Roman Period," *JBL* 98 (1979), 45–65.

DAVIES, WILLIAM D. and FINKELSTEIN, LOUIS, eds. *The Cambridge History of Judaism*, vol. 2: *The Hellenistic Age* (1989).

EDDY, SAMUEL K. *The King Is Dead: Studies in the Near Eastern Resistance to Hellenism 334–31 BC* (1961).

FELDMAN, LOUIS H. "The Orthodoxy of the Jews in Hellenistic Egypt," *JSoS* 22 (1960), 212–37.

——. *Josephus and Modern Scholarship (1937–1980)* (1984).

——. "Anti-Semitism in the Ancient World," in David Berger, ed., *History and Hate: The Dimensions of Anti-Semitism* (1986), 15–42.

——. "How Much Hellenism in Jewish Palestine?" *HUCA* 57 (1986), 83–111.

——. "A Selective Critical Bibliography of Josephus," in Louis H. Feldman and Gohei Hata, eds, *JBH* (1989), 330–448.

——. "Palestinian and Diaspora Judaism in the First Century," in Hershel Shanks, ed., *Christianity and Rabbinic Judaism: A Parallel History of Their Origins and Early Development* (1992), 1–39, 327–36.

——. "Some Observations on Rabbinic Reaction to Roman Rule in Third Century Palestine," *HUCA* 63 (1992), 39–81.

——. *Jew and Gentile in the Ancient World: Attitudes and Interactions from Alexander to Justinian* (1993).

——. *Studies in Hellenistic Judaism* (1996).

FELDMAN, LOUIS H. and HATA, GOHEI, eds. *Josephus, Judaism, and Christianity* (1987).

—— and HATA, GOHEI, eds. *Josephus, the Bible, and History* (1989).

FINKELSTEIN, LOUIS. *The Pharisees*, 2 vols (1962).

FISCHEL, HENRY A. *Rabbinic Literature and Greco-Roman Philosophy* (1973).

——, ed. *Essays in Greco-Roman and Related Talmudic Literature* (1977).

FREEDMAN, DAVID N., ed. *The Anchor Bible Dictionary*, 6 vols (1992).

FREY, JEAN-BAPTISTE. *Corpus Inscriptionum Iudaicarum*, 2 vols (1936–52) (reissued with a prolegomenon by Baruch Lifshitz [1975], 21–107).

FREYNE, SEAN. *Galilee from Alexander the Great to Hadrian 323 BCE to 135 CE: A Study of Second Temple Judaism* (1980).

FUKS, ALEXANDER. "Aspects of the Jewish Revolt in AD 115–17," *JRS* 51 (1961), 98–104.

GAGER, JOHN G. *Moses in Greco-Roman Paganism* (1972).

——. "The Dialogue of Paganism with Judaism: Bar Cochba to Julian," *HUCA* 44 (1973), 89–118.

——. *The Origins of Anti-Semitism: Attitudes toward Judaism in Pagan and Christian Antiquity* (1983).

GOLDSTEIN, JONATHAN A. "Jewish Acceptance and Rejection of Hellenism," in E. P. Sanders *et al.*, *Jewish and Christian Self-Definition*, vol. 2: *Aspects of Judaism in the Greco-Roman Period* (1981), 64–87, 318–26.

GOODENOUGH, ERWIN R. *The Politics of Philo Judaeus* (1938).

——. *An Introduction to Philo Judaeus* (1940).

——. *Jewish Symbols in the Greco-Roman Period*, 13 vols (1953–68).

GOODMAN, MARTIN. *State and Society in Roman Galilee AD 132–212* (1983).

——. *The Ruling Class of Judaea: The Origins of the Jewish Revolt against Rome AD 66–70* (1987).

——. *Mission and Conversion: Proselytizing in the Religious History of the Roman Empire* (1994).

GRABBE, LESTER L. *Judaism from Cyrus to Hadrian*, vol. 1: *The Persian and Greek Period*; vol. 2: *The Roman Period* (1991–2).

GRANT, MICHAEL. *Herod the Great* (1971).

——. *The Jews in the Roman World* (1973).

GRAY, REBECCA. *Prophetic Figures in Late Second Temple Jewish Palestine: The Evidence from Josephus* (1993).

GREEN, PETER. *Alexander to Actium: The Historical Evolution of the Hellenistic Age* (1990).

GUTMANN, JOSEPH, ed. *The Synagogue: Studies in Origins, Archaeology, and Architecture* (1975).

——, ed. *Ancient Synagogues: The State of Research* (1981).

HACHLILI, RACHEL. *Ancient Jewish Art and Archaeology in the Land of Israel* (1988).

HADAS, MOSES. *Hellenistic Culture: Fusion and Diffusion* (1959).

HALIVNI, DAVID W. *Midrash, Mishnah and Gemara* (1986).

HANSON, JOHN S. and HORSLEY, RICHARD A. *Bandits, Prophets, and Messiahs: Popular Movements in the Time of Jesus* (1985).

HARRIS, HAROLD A. *Greek Athletics and the Jews* (1976).

HEINEMANN, ISAAK. "The Attitude of the Ancient World toward Judaism," *RR* 4 (1939–40), 385–400.

HENGEL, MARTIN. *Judaism and Hellenism: Studies in their Encounter in Palestine during the Early Hellenistic Period*, trans. by John Bowden, 2 vols (1974).

——. *Jews, Greeks and Barbarians: Aspects of the Hellenization of Judaism in the Pre-Christian Period*, trans. by John Bowden (1980).

——. *The "Hellenization" of Judaea in the First Century after Christ* (1989).

HOLLADAY, CARL R. *Fragments from Hellenistic Jewish Authors*, vol. 1: *Historians* (1983); vol. 2: *Poets* (1989); vol. 3: *Aristobulus* (1995).

HORBORY, WILLIAM and NOY, DAVID. *Jewish Inscriptions of Graeco-Roman Egypt: With an Index of the Jewish Inscriptions of Egypt and Cyrenaica* (1992).

HORST, PIETER W. VAN DER. *Ancient Jewish Epitaphs. An Introductory Survey of a Millennium of Jewish Funerary Epigraphy (300 BCE–700 CE)* (1991).

——. *Hellenism, Judaism, Christianity: Essays on Their Interaction* (1994).

JACOBSON, HOWARD. *The Exagoge of Ezekiel* (1983).

——. *A Commentary on Pseudo-Philo's Liber Antiquitatum Biblicarum*, 2 vols (1996).

JEREMIAS, JOACHIM. *Jerusalem in the Time of Jesus: An Investigation into Economic and Social Conditions during the New Testament Period*, trans. by F. H. and C. H. Cave (1969).

KADMAN, LEO. *The Coins of the Jewish War of 66–73 CE* (1960).

KANAEL, BARUCH. "Ancient Jewish Coins and Their Historical Importance," *BA* 26 (1963), 38–62.

KASHER, ARYEH. *The Jews in Hellenistic and Roman Egypt: The Struggle for Equal Rights* (1985).

——. *Jews and Hellenistic Cities in Eretz-Israel: Relations of the Jews in Eretz-Israel with the Hellenistic Cities during the Second Temple Period (332 BCE–70 CE)* (1990).

KINDLER, ARIE. *Coins of the Land of Israel* (1974).

KRAABEL, ALF THOMAS. "The Diaspora Synagogue: Archaeological and Epigraphic Evidence since Sukenik," *ANRW* 2.19 (1979), 477–510.

KRAEMER, DAVID. *Responses to Suffering in Classical Rabbinic Literature* (1995).

KRAEMER, ROSS S. *Her Share of the Blessings. Women's Religions among Pagans, Jews, and Christians in the Greco-Roman World* (1992).

KRAFT, ROBERT and NICKELSBURG, GEORGE W. E., eds. *Early Judaism and Its Modern Interpreters* (1986).

LANGE, NICHOLAS R. M. DE. *Apocrypha. Jewish Literature of the Hellenistic Age* (1978).

LANGMUIR, GAVIN I. *History, Religion and Antisemitism* (1990).

LEON, HARRY J. *The Jews of Ancient Rome* (1960).

LEVINE, LEE I. A. *Ancient Synagogues Revealed* (1981).

——. "The Age of Hellenism: Alexander the Great and the Rise and Fall of the Hasmonean Kingdom," in Hershel Shanks, ed., *Ancient Israel: A Short History from Abraham to the Roman Destruction of the Temple* (1988), 177–204, 254–7.

——. *The Rabbinic Class of Roman Palestine in Late Antiquity* (1989).

——. "Judaism from the Destruction of Jerusalem to the End of the Second Jewish Revolt: 70–135 CE), in Hershel Shanks, ed., *Christianity* and Rabbinic Judaism: A Parallel History of Their Origins and Early Development (1992), 125–49, 338–40.

LIEBERMAN, SAUL. Greek in Jewish Palestine: Studies in the Life and Manners of Jewish Palestine in the II–IV Centuries CE (1942).

——. Hellenism in Jewish Palestine: Studies in the Literary Transmission, Beliefs and Manners of Palestine in the I Century BCE (1950).

——. "How Much Greek in Jewish Palestine?" in Alexander Altmann, ed., Studies and Texts, vol. 1: Biblical and Other Studies (1963), 123–41.

LIEU, JUDITH; NORTH, JOHN; and RAJAK, TESSA, eds. The Jews among the Pagans and Christians in the Roman Empire (1992).

LINDER, AMNON, ed. The Jews in Roman Imperial Legislation (1987).

MANTEL, HUGO. Studies in the History of the Sanhedrin (1961).

MARCUS, RALPH. "Antisemitism in the Hellenistic–Roman World," in Koppel S. Pinson, ed., Essays on Antisemitism, 2nd edn (1946), 61–78.

——. "A Selected Bibliography of the Jews in the Hellenistic–Roman Period," PAAJR 16 (1946–7), 97–181.

——. "The Hellenistic Age," in Leo W. Schwarz, ed., Great Ages and Ideas of the Jewish People (1956), 95–139.

MASON, STEVE. Flavius Josephus on the Pharisees (1991).

McCLAREN, JAMES S. Power and Politics in Palestine: The Jews and the Governing of Their Land: 100 BC–AD 70 (1991).

McKAY, HEATHER A. Sabbath and Synagogue: The Question of Sabbath Worship in Ancient Judaism (1994).

McKNIGHT, SCOT. A Light among the Gentiles: Jewish Missionary Activity in the Second Temple Period (1991).

MENDELSON, ALAN. Secular Education in Philo of Alexandria (1982).

——. Philo's Jewish Identity (1988).

MESHORER, YAAKOV. Jewish Coins of the Second Temple Period, trans. by I. H. Levine (1967).

——. Ancient Jewish Coinage, 2 vols (1983).

MILLAR, FERGUS. "The Background of the Maccabean Revolution: Reflections on Martin Hengel's 'Judaism and Hellenism,'" JJS 22 (1978), 1–21.

——. "The Jews of the Graeco-Roman Diaspora between Paganism and Christianity, AD 312–438," in Judith Lieu et al., eds, The Jews among Pagans and Christians in the Roman Empire (1992), 97–123.

——. The Roman Near East 31 BC–AD 337 (1993).

MODRZEJEWSKI, JOSEPH MÉLÈZE. The Jews of Egypt from Rameses II to Emperor Hadrian (trans. by Robert Cornman) (1995).

MOMIGLIANO, ARNALDO D. Alien Wisdom: The Limits of Hellenization (1975).

——. On Pagans, Jews, and Christians (1987).

MOORE, GEORGE F. Judaism in the First Centuries of the Christian Era: The Age of the Tannaim, 3 vols (1927–30).

MULDER, MARTIN J., ed. Mikra: Text, Translation, Reading and Interpretation of the Hebrew Bible in Ancient Judaism and Early Christianity (CRINT, Sect. 2, vol. 1) (1988).

MURPHY, FREDERICK J. Pseudo-Philo: Rewriting the Bible (1993).

MUSURILLO, HERBERT, ed. The Acts of the Pagan Martyrs. Acta Alexandrinorum (1954).

NEUSNER, JACOB. *The Rabbinic Traditions about the Pharisees before 70*, 3 vols (1971).

——. *From Politics to Piety: The Emergence of Pharisaic Judaism* (1973).

——, ed. *Judaism in Late Antiquity*: Part 1: *The Literary and Archaeological Sources*; Part 2: *Historical Syntheses* (1995).

NICKELSBURG, GEORGE W. E. *Jewish Literature between the Bible and the Mishnah: A Historical and Literary Introduction* (1981, rev. edn 1987).

NOY, DAVID. *Jewish Inscriptions of Western Europe*, vol. 1: *Italy (Excluding the City of Rome), Spain and Gaul*; vol. 2: *The City of Rome* (1993–5).

OESTERLEY, WILLIAM O. E. *The Jews and Judaism during the Greek Period: The Background of Christianity* (1941).

OPPENHEIMER, AHARON. *The Am Ha-Aretz: A Study in the Social History of the Jewish People in the Hellenistic-Roman Period* (1977).

OVERMAN, J. ANDREW and MACLELLAN, ROBERT S., eds. *Diaspora Jews and Judaism: Essays in Honor of and in Dialogue with A. Thomas Kraabel* (1992).

PARENTE, FAUSTO and SIEVERS, JOSEPH, eds. *Josephus and the History of the Greco-Roman Period: Essays in Memory of Morton Smith* (1994).

PARKES, JAMES W. *The Conflict of the Church and the Synagogue: A Study in the Origins of Antisemitism* (1934).

PEARLMAN, MOSHE. *The Maccabees* (1973).

PFEIFFER, ROBERT H. *History of New Testament Times with an Introduction to the Apocrypha* (1949).

PORTON, GARY G. *The Stranger within Your Gates: Converts and Conversion in Rabbinic Literature* (1994).

PRICE, JONATHAN J. *Jerusalem under Siege: The Collapse of the Jewish State 66–70 CE* (1992).

RABELLO, ALFREDO M. "The Legal Condition of the Jews in the Roman Empire," *ANRW* 2.13 (1980), 662–762.

RADIN, MAX. *The Jews among the Greeks and Romans* (1915).

RAJAK, TESSA. *Josephus: The Historian and His Society* (1984).

REIFENBERG, ADOLF. *Ancient Jewish Coins*, 4th edn (1965).

REINHOLD, MEYER. *Diaspora: The Jews among the Greeks and Romans* (1983).

RHOADS, DAVID. *Israel in Revolution 6–74 CE* (1976).

ROKEAH, DAVID. *Jews, Pagans and Christians in Conflict* (1982).

RUSSELL, DAVID S. *The Jews from Alexander to Herod* (1967).

RUTGERS, LEONARD V. "Archaeological Evidence for the Interaction of Jews and non-Jews in Late Antiquity," *AJA* 96 (1992), 101–18.

——. *The Jews in Late Ancient Rome: Evidence of Cultural Interaction in the Roman Diaspora* (1995).

SAFRAI, SAMUEL and STERN, MENAHEM, with FLUSSER, DAVID and VAN UNNIK, WILLEM C., eds, *The Jewish People in the First Century* (*CRINT*, 2 sections, 2 vols) (1974–6).

—— and TOMSON, P. J., eds. *The Literature of the Sages* (*CRINT* 2.3) (1987).

SANDERS, E. P. *Jewish Law from Jesus to the Mishnah* (1990).

——. *Judaism: Practice and Belief 63 BCE–66 CE* (1992).

—— et al., eds. *Jewish and Christian Self-Definition*, 3 vols (1980–2).

SANDMEL, SAMUEL. *The First Christian Century in Judaism and Christianity: Certainties and Uncertainties* (1969).

SANDMEL, SAMUEL. "Hellenism and Judaism," in Stanley M. Wagner and Allen D. Breck, eds, *Great Confrontations in Jewish History* (1977), 21–38.

——. *Philo of Alexandria: An Introduction* (1979).

SCHALIT, ABRAHAM, ed. *The World History of the Jewish People*, vol. 6: *The Hellenistic Age* (1972).

SCHIFFMAN, LAWRENCE H. *From Text to Tradition: A History of Second Temple and Rabbinic Judaism* (1991).

——. *Reclaiming the Dead Sea Scrolls* (1994).

SCHÜRER, EMIL. *The History of the Jewish People in the Age of Jesus Christ (175 BC–AD 135)*, ed. by Geza Vermes and Fergus Millar, 3 vols (1973–86).

SCHWARTZ, DANIEL R. *Agrippa I: The Last King of Judaea* (1990).

SCHWARTZ, SETH. *Josephus and Judaean Politics* (1990).

SEAVER, JAMES E. *Persecution of the Jews in the Roman Empire (300–438)* (1952).

SEGAL, ALAN F. *Two Powers in Heaven* (1977).

——. *The Other Judaisms of Late Antiquity* (1987).

SELTZER, ROBERT M. *Jewish People, Jewish Thought: The Jewish Experience in History* (1980).

SEVENSTER, JAN N. *Do You Know Greek? How Much Greek Could the First Jewish Christians Have Known?* (1968).

——. *The Roots of Pagan Anti-Semitism in the Ancient World* (1975).

SHANKS, HERSHEL, ed. *Ancient Israel: A Short History from Abraham to the Roman Destruction of the Temple* (1988).

——, ed. *Christianity and Rabbinic Judaism: A Parallel History of Their Origins and Early Development* (1992).

SIEVERS, JOSEPH. *The Hasmoneans and their Supporters: From Mattathias to the Death of John Hyrcanus I* (1990).

SIMON, MARCEL. *Verus Israel: A Study of the Relations between Christians and Jews in the Roman Empire (135–325)*, trans. by Henry McKeating (1986).

SMALLWOOD, EDITH MARY. *The Jews under Roman Rule: From Pompey to Diocletian* (1976).

SMITH, MORTON. "Palestinian Judaism in the First Century," in Moshe Davis, ed., *Israel: Its Role in Civilization* (1956), 67–81; reprinted in Henry A. Fischel, ed., *Essays in Greco-Roman and Related Talmudic Lierature* (1977), 183–97.

STERLING, GREGORY, E. *Historiography and Self-definition: Josephos, Luke–Acts and Apologetic Historiography* (1992).

Stern, Menahem. *Greek and Latin Authors on Jews and Judaism*, 3 vols (1974–84).

——. "The Jews in Greek and Latin Literature," in Samuel Safrai and Menahem Stern, with David Flusser and Willen C. van Unnik, eds, *The Jewish People in the First Century (CRINT)* (1976), 1101–59.

——. "The Period of the Second Temple," in Haim H. Ben-Sasson, ed., *A History of the Jewish People* (1976), 185–306.

——. *Studies in Jewish History: The Second Temple Period*, ed. M. Amit, Isaiah Gafni, and Moshe D. Herr (1991).

STONE, MICHAEL, E., *Scriptures, Sects and Visions* (1980).

STONE, MICHAEL, E., ed. *Jewish Writings of the Second Temple Period: Apocrypha, Pseudepigrapha, Qumran Sectarian Writings, Philo, Josephus* (*CRINT*, Sect. 2, vol. 2) (1984).

SULLIVAN, RICHARD D., "The Dynasty of Judaea in the First Century," *ANRW* 2.8 (1977), 296–354.

TALMON, SHEMARYAHAU, ed. *Jewish Civilization in the Hellenistic–Roman Period* (1991).

TCHERIKOVER, VICTOR. "Jewish Apologetic Literature Reconsidered," *Eos* 48 (1956), 169–93.

——. *Hellenistic Civilization and the Jews* (1959).

——. "The Decline of the Jewish Diaspora in Egypt in the Roman Period," *JJS* 4 (1963), 1–32.

——; FUKS, ALEXANDER; and STERN, MENAHEM, eds. *Corpus Papyrorum Judaicarum*, 3 vols (1957–64).

THACKERAY, HENRY ST. J. *Josephus the Man and the Historian* (1929).

TREBILCO, PAUL R. *Jewish Communities in Asia Minor* (1991).

URBACH, EPHRAIM E. "The Rabbinical Laws of Idolatry in the Second and Third Centuries in the Light of Archaeological and Historical Facts," *IEJ* 9 (1959), 149–65 and 229–45.

——. *The Sages: Their Concepts and Beliefs* (1975).

VANDERKAM, JAMES C. *The Dead Sea Scrolls Today* (1994).

VERMES, GEZA. *The Dead Sea Scrolls: Qumran in Perspective* (1981).

VILLALBA I VARNEDA, PERE. *The Historical Method of Flavius Josephus* (1986).

WACHOLDER, BEN ZION. *Eupolemus: A Study of Judaeo-Greek Literature* (1974).

WIRGIN, WOLF and MANDEL, SIEGFRIED. *The History of Coins and Symbols in Ancient Israel* (1958).

WOLFSON, HARRY A. *Philo: Foundations of Religious Philosophy in Judaism, Christianity, and Islam* (1947).

YADIN, YIGAEL. *Masada: Herod's Fortress and the Zealots' Last Stand* (1966).

——. *Bar-Kokhba: The Rediscovery of the Legendary Hero of the Second Jewish Revolt against Rome* (1971).

ZEITLIN, SOLOMON. *The Rise and Fall of the Judaean State: A Political, Social and Religious History of the Second Commonwealth*, 3 vols (1962–78).

Index of Ancient Authors, Tracts, and Documents

General Index

Abaye, Rabbi, on credibility of one witness when wife is charged with adultery, 156; on power of demons, 225

Abba bar Kahana, Rabbi, on coming of Messiah when Persia will overcome Rome, 188

Abba Benjamin, Rabbi, on power of demons, 225

Abba Joseph ben Ḥanin, Rabbi, on strife between high priest and ordinary priests, 210

Abba Qolon, makes possible founding of Rome, 189–90

Abba Saul, Rabbi, on strife between high priest and ordinary priests, 210

Abba Sikra, head of revolutionaries in Jerusalem in 66, 275

Abbahu, Rabbi, on Emperor "Antoninus" as a righteous proselyte, 141; on tremendous number of Jews killed in Bar Kochba rebellion, 300

Abimi, Rabbi, speculates on coming of Messiah, 221

Abraham, as astrologer, 114–15, 226, 228; on change of his name as viewed by Philo, 53; circumcision of, 129; Heracles connected to, 117–18, 229; as King of Damascus according to Pompeius Trogus, 105–6; and the Pergamenes, 166; praise of in poem by Philo the Epic Poet, 38–9; Sparta as descending from, 163–4

Adam and Eve, account of in Bible attacked by Julian, 364–5

Adiabenians, conversion of, 126–7; participation of in revolt against Rome, 266

Adonis, equated with Jewish God by Plutarch, 374–5

Afterlife, belief in, as described by 1 Enoch, 223; disagreement of Pharisees and Sadducees on, 242–3; Essene belief in, 251; Talmudic description of, 224–5

Agriculture, richness of Palestine in, 195–6

Agrippa, Marcus, son-in-law of Augustus, friend of Herod, 171, 175; reaffirms right of Jews in Ionia to be citizens, 86–7

Agrippa I, king of Judaea, appeals to Roman governor to protest desecration of synagogue by people of Dora, 88–9; arranges meeting of rulers of

several small kingdoms, 266; on his imprisonment by Tiberius and later elevation to kingship by Emperor Caligula, 178–80; lawsuit against brought by gymnasiarch Isidoros before Claudius, 359–60; meeting of with other rulers broken up by Roman governor of Syria, 332–3; persuades Caligula to give up plan of setting up his image in the Temple, 328–30; petitions Emperor Claudius to reaffirm Jewish rights in Alexandria, 90; on triumphal march in Alexandria in 38 CE, 321–2; writes Caligula on widespread Jewish settlements among many lands, 192–3

Agrippa II, convenes Sanhedrin to allow Levites to wear linen robes on equal terms with priests, 210; deposes high priest Ananus for high-handed action against James, brother of Jesus, 215; fights on side of Romans in revolt of 66 CE, 266; influences Claudius to rule against Samaritans, 336, 338; spies on proceedings in Temple, 140 n 2

Aha, Rabbi, on presence of proselytes at Sinai, 129–30

Albinus, Lucceius, Roman procurator of Judaea, releases prisoners, infesting land with brigands, 341

Alchemy, practiced by Maria, a Jewess, in Alexandria, 46

Alexander (son of Aristobulus II), revolt of against Rome crushed by Gabinius, 169

Alexander the Great, grants Jews in Alexandria privileges equal to those of Macedonians, 4–5; Jews refuse to obey his order to restore pagan temple, 11; on presence of Jews in his army, 10; shows reverence to high priest, 1–4

Alexander Severus, emperor, fondness of for Golden Rule, 96–7; keeps statue of Abraham in his sanctuary, 96

Alexandra, Salome (the Hasmonean), advised by her husband to make peace with the Pharisees, 158–9; assisted by Cleopatra VII, 315; death of results in civil war between her sons, 167; reign

Cleopatra II, receives petition from Onias to build temple in Egypt, 50

Cleopatra III, appoints two Jews, Chelkias and Ananias, commanders-in-chief of army, 80–1, 312–14; heeds advice of Ananias not to go to war against Alexander Jannaeus, 158

Cleopatra VII, said to have knowledge of Hebrew, 315

Colchians, circumcision practiced by, 5, 378

Commerce, Jewish, ancient Greek contacts with, 1; Hellenization of, 22–3, 31–2; in Pergamum, 79–80; Roman protection of autonomy in, 100

Commodus, Roman emperor, possibly identified with "Antoninus," 140 n 3; sentences anti-Jewish Alexandrian gymnasiarch to death, 94–5

Constantine the Great, Roman emperor, continues exemption of Jewish religious officials from public services, 97; punishes with death Jews who attack fellow-Jews who harm converts to Christianity, 347

Constantine II, Roman emperor, law promulgated by depriving Jews of possession of Christian slaves, 347

Conversion of Jews to Christianity, forbidding of Jews from disinheriting fellow-Jews in cases of, 349–50; forbidding of Jews to attack fellow-Jews in cases of, 347; protection of Jewish rights against missionaries in cases of, 100–1

Conversion to Judaism, of the Adiabenians, 126–7, 266; in Antioch, 64; of Aseneth, 51–2, 54–5; and circumcision, 126, 130, 138, 139; extent of, 123–4; forced, 124–5, 154; legal penalties for, 133–4, 346; as source of controversy in Rome, 306, 313–14, 317, 332. *See also* Proselytes; "Sympathizers"

Courts: Christians protected from Jewish witnesses in, 350; criticism of Jewish, 390; of Jews in Egypt, 22–3; of Jews in Sardis, 80; religious jurisdiction of according to *Theodosian Code*, 101; trial of Jews in Egypt before non-Jewish, 27–8. *See also* Sanhedrin

Cowardice: alleged of Jews, 391–2

Creation: biblical accounts criticized, 364–5; and the demiurge, 112, 112 n 20, 113; and Platonic Ideas, 45–6

Credulity: alleged of Jews, 390–1

Crete, Jewish settlements in, 192–3; origin of Jews from, according to Tacitus, 106, 106 n 3

Cumanus, Ventidius, Roman procurator of Judaea, use of force by in handling of insults to and Samaritan attacks on Jews, 335–8

Cutheans. *See* Samaritans

Cyprus, Jewish settlements in, 192–3; slaying by Jewish rebels of 240,000 in 115 CE in, 291–2

Cyrene, Jewish settlement in, 192; reaffirmation by Agrippa of right of Jews in to transmit money to Temple, 87; reaffirmation of Jewish privileges in by Augustus, 85–6; revolt in headed by Lukuas-Andreas in 115–17 CE, 291–5; status of Jews in, 61–2

Damascus: origin of Jews in, 105–6

Dead, judgment of the, description in *1 Enoch* of, 223; description in *4 Ezra* of, 224; Pharisaic view of, 242; Sadducean view of, 243

Dead Sea sect, Messianism of, 219, 221–2; requirements for joining and rules of, 255–9; similarities with and differences from Essenes, 256–7

Delos, inscription from invoking God to avenge death of innocent woman, 63–4

Delphi, manumission inscription from, 63

Demetrius I, king of Syria, offers concessions to Jews, 148; offers various privileges to Jews, 150–1; Roman protest against for mistreatment of Jews, 162

Demetrius II Nicator, king of Syria, abolishes payment of tribute by Jews, 148; offers Simon the Hasmonean complete independence, 151–2

Demetrius of Phalerum, administrator of royal Egyptian library, suggests translation of Pentateuch to Ptolemy Philadelphus, 19

Demiurge, equated with God by Galen, 111–12, 112 n 20; equated with God by Neo-Platonist philosophers, 113

Demons, rabbinic belief in, 225

Deucalion, equated with Noah by Celsus, 364

Dietary laws: martyrdom for the sake of, 98, 120, 310; permission granted Jews by people of Sardis for observance of, 80; permission granted Jews of Ephesus for observance of, 83; Roman hostility to, 327, 373–7; "sympathizers" and, 138, 139, 317–18

Dimi, Rabbi, on appointment of teachers, 204

Dionysus, associated with the Jewish God by Plutarch and Tacitus, 109–11, 314 n 12, 375; worship of forced upon Jews by Antiochus Epiphanes, 312

Divorce, deed of on papyrus, 34

Dolabella, Publius, Roman governor of Syria, grants privileges to Jews of Ephesus, 82–3

Domitian, emperor, condemns those who drift into Jewish ways, 145; enforces *Fiscus Judaicus*, 290, 345–6

Dosa, Rabbi, speculates on coming of Messiah, 221

Dositheus, apostate, becomes pagan priest, 57; saves life of Ptolemy Philopator from plot, 56